职业教育双语教材

Bilingual Textbooks of Vocational Education

汽车安全与舒适系统检修

Automotive Safety and Comfort System Maintenance

郑春光 主编

Edited by Zheng Chunguang

化学工业出版社
Chemical Industry Press

· 北 京 ·
Beijing

内容简介

本书以培养学生利用现代诊断和检测设备对汽车安全与舒适系统进行故障诊断、故障分析、零部件检测及维修更换等技能为目标，详细地介绍了汽车电子控制主动安全系统的检修、汽车空调系统的检修、汽车电子控制被动安全系统的检修、汽车电子控制悬架系统的检修、汽车防盗系统的检修、汽车定速巡航系统的检修、汽车电动助力转向系统的检修7个项目的操作内容。

本书可作为职业本科院校、高等职业技术学院各相关专业的教学用书，也可供汽车维修技术人员、汽车维修职业资格证书的申请人员参考、学习使用。

图书在版编目（CIP）数据

汽车安全与舒适系统检修/郑春光主编. —北京：化学工业出版社，2024.2
ISBN 978-7-122-44358-8

Ⅰ.①汽… Ⅱ.①郑… Ⅲ.①汽车-安全装置-维修-高等职业教育-教材 Ⅳ.①U472.41

中国国家版本馆CIP数据核字（2023）第201931号

责任编辑：韩庆利　　　　　　　　　　　文字编辑：宋　旋　温潇潇
责任校对：李雨函　　　　　　　　　　　装帧设计：刘丽华

出版发行：化学工业出版社（北京市东城区青年湖南街13号　邮政编码100011）
印　　装：大厂聚鑫印刷有限责任公司
787mm×1092mm　1/16　印张22¾　字数572千字　2024年2月北京第1版第1次印刷

购书咨询：010-64518888　　　　　　　　售后服务：010-64518899
网　　址：http://www.cip.com.cn
凡购买本书，如有缺损质量问题，本社销售中心负责调换。

定　　价：79.00元　　　　　　　　　　　　　　　　　　　　版权所有　违者必究

前言

　　汽车安全与舒适系统检修是汽车检测与维修技术人员的典型工作任务,是汽车检测与维修技术高技能人才必须掌握的技能,也是高职交通运输类、汽车制造类各专业的一门重要的专业核心课程。

　　本书是一本以培养学生利用现代诊断和检测设备对汽车安全与舒适系统进行故障诊断、故障分析、零部件检测及维修更换的操作技能为核心,以工作项目为导向,用工作任务进行驱动,以行动体系为框架,以典型案例为引导的教材。本书重点培养学生的专业能力,同时注重培养学生的社会能力和方法能力。

　　本书包含7个项目,每个项目由项目导读、若干个任务、项目小结、项目习题测试组成。每个任务由学习目标、任务导入、知识准备、任务实施、习题测试5部分组成。在项目导读部分,介绍每个项目的特点、作用、分类等;任务中的学习目标由知识要求和能力要求组成;任务导入以企业的典型案例为引导;知识准备包括学生需要学习的每个任务所涉及总成部件的作用、结构形式、工作原理;任务实施中介绍了故障诊断的注意事项、故障诊断的流程与故障修复的方法等,培养学生的动手操作能力,以及分析任务导入中典型故障的排除思路与修复方法;习题测试中精心筛选了一定数量的习题,供学生检测学习效果。

　　通过7个项目的学习和训练,学生不仅能够掌握汽车安全与舒适系统各总成的相关知识,而且能够掌握汽车安全与舒适系统故障诊断与修复的方法,达到高级汽车维修工的水平。

　　本书由天津交通职业学院郑春光主编,其中由天津交通职业学院郑春光编写项目二、项目六、项目七,天津交通职业学院李嘉泽编写项目一,天津交通职业学院刘冰月编写项目三、项目四、项目五。

　　由于编者水平和经验有限,书中难免有欠妥之处,恳请读者批评指正。

编者

目录

项目一 汽车电子控制主动安全系统的检修 ········ 001

项目导读 ················ 001
一、什么是主动安全技术 ······ 001
二、汽车主动安全技术主要内容 ··· 001

任务一 汽车防抱死制动系统的检修 ············ 002
任务导入 ················ 002
知识准备 ················ 002
一、概述 ················ 002
二、汽车防抱死制动系统的类型 ··· 002
三、ABS的理论基础 ·········· 003
四、ABS的功用 ············ 005
五、ABS的技术要求及评价方法 ············ 006
六、ABS的组成与工作原理 ····· 008
七、ABS的控制方式 ·········· 010
八、传感器结构原理 ·········· 013
九、制动压力调节器结构原理 ····· 016
十、电子控制单元（ECU） ····· 022
十一、ABS应用实例 ·········· 024
任务实施 ················ 027
一、ABS的使用与检修 ········ 027
二、ABS故障的一般检查方法 ···· 029
三、ABS制动液添加与补充 ····· 030
四、ABS的放气 ············ 030
五、ABS的故障案例诊断过程 ··· 031
习题测试 ················ 032

任务二 汽车驱动防滑系统的检修 ··· 032
任务导入 ················ 032
知识准备 ················ 032
一、概述 ················ 032
二、ASR的基本组成及工作原理 ············ 034
三、典型ASR结构 ············ 036
任务实施 ················ 037
一、ASR的故障检修 ·········· 037
二、ASR的故障案例诊断过程 ··· 042
习题测试 ················ 043

任务三 汽车车身电子稳定系统的检修 ············ 043
任务导入 ················ 043
知识准备 ················ 043
一、汽车车身电子稳定系统的作用 ··· 043
二、汽车车身电子稳定系统的结构与组成 ············ 043
三、汽车车身电子稳定系统子系统的工作过程 ············ 045
任务实施 ················ 047
汽车车身电子稳定系统的故障案例诊断过程 ············ 047
习题测试 ················ 047
项目小结 ················ 048
项目习题测试 ············ 048

项目二 汽车空调系统的检修 ········ 049

项目导读 ················ 049

一、汽车空调系统的组成 ······ 049

二、认识连接管路 ……………… 050
　　三、空调的工作过程简述 ………… 050
任务一　汽车空调系统识别 ………… 050
　任务导入 ……………………………… 051
　知识准备 ……………………………… 051
　　一、汽车空调的功能 ……………… 051
　　二、汽车空调的主要指标 ………… 051
　　三、汽车空调系统的组成与分类 … 051
　任务实施 ……………………………… 052
　习题测试 ……………………………… 052
任务二　汽车空调制冷系统的检修 … 052
　任务导入 ……………………………… 052
　知识准备 ……………………………… 053
　　一、汽车空调制冷系统压缩机结构
　　　　原理 ……………………………… 053
　　二、汽车空调制冷系统膨胀阀 …… 054
　　三、汽车空调冷凝器 ……………… 055
　　四、储液干燥器 …………………… 056
　任务实施 ……………………………… 057
　　一、电装压缩机的维修 …………… 057
　　二、空调制冷系统膨胀阀的检修 … 060
　　三、汽车空调冷凝器的检修 ……… 062
　　四、汽车空调制冷系统的故障案例
　　　　诊断过程 ……………………… 062
　习题测试 ……………………………… 063
任务三　汽车空调控制系统的检修 … 063
　任务导入 ……………………………… 063
　知识准备 ……………………………… 063
　　一、电源的控制 …………………… 063
　　二、压缩机电磁离合器的控制 …… 063
　　三、压力开关电路 ………………… 064
　　四、汽车空调电路中的典型控制
　　　　回路 …………………………… 064
　　五、速度控制电路 ………………… 064
　任务实施 ……………………………… 065

　　一、丰田花冠轿车空调电路故障检测
　　　　与排除步骤 …………………… 065
　　二、汽车空调的检查方法 ………… 067
　　三、汽车空调系统的定期维护 …… 070
　　四、汽车空调系统故障检测 ……… 071
　　五、汽车空调控制系统的故障案例
　　　　诊断过程 ……………………… 071
　习题测试 ……………………………… 072
任务四　充注与回收汽车空调制
　　　　冷剂 …………………………… 072
　任务导入 ……………………………… 072
　知识准备 ……………………………… 072
　　一、充注汽车空调系统制冷剂 …… 072
　　二、补充与排放汽车空调制冷系统制
　　　　冷剂 …………………………… 074
　　三、加注汽车空调制冷系统冷冻
　　　　润滑油 ………………………… 074
　　四、回收制冷剂 …………………… 075
　任务实施 ……………………………… 076
　　一、操作注意事项 ………………… 076
　　二、操作步骤 ……………………… 077
　习题测试 ……………………………… 079
任务五　汽车空调制热系统的检修 … 079
　任务导入 ……………………………… 080
　知识准备 ……………………………… 080
　　一、发动机余热式暖气装置 ……… 080
　　二、独立热源式暖气装置 ………… 084
　任务实施 ……………………………… 085
　　一、帕萨特暖风装置的结构 ……… 085
　　二、帕萨特暖风装置的拆卸与
　　　　装配 …………………………… 086
　习题测试 ……………………………… 088
　项目小结 ……………………………… 089
　项目习题测试 ………………………… 089

项目三　汽车电子控制被动安全系统的检修 …………………………………… 090

项目导读 ……………………… 090　　任务一　汽车电子控制被动安全

系统识别 …………………… 090
　　任务导入 ……………………… 090
　　知识准备 ……………………… 090
　　一、作用 ………………………… 091
　　二、结构分类 …………………… 091
　　三、组成及基本原理 …………… 092
　　任务实施 ……………………… 094
　　习题测试 ……………………… 094
　任务二　汽车电子控制被动安全
　　　系统的检修 ………………… 094
　　任务导入 ……………………… 095

　　知识准备 ……………………… 095
　　任务实施 ……………………… 095
　　一、安全气囊系统的检修 ……… 095
　　二、奥迪 A6 安全气囊系统自
　　　诊断 ………………………… 100
　　三、汽车电子控制被动安全系统的
　　　故障案例诊断过程 ………… 101
　　习题测试 ……………………… 101
　项目小结 ……………………… 101
　项目习题测试 ………………… 101

项目四　汽车电子控制悬架系统的检修 ………………………………………… 102

　项目导读 ……………………… 102
　任务一　汽车电子控制悬架系统
　　　识别 ………………………… 102
　　任务导入 ……………………… 102
　　知识准备 ……………………… 102
　　一、电子控制悬架系统的功能 …… 102
　　二、电子控制悬架系统的种类 …… 103
　　三、电子控制悬架系统的组成与
　　　工作原理 …………………… 103
　　任务实施 ……………………… 108
　　习题测试 ……………………… 108
　任务二　汽车电子控制变高度悬架
　　　系统的检修 ………………… 108
　　任务导入 ……………………… 109
　　知识准备 ……………………… 109
　　一、车身高度控制系统功用及
　　　分类 ………………………… 109
　　二、变高度控制悬架系统的组成 … 109
　　三、变高度控制悬架系统的控制
　　　过程 ………………………… 109
　　任务实施 ……………………… 110
　　一、电子控制变高度悬架系统
　　　检修 ………………………… 110
　　二、电子控制变高度悬架系统的
　　　故障案例诊断过程 ………… 111

　　习题测试 ……………………… 111
　任务三　汽车电子控制变刚度悬架
　　　系统的检修 ………………… 111
　　任务导入 ……………………… 112
　　知识准备 ……………………… 112
　　一、电子控制变刚度悬架系统的
　　　功用 ………………………… 112
　　二、电子控制变刚度悬架系统的
　　　组成 ………………………… 112
　　三、空气弹簧悬架刚度的调节
　　　原理 ………………………… 112
　　任务实施 ……………………… 113
　　一、空气弹簧的拆卸和安装 …… 113
　　二、电子控制变刚度悬架系统的
　　　故障案例诊断过程 ………… 114
　　习题测试 ……………………… 114
　任务四　汽车电子控制变阻尼悬架
　　　系统的检修 ………………… 114
　　任务导入 ……………………… 115
　　知识准备 ……………………… 115
　　一、变阻尼悬架系统的功用及控制
　　　方式 ………………………… 115
　　二、减振器阻尼控制机构的结构
　　　特点 ………………………… 115
　　三、减振器阻尼调整的控制过程 … 115

任务实施 ················ 116
　　一、电子控制变阻尼悬架系统诊断
　　　基本步骤 ················ 116
　　二、电子控制变阻尼悬架系统维修与
　　　检测 ··················· 116
　　习题测试 ·················· 117
　　项目小结 ·················· 117
　　项目习题测试 ··············· 117

项目五 汽车防盗系统的检修 ················ 118

　项目导读 ·················· 118
　任务一 汽车防盗系统的认知 ······ 118
　　任务导入 ·················· 118
　　知识准备 ·················· 118
　　一、机械式防盗装置 ············ 118
　　二、电子式防盗装置 ············ 118
　　三、网络式防盗系统 ············ 119
　　四、生物识别式防盗器 ·········· 119
　　五、芯片式防盗器 ············· 119
　　任务实施 ·················· 120
　　习题测试 ·················· 120
　任务二 汽车防盗系统的检修 ······ 120
　　任务导入 ·················· 120
　　知识准备 ·················· 120
　　一、汽车防盗系统类型 ·········· 120
　　二、第三代防盗系统特点 ········ 121
　　三、第三代防盗系统的组成与工作
　　　原理 ··················· 121
　　四、第四代防盗系统的工作原理 ··· 123
　　任务实施 ·················· 124
　　一、维修注意事项 ············· 125
　　二、技术要求 ················ 125
　　三、卡罗拉防盗系统检修 ········ 125
　　四、汽车防盗系统的故障案例诊断
　　　过程 ··················· 127
　　习题测试 ·················· 127
　　项目小结 ·················· 127
　　项目习题测试 ··············· 127

项目六 汽车定速巡航系统的检修 ················ 128

　项目导读 ·················· 128
　任务一 汽车定速巡航系统的结构与
　　工作原理 ················ 128
　　任务导入 ·················· 128
　　知识准备 ·················· 128
　　一、定速巡航系统的分类与功能 ··· 128
　　二、定速巡航系统的工作原理与
　　　组成 ··················· 129
　　任务实施 ·················· 132
　　习题测试 ·················· 134
　任务二 汽车自适应巡航控制系统的
　　检修 ··················· 134
　　任务导入 ·················· 134
　　知识准备 ·················· 134
　　一、自适应巡航系统的优点 ······ 134
　　二、自适应巡航系统的局限性 ···· 134
　　三、自适应巡航系统的工作原理 ··· 135
　　四、自适应巡航系统的组成 ······ 135
　　任务实施 ·················· 136
　　自适应巡航控制系统的故障诊断与
　　修复 ··················· 136
　　习题测试 ·················· 138
　　项目小结 ·················· 138
　　项目习题测试 ··············· 138

项目七 汽车电动助力转向系统的检修 ················ 139

项目导读 …………………………… 139
任务　电动助力转向系统的结构与
　　　工作原理 ………………… 139
任务导入 …………………………… 139
知识准备 …………………………… 139
　一、助力转向系统的分类 ………… 139
　二、电动助力转向系统的组成及工作
　　　原理 …………………………… 140

任务实施 …………………………… 144
　一、注意事项 ……………………… 145
　二、技术要求 ……………………… 145
　三、花冠助力转向系统检修 ……… 145
习题测试 …………………………… 148
项目小结 …………………………… 148
项目习题测试 ……………………… 148

参考文献 ………………………………………………………………… 149

项目一

汽车电子控制主动安全系统的检修

 项目导读

一、什么是主动安全技术

为预防汽车发生事故，避免人员受到伤害而采取的安全设计，称为主动安全技术。如ABS（防抱死制动系统）、EBD（电子制动力分配系统）、ASR（驱动防滑系统）、ESP（电子稳定系统）等都是主动安全技术。它们的特点是提高汽车的行驶稳定性，尽量防止车祸发生所带来的危害。

二、汽车主动安全技术主要内容

1. ABS（防抱死制动系统）

ABS通过传感器监测到的各车轮的转速，由计算机计算出当时的车轮滑移率，由此了解车轮是否已抱死，再命令执行机构调整制动压力，使车轮处于理想的制动状态（控制车轮将要抱死但未完全抱死）。ABS能在紧急制动状况下，保持车轮不被抱死而防止车辆失控，维持转向能力，避开障碍物。在一般状况下，它并不能缩短制动距离。

2. ASR（驱动防滑系统）

ASR是继防抱死制动系统之后应用于车轮防滑技术的电子控制系统，控制汽车行驶时的驱动轮"滑转"，主要用于汽车起步、加速及在光滑路面行驶时的牵引力控制和行驶稳定性控制。虽然ASR和ABS一样，通过控制车轮的制动力来控制驱动车轮相对地面的滑动，但ASR只对驱动轮实施制动力控制。ASR一般在车速很高（80～120km/h）时不起作用。

3. ESP（电子稳定系统）

电子稳定系统实际上也是一种牵引力控制系统，与其他牵引力控制系统比较，ESP不但控制驱动轮，而且控制从动轮。它通过主动干预危险信号来实现车辆平稳行驶。如后轮驱动的汽车常出现转向过度所引起的后轮失控而甩尾，ESP便会放慢外侧的前轮来稳定车辆；在转向不足时，为了校正运行方向，ESP则会放慢内后轮，从而校正行驶方向。

ESP包含ABS及ASR，是这两种系统功能上的延伸。因此，ESP称得上是汽车防滑装置的高级形式。ESP由控制单元及转向传感器（监测转向盘的转向角度）、车轮传感器（监测各个车轮的转动速度）、侧滑传感器（监测车体绕垂直轴线转动的状态）、横向加速度传感器（监测汽车转弯时的离心力）等组成。控制单元通过这些传感器的信号对车辆的运行状态进行判断，进而发出控制指令。

任务一　汽车防抱死制动系统的检修

【学习目标】

知识要求：掌握 ABS 的作用、组成、原理及检修方法；熟悉 ABS 的主要元件的结构与原理。

能力要求：能够依据维修手册并使用常用工具、量具对 ABS 进行基本检查；能够对 ABS 常见故障进行诊断与修复。

任务导入

一辆本田雅阁轿车出现故障：将点火开关置于 ON 位，ABS 灯亮；启动发动机，ABS 灯熄灭，同时 ABS 油泵电动机旋转；过 1~2min，ABS 油泵电动机停止运转，与此同时 ABS 灯点亮。

知识准备

防抱死制动系统是可以防止车轮完全抱死，制动效果优于常规制动系统的制动装置，是在常规制动系统的基础之上，经改进而成。整个制动系统在制动时既有常规制动系统的制动功能，又有防止车轮被完全抱死的功能；它将驾驶员施加在制动踏板上的力迅速、均匀地转化为车轮的制动力。而增加的 ABS 控制系统是由电子、机械和液压源、气压源组成的自动控制系统，它可以连续地监测车辆的制动状况，并及时将汽车的制动调整到最佳状态。如果常规制动系统出现故障，ABS 就会自动失去作用；如果 ABS 出现故障，常规制动系统仍会照常工作。

一、概述

1920 年英国人霍纳摩尔首先研制了 ABS 并申请了专利。1928 年防抱死制动系统理论被提出，20 世纪 30 年代，机械式 ABS 就开始在火车和飞机上应用。20 世纪 40 年代末，ABS 被应用于波音 B-47 飞机上。20 世纪 50 年代福特公司将飞机的 ABS 应用在林肯轿车上。1978 年，博世公司推出采用数字式电控装置的 ABS，揭开了现代 ABS 发展的序幕。进入 21 世纪，ABS 发展得越来越快，美国、日本、中国和欧洲等国家和地区均在高速发展 ABS，ABS 的普及使用是大势所趋。

二、汽车防抱死制动系统的类型

1. 整体式 ABS

整体式 ABS 的制动压力调节器与制动主缸以及制动助力器组合为一个整体，福特、别克、凯迪拉克、奥斯莫比尔、庞蒂克、绅宝等高级轿车采用该种方式，如图 1-1 所示。

2. 分离式 ABS

分离式 ABS 的制动压力调节器为独立总成，通过制动管路与制动主缸和制动轮缸相连，桑塔纳、捷达、红旗、宝马和沃尔沃等轿车采用该种方式。具体形式如图 1-2 所示。

另外，汽车防抱死制动系统按控制方式分，包括机械式和电子式两类。按动力源分为气

压式、液压式和气顶液压式。

按控制车轮的方式,分为轴控式和轮控式两种。轴控式又分为轴控低选控制式和轴控高选控制式。轴控低选控制 ABS 如图 1-3 所示。ϕ 为车轮与路面的附着系数。轴控高选控制 ABS 如图 1-4 所示。轮控独立式 ABS 如图 1-5 所示,每个车轮各占用一个控制通道。

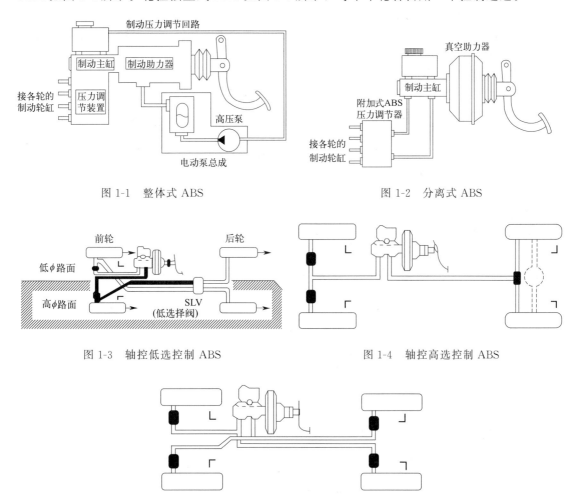

图 1-1 整体式 ABS

图 1-2 分离式 ABS

图 1-3 轴控低选控制 ABS

图 1-4 轴控高选控制 ABS

图 1-5 轮控独立式 ABS

三、ABS 的理论基础

汽车制动系统是在汽车行驶过程中,能够根据驾驶员的需要减速、停车的重要装置。良好的制动系统应具有制动距离短、制动时汽车行驶方向能够控制、轮胎损耗小等特点。随着汽车工业的发展,计算机技术在汽车上得到广泛的应用,用计算机控制制动力,使汽车在制动时,控制车轮不至于抱死,同时缩短了制动距离,解决了常规制动系统的不足。

1. 汽车的制动性

汽车的制动性指汽车在行驶过程中,强制地减速以至停车且维持行驶的方向稳定性的能力。对一辆汽车制动系统的性能有多方面的要求,主要评价指标有以下 3 个方面。

① 制动效能:制动效能主要指汽车在行驶中,强制减速以至停车的能力。其基本评价指标为制动距离、制动减速度以及制动时间。

② 制动时车辆的方向稳定性:指汽车在制动时仍能按指定方向的轨迹行驶,即不发生

跑偏、侧滑，以及失去转向能力。

③ 制动效能的恒定性：主要指抗热衰退性能。汽车在大负荷工作条件下制动，制动器性能会因温度升高而衰退。抗热衰退性指汽车保持制动效能的程度。它是设计制动器及选材中必须认真考虑的一个重要问题。

为了达到良好的制动性能指标，现代汽车采用了防抱死制动系统。在以上3个指标中，前两项指标在采用了 ABS 装置后，其性能都有明显的改善和提高，对避免交通事故的发生起到很好的作用，因此，ABS 是汽车上十分重要的主动安全装置。

2. 汽车制动时车轮受力分析

汽车在行驶过程中能够实施制动过程的根本原因是与轮胎接触的路面给相应车轮提供了路面制动力。一个是制动器内制动蹄摩擦片与制动鼓间的摩擦力，另一个是轮胎与路面间的附着力。图 1-6 所示为车轮在制动时的受力情况示意图。

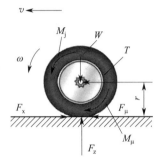

图 1-6　车轮在制动时的受力情况示意图
v—车轮中心的纵向速度；ω—车轮旋转角速度；M_j—惯性力矩；M_μ—制动阻力矩；W—车轮法向载荷；F_z—地面法向反力；T—车轴对车轮的推力；F_x—地面制动力；r—车轮的滚动半径；F_μ—制动器制动力

从力矩平衡可知：制动时地面对车轮的切向反作用力为 $F_x = M_j/r$。

制动蹄与制动鼓（盘）压紧时形成的摩擦力矩为制动阻力矩 M_μ，通过车轮作用于地面的切向力称为制动器制动力，以 F_μ 表示，制动器制动力 $F_\mu = M_\mu/r$。

大量实验证明，弹性车轮在地面上滚动，产生阻力和摩擦力（附着力），其中附着力是地面对轮胎切向反作用力的极限值，用 F_φ 表示，附着力取决于轮胎与路面之间的摩擦作用及路面的抗剪强度，即路面的附着系数 φ，由上可知 $F_\varphi = \varphi F_z$。

由于地面制动力受到附着力的限制，所以地面制动力最大不能超过附着力 F_φ，即 $F_x \leqslant F_\varphi$。

根据上述分析，在汽车制动过程中，制动器制动力 F_μ、地面制动力 F_x 及附着力 F_φ 之间的关系如图 1-7 所示。汽车制动过程中，地面制动力的大小首先取决于制动器的制动力，但又受地面附着条件的限制，所以为了达到最佳的制动效果，不仅需要足够的制动器制动力，同时又需要较高的附着力。在汽车制动时，通常将附着系数分为纵向附着系数和横向附着系数，汽车的加速运动和减速运动主要受纵向附着系数限制，抵抗外界横向作用力的能力则主要受车轮横向附着系数的限制。

3. 滑移率

（1）滑移率的定义

滑移率指车轮在制动过程中车速和车轮速度之差与车速的比值，用百分比来表示。其定义表达式为

$$S = [(v - \omega r)/v] \times 100\%$$

式中　S——车轮的滑移率，%；
　　　r——车轮的滚动半径，m；
　　　ω——车轮旋转角速度，rad/s；
　　　v——车轮中心的纵向速度，m/s。

由上式可知：当车轮为纯滚动时，汽车的实际车速与车轮滚动时的圆周速度相等，滑移率为零；当车轮边滚动边滑动时，滑移率为 0～100%；当车轮处于抱死状态，而车身又具

有一定的速度时，则滑移率为100%。

(2) 附着系数与滑移率的关系

在汽车的制动过程中，附着系数的大小随着滑移率的变化而变化。图1-8所示为在干路面上时附着系数与滑移率的关系曲线。对于纵向附着系数 ϕ_B，随着滑移率的迅速增加，并在 $S=20\%$ 左右时，纵向附着系数最大；然后随着滑移率的进一步增加，当 $S=100\%$，即车轮抱死时，纵向附着系数有所下降，制动距离会增加，制动效能下降。对于横向附着系数 ϕ_S，当 $S=0$ 时，横向附着系数最大；然后随着滑移率的增加，横向附着系数逐渐下降，并在 $S=100\%$，即车轮抱死时，横向附着系数下降到几乎为零。

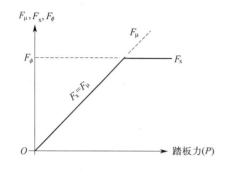

图1-7 制动器制动力 F_μ、地面制动力 F_x 及附着力 F_ϕ 之间的关系图

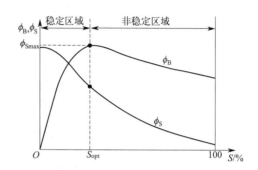

图1-8 附着系数与滑移率的关系曲线

从以上分析可知，如果制动时将车轮的滑移率 S 控制在20%左右，即如图1-8所示的 S_{opt} 处，此时纵向附着系数最大，可得到最好的制动效能；同时横向附着系数也保持较大值，使汽车也具有较好的制动方向稳定性。

(3) 横向附着系数过小的危害

① 方向稳定性变差。因为横向附着力较小，汽车失去抵抗横向外力的能力，后轮易产生横向滑移、甩尾等现象，使汽车方向稳定性变差。

② 转向控制能力丧失。在汽车转向行驶时，尽管驾驶员在操纵转向盘，由于前轮横向附着力丧失，汽车会按原来惯性方向行驶，而不按驾驶员的意愿行驶，从而使转向控制能力丧失。

4. 理想的制动控制过程

$S<20\%$ 为制动稳定区域；$S>20\%$ 为制动非稳定区域；车轮在制动过程中，以5~10次/s的频率进行增压、保压、减压的不断切换，将滑移率 S 控制在20%左右，便可获得最大的纵向附着系数和较大的横向附着系数，是最理想的控制效果。

四、ABS的功用

装有ABS的汽车制动时，ABS直接控制的车轮（依据自身的运动状态来调节其制动压力的车轮）不能抱死滑移，但允许有短暂的车轮抱死，也允许车速低于15km/h时车轮抱死。

ABS可控制实际制动过程接近于理想制动过程。其具体功能为缩短制动距离；防止车辆转向制动时，因转向内外轮横向附着力差所造成的侧滑；改善了轮胎的磨损状态；防止因制动油管漏油，造成制动完全失效的隔断功能；减轻制动踏板踩下时的力，提升制动辅助效果，驾驶员也没有必要用一连串的点制动方式进行制动。

1. 制动时缩短制动距离

有ABS的汽车制动时可缩短制动距离，因为在同样紧急制动的情况下，ABS将滑移率控制在20%左右，可获得最大的纵向制动力。在冰雪等光滑路面上，如果没有ABS，无论

怎么小心，制动力总是会显得太大，使轮胎抱死，从而使汽车制动距离过长。同样，在这种路面上，如果汽车装有 ABS，就能自动地使车轮与路面间产生最大的附着力，可以使制动距离变短。但不要错误地认为有了 ABS，汽车的制动就再也没有问题了，甚至错误地认为无论是附着冰雪等湿滑路面还是干燥路面，使用了 ABS 的汽车的制动距离都是一样的。

2. 制动时保持方向稳定性

制动时的方向稳定性指汽车制动时按预定方向行驶的能力，即不发生跑偏、侧滑的能力。

ABS 的最大优点是：当汽车紧急制动时，ABS 能最大限度地利用轮胎与路面之间的附着力来获得最大制动力，并且仍然可以控制汽车的方向，以保持整车的方向稳定性。

3. 制动时保持转向控制能力

制动时保持转向控制能力，如图 1-9、图 1-10 所示。

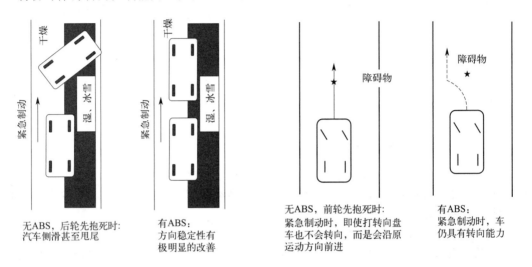

图 1-9　制动时保持方向稳定性　　　　图 1-10　制动时保持转向控制能力

当汽车转向时，如果汽车紧急制动，和汽车直线行驶时紧急制动一样会出现车轮抱死现象。由于车轮抱死，汽车的横向附着力变为零，车轮将出现横向滑动，汽车丧失了控制方向的能力，这是十分危险的。

如果汽车前轮抱死，驾驶员就无法控制汽车的行驶方向；倘若汽车的后轮先抱死，则会出现侧滑、甩尾，甚至使汽车出现整体掉头等严重事故。ABS 可以防止 4 个车轮制动时被完全抱死，使汽车在转弯过程中制动也不会影响汽车的转向性，提高了汽车行驶的稳定性。

4. 制动时能使轮胎磨损下降

事实上，车轮抱死会造成轮胎杯形磨损，轮胎面磨损也会不均匀，使轮胎磨损消耗费用增加。因此，装有 ABS 在一定程度上可使轮胎磨损成本下降。

5. 使用方便，工作可靠

ABS 的使用与普通制动系统的使用几乎没有区别。制动时只要把脚踏在制动踏板上，ABS 就会根据情况自动进入工作状态，ABS 工作十分可靠，并具有自诊断能力。

五、ABS 的技术要求及评价方法

1. 对 ABS 的设计要求

评价 ABS 的主要指标是转向能力、稳定性和最佳制动距离，由此对 ABS 提出以下

要求。

①在调节制动过程中，汽车转向能力和行驶稳定性必须得到保证。

②即使左右车轮的附着力系数不相等，也应保证无法避免的转向反应尽可能小。

③必须在汽车的整个速度范围内进行调节。

④调节系统应该最有效地利用车轮在路面上的附着性，这时对保持转向能力的考虑优先于缩短制动距离的目标。

⑤调节装置应极快地适应路面传递能力的变化。

⑥在波状路面上给以任意强度的制动，汽车都能被完全控制住。

⑦调节装置必须能识别出附着系数小的路面，并对此做出正确的反应。

⑧调节装置只能附加在常规制动装置上，如果出现损坏，安全通路必须自动断开调节装置而不出现不良作用，这时常规制动装置必须能全功能工作。

2. ABS 的质量准则

高质量的 ABS 必须有高的可靠性、广泛的适应性及良好的性能。评判一个 ABS 应该遵循的质量准则如下。

（1）良好的行驶稳定性

为使汽车有良好的行驶稳定性，ABS 必须在汽车制动时使后轮具有抵抗足够大的外界侧向力的能力，不至于发生后轴侧滑的不稳定制动工况。

（2）良好的转向能力

ABS 在汽车制动时，应使转向轮具有足够大的侧向控制力，而不至于发生侧滑，且转向轮不抱死滑移，使汽车保持良好的转向能力。

（3）高附着力系数利用率

汽车装用 ABS 制动时，应有高的附着力系数利用率，即合理的轮胎与路面间的潜在附着力。在一般情况下，装用 ABS 的汽车应具有良好的制动效能，即较短的制动距离和较高的制动减速度。

（4）良好的制动舒适性

在汽车制动时，若 ABS 对制动压力控制得不理想，发生严重的过制动或欠制动现象，会使汽车发生前后窜动的现象，制动舒适性很差，而且制动效能也不佳，这是不允许的。

3. 主要评价指标

安装有 ABS 的汽车制动性能的主要评价指标如下。

（1）良好的抗外界电磁场干扰的能力

ABS 是一个典型的电子控制系统，如不能抵抗外界电磁场的干扰，工作时就可能对制动压力进行误调节，从而出现危险情况。

（2）滑移率控制的能力

装有 ABS 的汽车制动时，ABS 直接控制的车轮（依据自身的运动状态来调节其制动压力的车轮）不能抱死滑移，但允许有短暂的车轮抱死，也允许车速低于 15km/h 时车轮抱死。

（3）附着系数利用率

装用 ABS 的汽车在附着系数均匀的路面上制动时，附着系数利用率不得小于 0.75。汽车在左、右车轮位于不同附着系数的路面上制动时，附着系数利用率也要足够大。

（4）对道路条件突变的适应性

装有 ABS 的汽车制动过程中，路面附着系数突变，附着系数由高（$\phi_1 \geqslant 0.5$）到低（$\phi_2 < \phi_1$，$\phi_1/\phi_2 \geqslant 2$）或由低到高，ABS 直接控制的车轮不得抱死，且制动减速度应急速

变化。一般要求制动行驶中通过附着系数突变分界线的车速在50km/h左右。

（5）产生电气故障可解除ABS的工作

如ABS出现故障后继续参与工作，可能对制动压力进行误调节，这是十分危险的。因此ABS一旦出现电气故障，必须迅速终止ABS的工作，而ABS的调节器必须保证常规制动管路畅通。

六、ABS的组成与工作原理

1. 组成

汽车制动系统随车型的不同而不同，同样，ABS也因车型而异。因此ABS的类型较多，但基本由常规制动系统（制动总泵、制动分泵）、电子控制单元ECU（加速度传感器）、轮速传感器、制动压力调节器（压力开关、储能器、动力装置和液压泵）、ABS警告灯和必需的导线等组成。

在图1-11所示的ABS中，在汽车的每个车轮上各安装了一个轮速传感器，将各个车轮的转速信号输入给电子控制单元，电子控制单元根据各轮速传感器输入的信号对各个车轮的运动状况进行分析判断，并形成相应的控制指令，发送给制动压力调节装置。制动压力调节装置主要由调压电磁控制阀总成、电动泵总成和储液器等组成，通过制动管路与制动主缸和各制动轮缸相连。制动压力调节装置受电子控制单元的控制，对各制动轮缸的制动压力进行调节。在正常工作时，所有ABS都和传统的助力制动系统相似。在强力制动时，ABS根据车轮的速度调节通向每个车轮的制动液压力。

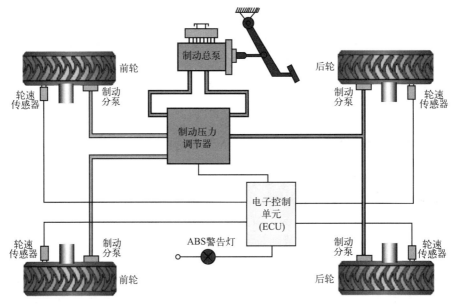

图1-11 电子控制防抱死制动系统（ABS）的组成

2. 工作原理

制动时ECU接收传感器的信号，当车轮将要被抱死时，ECU发出控制信号，通过执行机构控制制动器的制动力使车轮不被抱死。

（1）ABS的工作条件

① ABS是在常规制动的基础上工作，制动中车轮未抱死时，与常规制动相同；车轮趋于抱死时，ABS才工作，ECU控制制动压力调节器对分泵制动压力进行调节。

② ABS工作时，车速必须大于5km/h，若低于该车速，制动时车轮仍可能抱死。

③ 常规制动系统出现故障，ABS随之失去控制作用；ABS出现故障，ECU自动关闭ABS，同时ABS警告灯点亮并存储故障码，但常规制动系统仍可正常工作。

（2）典型ABS的调节原理

① 常规制动阶段。在常规制动阶段，ABS并不介入制动压力控制，调压电磁阀总成中的各进液电磁阀均不通电而处于开启状态，各出液电磁阀均不通电而处于关闭状态，电动泵也不通电运转，制动主缸至各制动轮缸的制动管路均处于畅通状态，而各制动轮缸至储液器的制动管路均处于封闭状态，各制动轮缸的压力将随制动主缸的输出压力而变化。此时的制动过程与一般制动系统的制动过程完全相同，如图1-12所示。

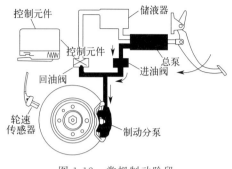

图1-12 常规制动阶段

② 制动压力保持阶段。在制动过程中，电子控制单元根据轮速传感器输入的车轮转速信号判定有车轮抱死时，ABS就进入防抱死制动压力调节过程。例如，电子控制单元发现左前轮趋于抱死时，电子控制单元就使控制左前轮制动压力的进液电磁阀通电，使左前进液电磁阀转入关闭状态，制动主缸输出的制动液不再进入左前制动轮缸。此时，左前出液电磁阀仍未通电而处于关闭状态，左前制动轮缸中的制动液也不会流出，左前制动轮缸的制动压力就保持一定，而其他未抱死车轮的制动压力仍会随制动主缸输出压力的增大而增大，维持在最大制动力，控制元件与传感器充分配合，使制动分泵的液压不会太大而导致滑移，也不会太小而导致制动力不足，如图1-13所示。

③ 制动压力减小阶段（车轮抱死时）。在左前制动轮缸的制动压力保持一定时，电子控制单元判定左前轮仍趋于抱死，电子控制单元又使左前出液电磁阀也转入开启状态，左前制动轮缸中的部分制动液就会经过处于开启状态的出液电磁阀流回储液器，使左前制动轮缸的制动压力迅速减小，左前轮的抱死趋势将开始消除，车轮被抱死时，传感器传送信号给控制元件，使进油阀关闭，回油阀打开，部分制动油流回储液器，降低制动分泵的液压，避免车轮被抱死，如图1-14所示。

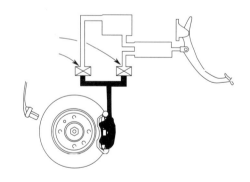

图1-13 保持最大制动力时

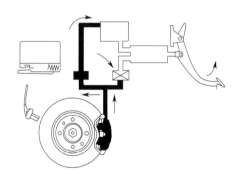

图1-14 车轮抱死时

④ 制动压力增大阶段。随着左前制动轮缸制动压力的减小，左前轮会在汽车惯性力的作用下逐渐加速，当电子控制单元根据轮速传感器输入的信号判断左前轮的抱死趋势已经完全消除时，电子控制单元就使左前进液电磁阀和出液电磁阀都断电，使进液电磁阀转入开启状态、出液电磁阀转入关闭状态，同时也使电动泵通电运转，向制动轮缸泵送制动液，由制

动主缸输出的制动液和电动泵泵送的制动液都经过处于开启状态的左前进液电磁阀进入左前制动轮缸，使左前制动轮缸的压力迅速增大，左前轮又开始减速转动。

ABS 使趋于抱死车轮的制动压力循环往复地经历保持—减小—增大过程，而将趋于抱死车轮的滑移率控制在峰值附着系数滑移率的范围内，直至汽车速度减小到很低或者制动主缸的输出压力不再使车轮趋于抱死时为止，一般制动压力调节循环的频率可达 3～20Hz。在四通道 ABS 中对应于每一个制动轮缸各有一对进液和出液电磁阀，可由电子控制单元分别进行控制。因此，各制动轮缸的制动压力能够被独立地调节，从而使 4 个车轮都不发生制动抱死现象。

七、ABS 的控制方式

ABS 中能够独立进行制动压力调节的制动管路称为控制通道，ABS 按控制通道数可分为单通道系统、双通道系统、三通道系统和四通道系统。

如果车轮的制动压力可以进行单独的调节，与其他车轮的控制无关，称该车轮为独立控制，独立控制方式能使每一个车轮都根据各自的防抱死控制算法达到最大的附着系数利用率，得到最佳的制动效果。但在综合 4 个车轮的控制时，在很多情况下不能得到最佳的制动效果，这主要是由于在分离附着系数路面上行驶时，左右车轮上产生的制动力不同，将导致附加的侧摆力矩，使汽车失去操纵稳定性。独立控制方式主要用于汽车的主要承载轴或驱动轴，对轿车主要应用于前轴，对中、重型汽车主要应用于后轴。

如果对两个或两个以上的车轮制动压力一同进行调节，则称该两个车轮为一同控制。如果对两个车轮一同进行控制，若以保证附着系数较大的车轮不发生制动抱死为原则进行防抱死制动控制，称这两个车轮是按高选原则一同控制的；若以保证附着系数较小的车轮不发生制动抱死为原则进行防抱死制动控制，称这两个车轮是按低选原则一同控制的。按高选原则控制的车辆，附着系数的利用率比较大，制动距离比较短，但同样在分离附着系数路面上行驶时会产生附加的侧摆力矩，使制动稳定性恶化，所以这种控制方式适用于轿车前轴。按低选原则进行控制的车辆，由于高附着系数一侧的车轮不能充分利用附着系数，从而使汽车制动距离加长，但由于这种控制方式可以消除和减少附加的侧摆力矩，因此汽车在附着系数均匀的路面上直线行驶时，其制动效果基本与独立控制的制动效果相同，制动距离也基本相同，只是在分离附着系数路面上行驶时，制动距离略长。这种控制方式常用于轿车的后轴。

① 四传感器四通道/四轮独立控制如图 1-15 所示。

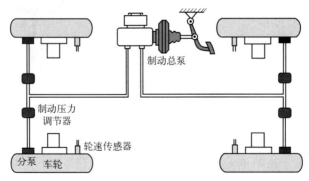

图 1-15　四传感器四通道/四轮独立控制

② 四传感器四通道/前轮独立-后轮选择控制方式。对应于双制动管路的 H 形（前后）或 X 形（对角）两种布置形式，如图 1-16 所示，四通道 ABS 也有两种布置形式。为了对 4 个车轮的制动压力进行独立控制，在每个车轮上各安装一个轮速传感器，并在通往各制动轮缸的制动管路中各设置一个制动压力调节分装置（通道）。由于四通道 ABS 可以最大程度地利用每个车轮的附着力进行制动，因此汽车的制动效能最好。但在附着系数分离（两侧车轮的附着系数不相等的路面上制动）时，由于同一轴上的制动力不相等，使得汽车产生较大的偏转力矩而产生制动跑偏。因此，ABS 通常不对 4 个车轮进行独立的制动压力调节。

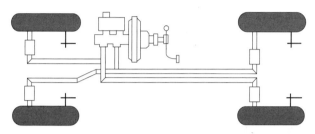

图 1-16 对应于双制动管路的 X 形（对角）布置形式

③ 四传感器三通道/前轮独立-后轮低选控制方式如图 1-17 所示。

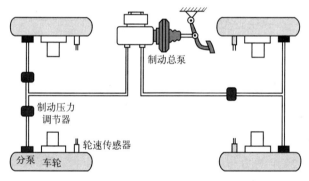

图 1-17 四传感器三通道/前轮独立-后轮低选控制方式

④ 三传感器三通道/前轮独立-后轮低选控制方式如图 1-18 所示。四轮 ABS 大多为三通道系统，而三通道系统都是对两前轮的制动压力进行单独控制，对两后轮的制动压力按低选原则一同控制。由于三通道 ABS 对两后轮进行一同控制，所以对于后轮驱动的汽车可以在变速器或主减速器中只设置一个转速传感器来检测两后轮的平均转速。

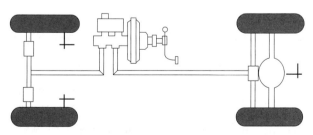

图 1-18 三传感器三通道/前轮独立-后轮低选控制方式

⑤ 四传感器二通道/前轮独立控制方式如图 1-19 所示。

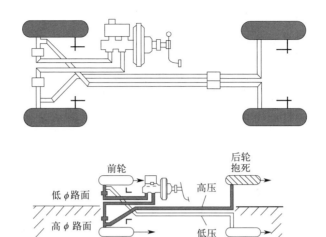

图 1-19　四传感器二通道/前轮独立控制方式

⑥ 四传感器二通道/前轮独立-后轮低选控制方式如图1-20所示。由于双通道ABS难以在方向稳定性、转向操纵能力和制动距离等方面得到兼顾，因此目前很少被采用。

⑦ 一传感器一通道/后轮近似低选控制系统制动方式如图1-21所示。所有单通道ABS都是在前后布置的双管路制动系统的后制动管路中设置一个制动压力调节装置，对于后轮驱动的汽车只需在传动系统中安装一个轮速传感器。由于前制动轮缸的制动压力未被控制，前轮仍然可能发生制动抱死，所以汽车制动时的转向操作能力得不到保障。但由于单通道ABS能够显著地提高汽车制动

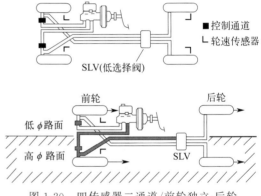

图 1-20　四传感器二通道/前轮独立-后轮低选控制方式

时的方向稳定性，又具有结构简单、成本低的优点，因此在轻型货车上得到广泛应用。

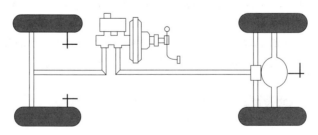

图 1-21　一传感器一通道/后轮近似低选控制系统制动方式

⑧ ABS的控制参数。目前，ABS控制方式很多，主要有逻辑门限值控制、最优控制和滑动模态变结构控制等。但绝大多数ABS都是采用逻辑门限值控制方式，即普遍采用以车轮滑移率为控制参数的ABS和以车角加速度和角减速度为控制参数的ABS，如图1-22所示。

在实际控制中，ABS一般以多种参数结合进行控制，若仅采用其中任何一种门限作为

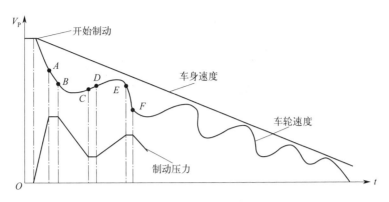

图 1-22 ABS 的控制参数

防抱死制动控制，都存在较大的局限性。

八、传感器结构原理

1. 车轮速度传感器

（1）车轮速度传感器的结构

在 ABS 控制系统中每个车轮都装有车轮速度传感器，来检测车轮的转速，前轮速度传感器装在转向节上，后轮速度传感器装在后轴托架上。有些后驱动的车辆，轮速传感器装在差速器内，通过后轴转速检测，称为轴速传感器。传感器由永久磁铁、线圈和齿圈组成，它对车轮的转速进行非接触式测量。齿圈与车轮同步转动，切割传感器的磁力线使磁通量交替变化，从而在传感器的输出端产生交变电压，其电压频率与车轮转速成正比变化，同时该脉冲信号输入 ABS 控制装置，就可以检测到车轮的瞬时转速变化，如图 1-23 和图 1-24 所示。

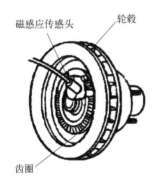

图 1-23　前轮速度传感器

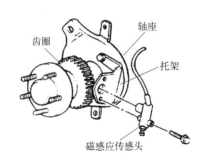

图 1-24　后轮速度传感器

（2）车轮速度传感器安装的不同位置

安装在驱动轮上和安装在非驱动轮上的车轮速度传感器，如图 1-25 所示。

安装在后驱动桥主减速器上，如图 1-26 所示，安装在变速器输出轴上，如图 1-27 所示。

（3）ABS 车轮速度传感器安装方式

① 轴向式安装，如图 1-28 所示。

② 径向式安装，如图 1-29 所示。

（4）车轮速度传感器的类型

车轮速度传感器主要有两种类型：电磁感应式和霍尔效应式。

项目一　汽车电子控制主动安全系统的检修　**013**

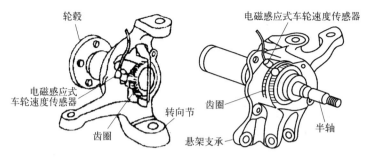

图 1-25　安装在驱动轮/非驱动轮上的车轮速度传感器

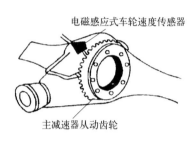

图 1-26　安装在后驱动桥主减速器上的车轮速度传感器

图 1-27　安装在变速器输出轴上的车轮速度传感器

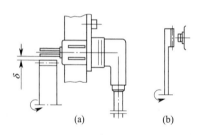

图 1-28　轴向式安装

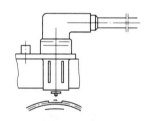

图 1-29　径向式安装

① 电磁感应式车轮速度传感器。电磁感应式车轮速度传感器主要由电缆、永磁体、外壳、感应线圈、极轴和齿圈组成，如图 1-30 所示。当齿圈的齿隙与传感器的极轴端部相对时，极轴端部与齿圈之间的空气间隙最大，通过感应磁线圈的磁通量最小，如图 1-31 所示。当齿圈的齿顶与传感器的极轴端部相对时，极轴端部与齿圈之间的空气间隙最小，通过感应磁线圈的磁通量最大，如图 1-32 所示。齿圈的齿顶和齿隙交替地与极轴端部相对，周围磁场发生强弱交替变化，感应出交变电压，如图 1-33 所示。

其特点为：结构简单，成本低；输出的信号电压的幅值随转速变化而变化，一般为 1～15V；若车速过慢，输出信号电压小于 1V 时，ABS 计算机无法检测。有效的控制速度范围较窄，一般为 15～160km/h；抗电磁波干扰能力差。

② 霍尔式车轮速度传感器。霍尔式车轮速度传感器主要由霍尔元件、永磁体、齿圈和电路等组成，如图 1-34 所示。其工作过程如下。

a. 齿圈的齿不正对永磁体时，穿过霍尔元件的磁力线分散，磁场相对较弱，如图 1-35 所示。

b. 齿圈的齿正对着永磁体时，穿过霍尔元件的磁力线集中，磁场相对较强，引起霍尔电压变化，将输出正弦波电压，如图 1-36 所示。

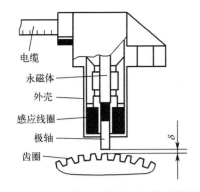

图 1-30 电磁感应式车轮速度传感器结构

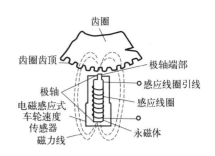

图 1-31 电磁感应式车轮速度传感器工作过程（1）

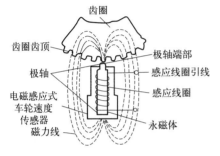

图 1-32 电磁感应式车轮速度
传感器工作过程（2）

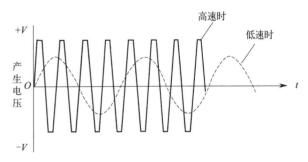

图 1-33 电磁感应式车轮速度
传感器工作过程（3）

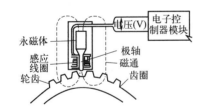

图 1-34 霍尔式车轮速度传感器结构

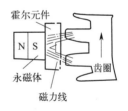

图 1-35 霍尔式车轮速度传感器工作过程（1）

2. 减速度传感器

（1）作用

减速度传感器也称为 G 传感器，用于测量汽车制动时的减速度，识别是否为雪路、冰路等易滑路面。

（2）类型

① 光电式减速度传感器。其基本结构如图 1-37 所示，由 2 个发光二极管、2 个光电三极管、1 个透光板和 1 个信号电路组成。

工作过程：当透光板上的开口位于发光二极管与光电三极管之间时，能使光电三极管导通，反之截止，计算机接收到传感器信号后，就可判定路面状况，如图 1-38 所示。

② 水银式减速度传感器。其基本结构如图 1-39 所示，由玻璃管和水银组成。

工作过程：当汽车在低附着系数路面上制动时，汽车减速度小，水银基本不动，开关在玻璃管内处于接通状态，计算机按低附着系数路面控制。反之，在高附着系数路面上制动时，汽车减速度大，水银在玻璃管内前移，使玻璃管内的电路开关断开，计算机按高附着系

数路面控制，如图 1-40 所示。

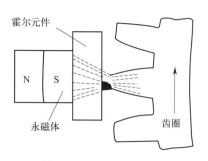

图 1-36 霍尔式车轮速度传感器工作过程（2）

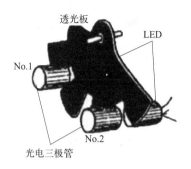

图 1-37 光电式减速度传感器结构

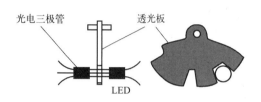

图 1-38 光电式减速度传感器工作过程

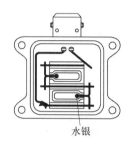

图 1-39 水银式减速度传感器结构

③ 差动变速器式减速度传感器。其基本结构如图 1-41 所示，由差动变压器和电子电路组成，其中差动变压器主要由一个初级绕组、两个串联的次级绕组和铁芯组成。

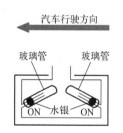

图 1-40 水银式减速度传感器工作过程

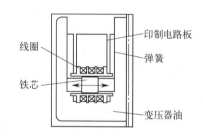

图 1-41 差动变速器式减速度传感器结构

工作过程：当汽车制动减速时，铁芯受惯性力作用向前移动，从而使差动变压器线圈内的感应电压发生变化，以此作为输出信号送入 ECU 用来控制 ABS 的工作，如图 1-42 所示。

九、制动压力调节器结构原理

制动压力调节器（见图 1-43）的功用是根据 ECU 的指令来调节各个车轮制动器的制动压力。制动系统不同，所采用的制动压力调节装置的结构和工作原理也不同。常用的制动系统主要有液压式、机械式、气压式和空气液压复合式等，在 ABS 中应用最广泛的是液压式制动系统，所以在这里主要介绍液压式制动压力控制装置。

液压式制动压力控制装置（制动压力调节器）主要由液压电动泵、液压控制电磁阀及储液器等组成。压力调节器安装在主缸和轮缸之间，通过电磁阀直接或间接地控制轮缸的制动压力。

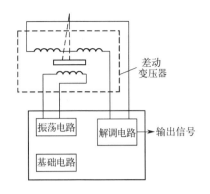

图 1-42　差动变速器式减速度传感器工作过程

图 1-43　制动压力调节器

1. 循环式制动压力调节器

循环式制动压力调节器的结构如图 1-44 所示。

（1）电磁阀

电磁阀直接控制轮缸的制动压力。

① 三位三通电磁阀。三位三通电磁阀的结构如图 1-45 所示，由进液阀、回液阀、主弹簧、副弹簧、固定铁芯及衔铁套筒等组成。三位三通电磁阀（由博世公司生产，应用于博世 ABS 中）在 ECU 控制下，使阀处于增压、保压、减压 3 种状态。工作过程如下。

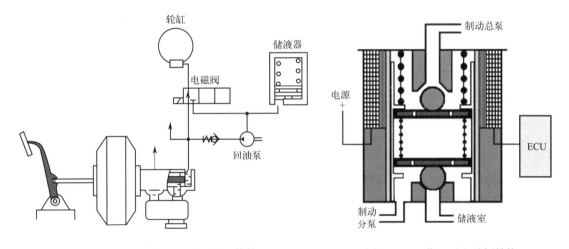

图 1-44　循环式制动压力调节器结构　　　图 1-45　三位三通电磁阀结构

增压（常规）制动状态：电磁线圈未通电时，在主弹簧张力作用下，进液阀打开，回液阀关闭，进液口与出液口保持畅通。

保压状态：如图 1-46 所示，电磁线圈通入较小电流（2A），产生的电磁吸力小，吸动衔铁上移量少，但能适当压缩主弹簧，使进液阀关闭，放松副弹簧，回液阀并不打开。

减压状态：如图 1-47 所示，电磁阀线圈通入较大电流（5A），产生的电磁吸力大，吸动衔铁上移量大，同时压缩主、副弹簧，使进液阀仍保持关闭，回液阀打开。

该电磁阀工作在 3 个状态（增压、保压、减压），称为"三位"。该电磁阀对外具有三个接口（进液口、出液口、回液口）分别通总泵、通分泵、通储液器，称为"三通"。所以该电磁阀称为三位三通电磁阀，常写成 3/3 电磁阀。

项目一　汽车电子控制主动安全系统的检修

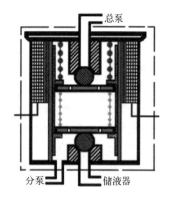
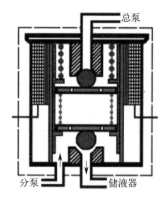

图 1-46 三位三通电磁阀保压状态　　　　　图 1-47 三位三通电磁阀减压状态

② 二位二通电磁阀。二位二通电磁阀的结构如图 1-48 所示，又分为二位二通常开电磁阀和二位二通常闭电磁阀。两种电磁阀均由阀门、衔铁、电磁线圈、回位弹簧等组成。

常态下，二位二通常开电磁阀阀门在弹簧张力作用下打开，二位二通常闭电磁阀阀门在弹簧张力作用下闭合。

二位二通常开电磁阀用于控制制动总泵到制动分泵的制动液通路，又称为二位二通常开进液电磁阀。

二位二通常闭电磁阀用于控制制动分泵到储液器的制动液回路，又称为二位二通常闭出液电磁阀。

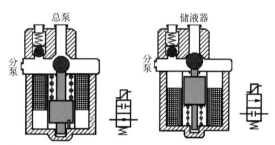

图 1-48 二位二通电磁阀结构

两个电磁阀配套使用，共同完成 ABS 工作中对制动压力调节的任务。

③ 二位三通电磁阀。二位三通电磁阀的结构如图 1-49 所示，由两个阀门（第一球阀和第二球阀）、衔铁、弹簧及电磁线圈等组成。二位三通电磁阀可用作戴维斯 MK II ABS 中的主电磁阀。

第一球阀（常闭阀门）用于控制助力室与内部储液室之间的制动液通路——高压控制。
第二球阀（常开阀门）用于控制储液筒与内部储液室之间的制动液通路——低压控制。
二位三通电磁阀的工作过程如下。

踏下制动踏板，ABS 不工作（电磁线圈未通电）时，第一球阀关闭，第二球阀打开，内部储液室与储液筒相通，低压制动液由制动总泵进入两前轮制动分泵，对两前轮实施低压制动。由于助力室在控制滑阀作用下且在踏下制动踏板的同时，储存了高压制动液，所以对两后轮实施高压制动。

ABS 工作（电磁线圈通电）时，第一球阀打开，接通助力室与内部储液室之间的高压制动液通路，第二球阀关闭，切断了储液筒与内部储液室之间的低压制动液通路，此时，前、后轮均为高压制动。

在制动过程中，增压、保压、减压的转换均由二位三通常开进液电磁阀和二位三通常闭出液电磁阀控制调节。

（2）回油泵与储液器

当电磁阀在减压过程中，从制动轮缸流出的制动液经储液器由回油泵泵回制动主缸。

储液器根据储存制动液压力的不同，分为低压储液器和高压储能器，分别配置在不同形

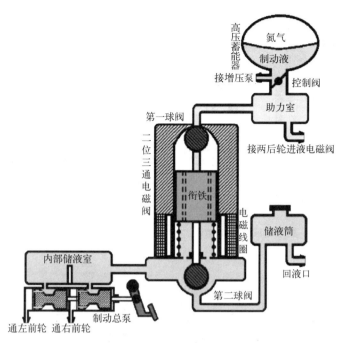

图 1-49 二位三通电磁阀结构图

式的制动压力调节系统中。

① 低压储液器与电动泵如图 1-50 所示。低压储液器，用来接纳 ABS 减压过程中从制动分泵回流的制动液，同时还对回流制动液的压力波动具有一定的衰减作用。

储液器内有一活塞和弹簧。减压时，回流的制动液压缩活塞克服弹簧张力下移，使容积增大，暂时存储制动液。

电动回液泵由直流电动机和柱塞泵组成。柱塞泵由柱塞、进出液阀及弹簧组成。当 ABS 工作（减压）时，根据 ECU 输出的指令，直流电动机带动凸轮转动，凸轮将驱动柱塞在泵筒内移动。柱塞上行时，储液器与制动分泵内具有一定压力的制动液进入柱塞泵筒。柱塞下行时，压开进液阀及泵筒底部的出液阀，将制动液泵回制动总泵出液口。

② 高压蓄能器与电动增压泵如图 1-51 所示。高压蓄能器下端，设有一个压力控制开关、一个压力警示开关，检测高能蓄压器下腔制动液压力。压力低于 15MPa 时，开关闭合，增压泵工作。压力达到 18MPa 时，开关打开，增压泵停止工作。

高能蓄压器用于储存制动中或 ABS 工作时所需的高压制动液。高压蓄能器多采用黑色气囊状球体。黑色气囊状球体被一个膜片分隔成两个互不相通的腔室。上腔为气室，充入氮气并具有一定的压力。下腔为液室，与电动增压泵液道相通，盛装由电动增压泵泵入的制动液。

压力警示开关设有两对开关触点，一对常开，一对常闭。当高压蓄能器下腔制动液压力低于 10.5MPa 时，常开触点闭合，点亮红色制动警示灯；同时常闭触点张开，该信号送给 ECU，关闭 ABS 并点亮黄褐色 ABS 警示灯。

循环式制动压力调节器的工作过程如下。

（1）增压（常规制动）过程

增压过程如图 1-52 所示。踏下制动踏板，由于电磁阀的进液阀开启，回液阀关闭，各电磁阀将制动总泵与各制动分泵之间的通路接通，制动总泵中的制动液将通过各电磁阀的进出液口进入各制动分泵，各制动分泵的制动液压力将随着制动总泵输出制动液压力的升高而升高。

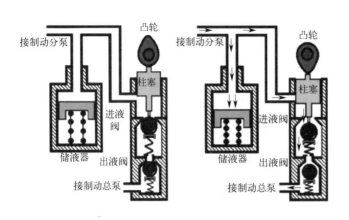

图 1-50 低压储液器与电动泵

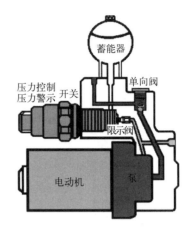

图 1-51 高压蓄能器与电动增压泵

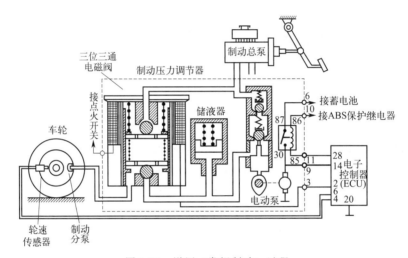

图 1-52 增压（常规制动）过程

（2）保压过程

如图 1-53 所示，当某车轮制动中，滑移率接近于 20% 时，ECU 输出指令，控制电磁阀线圈通过较小电流（约 2A），使电磁阀的进液阀关闭（回液阀仍关闭），保证该控制通道中的制动分泵制动压力保持不变。

（3）减压过程

如图 1-54 所示，当某车轮制动中，滑移率大于 20% 时，ECU 输出指令，控制电磁阀线圈通过较大电流（约 5A），使电磁阀的进液阀关闭、回液阀开启，制动分泵中的制动液将通过回液阀流入储液器，使制动压力减小。

与此同时，ECU 控制电动泵通电运转，将流入储液器的制动液泵回到制动总泵出液口。

2. 可变容积式制动压力调节器

液压控制可变容积式制动压力调节器如图 1-55 所示。

（1）特点

在汽车原有制动系统管路中增加一套液压控制装置，用于改变制动管路容积，实现增压—保压—减压的循环调节。这种制动压力调节系统的控制液压油路和 ABS 控制的制动液油路是相互隔开的。

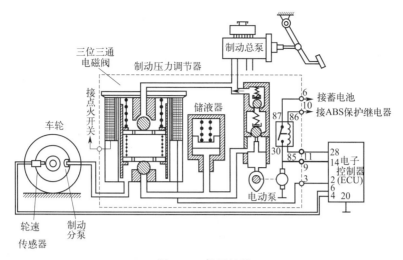

图 1-53 保压过程

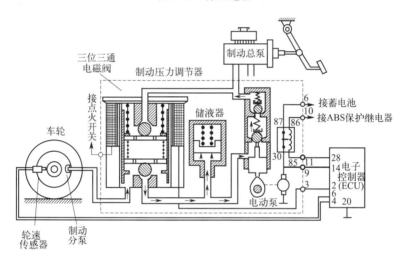

图 1-54 减压过程

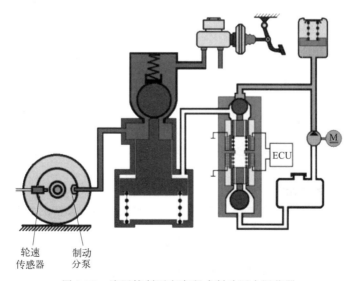

图 1-55 液压控制可变容积式制动压力调节器

（2）液压控制可变容积调压方式应用实例（本田车系 ABS）

液压控制可变容积调压方式应用如图 1-56 所示，4 个传感器、4 个通道、4 个车轮均为独立控制，制动压力调节器由电磁阀、调压缸、电动增压泵、储能器、压力开关组成。

液压控制可变容积调压方式的工作过程如下：踏下制动踏板，制动液由制动泵→A腔→开关阀→B腔→制动分泵。制动分泵制动液压力将随踏板力的增大而增大。

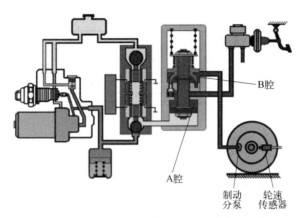

图 1-56　液压控制可变容积调压方式应用实例

滑移率趋近于 20% 时，ECU 控制输入电磁阀略通电后即关闭，输出电磁阀通电关闭。滑动活塞产生位移使开关阀关闭，A 腔与 B 腔隔断，B 腔容积不变，实现保压过程。

滑移率＞20% 时，ECU 控制输入电磁阀通电打开，输出电磁阀通电关闭。滑动活塞在控制液压作用下上移，使 B 腔容积增大，实现减压过程。

滑移率＜20% 时，ECU 控制输入电磁阀断电关闭，输出电磁阀断电打开。控制油液泄入储液罐，滑动活塞下移，使 B 腔容积减小，实现增压过程。

（3）微型电动机控制可变容积式制动压力调节器

微型电动机控制可变容积式制动压力调节器的特点是在汽车原有制动系统管路上增加一套控制装置，用于控制制动管路中容积的变化。这种制动压力的调节方式是由活塞在调压缸中所产生的位移直接改变制动管路的容积，实现增压—保压—减压的循环调节。其结构如图 1-57 所示，主要由调压缸和电磁阀组成。ABS 工作过程是单向阀、电磁阀均关闭，活塞在调压缸中运动，完成增压、保压、减压过程。

十、电子控制单元（ECU）

电子控制单元是汽车 ABS 防抱死制动系统的控制中心。它能够接收传感器的信号并进行分析，判断车轮是否抱死，然后向制动压力调节器发出制动压力控制指令。在某些车型上，为了使 ABS 系统结构紧凑，减少插头和线束，将电子控制单元就安装在制动压力调节装置上。

1. 电子控制单元的作用

当 ABS 起作用时，电子控制单元监测并控制制动系统的工作情况，即 ECU 具有对制动系统进行"监测"和"控制"两方面的功能。

（1）防抱死制动控制功能

对制动系统进行防抱死制动控制是电子控制单元的主要功能，ECU 接收各个车轮轮速传感器及其他传感器的输入信号，然后按照预先设置的控制逻辑进行处理和运算，从而形成

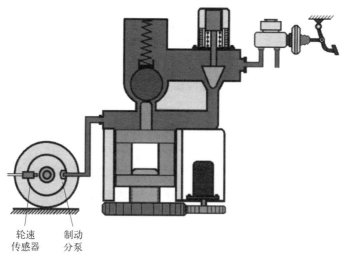

图 1-57 微型电动机控制可变容积式制动压力调节器

相应的控制指令,对执行机构进行控制,通过制动压力调节装置调节制动压力,防止各车轮抱死。

(2) 系统监测功能

对制动系统进行监测是电子控制单元的另一个功能,ECU 接收制动灯开关、压力开关以及其他各种信号来监测 ABS 工作是否正常,当 ECU 监测到 ABS 工作不正常时,会自动停止 ABS 工作并点亮 ABS 警告灯,以免因系统故障造成错误的控制结果。在部分利用液压制动的 ABS 中,ECU 还控制电动液压泵的工作。在正常情况下,发动机启动后,ABS 警告灯数秒后就应自动熄灭,否则说明 ABS 有故障。

2. ECU 的基本电路

ECU 内部电路结构主要由输入放大电路、运算电路、电磁阀控制电路以及安全保护电路等组成。

其中,电磁阀控制电路接收由运算电路输送来的电磁阀控制参数信号,由数字式控制指令转换为模拟式控制信号,并将控制信号放大后向电磁阀的电磁线圈提供不同的控制电流,以控制电磁阀的工作位置;安全保护电路主要包括稳压电源电路、电源监控电路、故障存储电路和继电器驱动电路 4 部分;稳压电源电路将汽车蓄电池或发电机提供的电源电压转变为 ECU 内部所需的稳定电压,并由电源监控电路对电源电压是否稳定在规定的范围进行监控;故障存储电路对向 ECU 各电路(输入电路、运算电路和电磁阀控制电路)输入的信号进行监控,并以故障码的形式将其检测到的故障存储在存储器中,以便诊断故障时调取;继电器驱动电路实际是一个报警电路,当故障存储电路检测到故障时,报警电路驱动相应的继电器,切断 ABS 电源电路使 ABS 停止工作,制动系统转入普通制动模式,同时点亮 ABS 警告灯提示驾驶员 ABS 出现故障。

3. ECU 软件简介

ABS 的电子控制单元的软件主要由防抱死控制和安全控制两部分组成。防抱死控制部分的功能是对经过输入电路预处理的车轮转速信号进行采样、计算和分析,并形成相应的控制指令。安全控制部分的功能是对系统的工作状态进行监控,将故障情况进行存储,并将系统自动关闭。

十一、ABS应用实例

ABS形式各异，但有两个方面是相同的。一方面，ABS工作车速必须达到一定值后，才会对制动过程中趋于抱死的车轮进行制动防抱死控制调节。另一方面，ABS都具有自诊断功能。一旦发生影响系统正常工作的故障时，ABS自动关闭，同时ABS警告灯点亮，常规制动仍可正常工作。

（一）博世ABS

1. 结构特点

制动压力调节器为分离式且独立安装；调压方式为循环式；控制方式为两前轮独立控制，两后轮按低选原则一同控制；电磁阀为三位三通电磁阀。

2. 制动压力调节过程

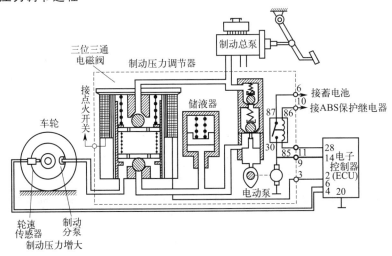

图1-58 制动压力增大过程

（1）制动压力增大

制动压力增大过程如图1-58所示，踏下制动踏板，由于电磁阀的进液阀开启，回液阀关闭，各电磁阀将制动总泵与各制动分泵之间的通路接通，制动总泵中的制动液将通过各电磁阀的进出液口进入各制动分泵，各制动分泵的制动液压力将随着制动总泵输出制动液压力的升高而升高，实现增压过程。

（2）制动压力保持

制动压力保持过程如图1-59所示，当某车轮制动中，滑移率接近于20%时，ECU输出指令，控制电磁阀线圈通过较小电流（约2A），使电磁阀的进液阀关闭（回液阀仍关闭），保证该控制通道中的制动分泵制动压力保持不变，实现保压过程。

（3）制动压力减小

制动压力减小过程如图1-60所示，当某车轮制动中，滑移率大于20%时，ECU输出指令，控制电磁阀线圈通过较大电流（约5A），使电磁阀的进液阀关闭回液阀开启，制动分泵中的制动液将通过回液阀流入储液器，使制动压力减小，实现减压过程。

与此同时，ECU控制电动泵通电运转，将流入储液器的制动液泵回到制动总泵出液口。

3. 电子控制系统控制过程

对图1-61所示的电子控制系统的控制过程分析如下。

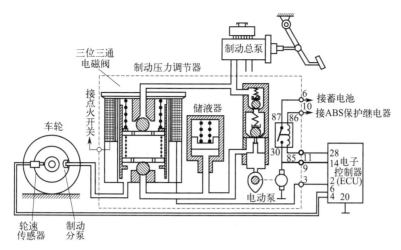

图 1-59 制动压力保持过程

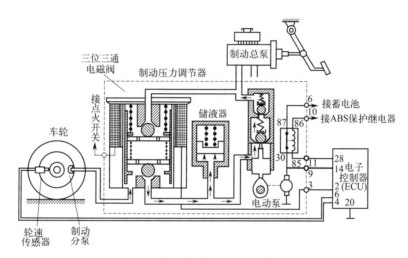

图 1-60 制动压力减小过程

（1）打开点火开关，ECU 进入自检

ABS 保护继电器线圈通电：蓄电池电压（12V）经触点送至 ECU 端子 1，触发自检，时间为 3~5s。自检中，ECU 端子 27、28 均未搭铁，电动泵继电器、电磁阀继电器常开触点均不闭合，电动泵及电磁阀均不工作。

（2）ABS 警告灯亮

ABS 警告灯亮后可能出现两种情况：灯亮 3~5s 后熄灭，说明系统正常；灯亮 3~5s 后不熄灭，说明系统有故障，ECU 关闭 ABS，汽车仅保持常规制动。

（3）自检正常，ABS 等待工作

ECU 端子 27 搭铁，接通电磁阀继电器线圈电路。电磁阀继电器线圈通电，铁芯产生吸力，常闭触点（30→87A）张开，ABS 警告灯熄灭；常开触点（30→87）闭合，蓄电池电压作用在 3 个三位三通电磁阀线圈及 ECU 端子 32 上。

（二）戴维斯 MK20-Ⅰ型 ABS

戴维斯 MK20-Ⅰ ABS 是戴维斯 MK Ⅱ ABS 的换代产品，是目前世界上比较新的一代 ABS 产品。以桑塔纳 2000GSi 轿车上装用的 MK20-Ⅰ ABS 为例说明其结构特点。

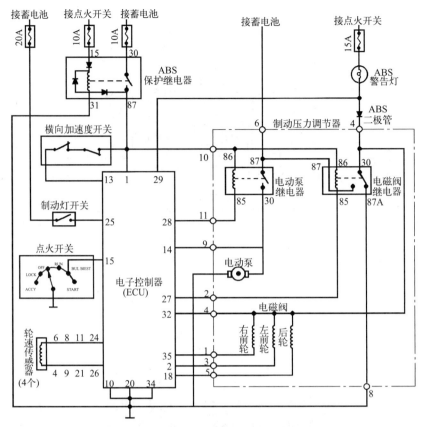

图 1-61　博世 ABS 电子控制系统

1. MK20-Ⅰ ABS 结构特点

① 采用模块式结构设计，将液压控制单元（储液器、电动回液泵、电磁阀）与电子控制单元集成为一体，使其结构更加紧凑。

② 电磁阀线圈设置于控制单元内部，节省连接导线。采用大功率集成电路直接驱动电磁阀及回液泵电动机，省去了电磁阀继电器。

③ 电子控制单元内部设有故障存储器，随车带有故障诊断接口，借助诊断仪调取故障码可以很方便地进行故障诊断。

④ MK20-Ⅰ ABS 采用四传感器、三通道控制系统，其控制原则是对两前轮进行独立控制，对两后轮按低选原则一同控制。

其目的是在制动过程中，确保后轮不会先于前轮抱死，从而获得良好的制动稳定性。

2. 主要组成与结构

（1）轮速传感器

桑塔纳 2000GSi 轿车上装有 4 个磁感应轮速传感器，每个轮速传感器均由传感器头和齿圈组成，如图 1-62 所示。

前轮轮速传感器齿圈（43 个凸齿）镶嵌在制动盘后，随制动盘一同旋转，传感器头安装在转向节上。后轮轮速传感器齿圈（43 个凸齿）安装在轮毂上，随轮毂一同旋转，传感器头则安装在固定支架上。

（2）控制模块

控制模块由液压控制单元和电子控制单元组成。液压控制单元由储液器、电动回液泵、

电磁阀等组成,如图1-63所示。

(3)故障警告灯

在仪表板及仪表板附加部件上装有两个故障警告灯,一个是ABS警告灯(K47),另一个是制动装置警告灯(K118)。

打开点火开关后,ABS警告灯亮约2s熄灭,说明自检结束的同时已启动ABS。若ABS警告灯常亮,说明ABS出现故障。

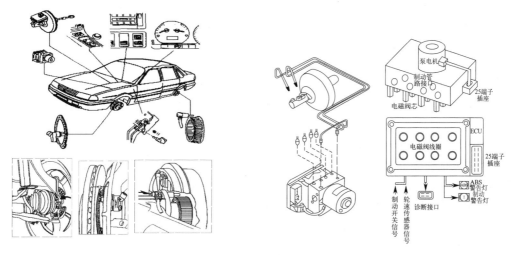

图1-62 桑塔纳2000GSi轿车上装用磁感应轮速传感器　　图1-63 桑塔纳2000GSi轿车ABS控制模块

3. 液压控制系统

桑塔纳2000GSi轿车上采用的MK20-Ⅰ ABS液压控制系统为对角线双回路控制系统,如图1-64所示。

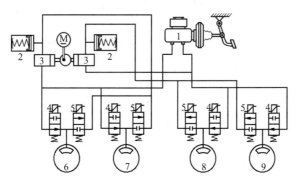

图1-64 桑塔纳2000GSi轿车MK20-Ⅰ ABS液压控制系统

任务实施

一、ABS的使用与检修

1. ABS的使用

(1)装有ABS的车辆容易出现的一些特殊现象

① 发动机启动后,有时发动机舱内会发出类似撞击的声音。

② 某些装有ABS的汽车在发动机启动时,踏下制动踏板会弹起,而在发动机熄火时,

制动踏板会下沉。

③ 制动时转动转向盘，会感到转向盘有轻微的振动。

④ 制动时，有时会感到制动踏板有轻微下沉或轻微振动，这是由于制动分泵在高速收放时高压的制动液被频繁挤压而产生的。

⑤ 高速行驶急转弯时，或在冰滑路面上行驶时，有时会出现制动警告灯亮起的现象。

⑥ 在积雪路面上制动时，有时制动距离较长。

⑦ 装有 ABS 的汽车在制动后期，车轮也会抱死，在地面留下拖滑的印痕，但与常规制动时的印痕有所不同。

（2）装备 ABS 的车辆的注意事项

① 要保持足够的制动距离。

② 切忌反复踩制动踏板。应在踩下制动踏板时，使施加在制动踏板上的力持续且稳定。

③ ABS 正常时，会产生液压工作噪声和制动踏板振动，这属于正常现象。在紧急制动时，应直接将制动踏板踩到底，且不放松。

④ 不要忘记控制转向盘。

⑤ 在行车中应留意仪表板上的 ABS 警告灯情况，如发现闪烁或长亮，说明已不具备 ABS 功能，但常规制动系统仍起作用，应尽快到修理厂检修。

⑥ 要保持装在车轮上的传感器探头及齿圈的清洁。

⑦ 应严格按规定的轮胎气压标准加气，同时要保持同轴轮胎气压的均衡，严禁使用不同规格的轮胎。

⑧ ABS 系统对制动液有严格的要求。添加或更换制动液应严格按照车辆使用说明书上的要求，禁止掺杂不同型号的制动液。

2. 检修 ABS 时应注意的事项

① 制动系统发生故障由 ABS 警告灯和制动装置警告灯指示。有时 ABS 警告灯和制动装置警告灯不亮，但制动效果仍不理想，则可能是系统放气不干净或在常规制动系统中存在故障。

② 制动不良时，先区分是机械故障还是 ABS 系统故障。鉴别方法：让汽车以常规制动方式工作，如制动不良故障消失，则说明为 ABS 系统故障，如制动不良故障依然存在，则为机械故障。

③ 确定为 ABS 故障后，应首先对 ABS 的外观进行检查，检查制动油路和泵及阀有无泄漏、导线的接头和插接器有无松脱、蓄电池是否亏电。在检查线路故障时，也不应漏检保险器。

④ 若外观检查正常，应用故障诊断仪或人工调取的方式查询故障代码，检查故障所在。

⑤ 不要轻易拆检 ECU 和液压控制器件，如果怀疑其有问题，可用替换法检查。

在拆检 ABS 液压控制器件时，应先进行卸压，以免高压油喷出伤人。卸压方法是先关闭点火开关，反复踩制动踏板 20 次以上，直到感觉踩制动踏板的力明显增加变得非常硬时为止。

⑥ 开始维修前，应关闭点火开关，从蓄电池上拆下负极线。特别注意拔出 ABS 电气插头之前，必须关闭点火开关。

⑦ 拆卸前必须彻底清洁连接点和支撑面，清洁时不要使用汽油、稀释剂等类似的清洁剂，拆下的零件必须放在干净的地方，并覆盖好。

⑧ 把 ABS ECU 和液压控制单元分开后，必须把液压控制单元放在专用支架上，以免在搬运中碰坏阀体。

⑨ 制动系统打开后不要使用压缩空气，也不要移动车辆。
⑩ 拆下的部件如果不能立刻完成修理工作，必须小心地盖好或者用塞子封闭，以保证部件的清洁。
⑪ 更换配件时，必须使用质量良好的配件。配件要在安装前才从包装内取出。
⑫ 一定要按维修手册的要求进行安装调整。
⑬ 维修 ABS 制动系统作业完成后，按规定加装制动液，并对系统进行放气。
⑭ 在试车中，至少进行一次紧急制动。当 ABS 正常工作时，会在制动踏板上感到有反弹，并可感觉到车速迅速降低而且平稳。

二、ABS 故障的一般检查方法

1. 车速传感器故障的检查

（1）故障现象

车轮速度传感器出现故障，传感器不一定损坏，往往是传感器磁头脏污，传感器与齿圈之间的气隙过大或过小，传感器插接件松动。

（2）检查方法

① 检查车轮速度传感器的电阻值：将点火开关置于关闭（OFF）位置；举升汽车；分别拆下前后轮及传感器的连接器；对应不同车型的维修手册，用数字多用表检查是否有异常。

② 检查车轮速度传感器的信号电压：举升汽车；将点火开关置于打开（ON）位置；以慢速度转动被检查车轮；对应不同车型的维修手册，用数字多用表检查是否有问题。如有问题就要按照不同车型维修手册的要求进行更换。

③ 车轮速度传感器的齿圈的检查：检查是否有变形、断齿等现象，是否有泥土、脏污、铁石等异物堵塞。应根据不同情况进行更换或清洁。

2. ECU 的检查

① 检查 ECU 线束插接器、连接导线有无松动。

② 检查 ECU 线束插接器各端子的电压值、波形或电阻，如与标准值不符且与之相连的部件和线路正常，应更换 ECU 后再试。

③ 直接采用替换法检验，即在检查其他部件无故障时，可用新的 ECU 代替原 ECU，如故障消失，则为 ECU 故障。

3. 压力调节器的检查

（1）常见故障

压力调节器的常见故障为电磁阀线圈不良和阀泄漏。

（2）检查方法

① 用电阻表检查电磁阀线圈的电阻，若电阻无穷大或过小，则电磁阀有故障。

② 给电磁阀加载其工作电压进行实验，如不能正常动作，则应更换。

③ 解体后检查。

4. ABS 控制继电器的检查

（1）常见故障

ABS 控制继电器的常见故障为触点接触不良和继电器线圈不良等。

（2）检查方法

① 对继电器施加正常工作电压，若能正常动作，再检测继电器触点间的电压和电阻，正常情况下，触点闭合时电压为零。电压大于 0.5V，说明触点接触不良。

② 继电器线圈电阻应在正常范围内。

三、ABS 制动液添加与补充

1. 要求原则

① 应选用厂家要求的制动液。
② 应选用具有抗氧化性的制动液。
③ 应选用对橡胶件有较好润滑作用的制动液，不能使橡胶件膨胀。
④ 应选用对金属腐蚀性小的制动液。
⑤ 应选用具有较低的凝固点、较高的沸点和吸水性的制动液，必须具有较好的润滑性能，适应液压系统的橡胶及金属件。

2. 选用制动液

ABS 制动液一般选用 DOT3、DOT4，不能使用 DOT5 硅铜制动液，制动液用错会造成制动元件过度磨损和其他情况。

3. 制动液的更换周期

ABS 系统的制动液建议每两年更换一次。

注意事项：要经常检查制动液储液室液面高度，液面应在允许最高液面与最低液面之间。

四、ABS 的放气

1. ABS 渗入空气的直观判断

若一次踏下制动踏板，软弱无力，连续踏下数次，制动踏板逐渐升高，感觉制动踏板很硬，说明 ABS 中渗入空气。

2. ABS 渗入空气的危害性

ABS 中若有空气，会严重干扰制动压力调节，而使 ABS 系统的作用丧失，会导致制动效果下降，制动反应迟钝，甚至制动失灵。

3. ABS 的放气

对 ABS 的放气，要按规定进行，放气的顺序如下。

① 使用专用橡胶管的一端接在某一放气螺钉下，而另一端插入盛有半瓶制动液的玻璃瓶中。
② 反复踏制动踏板，将制动踏板踏住不动，按顺序先远后近打开制动分泵放气螺钉后马上扭紧，玻璃瓶中应有气泡产生，多次重复这一过程，每次间隔 2~5s，直至玻璃瓶中没有气泡产生，制动踏板升至最高位置（约和加速踏板平齐），如图 1-65 所示。

(a) 反复踏制动踏板

(b) 有气泡产生

(c) 无气泡产生

图 1-65 放气操作过程

③ 补充制动液。

4. ABS 的放气原则

ABS 的放气原则通常是先远后近、先下后上逐个车轮进行放气。

5. ABS 的放气顺序

放气顺序为从右后轮缸到左后轮缸、从左后轮缸到右前轮缸、从右前轮缸到左前轮缸。

例如，达科（Ⅵ）ABS 的放气，一般程序如下。
① 找到前轮放气螺钉。
② 在前轮放气螺钉上安一泄油管。
③ 慢慢拧松放气螺钉 1/2～3/4 转。
④ 制动液流出，若没有气泡时就关闭。
⑤ 找到后轮放气螺钉按步骤进行放气，如图 1-66 所示。

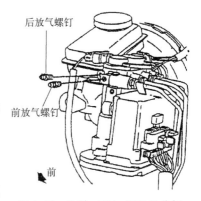

图 1-66 达科（Ⅵ）ABS 的放气

五、ABS 的故障案例诊断过程

根据任务资料中的故障现象，首先应检查 ABS 液压调节器储液器的制动液液面，如正常，将点火开关置于 OFF 位，短接杂物箱下方的诊断插座两端子，再将点火开关置于 ON 位，读取故障码，结果无代码输出。

本田雅阁 ABS 由 ABS ECU、液压调节器、轮速传感器、ABS 警告灯和诊断插座等组成。液压调节采用变容原理，液压调节器由油泵、蓄压器、压力开关、储液器、6 个电磁阀（3 个进油电磁阀的输入阀、3 个回油电磁阀）和 4 个滑动活塞组成。进油阀（输入阀）为常闭电磁阀，回油阀（输出阀）为常开电磁阀。在整个制动过程中，油泵产生的高压油液并不与制动轮缸相通，压力的调节是通过滑动活塞移动来实现的，滑动活塞的移动则是由控制活塞控制，而控制活塞的移动则是由 ECU 指令电磁阀动作，使高压油液进入或停止进入控制活塞下方，或是使控制活塞下腔内的高压油回到储液器来实现的；常规制动状态时，电磁阀均不通电，制动轮缸的压力随主缸的压力上升而上升；进、回油阀均通电，则为减压状态；进油阀断电关闭，同时回油阀通电关闭时为压力保持状态；ABS ECU 根据来自轮速传感器的信号确定车轮有无抱死，然后给液压调节器中的电磁阀发出指令，进行防抱死制动控制。当油压不足时，ABS ECU 同时指令油泵电动机运转。ABS ECU 还通过制动灯开关、手制动灯开关和压力开关来监视 ABS 的工作是否正常，并能进行自我诊断。

基于以上工作原理，考虑到该车每次启动后，ABS 油泵电动机都运转较长时间，油泵电动机停止运转后 ABS 警告灯点亮。这说明有两种可能：一是初次启动时，ABS 油压不足，所以油泵电动机运转，发动机熄火后接着再启动，油泵仍需工作，说明前一次油泵工作并没能给系统建立足够的油压，屡次启动都是如此，说明油压不能建立；二是压力开关在油压足够高时仍不能接通，ABS ECU 判定油压过低而使油泵在发动机每次启动后较长时间运转。

为确定是否油压过低，拧开 ABS 液压调节器上的放气螺钉，启动发动机，此时油泵电动机运转，放气螺钉处只能喷出高度约 30mm 的油柱，油泵工作一定时间后，再拧松放气螺钉，则几乎无油流出。从理论上来说，油泵能产生高达 20MPa 左右的压力，且有蓄压器，即使油泵电动机停止运转后，在一定时间内也能保持足够的油压。此种情况说明油压过低了。

观察储液器，油泵运转时，回油口不见回油，而进油口反而有反流的现象。问题很可能出在柱塞式油泵本身的进油阀或柱塞与柱塞套筒上。拆下液压调节器总成，分解柱塞泵，发现进、出油阀的钢球及阀座均已磨损，柱塞上的皮圈也老化了，于是更换柱塞泵组件，直接通电给油泵电动机，拧开放气螺钉，此时喷出油柱达 200mm 高，装复后放气，启动发动机，故障排除。

原来，这种 ABS 在油压达到标准时，油泵停止工作，油压过低时，油泵工作，而工作一定时间后如油压仍不足，ABS ECU 便令油泵停止工作，同时将 ABS 警告灯点亮，警告驾驶员 ABS 有故障，应检修。后来出厂的装有这种 ABS 的本田车如果出现此类故障，一般可

以读到故障码 10。

习题测试

选择题

1. 当滑移率为 100% 时，横向附着系数降为（　　）。
   A. 100%　　　B. 50%　　　C. 0　　　D. 都不正确
2. 为了避免灰尘与飞溅的水、泥等对传感器工作的影响，在安装前需对车速传感器加注（　　）。
   A. 机油　　　B. 工作液　　C. 润滑脂　　D. ATF 油
3. 循环式制动压力调节器是在制动总缸与轮缸之间（　　）一个电磁阀，直接控制轮缸的制动压力。
   A. 串联　　　B. 并联　　　C. A、B 都可以　　D. A、B 均不正确

任务二　汽车驱动防滑系统的检修

【学习目标】

知识要求：了解 ASR 的作用、组成、原理及检修方法。

能力要求：能够依据维修手册并使用常用工具、量具对 ASR 进行基本检查，能对 ASR 常见故障进行诊断与修复。

任务导入

皇冠 3.0 轿车，仪表板上 ASR 故障灯常亮。通过了解，故障现象在车辆行驶一段时间后出现，同时 ASR 故障灯点亮；关掉点火开关再重新启动，仪表板上的 ASR 故障灯又会熄灭；但再行驶一段路程，ASR 故障灯又会重新点亮。

知识准备

一、概述

1. ASR 与 ABS 的比较

ABS 和 ASR 都是用来控制车轮相对于地面的滑动，以提高车轮与地面之间的附着力。但 ABS 控制的是汽车制动时车轮的"滑移"，主要是用来提高汽车的制动效能和制动时的方向稳定性；而 ASR 是控制汽车行驶时驱动车轮的"滑转"，用于提高汽车起步、加速及在光滑路面行驶时的牵引力和确保行驶稳定性。

虽然 ASR 也可以和 ABS 一样，通过控制车轮的制动力来控制驱动车轮相对地面的滑动，但 ASR 只对驱动车轮实施制动控制。

ABS 一般在车速很低（<5km/h）时不起作用，而 ASR 一般在车速很高（80～120km/h）时不起作用。

2. 滑转率与附着系数的关系

汽车在驱动过程中，驱动车轮可能相对于路面发生滑转。滑转率与附着系数之间存在着密切关系，图 1-67 所示为滑转率与附着系数之间的关系曲线。从图中可以看出：

① 与汽车在制动过程中的滑转率相同，在汽车的驱动过程中，车轮与路面间的附着系数的大小随着滑转率的变化而变化。

② 附着系数随路面的不同呈大幅度变化。在干路面或湿路面上，当滑转率在 20% 左右时，车轮具有最大的附着系数。

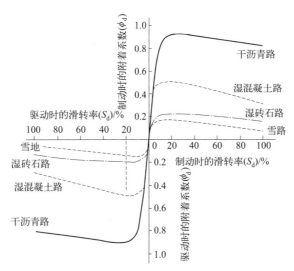

图 1-67 滑转率与附着系数之间的关系

上述趋势无论是制动还是驱动几乎一样。因此 ASR 也可以通过控制驱动车轮与路面的滑转率来控制其与路面间的附着系数，来实现汽车在行驶过程中的防滑控制，以保持汽车行驶过程中的操纵稳定性和最佳的驱动性能。

3. ASR 的作用

汽车驱动防滑系统（ASR）是继防抱死制动系统（ABS）之后用于车轮防滑的电子控制系统，其作用是防止汽车起步、加速和在光滑路面行驶时驱动轮的滑转。

当车轮转动而车身不动或是汽车的速度低于转动车轮的轮缘速度时，轮胎与地面之间就有相对的滑动，这种滑动称为"滑转"，以区别于汽车制动时车轮抱死而产生的车轮"滑移"。只有驱动车轮才会产生"滑转"，而所有车轮（包括驱动轮和从动轮）都可能产生"滑移"。

4. ASR 的类型

ASR 按控制方式可分为差速制动控制、发动机输出功率控制、差速制动控制和发动机输出功率综合控制 3 种类型。

（1）差速制动控制

当驱动车轮单边滑转时，控制计算机输出控制信号，使差速制动阀和制动压力调节器动作，对滑转车轮施加制动力，使车轮的滑转率控制在目标范围之内。这时，非滑转车轮仍有正常的驱动力，从而提高了汽车在滑溜路面的起步和加速能力及行驶方向的稳定性。

这种控制方式的作用类似于差速锁，在一边驱动车轮陷于泥坑或完全失去驱动能力时，对其制动后，另一边的驱动车轮仍能发挥其驱动力，使汽车能驶离泥坑。当两边的驱动车轮都滑转，但滑转率不同的情况下，则对两边驱动车轮施以不同的制动力。

（2）发动机输出功率控制

在汽车起步、加速时若加速踏板踩得过猛，会因为驱动力过大而出现两边的驱动车轮都滑转的情况，这时，ASR 控制计算机输出控制信号，控制发动机的功率输出，以抑制驱动车轮的滑转。发动机功率控制可以通过改变节气门的开度、调节喷油器的喷油量和改变点火

时间等方法来实现。

（3）差速制动和发动机输出功率综合控制

ASR 采用差速制动控制和发动机输出功率控制相结合的综合控制系统，控制效果更为理想。汽车在行驶过程中，路面的光滑程度千差万别，驱动力的状态也是不断变化的，综合控制系统可根据发动机的状况和车轮滑转的实际情况采取相应的控制措施。

二、ASR 的基本组成及工作原理

1. ASR 的基本组成

ASR 的基本组成如图 1-68 所示。

2. ASR 的工作原理

ASR 也被称为 TCS（牵引力控制系统）或 TRC，可以通过调节作用于驱动车轮的驱动力矩和制动力矩，在驱动过程中防止驱动车轮发生滑转。

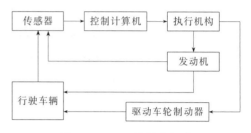

图 1-68　ASR 的基本组成

调节作用于驱动车轮的驱动力矩可以通过调节发动机的输出转矩、变速器传动比、差速器锁紧系数等方面实现。目前，调节变速器传动比和差速器锁紧系数的方式在 ASR 中尚少采用，而调节发动机的输出转矩可通过调节节气门开度、点火提前角、燃油喷射量以及中断燃油喷射和点火来实现。由于发动机已经实现了电子控制，因此，可以通过发动机电子控制系统对发动机的点火和供油进行控制，进而对发动机的输出转矩进行调节。目前在 ASR 中通常通过控制节气门开度和点火提前角的方式调节发动机的输出转矩，从而对作用于驱动车轮的驱动力矩进行调节。

为了使驱动车轮的转速迅速降低，或者使两侧驱动车轮获得不同的牵引力，通常 ASR 都可以通过对驱动车轮施加一定的制动力矩得以实现。在 ASR 中为了确定驱动车轮是否滑转，可以利用 ABS 中的车轮转速传感器获得车轮的转速信号。ASR 电子控制装置既可是独立的，也可与 ABS 共用。ASR 的制动压力调节装置通常与 ABS 的制动压力调节装置共用，为了控制节气门开度，通常设有电动控制的副节气门及节气门开度传感器。点火提前角的控制则通过发动机电子控制系统进行。因此，ASR 通常都与 ABS 和发动机电子控制系统交织在一起，此外 ASR 中都具有 ASR 关闭指示灯和 ASR 工作指示灯。

图 1-69 所示为一种较为典型的具有制动防抱死和驱动防滑转功能的 ABS/ASR 防滑控制系统。其中的 ASR 与 ABS 共用车轮速度传感器和电子控制装置，只在通往驱动车轮制动轮缸的制动管路中增设一个 ASR 制动压力调节装置，在由加速踏板控制的主节气门上方增设一个由步进电动机控制的副节气门，并在主、副节气门处各设置一个节气门开度传感器，即可实现驱动防滑转控制。

图 1-69 所示 ABS/ASR 中的 ASR 在汽车驱动过程中，ABS/ASR 电子控制装置根据各车轮转速传感器产生的车轮转速信号，确定驱动车轮的滑转率和汽车的参考速度。当 ABS/ASR 电子控制装置判定驱动车轮的滑转率超过设定的限值时，就使驱动副节气门的步进电动机转动，减小副节气门的开度。此时，即使主节气门的开度不变，发动机的进气量也会因副节气门开度的减小而减少，使发动机的输出转矩减小，驱动车轮上的驱动力矩就会随之减小。如果驱动车轮的滑转率仍未降低到设定的控制范围内，ABS/ASR 电子控制装置又会控制 ASR 制动压力调节装置和 ABS 制动压力装置，对驱动车轮施加一定的制动压力，就会有制动力矩作用于驱动车轮。

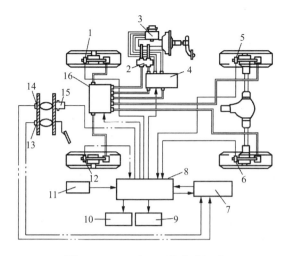

图 1-69 ABS/ASR 的典型组成

1—右前车轮转速传感器；2—比例阀和差压阀；3—制动主缸；4—ASR 制动压力调节装置；5—右后车轮转速传感器；6—左后车轮转速传感器；7—发动机/变速器电子控制装置；8—ABS/ASR 电子控制装置；9—ASR 关闭指示灯；10—ASR 工作指示灯；11—ASR 选择开关；12—左前车轮转速传感器；13—主节气门开度传感器；14—副节气门开度传感器；15—副节气门制动步进电动机；16—ABS 制动压力调节装置

图 1-70 所示 ABS/ASR 中的 ASR 制动压力调节装置主要包括制动供能装置和电磁控制阀总成两部分，制动供能装置主要由电动泵和蓄能器组成，电磁控制阀总成主要由 3 个二位二通电磁阀组成。它们与 ASR 制动压力调节装置共同组成制动液压系统。

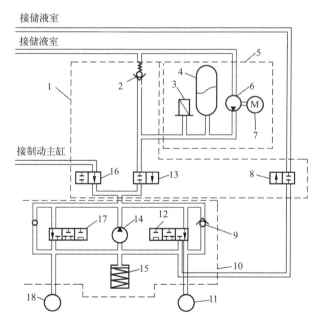

图 1-70 ASR 制动液压系统

1—ASR 电磁阀总成；2—单向阀；3—压力开关；4—蓄能器；5—制动供能装置；6—泵；7—电动机；8—电磁阀Ⅰ；9—单向阀；10—ABS 制动压力调节装置；11—左后驱动车轮；12—电磁阀Ⅳ；13—电磁阀Ⅱ；14—回液泵；15—储液器；16—电磁阀Ⅲ；17—电磁阀Ⅴ；18—右后驱动车轮

当 ABS/ASR 电子控制装置判定需要对驱动车轮施加制动力矩时，ABS/ASR 电子控制

装置就使 ASR 制动压力调节装置中的 3 个二位二通电磁阀都通电，电磁阀Ⅲ将制动主缸至后制动轮缸的制动管路封闭，电磁阀Ⅱ将蓄能器至 ABS 制动压力调节装置的制动管路连通，电磁阀Ⅰ将 ABS 制动压力调节装置至储液室的制动管路连通。

蓄能器中具有一定压力的制动液经过处于开启状态的电磁阀Ⅱ、电磁阀Ⅳ和Ⅴ进入两后制动轮缸，驱动车轮的制动力矩随着制动轮缸制动压力的增大而增大。当 ABS/ASR 电子控制装置判定需要保持两驱动车轮的制动力矩时，ABS/ASR 电子控制装置就使 ABS 制动压力调节装置中的两个三位二通电磁阀Ⅳ和Ⅴ的电磁线圈中通过较小的电流，使电磁阀Ⅳ和Ⅴ都处于中间位置，将两后制动轮缸的进、出液管路都封闭，两后制动轮缸的制动压力就保持一定。当 ABS/ASR 电子控制装置判定需要减小两驱动车轮的制动力矩时，就使电磁阀Ⅳ和Ⅴ的电磁线圈中都通过较大的电流，电磁阀Ⅳ和Ⅴ分别将两后制动轮缸的进液管路封闭，而将两后制动轮缸的出液管路连通，两后制动轮缸中的制动液就会经电磁阀Ⅳ和Ⅴ、电磁阀Ⅰ流回制动主缸储液室，两后制动轮缸的制动压力就会减小。在 ASR 制动压力调节过程中，ABS/ASR 电子控制装置根据车轮转速传感器输入的车轮转速信号，对驱动车轮的运动状态进行连续监测，通过控制电磁阀Ⅳ和Ⅴ的通电情况，使后制动轮缸的制动压力循环往复地进行增大—保持—减小过程，从而将驱动车轮的滑转率控制在设定的理想范围之内。如果 ABS/ASR 电子控制装置判定需要对两驱动车轮的制动力矩进行不同控制时，ABS/ASR 电子控制装置就对电磁阀Ⅳ和Ⅴ进行分别控制，使两后制动轮缸的制动压力进行各自独立调节。

当 ABS/ASR 电子控制装置判定无需对驱动车轮实施防滑转控制时，ABS/ASR 电子控制装置使各个电磁阀均不再通电，各电磁阀恢复到图 1-70 所示的状态。后制动轮缸中的制动液可经电磁阀Ⅳ和Ⅴ、电磁阀Ⅲ流回制动主缸，驱动车轮的制动力矩将完全消除，在解除驱动车轮制动的同时，ABS/ASR 电子控制装置还控制步进电动机转动，将副节气门完全开启。

目前，在各种车型上装备的 ASR 的具体结构和工作过程不尽相同，但在以下几个方面却是相同的。

① ASR 可以由驾驶员通过 ASR 选择开关对其是否进入工作状态进行选择，在 ASR 进行防滑转调节时，ASR 工作指示灯会自动点亮，如果通过 ASR 选择开关将 ASR 关闭，ASR 关闭指示灯会自动点亮。

② ASR 处于关闭状态时，副节气门将自动处于全开位置；ASR 制动压力调节装置将不会影响制动系统的正常工作。

③ 如果 ASR 处于防滑转调节过程中，驾驶员踩下制动踏板进行制动时，ASR 将会自动退出防滑转调节过程，而不影响制动过程的进行。

④ ASR 通常只在一定的车速范围内才进行防滑转调节，而当车速达到一定值以后（如 120km/h 或 80km/h），ASR 将会自动退出防滑转调节过程。

⑤ ASR 在其工作车速范围内通常具有不同的优先选择性，在车速较低时以提高牵引力作为优先选择。此时，对两驱动车轮施加的制动力矩可以不同，即对两后制动轮缸的制动压力进行独立调节。而在车速较高时则以提高行驶方向稳定性为优先选择，此时，对两驱动车轮施加的制动力矩将是相同的，即对两后制动轮缸的制动压力一同进行调节。

⑥ ASR 都具有自诊断功能，一旦发现存在影响系统正常工作的故障时，ASR 将会自动关闭，并向驾驶员发出警告信号。

三、典型 ASR 结构

1. 丰田 ASR 结构特点

丰田车系将 ASR 称为 TRC，丰田 ABS/TRC 具有制动防抱死和驱动防滑转功能。在制

动过程中，采用流通调压方式对 4 个控制通道进行防抱死制动压力调节，在驱动过程中，通过调节节气门的开度和对驱动车轮介入制动，进行驱动防滑转控制。

丰田 ABS/TRC 主要由车轮转速传感器、ABS/TRC 电子控制装置、制动压力调节装置、TRC 隔离电磁阀总成、TRC 制动供能总成、主副节气门开度传感器、副节气门控制步进电动机等组成，如图 1-71 所示。丰田 ABS/TRC 在汽车的 4 个车轮上各安装一个电磁感应式车轮转速传感器，将各个车轮的转速信号输入 ABS/TRC 电子控制装置。

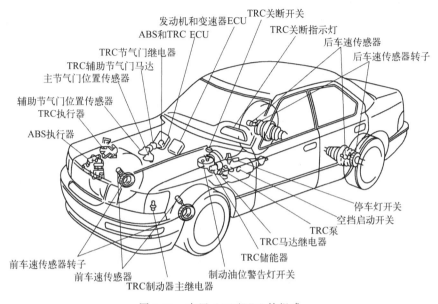

图 1-71 丰田 ABS/TRC 的组成

2. 丰田 TRC 工作原理

在驱动过程中，如果 ABS/TRC 电子控制装置根据车轮转速传感器输入的车轮转速信号判定驱动车轮的滑转率超过控制门限值时，ABS/TRC 防滑控制系统就进入驱动防滑转控制过程。ABS/TRC 电子控制装置将使副节气门控制步进电动机通电转动，将副节气门的开度减小，减少进入发动机的进气量，使发动机的输出转矩减小。当 ABS/TRC 电子控制装置判定需要对驱动车轮进行制动介入时，将使 TRC 隔离电磁阀总成中的 3 个隔离电磁阀通电，使制动主缸隔离电磁阀处于断流状态，而使蓄能器隔离电磁阀和储液室隔离电磁阀处于通流状态，蓄能器中具有压力的制动液就会进入后制动轮缸，后制动轮缸的制动压力随之增大。在驱动防滑转制动介入过程中，ABS/TRC 电子控制装置可以像制动防抱死控制一样，通过独立地控制两个后调压电磁阀的通过电流，对两个后制动轮缸的制动压力进行增大、保持和减小调节。

任务实施

一、ASR 的故障检修

1. ASR 检修注意事项

目前，大多数驱动防滑系统都具有很高的工作可靠性，通常无需对其进行定期的特别维护，但在使用、维护和检修过程中，应特别注意以下几个方面。

① 在点火开关处于点火位置时，不要拆装系统中的电气元件和线束插头，以免损坏电子控制装置。拆装系统中的电气元件和线束插头时，应先将点火开关断开。

② 不可向电子控制装置供给过高的电压，否则容易损坏电子控制装置，所以，切不可用充电机启动发动机，也不要在蓄电池与汽车电器连接的情况下，对蓄电池进行充电。

③ 电子控制装置受到碰撞和敲击也极容易引起损坏，因此，要注意使电子控制装置免受碰撞和敲击。

④ 高温环境也容易损坏电子控制装置，所以，在对汽车进行烤漆作业时，应将电子控制装置从车上拆下。另外，在对系统中的电气元件或线路进行焊接时，也应将线束插头从电子控制装置上拆下。

⑤ 不要让油污沾染电子控制装置，特别是电子控制装置的端子，否则会使线束插头接触不良，影响系统的正常工作。不要用砂纸打磨系统中各插头的端子，否则也会造成接触不良。

⑥ 在蓄电池电压过低时，系统将不能进入工作状态，因此，要注意对蓄电池的电压进行检查，特别是当汽车长时间停驶后初次启动时更要注意。

⑦ 不要使车轮转速传感器和传感器齿圈沾染油污或其他脏污；否则，车轮转速传感器产生的车轮转速信号就可能不够准确，影响系统的控制精度，甚至使系统无法正常工作。另外，不要敲击转速传感器；否则，很容易导致传感器发生消磁现象，从而影响系统的正常工作。

⑧ 由于在很多具有防滑制动功能的制动系统中，都有供给防抱死制动压力调节所需能量的蓄能器，所以，在对这类制动系统的液压系统进行维修作业时，应首先使蓄能器中的高压制动液完全释放，以免高压制动液喷出伤人。在释放蓄能器中的高压制动液时，先将点火开关断开，然后反复地踩下和放松制动踏板，直到制动踏板变得很硬时为止。另外，在制动液压系统完全装好以前，不能接通点火开关，以免电动泵通电运转。

⑨ 具有防滑控制功能的制动系统应使用专用的管路，因为制动系统往往具有很高的压力，如果使用非专用的管路极易损坏。

⑩ 大多数驱动防滑系统中的车轮转速传感器、电子控制装置和制动压力调节装置都是不可修复的，如果发生损坏，应该进行整体更换。

⑪ 在对制动液压系统进行维修以后，或者在使用过程中发觉制动踏板变软时，应按照要求的方法和顺序对制动系统进行空气排除。

⑫ 应尽量选用汽车生产厂家推荐的轮胎，如要换用其他型号的轮胎，应该选用与原车所用轮胎的外径、附着性能和转动惯量相近的轮胎，但不能混用不同规格的轮胎，因为这样会影响驱动防滑系统的控制效果。

2. ASR故障码的读取与清除

（1）系统的自诊断和故障保险功能

驱动防滑系统大都具有自诊断和故障保险功能，当点火开关开始处于点火位置时，电子控制装置将会自动地对自身、车轮转速传感器、制动压力调节装置中的电气元件（如电磁阀、电动机）、继电器等进行静态测试。在此期间，防抱死警告灯（或者包括防滑转警告灯）将会自动点亮，由此可以检查防抱死警示灯及其线路是否存在故障。系统静态自检持续的时间很短，一般只需3～5s。在自检过程中，如果电子控制装置发现系统中存在故障时，电子控制装置将会以故障码的形式存储、记忆故障情况，防抱死警告灯将会持续点亮，防滑控制系统将不进入工作状态，汽车的制动系统恢复为常规制动系统。在自检过程中如果电子控制装置未发现系统中有故障存在，在自检过程结束以后，防抱死警告灯将会自动熄灭。

在汽车的速度达到一定值时，例如5km/h或8km/h，驱动防滑系统的电子控制装置还

要对系统中的一些电气元件（如车轮转速传感器、电磁阀和电动泵等）进行动态测试。在动态测试时，如果发现系统中有故障存在，电子控制装置将会以故障码的形式存储、记忆故障情况，并使防抱死警告灯持续点亮，汽车的制动系统将恢复为常规制动系统。

此外，电子控制装置在系统处于工作状态期间对系统中的电气元件进行监测，检查系统中是否存在故障，一旦发现系统中存在故障，电子控制装置将会以故障码的形式存储、记忆系统的故障情况，并使系统退出工作状态，防抱死警告灯也会持续点亮。

总之，当防抱死警告灯持续点亮时就表明系统因故障已退出工作状态，已将故障情况以故障码的形式存储、记忆。但是，并非系统中的所有故障都可由电子控制装置检查出来，因此，即使防抱死警告灯未持续点亮，但发觉系统的工作不正常时，也需对系统进行检查。

（2）故障诊断仪器和工具

在多数驱动防滑系统中，可以通过跨接诊断插座中相应的端子，根据防抱死警告灯（或电子控制装置上的发光二极管）的闪烁情况读取故障码。所以，在故障码读取时，往往需要有合适的跨接线，跨接线是两端带有插接端子的一段导线，也有的跨接线在中间设有保险管，跨接线如图1-72所示。

故障码只是代表着故障情况的一系列代码，要确切地了解故障情况，还须根据维修手册查对故障码所代表的故障情况。另外，要正确地对系统进行故障诊断和排除也需维修手册作参考，因此，维修手册是故障诊断和维修过程中最为重要的工具。

对驱动防滑系统进行检查时，多用表是基本的测试工具，由于指针式多用表能够反映电参数的动态变化，所以更适合于防滑控制系统的电路检查。另外也可以使用一些更为专用的电参数测试仪器（如多踪示波器等），更为方便、深入地对系统进行检查。

在大部分汽车上，驱动防滑系统电子控制装置的端子没有标号，使确定所要测试的端子变得较为困难，特别是当向一些特定的端子加入电压时，如果电压加入有误，可能会损坏系统中的一些电气元件。另外，如果直接从线束插头的端子上对系统进行测试，不仅影响测试结果的准确性，可能还会使端子发生变形或损坏，为此，可以使用图1-73所示的接线端子盒。由于各种驱动防滑系统线束插头中的端子数目、端子号排列、插头形式不尽相同，因此，所用的接线端子盒也就不同。

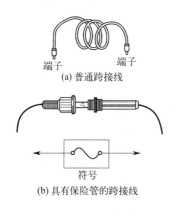

图1-72 跨接线

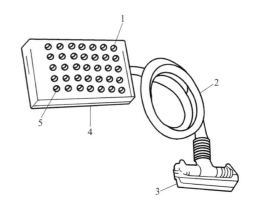

图1-73 接线端子盒

1—端子1；2—线束；3—接线盒线束端子；
4—接线端子盒束；5—端子35

如图1-74所示，对驱动防滑系统进行电路测试时，将系统的线束插头从电子控制装置上卸下，再将接线端子盒的线束插头与系统的线束插头插接，这样接线端子盒上的端子标号

就与系统线束插头中端子编号相对应。对接线端子盒上端子的测试，就相当于对系统线束插头中相应端子进行测试。

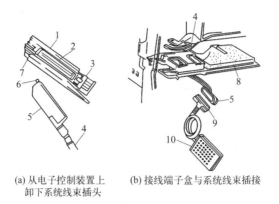

(a) 从电子控制装置上卸下系统线束插头　　(b) 接线端子盒与系统线束插接

图 1-74　接线端子盒的连接

1—电子控制装置；2—电子控制装置插头；3—弹簧卡；4—系统线束；5—系统线束插头；
6—挂钩；7—挂钩销；8—隔音板；9—接线端子盒线束插头；10—接线端子盒

在对驱动防滑系统的液压装置进行检查时，有时需要使用压力表，如图 1-75 所示。

对驱动防滑系统进行故障诊断时，也可以借助各种诊断测试仪器，有些系统甚至只有使用专用诊断测试仪器才能进行故障诊断。专用诊断测试仪器可以分为两大类，其中一类可以替代系统的电子控制装置，对系统的工作情况进行检查和模拟，这类仪器有图 1-76(a) 所示的 ABS 诊断测试器和图 1-76(b) 所示的丰田 ABS 诊断测试器。另一类诊断测试器则需要借

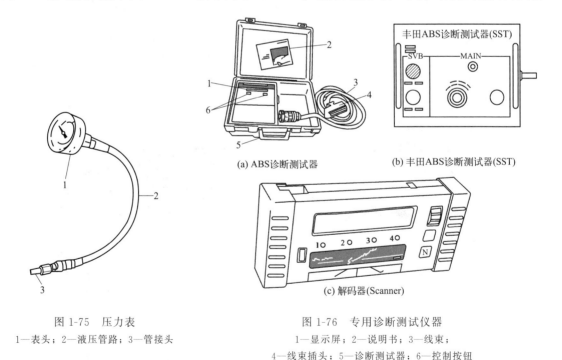

图 1-75　压力表

1—表头；2—液压管路；3—管接头

图 1-76　专用诊断测试仪器

1—显示屏；2—说明书；3—线束；
4—线束插头；5—诊断测试器；6—控制按钮

助系统的电子控制装置，通过与系统的电子控制装置进行双向通信来读取故障信息，系统电子控制装置因可以读解故障码，一般称为解码器，如图 1-76(c) 所示。解码器不仅可以对驱动防滑系统进行故障诊断，而且还可以对汽车的其他一些电控系统进行诊断测试，只是需要

选择相应的软件而已。

(3) 故障诊断与排除的一般步骤

当驱动防滑系统的警告灯（包括防抱死警告灯和防滑转警告灯）持续点亮时，或感觉驱动防滑系统工作不正常时，应及时对系统进行故障诊断和排除。在故障诊断和排除时应按照一定的步骤进行，才能取得良好的效果。故障诊断与排除的一般步骤如下。

① 确认故障情况和故障症状。

② 对系统进行直观检查，检查是否有制动液渗漏、导线破损、插头松脱、制动液液位过低等现象。

③ 读解故障码，既可以用解码器直接读解，也可以通过警告灯读取故障码后，再根据维修手册查找故障码所代表的故障情况。

④ 根据读解的故障情况，利用必要的工具和仪器对故障部位进行深入检查，确诊故障部位和故障原因。

⑤ 排除故障。

⑥ 清除故障码。

⑦ 检查警告灯是否仍然持续点亮，如果警告灯仍然持续点亮，可能是系统中仍有故障存在，也有可能是故障已经排除，而故障码未被清除。

⑧ 警告灯不再持续点亮后，进行路试，确认系统是否恢复正常工作。

在故障诊断和维修过程中，应当注意不仅不同型号的汽车所装备的驱动防滑系统可能不同，而且即使是同一型号的汽车，由于生产年份不同其装备的驱动防滑系统也可能不同。

驱动防滑系统的故障大多是由系统内的接线插头松脱或接触不良、导线断路或短路、电磁阀电磁线圈断路或短路、电动泵电路断路或短路、车轮转速传感器电磁线圈断路或短路、继电器内部断路或短路，以及制动开关、液位开关和压力开关等不能正常工作引起的，另外，蓄电池电压过低、车轮转速传感器与齿圈之间的间隙过大或受到泥污沾染、储液室液位过低等也会影响系统的正常工作。

3. ASR 的主要元件的检修

下面以丰田车系为例介绍 ASR 的主要元件的检修。

主继电器电路的故障诊断。TRC 主继电器电路出现断路或短路故障时，其故障码为 11 和 12。

① 当 TRC 计算机向主继电器输出接通（ON）信号时，若计算机端子 SRC、SMC 和 SAC 的电压均为 0V，计算机就储存故障码 11，说明 TRC 主继电器电路中有断路故障。可能的故障原因有以下几种。

a. TRC 主继电器不良（触点不能闭合或触点接触不良）。

b. TRC 主继电器与计算机之间的线路或连接器接触不良或松脱。

c. TRC 主继电器与 TRC 制动压力调节器之间的线路或连接器接触不良或松脱。

d. TRC 主继电器与蓄电池之间的线路或连接器接触不良或松脱。

e. TRC 计算机有故障。

② 当 TRC 计算机未向主继电器输出接通（ON）信号时，若计算机端子 SRC、SMC 和 SAC 中任一端子的电压为蓄电池电压，计算机就储存故障码 12，说明 TRC 主继电器电路中有短路故障。可能的故障原因有以下几种。

a. TRC 主继电器不良（触点不能张开或线圈与电源短路）。

b. TRC 主继电器与 TRC 制动压力调节器之间的线路和连接器与电源线路有短路。

c. TRC 计算机有故障。

③ TRC 主继电器电路如图 1-77 所示，检查方法如下。

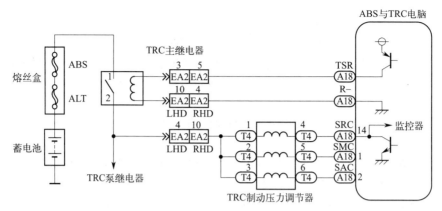

图 1-77 TRC 主继电器电路

a. 检查 TRC 主继电器电源端子的电压。拆下 TRC 主继电器连接器，在点火开关接通时，用直流电压表测量 TRC 主继电器连接器（线束侧）1 号端子与搭铁之间的电压，如图 1-78 所示，正常电压应为蓄电池电压。

若电压不正常，应检查 TRC 主继电器与蓄电池之间的线路、连接器及有关的熔丝。若电压正常，应检查主继电器。

b. 检查 TRC 主继电器。测量 TRC 主继电器连接器各端子之间的导通情况，正常情况应为 1—2 端子之间不导通（电阻∞）、2—4 端子之间导通（电阻很小）。

然后给继电器 2—4 端子之间施加蓄电池电压，再检查继电器 1—2 端子之间是否导通，如图 1-79 所示，正常情况应导通。

若上述检查结果不正常，应更换 TRC 主继电器。若检查结果正常，应检查 TRC 主继电器的有关线路和连接器，如果线路和连接器均良好，则应检查或更换 TRC/ABS 计算机。

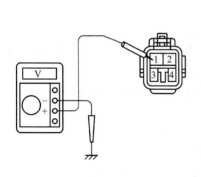

图 1-78 检查主继电器电源端子电压

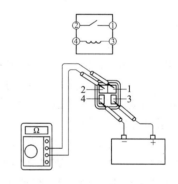

图 1-79 检查主继电器端子导通情况

二、ASR 的故障案例诊断过程

仪表板上的 ASR 故障灯常亮，说明该车 ASR 有故障。ASR 一般与 ABS 互为一体，统称为汽车驱动防滑系统。

先对 ASR 利用随车故障自诊断功能从故障检测插座上调取 ASR 故障码，故障码显示：ASR 计算机与 EGAS（电子节气门控制系统）计算机信号传输有问题。对 EGAS 进行故障自诊断，调取故障码，但读不出任何信息。因此怀疑其线路存在故障。经仔细检查 EGAS 计算机的线路系统，没有发现任何异常现象。打开 EGAS 计算机，发现 EGAS 计算机中有

个集成块已经烧毁，更换后试车，ASR 故障灯不再点亮，但路试一段距离后，ASR 故障灯又点亮了。再利用随车故障自诊断系统提取 ASR 的故障码，故障码显示怠速触点线路不良（原来 ASR 与 EGAS 信号传输不良）。

检查怠速触点线路（奔驰车怠速触点装在加速踏板下），发现怠速触点线路有一个线插断开，把该线插接上，试车，ASR 故障灯不再点亮，故障彻底排除。

习题测试

简答题

请分析 ASR 和 ABS 有哪些异同。

任务三　汽车车身电子稳定系统的检修

【学习目标】

知识要求：了解汽车车身电子稳定系统（ESP）的作用、组成及原理。

能力要求：能够依据维修手册并使用常用工具、量具对汽车车身电子稳定系统（ESP）进行故障诊断与修复。

 任务导入

一辆 2000 年款的奔驰 ML500 越野车，行驶里程 8 万多 km。行驶中仪表板上的 ESP、ETS 及 ABS 的 3 个仪表灯全部点亮。该车已经在特约维修站进行过检查，维修人员检查后认为是 ABS 泵、横向加速度传感器以及偏移率传感器都出现问题，需要更换 ABS 泵、横向加速度传感器以及偏移率传感器。车主认为维修价格过高，于是到修理厂检查。

 知识准备

一、汽车车身电子稳定系统的作用

汽车车身电子稳定系统（Electronic Stability Program，ESP），由德国博世公司（BOSCH）和梅赛德斯-奔驰（MERCEDES-BENZ）公司联合研制。1998 年 2 月，梅赛德斯-奔驰公司首次在其 A 级微型轿车中成批地安装该电控车辆稳定行驶系统。它集成了电子防抱死制动系统（ABS）、电子制动力分配（EBD）和牵引力控制（ASR）的基本功能；能够在几毫秒的时间内，识别出汽车不稳定的行驶趋势，恰当地消除这些不稳定行驶趋势，使汽车保持在所期望的行驶路线上。

二、汽车车身电子稳定系统的结构与组成

汽车车身电子稳定系统（ESP）是在原有电子防抱死制动系统（ABS）、电子制动力分配（EBD）和牵引力控制（ASR）的基础上发展起来的。该电子制动系统由电子控制单元（ECU）、液压调节器总成、车轮速度传感器、车轮速度传感器脉冲环、转向盘转角传感器、横向偏摆率传感器以及 ESP 控制开关等部件组成，其中电子控制单元与液压调节器是一体

的。ESP 系统组成如图 1-80 所示。

图 1-80　ESP 系统组成

1. 电子控制单元

电子控制单元是 ABS-ASR/ESP 系统的控制中心，它与液压调节器集成在一起组成一个总成。电子控制单元持续监测并判断的输入信号有：蓄电池电压、车轮速度、转向盘转角、横向偏摆率以及点火开关接通、停车灯开关、串行数据通信电路等信号。根据所接收的输入信号，电子控制单元将向液压调节器、发动机控制模块、组合仪表和串行数据通信电路等发送输出控制信号。

2. 液压调节器总成

液压调节器总成如图 1-81 所示。为了能独立控制各车轮的制动回路，该系统采用了前/后分离的 4 通道回路结构，每个车轮的液压制动回路都是隔离的，这样当某个制动回路出现泄漏时仍能继续制动。液压调节器总成根据电子控制单元（ECU）发送的控制信号调节制动液压力。液压调节器总成包括回程泵、电动机、储能器、进口阀、出口阀、隔离阀和后启动阀等部件。

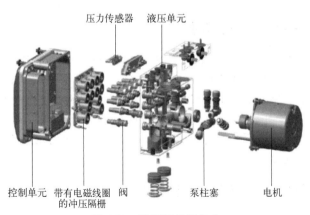

图 1-81　液压调节器总成

3. 前轮速度传感器

前轮速度传感器如图 1-82 所示，是一个电磁式传感器，是前轮轮毂总成的一部分，前

轮轮毂总成是一个永久性的密封装置。左前和右前轮轮毂装有车轮速度传感器和一个48齿的磁脉冲环。

4. 后轮速度传感器

后轮速度传感器如图1-83所示，位于主减速器后盖的支架上，也是电磁式传感器。后轮速度传感器脉冲环是主减速器内车桥法兰的一部分，不能单独维修。

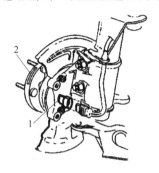

图1-82　前轮速度传感器
1—前轮速传感器；2—前轮毂总成

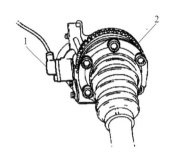

图1-83　后轮速度传感器
1—后轮速传感器；2—传感器脉冲环

5. ESP开关

ESP开关位于地板控制台上。该开关是一个瞬间接触开关，按一下ESP开关，电子稳定程序从接通转至关闭。当ESP关闭时，ABS-TCS系统仍能正常工作。当ESP处于关闭位置时，再次按一下ESP开关，将接通电子稳定程序。按下ESP开关超过60s将被视为短路，会记录故障诊断码，且电子稳定程序在该点火循环内将被禁用。如果没有记录牵引力控制系统当前故障诊断码，电子稳定程序将在下一个点火循环复位到接通状态。

6. 转向盘转角传感器

转向盘转角传感器位于转向盘下面，如图1-84所示。转向盘转角传感器提供表示转向盘旋转角度的输出信号。由于两只测量齿轮的齿数不同，故产生不同相位的两个转角信号，即能产生一个可表示±760°转向盘旋转角度的输出信号。电子控制单元利用这个信息计算出驾驶员所要求的方向。控制单元通过转向盘转角传感器与横向偏摆率传感器信号的比较，确定车辆实际行驶轨迹与驾驶要求是否一致，从而确定控制目标。

7. 横向偏摆率传感器

横向偏摆率传感器位于仪表板中央控制台下部，如图1-85所示。横向偏摆率传感器总成包括两个部件，一个是横向偏摆率传感器，另一个是横向加速度传感器。横向偏摆率传感器根据车辆绕其纵轴的旋转角度产生对应的输出信号电压；横向加速度传感器根据车轮侧向滑移量产生对应的输出信号电压。ESP控制单元利用横向偏摆率传感器和横向加速度传感器输出的信号，计算出车辆的实际行驶状态，再结合车轮速度传感器的输出信号和转向盘转角传感器的串行数据输出信号，确定控制目标。

三、汽车车身电子稳定系统子系统的工作过程

ESP在汽车高速转弯或湿滑路面上行驶时，提供最佳的车辆稳定性和方向控制。电子控制单元（ECU）通过转向盘转角传感器确定驾驶员想要的行驶方向；通过车轮速度传感器和横向偏摆率传感器来计算车辆的实际行驶方向。当电子稳定程序检测到车辆行驶轨迹与驾驶员要求不符时，电子稳定程序将首先利用牵引力控制系统中的发动机扭矩减小功能，向发动机控制模块（ECM）发送一个串行数据通信信号，请求减小发动机扭矩。如果电子稳

定程序仍然检测到车轮侧向滑移,则电子稳定程序将根据"从外部作用于车辆上的所有力(不管是制动力、推动力,还是任何一种侧向力)都会使车辆环绕其重心而转动"的原理,通过对前、后桥一个以上的车轮进行制动干预,迅速克服以下操作缺陷,使车辆不偏离正确的行驶轨迹,确保安全。

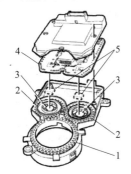

图 1-84 转向盘转角传感器
1—齿轮;2—测量齿轮;3—磁铁;4—判断电路;
5—各向异性磁阻(AMR)集成电路

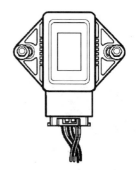

图 1-85 横向偏摆率传感器

1. 克服转向不足的操作

转向不足示意图如图 1-86 所示。转向盘转角传感器向电子控制单元发送一个驾驶员想要朝方向"A"转向的信号,横向偏摆率传感器"B"检测到车辆开始旋转,同时车辆前端开始向方向"C"滑移,说明车辆出现转向不足,电子稳定程序将实行主动制动干预。电子稳定程序利用 ABS-ASR 系统中已有的主动制动控制功能,对左后轮进行制动干预,此刻,由于左后轮被制动,而车子的重心因惯性作用继续向前运动,于是车子就只好以左后轮为支点,绕着它旋转,这样一来,车子就朝方向"A"转向,即朝驾驶员想要的方向转向,转向不足的操作缺陷就被克服了。

2. 克服转向过度的操作

转向过度示意图如图 1-87 所示,转向盘转角传感器向电子控制单元发送一个驾驶员想要朝方向"A"转向的信号,横向偏摆率传感器"B"检测到车辆开始旋转,同时车辆后端开始向方向"C"滑移。说明车辆开始转向过度,电子稳定程序将实行主动制动干预。电子稳定程序利用 ABS-ASR 系统中已有的主动制动控制功能,对右后轮进行制动干预,此刻由于右后轮被制动,而车子的重心因惯性作用继续向前运动,于是车子就只好以右后轮为支点,绕着它旋转,这样一来,车子就朝方向"A"转向,即朝向驾驶员想要的方向转向,转向过度的操作缺陷就被克服了。

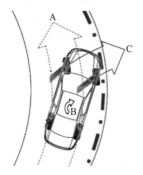

图 1-86 转向不足示意图

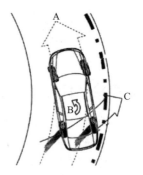

图 1-87 转向过度示意图

任务实施

汽车车身电子稳定系统的故障案例诊断过程

首先用故障诊断仪 STAR 进行检查，查询 ESP 系统后得到一个故障码 C1402，含义为"高压回流泵故障"。出现这个故障码的可能部位有 ABS 泵、ESP 控制单元以及相关电路。使用另一辆车上的 ABS 泵进行了替换试验，清除故障码后进行路试，只行驶了很短的距离，仪表板上的 ETS 就点亮了，调取故障码还是 C1402，这说明不是 ABS 泵的问题。奔驰 ML500 的 ESP 控制单元位于发动机舱内的熔丝盒内，紧靠着发动机控制单元，为了排除故障，又将两车的 ESP 控制单元进行了对调。由于更换了 ESP 控制单元，所以要用故障诊断仪对控制单元进行编码，然后激活驾驶测试，进行路试时发现 ETS 灯仍然会在起步时亮起，而 ABS 灯却在启动后常亮了。调取故障码，除故障码 C1402 之外又增加了一个故障码 C1200，含义为"驾驶测试被激活"，原来是进行完驾驶测试激活后没有退出。故障码 C1200 用故障诊断仪无法清除，于是继续进行试车。此时，仪表板上的 ESP、ETS 以及 ABS 灯全部熄灭，将发动机熄火后再打开点火开关，又发现仪表板上的故障灯全都不亮了，关掉点火开关，等待几分钟后再打开点火开关，故障灯又全部点亮。再仔细观察各个仪表的显示，里程表不显示公里数，燃油表指针转了 300 多度，转速表指针也不正常。

为了使仪表指示恢复正常，维修人员进行了多次通、断电试验，但是没有效果。这时车主反映这辆车的仪表曾经调校过，而且在第一次调表时没有调好，安装后燃油表指示就不正常，后来又重新调校了一次，燃油表指示才恢复正常。据此维修人员决定重新进行仪表调校，找到仪表备份数据，使用编程器重新写入一遍程序后，各个仪表的指示都恢复正常。

经过上面的检修过程，基本上可以排除 ABS 泵和 ESP 控制单元的问题。维修人员根据 ABS 系统电路图，发现 ABS 泵 A7/3 中的高压回流泵 M1 上只有两根连接线，一根线在左前照灯附近搭铁，另一根由 K25 继电器控制。K25 继电器有 5 个脚，1 号脚和 2 号脚分别连接到 ESP 控制单元 N47 的 10 号脚和 12 号脚。而 5 号脚则分两条线，一条线连接到 ESP 控制单元 N47 的 11 号脚，另一条线连接到 M1 高压回流泵，3 号脚则连接常正电源线。维修人员仔细检查了 ABS 泵和 ESP 控制单元上的线束插头，并测量了相关线路，但没有发现问题。因为继电器 K25 在 ESP 控制单元和 M1 高压回流泵的线路之间起着重要的连接作用，于是将 K25 继电器进行了替换，在路试的过程中，ETS 灯和 ESP 灯不再点亮，故障码 C1402 也没有再出现，看来故障点确实在于继电器 K25。接下来需要解决被故障诊断仪 STAR 激活的驾驶测试引起的 ABS 灯常亮的问题。

按照故障诊断仪 STAR 上的提示，在拔掉诊断插头后进行一段距离的行驶就会关闭被激活的驾驶测试，但是行驶了很长的距离 ABS 灯仍然没有熄灭。在奔驰的 WIS 中找到关于驾驶测试的说明，按照说明的规定进行行驶，ABS 灯自动熄灭了，到此故障彻底排除。

习题测试

简答题

1. 简述 ESP 工作原理。

2. ESP 的组成部件有哪些?

项目小结

电子控制技术、微电脑处理技术、传感技术的应用,使车辆控制精度提高的同时,也使安全技术得到了长足的发展。主动安全技术、被动安全技术的协调集成发展是势不可当的发展趋势,对减轻驾驶员的劳动强度,发生事故时有效地保护驾驶员、乘员及行人的安全方面也起到重要作用。

项目习题测试

一、填空题

1. 评价制动效能的主要评价指标有_____、_____和_____。
2. 电控 ABS 由_____、_____和_____组成。
3. 车速传感器主要由_____和_____组成。

二、单项选择题

1. 菱形极轴式传感器头安装位置是(　　)。
   A. 径向垂直于齿圈安装　　　　B. 轴向相切于齿圈
   C. 以上两个都正确　　　　　　D. 以上两个都错误
2. 凿式极轴式车速传感器头的安装位置是(　　)。
   A. 径向垂直于齿圈安装　　　　B. 轴向相切于齿圈
   C. 以上两个都正确　　　　　　D. 以上两个都错误
3. 为保证传感器无错误信号输出,安装车速传感器时应保证其传感器头与齿圈间留有一定的空气间隙,约为(　　)。
   A. 5mm　　　　B. 1mm　　　　C. 0.01mm　　　　D. 1μm

三、名词解释

1. 滑移率
2. 制动时汽车的方向稳定性

四、判断题

1. 评价制动性能的指标主要有制动效能和制动稳定性。(　　)
2. 制动效能主要取决于制动力的大小,而制动力仅与制动器的摩擦力矩有关。(　　)

五、简答题

按不同的分类方式,可将 ABS 分为哪些种类?

项目二

汽车空调系统的检修

项目导读

汽车空调系统是实现对车厢内空气进行制冷、加热、换气和空气净化的装置。它可以为乘车人员提供舒适的乘车环境,降低驾驶员的疲劳强度,提高行车安全。

空调装置已成为衡量汽车功能是否齐全的标志之一。

一、汽车空调系统的组成

1. 空调压缩机

汽车空调压缩机一般安装在汽车发动机旁边,由主发动机或副发动机通过带轮驱动。空调压缩机把制冷剂从低压区抽取来经压缩后送到高压区冷却凝结,通过散热片散发热量到空气中,制冷剂也从气态变成液态。制冷剂再从高压区流向低压区,通过膨胀阀喷射到蒸发器中,压力骤降,液态制冷剂立即变成气态,通过散热片吸收空气中大量的热量。这样,空调压缩机就不断地把低压区一端的热量吸收到制冷剂中,再送到高压区散发到空气中,起到调节气温的作用。

2. 空调冷凝器

空调冷凝器用于制冷空调系统,管内制冷液直接与管外空气强制进行热交换,以达到制冷空气的效果。

冷凝器在制冷时为系统的高压设备(冷暖热泵型在制热状态时为低压设备),装在压缩机排气口和节流装置(孔管或膨胀阀)之间,由空调压缩机中排出的高温高压气体,进入冷凝器,通过铜管和铝箔片散热冷却,空调器中都装有轴流式冷却风扇,采用的是风冷式,使制冷剂在冷却凝结过程中,压力不变,温度降低,由气体转化为液体。

在冷凝器内制冷剂发生变化的过程,在理论上可以看成等温变化过程。实际上它有3个作用:一是空气带走了压缩机送来的高温空调制冷剂气体的过热部分,使其成为干燥的饱和蒸气;二是在饱和温度不变的情况下进行液化;三是当空气温度低于冷凝温度时,将已液化的制冷剂进一步冷却到与周围空气相同的温度,起到冷却作用。

3. 空调蒸发器

空调蒸发器的作用是利用液态低温制冷剂在低压下易蒸发,转变为蒸气并吸收被冷却介质的热量,达到制冷目的。

4. 空调膨胀阀

膨胀阀是制冷系统中的一个重要部件,膨胀阀使中温高压的液体制冷剂通过其节流成为低温低压的湿蒸气,然后制冷剂在蒸发器中吸收热量达到制冷效果,膨胀阀通过蒸发器末端的过热度变化来控制阀门流量,防止出现蒸发器面积利用不足和敲缸现象。简单来说,膨胀阀主要起到根据温度变化自动调节节流,控制制冷剂流量的作用。

5. 空调储液干燥器

储液干燥器在空调发展过程中不断改进、更新，其功能主要是储液和干燥。储液干燥器是随着现代制冷技术的发展应运而生的。制冷原理中冷媒（制冷剂）通过物理形态的转化，达到吸热和放热的效果，在冷媒添加到空调器密封系统中时，不可避免地会掺入空气中的水分和管路中的杂质。水分在物理形态转化过程中会结成固态的冰，堵塞空调系统密闭管路，从而影响制冷剂流动，最终导致制冷失效，严重时会产生爆破。储液干燥器的作用就是吸走密封空调管路中的水分，同时过滤掉管路中的微小杂质。

二、认识连接管路

① 高压软管：高压软管是压缩机和冷凝器之间的连接管路。
② 液体管路：液体管路是冷凝器和蒸发器之间的连接管路。
③ 回气管路：回气管路是蒸发器和压缩机之间的连接管路。
④ 暖风管路：暖风管路是发动机和暖风散热器之间的连接管路。

三、空调的工作过程简述

为了分析汽车空调制冷系统的热力循环，必须首先分析汽车空调制冷系统理论循环。

1. 压缩过程

低温低压的制冷剂气体被压缩机吸入，并压缩成高温高压的制冷剂气体。该过程的主要作用是压缩增压，以便气体液化。这一过程是以消耗机械功作为补偿的。在压缩过程中，制冷剂状态不发生变化，而温度、压力不断增大，形成过热气体。

2. 冷凝过程

制冷剂气体由压缩机排出后进入冷凝器。此过程的特点是制冷剂的状态发生变化，即压力和温度不变的情况下，由气态逐渐向液态转变。冷凝后的制冷剂液体呈高温高压状态。

3. 节流膨胀过程

高温高压的制冷剂液体经膨胀阀节流降温降压后进入蒸发器。该过程的作用是使制冷剂降温、降压、调节流量、控制制冷能力。其特点是制冷剂经过膨胀阀时，压力、温度急速下降，由高温高压液体变成低温低压液体。

4. 蒸发过程

制冷剂液体经膨胀阀降温降压后进入蒸发器，吸热制冷后从蒸发器出口被压缩机吸入。此过程的特点是制冷剂由液态变化成气态，此时压力不变。节流后，低温低压液态制冷剂在蒸发器中不断吸收汽化热，吸收车内的热量后变成低温低压的气体，该气体又被压缩机吸入再次进行压缩。

任务一　汽车空调系统识别

【学习目标】

知识要求：掌握汽车空调系统的作用、组成及分类。

能力要求：能够在实车上找到空调系统各组成部件；能通过与客户交流、查阅相关维修技术资料等方式获取车辆信息。

任务导入

除了在车内用控制开关来调节车内冷气的温度外,大家能在汽车上找到汽车空调系统的其他组成部件吗?下面就来了解一下汽车空调系统的作用、分类、组成及基本原理。

 知识准备

一、汽车空调的功能

空调是空气调节器的简称。现代汽车空调有以下4种功能,都是为了使车上的人员感到舒适。

① 空调器能控制车厢内的气温,以把车内温度控制到舒适的水平。
② 空调器能够排除空气中的湿气。
③ 空调器可吸入新鲜空气,具有通风功能。
④ 部分空调器可过滤空气,排除空气中的灰尘和花粉。

二、汽车空调的主要指标

衡量汽车空调的主要指标有温度、湿度、流速和清洁度4项。

1. 温度

不同季节,人体的舒适温度不同,设计空调出风口时,应让冷风能吹到乘员头部,暖风能吹到乘员足部,即采取"头凉足暖"的布置方式。

2. 湿度

人觉得最舒适的相对湿度夏季是50%~60%,冬季则是40%~50%。在这种湿度环境中,人会觉得心情舒畅。湿度过高,人体皮肤的水分蒸发不出来,人会觉得闷。

3. 流速

夏季气流速度稍大,人在流动的空气中比在静止的空气中要舒适。冬季风速大了会影响人体保温,因而冬季取暖希望气流尽量小一点,空气流速在0.2 m/s以下较佳。

4. 清洁度

车室内的空气应是干净的,这就需要空调系统还有一套通风过滤设施及空气净化设备。

三、汽车空调系统的组成与分类

1. 汽车空调系统的组成

① 制冷系统:制冷系统对车室内空气或由外部进入车内的新鲜空气进行冷却或除湿,使车室内空气变得凉爽舒适。
② 暖风系统:暖风系统主要用于取暖,对车室内空气或由外部进入车内的新鲜空气进行加热,达到取暖、除湿的目的。
③ 通风系统:将外部新鲜空气吸进车内,起到通风和换气作用。同时防止风窗玻璃起雾。
④ 加湿系统:在空气湿度较低的时候,对车内空气进行加湿,以提高车内空气的湿度。
⑤ 空气净化系统:空气净化系统除去车室内空气中的尘埃、异味、烟气及有毒气体。
⑥ 控制系统:控制系统对制冷和暖风系统的温度、压力进行控制,同时对车室内空气的温度、风量、流向进行控制,完善空调系统的正常工作。

上述各部分全部或部分地组合在一起安装在汽车上,便组成了汽车空调系统。在一般的轿车和客货车上,通常只有制冷系统、暖风系统、通风系统和控制系统,在高级轿车和高级大客车上,除了制冷系统、暖风系统外,还有加湿系统和PM2.5空气净化系统。

2. 汽车空调系统的分类

(1) 按功能分类

汽车空调系统按功能分类,可分为单一功能式汽车空调系统和组合式汽车空调系统两种。

① 单一功能式汽车空调系统指制冷系统、暖风系统各自独立,一般用于大、中型客车上。

② 组合式汽车空调系统指制冷、暖风合用一个鼓风机、一套操纵机构的汽车空调系统。这种结构又分为制冷、暖风分别工作和制冷、暖风可同时工作两种方式,多用于轿车上。

(2) 按驱动方式分类

汽车空调系统按驱动方式分类,可分为非独立式汽车空调系统和独立式汽车空调系统两种。

① 非独立式汽车空调系统。空调制冷压缩机由汽车发动机驱动,汽车空调系统的制冷性受汽车发动机工况的影响较大,工作稳定性较差,低速时制冷量不足,而在高速时制冷量过剩,并且消耗功率较大,影响汽车发动机的动力性。这种类型的汽车空调系统一般用于制冷量相对较小的中、小型汽车上。

② 独立式汽车空调系统。空调制冷压缩机由专用的空调发动机(也称副发动机)驱动,汽车空调系统的制冷性能不受汽车发动机工况的影响,工作稳定,制冷量大,但由于加装了一台发动机,不仅成本增加,而且体积和质量增加。这种类型的汽车空调系统多用于大、中型客车上。

 任务实施

分组训练,在实车上找到空调系统各组成部件。

习题测试

简答题

1. 简述空调制冷的工作过程。
2. 简述空调的分类。

任务二　汽车空调制冷系统的检修

【学习目标】

知识要求:掌握汽车空调制冷系统各类型的结构、原理与检修方法。

能力要求:能根据故障现象制订正确的维修计划,并根据维修手册,使用常用的维修工具对汽车空调制冷系统的常见故障进行诊断与修复。

 任务导入

一辆上海通用别克君越轿车,装配自动空调,空调系统工作时会出现间歇性不制冷的现

象,该故障多出现在高速行驶时,怠速有时也出现,天气越热故障出现的频率越高。

知识准备

一、汽车空调制冷系统压缩机结构原理

制冷压缩机是汽车空调制冷系统的心脏,起着压缩和输送制冷剂、保证制冷剂正常循环工作的作用,是推动制冷剂在冷气系统中不断循环的动力。

1. 曲轴连杆式压缩机

曲轴连杆式压缩机是一种应用较为广泛的制冷压缩机。如图 2-1 所示,压缩机的活塞在气缸内不断地运动,改变了气缸的容积,从而在制冷系统中起到了压缩和输送制冷剂的作用。曲轴连杆式压缩机的机体由气缸体和曲轴箱组成,气缸体中装有活塞,曲轴箱中装有曲轴,通过连杆将曲轴与活塞连接起来。在气缸顶部装有进气阀和排气阀,通过吸气腔和排气腔分别与吸气管和排气管相连。当发动机带动曲轴旋转时,通过连杆的传动,活塞便在气缸内做上下往复运动,在吸、排气阀的配合下,完成对制冷剂气体的吸入、压缩和输送的任务。

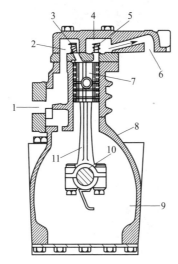

图 2-1 曲轴连杆式压缩机
1—进气管;2—进气腔;3—进气阀;4—排气腔;5—排气阀;
6—排气管;7—活塞;8—气缸体;9—曲轴箱;10—曲轴;11—连杆

2. 径向活塞式压缩机

径向活塞式压缩机是一种往复活塞式压缩机,它有两种类型。

一种类型是 4 个气缸位于同一径向平面,一根连杆连接两个活塞,曲柄在连杆槽中滑动,将曲轴的旋转运动转变为活塞的直线往复运动,如图 2-2 所示,称为连杆径向活塞式压缩机。

另一种类型是无连杆,称为滑环径向活塞式压缩机,如图 2-3 所示。

3. 斜盘式压缩机

斜盘式压缩机是一种轴向活塞式压缩机,其主要零件是主轴和斜板,结构如图 2-4 所示。

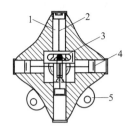 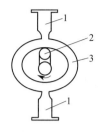

图 2-2 连杆径向活塞式压缩机　　　　　图 2-3 滑环径向活塞式压缩机
1—气缸；2—连杆；3—曲轴轴颈；4—活塞；5—基座　　　1—活塞；2—压缩机轴；3—滑环

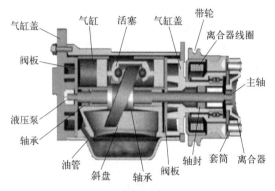

图 2-4 斜盘式压缩机

4. 压缩机离合器

汽车压缩机离合器一般是电磁式的。电磁离合器主要有装在轴承上的带轮、与压缩机主轴花键相连的驱动盘以及不转动的电气绕组或线圈 3 个组成部分，如图 2-5 所示。

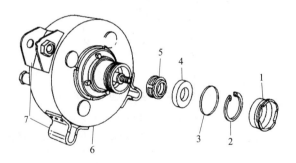

图 2-5 压缩机离合器的机构
1—防尘盖；2—弹性卡圈；3—密封圈；4—陶瓷密封座；5—密封；6—压缩壳体；7—安装吊耳

二、汽车空调制冷系统膨胀阀

膨胀阀也称节流阀，是汽车空调制冷系统的主要部件，安装在蒸发器入口处，如图 2-6 所示。膨胀阀有感温膨胀阀、H 形膨胀阀等。

1. 内平衡感温膨胀阀

图 2-7 所示为内平衡感温膨胀阀的结构示意图。针阀、阀座和孔口用以调节制冷剂流量，针阀由膜片驱动。

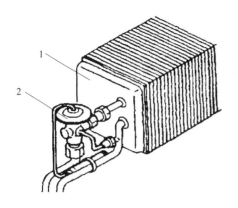
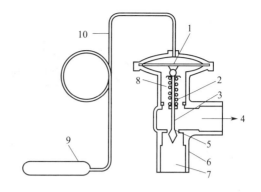

图 2-6 膨胀阀的安装位置
1—蒸发器；2—膨胀阀

图 2-7 内平衡感温膨胀阀
1—膜片；2—平衡口；3—针阀；4—接蒸发器出口；5—阀座；
6—阀体；7—通储液罐的出口；8—弹簧；9—遥控温包；10—毛细管

2. 外平衡感温膨胀阀

外平衡感温膨胀阀的结构如图 2-8 所示。

3. H 形感温膨胀阀

H 形感温膨胀阀外观为长方形，因其内部通路像字母 H 而得名。它有 4 个通往汽车空调系统的接口，其中两个接口和标准膨胀阀的一样，一个接储液干燥器出口，另一个接蒸发器进口。它还有两个接口，一个接蒸发器出口，另一个接压缩机进口，如图 2-9 所示。

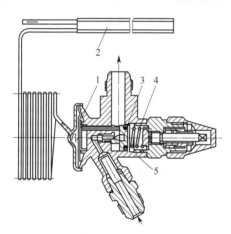
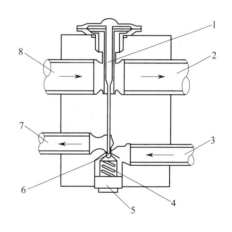

图 2-8 外平衡感温膨胀阀
1—膜片；2—感温筒；3—针阀；4—弹簧；5—阀体

图 2-9 H 形感温膨胀阀
1—感温器；2—接压缩机进口；3—接储液干燥器出口；
4—弹簧；5—调整螺栓；6—球阀；
7—接蒸发器进口；8—接蒸发器出口

4. 孔管

孔管的结构如图 2-10 所示。

三、汽车空调冷凝器

汽车空调制冷系统中的冷凝器是一种由管与散热片组合起来的热交换器。一般采用风冷式结构，其结构形式主要有管带式、管片式和鳍片式 3 种。

项目二　汽车空调系统的检修　055

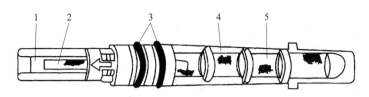

图 2-10 孔管

1—出口滤网；2—节流孔；3—密封圈；4—管外壳；5—进口滤网

1. 管带式

管带式结构如图 2-11 所示。

2. 管片式

管片式结构如图 2-12 所示。

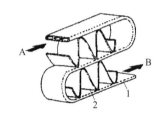 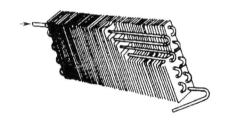

图 2-11 管带式冷凝器　　　　　　　　图 2-12 管片式冷凝器

1—盘管；2—铝片；A—气态制冷剂；
B—液态制冷剂

3. 鳍片式

鳍片式冷凝器是在扁平的多通管道表面直接铣出鳍片状散热片，然后装配成冷凝器，如图 2-13 所示。鳍片式冷凝器是较先进的汽车空调冷凝器。

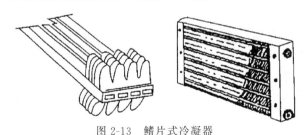

图 2-13 鳍片式冷凝器

四、储液干燥器

储液干燥器简称储液器，安装在冷凝器和膨胀阀之间。储液干燥器由储液器、干燥器、检视窗和安全装置（见图 2-14）组合装配在一起构成，也有分散安装的，图 2-15 所示为储液干燥器的结构。

储液器一般安装在冷凝器旁或其他通风良好的地方，便于连接和安装，且易从顶部玻璃视液镜观察制冷剂的流动情况。对直立式储液器，安装时若偏离垂直方向，倾斜度不得超过15°。在安装新的储液干燥器之前，不得过早地将其进出管口的包装打开，以免潮湿空气侵入储液器和系统内部，使之失去除湿的作用。安装前要先弄清楚储液器的进、出口端，以免装错，如果进、出口接反，则会导致制冷剂量不足。在储液器的进出口端一般都打有记号，如进口端用英文字母 IN，出口端用 OUT 表示，或直接打上箭头以表示进、出口端。

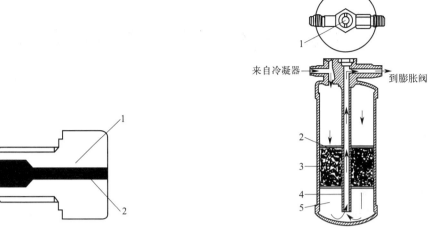

图 2-14 安全装置
1—易熔塞；2—焊锡

图 2-15 储液干燥器的结构
1—视液镜；2—过滤网；3—干燥剂；4—吸出管；5—储液罐

① 用手摸储液干燥器的进出管，并观察视液镜。如果进口很烫，而且出口管接近气温，从视液镜中看不到或很少有制冷剂流过，或者制冷剂很浑浊、有杂质，可能储液器中的滤网堵了或干燥剂散了并堵住出口。一般干燥剂使用 3 个月，吸湿能力要下降一半，所以每两年应更换一次干燥器。

② 检查易熔塞是否熔化，各接头处是否有油迹。

③ 检查视液镜是否有裂纹，周围是否有油迹。

任务实施

一、电装压缩机的维修

日本电装公司压缩机可能装有电装（Denso）离合器或者沃纳（Warner）离合器组件。尽管这两种离合器外形类似，但它们的零件是不可互换的。然而，整个离合器总成在这种压缩机上是可以互换的。这两种离合器的明显不同是电装离合器带轮（见图 2-16）有两个窄的单列轴承，这两个轴承用钢丝卡环定位。

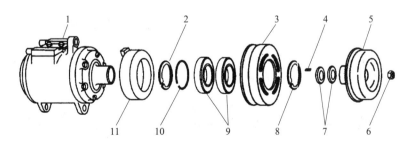

图 2-16 电装离合器
1—压缩机；2，8，10—卡环；3—离合器带轮；4—毂键；5—离合器毂；6—锁紧螺母；
7—调整垫圈；9—带轮轴承；11—励磁线圈

沃纳离合器（见图 2-17）只有一个宽的双列轴承，它通过冲铆翻边来定位。

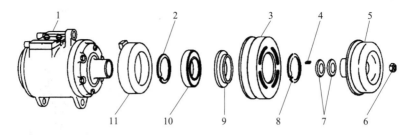

图 2-17 沃纳离合器

1—压缩机；2，8—卡环；3—离合器带轮；4—毂键；5—离合器毂；6—锁紧螺母；
7—调整垫圈；9—防尘护圈；10—带轮轴承；11—励磁线圈

① 使用离合器毂拆卸工具，拆卸离合器毂，如图 2-18 所示。

② 使用卡环钳，拆卸带轮定位卡环，然后使用三爪拉器拆下带轮和轴承组件，如图 2-19 所示。

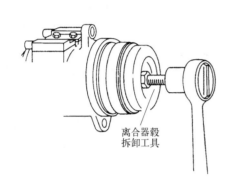

图 2-18 拆卸离合器毂

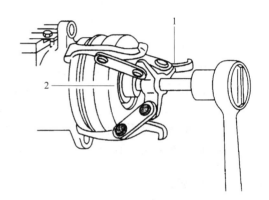

图 2-19 拆卸带轮和轴承组件
1—三爪拉器；2—轴保护器

③ 使用卡环钳，拆卸励磁线圈定位卡环，并从压缩机上取下励磁线圈，如图 2-20 所示。

④ 使用合适的工具从前盖上拆下 6 个贯穿螺栓，如图 2-21 所示。

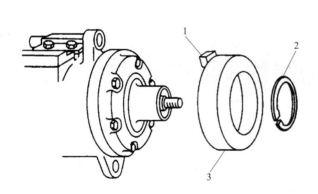

图 2-20 拆卸励磁线圈
1—导线连接器；2—卡环；3—励磁线圈

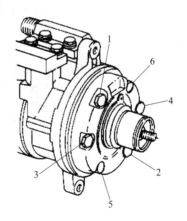

图 2-21 拆卸贯穿螺栓
1，2，3，4，5，6—螺栓

⑤ 用塑料锤轻轻敲击前盖，使前盖与压缩机壳脱离。

⑥ 拆卸压缩机壳与前盖之间的O形圈以及前盖与阀板之间的衬垫，并将它们报废（一次性零件）。

⑦ 使用轴封座拆卸工具，拆卸轴封座和轴封，如图2-22所示。

⑧ 用塑料锤轻轻敲击后盖，并拆下后盖。将后盖与壳体之间的O形圈拆下，然后将它报废（一次性零件）。使用阀板拆卸工具拆下阀板，如图2-23所示。

⑨ 敲击压缩机壳体上的凸耳，使前、后壳分离。

⑩ 检查吸气阀是否损坏。

⑪ 检查两个排气阀是否损坏。

⑫ 检查所有的配合表面是否有刻痕和起毛刺现象。

⑬ 检查压缩机活塞腔内和压缩机体内是否有异物。

⑭ 使用洁净的矿物基冷冻润滑油或O形圈润滑剂，对所有的O形圈和衬垫进行充分润滑。放上前、后壳O形圈，并将两半壳体向一起滑动。

图2-22 拆卸轴封

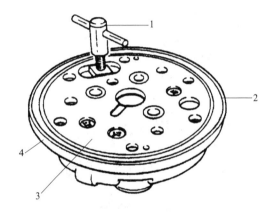

图2-23 使用阀板拆卸工具拆下阀板
1—阀板拆卸工具；2—O形圈；3—阀板；4—前盖

⑮ 将后盖安装到阀板衬垫上。

⑯ 安装排气阀板和吸气阀板，并确保衬垫和阀板与后盖上的定位销对正。

⑰ 安装后盖O形圈，并将后盖和阀板组件安装到压缩机壳上。

后盖定位销必须插入压缩机壳上的相应的孔中。将压缩机放在后盖上，并安装吸气阀、排气阀和阀板衬垫，并确保阀板和衬垫与压缩机壳上的定位销对正。安装压缩机轴封，确保将轴封转入曲轴环槽中。

⑱ 安装前盖和压缩机壳O形圈，并小心地将前盖滑到压缩机壳体上。

使用6只新的黄铜垫圈（如果需要的话），安装6个压缩机贯穿螺栓。根据需要，使用一只10mm六角套筒，将这些螺栓拧紧到29N·m。使用交替拧紧的方法（见图2-24）来拧紧螺栓。

⑲ 安装励磁线圈。应确保压缩机上的定位销插入离合器线圈上的孔中。安装卡环，确保卡环的锥形边缘朝外。将转子和轴承组件滑到盖上。使用轴承拆卸/带轮安装工具（见图2-25），轻轻地敲击带轮，将其安装到盖上。

⑳ 安装转子和轴承卡环。卡环的锥形边缘必须朝外。检查轴和毂键，确保正确安装到位。将轮毂上的键槽与轴上的键对正。使用轮毂安装工具，将轮毂压到压缩机轴上，如

图 2-26 所示。

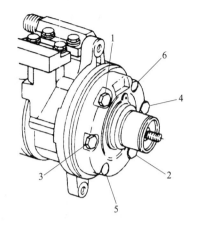

图 2-24 拧紧螺栓
1, 2, 3, 4, 5, 6—螺栓

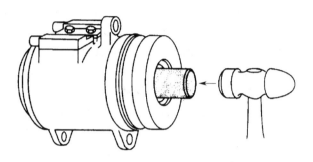

图 2-25 安装带轮

㉑ 使用非磁性塞尺，检查轮毂与转子之间的间隙，如图 2-27 所示。将轴（毂）转动半圈，再重新检查间隙。如间隙不正确，应按需更换合适的调整垫圈。安装锁紧螺母，并拧紧到 13.6～19.0N·m。

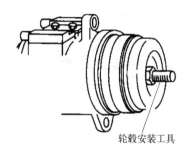

图 2-26 安装轮毂

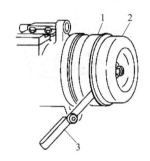

图 2-27 检查间隙
1—转子；2—轮毂；3—非磁性塞尺

二、空调制冷系统膨胀阀的检修

1. 检修 L 形膨胀阀

① 使用两个扳手拆卸膨胀阀，如图 2-28 所示。

② 将膨胀阀装在歧管和压力表上，并注入制冷剂，如图 2-29 所示。将膨胀阀的毛细管放入水箱中，打开高压手动阀门，使高压表指针达到 490kPa，制冷剂通过膨胀阀以气体排出。

③ 观察水箱中水温的变化（横坐标）与高压表上的读数（纵坐标），两数值的交点应落在图 2-30 中的两曲线之间，否则应更换膨胀阀。

2. 检修空调制冷系统孔管

① 将歧管压力表组安装到汽车空调系统上。

② 启动发动机，并将发动机转速调到 1000～1200r/min。

③ 将所有的空调控制开关调到最冷（MAX）位置。

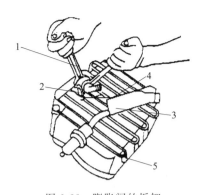

图 2-28　膨胀阀的拆卸
1—扳手；2—膨胀阀；3—感温包；4—毛细管；5—蒸发箱

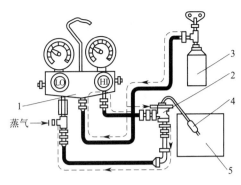

图 2-29　膨胀阀的连接
1—压力表；2—膨胀阀；3—压缩制冷剂；
4—毛细管；5—水箱

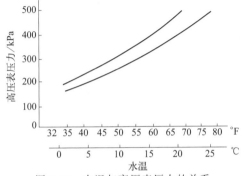

图 2-30　水温与高压表压力的关系

让空调系统运转 10～15min。观察低压侧压力表。低压侧压力表读数不正常，表明孔管不能让足够数量的制冷剂进入蒸发器。确定问题是由系统进水引起还是由系统堵塞所引起。将一块温热（约 52℃）的布放在固定孔管的周围，观察低压侧压力表，如果压力读数上升到正常值或者接近正常值，表明系统内有水分。如果系统中有水分，必须更换储液器。如果无变化则可能是孔管堵塞，必须更换孔管。更换孔管时将孔管拆卸工具安装到孔管上，顺时针转动 T 形手柄，使工具与孔管的舌片刚好啮合，握住 T 形手柄，并顺时针转动孔管拆卸工具的外套壳，拆下孔管，如图 2-31 所示。

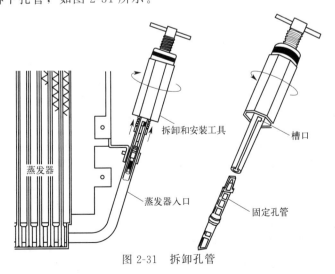

图 2-31　拆卸孔管

三、汽车空调冷凝器的检修

① 检查冷凝器表面及冷凝器与发动机水箱之间（停机检查）是否有碎片、杂物、泥污，并进行清理和用水清洗。

② 检查冷凝器表面有无脱漆，注意及时补漆，以免锈蚀。

③ 检查冷凝器表面及管接头处（包括储液器接头处）有无油迹。若有，判断是否有制冷剂泄漏。

④ 若翅片弯曲，要用尖嘴钳小心扳直，或用专用翅片梳子梳直。

⑤ 若冷凝器管被石头等外力击打而折弯、压扁、破损，应及时修理。

⑥ 检查导风罩是否完好、冷凝器与水箱之间的距离是否合理（二者距离不应超过 5mm，否则空气在其之间循环会产生紊流，影响散热）。

四、汽车空调制冷系统的故障案例诊断过程

遇此故障（见任务二任务导入），应首先用歧管压力表检查系统压力，如果高压低于 0.883MPa，低压低于 0.078MPa，同时，从玻璃检测窗中发现有气泡，出风口出风不冷，表明制冷剂不足或有严重泄漏，应予检查并补充制冷剂。检修后，使发动机以 2000 r/min 的转速运转，直至气泡消失，用歧管压力表检查，低压侧压力应为 0.118～0.216MPa，高压侧压力应为 1.274～1.596MPa。

接着，检查系统是否脏堵。系统脏堵，是指压缩机运转中产生的机械杂质和制冷剂对系统内壁作用而脱落的杂质。该杂质将储液干燥罐或膨胀阀堵住，使制冷剂流动受阻。对此，可用歧管压力表检查，如果低压侧呈真空，高压侧压力很低，同时，储液干燥罐或膨胀阀前后管路上挂霜或有结冰现象，出风口出风不冷，并且关机后再开机也没有多大变化，即说明系统脏堵。处理方法是更换储液干燥器或用酒精清洗膨胀阀。

冷凝器风机不转，多半是由滑动轴承缺油、轴承烧坏或电动机绕组断路、短路所致。经检查，如果轴承缺油，可在电动机后部滑动轴承含油毛毡的上端钻一小孔，用油壶注入几滴 30 号机油进行润滑；如果滑动轴承烧坏，可将电动机后盖拆下，按规定要求，换装新轴承；如果电动机绕组有断路或短路故障，应分解电动机进一步检修或换装新风机。

冷凝器周围空气流通不畅，冷却不良，可用歧管压力表进行检查。如果高压侧压力较高，而且发动机冷却系统散热片和冷凝器散热片处积存灰尘、杂物较多，应清除杂物和灰尘并用自来水冲洗干净，使其通风散热良好。蒸发器通风道被杂物和灰尘堵塞，可打开空调进行检查。如果出风口风量很小，出风不冷，即表明蒸发器通风道被灰尘和杂物堵塞，应取出杂物、清除灰尘，并用一块合适的铁丝网装在蒸发器进风侧，以防灰尘和杂物被大量吸入。

压缩机电磁离合器打滑，可启动发动机，打开空调进行检查。如果电磁离合器有异响或出现打滑现象，应拆下电磁离合器进行分解检查。若离合器压板和带轮工作面磨损不严重，可在磨床上磨平；若磨损严重，则应换装新电磁离合器。压缩机损坏，内部泄漏，可用歧管压力表检查。如果低压侧压力过高，高压侧压力过低，而且压缩机运转时有不正常的敲击声，压缩机的高、低压侧温差不大，表明压缩机存在阀片破碎、轴承损坏或密封垫破损等故障，应解体检修或更换压缩机。

外循环风门未关，使车外热空气进入车内，应查看真空电磁阀上的真空导管是否破损或断裂，使外循环风门无法关闭。必要时，换装新的真空导管。

习题测试

填空题

1. 在冷凝器内，制冷剂从_____变成_____。
2. 空调系统高压部分压力过高可能是由于_____过量，或系统内有_____。
3. 当空调系统从 R-12 替换为 R-134a 后，原储液干燥器因含有_____干燥剂，应被含有_____或_____的干燥器替换。

任务三　汽车空调控制系统的检修

【学习目标】

知识要求：掌握汽车空调控制系统的结构、原理、故障诊断的思路及方法。

能力要求：

1. 能根据维修计划，选择正确的检测和诊断设备对汽车空调控制系统进行故障诊断；
2. 能使用多用表、故障诊断仪、制冷剂检测仪及常用检测和诊断设备对汽车空调系统传感器、控制器、执行器进行检测；
3. 能正确记录、分析各种检测结果并做出故障判断；
4. 能按照正确的操作规范进行传感器、执行器和控制器的更换，并能进行系统匹配设定；
5. 能对车辆进行测试，检查和评估汽车空调系统的修复质量；
6. 能根据环保要求，正确处理对环境和人体有害的辅料、废弃液体和损坏的零部件。

任务导入

一辆华普轿车，制冷剂为 R-134a，开启空调后空调不制冷，电磁离合器不吸合，有时能吸合一下，但立即脱开，无法正常工作。

知识准备

汽车的空调控制系统有压缩机、冷凝器、膨胀阀、蒸发器、鼓风电动机等主要部件。而汽车空调电路的任务便是对上述配置的工况进行调节和控制，这其实便是汽车空调电路的基本特点。图 2-32 所示为一种普通轿车的空调装置电气线路图。

一、电源的控制

这部分包括了蓄电池、点火开关、熔丝继电器以及鼓风电动机开关、鼓风电动机、压力开关、电磁离合器等。当点火开关接通时，只要鼓风电动机开关闭合，空调电路便开始正常工作，此时，电磁离合器吸合→压缩机运转→制冷系统进行循环，开始制冷。由于鼓风电动机的运转，被蒸发器制冷的空气也被送入车厢内。

二、压缩机电磁离合器的控制

由于轿车的压缩机是由发动机直接驱动，所以当电磁离合器吸合后压缩机才会随之运转

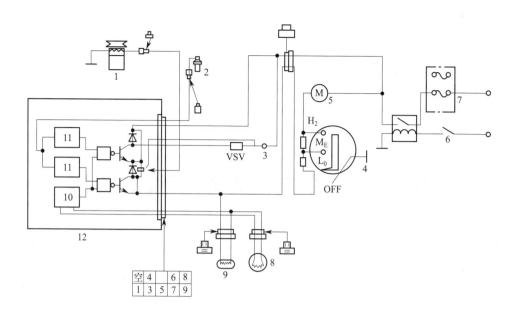

图 2-32　普通轿车空调电气线路

1—压缩机电磁离合器；2—点火线圈；3—压力开关；4—鼓风电动机开关；5—鼓风电动机；
6—点火开关；7—熔断器；8—温度调节旋钮；9—热敏电阻；10—温度检测电路；
11—发动机转速检测电路；12—放大器

作动力输出，而电磁离合器的吸合必须是它的线圈通电，产生电磁吸力，使动力压板吸合在带轮上，再通过带轮来带动压缩机运转。

作为控制电路而言，一般只要点火开关在接通位置，鼓风电动机开关打开，鼓风电动机电路被接通的同时，就会供给一放大电路电流，通过该电路将电磁离合器线圈接通而产生吸合。

三、压力开关电路

压力开关电路是制冷系统正常安全运行的必备电路。因为当制冷系统由某种原因而导致压力升高时，如果没有保护装置，将会引起制冷系统的运行事故。在这时，采用压力开关将系统断开，使压缩机停止运行，从而保护压缩机和制冷系统。

在压力开关中，一般采用将空调系统压力导入开关内，让开关的触点在机械力的作用下强行分离，从而切断开关回路，电磁离合器分离，使压缩机停止运行。

从上面所述可以看出，整个电路系统中，汽车空调电气系统的基本元件和电路主要是围绕着压缩机电磁离合器的开停线路为控制中心。

四、汽车空调电路中的典型控制回路

一般电器电路都是由它的各种控制功能的需要而配置各种控制回路，汽车空调电路也是如此。

五、速度控制电路

汽车空调速度控制电路主要是对发动机处于怠速和高速时的控制，以防止发动机负荷过

大和车厢内供冷量过剩。

任务实施

一、丰田花冠轿车空调电路故障检测与排除步骤

1. 电控元件位置

丰田花冠轿车空调电路的电控元件位置如图 2-33 所示。

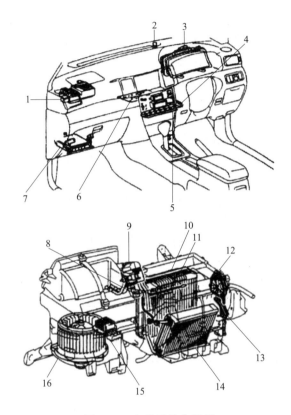

图 2-33 电控元件位置图

1—仪表板接线盒；2—日光传感器；3—组合仪表；4—车内温度传感器；5—中心组合板（空调控制总成）；
6—空调放大器；7—发动机（和 ECT）ECU；8—膨胀阀；9—网状风挡伺服电动机；10—蒸发器；
11—蒸发器温度传感器；12—出风口风挡控制伺服电动机；13—空气混合风挡控制伺服电动机；
14—加热器散热器；15—鼓风机电动机线性控制器；16—鼓风机电动机

2. 电路检查及故障码的调取和清除

① 将点火开关转至 ON 位置，同时按下 AUTO 和 R/F 开关，进行指示灯检查。如果 AUTO 和 R/F 开关没有同时按下，则取消检查模式并开始 A/C 控制。

② 指示灯检查结束后，则自动进入故障码检查（传感器检查）连续操作模式。在这种模式下，按下 R/F 开关，则进入调节器检查连续操作模式；按下 OFF 开关，则取消检查模式并能开始 A/C 控制；按下 DEF 开关，则进入故障码检查（传感器检查）分步操作模式。

③ 在故障码检查（传感器检查）分步操作模式下，按下 R/F 开关，则进入调节器检查

连续操作模式，按下 AUTO 开关，则返回到故障码检查（传感器检查）连续操作模式；按下 DEF 开关，则进行分步操作；按下 OFF 开关，则取消检查模式并能开始 A/C 控制。

④ 在调节器检查连续操作模式下，按下 AUTO 开关，则进入故障码检查（传感器检查）连续操作模式；按下 OFF 开关，则取消检查模式并能开始 A/C 控制；按下 DEF 开关，则进入调节器检查分步操作模式。

⑤ 在调节器检查分步操作模式下，按下 R/F 开关，则返回到调节器检查连续操作模式；按下 AUTO 开关，则返回到故障码检查（传感器检查）连续操作模式；按下 DEF 开关，则进行分步操作；按下 OFF 开关，则取消检查模式并能开始 A/C 控制。

⑥ 指示灯检查。同时按下 AUTO 和 R/F 开关，将点火开关转至 ON 位置，所有的指示灯在 1s 内应亮灭 4 次。完成指示灯检查后，系统自动进入故障码检查模式。

⑦ 故障码检查（传感器检查）。在结束指示灯检查后，系统自动进入到故障码检查模式，这时可通过控制面板读取故障码。如果要求显示变慢，则按下 DEF 开关，转换至分步操作模式。每按 DEF 开关一次，故障码变化一次。

⑧ 故障码清除。

a. 在进行传感器检查期间，同时按下 DEF 开关和 R/F 开关，即可清除故障码。

b. 从发动机室中继电器盒内拔出 DOME 保险丝至少 20s 或更长时间，即可清除故障码。

⑨ 调节器检查。

a. 进入故障码检查模式后，按下 R/F 开关，便进入到调节器检查模式。

b. 由于每个风挡、电动机和继电器以 1s 为时间间隔，在温度显示屏上按顺序显示，用手检查温度和空气流量。如果要求显示变慢，则按下 DEF 开关，转换至分步操作模式。每按 DEF 开关一次，显示屏变化一次。

⑩ 空调放大器端子电压。检测空调放大器端子间的电压，检查结果应符合表 2-1 中的要求，否则应检查相关传感器和电气配线。空调放大器连接器如图 2-34 所示。

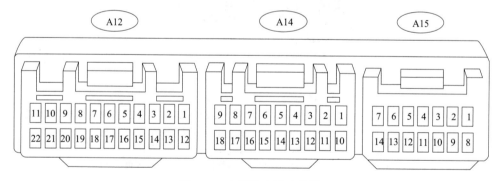

图 2-34 空调放大器连接器

表 2-1 空调放大器端子电压列举

测试端子	配线颜色	测试条件	标准值
TP—SG-1(A12-4—A12-12)	白蓝色—棕黄色	点火开关在 ON 位置,温度开关最冷位置→最热位置	3.5～4.5V→0.5～1.5V
TPM—SG-2(A12-5—A12-3)	蓝橙色—蓝黄色	点火开关在 ON 位置,出风口 FACE→DEF 位置	3.5～4.5V→0.5～1.5V
S5-1—SG-1(A12-6—A12-2)	白红色—棕黄色	点火开关在 ON 位置	4.5～5.5V
S5-2—SG-2(A12-7—A12-3)	淡绿色—蓝黄色	点火开关在 ON 位置	4.5～5.5V

3. 手动空调部件检查

（1）检查空调放大器电路

不要脱开空调放大器连接器，检测空调放大器配线侧连接器端子间的电压，检查结果应符合标准要求，否则应检查相关传感器和电气配线。后侧空调放大器连接器如图2-35所示。

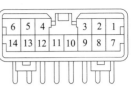

图2-35 后侧空调放大器连接器

（2）检查鼓风机开关

检查鼓风机开关的导通性。如图2-36所示，鼓风机开关在OFF位置时，端子间不导通；鼓风机开关在LO位置时，端子1与8间应导通；鼓风机开关在M1位置时，端子1、6、8三者间应导通；鼓风机开关在M2位置时，端子1、5、8三者间应导通；鼓风机开关在HI位置时，端子1、4、8三者间应导通。若导通性不符合要求，则应更换鼓风机开关。将蓄电池正极与鼓风机开关端子2相连，负极与端子3相连，照明灯应亮。

（3）检查空调开关

检查空调开关的导通性，如图2-37所示，按下空调开关时，端子2与5间应导通。若导通性不符合要求，则应更换空调开关。

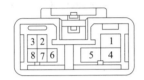

图2-36 鼓风机开关

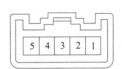

图2-37 空调开关

将蓄电池正极与空调开关端子4相连，负极与端子3相连，照明灯应亮。若照明灯不亮，则应更换空调开关。

将蓄电池正极与空调开关端子2相连，负极与端子1相连，按下空调开关，A/C指示器应亮。若A/C指示器不亮，则应更换空调开关。

按下空调开关时，将蓄电池正极与空调开关端子2相连，负极与端子1相连，再将蓄电池正极与空调开关端子4相连，A/C指示器亮度应变化。若亮度不变，则应更换空调开关。

图2-38 鼓风机电阻器连接器

（4）检查鼓风机电阻器

检测鼓风机电阻器端子间的电阻，端子1与2间的电阻为1.398～1.605Ω，端子1与3间的电阻为0.465～0.535Ω，端子1与4间的电阻为3.069～3.531Ω。鼓风机电阻器连接器如图2-38所示。

二、汽车空调的检查方法

汽车空调在检查过程中，要做到一听、二看、三摸、四检查。

启动发动机并稳定在1500r/min左右，将空调系统的鼓风机启动并置于高速挡，功能键置于A/C挡，并移动调温键从冷至热，再由热至冷慢慢移动，测定或手感空调出风口的温度变化以及各控制键的操纵是否灵活、轻便。

1. 一听

从压缩机的运行声音状况来判断其运转状况。

① 听到压缩机传出清脆而均匀的阀片跳动声，即为正常。

② 听到有敲击声，即表明制冷剂有"液击"声或者奔油（油量过多）敲缸等故障。

③ 听到机体内有较严重的摩擦声，以及离合器时而发出摩擦声，表明压缩机负荷太重，润滑油不足以及离合器打滑。

④ 听到外部有拍击声，是V带太松或者严重磨损。

⑤ 听一下空调器内的风扇转动是否有响声。如果风扇有响声，表明是叶片碰击异物、风扇轴承磨损或者缺油。

⑥ 在停机过程中，更清晰地听到机体内运动部件的连续撞击声，则是内部的运动部件磨损严重引起的轴与轴承之间，活塞与缸体之间，连杆与轴之间间隙过大或者松动。

2. 二看

① 观察冷凝器表面是否清洁，因为杂物和泥土附在冷凝器上，会影响制冷效果。平时要经常用水清洗冷凝器。但是应注意，在清洗冷凝器时，不要损伤翅片。对于已变形的翅片，应细心地用尖嘴钳矫正过来。

② 汽车空调器的蒸发器进风处，一般汽车都装有空气过滤网，所以要定期观察空气过滤网。

③ 观察空调制冷系统的所有连接部位是否有油渍。一旦有油渍，说明此处有制冷剂渗漏，此时应用电子检漏仪或其他类检漏装置进行检查。一旦发现或确定有制冷剂泄漏，必须马上排除故障。

④ 检查压缩机轴封是否渗漏。

⑤ 仔细检查各软管有无磨损、老化、鼓泡、裂纹和渗漏等现象。由于汽车的冷、暖系统采用了大量的橡胶管，在汽车行驶过程中易与汽车车身摩擦产生磨损，在发动机室内因经受高温容易老化，制冷管遇低温容易龟裂，结果导致制冷剂和冷冻润滑油泄漏，使水分、空气和灰尘渗入制冷系统，使压缩机及各个部件受到损害。因此，一旦发现橡胶管和发动机接触，要及时隔开并固定好橡胶管。橡胶管穿过金属板，一般都应有防护套，并注意防护套要牢固，否则金属会割破橡胶管。

3. 三摸

用手触摸正在运行中的空调系统管路和各部件的温度。一般在正常情况下，高压端的管路温度应在55℃以下，而低压端管路因处于低温状态，所以低压端的部件和管路，连接部分表面都会结有水露。

① 用手小心摸触高压区，特别是高压端金属部件，如压缩机的出口阀、冷凝器、储液干燥器等。这些部分应都是热的，正常为手感觉热而不烫手。若感觉烫手，则应先检查冷凝器的冷却是否良好，冷凝器表面是否清洁而无杂物，风扇的风量是否过小。此时可以试着用大风扇对着冷凝器吹，若还是烫手，则可能是制冷剂过多。若高压端手感热度不够，则为制冷剂过少；若没有温度，则为制冷剂漏光。

② 低压管的手感为冰凉，有水露，但不应该有霜。若有霜说明系统有故障，可能是膨胀阀的故障，也可能是制冷剂充注太多，需要放掉一些；或者是蒸发器的温度传感器或恒温器出现了故障。

③ 如果在储液干燥器上出现霜或水露，这说明干燥剂已破碎堵住了制冷剂流动管道，而且此处的前端高压区表现为温度高且很烫手。此时必须尽快排除堵塞问题，换上一只新的储液干燥器。

④ 膨胀阀的手感温度是比较特殊的，它的制冷剂进口连接处是热的，而其出口连接处是凉的，有水露。

⑤ 用双手触摸压缩机的进气口和排气口，手感温度应该有明显的差别。若没有温度差

别，则说明制冷剂已经全部漏光；若差别不大，则说明制冷剂不足。

⑥ 用手触摸各个接头，检查是否已经松动等。特别是一些电器插接器的连接是否松动，这些对空调系统的正常工作都有极大的影响。所以，正常的检查必须包括对电器连接件的固定、紧固和清洁等。

4. 四检查

对系统进行了上述 3 个步骤的初检后，还需做进一步的检查，以准确判断空调系统的故障所在。

① 检查 V 带的张力：空调带轮直径不同，中心距不同，所要求的张力也不同；新、旧 V 带的张力也不同；即使是新 V 带，用上 5min 后，其张力也会发生较大的变化。所以对新安装的 V 带必须进行两次调整。第一次为新安装后，调整到规定值。运行 30min 后新 V 带两边的毛边已经磨去，再进行第二次调整。

② 检查电磁离合器：接通离合器电源开关，此时压缩机应马上运行；断开电源，压缩机应立即停止运行。若不是这样，应先检查开关是否损坏，再检查电磁线圈是否正常。

③ 检查风扇电动机的调速器：打开风扇电动机开关后，从低挡到高挡进行转速调节，以检查其送出的风量是否有变化，若没有变化，则可能是调速器的电阻损坏。

④ 检查高、低压保护开关和过热保护器：高、低压保护开关和过热保护器的功能是在制冷系统发生故障时，保护压缩机和制冷系统不会损坏。它们都和空调开关、风扇开关串联在一起。当系统工作压力太高，或者当环境温度太低，制冷剂泄漏过多，高、低压力开关便会切断压缩机离合器电路。

⑤ 检查供暖系统：首先应保证有足够的冷却液，冷却液若不干净或有铁锈，液色变黄，都应该将冷却液放掉，再用化学清洗剂清洗冷却系统，用清水清洗干净，然后加满冷却液。启动发动机至冷却液温度正常。拨动调温键至取暖位置，这时出风口应有温暖空气吹出。

⑥ 检查膨胀阀：膨胀阀的毛细管应牢固地夹紧并用绝缘布包捆在蒸发器出口处，有的毛细管应准确地插入制冷管路的插孔中，并用感温包包裹。

⑦ 检查视液镜：汽车空调一般装配有视液镜，来观察制冷系统内部制冷剂的流动情况，大多数轿车的视液镜设置在储液干燥器的出口处，只有个别轿车或大、中型客车视液镜设置在储液干燥器和膨胀阀之间的管道上。视液镜的设置为保养汽车空调带来了许多方便。在检查汽车空调时，可以通过观察视液镜中制冷剂的流动状况来确定制冷系统的制冷工况是否正常。通过视液镜来检查制冷系统制冷工况的步骤如下：启动发动机，并将转速稳定在 1500～1700r/min，让制冷压缩机运行 5min；擦干净视液镜的玻璃，把空调功能选择键置于最大制冷状态，且使送风机（包括空调器和冷凝器送风机）达到最高转速。这时可以通过视液镜观察到以下几种情况，如图 2-39 所示。

a. 清晰：图 2-39(a) 所示的视液镜内没有气泡出现，也看不见液体流动。这种状况表明系统有以下 3 种故障。

(a) 表示系统内制冷剂已全部泄漏。这时若用手触摸压缩机进、排气口，没有温度差异，空调器出风口的空气温度也不低。这时应立即关闭制冷系统，检查制冷系统制冷剂泄漏的原因，并进行维修。

(b) 制冷剂过多。两手分别触摸压缩机进气管和排气管口，温差明显，而且高压侧有烫手感，低压侧能看到冰霜；空调器出风口的温度比正常制冷剂量时高 3～5℃；关闭空调系统压缩机 45s 以后，视液镜内仍然清晰无气泡流过，便可以判断是系统内制冷剂量过多，此时必须把多余的制冷剂排出。否则，会出现制冷性能降低、能耗上升等故障。此时用压力表测量高压端，其压力超过正常值。

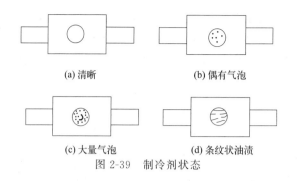

(a) 清晰　　　　　　(b) 偶有气泡

(c) 大量气泡　　　　(d) 条纹状油渍

图 2-39　制冷剂状态

(c) 制冷剂适量。此时的现象和制冷剂量过多时相比较,首先是高压不烫手,出风口的温度较低。

b. 偶有气泡。图 2-39(b) 所示为偶尔或者缓慢地看到有少量气泡流过,此状态说明制冷剂量稍有不足或制冷系统的干燥剂已经饱和,制冷剂内有水分混入。区分上述情况的方法如下。

(a) 当膨胀阀有结霜现象出现,并且视液镜有时能看到变颜色的干燥剂,则说明系统制冷剂含有水分,应马上更换干燥瓶。

(b) 当膨胀阀没有结霜现象出现,则说明制冷剂量不足,必须加入适量的制冷剂,并检查有无泄漏之处。

c. 有大量气泡或泡沫状。如图 2-39(c) 所示,此状态说明系统内制冷剂量严重不足,并伴有大量水分和空气进入系统。此时必须采用制冷剂检测仪查漏维修。然后将制冷系统抽真空,加入足量的冷冻润滑油和制冷剂。

d. 视液镜的玻璃上有条纹状的油渍或黑油状泡沫。如图 2-39(d) 所示,表明系统有以下 3 种故障。

(a) 如果压缩机进、排气管有明显温差,此时关闭空调系统压缩机,视液镜内玻璃的油渍干净,说明系统制冷剂量略少,而冷冻润滑油量过多。此时应从系统内释放一些冷冻润滑油,再加入适量的制冷剂。

(b) 如果压缩机进、排气管有明显温差,此时关闭空调系统压缩机,玻璃上留下的油渍是黑色的或有其他杂物,则说明空调系统内的冷冻润滑油已变质、受污染。此时在清洗制冷系统后,应重新注入冷冻润滑油和制冷剂。

(c) 如果压缩机进、排气阀门没有明显的温差,空调器出口也没有冷气出来,则说明制冷剂已全部漏完,视液镜上的是冷冻润滑油。

三、汽车空调系统的定期维护

(1) 制冷循环系统

① 检视高、低压管道。高低压管道的管类码应齐全,螺栓紧固不松动。软管表面无起泡、老化或破损现象;硬管焊接处无裂纹或渗漏现象。没有与其他机件发生碰擦干涉现象。用检漏仪检测各管道接头处有无泄漏。

② 检视膨胀阀。膨胀阀应无堵塞,感温包作用正常,膨胀阀能根据温度的变化而自动调节制冷剂的供给量。

③ 检视储液干燥过滤器。在制冷系统正常工作时,其表面应无露珠或挂霜现象。更换干燥剂(可拆式)或根据需要更换储液干燥过滤器总成(不可拆式)。

④ 检查、清洁蒸发器和冷凝器,检查全部固定螺栓、螺母。蒸发器、冷凝器应无渗漏,散热片应无折弯、无尘土杂物堵塞现象,蒸发器、冷凝器座应无裂纹,各固定螺栓、螺母应

齐全、紧固、可靠。

⑤ 检视制冷剂量。制冷系统工作时，观察视液镜，应无气泡流动现象。发动机转速为 2000r/min，送风机以最高速旋转和制冷选用最强挡的条件下，系统的工作压力应为低压侧 0.147～0.2MPa，高压侧 1.4～1.5MPa。

（2）压缩机

① 更换压缩机润滑油，并清洁或更换油滤网。压缩机润滑油面高度应达到视液镜的上部边缘或原厂规定标准，油滤网应清洁，无杂物堵塞或缺损现象。

② 检视进、排气阀。进、排气阀开闭灵活，作用正常。

③ 检视轴衬。轴衬处不应有渗漏现象。

（3）电气系统

① 检视冷凝器和蒸发器的风机。各风机工作正常无异响，叶片无裂损，固定螺栓、螺母齐全、牢固、有效。冷凝器风机与冷凝器散热片无干涉现象。

② 检视高、低压压力开关。高压开关在压力大于 2.2MPa 时应能切断通向电磁离合器的供电，当压力小于 2MPa 时能自动复位；低压开关在压力小于 0.2MPa 时应能切断通往电磁离合器的供电，当压力大于 0.2MPa 时能自动复位。

③ 检视电磁离合器。电磁离合器应离合良好，无打滑现象，离合器轴承在旋转时无偏摆拖滞现象。

④ 检查送风机工作是否正常、可靠。

（4）其他

① 紧固件：检查有无损伤，如发现松动则要加以紧固。

② V 带：检查其张力和磨损程度。

③ V 带张紧轮：检查其能否圆滑旋转。

④ 空气过滤网：如发现堵塞应更换空气过滤网。

四、汽车空调系统故障检测

① 利用解码器对汽车空调系统进行故障检测并读取故障码。

② 根据故障码对所测得的故障内容进行分析。

③ 根据维修手册进行故障排除。

五、汽车空调控制系统的故障案例诊断过程

连接车辆故障诊断仪后进行测试。测试过程中发现间歇性不制冷时压缩机没有吸合。根据别克轿车自动空调的控制原理分析，造成压缩机不吸合的原因除压缩机本身故障以外，还有可能是动力系统控制计算机 PCM、空调开关的请求信号、压力传感器信号以及室内/室外温度传感器等出现故障。

连接空调压力表，测量空调管路压力，结果显示高压为 2000 kPa，低压为 350 kPa 左右，这说明空调系统压力正常。打开发动机舱内右侧的继电器盒，找到压缩机继电器。检查继电器的吸合线圈未发现异常。用多用表检测压缩机继电器的控制线（继电器吸合时为低电位，断开时为高电位），发现当空调不制冷时从控制计算机 PCM 到压缩机继电器的控制线没有低电位。因而可以认定该车空调系统间歇性不制冷的故障并非由执行部分所引起，故障原因可能是 PCM 本身故障、空调相关信号或线路不正常。

检测 PCM 到压缩机继电器之间的相关线路，发现故障出现时 PCM 第 39 号线没有低电位信号。接上诊断仪监测空调系统的空调开关请求信号、压力传感器信号以及室内/室外温

度传感器信号，结果发现在有故障现象出现时压力传感器数据异常，而其他传感器数据没有明显变化。根据检测结果判断该故障为压力开关出现间歇性卡滞，导致PCM控制压缩机离合器间断吸合。更换压力开关，间歇性不制冷故障消失，系统恢复正常。

习题测试

简答题

请演示空调系统压力的检查方法。

任务四　充注与回收汽车空调制冷剂

【学习目标】

知识要求：掌握汽车空调制冷剂的基础知识。

能力要求：

1. 汽车空调制冷剂的充注与回收方法。
2. 汽车空调制冷剂的充注与回收工具的使用。

 任务导入

一辆大众迈腾轿车，该车配备自动空调，开启空调后空调出风口温度不太冷。

 知识准备

安装、检修空调制冷系统时，会有一定量的空气进入制冷系统，空气中含有的水蒸气会导致制冷系统的膨胀阀冰堵、冷凝压力升高、系统零部件发生腐蚀等。因此，在加注新制冷剂之前，必须先对制冷系统抽真空，然后再加注制冷剂。

一、充注汽车空调系统制冷剂

当制冷系统抽真空达到要求，并且经检漏确定制冷系统不存在泄漏部位后，才能向制冷系统充注制冷剂。

真空泵用于制冷系统安装、维修后的抽真空，排除系统内的空气和水分。抽真空并不能将制冷系统内的水抽出，而是使制冷系统内产生真空后降低了水的沸点，水在较低温度下沸腾，以蒸气的形式从系统中抽出。

常用的真空泵，用油密封的有滑阀式和刮片式两种，用水密封的有水环式，用油密封的真空泵真空度较高。常用的刮片式真空泵的结构如图2-40所示。

它主要由定子、转子、排气阀和刮片等组成。工作时弹簧弹力使两只刮片紧贴在定子的缸壁上，以保证其密封性，而定子上的进、排气口被转子和刮片分隔成两部分，形成吸气腔和压缩腔。当转子旋转时，进气腔容积逐渐扩大，腔内的压力下降，从而吸入气体，压缩腔容积逐渐减小，压力升高，气体从排气阀排到空气中。经过反复循环，把容器内的空气抽空，从而达到真空的目的。

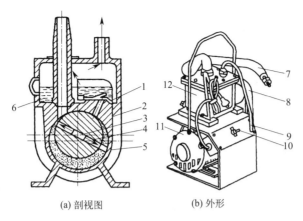

图 2-40 刮片式真空泵结构
1—排气阀；2—转子；3—弹簧；4—刮片；5—定子；6—润滑油；7—吸气管；
8—传动带保护罩；9—排气嘴；10—开关；11—真空泵；12—电动机

充注制冷剂的方法有两种，一种方法是高压端充注，从压缩机排气阀（高压阀）的旁通孔（多用通道）充注，充入的是制冷剂液体。这种充注方法安全、快速，适用于制冷系统的第一次充注，即经检漏、抽真空后的系统充注。但使用这种方法时必须注意，充注时不可开启压缩机（发动机停转），且制冷剂罐要求倒立，如图 2-41 所示。另一方法是低压端充注，从压缩机吸气阀（低压阀）的旁通孔（多用通道）充注，充入的是制冷剂气体，这种充注方法充注速度慢，适用于制冷系统补充制冷剂，其充注方法如图 2-42 所示。

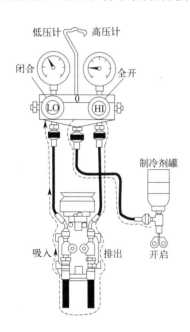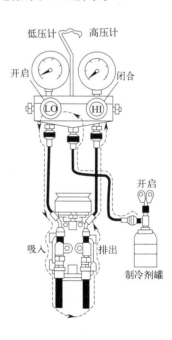

图 2-41 高压端充注液态制冷剂　　　　图 2-42 低压端充注气态制冷剂

充注前，须先确定注入制冷剂的数量，充注量过多或过少，都会影响空调制冷效果。压缩机的铭牌上一般都标有所用的制冷剂的种类及充量。

为便于维修汽车空调和随车携带，制冷剂厂商制作了一种小罐制冷剂（一般为 400g 左

右），如果要将制冷剂注入汽车空调制冷系统中，就必须使用注入阀。如图 2-43 所示，制冷剂注入阀利用蝶形手柄前部的针阀刺破制冷剂罐，通过螺纹接头把制冷剂引入歧管压力表组。

二、补充与排放汽车空调制冷系统制冷剂

① 制冷剂的补充。汽车空调系统经过一段时间运行后，由于汽车颠簸振动等原因，某些部位的接头松动，制冷剂泄漏，制冷效果变差。经过查漏、排漏后，从低压侧向系统补充制冷剂，如图 2-44 所示。

② 制冷剂排放。由于修理或其他原因，需将系统内的制冷剂排放掉，其排放方法有两种：一是将制冷剂放到大气中，但此方法污染环境；二是回收制冷剂，但要有回收装置。排放时，周围环境一定要通风良好，不能接近明火，否则会产生有毒气体。

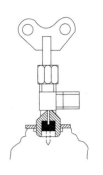

图 2-43 制冷剂注入阀结构

三、加注汽车空调制冷系统冷冻润滑油

汽车空调制冷系统的冷冻润滑油消耗很少，每两年更换一次即可，每次更换应按规定数量加注（一般压缩机的铭牌上会标注润滑油的型号和数量）。加注时要使用同一牌号的冷冻润滑油，不同牌号的冷冻润滑油混用会生成沉淀物污染空调制冷系统。

汽车空调压缩机是高速运转装置，其工作是否正常，取决于润滑是否充分，但过多的润滑油会影响制冷效果。当更换压缩机和制冷系统某一部件时，需检查压缩机内的油量。

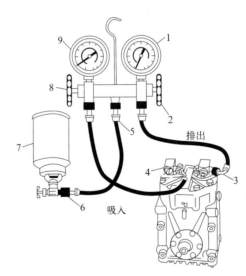

图 2-44 制冷剂的补充

1—压力表；2—高压侧手动阀；3—高压侧压缩机检修阀；4—低压侧压缩机检修阀；5—充注软管；
6—制冷剂罐开关；7—制冷剂；8—低压侧手动阀；9—复合压力表

1. 压缩机冷冻润滑油量的检查

如图 2-45 所示，卸下加油塞，通过加油孔察看并旋转离合器前板，把油尺擦干净，插入压缩机内，直到油尺端部碰到压缩机内壳体为止，取出油尺，观察油尺浸入深度。冷冻润滑油量合适时，压缩机内油面应在前 4~6 格之间，如果少需加入，如果多需放出，然后拧紧加油塞。

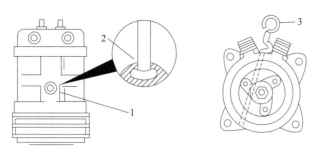

图 2-45 空调压缩机冷冻润滑油油量的检查
1—加油塞；2—加油孔；3—油尺

2. 冷冻润滑油加注

维修汽车空调制冷系统时不需加注冷冻润滑油，但在更换制冷系统部件以及发现系统有严重泄漏时，必须补充冷冻润滑油。补充冷冻润滑油的方法有以下两种。

① 利用压缩机本身的抽吸作用，将冷冻润滑油从低压阀处吸入，这时发动机要保持低速运转。

② 利用抽真空加注冷冻润滑油。

四、回收制冷剂

制冷剂本身对于人类来说是无毒无害的，但对于环境来说却是一个重要的污染源。R-12 就是导致全球臭氧空洞的罪魁祸首，它的代替产品 R-134a 虽然在对臭氧层的破坏上不如 R-12 那样严重，但也会污染大气。

回收装置体积小，使用轻便，只用于为其设计的那些制冷剂。它的润滑油、软管和密封适合用于有限范围的制冷剂。如果用于不匹配的制冷剂，回收设备就会被损坏。R-12 和 R-134a 两种回收装置如图 2-46 所示。回收制冷剂的方法有冷却法、压缩法两种。

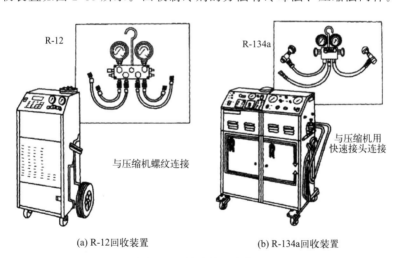

(a) R-12回收装置　　(b) R-134a回收装置

图 2-46 制冷剂回收装置

① 冷却法。冷却法是使制冷剂蒸气冷却液化，回收时，可利用干冰等使制冷剂冷却、液化后回收，回收容器需冷却到 −30℃，这种方法适合于干净的制冷剂，图 2-47 所示为冷却法回收装置的示意图。冷却法有一套独立的冷冻循环系统，回收容器中的制冷剂在蒸发器中冷凝成液体。从汽车空调系统排出的制冷剂通过过滤干燥器，除去水分和杂质；通过分油

器除去制冷剂中的润滑油。对于制冷剂纯度要求不太严格的场合,被回收的制冷剂可重新加到制冷系统中。

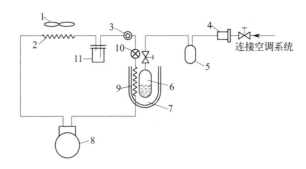

图 2-47　冷却法回收装置

1—风机;2—冷凝器;3—视液窗;4—过滤干燥器;5—分油器;6—回收容器;7—隔热容器;
8—压缩机;9—蒸发器;10—膨胀阀;11—储液干燥器

② 压缩法。压缩法是用压缩的方法将制冷剂蒸发变成液体,其工作原理如图 2-48 所示。从空调系统排出的制冷剂通过过滤干燥器,除去水分和杂质,受吸气压力调节阀控制,部分液态制冷剂存留在储液罐中,气态制冷剂进入压缩机被压缩成高温高压气体,通过分油器时,与制冷剂混合的冷冻润滑油被分离出来,流回压缩机,制冷剂则进入冷凝器被冷却,通过气液分离器,被冷凝的液态制冷剂流到回收容器,回收容器中的气态制冷剂通过毛细管部分被压缩机吸入。

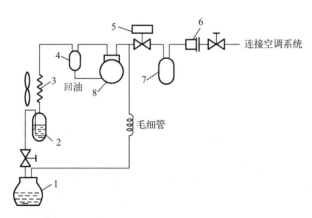

图 2-48　压缩法回收装置

1—回收容器;2—气液分离器;3—冷凝器;4—分油器;5—吸入压力调节器;
6—过滤干燥器;7—储液罐;8—压缩机

任务实施

一、操作注意事项

① 汽车空调制冷系统的冷冻润滑油消耗很少,每两年更换一次即可,充注制冷剂时要按照压缩机的铭牌上标注的制冷剂的种类及其充量进行加注。

② 如果要将制冷剂注入汽车空调制冷系统中,就必须使用注入阀。

③ 制冷剂排放时,周围环境一定要通风良好,不能接近明火,否则会产生有毒气体。

二、操作步骤

1. 放空制冷剂

（1）准备工作

① 将压力表组接入系统。

② 启动发动机，运行汽车空调系统。

③ 将发动机转速调至 1000~1200r/min，并运行 5min。

（2）制冷剂的排放

① 恢复发动机正常转速，然后关闭发动机。

② 慢慢打开高压手动阀，让制冷剂经中间软管排出，中间软管开口端应裹上白抹布，如果有冷冻油排出，应调整手动阀，至刚好无冷冻润滑油排出。

③ 当压力表读数降到 0.35MPa 以下时，慢慢打开低压手动阀，让制冷剂从高、低压两侧同时排出。

④ 观察压力表读数，随着压力下降，逐渐开大高、低压手动阀，直至高、低压表的读数指示为零。

2. 加注冷冻润滑油

选择一个有刻度的量筒，盛入比要补充的冷冻润滑油还要多的冷冻润滑油；将连接在压缩机上的低压软管从歧管压力计上拧下来，将其插入盛有冷冻润滑油的量筒内，如图 2-49 所示；启动真空泵，打开歧管压力计上的高压手动阀，补充的冷冻润滑油从压缩机的低压侧进入压缩机中，当冷冻润滑油量达到规定量时，停止真空泵的抽吸，并关闭高压手动阀。

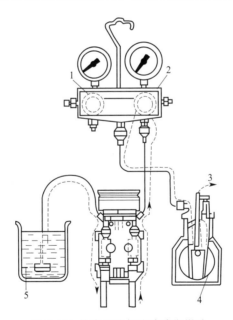

图 2-49 抽真空法加注冷冻润滑油

1—低压手动阀关闭；2—高压手动阀开启；3—排出空气；4—真空泵；5—冷冻润滑油

3. 系统抽真空

（1）准备工作

① 打开压力表组上的高、低压手动阀，中间软管连接到真空泵进口上。

② 拆除真空泵排气口护盖。

(2) 抽真空

① 启动真空泵。

② 观察压力表，表针应向下偏摆，显示略有真空。

③ 真空泵运转过 10min 之后，检查低压表读数是否高于 79.8kPa。如果真空度低于 79.8kPa，应关闭高、低压手动阀，使真空泵停转，检查系统是否有泄漏，根据情况修理。

④ 放置 5~10min，如果压力上升则说明系统有泄漏，应检查排除后，再进行抽真空工序。

⑤ 如果低压表指针保持不动，继续进行抽真空 30min 以上，关闭高、低压手动阀后，再关闭真空泵。

4. 加注制冷剂

(1) 准备工作

① 在制冷剂罐安装制冷剂注入阀之前，先以逆时针方向旋转蝶形手柄，直到阀针退回为止，再以逆时针方向旋转板状螺母直到最高位置。

② 将注入阀装到制冷剂罐顶部的螺纹槽内，然后将制冷剂注入阀顺时针拧动，直到注入阀嵌入制冷剂密封塞。

③ 将盘形螺母按顺时针方向旋转到底，再将歧管压力计上的中间软管固定到注入阀的接头上。

④ 拧紧盘形螺母。

(2) 系统停止时充注制冷剂

① 顺时针方向旋转手柄，使阀针刺穿密封塞，再逆时针方向旋转手柄，使阀针抬起。

② 松开表座上中间软管接头，直至有制冷剂流出后拧紧接头（将中间软管中的空气排出）。

③ 打开表座上高压侧手阀，观察低压表，表针应从真空范围转至压力范围。

④ 倒置制冷剂罐，使液态制冷剂进入系统。

⑤ 用手指敲击罐底，如果出现空筒声，说明罐已空。如制冷剂不足，第二罐应从低压侧进行加注。

⑥ 关闭表座上高压侧手阀，从中间软管上拆除注入阀，从系统上拆除压力表组，重新盖上所有的盖和帽。

(3) 系统运行时充注制冷剂

① 将压力表组接入系统并启动发动机，调整发动机转速到 1250r/min，保证表座上高低压阀均处于关闭状态。

② 将空调控制板上温度键调整到最冷位置，鼓风机调至高速。

③ 松开表座上中间软管接头，直至有制冷剂流出后拧紧接头（将中间软管中的空气排出）。

④ 打开表座上低压侧手阀，使气态制冷剂进入系统。

⑤ 用手指敲击罐底，如果出现空筒声，说明罐已空。如制冷剂不足，可按上述步骤再注入另一罐，直到达到规定压力为止。

⑥ 关闭表座上低压侧手阀，从中间软管上拆除注入阀；从系统拆除压力表组，重新盖上所有的盖和帽。

5. 空调系统加注制冷剂后的性能测试

① 如图 2-50 所示，将压力表组接入系统。连接时，先关闭高、低压手动阀，并在接好管后，排除管内的空气（否则管内空气会跑到制冷系统内）。

② 启动发动机，打开空调，将空调控制板上的温度键调至最冷位置，鼓风机调至高速。

③ 将发动机的转速保持在 2000r/min。

④ 将温度计放在空调出风口。

⑤ 干湿温度计放在车内空气循环进气口处（注：湿温度计的球都要覆盖饱蘸水的棉花）。
⑥ 观察温度计和干湿温度计来检测空调系统的工作性能。

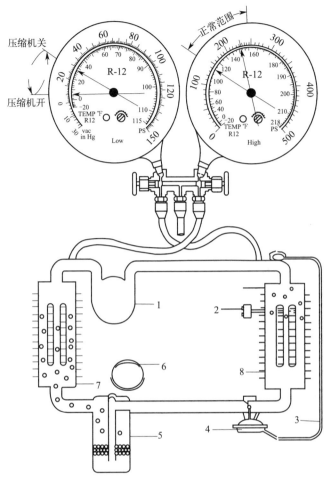

图 2-50　空调制冷系统高低压力正常值
1—压缩机；2—恒温器；3—温包毛细管；4—膨胀阀；5—储液干燥器；
6—视液镜；7—冷凝器；8—蒸发器

习题测试

简答题

制冷系统抽真空采用何设备？如何进行抽真空？

任务五　汽车空调制热系统的检修

【学习目标】

知识要求：掌握汽车空调制热系统的结构、原理、故障诊断的思路及方法。

能力要求：

1. 能根据维修计划，选择正确的检测和诊断设备对汽车空调制热系统进行故障诊断；
2. 能对汽车空调制热系统主要零部件进行维护、拆装，能使用多用表及常用检测设备对空调制热系统进行检测；
3. 能正确记录、分析各种检测结果并做出故障判断；
4. 能对车辆进行测试，检查和评估汽车空调制热系统修复质量。

任务导入

一辆大众帕萨特轿车，该车配备自动空调，冬天开启暖风后空调出风口无热风吹出。

知识准备

汽车暖气用来向驾驶车厢供热，一般在冬季寒冷时使用。暖气设备按所使用的热源可分为发动机余热式和独立热源式两种。按空气循环方式可分为内循环式、外循环式和内、外混合式 3 种。按照热载体又可分为水暖式和气暖式 2 类。

一、发动机余热式暖气装置

1. 气暖式暖气装置

气暖式暖气系统是利用发动机的排气余热进行车厢采暖。在汽油机中，发动机排气带走的热量约占 36％，在柴油发动机中，则占有 30％左右。气暖式暖气系统是最早采用的空调形式之一，它是让排气管通过驾驶室直接供暖，例如，早期的北京吉普车，以及北方寒冷地带的长途客车。

图 2-51 所示为轿车气暖式暖气装置布置。热交换器 1 接在发动机后，由进气管 10 将混合气引入热交换器加热，加热的空气通过排热风管 3，由鼓风机 5 将加热的空气送入车厢内采暖。

控制板在仪表板上，它可改变风门位置使部分热风进入除霜器 7，对车前窗玻璃除霜。若需要，可通过专用排气管 2 对后窗玻璃、侧位玻璃、脚下等部位供暖。夏季空调制冷时，从蒸发器吹出的冷风温差较大，会使人感到不舒服，这时可通过其与热风泄出阀 9 吹出的热风相混合，混合比例可根据舒适度要求由风门控制冷热风量，这样就可以得到舒适的凉风。截止阀 12 是用来关闭热风的。

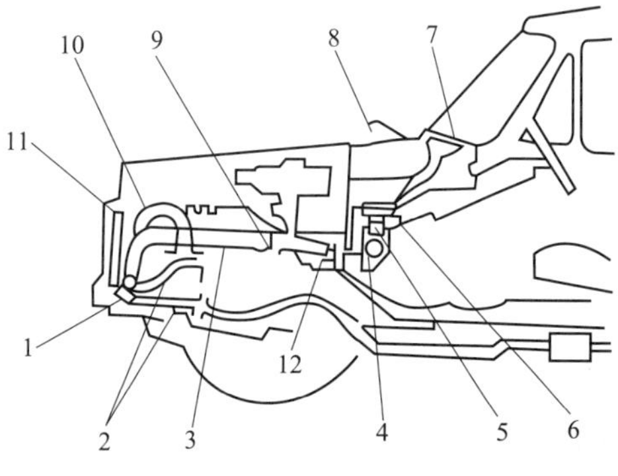

图 2-51 轿车空调余热气暖式暖风装置布置
1—热交换器；2—专用排气管（除霜、去雾）；
3—排热风管；4—转换阀；5—鼓风机；6—电动机；
7—除霜器；8—通风口；9—夏季用热风泄出阀；
10—进气管；11—挡风栅；12—截止阀

热交换器的热源为空冷后的热风，分流进入热交换器空气侧，热交换器管侧空气加热后送入车厢。气暖式暖气的传热效果是随车速变化而变化的。车速高，传热效果好；车速低，传热效果差，如图 2-52 所示。

热交换器铸成带散热翅片的管子装在发动机排气管上，一方面内腔作排气管用，另一方面外侧加热空气并将加热后的空气汇集起来，送到车内供暖用，热交换器的结构如图 2-53 所示。

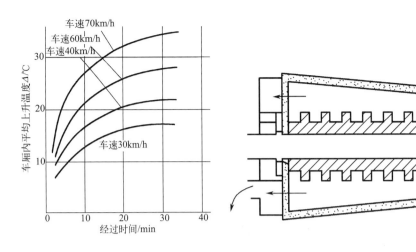

图 2-52 气暖式暖气效果　　　　　　图 2-53 气暖式热交换器
1—空气保温管；2—热变换管；3—排气管

气暖式暖风装置示意图如图 2-54 所示。它是在发动机的排气管上安装一个热交换器用于加热空气。工作时，将通往消声器的阀门关闭，汽车废气就进入热交换器内，用于加热交换器外的冷空气，冷空气通过热交换器吸收热量后温度升高，由风机吹入车厢内用于采暖和除霜。

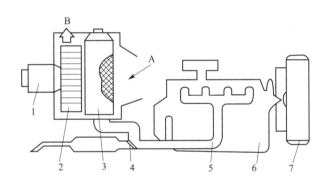

图 2-54 气暖式暖风装置示意图
1—鼓风机电动机；2—暖风鼓风机；3—热交换器；4—废气阀门；5—发动机排气管；
6—发动机；7—发动机散热器；A—新鲜空气；B—暖风

由于发动机的废气含热量较高，能够提供足够暖气来调节车内的温度，所以特别适合于北方寒冷地方解决车内供暖问题。但它的供热效果受车速、发动机工况的影响，供暖温度不稳定。其次，由于废气中含腐蚀性气体以及有毒气体和微粒，这种取暖器必须采用耐腐蚀材料，连接的密封性必须可靠，否则一旦穿孔，后果不堪设想。另外，在排气管道中加装的换热装置使排气阻力加大，对发动机工况有一定的影响。而且，这种装置的结构比较复杂，体积较大，它的应用在一定程度上受到了限制。

2. 水暖式暖气装置

水暖式暖气装量一般以水冷式发动机冷却系统中的冷却液作为热源，将冷却液引入车辆内的热交换器中，使鼓风机送来的车厢内空气（内气式）或外部空气（外气式）与热交换器中的冷却液进行热交换，鼓风机将加热后的空气送入车厢内。

轿车、载货车和中小型客车，需要的热量较少，可以用发动机冷却液的余热来直接供

暖。余热供暖设备简单,使用安全,运行经济。但其缺点是热量较小,受汽车运行工况的影响,发动机停止运行时,即没有暖气提供。

水暖式暖气系统工作原理如图 2-55 所示。从发动机出来的冷却液经过节温器 11,在温度达到 80℃时,节温器开启,让发动机冷却液流到供暖系统的加热器 5,在节温器和加热器之间设置了一个热水开关 8,用来控制热水的流动,冷却液的另一部分流到散热器。冷却液在加热器散热,加热周围的空气,然后再用风扇 4 送到车内;冷却液从加热器出来,在水泵 14 的泵吸下,又重新进入发动机的散热器内,冷却发动机,完成一次供暖循环。

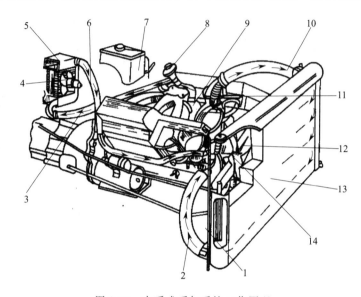

图 2-55 水暖式暖气系统工作原理
1—溢流管;2—回液管;3—加热器送水管;4,12—风扇;5—加热器;6—加热器出水管;7—溢流罐(副水箱);
8—热水开关;9—发动机;10—出液管;11—节温器;13—散热器;14—水泵

图 2-56 所示为独立式水暖暖气装置的结构,它由暖风热交换器、风机及外壳组成一个完整的总成。壳体上有吹向脚部、前部的出风口及吹向车窗起除霜作用的出风口。此种结构通常用于普通轿车、货车和小型客车。

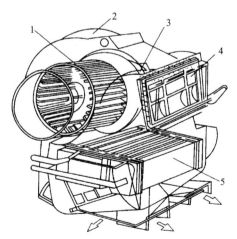

图 2-56 独立式水暖暖气装置结构
1—风机叶轮;2—壳体;3—电动机;4—暖风加热器;5—调节风门

暖风加热器目前结构形式主要有管片式和管带式两种。管带式的加热器散热效率高、体积小、重量轻，但其制造工艺要复杂些；现在用得最多的还是管片式加热器，可以采取减小管壁厚度、在散热翅片上开槽等措施，以提高其传热效率。

图 2-57 所示为水暖式内外混合循环暖风装置。由外部空气吸入口 7 吸进新鲜空气，内部空气吸入口 5 吸入内部空气，它们在混合室 4 混合后，由鼓风机 8 送入热交换器 1 空气侧，热交换器管内侧由发动机循环水提供热源，混合气体被加热后被送往前座脚下，通过前窗、侧窗除霜的连接管输送到前窗除霜或除雾。这种结构的暖风装置效果较好，一般用在中、高档轿车上。

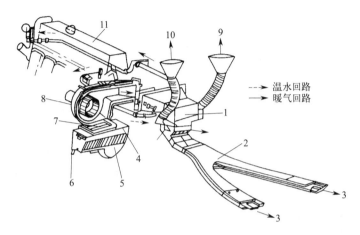

图 2-57 水暖式内外混合循环暖风装置
1—热交换器；2—后座导管；3—管道；4—混合室；5—内部空气吸入口；6—风门操纵杆；
7—外部空气吸入口；8—鼓风机；9—前窗除霜；10—侧窗除霜；11—发动机

另一种结构形式如图 2-58 所示，它是将加热器和蒸发器组装在一个箱体内，共用一个风机和壳体，可以实现全功能空调，大多数高级豪华轿车采用这种结构形式。

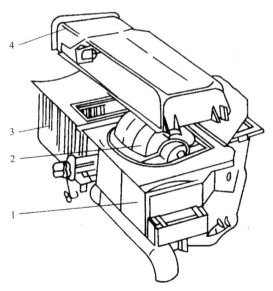

图 2-58 整体式空调器
1—加热器芯；2—轴流风机；3—蒸发器；4—进风口

二、独立热源式暖气装置

旅游车、高寒地区用车等，常常采用专用燃烧式暖气装置。它供热量大，不受发动机功率影响，其燃烧物质为汽油、煤油、轻质燃料油等，在热交换器中加热空气或水（暖气装置也分为空气加热式和热水加热式），燃烧后的气体在热交换后排出车外，对车内空气没有污染。

1. 热水加热式暖气装置

这种装置也称沸水式，先作为发动机的预热器，加热发动机的冷却水，提高发动机的启动性和耐久性；然后又作为暖气装置。热水加热式暖气装置仅在发动机功率小时作用良好，其燃料费用较少，一般使用煤油、轻质燃料油作燃料，发热量为1512～23260W，送风量为80～800m^3/h。

2. 空气加热式暖气装置

图2-59所示为空气加热独立燃烧式暖气装置结构图。当运转开关接通"点火"位置时，电流接通火花塞3，此时镍铬合金线前端加热变红，接着加热器开始燃烧，电动机1开始运转。电机上装有燃料泵2、燃料分布器4、燃烧空气送风机12和暖房空气送风机7。当送风机7回转时，燃料由燃料泵2从燃料箱中经燃烧过滤器、电磁阀燃料吸入管11吸出，燃料泵吸出的燃料由分布器4内部滴下，由于离心力的作用使其分散雾化，当送风机12将被燃烧空气由吸入管10吸进与燃料混合时，由火花塞点火在燃烧室5中进行燃烧。一旦燃烧开始，电火花塞即行断电，之后就是燃烧室和燃烧环14保持燃烧。燃烧后的高温气体由排气管8作为废气排到大气中；而电机轴前端安装的空气送风机送入的空气，经过燃烧室和外筒间壁以及外筒外侧被加热。加热的空气由温气排出口16排出而进入车室内的管道，由管道通入各喷口供暖。

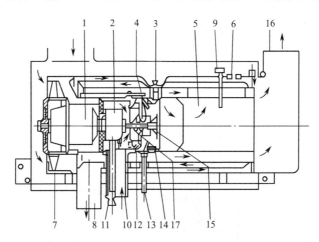

图2-59 空气加热独立燃烧式暖气装置

1—电动机；2—燃料泵；3—火花塞；4—燃料分布器；5—燃烧室；6—热熔丝；7—暖房空气送风机；8—排气管；9—燃烧指示器；10—燃烧室空气吸入管；11—燃烧吸入管；12—燃烧空气送风机；13—排气管；14—燃烧环；15—分布器帽；16—温气排出口；17—油分布器管

3. 加热器的日常维护

进入冬季，开始使用加热器之前应对以下项目进行检查。

① 燃油箱内是否有燃油。

② 暖气空气吸进口和车内暖气输送管出口是否堵塞。

③ 燃油系统内是否有漏气现象。如有，燃油泵吸进燃油时，空气会从漏气处混进，引

起燃油中断。检查泄漏现象时,应仔细检查燃油系统各连接部分是否拧紧,管道有无破裂现象。

④ 燃油箱是否有泄漏现象。油箱盖、油计软管、排泄栓等是否漏油。如有,应及时修理,以免发生火灾。

⑤ 检查燃油滤清器。视其内部是否有积水和杂物。如有,应拆除滤清器玻璃杯清洗或更换滤清器元件。玻璃杯如有损坏则应更换。密封圈老化应予更换。

⑥ 检查电气线路。打开配线盖,观察线路是否损坏或脱落。如有,则应修理。旋出电热塞,用钢丝刷清除积炭,防止因积炭过多导致点火不良、绝缘不良,使电热塞寿命缩短。

⑦ 检查燃烧空气系统。必须经常检查该系统的燃烧空气吸进管及排气管,是否因泥沙灰尘堵塞而造成燃烧空气减少或燃烧不良。

任务实施

一、帕萨特暖风装置的结构

在所有电气设备进行修理工作之前,先调取收音机的防盗密码,然后将蓄电池的接地线断开。在重新接上蓄电池的时候要对汽车的设备(收音机、时针、电动摇窗机)进行检验。

帕萨特暖风装置的结构如图 2-60 所示。

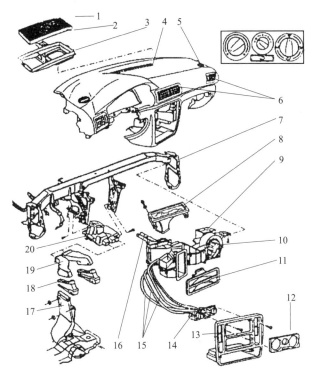

图 2-60　暖风装置零件图

1—夹子;2—灰尘和花粉滤清器;3—吸气罩;4—除霜喷嘴;5—侧窗出风口;6—出风口;7—仪表板横梁;8—除霜器中间件;9—暖风装置;10—新鲜空气鼓风机 V2;11—中间件;12—调节饰板;13—中间饰板;14—暖风和新鲜空气的调节;15—拉索;16—热交换器;17—后座左侧通道;18—下方的连接件;19—上方的连接件;20—脚部空间出风口

二、帕萨特暖风装置的拆卸与装配

1. 拆卸新鲜空气鼓风机

新鲜空气鼓风机 V2 的拆卸如图 2-61 所示,先拆卸副驾驶员侧的杂物盒,然后拆下鼓风机。

2. 暖风和新鲜空气调节装置的拆装

暖风和新鲜空气调节装置的组成如图 2-62 所示。

暖风和新鲜空气调节装置的拆卸如图 2-63 所示。推下暖风调节饰板 3,卸下中间饰板 2,将调节装置 1 连同拉索从仪表板上拔出来。

3. 出风口的拆装

① 拆卸对侧窗边的出风口,如图 2-64 所示。可用钳子拔出侧窗边的出风口。

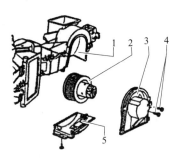

图 2-61 新鲜空气鼓风机
1—暖风机;2—新鲜空气鼓风机 V2;
3—鼓风机壳体;4—螺栓;
5—新鲜空气鼓风机串联电阻器
(带有过热熔丝)N24

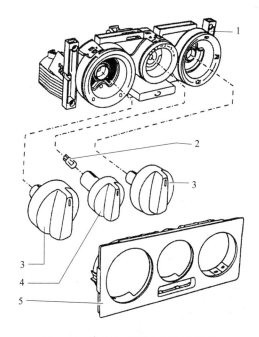

图 2-62 暖风和新鲜空气调节装置
1—新鲜空气调节装置;2—照明灯;3、4—旋钮;5—饰板

② 拆卸驾驶员侧和副驾驶员侧的出风口方法是一样的,只是换了一个侧面,如图 2-65 所示,仪表板侧面的盖板用适当的螺丝刀撬开后取出。

如图 2-66 所示,将一把适用的一字螺丝刀,交替通过侧面的孔 A 和 B 插入出风口与密封件之间,用螺丝刀交替沿 C 的方向向外撬出水平出风口 1。

如图 2-67 所示,在沿着 C 的方向取出出风口 1 时,分开背面的插接器 2。

③ 拆卸中央出风口的方法如下。如图 2-68 所示,双手的手指放到最下面的横条 A 上,用力往下压中央出风口 1,使定位钩 B 从其固定位上脱开。

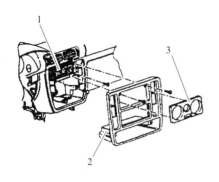  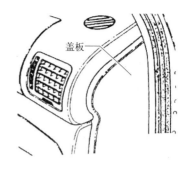

图 2-63　暖风和新鲜空气调节装置的拆卸
1—调节装置；2—中间饰板；3—调节饰板

图 2-64　拆卸对侧窗边的出风口

图 2-65　拆卸盖板

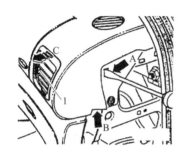 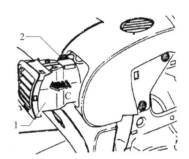

图 2-66　拆卸水平出风口
1—水平出风口；A、B—出风口

图 2-67　取出出风口
1—出风口；2—插接器

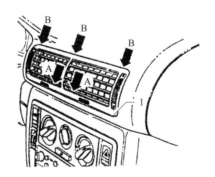

图 2-68　拆卸中央出风口
1—中央出风口；A—横条；B—定位钩

如图 2-69 所示，中央出风口 1 被从仪表板上拔出一点后，两手抓在 C 点上，沿着 D 的方向压中央出风口，使下方的定位钩脱开，然后将出风口稍拔出一点。

如图 2-70 所示，在沿箭头方向取出出风口之前，先将背面中央出风口的插接器分开。

4. 中央活门杠杆的安装和调节

如图 2-71 所示，中央活门小齿轮上有一个调整记号，在安装杠杆时注意让杠杆的调整记号与小齿轮上的调整记号对在一起（图中箭头所示）。

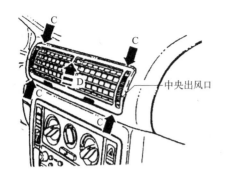
图 2-69 拔出中央出风口

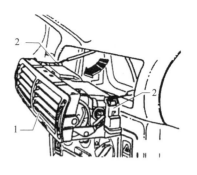
图 2-70 分开中央出风口插接器
1—中央出风口；2—插接器

5. 拉索的安装和调整

拉索的安装和调整方法如图 2-72 所示。

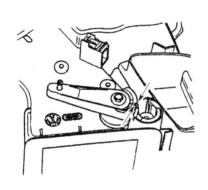
图 2-71 中央活门杠杆的安装

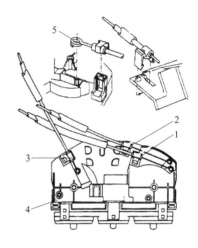
图 2-72 拉索的分解图
1—脚部空间和除霜器拉索；2—中央活门拉索；
3—温度活门拉索；4—暖风和新鲜空气的调节装置；
5—调节装置拉索的芯线

拉索的安装和调整要注意以下几点。

① 拉索先安装到卸下来的调节装置上，然后再把拉索固定到暖风装置上。

② 拉索护套的端部有颜色标记。上海帕萨特 B5 脚部空间和除霜器拉索护套固定器为白色；中央活门拉索护套固定器为黑色；温度活门拉索护套固定器为红色。

③ 旋转旋钮时，所有的活门都必须能听出达到止挡位。

④ 在插入调节装置拉索芯线时，将线的端部箭头对着调节杠杆压入。

习题测试

选择题

1. 下列汽车空调部件中，不是热交换器的是（　　）。
   A. 供暖水箱　　　B. 冷凝器　　　C. 蒸发器　　　D. 鼓风机

2. 小轿车采暖量的强度一般是通过（　　）进行调节的。

A. 风量大小　　　　B. 发动机水温　　　　C. 暖水阀　　　　D. 真空膜盒

项目小结

　　汽车空调故障现象可能会出现很多种，主要由制冷剂故障（包括制冷剂加注过多或过少、制冷剂存在水分或加注存在空气等）、管路系统故障（包括管路泄漏、管路堵塞）、压缩机和蒸发器故障等原因引起。在处理各种汽车空调故障时可以检查各个系统来进行排除。

　　在汽车空调系统使用过程中，由于部件损坏或管路泄漏等原因，使系统内的制冷剂排空或存量不足，需要重新加注或补充制冷剂，以恢复汽车空调系统的正常工作性能。在汽车空调制冷系统具体的检修过程中，离不开制冷剂的排放或回收、抽真空与加注等基本操作。

　　对于拆开修理的空调系统或者发现其制冷剂太少的空调系统，在添加新的制冷剂之前用真空泵完全抽空空调系统，清除空调系统内的空气和水分。完成抽真空后，在确认系统无泄漏的情况下，对空调系统进行定量充注。

　　汽车空调制暖系统故障现象可能会出现很多种，主要由供暖源故障（包括发动机冷却液温度过低、发动机冷却系统水泵故障）、管路系统故障（包括管路泄漏、管路堵塞）等原因引起。在处理空调制暖系统故障时可以依次检查来进行故障排除。

项目习题测试

一、判断题

1. 空调制冷系统中，制冷剂越多，制冷能力越强。　　　　　　　　　　　　　　（　　）
2. 蒸发器表面的温度越低越好。　　　　　　　　　　　　　　　　　　　　　　（　　）
3. 如果制冷系统内有水分，将造成系统间歇制冷。　　　　　　　　　　　　　　（　　）

二、单项选择题

1. 当空调系统改换了制冷剂时，甲说：用于 R-12 的 O 形圈不需更换；乙说：用于 R-134a 系统的 O 形圈也可用于 R-12 系统。谁的说法正确？（　　）

　　A. 甲正确　　　　B. 乙正确　　　　C. 两人均正确　　　　D. 两人均不正确

2. 甲说：真空泵用来清除系统中的湿气；乙说：真空泵用来抽出系统中的空气。谁的说法正确？（　　）

　　A. 甲正确　　　　B. 乙正确　　　　C. 两人均正确　　　　D. 两人均不正确

3. 当空调系统内有空气时，甲说：空气不会被冷凝；乙说：当空调循环停止时空气会聚集在蒸发器内。谁正确？（　　）

　　A. 甲正确　　　　B. 乙正确　　　　C. 两人均正确　　　　D. 两人均不正确

三、简答题

1. 空调系统的主要部件有哪些？
2. 空调系统的工作原理是什么？

项目三

汽车电子控制被动安全系统的检修

项目导读

当汽车车速低于 30km/h 发生碰撞时,碰撞产生的减速度和惯性力较小,安全传感器和中央传感器将此信号送到安全气囊 ECU,安全气囊 ECU 判断结果为不引爆安全气囊,只引爆安全带收紧器的点火器。与此同时,向左、右安全带点火器发出点火指令使安全带收紧,防止驾驶员和乘客受伤。

当汽车车速高于 30km/h 发生碰撞时,碰撞产生的减速度和惯性力较大,安全传感器和中央传感器将此信号送到安全气囊 ECU,安全气囊 ECU 判断结果为需要引爆安全气囊和安全带收紧器共同保护驾驶员和乘员。与此同时,向左、右安全带点火器和安全气囊点火器发出点火指令,在安全带收紧的同时,驾驶员安全气囊和乘员安全气囊同时打开,达到保护驾驶员和乘员的目的。

任务一 汽车电子控制被动安全系统识别

【学习目标】

知识要求:掌握汽车电子控制被动安全系统的作用、组成及基本原理。
能力要求:能够在实车上识别汽车电子控制被动安全系统的各组成部件。

任务导入

汽车电子控制被动安全系统对行车安全非常重要,大家能否在车上找到各组成部件?

知识准备

发生交通事故时,汽车不可避免地会发生碰撞。汽车发生碰撞分为两个阶段:没有人参与的汽车与汽车或汽车与障碍物之间的碰撞作为碰撞的第一阶段。碰撞第一阶段必然导致汽车产生减速度,车内人员由于惯性就会以一定的加速度向撞击发生的方向运动,如果这个加速度足够大,将造成人员与车内构件相碰,把这个碰撞称为碰撞的第二阶段,即伤人阶段。安全气囊的作用即在碰撞的第一阶段和第二阶段之间,迅速在车内人员与汽车构件之间产生一个充满气体的气垫,在碰撞过程中通过气囊的阻尼排气等过程吸收乘员的动能,使碰撞的第二阶段得以减缓,以减轻碰撞对人员的伤害程度。安全气囊属于汽车乘员"被动安全性保护装置"。其中,安全带在被动保护过程中起主要作用,而安全气囊属于辅助约束系统

(Supplemental Restraint System，SRS)。

气囊作为车身被动安全性的辅助配置，日渐受到人们的重视。当汽车碰撞后，乘员与车内构件尚未发生"二次碰撞前"迅速在两者之间打开一个充满气体的气垫，使乘员因惯性而移动时"扑在气垫上"，从而缓和乘员受到的冲击并吸收碰撞能量，减轻乘员的受伤程度。

一、作用

当汽车以大于 30km/h 的速度发生碰撞时，安全气囊就会自动充气弹开，瞬间在驾驶员和转向盘之间充起一个很大的气囊，减轻驾驶员头部及胸部的伤害。

驾驶员安全气囊组件位于转向盘中心处，乘员安全气囊组件位于仪表板右侧杂货箱上方。驾驶员安全气囊多采用尼龙布涂氯丁橡胶或有机硅制成。橡胶涂层起密封和保护作用，气囊背面有 2 个泄气孔。乘员安全气囊没有涂层，靠尼龙布本身的孔隙泄气。安全气囊系统各部件在车辆上的安装位置及线路连接如图 3-1 所示。

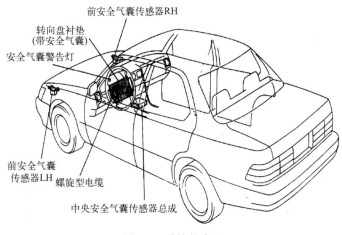

图 3-1 系统的布置

二、结构分类

1. 碰撞传感器

检测汽车碰撞强度的信号，并将信号输入安全气囊 ECU，安装于汽车前部的碰撞传感器称为前碰撞传感器；安装于安全气囊 ECU 内部的碰撞传感器称为中央传感器。

① 偏心锤式前碰撞传感器：安装在保险杠与挡泥板之间，装在一个防振保护盒内，用来感测低速碰撞信号。

② 应变仪式传感器：是汽车悬臂减速度产生的惯性力引起动态应变仪输出电压变化的一种传感器。碰撞的惯性力越大，输出电压越高。

③ 阻尼式传感器：强烈冲击时钢球传感器使触点闭合，发出碰撞信号。

2. 安全传感器

安全传感器用来防止系统在非冲撞时引起气囊的误动作。它们一般装在中央控制器内，是一个水银常开开关。当发生冲撞时，足够大的减速度力将水银抛上，接通电雷管电路。安全传感器传送的不是信号，它直接控制气囊展开时所需要的电源电路的通断。

三、组成及基本原理

安全气囊系统主要由传感器、气体发生器、点火器、安全气囊 ECU 和安全气囊 SRS 指示灯等部件组成。传感器和微处理器用以判断撞车程度，传递及发送信号；气体发生器根据信号指示产生点火动作，点燃固态燃料并产生气体向气囊充气，使气囊迅速膨胀。气囊装在转向盘毂内紧靠缓冲垫处，其容量为 50～90L，做气囊的布料具有很高的抗拉强度，多以尼龙材质制成，折叠起来的表面附有干粉，以防安全气囊粘在一起在爆发时被冲破；为了防止气体泄漏，气囊内层涂有密封橡胶；同时气囊设有安全阀，当充气过量或囊内压力超过一定值时会自动泄放部分气体，避免将乘客挤压受伤；气囊中所用的气体多是氮气。

1. 气体发生器

气体发生器的作用是在有效的时间内产生气体，使气囊张开。气体发生器由上盖、下盖、充气剂和金属滤网组成。金属滤网安装在气体发生器的内表面，用以过滤充气剂和点火剂燃烧产生的渣粒。

气体发生器是利用热效应产生氮气而充入气囊。在点火器引爆点火剂瞬间，点火剂会产生大量热量，充气剂受热立即分解，产生氮气并从充气孔充入气囊。虽然氮气是无毒气体，但是充气剂的副产品有少量的氢氧化钠和碳酸氢钠（白色粉末）。这些物质是有害的，因此在清洁膨胀后的气囊时，应保持良好的通风并采取防护措施。

2. 点火器

点火器主要由电雷管组成，其作用是当碰撞发生后，电雷管引爆火药，产生大量高温气体，冲撞或粉碎气体发生剂（叠氮化钠），同时使高温气体降温并继续产生气体。

3. 安全气囊 ECU

安全气囊 ECU 由中央处理器 CPU、只读存储器 ROM、随机存储器 RAM、I/O 接口、驱动器等电子电路组成，如图 3-2 所示。同时，安全气囊 ECU 内部还有安全传感器、备用电源、稳压电路和故障自诊断电路等，安全气囊 ECU 电控系统的原理如图 3-3 所示。

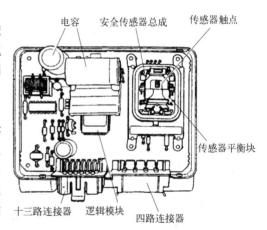

图 3-2 安全气囊 ECU 结构

4. 安全气囊 SRS 指示灯

SRS 指示灯位于仪表板上，接通点火开关时，诊断单元对系统进行自检，若点亮 6s 后熄灭，表示安全气囊系统正常；若 6s 后 SRS 指示灯依然闪烁或一直不熄灭，表示安全气囊系统有故障。

5. 奥迪 A3 Sportback 的安全系统组成

（1）安全气囊控制单元 J234

安全气囊控制单元连接在 CAN 驱动数据总线上，如图 3-4 所示。

（2）侧面防护系统碰撞传感器

侧面安全气囊碰撞传感器 G179、G180（在前门）如图 3-5 所示。

在奥迪 A3 Sportback 的两个前门内，安装了压力传感器。如果发生侧面碰撞，在车门内由于汽车的变形将会产生短暂的气压升高。传感器采集到压力升高的信息，传输给安全气囊控制单元。

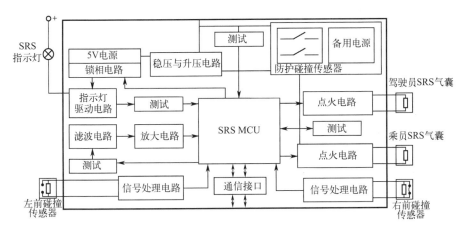

图 3-3 安全气囊 ECU 电控系统的原理

图 3-4 安全气囊控制单元

图 3-5 侧面安全气囊碰撞传感器

侧后安全气囊碰撞传感器 G256、G257（C 柱）分别安装在 C 柱左部和右部，侧后安全气囊碰撞传感器 G256、G257 是传统的照明传感器，在 3 门型奥迪 A3 上也安装了该型传感器。

（3）驾驶员安全气囊

驾驶员安全气囊上使用了双级式气体发生器。安全气囊是呈辐射状弹开的，与点火触发的时间是错开的，这样在发生交通事故时，作用到驾驶员身上的负荷也就减小了。根据事故的严重程度和种类不同，安全气囊控制单元控制两次点火的时间间隔。两次点火的时间间隔可能在 5~40ms 之间。

安全气囊控制单元激活第 1 个充气器的电子触发器，如图 3-6 所示。这样就点燃了点火器，再重新通过喷嘴孔触发自身的充气器。充气器点燃使气体发生器内产生压力。如果气体压力超过设定的界限，气体发生器变形，穿过金属过滤器通向气囊的通路打开。第 2 个充气器点燃，将安全气囊展开和充气。在确定的一段时间后，安全气囊控制单元向第 2 个电子点火器供电，点火器直接点燃第 2 个充气器，如图 3-7 所示。超过一定压力后，产生的气体将第 2 级的盖子抬起，流入第 1 级的燃烧室，从这里通过过滤器进入气囊。

与驾驶员安全气囊相反，副驾驶员安全气囊中的气体发生器是按混合气体技术原理工作的，如图 3-8 所示。该气体发生器由内置在一个高压气瓶中的两个烟火式充气器组成。安全气囊控制单元激活触发器，再通过点火装置点燃第 1 个充气器。如果气瓶中产生的压力超过一个设定值，则安全膜片断裂，混合气体可以充满气囊。第 2 个充气器点燃后产生的气体会

给安全气囊再次充气。螺旋弹簧的作用是按照设定压力点燃充气器。

使用烟火式管道气体发生器作为气体发生器。如果安全气囊控制单元检测到一个足以触发气囊的侧面碰撞，就向相应的侧面安全气囊触发器供电。通过点火器触发主充气器。产生的气体通过过滤器流入安全气囊。

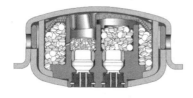  

图 3-6　第 1 个充气器触发　　　图 3-7　第 2 个充气器触发　　　图 3-8　副驾驶员安全气囊 N131、N132

侧面安全气囊如图 3-9 所示，头部安全气囊挡住几乎整个侧面玻璃，如图 3-10 所示。该车型的混合气发生器安装在车顶后部，通过一个喷气管向气囊充气。通过点燃充气器，用机械方法将支柱从其位置上射出。以 600 MPa 压力储存在高压气瓶中的氦气使安全膜片破裂。气体通过过滤器流入连接气囊与气体发生器的喷气管。

图 3-9　侧面安全气囊 N199、N200　　　图 3-10　头部安全气囊 N251、N252

任务实施

分组训练，在实车上找到汽车电子控制被动安全系统的各组成部件。

习题测试

简答题

1. 简述碰撞传感器的分类。
2. 简述气体发生器的功能。

任务二　汽车电子控制被动安全系统的检修

【学习目标】

知识要求：掌握汽车电子控制被动安全系统的故障诊断的思路及方法。

能力要求：

1. 能使用多用表、故障诊断仪、示波器及常用检测和诊断设备对汽车电子控制被动安全系统传感器、控制器、执行器进行检测；
2. 能正确记录、分析各种检测结果并做出故障判断；
3. 能按照正确操作规范进行传感器、执行器和控制器的更换，并能进行系统匹配设定；

4. 能对车辆进行测试，检查和评估汽车电子控制被动安全系统修复质量。

任务导入

一辆广州本田 2.3L 雅阁轿车安全气囊指示灯亮不熄，行驶里程 3.2 万 km。

知识准备

安全气囊系统的所有线束都套装在黄色的波纹管内，并与车颈线束连成一体，以便于区别。为了保证转向盘具有足够的转动角度而又不致损伤驾驶员气囊组件的连接线束，在转向盘与转向柱管之间采用了螺旋线束，即将线束安装在螺旋形弹簧内，再将螺旋弹簧放到弹簧壳体内。

电喇叭线束也安装在螺旋弹簧内，螺旋弹簧安装在转向盘与转向柱之间，安装时应注意其安装位置和方向，否则将导致螺旋线束和电喇叭线束折断、转向盘转向角度不足或转向沉重。

螺旋电缆用于保证电源连线的连接。安全气囊系统的所有线束都套装在黄色的波纹管内，并与车颈线束连成一体，以便于区别。

任务实施

一、安全气囊系统的检修

安全气囊应注意日常的检修。安全气囊的一般检查，应按故障代码显示的故障进行检修，可以由驾驶员或专业修理工严格按照维修手册操作规程进行。不允许非专业人员对安全气囊系统进行拆开和检修。

1. 检修安全气囊的安全规则

安全气囊的检测、安装和维修工作必须由专业人员来进行。检测时不可使用检测灯、电压表和欧姆表。安全气囊只可在安装好后用汽车专用诊断仪来检查。检查安全气囊时，必须断开蓄电池地线。断开蓄电池后不需等待。将安全气囊与电源相连时，车内不可有人。安全气囊从运输器具内取出后必须马上装车。如需中止工作，应将安全气囊放回运输器具内。不可将安全气囊放到无人照管的地方。存放拆开安全气囊时，起缓冲作用的面应朝上。安全气囊不可打开及修理，必须使用新件。掉到过坚硬地面上的或有损伤的安全气囊不可再用。

更换安全气囊的步骤：拆下旧安全气囊，缓冲面朝上放置；从运输器具中取出新安全气囊，缓冲面朝上放置；将旧安全气囊装入运输器具；将新安全气囊装到车上。

安全气囊有一定的使用寿命（见 B 柱上不干胶标签）。如更换安全气囊，应将新标签取下并贴到 B 柱的旧标签上面。每 14 年必须更换安全气囊和不干胶标签。如果车的 B 柱上无标签，应在保养手册中注明更换安全气囊。

安全气囊上不能沾油脂、清洁剂等，也不能置于温度在 100℃ 以上的地方（短时间也不可）。

2. 安全气囊的更换与处理

（1）事故后触发了的安全气囊的更换

在车辆发生交通事故，安全气囊和安全带张紧器工作后，车辆的显示屏会显示"安全气囊，前部和侧面"或"安全气囊，前面和头部"的警告信息。安全气囊控制单元最多可用于控制 3 个侧面/头部安全气囊和/或张紧器的触发。

3次触发后，故障阅读仪上显示"控制单元损坏"。在下述情况下必须更换安全气囊控制单元。

① 驾驶员/副驾驶员安全气囊触发一次。
② 壳体损坏。
③ 控制单元周围 200mm 内通道变形。
④ 安全气囊触发 3 次后。
⑤ 所有已触发的安全气囊总成。
⑥ 如果副驾驶员安全气囊已触发，还要更换仪表板。
⑦ 副驾驶员一侧的支架已变形（不允许二次变形）。
⑧ 横向加速度传感器故障（如果传感器周围地板已变形）。
⑨ 驾驶员安全气囊触发后，要更换带滑环的回位弹簧，要更换张紧器已触发的安全带。

(2) 可触发的安全气囊控制单元

对于已触发的前座张紧器，显示屏显示"zu groβ"（电阻过大）；对于已触发的后座张紧器，显示屏显示"zu groβ"（电阻过大）。

(3) 更换了安全气囊控制单元

查询故障存储器。对于已触发的张紧器，故障记录为"张紧触发器—电阻过大"。如需要（目视检查），还要更换所有损伤件。

(4) 事故后未触发安全气囊的处理

如果安全气囊报警灯 K75 未指示故障，那么就不必更换安全气囊部件，单独检查安全带即可。

3. 安全气囊的存放和运输

安全气囊是用一级聚乙烯制成的烟火式装置，其存放和运输应按易爆危险品对待（炸药管理规定）。安全气囊存放时间不可超过 3 个月。

4. 安全气囊的报废

安全气囊报废前，应按相应的安全规程使其触发。

5. 安全气囊部件的拆装

(1) 安全气囊安装位置

安全气囊主要部件的安装位置如图 3-11 所示。

(2) 驾驶员安全气囊的拆装

驾驶员安全气囊的分解如图 3-12 所示。

① 驾驶员安全气囊的拆卸。松开转向柱调节装置。向上尽量拉出转向盘。将转向盘置于垂直位置。按图 3-12 所示箭头方向转动 Torx 扳手（T30）90°（从前看为顺时针），以松开定位爪 7。将转向盘回转半圈，以松开另一个定位爪。拔下安全气囊插头 3 和除静电插头 4，缓冲面朝上放置安全气囊。

② 驾驶员安全气囊的安装。安装驾驶员安全气囊时要保证插头和安全气囊正确入位（可听见），注意车内不可有人。最后，打开点火开关并接上蓄电池地线。

③ 转向盘的拆装。拆卸转向盘时，先拆下安全气囊，将转向盘置于中央位置（车轮摆正），拧下螺栓 5，拔下插头 2 和插头 10。安装转向盘时，使转向盘在中央位置时（车轮摆正）装上。要确保插头正确入位（可听见）。更换螺栓 5，以 60N·m 拧紧，最后装上安全气囊。

(3) 带滑环的回位弹簧的拆装

将驾驶员安全气囊和转向盘拆下。将转向柱完全拉出并向下。如图 3-13 所示，拧下螺栓 1（2个，拧紧力矩为 2.8N·m），取下夹块 2。

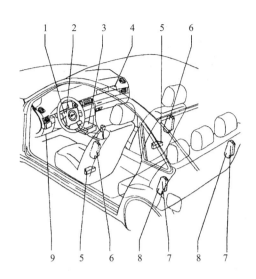 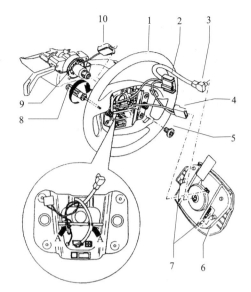

图 3-11 安全气囊主要部件安装位置示意图

1—驾驶员安全气囊；2—驾驶员安全气囊（赛车转向盘）；
3—安全气囊控制单元；4—副驾驶员安全气囊；
5—横向加速度传感器；6—侧面安全气囊；
7—后座侧面安全气囊（折叠式靠背）；
8—后座侧面安全气囊（固定式靠背）；9—自诊断插头

图 3-12 驾驶员安全气囊分解

1—转向盘（将松开的线固定到箭头，A—所示的位置）；
2—螺旋弹簧插头；3—安全气囊插头；4—除静电插头；
5—内多角螺栓（60N·m）；6—安全气囊；7—定位爪；
8—Torx扳手（T30）；9—带滑环的回位弹簧；
10—转向盘加热插头

拧下图3-14箭头所示的两个十字头螺栓，螺栓的拧紧力矩为0.6N·m。拆下转向开关上部装饰件。安装时，将上半部插入下半部的定位爪内，向下摆动并拧紧，如图3-14所示。

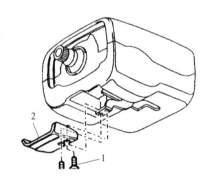 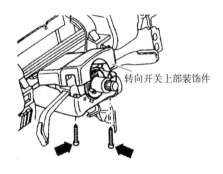

图 3-13 拆卸夹块

1—螺栓；2—夹块

图 3-14 拆卸转向开关上部装饰件

拧下螺栓2（2个），螺栓的拧紧力矩为0.6N·m。拆下转向开关下部装饰件3，如图3-15所示。拔下插头1，松开定位爪（箭头），从转向开关上拉下带滑环的回位弹簧，如图3-16所示。

（4）副驾驶员安全气囊的拆装

副驾驶员安全气囊分解如图3-17所示。副驾驶员安全气囊有不同型号，仪表板与副驾驶员安全气囊应匹配。拆卸副驾驶员安全气囊时，要断开蓄电池地线，拆下杂物箱，拔下插头6。注意千万不要拔下副驾驶员安全气囊上的红色脚插头。拧下螺母4（4个），拆下安全气囊，要将缓冲面朝上放置安全气囊。

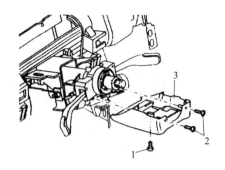

图 3-15　拆卸转向开关下部装饰件
1，2—螺栓；3—转向开关下部装饰件

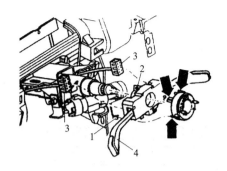

图 3-16　拆卸带滑环的回位弹簧
1，3—插头；2—螺栓；4—转向开关

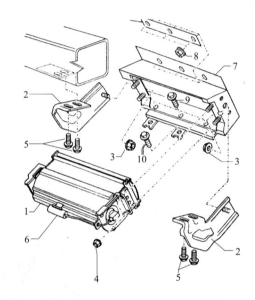

图 3-17　副驾驶员安全气囊分解图
1—副驾驶员安全气囊；2—支架；3—螺母（2个，18N·m）；4—螺母（4个，9N·m）；
5—螺栓（4个，9N·m）；6—插头；7—安全气囊支架；8—螺母（3个，4.5N·m）；
9—螺栓（3个，4.5N·m）；10—螺栓（1个，4.5N·m）

安装副驾驶员安全气囊时确保插头 6 入位（可听见），装上安全气囊。打开点火开关，接上蓄电池地线。注意操作过程中车内不得有人。安全气囊触发后必须更换的部件有支架 2、螺母 3 和螺母 4、螺栓 5、安全气囊支架 7。

如图 3-18 所示，用螺丝刀撬起插头 1 的定位凸起 2，按箭头 3 方向拔下插头。断开蓄电池地线。拆下中央副仪表板前部。

拆下左后和右后脚下出风口导流板的插入件。如图 3-19 所示，松开插头 2 的定位卡夹，从控制单元 1 上拔下插头 2，拧下螺栓 3（3个），拆下控制单元。更换控制单元后需重新编码。

（5）侧面安全气囊的拆装

侧面安全气囊的分解如图 3-20 所示。拆卸驾驶员/副驾驶员侧面安全气囊时，断开蓄电池地线，拆下靠背装饰件，松开侧面安全气囊 1 周围的面罩，松开插头 3 的定位，从侧面插头上拔下插头 3，拧下两个螺栓 2。为了表达清楚，图 3-20 中未画消音垫。小心地松开侧面

安全气囊的定位爪5，拆下侧面安全气囊1，缓冲面向上放置安全气囊。

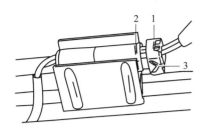 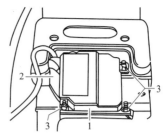

图 3-18 拆卸安全气囊插头　　　　　　　　　图 3-19 拆卸安全气囊控制单元
1—插头；2—定位凸起；3—箭头　　　　　　1—控制单元；2—插头；3—螺栓（6N·m）

安装驾驶员/副驾驶员侧面安全气囊时，不要切开定位爪5周围的消音垫，抬起消音垫，将安装孔扩大5.5mm，将消音垫铺到靠背支架上，将侧面安全气囊1固定到消音垫上，插入螺栓2，抬起消音垫，装上螺母并拧至5.5N·m。从安全气囊上揭下标有使用寿命的标签，并将其贴到B柱的旧标签上面。从安全气囊上揭下数据标签，将其贴到座椅的标签上。最后接上蓄电池地线。注意操作过程中车内不得有人。

（6）后座侧面安全气囊的拆装

如图3-21所示，拆下后座椅。拧下螺栓2（2个），取下侧面安全气囊1。

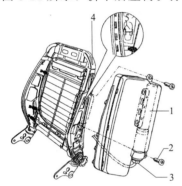 

图 3-20 侧面安全气囊分解　　　　　　　　　图 3-21 拆卸后座侧面安全气囊
1—驾驶员/副驾驶员侧面安全气囊；2—螺栓（5.5N·m）；　　　1—侧面安全气囊；2—螺栓
3—插头；4—靠背框架；5—定位爪

（7）横向加速度传感器的拆装

横向加速度传感器装在前座椅上，左右安装一个，两个传感器是相同的。安装时箭头指向外侧。断开蓄电池地线，拆下前座椅，拆下A柱下部装饰板，松开门槛内侧装饰件，拔下横向加速度传感器1的插头2，拧下螺栓3（2个），拆下横向加速度传感器，如图3-22所示。横向加速度传感器的安装按拆卸的相反顺序进行。打开点火开关，关上车门，接上蓄电池地线。注意车内不可有人。

（8）后座侧面安全气囊的断开/接通

① 后座侧面安全气囊的断开。拆下后座椅，左右侧面安全气囊只能同时切断，单独切断一个是不可能的。左、右C柱上各有一个插头，拔下定位凸起2，按箭头方向拔下插头1，如图3-23所示。用扎带固定松开的插头。装上后座椅，贴上已断开的侧面安全气囊标签。将安全气囊控制单元编码从204或206改为104或106。填上登记卡，并将卡交给经销商存档。将登记卡第三联交给用户，放在随车文件里。

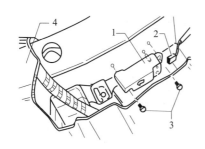
图 3-22 拆卸横向加速度传感器
1—横向加速度传感器；2—插头；3—螺栓（6N·m）；4—装饰件

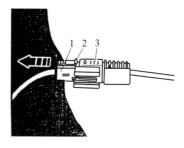
图 3-23 断开后座侧面安全气囊
1—插头；2—定位凸起；3—插座

② 后座侧面安全气囊的接通。拆下后座椅，左、右侧面安全气囊只能同时接通，单独接通一个是不可以的。左、右 C 柱各有一个插头均应接通。割断插头扎带。

二、奥迪 A6 安全气囊系统自诊断

1. 概述

奥迪 A6 安全气囊系统包括驾驶员安全气囊、副驾驶员安全气囊、两个前座安全带张紧器、两个前座侧面安全气囊、两个后座侧面安全气囊、两个或三个后座安全带张紧器。在撞车时，如达到给定的条件，以上装置由安全气囊控制单元（J234）来触发。可以通过自诊断来关闭或接通副驾驶员安全气囊。安全气囊和安全带张紧器触发后，控制单元将记录故障"已存入撞车数据"，这时需更换控制单元。根据撞车性质和强度，安全气囊控制单元向中央门锁控制单元发送一个"撞车信号"。该功能具有被动安全特点，即当一个安全气囊触发后，中央门锁机构将车门锁和行李箱锁锁止，并锁止车内开关，车内照明灯被接通。可用执行元件诊断来检查"撞车信号"。使用新的安全气囊控制单元前，需要进行编码。安全气囊控制单元（J234）在驾驶员或副驾驶员安全气囊触发一次后、前座安全带张紧器或侧面安全气囊触发三次后，必须更换。注意安全气囊只可目视检查导线，不可对触发线路进行电气检测。检查导线时必须关闭点火开关。

2. 自诊断功能

（1）自诊断条件

进行安全气囊系统自诊断时应满足以下条件。

① 相关系统的供电及熔丝正常。

② 故障阅读器 V.A.G1551 已接好。

③ 点火开关已打开。

（2）自诊断功能的使用

短时出现的故障是偶然故障，在显示屏上用"/SP"提示。为了排除这些故障，修理前应清除故障码。

① 关闭点火开关，连接故障阅读器 V.A.G1551，打开点火开关，按 1 键选择"快速数据传输"。

② 安全气囊系统地址码为 15，按 1 和 5 键。

③ 按 Q 键确认输入。

④ 5s 后屏幕显示前侧的安全气囊。

```
4B0959655G 安全气囊 前+侧      0001          →
编码 01106                    服务站代码 06812
```

⑤ 按→键。
⑥ 按 HELP 键可打印出可选功能一览表。

三、汽车电子控制被动安全系统的故障案例诊断过程

1. 读取故障码

将安全气囊短路插头与仪表板左侧维修插头连接。安全气囊指示灯不显示任何故障码，指示灯常亮不熄。安全气囊指示灯常亮不熄，通常是因为仪表总成中安全气囊指示灯电路故障或者插头之间线路短路或断路，另外结合该车症状，安全气囊装置本身或其电源电路装置出现故障导致故障灯常亮不熄的可能性极大。

2. 清除故障码

接通点火开关，如果指示灯亮并在 6s 后熄灭，说明只是间歇性故障，结果灯不熄灭。关闭点火开关，检查驾驶席仪表板下熔丝/继电器盒内 2 号熔丝 10A 是否熔断，结果没问题。该车因 SRS 事故后只换安全气囊没换 SRS 装置，新的安全气囊组件与原来的 SRS 装置在程序设定上不相匹配，从而导致该车在不该引爆时，安全气囊起爆伤人。不换 SRS 装置有时可能会侥幸消掉故障码，但这样具有极大的安全隐患。经更换匹配的 SRS 装置，故障灯熄灭，SRS 恢复正常。

习题测试

简答题

简述安全气囊系统的作用。

项目小结

气囊系统可以判断出车辆当前经历的碰撞形式，形成对乘客的最佳保护。智能化、多安全气囊是今后安全气囊系统发展的必然趋势。

项目习题测试

填空题

1. 汽车的安全系统可分为两大类，第一类制动系统属于_____安全系统；第二类安全气囊系统属于_____安全系统。
2. 安全气囊系统必须与_____配合使用，才能有效地保护乘员的安全。

项目四

汽车电子控制悬架系统的检修

项目导读

随着人们对汽车操纵性和舒适性要求的不断提高,以及电子技术的飞速发展,电子控制技术被有效应用于现代汽车悬架系统。电子控制悬架系统的最大优点就是它能使悬架随不同的路况和行驶状态做出不同的反应,既能使汽车的乘坐舒适性达到令人满意的状态,又能使汽车的操纵稳定性达到最佳状态。

任务一 汽车电子控制悬架系统识别

【学习目标】

知识要求:掌握汽车电子控制悬架系统的功能、组成及基本原理。
能力要求:能够在实车上识别汽车电子控制悬架系统的各组成部件。

 任务导入

了解汽车电子控制悬架系统在汽车行驶过程中起到的辅助作用,找出电子控制悬架系统与传统悬架在结构上有哪些不同。

知识准备

汽车悬架类型可分为被动悬架、半主动悬架和主动悬架。其中,被动悬架是由弹簧和减振器组成的机械式悬架系统,半主动悬架和主动悬架都属于电子控制悬架系统。

一、电子控制悬架系统的功能

电子控制悬架系统的基本作用是通过控制悬架的刚度和阻尼力来突破传统被动悬架的局限性,使汽车的悬架特性与道路状况和行驶状态相适应,从而保证汽车行驶的平顺性和操纵的稳定性要求都能得到满足。其基本功能有以下几方面。

1. 车高调整

无论车辆的负载多少,都可以保持汽车的高度一定,车身保持水平,从而使前照灯光束方向保持不变;当汽车在坏路面上行驶时,可以使车高升高,防止车桥与路面相碰;当汽车高速行驶时,又可以使车高降低,以便减少空气阻力,提高操纵稳定性。

2. 减振器阻尼力控制

通过对减振器阻尼系数的调整,防止汽车急速起步或急加速时车尾下蹲;防止紧急制动

时的车头下沉；防止汽车急转弯时车身横向摇动；防止汽车换挡时车身纵向摇动等，提高行驶平顺性和操纵稳定性。

3. 弹簧刚度控制

与减振器一样在各种工况下，通过对弹簧弹性系数的调整，来改善汽车的乘坐舒适性与操纵稳定性。

有些车型只具有其中的一个或两个功能，而有些车型同时具有以上三个功能。

二、电子控制悬架系统的种类

现代汽车装用的电子控制悬架系统种类很多。

1. 按传力介质不同分类

按传力介质的不同，电子控制悬架系统可分为气压式和油压式两种。

2. 按控制理论不同分类

按控制理论不同，电子控制悬架系统可分为半主动式、主动式两大类。其中，半主动式又分为有级半主动式（阻尼力有级可调）和无级半主动式（阻尼力连续可调）两种；主动式悬架根据频带和能量消耗的不同，分为全主动式（频带宽大于 15 Hz）和慢全主动式（频带宽 3～6 Hz）；而根据驱动机构和介质的不同，可分为电磁阀驱动的油气主动式悬架和由步进电动机驱动的空气主动式悬架。

无级半主动悬架可以根据路面的行驶状态和车身的响应对悬架阻尼力进行控制，并在几毫秒内由最小到最大，使车身的振动响应始终被控制在某个范围内。但在转向、起步、制动等工况时不能对阻尼力实施有效的控制。它比全主动式悬架优越的地方是不需要外加动力源，消耗的能量很小，成本较低。

主动式悬架是一种能供给和控制动力源（油压、空气压）的装置。根据各种传感器检测到的汽车载荷、路面状况、行驶速度、启动、制动、转向等状况的变化，自动调整悬架的刚度、阻尼力以及车身高度等。它能显著提高汽车的操纵稳定性和乘坐舒适性。

三、电子控制悬架系统的组成与工作原理

电子控制悬架系统由传感器、电子控制单元（ECU）、执行器 3 部分组成。传感器将汽车行驶的路面情况（汽车的振动）和车速及启动、加速、转向、制动等工况转变为电信号，输送给 ECU，ECU 将传感器送入的电信号进行综合处理，输出对悬架的刚度、阻尼、车身高度进行调节的控制信号。执行器按照 ECU 的控制信号，准确地动作，及时地调节悬架的刚度、阻尼系数及车身的高度，如图 4-1 所示。

1. 传感器

传感器的作用是将汽车行驶的速度、启动、加速度、转向、制动和路面状况、汽车振动状况、车身高度等信号输送给悬架 ECU。汽车悬架系统所用的传感器主要有转向盘转角传感器、车身加速度传感器、车身高度传感器、车速传感器、节气门位置传感器等。下面具体介绍这几种传感器。

（1）转向盘转角传感器

转向盘转角传感器用于检测方向盘的中间位置、转动方向、转动角度和转动速度。在电控悬架中，悬架 ECU 根据车速传感器信号和转向盘转角传感器信号，判断汽车转向时侧向力的大小，以控制车身的倾斜。转向盘转角传感器用于检测汽车转向轮的偏转方向。

光电式转向盘转角传感器是电控悬架中比较常用的转向盘转角传感器，其结构和工作原理如图 4-2 所示。在压入转向轴的遮光盘上有一定数量的窄槽，遮光盘的两端分别有两个发

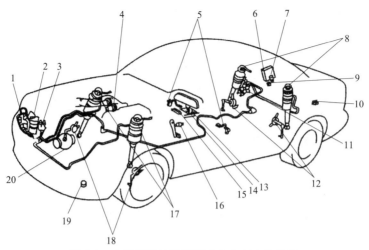

图 4-1 电子控制悬架系统元件在车上的位置

1—干燥器和排气阀；2—高度控制压缩机；3—1 号高度控制阀；4—节气门位置传感器；5—门控灯开关；6—悬架 ECU；7—2 号高度控制继电器；8—后悬架控制执行器；9—高度控制连接器；10、14—高度控制开关；11—2 号高度控制阀和溢流阀；12—后车身高度传感器；13—模式开关；15—转向传感器；16—制动灯开关；17—前悬架控制执行器；18—前车身高度传感器；19—1 号高度控制继电器；20—IC 调节器

光二极管和两个光敏三极管，组成两对光电耦合器（信号发生器）。当转动转向盘时，转向轴带动遮光盘旋转，当转到窄槽处时，光敏三极管感受到发光二极管发出的光，就会输出"ON"信号；当遮光盘转到除窄槽以外的其他位置时，光敏三极管感受不到发光二极管的光线，就会输出"OFF"信号。这样随着转向盘的转动，两个光电耦合器的输出端就形成"ON/OFF"的变换。悬架 ECU 根据两个光电耦合器输出"ON/OFF"变换的速度，检测出转向轴的转向速度。此外由于两个光电耦合器变换的相位错开约 90°，所以通过判断哪个遮光盘首先转变为"ON"状态，就可以检测出转向轴的转动方向。

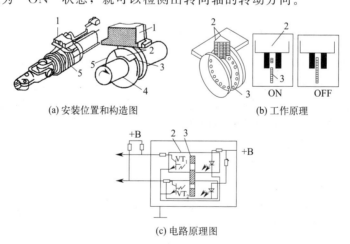

图 4-2 光电式转向盘转角传感器

1—转角传感器；2—光电耦合器；3—遮光盘；4—转向轴；5—传感器圆盘

（2）车身加速度传感器

一般来说，电控悬架系统不用设置专门的加速度传感器。通常利用发动机节气门位置传感器信号来判断汽车是否在进行急加速。

悬架系统中的传感器（车速传感器、高度传感器等）都是将信号直接输入悬架 ECU，

但节气门位置传感器信号则是输入发动机电子控制系统，然后发动机电子控制系统再将此信号输入悬架 ECU。当汽车启动或突然加速时，动力传动控制模块根据节气门位置传感器信号（探测到节气门开度超过 90%）或质量式空气流量传感器信号生成加速信号，然后将加速信号提供给悬架 ECU，悬架 ECU 控制执行器使其转换到硬阻尼状态，以便减少汽车"抬头"（"后坐"）。

少数情况下也采用加速度传感器来采集加速度信号，如车轮打滑时。加速度传感器一般有差动变压式和钢球位移式两种。

(3) 车身高度传感器

车身高度传感器的作用是把车身高度（汽车悬架装置的位置量）转换为电信号送给悬架 ECU。车身高度传感器的数量与车上装备的电控空气悬架系统的类型有关。车身高度传感器的一端与车架连接，另一端装在悬架系统上。在电控悬架上，车身高度传感器用于采集车身高度信息；在某些行驶平顺性控制系统上，车身高度传感器还用来探测悬架运动情况以确定是否需要硬阻尼。

车身高度传感器可以是模拟式，也可以是数字式；可以是线位移式，也可以是角位移式。

现在应用最广泛的是光电式数字车身高度传感器。在传感器内部有一个传感器轴，轴外端安装的连接杆与悬架臂相连接，轴上固定一个开有一定数量窄槽的遮光盘。遮光盘两侧对称安装有 4 组发光二极管和光敏三极管，组成 4 对光电耦合器（信号发生器）。当车身高度变化时，车身与悬架臂做相对运动，连接杆带动传感器轴和遮光盘一起转动。当遮光盘上的槽对准耦合器时，光敏三极管通过该槽感受到发光二极管发出的光线，光电耦合器输出导通（ON）信号，反之则输出截止（OFF）信号。只要使遮光盘上的槽适当分布，就可以利用这 4 对光电耦合器导通和截止的组合，把车身高度的变化分成 16 个区域进行检测。这种高度传感器有一个六线连接器，包括电源线、地线及 4 个信号线。

悬架 ECU 根据传感器输入的"ON""OFF"信号得到车身位移信息。根据车身高度变化的幅度和频率，可以判断车身的振动情况，根据一段时间（一般为 10ms）车身高度在某一区域的百分比来判断车身高度。

(4) 车速传感器

悬架 ECU 可从车速传感器、各种其他模块或多路传输网络接收车速信号输入，用于实现系统的各种控制功能。

变速器、驱动轴或分动箱的输出通过齿轮驱动车速传感器。车速传感器信号是交流波形信号，其频率和电压随车速提高而增加，由信号频率便可获知车速。

车速信号也可以由其他模块直接提供给悬架 ECU（直接连接），此信号为直流变化信号。

车速信号还可以以数据信号形式从汽车多路传输网络提供给悬架 ECU。

(5) 车门信号

悬架 ECU 利用车门信号实现系统的某些功能，如在车门打开时防止排气或保持目前行驶高度等。当车门关闭时，系统恢复正常工作状态。

(6) 制动信号

当汽车制动时，制动开关给悬架 ECU 一个制动信号，悬架 ECU 收到制动信号后，控制执行器将悬架由软转换到硬的状态，以防止汽车"点头"（"翘尾"）。

(7) 悬架控制开关

悬架控制开关包括悬架刚度和阻尼选择（LRC）开关、高度控制开关和锁止开关（高度

控制 ON/OFF 开关），前两个开关一般都装在驾驶室内选挡操纵手柄旁边（见图 4-3），锁止开关一般装在后备箱内（见图 4-4）。

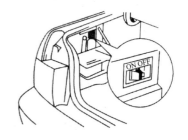

图 4-3　悬架刚度和阻尼选择（LRC）开关　　　　图 4-4　锁止开关（高度控制 ON/OFF 开关）
　　　　以及高度控制开关的安装位置　　　　　　　　　　　　　的安装位置

① 悬架刚度和阻尼选择（LRC）开关。LRC 开关用于选择悬架的刚度和阻尼力参数，它有两个挡位：当 LRC 开关处于 "NORM"（软）位置时，系统进入"常规行驶自动控制"；当 LRC 开关处于 "SPORT"（硬）位置时，系统进入"高速行驶自动控制"。每一种模式下按照刚度与阻尼的大小依次又有低、中、高 3 种状态。当 "NORM"（软）和"SPORT"（硬）模式通过 LRC 选定后，就由悬架 ECU 根据传感器的输入信号在低、中、高 3 种状态间自动调节刚度和阻尼系数。

② 高度控制开关。高度控制开关也有两种控制模块，即 "NORM" 和 "HIGH"，按照车身的高度从低到高的顺序，每一种模式又有低、中、高 3 种状态。在 "NORM" 模式时，车身高度常处于"低"状态，系统对车身高度进行"常规值自动控制"；在 "HIGH" 模式时，车身高度常处于"高"状态，系统对车身高度进行"高值自动控制"。

③ 锁止开关（高度控制 ON/OFF 开关）。锁止开关（高度控制 ON/OFF 开关）一般装在后备箱内。当锁止开关位于 "ON" 时，系统按照驾驶员通过高度控制开关选定的模式进行车身高度控制；当锁止开关位于 "OFF" 时，系统不进行车身高度的调节。

2. 电子控制单元 ECU

（1）电子控制单元 ECU 的功能

控制悬架系统的电子控制模块（悬架 ECU）是悬架控制系统的中枢，它具有多种功能。

① 传感器信号放大。用接口电路将输入信号（如传感器的信号、开关信号）中的干扰信号除去，然后放大、变换极值、比较极值，变换为适合输入悬架 ECU 的信号。

② 输入信号的计算。悬架 ECU 根据预先写入只读存储器 ROM 中的程序对各输入信号进行计算，并将计算结果与内存中的数据进行比较后，向执行器（电机、电磁阀、继电器等）发出控制信号。输入悬架 ECU 的信号除了开关信号外，还有电压值，还应进行 A/D 变换。

③ 驱动执行器。悬架 ECU 用输出驱动电路将输出驱动信号放大，然后输送到各执行器，如电机、电磁阀、继电器等，以实现对汽车悬架参数的控制。

④ 故障检测。悬架 ECU 用故障检测电路来检测传感器、执行器和线路的故障。

（2）电控空气悬架系统电子控制模块（悬架 ECU）的结构

电控空气悬架系统悬架 ECU 同时给出了所有的输入和输出信号。悬架 ECU 包括一个 8 位微处理器、输入接口和输出驱动电路，同时还包括一个失效保护电路，也用于诊断模块的接口。悬架 ECU 根据接收的各传感器信号，选择一个预先编好的控制模式。

（3）电控空气悬架系统电子控制模块（悬架 ECU）的工作原理

预先将悬架 ECU 的控制程序写入只读存储器 ROM，悬架控制过程中，按控制程序规

定的顺序进行计算、分析和比较。

系统启动后,首先对悬架 ECU 内存储器 RAM、执行器进行初始化,然后读取各种传感器输入信号和各种开关信号,根据驾驶员所选择的系统控制模式,对输入信号进行计算、分析,并发出控制信号进行汽车行驶姿态控制,随后再读取各种输入信号,如此反复循环。

悬架 ECU 对信号的处理速度快于汽车的运动,以微秒级进行 1 次运算,所以,按照以上顺序进行处理,在控制上没有任何问题。

3. 电控空气悬架系统执行器

(1) 执行器的作用

悬架执行器的作用是驱动主、副气室的空气阀阀芯和减振器阻尼孔的回转阀,使其转动,从而实现对悬架刚度和阻尼参数的控制,如图 4-5 所示。

电控空气悬架系统的控制功能主要包括以下 3 方面的控制。

① 车速与路面感应控制。这种控制主要是随着车速和路面的变化,改变悬架的刚度和阻尼系数,使之处于低、中、高 3 种状态。车速和路面感应主要有以下 3 种。

a. 高速感应。当车速很高时,控制模块输出控制信号,使悬架的刚度和阻尼系数相应增大,以提高汽车高速行驶时的操纵稳定性。

b. 前后车轮关联感应。当汽车前轮在遇到路面单个的凸起时,控制模块输出控制信号,相应减少后轮悬架的刚度和阻尼系数,以减小车身的振动和冲击。

c. 差路面感应。当汽车进入差路面行驶时,为了控制车身产生大的振动,控制模块输出控制信号,相应增大悬架的刚度和阻尼系数。

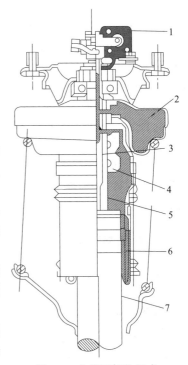

图 4-5 电控悬架的组成
1—执行器;2—副气室;
3—减振器调整杆;4—主气门;
5—减振器活塞杆;6—滚动膜;
7—减振器

② 车身姿态控制。当汽车起步、制动和转向时,会造成车身姿态的急剧改变。这种车身姿态的改变既降低了汽车的乘坐舒适性,又由于车身的过度倾斜容易使汽车失去稳定性,所以应该对其进行控制。这种控制主要包括以下 3 个方面。

a. 转向时车身的倾斜控制。

b. 制动时车身的点头控制。

c. 起步或者加速时车身的后坐控制。

③ 车身高度控制。车身高度控制是在汽车行驶速度和路面变化时,悬架 ECU 对执行元件输出控制信号,控制调节车身的高度,以确保汽车行驶的稳定性和通过性。

(2) 电控空气悬架系统执行器的结构、工作原理

电控悬架系统执行器的结构如图 4-6 所示。当悬架 ECU 控制步进电动机动作时,带动小齿轮转动,小齿轮驱动扇形齿轮转动。与扇形齿轮同轴的阻尼调节杆带动回转阀旋转,从而使阻尼孔开闭的数量发生变化,达到调节减振器阻尼的目的。同时阻尼调节杆上通过齿轮带动空气阀控制杆转动,使空气阀阀芯转动,随着阀芯转动角度的改变,使空气弹簧的刚度也得到调节。

悬架系统执行器上还有一个电磁线圈,当电磁线圈不通电时,由它控制的制动开关松开,制动杆处于扇形齿轮的滑槽内,扇形齿轮可以转动;当电磁线圈通电而吸合制动开关时,制动杆往

回拉，各齿轮处于锁止状态，阻尼调节杆和空气阀控制杆都不能转动，此时悬架的刚度参数和阻尼参数都为固定值，悬架系统处于相对稳定的状态。

（3）电控空气悬架系统执行器的分类

常见的有 3 种电控悬架系统执行器，分别为 4 线执行器、3 线执行器和 2 线执行器。

① 4 线执行器。4 线执行器是一个双向直流电动机。执行器安装在减振器的顶部，执行器驱动减振器内的一根轴来改变减振器阀门。这类执行器由悬架 ECU 通过一对称为硬/软继电器的部件来控制。4 线执行器可以从减振器总成上取下单独更换，4 线执行器内带位置传感器。

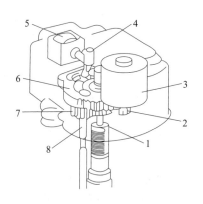

图 4-6 悬架系统执行器的结构
1—阻尼调节杆；2—小齿轮；3—步进电动机；
4—制动杆；5—电磁线圈；6—扇形齿轮；
7—空气阀驱动齿轮；8—空气阀控制杆

② 3 线执行器。3 线执行器是一个直流电动机，位于减振器顶部，只能单向旋转。电动机转动时，通过减速齿轮总成带动减振器活塞杆改变减振阻尼。

③ 2 线执行器。2 线执行器是一个 on/off 电磁阀。如果电磁阀处于 off 位置，减振器处于硬阻尼状态；如果电磁阀处于 on 位置，减振器处于软阻尼状态。2 线执行器与减振器为一体式，不可单独维护。

任务实施

学生分组训练，在实车上找出电子控制悬架系统与传统悬架在结构上的不同之处。

习题测试

简答题

1. 简述电子控制悬架系统的功能。
2. 简述电控空气悬架系统执行器的分类。

任务二　汽车电子控制变高度悬架系统的检修

【学习目标】

知识要求：
1. 了解汽车电子控制变高度悬架系统的作用、分类、组成；
2. 掌握汽车电子控制变高度悬架系统的结构、原理与检修；
3. 理解汽车电子控制变高度悬架系统的故障诊断的思路及方法。

能力要求：
1. 能通过与客户交流、查阅相关维修技术资料等方式获取车辆信息；
2. 能根据故障现象制订正确的维修计划；
3. 能根据维修计划，选择正确的检测和诊断设备对汽车电子控制变高度悬架系统进行故障诊断；

4. 能使用多用表、故障诊断仪、示波器及常用检测和诊断设备对汽车电子控制变高度悬架系统传感器、控制器、执行器进行检测；

5. 能按照正确操作规范进行传感器、执行器和控制器的更换，并能进行系统匹配设定；

6. 能对车辆进行测试，检查和评估汽车电子控制变高度悬架系统的修复质量。

 任务导入

有一辆轿车仪表板灯光系统警告灯点亮，中央控制面板的悬架升高按键上的LED灯不停闪烁，电控空气悬架升高系统不工作。

 知识准备

一、车身高度控制系统功用及分类

车身高度控制系统的主要功用是当车身载荷变化或车辆行驶速度变化时，自动调节车身高度，使汽车行驶姿态稳定，从而提高乘坐舒适性和安全性。

1. 自动水平调节

系统可把车辆保持在一个不变的高度面，与乘员及重量无关，把车辆高度置于正常或高位置。

2. 高速时的调节

把车辆悬挂高度开关置于SPORT位置时，车高略低于正常时的位置。该位置可改善高速行驶的稳定性和空气动力性。

3. 点火开关关闭时的悬挂位置调节

为防止在点火开关关闭后改变乘客人数和行李重量而引起的车辆高度的变化，可调节车高到所设置的位置，该功能可改善汽车行车时的车辆姿态。

车身高度控制系统分为两大类型，一类是仅对两个后轮悬架进行控制；另一类是对全部4个车轮的悬架进行高度控制。两种类型的控制原理基本相同。

二、变高度控制悬架系统的组成

目前，汽车普遍采用的车身高度控制系统由4只高度传感器（每个减振器下面各设1只）、控制开关、悬架控制电控单元EMS ECU、高度调节执行器（包括4个气压缸、两只高度控制电磁阀、空气压缩机、干燥器和空气管路）等组成。

三、变高度控制悬架系统的控制过程

变高度控制悬架系统在汽车乘员或载荷变化时，能够自动调节车身高度。当乘员或载荷增加时，系统将自动调高车身高度；反之，当乘员或载荷减小时，系统将自动调低车身高度。

1. 车身高度不变时悬架系统的控制过程

当车身高度传感器输入电控单元ECU的信号表示车身高度在设定高度范围内时，ECU将发出指令使空气压缩机停止转动，空气减振器内空气量保持不变，车身高度保持在正常位置。

2. 车身高度降低时悬架系统的控制过程

当汽车乘员或载荷增加使车身高度"偏低"或"过低"时，高度传感器将向悬架控制电

控单元 EMS ECU 输入车身"偏低"或"过低"的信号。EMS ECU 接收到车身高度降低的信号时，立即向压缩机继电器和高度控制电磁阀发出电路接通指令，在接通高度控制空气压缩机继电器电路使压缩机运转的同时，接通高度控制电磁阀线圈电路使电磁阀打开，压缩空气进入空气弹簧的气压腔（气室），气压腔充气量增加便使车身高度上升。

空气压缩机继电器触点接通时，直流电动机带动空气压缩机运转，从压缩机输出的压缩空气进入干燥器干燥后进入储气罐，储气罐的气体压力由调压阀进行调节。

3. 车身高度升高时悬架系统的控制过程

当汽车乘员或载荷减少使车身高度"偏高"或"过高"时，高度传感器将向悬架控制电控单元 EMS ECU 输入车身升高的信号。EMS ECU 接收到车身高度升高的信号时，立即向空气压缩机继电器发出电路切断指令，并向排气阀和高度控制电磁阀发出电路接通指令，压缩机继电器触点迅速断开使电动机电路切断而停止运转，排气阀和高度控制电磁阀线圈电路接通使电磁阀打开，空气从减振器气压腔，经高度控制电磁阀、空气软管、干燥器、排气阀排出，气压腔空气量减少使车身高度降低。

4. 系统保护措施

从减振器中放出的空气经过干燥器时，带走了干燥剂中的湿气。这样，干燥剂经过一段时间使用后不会被湿气浸透。这种保护干燥剂的再生干燥系统为许多电控悬架系统所采用。干燥器中空气的压力保持在 55～165kPa，从而保证系统中有一定的空气。这样在乘员或载荷减少使减振器伸长时，空气弹簧的气压腔不致凹瘪。

 任务实施

一、电子控制变高度悬架系统检修

1. 检修调高后电控悬架的故障

故障检修时使用能够显示和翻译故障码的专用数字检测仪。将专用检测仪连接在悬架控制和转向动力控制模块的检测接口上，接收系统控制模块自检系统传输的故障码，完成以下诊断检测。

① 自动/手工故障检查。
② 故障码显示。
③ 详细检查。
④ 功能检查。

在自动/手工检查中，控制模块自检系统检测系统元件是否有故障。检查元件故障后，控制器升起和降低车辆以检查 3 个高度传感器状态。高度传感器检查完成后为手工检查。此过程中，使车门打开数次、转向盘向左右两边分别转动半圈，控制模块监测到车门开关和转向传感器工作。

在生产厂家提供的维修信息中，给每种故障码均提供了详细检查。详细检查是用电压表和电阻表检查，从而确定故障码是何原因造成的。

功能检查用在自动/手工检查的最后，以找出故障码所代表的元件。除非详细检查指出需要进行功能检查，否则不进入功能检查。如果没有这种专门指导而进行功能检查，会造成控制模块损坏。生产厂家维修手册提供了详细检查的步骤。

2. 空气弹簧的充气操作步骤

① 用起重机吊起车架，缓慢降下起重机，直到轻微的车重作用在悬架上。

② 使电控悬架系统的控制开关至打开状态。
③ 使点火开关从断开到接通保持 5s，并使驾驶员一侧车门打开，其他车门关闭，断开点火开关。
④ 将系统检测诊断引线接搭铁（接地）。
⑤ 踩下制动踏板，并使点火开关在接通状态。
⑥ 给后悬架弹簧充气时，关闭、打开驾驶员门各一次，延时 6s 后，后悬架弹簧充气。
⑦ 给前悬架弹簧充气时，关闭、打开驾驶员门各两次，延时 6s 后，前悬架弹簧充气。
⑧ 当前后悬架弹簧均需充气时，先充后悬架弹簧。后悬架弹簧充气后，再关闭、打开驾驶员一侧的车门各一次，使前悬架弹簧开始充气。
⑨ 如果诊断引线与搭铁脱离，弹簧充气状态停止。如果点火开关断开，或制动踏板踩下，也会停止充气。

二、电子控制变高度悬架系统的故障案例诊断过程

连接故障检测仪对空气悬架系统进行检测，发现了故障为加注中央蓄压器时间异常。利用故障检测仪的动作测试功能为中央蓄压器充气，发现控制单元的指令可以发出但充气泵不工作。根据动作测试结果可以判定造成该故障的原因既可能是线路问题，也有可能是元件问题。首先用多用表电压挡检查充气泵的电源线，测试结果为无工作电压。对照电路图进行线路检查发现，提供电源的 40A 熔丝已经熔断。但继续检查充气泵及线路发现无短路现象。于是更换熔断的熔丝后启动发动机进行试车，但进行试车后故障还是存在。于是又用导线直接将蓄电池的正负极电源引至充气泵，发现充气泵不工作。根据以上检查结果，可以确定充气泵损坏。在更换新的充气泵后悬架系统升降功能恢复，升降开关上的 LED 灯在车辆悬架达到预定高度后熄灭，电控空气悬架系统恢复正常。

习题测试

填空题

1. 车轮和车身状态只能被动地取决于路面及行驶状况以及汽车的弹性支撑元件、减振器和导向机构的悬架是_____悬架。
2. 根据行驶条件，随时对悬架系统的刚度、减振器的阻尼力以及车身的高度和姿态进行调节，使汽车的有关性能始终处于最佳状态的悬架是_____悬架。

任务三　汽车电子控制变刚度悬架系统的检修

【学习目标】

知识要求：理解汽车电子控制变刚度悬架系统的故障诊断的思路及方法。
能力要求：
1. 能根据维修计划，选择正确的检测和诊断设备对汽车电子控制变刚度悬架系统进行故障诊断；
2. 能使用多用表、故障诊断仪、示波器及常用检测和诊断设备对汽车电子控制变刚度悬架系统传感器、控制器、执行器进行检测；

3. 能正确记录、分析各种检测结果并做出故障判断；
4. 能按照正确操作规范进行传感器、执行器和控制器的更换，并能进行系统匹配设定；
5. 能对车辆进行测试，检查和评估汽车电子控制变刚度悬架系统的修复质量。

任务导入

一辆马自达轿车的悬架系统，无论在什么车况下，都只能以一种模式运行，不能根据行驶路况进行调节。该车装有马自达电控悬架系统 TEMS。正常情况下，驾驶员可根据行车状况选择悬架的控制方式，从而决定衰减力的大小，而该车却只能以"正常手动状态"运行。

知识准备

一、电子控制变刚度悬架系统的功用

影响汽车乘坐的舒适性和行驶安全性的一个主要因素就是汽车悬架弹性元件的刚度，悬架弹性元件的刚度将直接影响车身的振动强度和对路况及车速的感应程度。目前，中、高档汽车倾向于利用可调刚度的空气弹簧或油气弹簧，通过调节这些元件的空气压力的办法来调整弹性元件的刚度。

二、电子控制变刚度悬架系统的组成

电子控制变刚度悬架系统也是由高度传感器、控制开关、悬架控制电控单元 EMS ECU、刚度调节执行器（气压缸、高度控制电磁阀、空气压缩机、干燥器和空气管路）等组成的。

三、空气弹簧悬架刚度的调节原理

在汽车行驶过程中，为了防止或抑制车身出现"点头""侧倾""后坐"等现象，需要调节相应悬架的高度和减振器的阻尼。例如，当汽车紧急制动时，为了抑制点头现象，悬架控制电控单元 EMS ECU 将根据制动灯开关接通信号和车速传感器提供的车速高低信号，向前空气弹簧执行元件发出指令使其气压升高，增大前空气弹簧的刚度，同时控制后空气弹簧执行元件使后空气弹簧放气，减小其刚度。当控制单元计算的车速变化量表明无须抑制点头控制时，就使前、后空气弹簧恢复到原来的压力。

在部分小轿车、越野汽车和大型豪华客车上采用的电子控制悬架系统中，每个车轮上都采用了空气弹簧和普通减振器。改变空气弹簧气压腔中压缩空气的压力（实际上是改变空气密度），即可改变空气弹簧悬架的刚度。

空气弹簧由封入低压惰性气体和阻尼力可调的减振器、旋转式膜片、主气室、副气室和悬架执行元件组成。主气室的容积是可变的，在它的下部有一个对向伸展的隔膜。压缩空气进入主气室后可以升高悬架的高度，反之使悬架高度下降，主、副气室设计为一体，既节省空间，又减轻了重量。悬架的上方与车身相连，下方与车轮相连，如图 4-7 所示，随着车身与车轮的相对运动，主气室的容

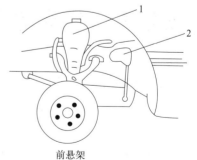

前悬架

图 4-7 悬架安装位置
1—空气悬架；2—车身高度传感器

积在不断变化。主气室与副气室之间有一个通道，气体可相互流通。改变主、副气室间的气体通道的大小，就可以改变电控悬架的刚度。减振器的活塞通过中心杆（阻尼调整杆）和齿轮系与直流步进电动机相连接。步进电动机转动可改变活塞阻尼孔的大小，从而改变减振器的阻尼系数。

悬架刚度的自动调节原理：主、副气室间的气阀体上有大小两个通道。步进电动机带动空气阀控制杆转动，使空气阀阀芯转过一个角度，改变气体通道的大小，就可以改变主、副气室之间的气体流量，使悬架的刚度发生变化。

悬架刚度可以在低、中、高3种状态下改变。

当阀芯的开口转到对准图4-8所示的低位置时，气体通道的大孔被打开。主气室的气体经过阀芯的中间孔、阀体侧面通道与副气室的气体相通，两气室之间空气流量越大，相当于参与工作的气体容积增大，悬架刚度处于低状态。

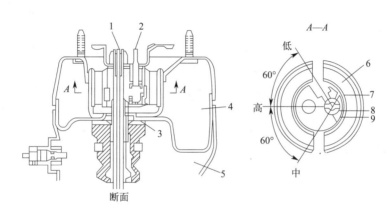

图4-8 悬架刚度的自动调节原理
1—阻尼调节杆；2—空气阀控制杆；3—主、副气室通道；4—副气室；5—主气室；
6—气阀体；7—气体小通道；8—阀芯；9—气体大通道

当阀芯的开口转到对准图4-8所示的中间位置时，气体通道的小孔被打开，两气室之间的流量小，悬架刚度处于中间状态。

当阀芯的开口转到对准图4-8所示的高位置时，两气室之间的气体通道全部被封住，两气室之间的气体相互不能流动，压缩空气只能进入主空气室，悬架在振动过程中，只有主气室的气体单独承担缓冲工作，悬架高度处于高状态。

 任务实施

一、空气弹簧的拆卸和安装

空气弹簧的拆装应参考生产厂家的维修手册进行，一般的操作步骤如下。
① 断开电控悬架开关。
② 吊起车辆后悬架自然下垂，或用千斤顶顶起车辆并将千斤顶支架放在车架下，使车辆降在架上，并使悬架自然下垂。
③ 从空气弹簧的电磁阀上拆下尼龙空气管路。将阀门旋转至第一挡，使空气从弹簧中完全排出，空气排完之前不要将阀门旋至第二挡。
④ 卸下空气弹簧下的保持架，将弹簧从车架上拆下。

⑤ 在空气弹簧安装前，应将其正确折叠在皮腔底部活塞上。将空气弹簧安在车架上，并安上弹簧下的保持架。确保弹簧顶部正确安装在弹簧内，安装悬架或悬架弹簧时，弹簧必须正确放置。

注意：在修理系统元件时，系统控制开关必须在断开状态。

拆卸空气弹簧阀门时旋转阀门至第一挡，直到空气弹簧内的空气完全排放。空气未完全排放之前，不要将阀门旋至第二挡。

电控空气悬架系统中许多零件，如减振器、横向稳定杆等的诊断和维修与普通悬架系统中的方法相同。

二、电子控制变刚度悬架系统的故障案例诊断过程

在检修过程中发现该车刚刚铺设了地胶。而车辆的模式选择开关在自动变速器选挡杆的前方，如果要铺地胶就需要揭开模式选择开关附近的胶皮，并且拆下开关护板。所以怀疑造成故障的原因是在拆装过程中，模式选择开关的接线受到损伤。将模式选择开关拆下，开关有4根引线，其中有两根分别通向悬架控制系统电控单元的A1脚和A13脚，一根线搭铁，另外一根通向TEMS电源的20A熔丝。这根线在点火开关打开之后一直有电，然而用多用表测量，发现该线电压始终为0V。仔细检查各插脚，发现该线伸入插头内的部分已经脱开。将该线接好，将模式选择开关装复试车，一切恢复正常。无论按压哪一个模式选择开关的按钮，悬架控制系统都能根据相应的选择自动进行"正常手动""正常自动""运动手动"和"运动自动"的相应调节。

习题测试

判断题

1. 主动悬架可以根据路面的行驶状态和车身的响应对悬架阻尼力进行控制，并在几秒内由最小到最大，使车身的振动响应始终被控制在某个范围之内。（   ）
2. 主动悬架需要外加动力源，消耗的能量多。（   ）

任务四　汽车电子控制变阻尼悬架系统的检修

【学习目标】

知识要求：理解汽车电子控制变阻尼悬架系统的故障诊断的思路及方法。

能力要求：

1. 能根据维修计划，选择正确的检测和诊断设备对汽车电子控制变阻尼悬架系统进行故障诊断；

2. 能使用多用表、故障诊断仪、示波器及常用检测和诊断设备对汽车电子控制变阻尼悬架系统传感器、控制器、执行器进行检测；

3. 能按照正确操作规范进行传感器、执行器和控制器的更换，并能进行系统匹配设定；

4. 能对车辆进行测试，检查和评估汽车电子控制变阻尼悬架系统的修复质量。

任务导入

电动汽车在行驶时,悬架刚度和阻尼系数不随着行驶状况、路况、汽车姿态变化而调节。

 知识准备

一、变阻尼悬架系统的功用及控制方式

在电子控制悬架系统中,最常用的是变阻尼悬架系统。改变减振器阻尼的悬架系统相对于使用空气弹簧的悬架系统有许多优点,最突出的优点是质量轻,变阻尼悬架系统只增加了电子控制元件和改变了减振器阻尼的执行元件的质量。

变阻尼悬架系统采用的控制方式分为以下 3 种。

① 根据汽车行驶状况进行控制。
② 根据驾驶员选择的运行模式进行控制。
③ 根据汽车行驶状况和驾驶员选择的运行模式进行控制。

二、减振器阻尼控制机构的结构特点

1. 运行模式选择开关

电子控制悬架系统减振器阻尼的工作模式选择开关又称为运行模式选择开关,用于选择减振器阻尼的工作模式。驾驶员选择的工作模式不同,减振器阻尼的状态也不相同。减振器阻尼的状态一般设有"标准""中等硬度"和"坚硬"3 种。

2. 变阻尼执行元件

丰田汽车电子调节悬架系统的执行元件安装在减振器支柱的顶部。

三、减振器阻尼调整的控制过程

1. 阻尼"标准"的控制过程

当悬架控制电控单元 EMS ECU 根据传感器和控制开关信号确定阻尼为"标准"状态时,控制单元向步进电动机发出控制指令使其沿顺时针方向旋转,因此小齿轮驱动扇形齿轮沿逆时针方向转动,直到扇形齿轮凹槽的一边靠在挡块上为止。

2. 阻尼"中等"的控制过程

当电控单元 ECU 根据传感器和控制开关信号确定阻尼为"中等"状态时,控制单元向步进电动机发出控制指令使其沿逆时针方向旋转,因此小齿轮便驱动扇形齿轮沿顺时针方向转动,直到扇形齿轮凹槽的另一边靠在挡块上为止(从"柔软"位置开始计算,其转角约为 120°)。与此同时,扇形齿轮带动回转阀控制杆和回转阀旋转,使回转阀上的阻尼孔与活塞杆上的减振油液孔的位置相对应。由于只有第二个截面上的阻尼孔打开,允许减振油液流过活塞的流动速度不快也不慢,因此减振器能以缓慢速度伸缩,使阻尼处于"中等"状态。

3. 阻尼"坚硬"的控制过程

当电控单元 ECU 根据传感器和控制开关信号确定阻尼为"坚硬"状态时,控制单元将同时向步进电动机和电磁线圈发出控制指令,使步进电动机和扇形齿轮从阻尼"柔软"或"中等"的极限位置旋转约 60°(从"柔软"的极限位置顺时针旋转 60°,从"中等"的极限位置逆时针旋转 60°),接通电磁线圈电流,其电磁吸力将挡块吸出,使挡块进入扇形齿轮凹槽中间部位的一个凹坑内。与此同时,扇形齿轮带动回转阀控制杆和回转阀旋转,使回转

阀上的阻尼孔与活塞杆上的减振油液孔的位置相对应。由于3个阻尼孔全部关闭，减振油液不能流动，因此减振器伸缩非常缓慢，使阻尼处于"坚硬"状态。

4. 变阻尼悬架系统指示灯的控制

电控单元除了向执行元件发出控制信号外，同时还向汽车仪表盘上的3只悬架系统指示灯发出控制指令。当减振器处于"柔软"阻尼状态时，控制左边一只指示灯发亮；当减振器处于"中等"阻尼位置时，控制左边和中间共两只指示灯发亮；当减振器处于"坚硬"阻尼位置时，控制3只指示灯全部发亮。悬架系统指示灯在接通点火开关时，大约发亮2s后熄灭，以便驾驶员检查指示灯及其线路是否完好。如果控制单元发现系统有故障，将使这些指示灯闪烁提示驾驶员系统有故障。

电控悬架的电控模块内部一般都有自诊断检测功能，检修时，需要按照对应车型的维修手册，对照检测流程进行检测维修。除此之外，还需要一些基本工具，如常用五金工具、千斤顶、千斤顶支架、尺子等。

任务实施

一、电子控制变阻尼悬架系统诊断基本步骤

如果电控悬架的警告灯在发动机运转条件下亮了，说明控制模块检测出电控悬架系统有故障。电控悬架系统的故障诊断和维修步骤由于车辆型号的不同而不同，应按生产厂家提供的维修手册中所述步骤进行维修。

林肯大陆轿车中的电控悬架系统，当电控悬架警报灯显示系统有故障时，诊断步骤如下。

① 确保电控悬架系统开关在开的位置。
② 打开点火开关，5s后关闭。驾驶员一侧车门打开，其他车门关闭。
③ 将控制模块附近的诊断引线搭铁接地，关闭驾驶员一侧车门，并将车窗玻璃降下。
④ 打开点火开关，警报灯会以1.8次/s连续闪烁，表示系统进入故障诊断状态。

二、电子控制变阻尼悬架系统维修与检测

1. 试车检测

试车检测可显示出上一次行车时的故障码。试车检测可检测出在其他检查中不能被检测出的故障（有的故障是中断性的）。

试车应在不同车速、不同道路状况的条件下进行，行驶最少5km或仪表板内的模式信号灯亮为止。经过试车后，应将车直接开至维修地点，停下后断开点火开关，故障码就储存在电控悬架的控制模块中，存储时间为点火开关断开后1h以内（或直到再次接通点火开关）。如在1h后接通点火开关，故障码会被从电控悬架控制模块的内存中删除。在检测中，电控悬架的开关必须保持"接通"的状态。

将能进行电控悬架检测的检测仪连接到控制模块附近的诊断接口上。应按汽车生产厂家维修手册和检测仪操作说明的程序进行检测。检测仪会显示一个"通过"代码或显示一个或多个故障码。记下故障码以备故障排除中应用。

2. 分级诊断检测

（1）自动/手动诊断检测

在自动/手动检测中，电控悬架控制模块进行自我检测，并检查其他系统零件。检查后，

手动检查是让维修人员检查控制模块的各种输入。

（2）故障码显示

完成自动/手动检查后，故障码可通过按下相应的检测仪按钮来显示。每个故障码大约显示15s，并且此故障码会持续显示下去，直到下一检测模式的输入。要将试车检测中得到的故障信号与维修间检测中得到的故障码进行对比。当一种信号在两种状态下均出现时，表明此故障为"实"故障；如果故障信号仅在行车、试车检测时出现，此故障为"时有时无"类型的故障。

（3）详细检测

详细检测是一个具体排除故障的过程，应按照优先级从高到低的顺序进行。故障码按优先级提供，排除一项故障后，一定要重新检查系统。有的系统模块中的计算机可能只能按优先级存储一定数量的代码。如果只显示了一个故障码，在系统中可能存在优先级更低的另一个故障代码。

3. 弹簧充气诊断

弹簧的充气诊断允许维修人员利用电控悬架控制模块给每个空气弹簧充气或排气。

此过程可显示已经失效的零件，例如空气弹簧电磁阀或对应的触发电路。在弹簧充气过程中，维修人员可检测空气管路是否泄漏。

习题测试

填空题

1. 汽车电子控制悬架系统应用的开关有_____、_____、_____和_____等。
2. 汽车电子控制悬架系统的执行机构有_____，可调节弹簧高度和弹性大小的弹性元件等。

项目小结

电子控制悬架代表了目前汽车悬架的发展方向，半主动是今后悬架系统的主要发展方向。研究性能可靠、调节方便的可调阻尼减振器将是半主动悬架走向大众的必经之路。

项目习题测试

一、填空题

1. 主动悬架根据频带和能量消耗的不同，可分为_____和_____。按驱动机构和介质不同可分为_____和_____。
2. 汽车电子控制悬架系统主要由感应汽车运行状况的各种传感器、开关、_____及_____组成。

二、判断题

1. 装有电子控制悬架系统的汽车无论车辆负载多少，都可以保持汽车高度一定，车身保持水平。（　　）

项目五

汽车防盗系统的检修

项目导读

汽车防盗系统是一种安装在车上,用来增加盗车难度,延长盗车时间的装置。它通过将防盗系统与汽车电路配接在一起,从而可以达到防止车辆被盗、被侵犯、保护汽车的目的。随着科学技术的进步,为对付不断升级的盗车手段,人们研制出各种形式、不同结构的防盗器。

任务一 汽车防盗系统的认知

【学习目标】

知识要求:了解汽车防盗系统的种类和功能。
能力要求:能够在实车上识别各种类型的防盗系统。

任务导入

汽车防盗系统的种类有哪些?各车系的防盗系统有何不同?

 知识准备

目前汽车防盗装置已经由初期的机械控制,发展成为电子密码、遥控呼救、信息报警等高科技产品,早期的防盗装置主要用于控制门锁、门窗等联锁机构。随着科技的发展,汽车防盗装置日趋严密和完善,目前防盗器按其结构与功能可分五大类:机械式、电子式、网络式、生物识别式和芯片式,各有优劣,但汽车防盗的发展方向是向智能程度更高的芯片式和网络式发展。

一、机械式防盗装置

机械式防盗装置是采用金属材料制作的各种防盗锁具,包括转向柱锁、转向盘锁、变速杆锁、踏板锁(离合器踏板锁、制动踏板锁)、车轮锁等,这些防盗锁的作用是锁住汽车的操纵部件,使盗窃者无法将汽车开走。早期的汽车防盗器材主要是机械式的防盗锁,只防盗不报警。

二、电子式防盗装置

电子式防盗装置也称微电脑防盗装置,主要有插片式、按键式和遥控式等种类。该防盗

装置安装隐蔽，功能齐全，无线遥控，操作简便。

1. 防盗报警功能

电子式防盗装置通过电子设备控制汽车的启动、点火等电路，当整个系统开启之后，如果有非法移动汽车、开启车门、油箱门、发动机盖、行李箱盖、连接点火线路时，防盗装置立刻进入警报状态，控制车辆灯光闪烁、鸣响喇叭，同时切断启动电路、点火电路、喷油电路、供油电路，甚至切断自动变速器电路，使汽车处于完全瘫痪状态。电子式防盗器系统的缺点是误报率较高。

2. 车门未关安全提示功能

行车时车门未关妥，警告灯会连续闪烁数秒。汽车熄火遥控锁门后，若车门未关妥，车灯会不停闪烁，喇叭鸣叫，直至车门关好为止。

3. 寻车功能

车主用遥控器寻车时，喇叭断续鸣叫，同时伴有车灯闪烁提示。

4. 遥控中央门锁

当遥控器发射正确信号时，中央门锁自动开启或关闭。电子遥控防盗装置的遥控器、电子钥匙都有相对应的密码。遥控器发射部分采用微波/红外线系统。利用遥控器将密码信号发送至车辆，车辆门锁系统工作。

三、网络式防盗系统

网络式汽车防盗系统是目前国际上比较流行而且比较先进实用的一种新型的防盗方式。其主要有两种：一种是GPS卫星定位防盗系统，另外一种是GSM移动防盗器。

1. GPS卫星定位防盗系统

GPS即全球卫星定位系统，属网络式防盗器，是一种主动监护式防盗器，它通过GPS卫星定位系统，确定车辆的位置，再将位置和报警信息传送到报警中心。如果GPS防盗器被非法拆卸，还会发出报警信息，与此同时，还可以对汽车进行实时跟踪和定位，利用GPS定位功能，能迅速准确地找到被盗车辆的位置。

GPS卫星定位防盗系统缺点是需要经常支付服务费，系统运行的功率较大。

2. GSM移动防盗器

GSM移动防盗器依托GSM通信网络，进行手机与汽车的智能联动防盗，具有防盗、监控、远程控制、远程报警、定位、反劫持等多种功能，是维护社会治安、保护车主利益的有效手段。与同类产品相比，该系统还具有安装更隐蔽、技术更先进、性能更可靠等特性。GSM移动防盗器具有不须建基站、报警不受距离限制的优点。

GSM移动防盗器的缺点是需要缴纳GSM号码的月租费，依赖GSM网的覆盖。盗窃者的手段也是使用信号干扰器，阻断车辆与报警中心的联系，使防盗系统失效。

四、生物识别式防盗器

生物识别式防盗系统现在应用在车辆上的是汽车指纹识别防盗系统，也是防盗效果最好的防盗系统。生物识别式防盗器的缺点是价格较高，而且启动汽车之前多一个比对指纹的动作。

五、芯片式防盗器

芯片式数码防盗器是现代汽车防盗器发展的重点，大多数轿车均采用这种防盗方式作为

原装防盗器。芯片式防盗器的基本原理是锁住汽车发动机的电路和油路，在没有芯片钥匙的情况下无法启动车辆。数字化的密码重码率极低，而且要用密码钥匙接触车上的密码识别线圈才能开锁，杜绝了被扫描的可能。现在很多中高档车型已装有原厂的芯片防盗系统。

任务实施

学生分组识别各种车型的防盗系统类型。

习题测试

简答题
1. 电子防盗装置有哪些功能？
2. 网络式防盗装置的分类

任务二　汽车防盗系统的检修

【学习目标】

知识要求：
1. 了解汽车防盗系统的作用、分类、组成；
2. 掌握汽车防盗系统的结构、原理与检修；
3. 理解汽车防盗系统的故障诊断的思路及方法。

能力要求：
1. 能通过与客户交流、查阅相关维修技术资料等方式获取车辆信息；
2. 能根据故障现象制订正确的维修计划；
3. 能根据维修计划，选择正确的检测和诊断设备对汽车防盗系统进行故障诊断。

任务导入

一辆丰田卡罗拉轿车无法启动，打开点火开关观察各仪表及警告灯工作正常，但是启动时检测发动机无点火和喷油，同时发现防盗系统安全指示灯点亮。根据此现象，基本确定该故障为车辆防盗系统的故障。

 知识准备

目前汽车防盗系统已经发展到第五代，第五代防盗系统除了比以往的防盗系统更有效地起到防盗效果外，还具有其他先进之处，独特的射频识别技术可以保证系统在任何情况下都能正确地识别驾驶者，在驾驶者接近或远离车辆时可以自动识别其身份，自动打开或关闭车辆。

一、汽车防盗系统类型

单独防盗系统控制单元的结构如图5-1所示；防盗系统控制单元可集成在组合仪表内，

如图 5-2 所示；防盗系统控制单元也可集成在舒适系统控制单元内，如图 5-3 所示。

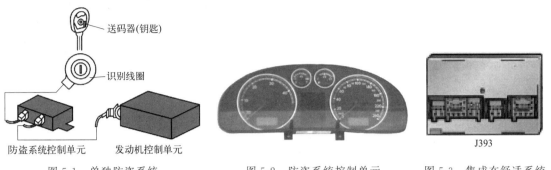

图 5-1　单独防盗系统控制单元　　　图 5-2　防盗系统控制单元集成在组合仪表内　　　图 5-3　集成在舒适系统控制单元内

第二、三代防盗系统由送码器（点火钥匙）、点火开关上的识别线圈（天线）、仪表内的防盗系统控制单元、发动机控制单元（只有在第三代系统上才参与防盗码的计算）、仪表板上的故障警告灯组成，如图 5-4 所示。

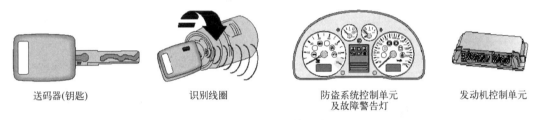

图 5-4　防盗系统组成

二、第三代防盗系统特点

第三代防盗系统的发动机控制单元是防盗系统的一部分，钥匙在自适应后被锁止，不能再用于其他车辆。第三代防盗系统提供对第二代防盗系统的功能支持，由 CAN 总线进行数据传递。

三、第三代防盗系统的组成与工作原理

防盗器由以下部件组成：完成自适应的防盗器控制单元（集成在仪表盘上）、组合仪表盘上的一个故障警报灯、点火锁上的一个读出线圈、已完成自适应的发动机控制单元、已配好的点火钥匙（带脉冲转发器）。

防盗器控制单元与组合仪表一体，该控制单元如损坏，必须更换组合仪表。其中的脉冲转发器编码是由一个固定码和一个可变码组成的。该码每次启动都变化，这样可防止他人复制钥匙。此外，每个防盗器还有一套可变码的计算规则，该规则在使用寿命内保持不变。在适配车钥匙时，防盗器将计算规则写入钥匙的脉冲转发器，同时学习相应的脉冲转发器的固定码。固定码可识别各个不同的钥匙，因此丢失的钥匙可被锁止。每次打开点火开关时，防盗器读出线圈读取钥匙中的脉冲转发器固定码，紧接着又读取可变码并检查这把钥匙是否有资格来启动。

在使用已授权的钥匙时，警报灯短时亮（最长 3s），然后熄灭。当使用未经授权的钥匙或系统有故障时，如打开点火开关，警报就一直亮着。

1. 固定码传输（从钥匙到防盗系统控制单元）

如图 5-5 所示，点火开关打开后，防盗系统控制单元通过改变天线中的磁场能量，向送码器（钥匙）传输数据提出质询。此时，钥匙发送回来它的固定码（首次匹配中这个固定码就存储在防盗系统控制单元中）。传送回来的固定码与存储在防盗系统控制单元中的码进行比较，如果相同则开始传输可变码。

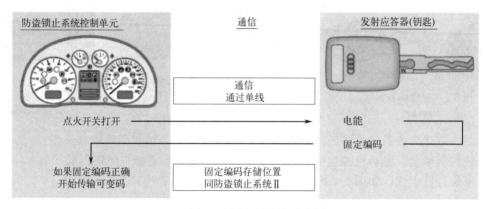

图 5-5　固定码传输图

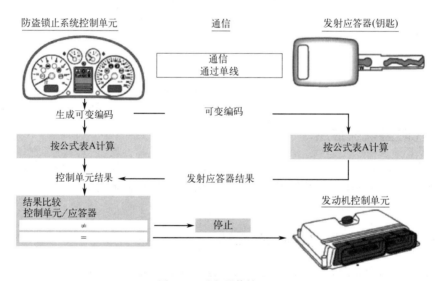

图 5-6　可变码传输（1）

2. 可变码传输（从防盗系统控制单元到钥匙）

如图 5-6 所示，防盗系统控制单元随机产生一变码。在钥匙内和防盗系统控制单元内有一套公式表和一个相同且不可改写的 SKC（隐秘的钥匙代码）。在钥匙和防盗系统控制单元中分别计算结果，钥匙发送结果给防盗系统控制单元，防盗系统控制单元把这个结果和自己的计算结果进行比较。如果相同，钥匙确认完成。

3. 可变码传输（从发动机控制单元到防盗系统控制单元）

如图 5-7 所示，发动机控制单元随机产生一变码。在发动机控制单元和防盗系统控制单元内有另一套公式表和一个相同的 SKC（公式指示器）。防盗系统控制单元返回这个计算结果到发动机控制单元内与其计算结果进行比较。这个数据由 CAN 总线传输。如果结果相同，发动机被允许启动。发动机控制单元每次启动后按照随机选定原则产生一变码，并把这

个变码储存在发动机控制单元和防盗系统控制单元内，用于下次发动机启动时计算。

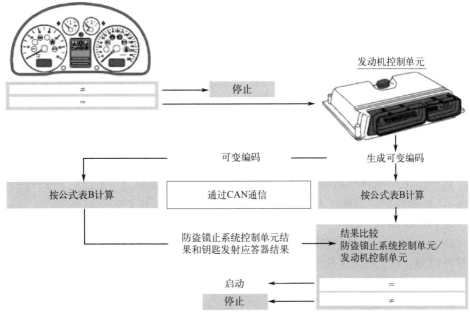

图 5-7　可变码传输（2）

四、第四代防盗系统的工作原理

第四代防盗系统并不是一个常规、简单的车辆防盗控制系统，而是一种具有网络数据交换功能的防盗系统。第四代防盗系统最重要的组成部分是中央数据库（Fahrzeugauskunft-und Zentrales Identifikations-Tool，FAZIT）。

1. 第四代防盗系统的特点

① 功能形式与第三代防盗器一致，只是所有与防盗器有关的元件均需在线进行匹配。

② 只能通过诊断仪"在线查询"，可确保安全、快速并可靠地将数据传送至车辆。通过传真来查询防盗器部件 PIN 码是否存在。

③ 所有车钥匙（包括补订的）在出厂前均已针对某一辆车编制了代码，因此这些钥匙只能与该车进行适配。

2. 第四代防盗系统的组成

（1）防盗系统控制单元

目前，一般车辆防盗系统控制单元有的是独立配备的，有些则安装在组合仪表总成中。第四代防盗系统则是两者的结合。

（2）发动机控制单元

所有发动机控制单元都是防盗系统的组成部分，必须在线接通。

（3）车钥匙

钥匙带有一个经过机械编码处理的钥匙齿，它只能用于（驾驶员车门、行李箱盖）锁芯处。钥匙发射器与电子部件连成一体，并且在钥匙电池无电压的情况下也能工作。这种高级钥匙增设了一个电子部件，该电子部件可以实现与进入和启动许可控制单元之间的无线双向通信。

（4）进入和启动许可开关

第四代防盗轿车上配用的是一种不同寻常的点火开关。进入和启动许可开关不是机械编

码钥匙。开关装有读取线圈，它可以将点火钥匙传输的密码数据经由双向数据电缆传送到进入和启动控制单元。进入和启动许可开关不需要匹配到防盗系统中。

（5）方向盘锁执行元件

方向盘锁执行元件受进入和启动许可开关的控制。它对方向盘进行闭锁或开锁。

（6）其他部件

所有其他电子部件，如车门把手、天线、启动/停止按钮等都没有安装微型控制装置，它们不属于 WFS 防盗系统和部件保护系统。

任务实施

卡罗拉防盗系统（发动机停机系统）使用收发器钥匙 ECU 总成来存储经授权的点火钥匙代码。如果试图使用未经授权的钥匙启动发动机，收发器钥匙 ECU 将向发动机计算机 ECM 发送信号以禁止供油和点火，从而有效地禁止发动机工作。

收发器钥匙线圈/放大器：当有钥匙插在点火锁芯中时，钥匙线圈接收到一个钥匙代码。然后放大器放大 ID 代码并把它输出至收发器钥匙 ECU 总成。

卡罗拉防盗系统如图 5-8 所示。

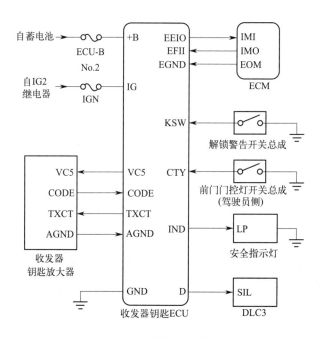

图 5-8　卡罗拉防盗系统

解锁警告开关总成的作用是检查是否有钥匙插入点火锁芯中，并将结果输出至收发器钥匙 ECU 总成。

ECM 的作用是从收发器钥匙 ECU 总成接收 ID 代码，验证该 ID 代码是否为合法代码；验证 ECU 是否为合法部件；经过运算后决定启动或停止发动机。

根据收发器钥匙 ECU 总成的操作，车内安全指示灯亮起或开始闪烁。当收发器钥匙 ECU 总成检测到钥匙解锁警告开关置于 ON 位置时，ECU 向发射器钥匙线圈提供电流并产生一个电波。钥匙柄中的发射应答芯片接收到电波后，发射应答芯片输出一个钥匙识别码信号。该信号通过收发器钥匙放大器放大，由发射器钥匙线圈接收，并被发送

到 ECU。

ECU 将钥匙识别码与先前在 ECU 中注册的车辆识别码匹配，并将结果发送到 ECU。在识别结果显示钥匙识别码与车辆识别码匹配，且 ECU 已确认二者匹配后，发动机启动控制进入准备模式（燃油喷射控制和点火控制）。同时 ECU 发送一个指示灯熄灭指令使安全指示灯熄灭。

一、维修注意事项

故障诊断仪的连接顺序为将诊断仪 OBD2 插头连接到车辆诊断座上，打开点火开关，打开诊断仪电源开关。钥匙为精密装置，所以在操作过程中切勿掉落或敲击钥匙，并将钥匙远离高温、磁铁或磁化物体。操作时按维修手册的规定进行。

二、技术要求

通过实习了解防盗系统的组成部件、安装位置及工作情况，熟悉系统检测方法。掌握诊断仪提取故障码、清除故障码和数据流的操作方法，并根据诊断仪提供的信息参阅维修手册提供的检测方法，准确地排除故障。

三、卡罗拉防盗系统检修

1. 故障诊断仪的使用

在仪表台左下侧找到车辆诊断座，如图 5-9 所示。将诊断仪诊断接头连接到车辆诊断座，如图 5-10 所示。打开诊断仪电源开关，选择车系，如图 5-11 所示。选择"车型系统"选项，如图 5-12 所示。选择"防盗系统"选项，如图 5-13 所示。使用"读取故障码"功能，如图 5-14 所示。选择"数据清单"读取数据流，如图 5-15 所示。

图 5-9　车辆诊断座

图 5-10　连接车辆诊断座

2. 拆装操作步骤

拆卸转向柱衬套，如图 5-16 所示。

图 5-11　选择车系

图 5-12　车型系统图

图 5-13　防盗系统

拆下点火开关下部的收发器钥匙线圈放大器线束插接器，如图 5-17 所示。

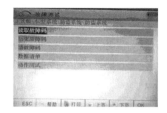 

图 5-14　读取故障码

 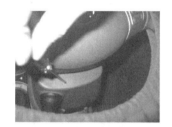

图 5-15　读取数据流

图 5-16　拆卸转向柱衬套

图 5-17　收发器钥匙线圈放大器线束插接器

3. 检测方法

检测收发器钥匙线圈放大器，如图 5-18 所示。

检测 E29-7♯—车身搭铁之间电阻始终小于 1Ω。如果检测结果不符合规定，则可能是线束侧有故障。下一步重新连接收发器钥匙线圈放大器连接器 E29，并根据以下数值检测。

E29-1♯—E29-7♯钥匙不在点火锁芯中时电压低于 1V，钥匙在点火锁芯中时电压为 4.6～5.4V。

E29-4♯—E29-7♯钥匙不在点火锁芯中时电压低于 1V。

E29-5♯—E29-7♯钥匙不在点火锁芯中时电压低于 1V。

图 5-18　收发器钥匙线圈放大器

使用"清故障码"功能，如图 5-19 所示。

图 5-19　清故障码

选择"数据清单"读取数据流，确认故障排除，如图 5-20 所示。

图 5-20　读取数据流

四、汽车防盗系统的故障案例诊断过程

通过故障现象，确定故障范围后，要准确地分析、诊断故障，就必须全面深入地了解出现故障的系统结构及控制原理。既然此车故障现象表明由防盗系统所致，那么必须了解此车的防盗系统结构、组成、工作原理以及电路图。这些都是在诊断此故障之前必须搞清楚的。在维修过程中通过查询维修手册及相关维修资料，合理使用故障诊断仪和检测工具，就可以快速、准确地确定故障点。

习题测试

简答题
奥迪 A3 防盗系统由哪些装置组成？

项目小结

针对目前世界范围内汽车盗窃案的上升趋势，汽车制造商都在不断地改进防盗技术，尤其是随着微电子技术的进步，汽车防盗技术已向着自动化、智能化方向发展。

项目习题测试

填空题
1. 用电脑控制的中控门锁系统包括_____、_____和_____。
2. 信号输入装置由_____、_____、_____、_____、_____和_____组成。

项目六

汽车定速巡航系统的检修

项目导读

汽车在高速公路上长时间行驶时,驾驶员长时间操纵加速踏板,容易造成腿部肌肉疲劳。汽车巡航控制系统就是为解决此问题而诞生的。汽车巡航控制系统经历了机械控制系统、晶体管系统、模拟集成电路控制系统和微机控制系统等几个过程。微机控制的汽车巡航控制系统自从 1981 年开始应用于汽车后,发展迅速。现在新型汽车基本上都采用了微机控制的汽车巡航控制系统。

任务一 汽车定速巡航系统的结构与工作原理

【学习目标】

知识要求:了解汽车定速巡航系统的组成、结构及原理。
能力要求:能够在实车上识别定速巡航系统各组成部件。

 任务导入

一台 2007 年制造的凯美瑞轿车,在按下定速巡航系统的开关后,定速巡航系统 CRUISE 指示灯点亮,但是不能设定车速。

 知识准备

一、定速巡航系统的分类与功能

汽车巡航控制系统(Cruise Control System,CCS)又称为定速巡航系统,是利用先进的电子技术对汽车的行驶速度进行自动调节,从而实现以事先设定速度行驶的一种电子控制装置。接通巡航控制开关,巡航控制系统将根据汽车行驶阻力的变化,自动加大或减小节气门开度,而不必控制加速踏板。采用这种装置后,在高速公路上长时间行车时,驾驶员不会因长时间控制加速踏板来稳定车速而产生疲劳。同时,使用这种速度稳定装置后,由于是定速行驶,加速踏板及制动踏板的踩放次数减少,可使汽车燃油的供给与发动机功率间的配合处于最佳状态,有效降低燃油消耗,减少有害气体排放。

1. 巡航系统的分类

目前,CCS 一般分为两大类,一类是电子式巡航控制系统,另一类是电控真空控制式

巡航控制系统。前者主要由指令开关、车速传感器、电子控制器和油门执行器4部分组成。后者一般由控制开关、真空系统和控制电路等组成。

2. 巡航系统的功能

（1）设定功能

当主开关接通，车辆在巡航控制车速范围（40~120km/h）内行驶时，若巡航控制开关接通后，巡航控制 ECU 便将此车速存储于 ECU 存储器内，并使汽车保持该速度行驶。

（2）手动取消功能

当汽车以巡航控制模式行驶时，如果步进电动机执行器切断电磁离合器，巡航控制模式即取消。

（3）自动取消功能

当汽车以巡航控制模式行驶时，踩下制动踏板或出现步进电动机驱动电流过大，步进电动机始终向节气门打开方向转动时，存储器中设置的车速被清除，巡航控制方式取消，主控开关同时关闭。

（4）恢复功能

当路面车流情况又可稳定运行时，可按"恢复"功能开关，这样汽车又自动按上述设定的车速稳定均匀运行。

（5）车速下限控制功能

车速下限是巡航控制所能设定的最低车速，其值为40km/h，巡航控制不能低于这个速度。当汽车以巡航控制模式行驶时，若车速降至40km/h以下，巡航控制就会自动取消，设置在存储器内的车速也被清除。

（6）车速上限控制功能

车速上限是巡航控制所能设定的最高车速，一般不会超过200km/h。汽车在巡航控制模式下行驶时，出于安全的需要，即使操作加速开关也不能使车速超过200km/h。

（7）匀速控制功能

ECU 将实际车速与设定车速进行比较，若车速高于设定车速，控制执行器将节气门适当减小，若车速低于设定车速，控制执行器将节气门适当增大。

（8）设定车速调整功能

当车辆以巡航控制模式行驶时，若操作加速或减速开关，执行器就会将节气门适当增大或减小，使汽车改变车速。巡航控制 ECU 将记忆改变后的车速，并按改变后的车速进行巡航控制。

（9）自动变速器控制功能

当具有自动变速器的汽车以巡航控制模式行驶时，如果上坡时变速器在超速挡，车速降至比设定车速低4km/h以上时，巡航控制 ECU 将超速挡取消信号送至自动变速器 ECU，取消自动变速器超速挡；当车速升至比设定车速低2km/h时，巡航控制 ECU 将超速挡恢复信号送至自动变速器 ECU，恢复自动变速器超速挡。

二、定速巡航系统的工作原理与组成

定速巡航系统工作原理是由巡航控制组件读取车速传感器发来的脉冲信号，并与设定的速度进行比较，从而控制执行器来调整节气门开度的增大或减小，节气门位置传感器将节气门开度信号传给发动机 ECU，由发动机 ECU 控制喷油量，以使车辆始终保持所设定的速度。

定速巡航系统主要由电控单元（ECU）、传感器、控制开关以及执行器等组成。

1. 定速巡航 ECU

定速巡航 ECU 是控制系统的中枢，一般装在一金属薄板制成的封闭壳体内。其主要作用是根据传感器、控制开关等输入的信号进行运算和判断。当定速巡航 ECU 判断实际车速偏离目标车速时，便向控制节气门开度的执行器（电动机或压力控制阀的电磁线圈）发出控制信号，控制执行器动作，调节节气门开度大小从而改变车速，最终将实际车速与目标车速的误差控制在许可范围内。CCS 系统采用的 ECU 可以是单独供巡航系统使用的，也可以与其他控制系统共用一个 ECU。此外，定速巡航 ECU 还起着记忆设定的巡航车速、对定速巡航系统进行故障自诊断等作用。定速巡航 ECU 的原理框图如图 6-1 所示。

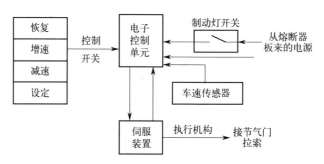

图 6-1　定速巡航 ECU 的原理框图

定速巡航 ECU 由线性放大器和积分放大器组成，如图 6-2 所示。它有两个输入信号，一个是实际车速的反馈信号，由车速传感器检测后反馈给控制器，另一个是驾驶员按要求直接设定车速，控制器检测辨别不同信号后，产生一个控制信号送至节气门执行器，节气门执行器根据所接收到的信号调节发动机节气门开度，从而保证车速稳定性。定速巡航 ECU 作为巡航控制系统的核心部件，其所采用的控制技术直接决定控制结果。

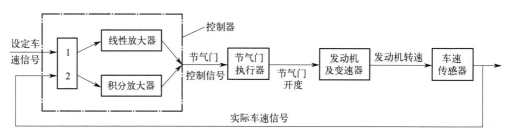

图 6-2　定速巡航 ECU 的组成

2. 定速巡航系统传感器

定速巡航系统采用的传感器主要有车速传感器、节气门位置传感器以及节气门控制摇臂位置传感器。定速巡航 ECU 根据这些信号控制节气门开度，稳定车速。

（1）车速传感器

车速传感器一般安装在变速器的输出轴上，这是因为实际车速与变速器输出轴转速成正比。车速传感器有磁感应式、霍尔式、光电式等多种结构形式，常用的是磁感应式。车速传感器的作用是将汽车行驶的实际车速转变为电信号并输送给巡航控制系统的定速巡航 ECU。

（2）节气门位置传感器

节气门位置传感器的信号可同时用于发动机控制、自动变速器控制和定速巡航控制。定速巡航系统节气门位置传感器的作用是将节气门开度的变化转变为电信号并输送给定速巡

航 ECU。

(3) 节气门控制摇臂位置传感器

节气门控制摇臂位置传感器的作用是将节气门控制摇臂的位置转变成电信号并输送给定速巡航 ECU。

3. 定速巡航系统的控制开关

定速巡航系统的控制开关是由驾驶者用来操作车辆进入或者取消巡航系统的。它主要由主控开关、制动开关、空挡启动开关、离合器开关、驻车制动开关等组成，主要用来启动、关闭巡航控制系统，并调节巡航控制系统的工作状态。

(1) 巡航控制主控开关

巡航控制主控开关一般为杆式开关，安装在转向柱上驾驶员容易接近的地方，或将组合开关设计在转向盘上。大多数开关有3个挡位：设置/减速（SET/COAST）、取消（CANCEL）和恢复/加速（RES/ACC）挡。通常情况下，当车速超过40km/h时，只要按下设定键，车辆就会记住当前的车速并保持定速行驶，当按下取消键时，恒速行驶立即停止。"恢复/加速"挡用于制动或断开电路后，使车辆重新按设定速度行驶。汽车在自动巡航控制状态下，可以通过按加速键提高车速，或按减速键来降低车速。

(2) 制动开关

制动开关用于向巡航控制 ECU 传送制动信号（即驾驶员踩下制动踏板的信号），以使汽车迅速退出巡航控制状态。

(3) 空挡启动开关

空挡启动开关用于向巡航控制 ECU 传送空挡信号（即变速器操纵杆处于空挡位置的信号），以使汽车立即退出巡航控制状态。

(4) 驻车制动开关

当拉起驻车制动操纵杆时，驻车制动开关就接通，接通信号传送至巡航控制 ECU，以使汽车退出巡航控制状态。

(5) 离合器开关

当踩下离合器踏板时，开关即接通，接通信号传送至巡航控制 ECU，以使汽车退出巡航控制状态。

4. 执行器

执行器又称伺服器，其作用是受巡航控制 ECU 的控制驱动与节气门拉索并联的拉线盘，用于调整节气门的开度，使车辆做加速、减速及定速行驶。执行器常分为电动式和真空式（气动式）两种。

(1) 真空式执行器

真空式执行器的结构如图 6-3 所示。密封圆筒内装有膜片、膜片弹簧、两个空气电磁阀和一个真空电磁阀。真空电磁阀和空气电磁阀的搭铁线分别接到巡航控制 ECU 的端子上，在 ECU 内部搭铁时，电磁阀起作用。真空电磁阀内部有一个真空管接头，通过一根橡胶管与进气歧管相连。在膜片的中间装有拉动节气门的拉索。真空式执行器利用发动机进气歧管的真空度吸引膜片，通过节气门拉索，使节气门开度增大，并可保持固定位置不动。如果空气电磁阀打开，则由于膜片弹簧的弹力，使节气门拉索放松，节气门开度减小。

图 6-4 所示为真空式巡航控制系统的结构原理。在巡航控制系统未工作时，真空电磁阀保持关闭，空气电磁阀打开，密封圆筒与大气相通。当汽车加速时，真空电磁阀打开，与进气歧管相通，而两个空气电磁阀则关闭，密封圆筒内真空度增大，吸动膜片，克服弹簧力，通过拉索使节气门开度增大，车辆加速行驶。当加速到一定车速时，真空电磁阀与空气电磁

阀同时关闭，此时密封圆筒内的真空度不变，汽车保持恒速行驶。当汽车减速时，空气电磁阀又恢复为打开状态，此时空气进入密封圆筒，膜片弹簧把膜片压回原位，节气门开度减小，汽车减速。

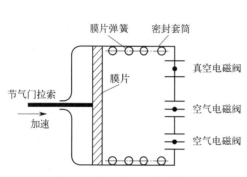

图 6-3 真空式执行器的结构

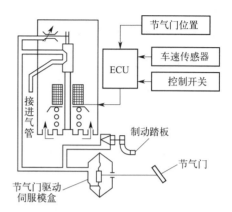

图 6-4 真空式巡航控制系统结构原理

（2）电动式执行器

电动式执行器主要由电动机、安全电磁离合器和位置传感器组成。电动机采用直流永磁式电动机，通过改变电动机中电流方向即可改变节气门转动方向。电动机转动时可带动执行元件控制臂转动，控制臂通过控制拉索改变节气门开度。为限定控制臂转动角度，电动机电路装有限位开关。在电动机与控制臂间装有安全电磁离合器。当进行巡航控制时，安全电磁离合器接合，此时电动机旋转可使节气门开度改变。若在巡航控制行驶阶段执行器或车速传感器发生故障，安全电磁离合器立即分离。在电动式执行器中还装有位置传感器，它是一个由滑动变阻器构成的电位计，用于检测执行器控制臂的转动位置，并将信号输入巡航控制ECU中。

任务实施

凯美瑞的定速巡航系统由车辆 ECM 控制。当定速巡航系统工作时，ECM 接收到定速巡航系统控制主开关的 ON 信号时，ECM 将点亮组合仪表内的 CRUISE 主指示灯，定速巡航系统开始工作。ECM 对车速传感器传送的行驶车速和通过定速巡航系统控制主开关设定的储存车速进行比较。当行驶速度大于储存车速时，ECM 控制节气门总成中的节气门马达减小节气门开度；当行驶速度小于储存车速时，ECM 控制节气门总成中的节气门马达增大节气门开度。如果在定速巡航系统工作中，变速器换挡杆的位置从 D 移动到 N，ECM 接收到驻车/空挡位置开关信号，ECM 将取消定速巡航系统的工作。

凯美瑞定速巡航系统的原理如图 6-5 所示。

① 连接诊断仪检测到 P0571 故障码。

② 查阅维修手册，该故障码的含义为制动灯开关 A 电路，可能的故障部位为制动灯开关、制动灯电路或 ECM。

③ 根据维修手册分析制动开关电路图，如图 6-6 所示。当 ECM 的 STP 端子接收到 12V 电源时定速巡航系统将不工作。

④ 进入诊断仪的数据流测试功能，发现在踩下和松开制动踏板时制动灯开关 S1 的信号一直为 ON。

⑤ 将 A19 号线束端子从制动灯开关上断开，用多用表电压挡检测 A19 号端子 2 号脚与

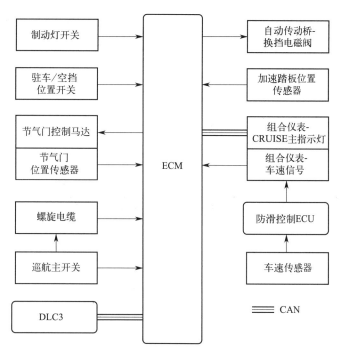

图 6-5 凯美瑞定速巡航系统原理

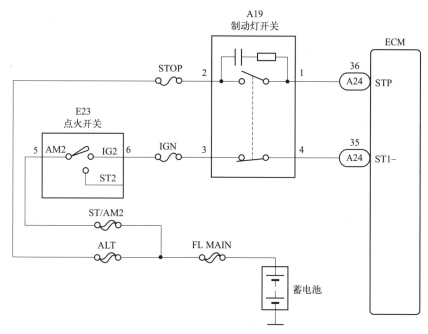

图 6-6 制动开关电路图

车身负极之间电压为 12V。打开点火开关至 ON 挡检测 A19 号端子 3 号脚与车身负极之间电压为 12V。从检测结果分析出制动灯开关电源线路没有故障。

⑥ 拆卸制动灯开关,用多用表电阻挡检测制动灯开关 1 号与 2 号脚,在开关销按下和未按下两种工况下电阻都为 0.8Ω。检测 3 号与 4 号脚开关销未按下时电阻为无穷大,开关销按下时电阻为 0.6Ω。从检测结果分析出制动灯开关 1 号与 2 号脚为短路故障。

经以上检测确定造成该故障的原因是制动灯开关短路,因为 ECM 的 STP 端子一直接收到制动灯开关的 12V 电压,ECM 接收到该信号后会认为车辆在制动工况,所以 ECM 程序会取消定速巡航控制。

习题测试

简答题
定速巡航系统的工作原理是什么?

任务二　汽车自适应巡航控制系统的检修

【学习目标】

知识要求:了解自适应巡航系统的组成、结构及工作原理。
能力要求:能够在实车上识别自适应巡航系统各组成部件。

任务导入

一辆迈腾轿车在使用仪表多功能菜单选择主动巡航系统时,仪表提示"故障自适应巡航",ACC 主动巡航系统不能使用。

知识准备

自适应巡航系统(也叫主动巡航系统,缩写为 ACC)是一种新开发的驾驶员辅助系统,它与传统的车速控制系统相比,在功能上有很大扩展。

一、自适应巡航系统的优点

① 通过车距传感器的反馈信号,ACC 控制单元可以根据靠近车辆物体的移动速度判断道路情况,并控制车辆的行驶状态;通过反馈式加速踏板感知驾驶者施加在踏板上的力,ACC 控制单元可以决定是否执行巡航控制,以减轻驾驶者的疲劳。

② 自适应巡航控制系统一般在车速大于 25km/h 时才会起作用,而当车速降低到 25km/h 以下时,就需要驾驶者进行人工控制。通过系统软件的升级,自适应巡航控制系统可以实现"停车/起步"功能,以应对在城市中行驶时频繁的停车和起步情况。自适应巡航控制系统的这种扩展功能,可以使汽车在非常低的车速时也能与前车保持设定的距离。当前方车辆起步后,自适应巡航控制系统会提醒驾驶者,驾驶者通过踩加速踏板或按下按钮发出信号,车辆就可以起步行驶。

③ 自适应巡航控制系统使车辆的编队行驶更加轻松。ACC 控制单元可以设定自动跟踪的车辆,当本车跟随前车行驶时,ACC 控制单元可以将车速调整为与前车相同。

④ 保持稳定的车距,而且这个距离可以通过转向盘附近的控制杆上的设置按钮进行选择。

二、自适应巡航系统的局限性

① 自适应巡航系统是一个驾驶辅助系统,而不是安全系统。该系统不能实现全自动驾驶。

② 自适应巡航系统只能够在 30～200km/h 的速度范围内发挥控制作用。
③ 自适应巡航系统不能感应静止物体。
④ 雷达的感应效果会因雨、水花及融雪的影响而变差。
⑤ 在小转弯半径处由于雷达探测区域的限制，系统功能会受到影响

三、自适应巡航系统的工作原理

自适应巡航控制系统的基本功能是保持驾驶员所选定的与前车的距离。因此，自适应巡航控制系统就是定速巡航系统的进一步发展。车上装有一个雷达传感器，它用于测定与前车的车距和前车的车速。如果车距大于驾驶员设定的值，那么车就会加速，直至车速达到驾驶员设定的车速值，如图 6-7 所示蓝车的驾驶员激活自适应巡航控制，设定好期望速度 v 及期望距离 D_w。车辆一直加速到设定的期望速度。如果车距小于驾驶员设定的值，那么车就会减速，减速可通过降低输出功率、换挡或必要时施加制动来实现，如图 6-8 所示蓝车识别出在前方同一车道内行驶的红车。系统通过减小油门及在必要情况下的制动使蓝车速度降低，使两车的距离调整到期望距离。出于舒适性的考虑，制动效果只能达到制动系统最大制动减速能力的 25%。当与前车的距离增加到安全距离时，ACC 控制单元控制车辆按照设定的车速行驶。如果需要更大的减速度时，ACC 控制单元会发出声光信号通知驾驶员主动采取制动操作。

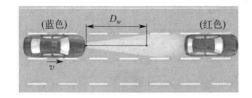

图 6-7　加速到设定的期望速度

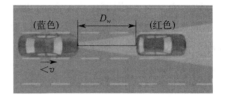

图 6-8　减速到设定的期望速度

虽然自适应巡航控制系统可以自动控制车速，但在任何时候驾驶员都可以主动进行加速或制动。当驾驶员在巡航控制状态下进行制动后，ACC 控制单元就会终止巡航控制；当驾驶员在巡航控制状态下进行加速，停止加速后，ACC 控制单元会按照原来设定的车速进行巡航控制。这个调节过程可以减轻驾驶员的劳累程度，因此可以间接提高行车安全性。

四、自适应巡航系统的组成

自适应巡航控制系统主要由雷达传感器、轮速传感器、转向角传感器以及 ACC 控制单元等组成。在前后车轮上装有轮速传感器（与 ABS 系统共用），可以感知车辆的行驶速度；转向角传感器用来判断车辆行驶的方向。

1. 雷达传感器

ACC 系统的关键部件是雷达传感器，雷达传感器一般安装在散热器格栅内或前保险杠的内侧，它可以探测到汽车前方 200m 左右的距离。其主要作用是测量目标车辆的距离、车速和测定前方车辆位置。

（1）车距测量

发射信号和接收（反射）信号的频率差取决于物体之间的距离，物体之间的距离越大，反射信号被接收前所运行的时间就越长，于是发射频率和接收频率之间的差就越大。

（2）车速测量

要想确定前车的车速，需要应用一种物理效应，这种效应被称为"多普勒效应"。对于反射波的物体来说，它相对于发射波的物体是处于静止状态还是运动状态，是有本质区别的。如果发射波的物体与反射波的物体之间的距离减小了，那么反射波的频率就提高了，反之若距离增大，那么这个频率就降低。电子装置会分析这个频率变化，从而得出前车的车速。

（3）测定前方车辆位置

雷达探测信号以波瓣状向外发射。信号强度随离发射器距离的增大而逐渐减弱，如图6-9所示。确认前方车辆的位置，必须附加一个信息，即前方车辆在本车前方以何种角度运动。此信息可通过运用三波束雷达探测技术来获得。通过每个雷达波瓣接收（反射）信号的振幅（信号强度）关系可确定角度信息，如图6-10所示。

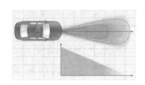

图6-9　波瓣状探测信号

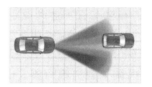

图6-10　三波束雷达探测

2. ACC控制单元

ACC控制单元是ACC系统的中央处理器，是系统的核心部分。它负责将传感器送来的数据（包括相对距离、相对速度）进行处理，然后按照控制算法进行计算，最后形成指令控制作动器工作。它主要包含目标车头距离计算，决定自车与前车的距离；车头距控制器，它计算获得目标车头距的车速、加速度命令；车速控制器，它决定制动作动器和节气门作动器的工作。

3. 其余组成部分

其余组成部分包括巡航控制开关、车速设定器、车距设定器、状态显示器和报警器等。

任务实施

自适应巡航控制系统的故障诊断与修复

1. 自适应巡航控制系统的组成

大众车型自适应巡航控制系统的组成如图6-11所示。

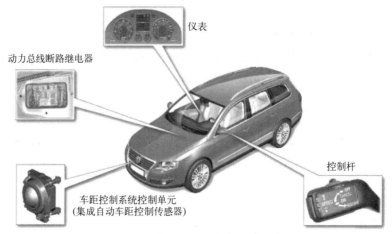

图6-11　自适应巡航控制系统组成

(1) ACC 传感器

迈腾轿车 ACC 传感器用来决定与前车的距离和相对车速,如果距离大于设定的距离,车辆加速到驾驶员设定车速。如果距离小于设定距离,ACC 系统会自动减小发动机的扭矩,并在必要时采取制动,以此将两车车距调节到驾驶员预设的值,该值为受时间控制的值。出于安全性考虑,制动减速度被限定在 0.3g(大约 3m/s^2)。如果这样的减速度不能制动停车,则系统通过仪表发出声音以及文字提示,要求驾驶员介入。

ACC 传感器的发射频率为 76.5GHz,可探测范围为 150m,水平视角为 12°,垂直视角为 ±4°,车速探测范围为 30～210km/h,如图 6-12 所示。

(2) ACC 控制杆

ACC 控制杆在不同的位置有不同的功能,如图 6-13 所示。ACC 控制杆在 ACC OFF 位置时代表 ACC 功能关闭。ACC 控制杆在 CANCEL 位置时代表"待命模式",同时在存储器中保存期望车速值。ACC 控制杆在 ACC ON 位置时代表 ACC 总是处在"打开"状态,必须按 ON/OFF 按钮切换到"待命模式"。ACC 控制杆在 RESUME 位置时代表恢复到预定车速,每向后拉一次,车速增加 1km/h。

图 6-12 ACC 传感器

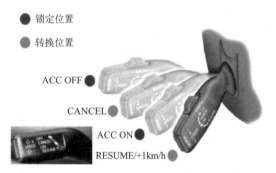

图 6-13 ACC 控制杆功能

2. 自适应巡航控制系统的功能

迈腾轿车装备 ACC 的车辆行驶速度达到 30km/h 以上时,ACC 开始进入工作状态。如果 ACC 传感器检测范围内没有车辆,则保持设定车速行驶,如图 6-14 所示。

如果车辆前方遇到一辆慢车行驶在同一条车道上,则发动机降低扭矩,如果有必要,车辆采取柔和的制动措施,将两车车距调节到驾驶员预设的值,该值为受时间控制的值。制动介入是通过 ABS 液压泵的方式,出于计算的原因,只能选择同方向行驶的情况为参考,如图 6-15 所示。

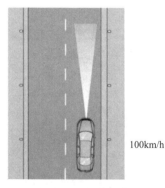

图 6-14 设定车速行驶

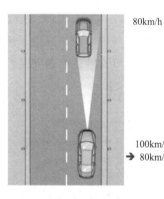

图 6-15 降低车速

3. 故障检测

使用 VAS5052A 进行检测，发动机和自适应巡航系统有故障，故障显示如图 6-16 和图 6-17 所示。

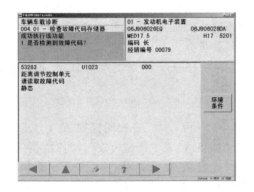 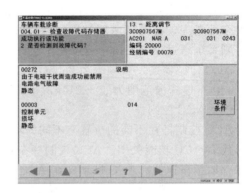

图 6-16　发动机系统故障　　　　　　图 6-17　自适应巡航系统故障

对故障进行分析，发动机系统存储的故障是因为 ACC 自适应巡航系统有故障，所以只需要排除自适应巡航系统的故障即可。ACC 自适应巡航系统故障可能原因有以下几种。

① 其他线路或电器信号干扰。
② ACC 自适应巡航系统线路故障。
③ ACC 雷达传感器错误调整。
④ ACC 雷达传感器本身故障。

4. 故障判断

参照电路图进行相关线路检查，没有发现有任何的异常，特别对车上可能造成信号干扰的音响系统进行检查，未发现电线有磨破或线间短路、断路现象，所以排除线路故障的可能性。使用 VAS5052A 读取 ACC 自适应巡航系统 006 组数据块，根据检查判断，主动巡航系统故障的根本原因是 ACC 雷达传感器本身的故障。

习题测试

填空题

自适应巡航控制系统主要由_____、_____、_____以及_____等组成。

项目小结

当今社会对汽车智能化的要求更加迫切，汽车自动巡航控制系统可以有效地减轻长途驾驶的疲劳，是提高舒适性和趣味性的重要方法之一，所以 ACC 系统在未来会成为主流。

项目习题测试

一、填空题

1. 定速巡航系统的控制开关主要由_____、_____、_____、_____、_____等组成。
2. 巡航控制主控开关大多数有_____、_____和_____3 个挡位。

二、判断题

1. 定速巡航系统的控制开关是驾驶员用来操作车辆进入或者取消巡航系统的。　　　　（　　）
2. 巡航控制系统将根据汽车行驶阻力的变化，自动加大或减小节气门开度，而不必控制加速踏板。
　　　　（　　）

项目七

汽车电动助力转向系统的检修

项目导读

助力转向系统可协助驾驶员做汽车方向调整，为驾驶员减轻打转向盘的用力强度。汽车电动助力转向系统（EPS，Electric Power Steering）与传统的机械、液压助力转向系统相比具有转向灵敏、能耗低、与环境的兼容性好、成本低等优点。在很多高端车上都装有 EPS，因此，开发 EPS 具有很大的实际意义和商业价值。

任务 电动助力转向系统的结构与工作原理

【学习目标】

知识要求：了解汽车电动助力转向系统的组成、结构及原理。
能力要求：能够在实车上识别电动助力转向系统各组成部件。

 任务导入

一台花冠汽车转向时转向盘沉重，仪表盘上电动助力转向故障灯点亮。

知识准备

一、助力转向系统的分类

1. 液压助力转向系统

液压助力转向系统（Hydraulic Power Steering，HPS），一般由液压泵、油管、压力流量控制阀体、V 形传动带、储油罐等部件构成。无论车是否转向，这套系统都要工作，而且在大角度转向、车速较低时，需要液压泵输出更大的功率以获得比较大的助力。所以，也在一定程度上浪费了资源。装备液压助力转向系统的车辆，在低速转弯的时候，转向盘比较沉，发动机动力损失也比较大。由于液压泵的压力很大，也比较容易损害助力系统。还有，液压助力转向系统由液压泵及管路和油缸组成，为保持压力，不论是否需要转向助力，系统总要处于工作状态，所以能耗较高。

2. 电动助力转向系统

电动助力转向系统（Electric Power Steering，EPS）利用电动机产生的动力协助驾车者进行动力转向。EPS 一般由转矩（转向）传感器、电子控制单元、电动机、减速器、机械转向

器，以及蓄电池电源所构成。电动助力转向系统根据动力源不同又可分为液压式电动助力转向系统（液压式 EPS）和电动式电动助力转向系统（电动式 EPS）。液压式 EPS 是在传统的液压助力转向系统的基础上增设了控制液体流量的电磁阀、车速传感器和电子控制单元等，电子控制单元根据检测到的车速信号，控制电磁阀使转向动力放大倍率实现连续可调，从而满足高、低速时的转向助力要求。电动式 EPS 是利用直流电动机作为动力源，电子控制单元根据转向参数和车速等信号，控制电动机扭矩的大小和方向。电动机的扭矩由电磁离合器通过减速机构减速增扭后，加在汽车的转向机构上，使之得到一个与工况相适应的转向作用力。

电动助力转向系统（EPS）可以在低速时减轻转向力以提高转向系统的操纵性；在高速时则可适当加大转向力，以提高操纵稳定性。液压式电子控制动力转向系统是在传统的液压动力转向系统的基础上增设电子控制装置而构成的。根据控制方式的不同，液压式电子控制动力转向系统又可分为流量控制式、反力控制式和阀灵敏度控制式 3 种形式。

3. 电控液压助力转向系统

电控液压助力转向系统（Electro Hydraulic Power Steering，EHPS），其助力原理与机械式液压助力完全相同，而与机械式液压助力最大的区别就是不再使用由发动机通过传动带驱动的液压泵，而是换成了电力驱动的电子泵。其主要构件包括储油罐、助力转向控制单元、电动泵、转向机、助力转向传感器等，其中助力转向控制单元和电动泵是一个整体结构。

电控液压助力转向系统克服了传统的液压助力转向系统的缺点。它所采用的液压泵不再靠发动机传动带直接驱动，而是采用一个电子泵驱动，它所有的工作的状态都是由电子控制单元根据车辆的行驶速度、转向角度等信号计算出的最理想状态。

汽车在低速大角度转向时，电子控制单元驱动电子液压泵以高速运转输出较大功率，使驾驶员打方向省力；汽车在高速行驶时，液压控制单元驱动电子液压泵以较低的速度运转，在不影响高速打转向需要的同时，节省一部分发动机功率。

电控液压助力转向系统的优势首先体现在能耗上，由电能驱动的电子泵，使用发电机和电池输出的电能，不再消耗发动机本身的动力，电子泵的启动和关闭全部由电子系统控制，在不做转向动作的时候，电子泵关闭，不像机械液压助力泵那样，始终与发动机联动，进一步减小能耗。其次，电控液压助力转向系统的电子控制单元，能够对车速传感器、横向加速度传感器、转向角度传感器等传感器的信息进行处理，通过实时改变电子泵的流量来改变转向助力的力度大小，也就是随速可变助力功能。当然，并不是只有电控液压助力转向系统能够实现助力随速可变。

电控液压助力转向系统的特点：无论是从技术、功能，还是从经济性方面来看，电控液压助力转向系统都较机械式液压助力更具优势，但是，目前电控液压助力转向系统并没能够取代机械式液压助力，主要原因是电控液压助力转向系统成本更高、可靠性不及机械液压助力、助力力度有限等。

二、电动助力转向系统的组成及工作原理

1. 电动助力转向系统的优点

相比传统液压助力转向系统，电动助力转向系统具有以下优点。

① 只在转向时电机才提供助力，可以显著降低燃油消耗。传统的液压助力转向系统由发动机带动转向油泵，不管转向或者不转向都要消耗发动机部分动力。而电动助力转向系统只是在转向时才由电机提供助力，不转向时不消耗能量。

② 转向助力大小可以通过 ECU 中的软件调整，能够兼顾低速时的转向轻便性和高速时的操纵稳定性，回正性能好。

电动助力转向系统提供的助力大小可以通过 ECU 中的软件调整。在低速时，电动助力转向系统可以提供较大的转向助力，提供车辆的转向轻便性；随着车速的提高，电动助力转向系统提供的转向助力可以逐渐减小，转向时驾驶员所需提供的转向力将逐渐增大，这样驾驶员就感受到明显的"路感"，提高了车辆稳定性。

③ 结构紧凑，质量轻，生产线装配好，易于维护保养。电动助力转向系统取消了液压转向油泵、油缸、液压管路、油罐等部件，而且电机及减速机构可以和转向柱、转向器做成一个整体，使得整个转向系统结构紧凑，质量轻，在生产线上的装配性好，节省装配时间，易于维护保养。

④ 通过程序的设置，电动助力转向系统容易与不同车型匹配，可以缩短生产和开发的周期。

2. 电动助力转向系统的种类

EPS 按照辅助电机的布置方式，可分为转向轴助力式（Column-assist type）EPS、齿轮助力式（Pinion-assist type）EPS 和齿条助力式（Rack-assist type）EPS。

（1）转向轴助力式转向系统

转向轴助力式转向系统其转矩传感器、电动机、离合器和转向助力机构组成一体，安装在转向柱上。其特点是结构紧凑，电动机助力的响应性较好。但由于助力电机安装在驾驶舱内，受到空间布置和噪声的限制，电机的体积较小，输出扭矩不大，一般只用在小型及紧凑型车辆上，如图 7-1 所示。

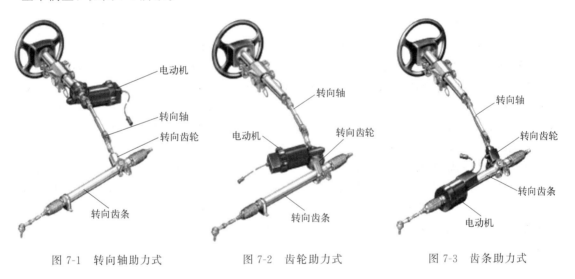

图 7-1　转向轴助力式　　　图 7-2　齿轮助力式　　　图 7-3　齿条助力式

（2）齿轮助力式转向系统

齿轮助力式转向系统的转矩传感器、电动机、离合器和转向助力机构仍为一体，只是整体安装在转向齿轮处，直接给齿轮助力，能够获得较大的转向力，可用于中型车辆，提供较大的助力值。该形式可使各部件布置更方便，但当转向盘与转向器之间装有万向传动装置时，转矩信号的取得与助力车轮部分不在同一直线上，助力控制特性难以保证准确，如图 7-2 所示。

（3）齿条助力式转向系统

齿条助力式转向系统的转矩传感器单独地安装在转向齿轮处，电动机与转向助力机构一起安装在转向齿轮另一端的齿条处，用以给齿条助力。齿条助力式系统的动力辅助单元，如图 7-3 所示。

3. 电动助力转向系统的组成

EPS 主要由扭矩传感器、车速传感器、电动机、减速机构和电子控制单元（ECU）等组成。通过传感器探测司机在转向操作时转向盘产生的扭矩或转角的大小和方向，并将所需信息转化成数字信号输入控制单元，再由控制单元对这些信号进行运算后得到一个与行驶工况相适应的力矩，最后发出指令驱动电动机工作，电动机的输出扭矩通过传动装置的作用而助力。电动助力转向系统如图 7-4 所示。

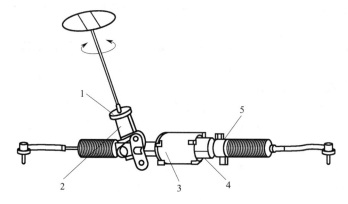

图 7-4 电动助力转向系统结构图
1—输入轴；2—扭矩传感器；3—电动机；4—循环球螺杆；5—齿条

4. 电动助力转向系统的工作原理

电动助力转向系统在不同车上的结构部件尽管不尽一样，但是基本原理是一致的。它一般是由扭矩（转向）传感器、电子控制单元 ECU、电动机、电磁离合器以及减速机构构成的。

其基本工作原理：当转向轴转动时，扭矩传感器将检测到的扭矩信号转化为电信号送至电子控制单元 ECU，ECU 再根据扭矩信号、车速信号、轴重信号等进行计算，得出助力电动机的转向和助力电流的大小，完成转向助力控制。当汽车点火开关闭合时，ECU 开始对 EPS 系统进行自检，自检通过后，闭合继电器和离合器，EPS 系统便开始工作。当转向盘转动时，位于转向轴上的转角传感器和扭矩传感器把测得转向盘上的角位移和作用于其上的力矩传递给 ECU，ECU 根据这两个信号并结合车速等信息，控制电机产生相应的助力，实现在全速范围内的最佳控制：在低速行驶时，减轻转向力，保证汽车转向灵活、轻便；在高速行驶时，适当增加阻尼控制，保证转向盘操作稳重、可靠。电动助力转向系统的工作原理图如图 7-5 所示。

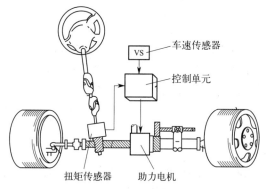

图 7-5 电动助力转向系统的工作原理图

(1) 电动助力转向 ECU

整个系统由车载 12V 蓄电池供电，ECU 工作时，扭矩、转角、车速、温度等传感器把采集到的信号经过输入接口电路处理后送至单片机的相应端口，单片机根据系统助力特性和相应算法对这些数据分析处理，以确定助力电流的大小和方向，并通过单片机的 PWM 口发出脉冲指令和相应的换向控制端口发出换向指令，通过驱动电路和 H 桥电路控制直流电动机工作。在电动机的驱动电路上设有电流传感器，该传感器把检测到的电机实际工作电流通过电流探测电路反馈到单片机，单片机再根据相应的控制算法对电机实现闭环控制。如 EPS 系统工作出现异常，单片机将驱动 EPS 灯亮进行报警提示，同时断开继电器、离合器，退出电动助力工作模式，转为人工手动助力模式。

(2) 扭矩传感器

扭矩传感器用来检测转向盘扭矩的大小和方向，以及转向盘转角的大小和方向，它是 EPS 的控制信号之一。扭矩传感器主要有接触式和非接触式两种。常用的接触式（主要是电位计式）传感器有摆臂式、双排行星齿轮式和扭杆式三种类型，而非接触式扭矩传感器主要有光电式和磁电式两种。前者的成本低，但受温度与磨损影响易发生漂移、使用寿命较短，需要对制造精度和扭杆刚度进行折中，难以实现绝对转角和角速度的测量。后者的体积小，精度高，抗干扰能力强，刚度相对较高，易实现绝对转角和角速度的测量，但是成本较高。

① 光电式扭矩传感器。光电式扭矩传感器由两个带孔的遮光圆盘和一个弹性扭力杆组成。圆盘随转向盘一起转动，每个遮光器是由一个发光二极管 LED 和一个光敏晶体管组成的，如图 7-6 所示。彼此相对安装，中间有扭力杆弹性连接。当转向盘转动时，因转向阻力的存在，扭杆变形，两个光电元件之间的光电信号值即出现差值，此差值即为转向助力的度量值。转向力矩越大，扭杆变形越大，差值角度就越大。此扭矩和方向信号传送到 ECU，ECU 再根据车速传感器信号以及车辆状态信号（静态或动态），经过编程处理，通过助力电动机，提供转向助力量化控制。

② 磁电式扭矩传感器。磁电式扭矩传感器中，有两对磁极环，相对安装，连接输入和输出轴，以磁性连接替代了弹性连接的扭力杆，它为非接触式扭矩传感器，体积小、输出的信号值精度高。当输入轴与输出轴之间产生扭转角度差值时，磁极环之间的空气间隙发生变化，从而引起电磁感应线圈中磁感应量发生变化，它就是转向助力的度量值，此信号输出给电脑 EPS/ECU，作为转向助力的依据，如图 7-7 所示。

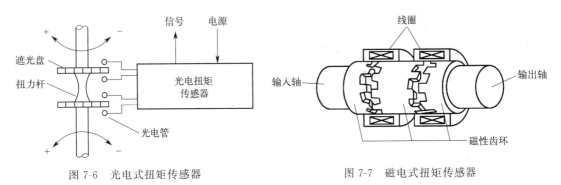

图 7-6 光电式扭矩传感器　　图 7-7 磁电式扭矩传感器

(3) 电动机

电动机根据 ECU 的指令输出适宜的扭矩，一般采用无刷永磁电动机，无刷永磁电动机具有无激磁损耗、效率较高、体积较小等特点。电动机是 EPS 的关键部件之一，对 EPS 的性能有很大的影响。由于控制系统需要根据不同的工况产生不同的助力转矩，具有良好的动

态特性并容易控制,这些都要求助力电动机具有线性的机械特性和调速特性。此外还要求电动机低转速大扭矩、波动小、转动惯量小、尺寸小、质量轻、可靠性高、抗干扰能力强。

(4) 电磁离合器

电磁离合器是保证电动助力只在预定的范围内起作用。当车速、电流超过限定的最大值或转向系统发生故障时,离合器便自动切断电动机的电源,恢复手动控制转向。此外,在不助力的情况下,离合器还能消除电动机的惯性对转向的影响。为了减少与不加转向助力时驾驶车辆感觉的差别,离合器不仅具有滞后输出特性,同时还具有半离合器状态区域。

(5) 减速机构

减速机构用来增大电动机传递给转向器的扭矩。它主要有两种形式:行星齿轮减速机构和蜗杆减速机构。由于减速机构对系统工作性能的影响较大,因此在降低噪声、提高效率和左右转向操作的对称性方面对其提出了较高的要求。

任务实施

花冠电动助力转向系统是通过安装在转向柱上的电动机和减速齿轮的运作,产生扭矩以增大转向扭矩。根据车速信号和内置于转向柱总成的扭矩传感器信号,助力转向 ECU 决定辅助助力的方向和转向力矩的大小,从而在低速行驶时控制转向力矩变小,在高速行驶时控制转向力矩适度增大。

花冠电动助力转向系统组成如图 7-8 所示。

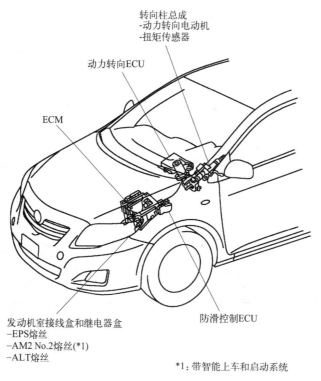

图 7-8 花冠电动助力转向系统组成

助力转向 ECU:根据扭矩传感器的转向扭矩信号和来自防滑控制 ECU 的车速信号,动力转向 ECU 计算辅助动力。

助力转向电机:助力转向电机由动力转向 ECU 的电流激活,并产生扭矩以辅助转向扭矩。

一、注意事项

① 故障诊断仪的连接顺序：将诊断仪 OBD2 插头连接到车辆诊断座上→打开点火开关→打开诊断仪电源开关。

② 操作过程中不要触碰车辆连接器端子，以防端子变形或因静电引起的故障。

③ 操作过程中要避免撞击转向柱总成，特别是电动机或扭矩传感器。

④ 断开 EPS 系统相关的连接器时，将点火开关置于 ON 位置并使转向盘回正，再将点火开关置于 OFF 位置后断开连接器。

⑤ 操作时参照维修手册，按维修手册规定操作。

二、技术要求

通过实习了解电动助力转向系统的组成部件、安装位置及工作情况，熟悉静态及动态状态下系统检测方法。掌握扭矩放大传感器工作时的电压、电流变化情况，电动机的检测方法，准确地排除故障。

三、花冠助力转向系统检修

1. 故障诊断仪的使用

在仪表台左下侧找到车辆诊断座，如图 7-9 所示。

将故障诊断仪连接到车辆诊断座，如图 7-10 所示。

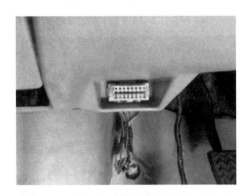 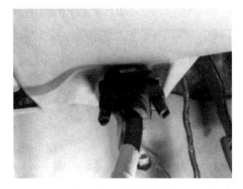

图 7-9　车辆诊断座　　　　　　　　图 7-10　连接诊断仪

打开诊断仪电源开关，选择车型，如图 7-11 所示。选择"车型系统"选项如图 7-12 所示。

选择"电子辅助动力转向"，如图 7-13 所示。

使用"当前故障码"功能，读取当前故障码，如图 7-14 所示。

使用"清故障码"功能，如图 7-15 所示。选择"电子辅助动力转向"读取数据流。

在车辆停止，不动转向盘（无负载）工况下观察扭矩传感器 1、2、3 的输出电压，参照维修手册判断是否为标准值，如图 7-16 所示。

车辆停止、向右转动转向盘工况下观察扭矩传感器 1、2、3 的输出电压，参照维修手册判断是否为标准值，如图 7-17 所示。

车辆停止、向左转动转向盘工况下观察扭矩传感器 1、2、3 的输出电压，参照维修手册判断是否为标准值，如图 7-18 所示。

图 7-11　打开诊断仪

图 7-12　选择车型

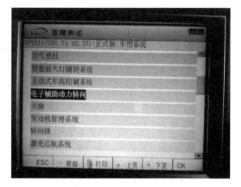

图 7-13　选择系统

图 7-14　读取当前故障码

图 7-15　清故障码

图 7-16　观察扭矩传感器

图 7-17　观察右转转向盘扭矩传感器

图 7-18　观察左转转向盘扭矩传感器

2. 检测与检修方法

用十字螺丝刀将固定仪表螺钉拆卸，如图 7-19 所示。

将仪表拆下找到动力转向 ECU，如图 7-20 所示。

图 7-19　螺钉位置

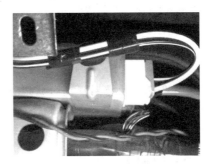

图 7-20　动力转向 ECU

动力转向 ECU 端子示意图如图 7-21 所示。

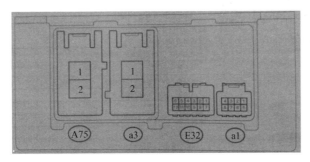

图 7-21　ECU 端子示意图

根据维修手册用多用表检测各端子的电压或电阻，如图 7-22 所示。

端子号（符号）	配线颜色	端子描述	状态	规定状态
a75-1(PIG)-A75-2(PGND)	L-W-B	电源	始终	11～14V
a75-2(PGND)-本身搭铁	W-B-本身搭铁	电源搭铁	始终	小于1Ω
a3-1(M1)-A75-2(PGND)	R-W-B	动力转向电动机	点火开关置于 ON(1G) 位置时向左转动方向盘	11～14V
			点火开关置于 ON(1G) 位置时向右转动方向盘	低于1V
a3-2(M2)-A75-2(PGND)	B-W-B	动力转向电动机	点火开关置于 ON(1G) 位置时向左转动方向盘	低于1V
			点火开关置于 ON(1G) 位置时向右转动方向盘	11～14V
E32-1(CANH)-E32-72(CANL)	SB-W	CAN 通信线路	点火开关置于 OFF 位置	54～69Ω
E32-6(IG)-A75-2(PGND)	L-W-B	IG 电源	点火开关置于 ON(1G) 位置	11～14V
a1-5(TRO1)-A75-2(PGND)	W-W-B	扭矩传感器信号	点火开关置于 ON(1G) 位置时左右转动方向盘	0.3～4.7V
a1-6(TROV)-A75-2(PGND)	R-W-B	扭矩传感器电源电压	点火开关置于 ON(1G) 位置	7.5～8.5V
a1-7(TRO2)-A75-2(PGND)	Y-W-B	扭矩传感器信号	点火开关置于 ON(1G) 位置时左右转动方向盘	0.3～4.7V
a1-8(TROG)-A75-2(PGND)	B-W-B	扭矩传感器搭铁	始终	小于1Ω

图 7-22　各端子数据

习题测试

简答题
1. 电动助力转向系统的组成是什么？
2. 电动助力转向系统的优点是什么？

项目小结

随着近年来电子控制技术的成熟和成本的降低，EPS越来越受到人们的重视，并以其具有传统动力转向系统不可比拟的优点，迅速迈向了应用领域，部分取代了液压动力转向系统（Hydraulic Power Steering，HPS）。EPS将成为汽车传统转向系统理想的升级换代产品。

项目习题测试

简答题
1. 磁电式扭矩传感器的组成和作用是什么？
2. 电动助力转向系统的优点是什么？
3. 电控液压助力转向系统的特点是什么？

参考文献

[1] 周志立. 汽车 ABS 原理与结构 [M]. 北京：机械工业出版社，2005.
[2] 郝军. 汽车空调 [M]. 北京：机械工业出版社，2010.
[3] 麻友良，赵英勋. 广州本田雅阁轿车维修手册 [M]. 北京：机械工业出版社，2001.
[4] L. 埃克霍恩，D. 克林恩乔克. 汽车制动系统 [M]. 叶淑贞，等译. 北京：机械工业出版社，1998.
[5] 郭伟. 通用鲁米娜汽车维修手册 [M]. 沈阳：辽宁科学技术出版社，2000.
[6] Steven Daly. 汽车空调与气候控制系统 [M]. 杨占鹏，等译. 北京：机械工业出版社，2009.
[7] 冯渊. 汽车电子控制技术 [M]. 北京：机械工业出版社，2002.
[8] 张西振，惠有利. 轿车 ABS/ASR 系统检修培训教程 [M]. 北京：机械工业出版社，2004.
[9] 黎军. 汽车制动电子控制系统检测与维修 [M]. 北京：人民交通出版社，2004.
[10] 幺居标. 汽车底盘构造与维修 [M]. 北京：机械工业出版社，2002.
[11] 鲁植雄. 汽车防抱死制动系统故障诊断图解 [M]. 南京：江苏科学技术出版社，2003.
[12] 戴冠军. 欧宝轿车电控系统维修手册 [M]. 北京：机械工业出版社，2003.
[13] 戴冠军. 丰田轿车电控系统维修手册 [M]. 北京：机械工业出版社，2002.
[14] 戴冠军. 宝马轿车电控系统维修手册 [M]. 北京：机械工业出版社，2003.
[15] 席金波，贾青. 一汽奥迪 A6 轿车维修手册 [M]. 沈阳：辽宁科学技术出版社，2001.
[16] 尹力会. 一汽花冠轿车维修手册 [M]. 沈阳：辽宁科学技术出版社，2005.
[17] B. H. 德维金斯. 汽车空调原理与维修 [M]. 北京：机械工业出版社，2006.
[18] 朱建风. 汽车自动空调系统检测与维修 [M]. 北京：人民交通出版社，2003.
[19] 田小农. 汽车空调检修 [M]. 北京：人民交通出版社，2007.
[20] 夏云铧，齐红. 汽车空调应用与维修 [M]. 北京：机械工业出版社，2007.
[21] 李祥峰. 汽车空调 [M]. 西安：西安电子科技大学出版社，2006.
[22] 徐昭. 日产轿车电气系统维修手册 [M]. 沈阳：辽宁科学技术出版社，2002.
[23] 董安，李显树. 国产中高档轿车空调装置保养和维修 [M]. 北京：北京理工大学出版社，2002.
[24] 于春鹏. 空调系统 [M]. 北京：化学工业出版社，2005.
[25] 李春明. 汽车底盘电控技术 [M]. 北京：机械工业出版社，2010.

Bilingual Textbooks of Vocational Education
职业教育双语教材

Automotive Safety and Comfort System Maintenance

汽车安全与舒适系统检修

英汉
双语教材

Edited by Zheng Chunguang

郑春光 主编

Chemical Industry Press
化学工业出版社

Beijing
· 北 京 ·

Preface

Maintenance of automobile safety and comfort system is a typical work task for automobile inspection and maintenance technicians, a skill that must be mastered by highly skilled personnel in automobile inspection and maintenance technology, and an important core course for transportation and automobile manufacturing majors in higher vocational colleges.

This book focuses on training students' operation skills of fault diagnosis, fault analysis, component detection and repair and replacement of automobile safety and comfort system by modern diagnosis and detection equipment. This book is guided by work items, driven by tasks, under the framework of action system and guided by typical cases. This book focuses on developing students' professional abilities, as well as their social and methodological abilities.

This book consists of 7 items, each consisting of item guide, several tasks, item summary and item exercise. Each task consists of five parts: learning goal, task introduction, knowledge preparation, task implementation and exercise. In the item guide, the characteristic, functions and classification of each item are introduced; the learning goal in the task is composed of knowledge requirements and capability requirements; the task introduction is guided by typical cases of the enterprises; knowledge preparation includes the function, structure form and working principle of the assembly parts involved in each task that students need to learn; precautions for fault diagnosis, fault diagnosis process and fault repair methods are introduced during task implementation to cultivate the students' hands-on operation ability, as well as the troubleshooting ideas and repair methods for analyzing typical faults in the task introduction; a certain number of exercises are carefully selected in the exercise part for students to test the learning effect.

Through the study and training of 7 items, the students can not only master the relevant knowledge of each assembly of automobile safety and comfort system, but also master the fault diagnosis and repair method of automobile safety and comfort system, reaching the level of senior automobile maintenance worker.

This book is edited by Zheng Chunguang of Tianjin Communications vocational college, of which Zheng Chunguang of Tianjin Communications Vocational College compiles project 2, project 6 and project 7, Li Jiaze of Tianjin Communications Vocational College compiles project 1, and Liu Bingyue of Tianjin Communications Vocational College compiles project 3, project 4 and project 5.

Due to the editor's limited level and experience, there are inevitably defects in the book, please don't hesitate to correct me.

Editor

Contents

Item I Maintenance of Automobile Electronic Control Active Safety System ················ 001

Item Guide ·· 001

I. What is Active Safety Technology ································ 001

II. Main Contents of Automobile Active Safety Technology ·········· 001

Task I Maintenance of Anti-lock Braking System ················ 002

Task Import ·· 002

Knowledge Preparation ·· 002

I. Overview ·· 003

II. Types of Anti-lock Braking System ································ 003

III. Rationale of ABS ·· 004

IV. Functions of ABS ·· 007

V. Technical Requirements and Evaluation Method of ABS ·········· 008

VI. Composition and Working Principle of ABS ······················ 010

VII. ABS Control Mode ·· 013

VIII. Sensor Structure Principle ·· 016

IX. Structural Principle of Brake Pressure Regulator ················ 021

X. Electronic Control Unit (ECU) ······································ 029

XI. ABS Application Examples ·· 031

Task Implementation ·· 035

I. Use and Maintenance of ABS ·· 035

II. General Check Methods for ABS Faults ···························· 037

III. Adding and Supplementing ABS Brake Fluid ···················· 038

IV. Bleeding of ABS ·· 039

V. Fault Case Diagnosis Process of ABS ······························ 040

Exercises ·· 041

Task II Maintenance of Automobile Acceleration Slip Regulation ·········· 041

Task Import ·· 042

Knowledge Preparation ·· 042

I. Overview ·· 042

II. Basic Composition and Working Principle of ASR ················ 044

III. Typical ASR System Structure ······································ 047

Task Implementation ·· 049

I. Troubleshooting of ASR ·· 049

Ⅱ. Fault Case Diagnosis Process of ASR ··· 055

Exercises ·· 056

Task Ⅲ Maintenance of Electronic Stability Program ························· 056

Task Import ·· 056

Knowledge Preparation ··· 056

Ⅰ. Function of Electronic Stability Program ··· 056

Ⅱ. Structure and Composition of ESP ··· 056

Ⅲ. Working Process of ESP Subsystem ··· 059

Task Implementation ·· 060

Fault Case Diagnosis Process of Electronic Stability Program ················ 060

Exercises ·· 061

Item Summary ·· 062

Item Exercises ·· 062

Item Ⅱ Maintenance of Automobile Air Conditioning System ······ 063

Item Guide ··· 063

Ⅰ. Composition of Automobile Air Conditioning System ······················ 063

Ⅱ. Know the Connecting Lines ·· 064

Ⅲ. Brief Description of Working Process of Air Conditioner ·················· 065

Task Ⅰ Automobile Air Conditioning System Identification ··············· 065

Task Import ·· 066

Knowledge Preparation ··· 066

Ⅰ. Functions of Automobile Air Conditioner ······································· 066

Ⅱ. Main Indicators of Automobile Air Conditioner ······························ 066

Ⅲ. Composition and Classification of Automobile Air Conditioning System ········· 067

Task Implementation ·· 068

Exercises ·· 068

Task Ⅱ Maintenance of Automobile Air Conditioning Refrigeration System ·············· 068

Task Import ·· 068

Knowledge Preparation ··· 068

Ⅰ. Structural Principle of Compressor in Automobile Air Conditioning
Refrigeration System ·· 068

Ⅱ. Expansion Valve of Automobile Air Conditioning Refrigeration System ········ 070

Ⅲ. Automobile Air Conditioning Condenser ······································· 071

Ⅳ. Receiver Dryer ·· 072

Task Implementation ·· 074

Ⅰ. Maintenance of Denso Compressor ·· 074

Ⅱ. Maintenance of Expansion Valve on Air Conditioning Refrigeration System ··· 077

Ⅲ. Maintenance of Automobile Air Conditioner Condenser ···················· 079

Ⅳ. Fault Case Diagnosis Process of Automobile Air Conditioning Refrigeration
System ······ 079

Exercises ······ 080

TaskⅢ Maintenance of Automobile Air Conditioning Control System ······ 081

Task Import ······ 081

Knowledge Preparation ······ 081

Ⅰ. Control of Power Supply ······ 081

Ⅱ. Control of Compressor Electromagnetic Clutch ······ 082

Ⅲ. Pressure Switch Circuit ······ 082

Ⅳ. Typical Control Circuit in Automobile Air Conditioning Circuit ······ 083

Ⅴ. Speed Control Circuit ······ 083

Task Implementation ······ 083

Ⅰ. Fault Detection and Troubleshooting Procedures for Air Conditioning Circuit of
Toyota Corolla Car ······ 083

Ⅱ. Inspection Method of Automobile Air Conditioner ······ 086

Ⅲ. Regular Maintenance of Automobile Air Conditioning System ······ 091

Ⅳ. Fault Detection of Automobile Air Conditioning System ······ 092

Ⅴ. Fault Case Diagnosis Process of Automobile Air Conditioning Control
System ······ 092

Exercises ······ 093

TaskⅣ Filling and Reclaiming Refrigerant for Automobile Air Conditioner ······ 093

Task Import ······ 093

Knowledge Preparation ······ 093

Ⅰ. Filling the Refrigerant of Automobile Air Conditioning System ······ 093

Ⅱ. Replenishment and Discharge of Refrigerant for Automobile Air Conditioning
Refrigeration System ······ 095

Ⅲ. Filling Refrigeration Lubricating Oil of Automobile Air Conditioning
Refrigeration System ······ 095

Ⅳ. Reclaiming Refrigerant ······ 097

Task Implementation ······ 098

Ⅰ. Precautions for Operation ······ 098

Ⅱ. Operating Steps ······ 098

Exercises ······ 102

TaskⅤ Maintenance of Automobile Air Conditioning Heating System ······ 102

Task Import ······ 102

Knowledge Preparation ······ 102

Ⅰ. Engine Waste Heat Heating Device ······ 102

Ⅱ. Independent Heat Source Heating Device ······ 107

Task Implementation ······ 109

Ⅰ. Structure of Passat Heating Device ······ 109

Ⅱ. Disassembly and Assembly of Passat Heating Device ········· 109

Exercises ········· 112

Item Summary ········· 112

Item Exercises ········· 113

Item Ⅲ Maintenance of Automobile Electronic Control Passive Safety System ········· **114**

Item Guide ········· 114

Task Ⅰ Identification of Automobile Electronic Control Passive Safety System ········· 114

Task Import ········· 114

Knowledge Preparation ········· 115

Ⅰ. Function ········· 115

Ⅱ. Structure Classification ········· 115

Ⅲ. Composition and Basic Principles ········· 116

Task Implementation ········· 119

Exercises ········· 119

Task Ⅱ Maintenance of Automobile Electronic Control Passive Safety System ········· 120

Task Import ········· 120

Knowledge Preparation ········· 120

Task Implementation ········· 120

Ⅰ. Maintenance of Airbag System ········· 120

Ⅱ. Self-Diagnosis of Audi A6 Airbag System ········· 126

Ⅲ. Fault Case Diagnosis Process of Automobile Electronic Control Passive Safety System ········· 127

Exercises ········· 128

Item Summary ········· 128

Item Exercises ········· 128

Item Ⅳ Maintenance of Automobile Electronic Control Suspension System ········· **129**

Item Guide ········· 129

Task Ⅰ Identification of Automobile Electronic Control Suspension System ········· 129

Task Import ········· 129

Knowledge Preparation ········· 129

Ⅰ. Functions of Electronic Control Suspension System ········· 130

Ⅱ. Types of Electronic Control Suspension Systems ········· 130

Ⅲ. Composition and Working Principle of Electronic Control Suspension System ········· 131

Task Implementation ········· 138

Exercises ········· 138

Task Ⅱ Maintenance of Automobile Electronic Control Variable Height Suspension System ······ 138

Task Import ······ 139

Knowledge Preparation ······ 139

Ⅰ. Functions and Classification of Body Height Control System ······ 139

Ⅱ. Composition of Variable Height Control Suspension System ······ 139

Ⅲ. Control Process of Variable Height Control Suspension System ······ 139

Task Implementation ······ 141

Ⅰ. Maintenance of Electronic Control Variable Height Suspension System ······ 141

Ⅱ. Fault Case Diagnosis Process of Electronic Control Variable Height Suspension System ······ 142

Exercises ······ 142

Task Ⅲ Maintenance of Automobile Electronic Control Variable Stiffness Suspension System ······ 142

Task Import ······ 143

Knowledge Preparation ······ 143

Ⅰ. Functions of Electronic Control Variable Stiffness Suspension System ······ 143

Ⅱ. Composition of Electronic Control Variable Stiffness Suspension System ······ 143

Ⅲ. Adjustment Principle of Air Spring Suspension Stiffness ······ 143

Task Implementation ······ 145

Ⅰ. Removal and Installation of Air Spring ······ 145

Ⅱ. Fault Case Diagnosis Process of Electronic Control Variable Stiffness Suspension System ······ 146

Exercises ······ 146

Task Ⅳ Maintenance of Automobile Electronic Control Variable Damping Suspension System ······ 146

Task Import ······ 147

Knowledge Preparation ······ 147

Ⅰ. Functions and Control Modes of Variable Damping Suspension System ······ 147

Ⅱ. Structural Features of Damping Control Mechanism of Shock Absorber ······ 147

Ⅲ. Control Process of Damping Adjustment of Shock Absorber ······ 147

Task Implementation ······ 149

Ⅰ. Basic Steps for Diagnosis of Electronic Control Variable Damping Suspension System ······ 149

Ⅱ. Maintenance and Detection of Electronic Control Variable Damping Suspension System ······ 149

Exercises ······ 150

Item Summary ······ 150

Item Exercises ······ 150

Item V　Maintenance of Automobile Anti-theft System ·············· 151

Item Guide ··· 151
Task I　Cognition of Automobile Anti-theft System ······························ 151
Task Import ··· 151
Knowledge Preparation ··· 151
Ⅰ. Mechanical Anti-theft Device ·· 152
Ⅱ. Electronic Anti-theft Device ··· 152
Ⅲ. Network Anti-theft System ·· 153
Ⅳ. Biometric Anti-theft Device ··· 153
Ⅴ. Chip Anti-theft Device ··· 153
Task Implementation ··· 154
Exercises ·· 154
Task Ⅱ　Maintenance of Automobile Anti-theft System ························· 154
Task Import ··· 154
Knowledge Preparation ··· 154
Ⅰ. Type of Automobile Anti-theft System ·· 155
Ⅱ. Features of the Third Generation Anti-theft System ·························· 155
Ⅲ. Composition and Working Principle of the Third Generation Anti-theft System ····· 156
Ⅳ. Working Principle of the Fourth Generation Anti-theft System ·············· 157
Task Implementation ··· 159
Ⅰ. Precautions for Maintenance ··· 160
Ⅱ. Technical Requirements ··· 160
Ⅲ. Maintenance of Corolla Anti-theft System ···································· 160
Ⅳ. Fault Case Diagnosis Process of Automobile Anti-Theft System ············· 162
Exercises ·· 163
Item Summary ··· 164
Item Exercises ··· 164

Item VI　Maintenance of Automobile Cruise Control System ······· 165

Item Guide ··· 165
Task I　Structure and Working Principle of Automobile Cruise Control System ········· 165
Task Import ··· 165
Knowledge Preparation ··· 165
Ⅰ. Classification and Function of Cruise Control System ························· 165
Ⅱ. Working Principle and Composition of Cruise Control System ··············· 167
Task Implementation ··· 171
Exercises ·· 173

Task II Maintenance of Automobile Adaptive Cruise Control System ·················· 173

Task Import ··· 173

Knowledge Preparation ·· 173

Ⅰ. Advantages of Adaptive Cruise Control System ································· 173

Ⅱ. Limitations of Adaptive Cruise Control System ································· 174

Ⅲ. Working Principle of Adaptive Cruise Control System ······················ 174

Ⅳ. Composition of Adaptive Cruise Control System ······················· 175

Task Implementation ··· 176

Exercises ··· 178

Item Summary ··· 178

Item Exercises ··· 179

Item Ⅶ   Maintenance of Automobile Electric Power Steering ··· 180

Item Guide ··· 180

Task Structure and Working Principle of Electric Power Steering ·················· 180

Task Import ··· 180

Knowledge Preparation ·· 180

Ⅰ. Classification of Power Steering ·· 180

Ⅱ. Composition and Working Principle of Electric Power Steering ··················· 182

Task Implementation ··· 187

Ⅰ. Precautions ··· 187

Ⅱ. Technical Requirements ··· 188

Ⅲ. Maintenance of Corolla Power Steering System ··························· 188

Exercises ··· 192

Item Summary ··· 192

Item Exercises ··· 192

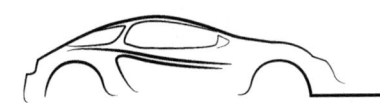

Item I

Maintenance of Automobile Electronic Control Active Safety System

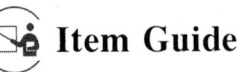 **Item Guide**

I. What is Active Safety Technology

The safety design adopted to prevent automobile accidents and avoid personal injury is called active safety technology, such as ABS (Anti-lock Braking System), EBD (Electronic Brake Force Distribution), ASR (Acceleration Slip Regulation), ESP (Electronic Stability Program), etc., with characteristics of improving the driving stability of the car and preventing damages caused by car accidents as far as possible.

II. Main Contents of Automobile Active Safety Technology

1. ABS (Anti-lock Braking System)

When ABS detects the speed of each wheel through the sensor, the computer will calculate the wheel slip ratio at that time, to know whether the wheel has locked or not, and then command the actuator to adjust the brake pressure to make the wheel in ideal braking state (to control wheel to lock but not fully locked). Under emergency braking condition, ABS can keep the wheels from being locked to prevent the vehicle from getting out of control, maintain steering ability and avoid obstacles. Under normal conditions, it does not shorten the braking distance.

2. ASR (Acceleration Slip Regulation)

ASR is an electronic control system applied to wheel anti-slid technology after anti-lock braking system. ASR is used to control the "skid" of driving wheels when the vehicle is running. ASR is mainly used for traction control and driving stability control when the vehicle starts, accelerates and runs on a smooth road. ASR, like ABS, controls the slip of the driving wheels relative to the ground by controlling the braking force of the wheels, but ASR only controls the braking force of the driving wheels. ASR generally does not work at very high speeds (80-120km/h).

3. ESP (Electronic Stability Program)

The ESP is actually a traction control system, and ESP controls not only the driving wheels but also the driven wheels compared to other traction control systems. It can realize smooth driving by actively interfering with danger signal. In case that the car driven by rear wheels often has rear wheels out of control and tail swing caused by excessive steering, ESP

will slow down the outer front wheel to stabilize the car; in case of understeer, in order to correct the running direction, ESP will slow down the inner rear wheel to correct the driving direction.

ESP includes ABS and ASR, which is the functional extension of these two systems. Therefore, ESP can be called advanced form of automobile anti-slid device. ESP system consists of control unit and steering sensor (monitoring steering angle of steering wheel), wheel sensor (monitoring the speed rotation of each wheel), sideslip sensor (monitoring the rotation state of vehicle body around vertical axis), lateral acceleration sensor (monitoring centrifugal force during cornering), etc. Based on the signals from these sensors, the control unit judges the operation state of the vehicle and issues a control command.

Task Ⅰ Maintenance of Anti-lock Braking System

〔Learning Objectives〕

Knowledge requirements: Master the function, composition, principle and maintenance method of ABS system; be familiar with the structure and principle of main components of ABS system.

Capability requirements: Be able to perform basic inspection on ABS system according to maintenance manual and by using common tools and measuring tools; be able to diagnose and repair common faults of ABS system.

 ## Task Import

A Honda Accord is out of order: Turn the ignition switch to ON position, ABS light is on; start engine, ABS light goes out and ABS oil pump motor rotates at the same time; after 1-2min, ABS oil pump motor stops running and ABS light turns on at the same time.

 ## Knowledge Preparation

The anti-lock braking system can prevent the wheels from being locked completely, and its braking effect is better than that of the braking device of the conventional braking system. It is improved on the basis of the conventional braking system. The whole braking system has both the braking function of the conventional braking system and the function of preventing the wheels from being locked completely during braking. It rapidly and evenly converts the force exerted by the driver on the brake pedal into the braking force of the wheels. The added ABS control system is an automatic control system composed of electronic, mechanical, hydraulic and pneumatic sources, which can continuously detect the braking status of the vehicle and adjust the braking of the vehicle to the optimum state in time. If the conventional braking system fails, the ABS system will automatically lose its

function; if the ABS system fails, the conventional braking system will still operate as usual.

Ⅰ. Overview

In 1920, the British Horner Moor first developed ABS and applied for a patent. The theory of anti-lock braking system was put forward in 1928. In the 1930s, mechanical ABS began to be used on trains and airplanes. In the late 1940s, ABS was used on Boeing B-47 aircraft. In the 1950s, Ford applied ABS to the Lincoln sedan. In 1978, Bosch introduced ABS with digital electronic control unit, which opened the prologue of the development of modern ABS system. In the 21st century, ABS develops more and more rapidly. America, Japan, China, Europe and other countries and regions are developing ABS at a high speed. The popularization and use of ABS is the general trend.

Ⅱ. Types of Anti-lock Braking System

1. Integrated ABS

The brake pressure regulator of the integrated ABS is integrated with the brake master cylinder and the brake booster, which is adopted in Ford, Buick, Cadillac, Oldsmobile, PONTIAC and SAAB, as shown in Fig. 1-1.

2. Separated ABS

The brake pressure regulator of the separated ABS is an independent assembly, which is connected with the brake master cylinder and the brake wheel cylinder through the brake pipeline, which is adopted in SANTANA, Jetta, Hong Qi, BMW and Volvo cars. The specific form is shown in Fig. 1-2.

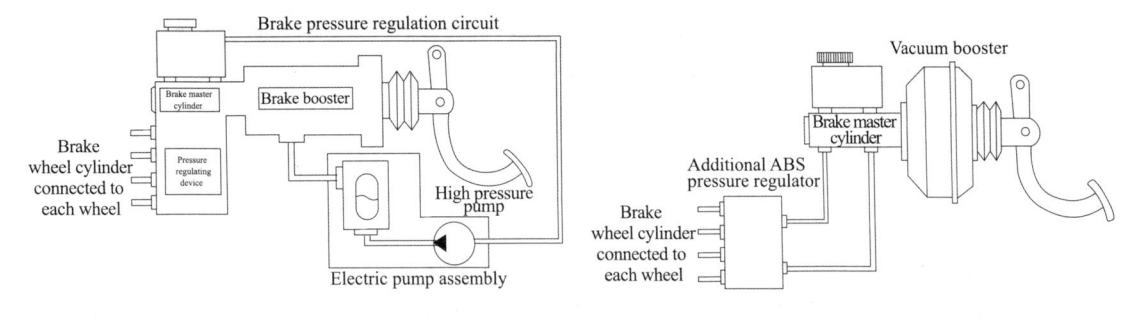

Fig. 1-1　Integrated ABS   Fig. 1-2　Separated ABS

In addition, the automobile anti-lock braking system is divided into mechanical type and electronic type by the control mode. By the power source, it is divided into pneumatic type, hydraulic type and gas cap hydraulic type.

By the way of controlling wheels, it can be divided into axle-controlled type and wheel-controlled type. The axle-controlled type is divided into axle-controlled low-selection control type and axle-controlled high-selection control type. The axle-controlled low-selection control ABS is shown in Fig. 1-3. ϕ is the adhesion coefficient between the wheel and the road surface. The axle-controlled high-selection control ABS is shown in Fig. 1-4. The wheel-controlled stand-alone ABS is shown in Fig. 1-5, with each wheel occupying one control channel.

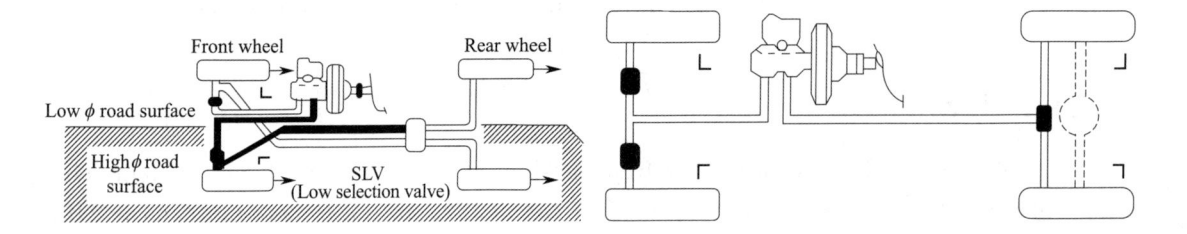

Fig. 1-3 Axle-controlled Low-selection Control ABS Fig. 1-4 Axle-controlled High-selection Control ABS

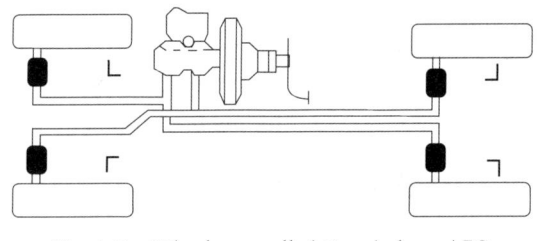

Fig. 1-5 Wheel-controlled Stand-alone ABS

Ⅲ. Rationale of ABS

Automobile braking system is an important device which can decelerate and stop according to the driver's need during the driving process. A good braking system shall be characterized by short braking distance, controllable driving direction and low tire loss when braking. With the development of automobile industry, computer technology has been widely used in automobile. The braking force is controlled by computer, so that the wheel is not locked when the automobile is braking, and the braking distance is shortened, and the deficiency of the conventional braking system is solved.

1. Braking performance of automobile

The braking performance of automobile refers to the ability of automobile to decelerate compulsorily so as to stop and maintain the stability of driving direction when driving. There are many requirements for the performance of a vehicle braking system, and the main evaluation indexes include the following three aspects.

① Braking efficiency: The braking efficiency mainly refers to the capacity of forced deceleration and even stop during driving. The basic evaluation indexes are braking distance, braking deceleration and braking time.

② Vehicle directional stability during braking: It refers to that the vehicle can still run along the track in the specified direction when braking, i. e. there is no deviation, sideslip and loss of steering ability.

③ Constancy of braking efficiency: It mainly refers to the resistance to thermal decay. When a car is braked under heavy load conditions, the performance of the brake deteriorates due to the increase of temperature. The resistance to thermal decay refers to the degree to which an automobile maintains braking efficiency. It is an important problem that must be seriously considered in designing brake and selecting material.

In order to achieve good braking performance indexes, modern automobile adopts anti-

lock braking system. Among the above three indexes, the performance of the first two indexes has been obviously improved after the adoption of ABS device, which plays a good role in avoiding the occurrence of traffic accidents. Therefore, ABS is a very important active safety device on the automobile.

2. Force analysis of wheel in automobile braking

The fundamental reason why the vehicle can perform the braking process during driving is that the road surface in contact with the tire provides the corresponding wheel with road braking force. One is the friction between the brake shoe lining and the brake drum in the brake, and the other is the adhesion between the tire and the road surface. Fig. 1-6 shows the schematic diagram of the force on the wheel during braking.

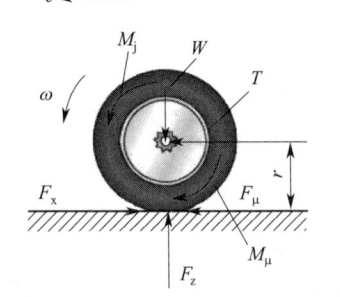

Fig. 1-6　Schematic Diagram of
Force on the Wheel During Braking
v—Vehicle speed; ω—Angular velocity of
wheel rotation; M_j—Moment of inertia;
M_μ—Braking resistance torque;
W—Normal wheel load; F_z—Ground
normal reaction; T—Axle thrust on wheel;
F_x—Ground braking force; r—Wheel
radius; F_μ—brake braking force

It can be seen from the moment balance that: The tangential reaction of the ground to the wheel during braking is $F_x = M_j/r$.

The friction moment formed when the brake shoe is pressed tightly with the brake drum (disc) is M_μ. The tangential force acting on the ground by the wheel is called brake braking force, which is represented by F_μ. The braking force of the brake $F_\mu = M_\mu/r$.

It has been proved by a large number of experiments that the elastic wheel rolls on the ground and generates resistance and friction force (adhesion), where the adhesion is the limit value of the tangential reaction of the ground on the tire, expressed by F_ϕ. The adhesion depends on the friction between the tire and the road surface and the shear strength of the road surface, i. e. , the adhesion coefficient of the road surface ϕ. From the above, it can be known that $F_\phi = \phi F_z$.

As the ground braking force is limited by adhesion, the maximum ground braking force cannot exceed the adhesion F_ϕ, i. e. $F_x \leqslant F_\phi$.

According to the above analysis, the relationship among brake braking force F_μ, ground braking force F_x and adhesion F_ϕ during vehicle braking is shown in Fig. 1-7. During braking, the ground braking force depends on the braking force of the brake first, but is limited by the adhesion condition of the ground. Therefore, in order to achieve the best braking effect, not only sufficient braking force but also high adhesion are needed. When braking, the adhesion coefficient is usually divided into longitudinal adhesion coefficient and lateral adhesion coefficient. The acceleration motion and deceleration motion of the vehicle are mainly limited by the longitudinal adhesion coefficient, and the ability of resisting external lateral force is mainly limited by the lateral adhesion coefficient of the wheel.

3. Slip ratio

(1) Definition of slip ratio

Slip ratio refers to the ratio of the difference between the vehicle speed and the wheel speed to the vehicle speed during braking, expressed as a percentage. Its definition expression is

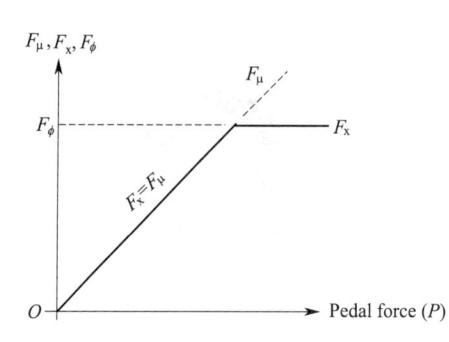

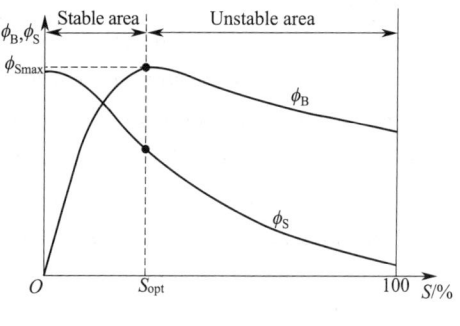

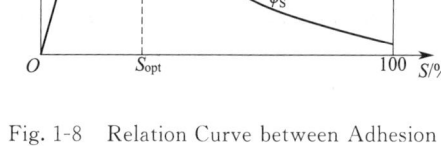

Fig. 1-7　Relationship among Brake Braking Force F_μ, Ground Braking Force F_x and Adhesion F_ϕ

Fig. 1-8　Relation Curve between Adhesion Coefficient and Slip Ratio

$$S=[(v-\omega r)/v]\times100\%$$

Where　S——wheel slip ratio, %;

　　　　r——rolling radius of wheel, m;

　　　　ω——rotational angular velocity of wheel, rad/s;

　　　　v——longitudinal speed at wheel center, m/s.

According to the above formula: When the wheel is just rolling, the actual vehicle speed is equal to the circumferential speed when the wheel is rolling, and the slip ratio is zero; when the wheel is rolling while sliding, the slip ratio is 0-100%; when the wheel is locked and the vehicle body has a certain speed, the slip ratio is 100%.

(2) Relationship between adhesion coefficient and slip ratio

In the braking process, the adhesion coefficient varies with the change of slip ratio. Fig. 1-8 shows the relationship curve of the adhesion coefficient versus the slip ratio on a dry pavement. As for the longitudinal adhesion coefficient ϕ_B, with the rapid increase of the slip ratio, the longitudinal adhesion coefficient is maximum when $S=20\%$; then with the further increase of slip ratio, when $S=100\%$, i. e. when the wheel is locked, the longitudinal adhesion coefficient decreases, the braking distance increases and the braking efficiency decreases. For the lateral adhesion coefficient ϕ_S, when $S=0$, the lateral adhesion coefficient is the maximum; then with the increase of the slip ratio, the lateral adhesion coefficient decreases gradually, and when $S=100\%$, i. e. when the wheel is locked, the lateral adhesion coefficient decreases to about zero.

According to the above analysis, if the wheel slip ratio S is controlled at about 20% during braking, i. e. at S_{opt} as shown in Fig. 1-8, the longitudinal adhesion coefficient is the largest and the best braking efficiency can be obtained; meanwhile, the lateral adhesion coefficient is also kept at a large value, so that the vehicle also has better braking direction stability.

(3) Hazards of too small lateral adhesion coefficient

① The direction stability becomes worse. Because the lateral adhesion is small, the car loses the ability to resist the lateral external force, and the rear wheel is easy to produce lateral slip, tail flick and other phenomena, which makes the direction stability worse.

② Loss of steering control ability. Even though the driver is manipulating the steering wheel, the vehicle will still drive in the original inertia direction instead of the driver's will

due to the loss of the lateral adhesion of the front wheel, which results in the loss of steering control ability.

4. Ideal braking control process

$S<20\%$ refers to the stable braking area; $S>20\%$ refers to the unstable braking area; during the braking process of the wheel, continuously switching the pressurization, pressure holding and depressurization at the frequency of 5-10 times/s, and controlling the slip ratio S at about 20%, the maximum longitudinal adhesion coefficient and large lateral adhesion coefficient can be obtained, which is the most ideal control effect.

IV. Functions of ABS

When the vehicle equipped with ABS is braked, the wheels directly controlled by ABS (the wheels whose brake pressure is adjusted according to their own motion state) shall not lock and slip. However, short wheel lockup is allowed, and wheel lockup is also allowed when the vehicle speed is lower than 15km/h.

ABS can control the actual braking process close to the ideal braking process. Its specific functions are to shorten the braking distance; prevent the side slip caused by the lateral adhesion difference between the inner and outer wheels during steering braking of the vehicle; improve the wear state of tires; prevent the braking failure caused by oil leakage of the brake oil pipe; reduce the force when the brake pedal is stepped down, improve the auxiliary braking effect, and it is unnecessary for the driver to apply a series of point braking methods for braking.

1. Shorten braking distance during braking

The braking distance of the vehicle with ABS is shortened, because under the same emergency braking condition, ABS can control the slip ratio to about 20%, and the maximum longitudinal braking force can be obtained. For example, on smooth roads such as ice-snow pavement, if there is no ABS, no matter how careful, the braking force will always appear too large, make the tire lock, thus make the braking distance of the car too long. Also, on this type of road, if the vehicle is equipped with ABS, it automatically maximizes the adhesion between the wheels and the road surface, reducing the braking distance. But don't mistakenly think that with ABS, the car's braking will be no longer a problem, or even mistakenly think that no matter on the ice-snow pavements and other slippery roads or dry roads, the braking distance of the car using ABS is the same.

2. Maintain direction stability during braking

The direction stability during braking refers to the ability of a car to drive in a predetermined direction during braking, i. e. , the ability not to deviate and sideslip, as shown in Fig. 1-9.

The greatest advantages of ABS are: When the vehicle is in emergency braking, ABS can maximize the adhesion between the tire and the road surface to obtain the maximum braking force, and can still control the direction of the vehicle to maintain the direction stability of the vehicle.

3. Maintain steering control during braking

Maintain steering control during braking, as shown in Fig. 1-10.

When the car is steering, if the car brakes hard, the wheel lock-up will occur as well as the emergency braking when the car is driving in a straight line. As the wheels lock up, the lateral adhesion of the car becomes zero, the wheels will slip laterally and the vehicle will lose the ability to control direction, which is very dangerous.

If the front wheels of the car are locked, the driver cannot control the driving direction of the car; if the rear wheels of the car are locked first, there will be serious accidents such as sideslip, tail flick and even the overall turning of the car. ABS can prevent the four wheels from being locked completely when braking, so that the braking will not affect the steering performance of the vehicle during cornering, thus improving the stability of the vehicle.

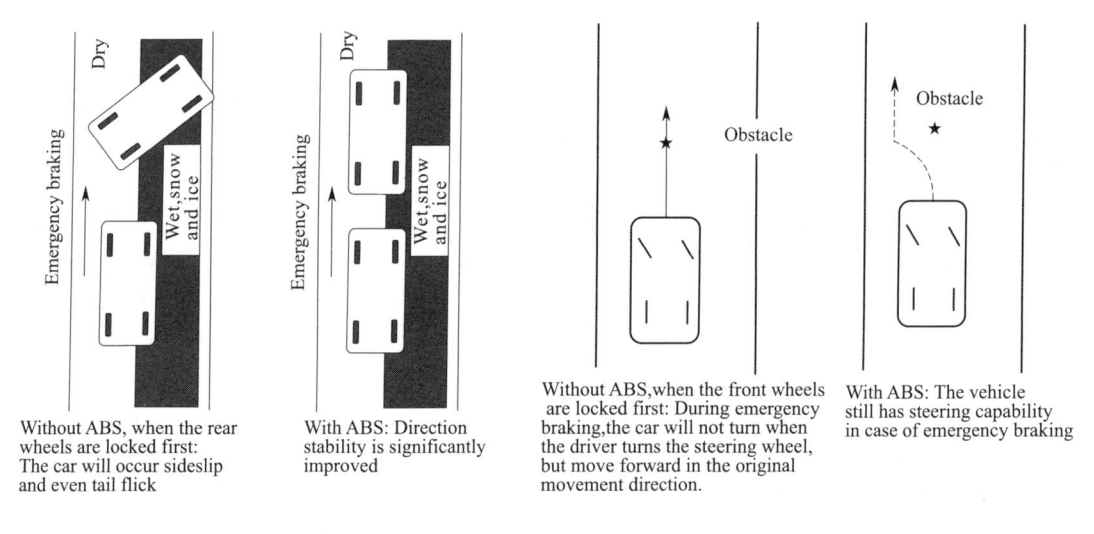

Fig. 1-9　Maintain Direction Stability during Braking　　Fig. 1-10　Maintain Steering Control during Braking

4. Reduce tyre wear when braking

In fact, the wheel lock-up will cause cup-shaped tire wear and uneven tire wear, which will increase the expense of tire wear consumption. Therefore, the tire wear cost can be reduced by using ABS to a certain extent.

5. Easy use and reliable operation

There is little difference between the use of ABS and the use of conventional brake systems. When braking, as long as the foot is placed on the brake pedal, ABS will automatically enter into working state according to the situation. ABS works reliably and has self-diagnosis capability.

V. Technical Requirements and Evaluation Method of ABS

1. Design requirements for ABS

The main indexes to evaluate ABS are steering capacity, stability and optimum braking distance. Therefore, the following requirements are put forward for ABS.

① In the process of adjusting braking, the steering capacity and driving stability of the vehicle must be guaranteed.

② Even if the adhesion coefficients of the left and right wheels are not equal, the unavoidable steering reaction shall be kept as small as possible.

008　Automotive Safety and Comfort System Maintenance

③ It must be adjusted within the whole speed range of the vehicle.

④ The adjustment system shall make the most effective use of the adhesion of wheels on the road surface, in which case the consideration of maintaining steering capacity takes precedence over the goal of shortening the braking distance.

⑤ The regulating device shall adapt to the change of the road surface transmission capacity very quickly.

⑥ The vehicle can be completely controlled by applying any strength of braking on the wavy road.

⑦ The regulating device must be able to identify the road surface with low adhesion coefficient and react correctly to this.

⑧ The regulating device can only be attached to the conventional braking device. In case of damage, the regulating device must be automatically disconnected by safe circuit without any adverse effect. In this case, the conventional braking device must be able to work with full functions.

2. Quality criteria for ABS

High quality ABS must have high reliability, wide adaptability and good performance. The following quality criteria should be followed to judge an ABS.

(1) Good driving stability

In order to make the vehicle have good driving stability, ABS must make the rear wheel have enough lateral resisting capacity when braking, so as to resist enough external lateral force to avoid the unstable braking condition of rear axle sideslip.

(2) Good steering capacity

When the vehicle brakes, ABS should provide the steering wheel enough lateral control force to avoid sideslip, and the steering wheel should not lock and slip, so that the vehicle can keep good steering capacity.

(3) High adhesion coefficient utilization rate

When ABS braking is used on the vehicle, it should have a high utilization rate of adhesion coefficient, i. e. reasonable potential adhesion between tire and road surface. In general, the vehicle equipped with ABS should have good braking effect, i. e. shorter braking distance and higher braking deceleration.

(4) Good comfort

During braking, if ABS does not control the brake pressure satisfactorily, severe over-braking or under-braking will cause the vehicle to move forward and backward. The braking comfort is poor, and the braking effect is also poor, which is not allowed.

3. Main evaluation indexes

The main evaluation indexes of braking performance of vehicles equipped with ABS are as follows.

(1) Good ability to resist external electromagnetic field interference

ABS is a typical electronic control system. If it cannot resist the interference of external electromagnetic field, the brake pressure may be misadjusted during operation, resulting in dangerous situations.

(2) Slip ratio control capability

When the vehicle equipped with ABS is braked, the wheels directly controlled by ABS (the wheels whose brake pressure is adjusted according to their own motion state) shall not lock and slip. However, temporary wheel locking is allowed, and wheel locking is also allowed when the vehicle speed is lower than 15km/h.

(3) Utilization rate of adhesion coefficient

When the vehicle equipped with ABS is braked on the road with uniform adhesion coefficient, the utilization rate of adhesion coefficient shall not be less than 0.75. When the left and right wheels are braked on the road with different adhesion coefficient, the utilization rate of adhesion coefficient should be large enough.

(4) Adaptability to abrupt change in road condition

During the braking of the vehicle equipped with ABS, when the adhesion coefficient of the road surface changes suddenly from high ($\phi_1 \geqslant 0.5$) to low ($\phi_2 < \phi_1$, $\phi_1 / \phi_2 \geqslant 2$) or from low to high, the wheels directly controlled by ABS shall not lock up, and the braking deceleration shall change rapidly. It is generally required that the speed passing through the sudden change boundary of adhesion coefficient shall be about 50km/h during braking driving.

(5) If electrical fault occurs, ABS can be removed from operation.

If the ABS continues to work after failure, misadjustment of the brake pressure may occur, which is very dangerous. Therefore, in case of electrical failure of ABS, ABS must be terminated quickly, and the regulator of ABS must ensure that the conventional brake pipeline is unblocked.

Ⅵ. Composition and Working Principle of ABS

1. Composition

The braking system varies from vehicle model to vehicle model, so does ABS. Therefore, there are many types of ABS, but they basically consist of conventional braking system (brake master cylinder, brake wheel cylinder), electronic control unit (ECU) (acceleration sensor), wheel speed sensor, brake pressure regulator (pressure switch, accumulator, power unit and hydraulic pump), ABS warning light and necessary wires, etc.

In the ABS shown in Fig. 1-11, one wheel speed sensor is installed on each wheel of the vehicle, and the wheel speed signal of each wheel is input to the ECU. The ECU analyzes and judges the movement condition of each wheel according to the input signal of each wheel speed sensor, forms corresponding control command, and sends it to the brake pressure regulator. The brake pressure regulator is mainly composed of pressure regulating solenoid control valve assembly, electric pump assembly and reservoir, etc., which is connected with brake master cylinder and each brake wheel cylinder through brake pipelines. The brake pressure regulator is controlled by the ECU and regulates the brake pressure of each brake wheel cylinder. In normal operation, all ABSs are similar to conventional power-assisted braking systems. During heavy braking, the ABS adjusts the brake fluid pressure to each wheel according to the speed of the wheel.

2. Working principle

When braking, ECU receives signal from sensor. When wheel is about to lock, ECU

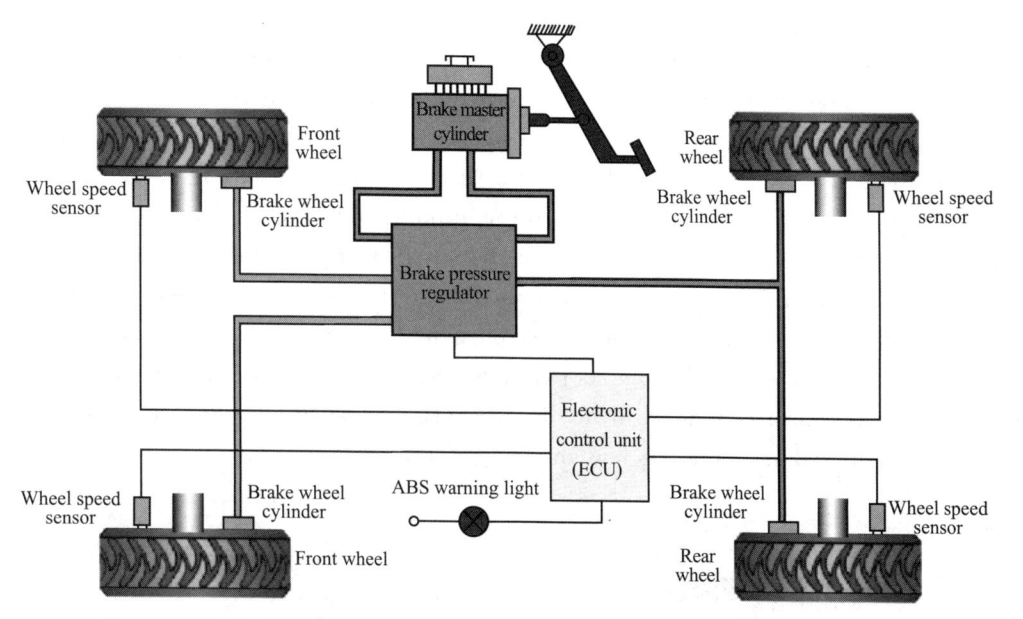

Fig. 1-11　Composition of Electronic Controlled Anti-lock Braking System （ABS）

sends control signal to control braking force of brake through actuator so that wheel is not locked.

（1）Working conditions of ABS

① ABS works on the basis of conventional braking. When the wheel is not locked during braking, it is the same as the conventional braking. When the wheel tends to lock up, the ABS works. ECU controls the brake pressure regulator to adjust the brake pressure of the wheel cylinder.

② When ABS works, the vehicle speed must be more than 5km/h. If the speed is lower than this speed, the wheel may still lock up during braking.

③ In case of failure of the conventional braking system, ABS loses its control function; in case of ABS failure, the ECU will automatically close ABS, meanwhile the ABS warning light lights up and stores the DTC, but the conventional braking system can still work normally.

（2）Regulation principle of typical ABS

① Normal braking stage. In the normal braking stage, ABS is not involved in the brake pressure control. Each inlet solenoid valve in the pressure regulating solenoid valve assembly is not energized but is opened, and each outlet solenoid valve is not energized but is closed. The electric pump is not powered on. The brake pipeline from the brake master cylinder to each brake wheel cylinder is in unblocked state, while the brake pipeline from each brake wheel cylinder to the accumulator is in closed state. The pressure of each brake wheel cylinder will change with the output pressure of the brake master cylinder. The braking process at this time is exactly the same as that of the general braking system, as shown in Fig. 1-12.

② Brake pressure holding stage. During the braking, when the ECU determines that there is wheel lock according to the wheel speed signal input by the wheel speed sensor, the

Item I　Maintenance of Automobile Electronic Control Active Safety System　**011**

ABS enters the anti-lock brake pressure adjustment process. For example, when the ECU finds that the left front wheel tends to lock up, the ECU energizes the inlet solenoid valve controlling the brake pressure of the left front wheel to turn the left front inlet solenoid valve into the closed state, and the brake fluid output from the brake master cylinder no longer flows into the left front brake wheel cylinder. At this time, the left front outlet solenoid valve is still not energized and is closed, and the brake fluid in the left front brake wheel cylinder will not flow out. The brake pressure of the left front brake wheel cylinder will remain constant, while the brake pressure of other unlocked wheels will still increase with the increase of the output pressure of the brake master cylinder to maintain the maximum braking force. The control element shall fully cooperate with the sensor, so that the hydraulic pressure of the brake wheel cylinder will not be too large to cause slippage, nor too small to cause insufficient braking force, as shown in Fig. 1-13.

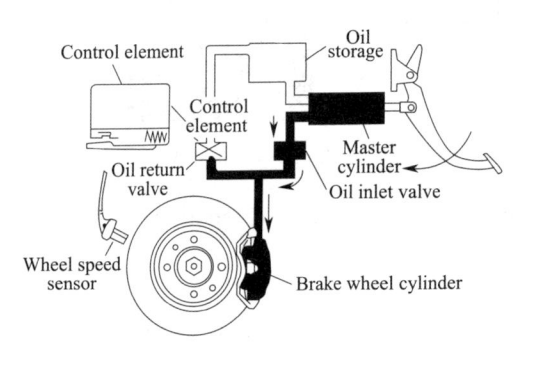

Fig. 1-12　Normal Braking Phase

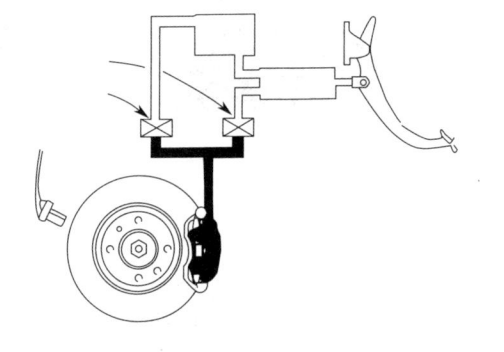

Fig. 1-13　When Maintaining Maximum Braking Force

③ Brake pressure reduction stage (when the wheel is locked). If the ECU determines that the left front wheel is still locked when the brake pressure of the left front brake wheel cylinder is kept constant, the ECU also turns the left front outlet solenoid valve into the open state, part of the brake fluid in the left front brake wheel cylinder will flow back to the reservoir through the outlet solenoid valve in the open state, so that the brake pressure of the left front brake wheel cylinder will decrease rapidly, and the locking tendency of the left front wheel will begin to be eliminated. When the wheel is locked, the sensor sends a signal to the control element to close the oil inlet valve, open the oil return valve, and part of the brake oil flows back to the reservoir to reduce the hydraulic pressure of the brake wheel cylinder to avoid wheel locking, as shown in Fig. 1-14.

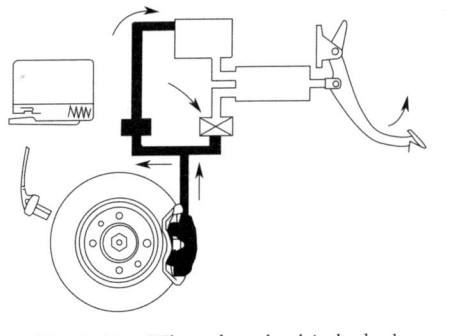

Fig. 1-14　When the wheel is locked

④ Brake pressure increase stage. With the decrease of brake pressure of left front brake wheel cylinder, the left front wheel will accelerate gradually under the action of vehicle inertia force. When the ECU judges that locking tendency of the left front wheel has been completely eliminated according to signal input by the wheel speed sensor, the ECU will cut off power of the left front inlet solenoid valve and

012　Automotive Safety and Comfort System Maintenance

the outlet solenoid valve, turn the inlet solenoid valve into open state, turn the outlet sole-noid valve into closed state, meanwhile, power on the electric pump to pump brake fluid to the brake wheel cylinder, brake fluid output from the brake master cylinder and brake fluid pumped by the electric pump enter the left front brake wheel cylinder through the left front inlet solenoid valve in open state, making pressure of the left front brake wheel cylinder in-crease rapidly, and the left front wheel begin to decelerate and rotate again.

ABS makes the brake pressure which tends to lock the wheel go through the process of holding-decreasing-increasing, and controls the slip ratio of the wheel tending to lock-up in the range of the peak adhesion coefficient slip ratio until the vehicle speed decreases to a very low speed or the output pressure of the brake master cylinder no longer makes the wheel tend to lock-up. Generally, the frequency of the brake pressure regulation cycle can reach $3\sim20$Hz. A pair of inlet and outlet solenoid valves corresponding to each brake wheel cylin-der in the four-channel ABS can be individually controlled by the ECU. Therefore, the brake pressure of each of the brake wheel cylinders can be independently adjusted so that there is no locking phenomenon of the four wheels.

VII. ABS Control Mode

The brake pipeline in ABS that can independently adjust the brake pressure is called control channel. ABS can be divided into single-channel system, two-channel system, three-channel system and four-channel system according to the number of control channels.

If the brake pressure of the wheel can be adjusted independently of the control of other wheels, the wheel is called independent control. The independent control mode can make each wheel achieve the maximum utilization rate of adhesion coefficient according to its own anti-lock control algorithm, and obtain the best braking effect. However, when the control of four wheels is integrated, the best braking effect can not be obtained in many cases, which is mainly due to the difference of braking force on the left and right wheels when driv-ing on the road with separated adhesion coefficient, which will lead to additional yaw mo-ment and make the vehicle lose the handling stability. The independent control mode is main-ly used for the main bearing axle or drive shaft of the vehicle. For cars, it is mainly applied to the front axle, while for the medium weight and heavy-duty vehicles, it is mainly applied to the rear axle.

Two or more wheels are said to be controlled together if the brake pressures of the two or more wheels are adjusted together. If the two wheels are controlled together, if the anti-lock braking control is carried out on the principle of ensuring that the wheel with large ad-hesion coefficient will not be locked, it is said that the two wheels are controlled together ac-cording to the principle of high selection; if the anti-lock braking control is carried out on the principle of ensuring that the wheel with small adhesion coefficient will not be locked, it is said that the two wheels are controlled together according to the principle of low selec-tion. When the vehicle is controlled according to the principle of high selection, the utiliza-tion rate of adhesion coefficient is relatively large and the braking distance is shorter, but the additional yaw moment will be produced when driving on the road with separated adhe-sion coefficient, which deteriorates the braking stability. This kind of control mode is appli-

cable to the front axle of a car. When the vehicle is controlled according to the principle of low selection, the braking distance is lengthened because the wheel on the side of high adhesion coefficient cannot make full use of the adhesion coefficient. However, this control mode can eliminate and reduce the additional yaw moment. Therefore, when the vehicle runs straight on the road with uniform adhesion coefficient, the braking effect is basically the same as that of independent control, and the braking distance is basically the same, except that the braking distance is slightly longer when driving on the road with separated adhesion coefficient. This type of control is commonly used on the rear axle of a car.

① Four-sensor four-channel/four-wheel independent control is shown in Fig. 1-15.

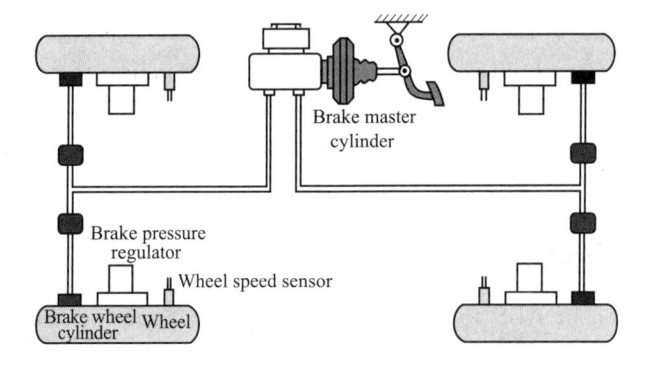

Fig. 1-15　Four-sensor Four-channel/Four-wheel Independent Control

② Four-sensor four-channel/front wheel independent-rear wheel selective control mode. Corresponding to H-shape (front and rear) or X-shape (diagonal) arrangements of double brake lines, as shown in Fig. 1-16, there are also two layout forms of four-channel ABS. For independent control of the brake pressure of the four wheels, one wheel speed sensor is installed on each wheel and a brake pressure regulating sub-unit (channel) is provided in each brake line to each brake wheel cylinder. Because the four-channel ABS makes the greatest use of the traction of each wheel for braking, the car has the best braking effect. However, when the adhesion coefficient is separated (braking on the road where the adhesion coefficients of the wheels on both sides are unequal), the braking force on the same axle is not equal, resulting in large yaw torque and brake deviation. Therefore, ABS does not normally perform independent brake pressure adjustment for 4 wheels.

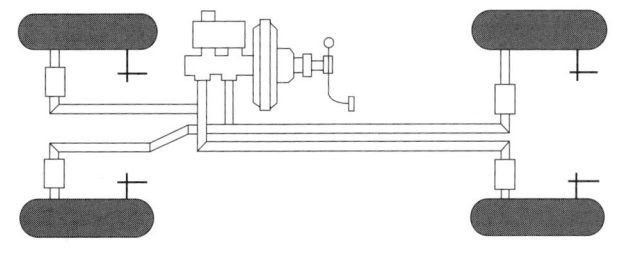

Fig. 1-16　X-shaped (Diagonal) Arrangement Corresponding to Double Brake Lines

③ Four-sensor three-channel/front wheel independent-rear wheel low selection control mode is shown in Fig. 1-17.

014　Automotive Safety and Comfort System Maintenance

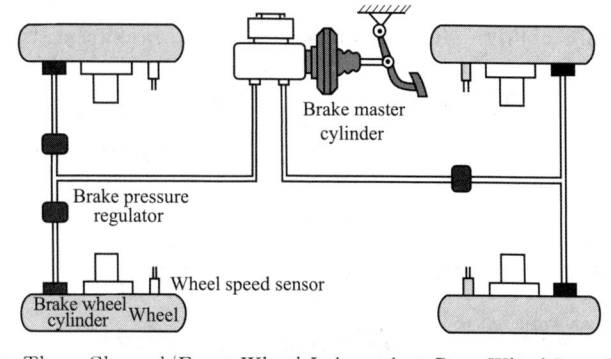

Fig. 1-17   Four-sensor Three-Channel/Front Wheel Independent-Rear Wheel Low Selection Control Mode

④ Three-sensor three-channel/front wheel independent-rear wheel low selection control mode is shown in Fig. 1-18. Most four-wheel ABS is a three-channel system, and the three-channel system controls the brake pressure of the two front wheels independently, and the brake pressure of both rear wheels is controlled together according to the principle of low selection. Because the three-channel ABS controls both rear wheels together, only one speed sensor can be installed in the transmission or final drive to detect the average speed of both rear wheels for a rear-wheel-driven vehicle.

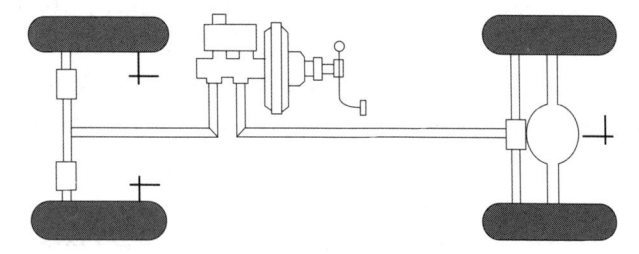

Fig. 1-18   Three-sensor Three-Channel/Front Wheel Independent-Rear Wheel Low Selection Control Mode

⑤ Four-sensor two-channel/front wheel independent control mode is shown in Fig. 1-19.

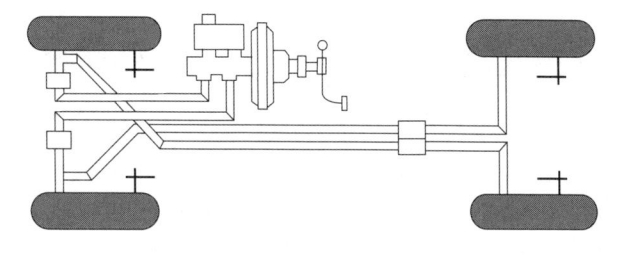

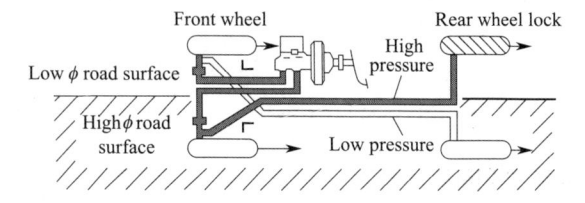

Fig. 1-19   Four-sensor Two-channel/Front Wheel Independent Control Mode

⑥ Four-sensor two-channel/front wheel independent-rear wheel low selection control mode is

Item Ⅰ   Maintenance of Automobile Electronic Control Active Safety System   **015**

shown in Fig. 1-20. Two-channel ABS is seldom used because it is difficult to give consideration to the aspects of directional stability, steering control ability and braking distance.

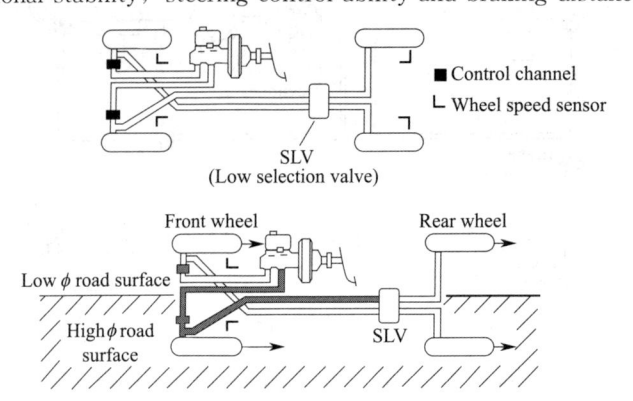

Fig. 1-20　Four-sensor Two-Channel/Front Wheel Independent-Rear Wheel Low Selection Control Mode

⑦ The braking mode of one-sensor one-channel/rear wheel approximate low selection control system is shown in Fig. 1-21. All single-channel ABSs are equipped with a brake pressure regulator in the rear brake line of the front-rear dual-line brake system. For rear-wheel-driven vehicles, only a speed sensor is required in the transmission system. Because the brake pressure of the front brake wheel cylinder is not controlled, the front wheel may still be locked, so the steering operation capability of the vehicle during braking cannot be guaranteed. However, single-channel ABS is widely used in light trucks because of its advantages of significant improvement of the direction stability of the vehicle when braking, simple structure and low cost.

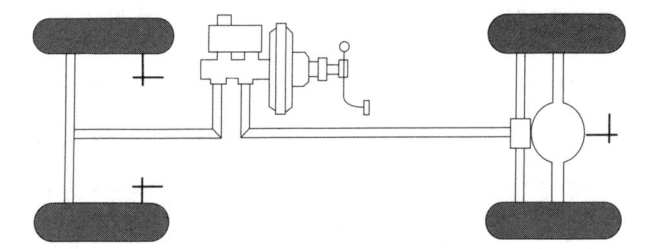

Fig. 1-21　Braking Mode of One-Sensor One -Channel/Rear Wheel Approximate Low Selection Control System

⑧ ABS control parameters. At present, there are many kinds of ABS control modes, such as logic threshold control, optimal control and sliding mode variable structure control. However, most ABSs adopt logic threshold control mode, i. e. ABS with wheel slip ratio as control parameter and ABS with angular acceleration and angular deceleration as control parameters, as shown in Fig. 1-22.

In actual control, ABS is usually controlled by the combination of many parameters. If only any one of the thresholds is used as anti-lock braking control, there is a great limitation.

Ⅷ. Sensor Structure Principle

1. Wheel speed sensor

(1) Structure of wheel speed sensor

In ABS control system, each wheel is equipped with a wheel speed sensor to detect the

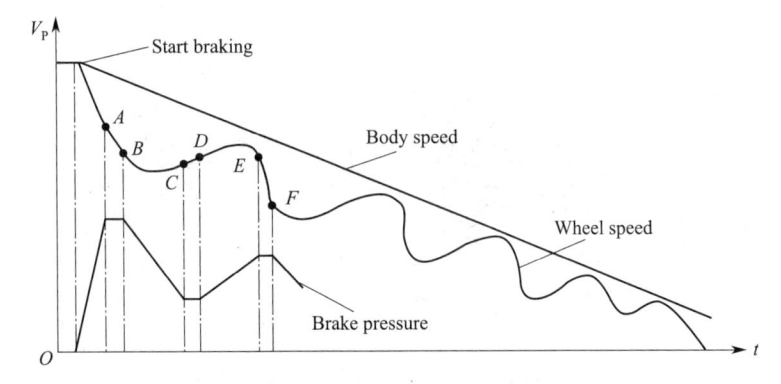

Fig. 1-22　ABS Control Parameters

speed of the wheel. The front wheel speed sensor is installed on the knuckle, and the rear wheel speed sensor is installed on the rear axle bracket. For some rear-driven vehicles, the wheel speed sensor is installed in the differential and is called axle speed sensor through rear axle speed detection. The sensor consists of a permanent magnet, a coil and a ring gear. It measures the speed of the wheel in a non-contact way. When the ring gear rotates synchronously with the wheel, the magnetic flux changes alternately by cutting the magnetic line of force of the sensor to generate alternating voltage at the output end of the sensor. The voltage frequency is proportional to the wheel speed. At the same time, this pulse signal is input to the ABS control device to detect the instantaneous speed change of the wheel, as shown in Fig. 1-23 and Fig. 1-24.

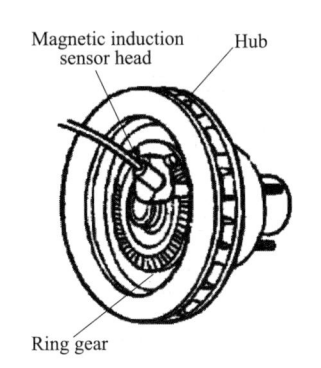

Fig. 1-23　Front Wheel Speed Sensor

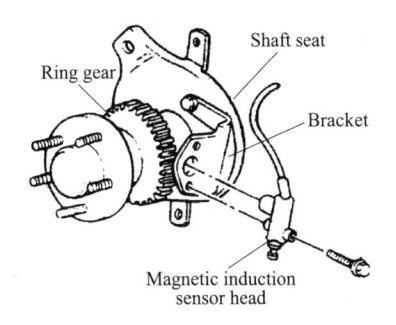

Fig. 1-24　Rear Wheel Speed Sensor

（2）Different installation position of wheel speed sensor

The wheel speed sensors are mounted on the driving wheel and on the non-driving wheel, as shown in Fig. 1-25.

Install on the rear drive axle final drive, as shown in Fig. 1-26, and on the transmission output shaft, as shown in Fig. 1-27.

（3）Installation method of ABS wheel speed sensor

① Axial installation, as shown in Fig. 1-28. ② Radial installation, as shown in Fig. 1-29.

（4）Type of wheel speed sensor

There are two main types of wheel speed sensors: electromagnetic induction type and Hall effect type.

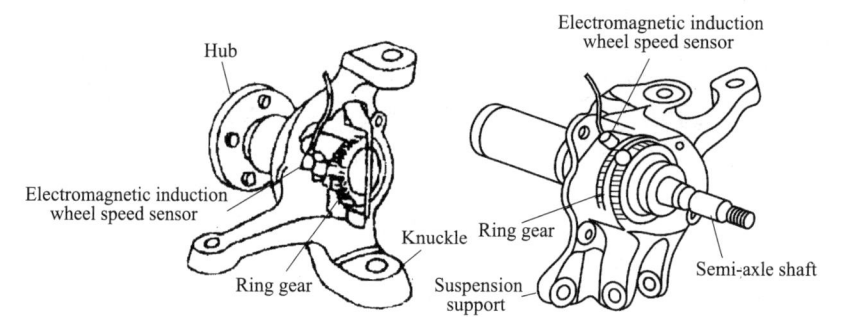

Fig. 1-25　Wheel Speed Sensor Mounted on Drive/Non-driving wheel

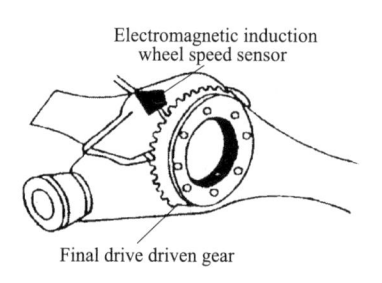

Fig. 1-26　Wheel Speed Sensor Mounted on Rear Drive Final Drive

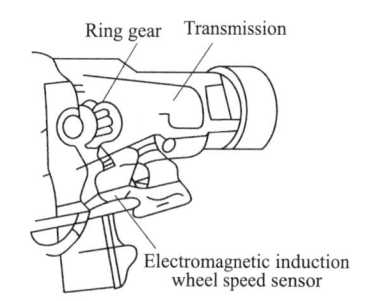

Fig. 1-27　Wheel Speed Sensor Mounted on Transmission Output Shaft

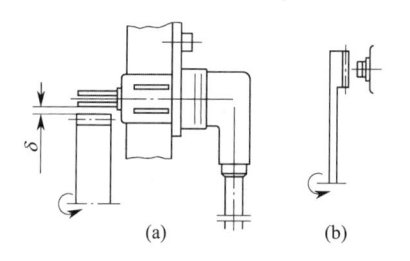

Fig. 1-28　Axial Installation

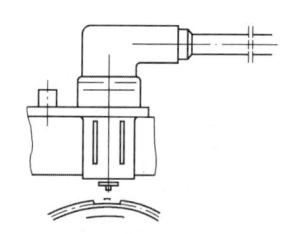

Fig. 1-29　Radial Installation

① Electromagnetic induction wheel speed sensor. Electromagnetic induction wheel speed sensor mainly consists of cable, permanent magnet, housing, induction coil, pole axis and ring gear, as shown in Fig. 1-30. When the tooth clearance of the ring gear is opposite to the pole axis end of the sensor, the air gap between the pole axis end and the ring gear is the largest, and the magnetic flux passing through the induction magnetic coil is minimum, as shown in Fig. 1-31. When the tooth top of the ring gear is opposite to the pole axis end of the sensor, the air gap between the pole axis end and the ring gear is minimum, and the magnetic flux passing through the induction magnetic coil is maximum, as shown in Fig. 1-32. The tooth top and tooth clearance of the ring gear are alternately opposite to the top of pole axis, and the surrounding magnetic field changes alternately, inducing alternating voltage, as shown in Fig. 1-33.

Its features are as follows: It has simple structure and low cost; the amplitude of output signal voltage varies with rotating speed, generally 1-15V; if the vehicle speed is too

slow and the output signal voltage is less than 1V, ABS computer cannot detect it. The effective control speed range is narrow, typically 15-160km/h; The ability to resist electromagnetic wave interference is poor.

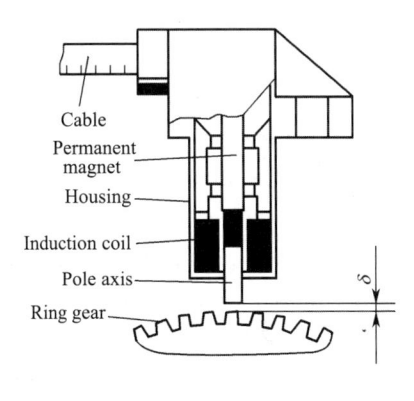

Fig. 1-30　Structure of Electromagnetic
Induction Wheel Speed Sensor

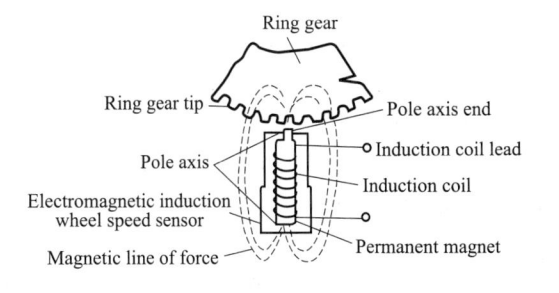

Fig. 1-31　Working Process of Electromagnetic
Induction Wheel Speed Sensor （1）

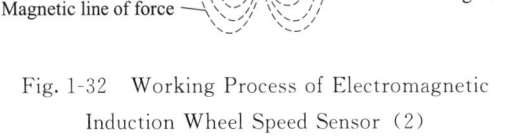

Fig. 1-32　Working Process of Electromagnetic
Induction Wheel Speed Sensor （2）

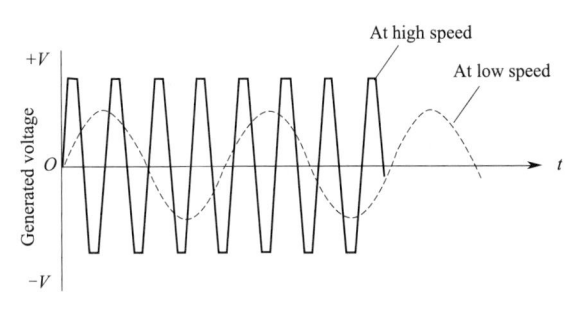

Fig. 1-33　Working Process of Electromagnetic
Induction Wheel Speed Sensor （3）

② Hall wheel speed sensor. Hall wheel speed sensor is mainly composed of Hall element, permanent magnet, gear ring and circuit, as shown in Fig. 1-34. The working process is as follows.

a. When the teeth of the gear ring are not aligned with the permanent magnet, the magnetic line of forces passing through the Hall element are dispersed, and the magnetic field is relatively weak, as shown in Fig. 1-35.

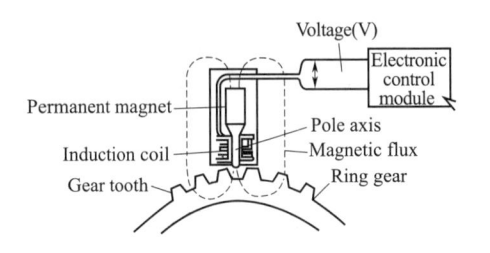

Fig. 1-34　Structure of Hall Wheel
Speed Sensor

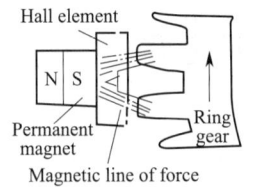

Fig. 1-35　Working Process of Hall
Wheel Speed Sensor （1）

b. When the teeth of the gear ring face the permanent magnet, the magnetic lines passing through the Hall element are concentrated and the magnetic field is relatively strong, which causes the Hall voltage to change and the sine wave voltage will be output, as shown in Fig. 1-36.

2. Deceleration sensor

(1) Function

The deceleration sensor, also called G sensor, is used to measure the deceleration of a car when braking and identify whether it is a slippery road such as snow road or ice road.

(2) Type

① Photoelectric deceleration sensor. Its basic structure is shown in Fig. 1-37. It consists of two light emitting diodes, two phototriodes, one light transmission board and one signal circuit.

Working process: When the opening on the light transmission board is located between the light-emitting diode and the phototriode, the phototriode can be turned on, otherwise cut off, and the computer can judge the road condition after receiving the sensor signal, as shown in Fig. 1-38.

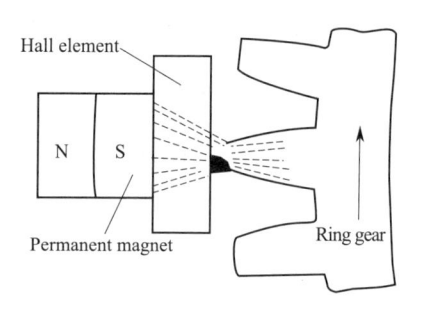

Fig. 1-36　Working Process of Hall Wheel Speed Sensor (2)

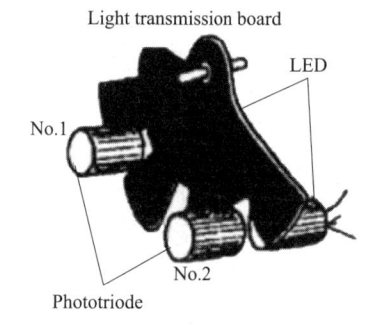

Fig. 1-37　Structure of Photoelectric Deceleration Sensor

② Mercury deceleration sensor. Its basic structure is shown in Fig. 1-39 and it consists of glass tube and mercury.

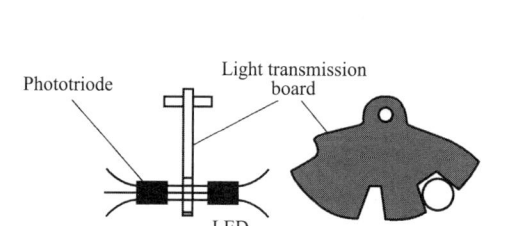

Fig. 1-38　Working Process of Photoelectric Deceleration Sensor

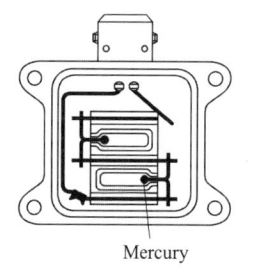

Fig. 1-39　Structure of Mercury Deceleration Sensor

Working process: When the car is braked on the road with low adhesion coefficient, the deceleration of the car is small, the mercury basically does not move, the switch is on in the glass tube, and the computer controls the road surface with low adhesion coefficient. On

the contrary, when braking on the road with high adhesion coefficient, the deceleration of the car is large, and the mercury moves forward in the glass tube, so that the circuit switch in the glass tube is disconnected, and the computer controls the road surface with high adhesion coefficient, as shown in Fig. 1-40.

③ Differential transmission deceleration sensor. Its basic structure, as shown in Fig. 1-41, consists of differential transformer and electronic circuit. The differential transformer mainly consists of one primary winding, two secondary windings in series and iron core.

Working process: When the vehicle brakes and decelerates, the iron core moves forward under the action of inertia force, so that the induced voltage in the coil of the differential transformer changes, which is sent to ECU as output signal to control the operation of ABS, as shown in Fig. 1-42.

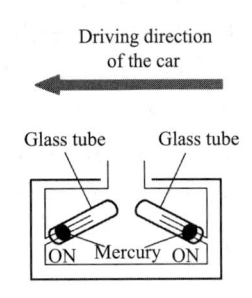

Fig. 1-40   Working Process of Mercury
Deceleration Sensor

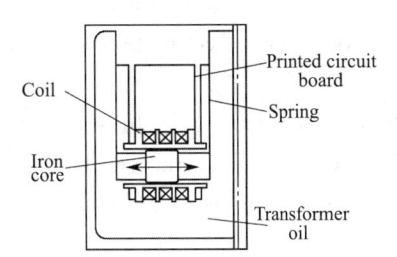

Fig. 1-41   Structure of Differential
Transmission Deceleration Sensor

IX. Structural Principle of Brake Pressure Regulator

The function of the brake pressure regulator (see Fig. 1-43) is to adjust the brake pressure of each wheel brake according to the command of ECU. The structure and working principle of the brake pressure regulator are different for different braking systems. The commonly used braking system mainly includes hydraulic braking system, mechanical braking system, pneumatic braking system and air hydraulic braking system, etc. The hydraulic braking system is most widely used in ABS, so the hydraulic brake pressure regulator is mainly introduced here.

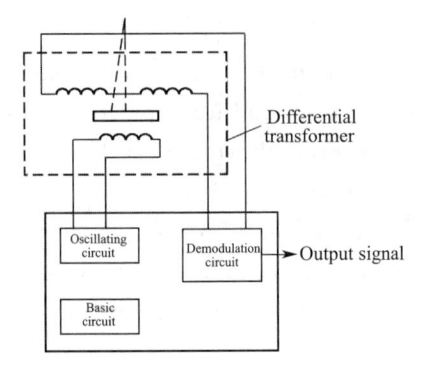

Fig. 1-42   Working Process of Differential
Transmission Deceleration Sensor

Fig. 1-43   Brake Pressure Regulator

The hydraulic brake pressure regulator (brake pressure regulator) is mainly composed of hydraulic electric pump, hydraulic control solenoid valve and reservoir. The pressure regulator is installed between the master cylinder and the wheel cylinder, and the brake pressure of the wheel cylinder is controlled directly or indirectly by the solenoid valve.

1. Circulating brake pressure regulator

The structure of the circulating brake pressure regulator is shown in Fig. 1-44.

(1) Solenoid valve

The solenoid valve directly controls the brake pressure of the wheel cylinder.

① Three-position three-way solenoid valve. The structure of the three-position three-way solenoid valve is shown in Fig. 1-45, which consists of inlet valve, return valve, main spring, auxiliary spring, fixed iron core and armature sleeve, etc. Three-position three-way solenoid valve (produced by BOSCH and applied in BOSCH ABS), under the control of ECU, makes the valve in three positions of pressurization, pressure holding and depressurizing.

Pressurized (normal) braking state: When the solenoid coil is not energized, the inlet valve is opened and the return valve is closed under the tension of the main spring, and the inlet and outlet are kept unblocked.

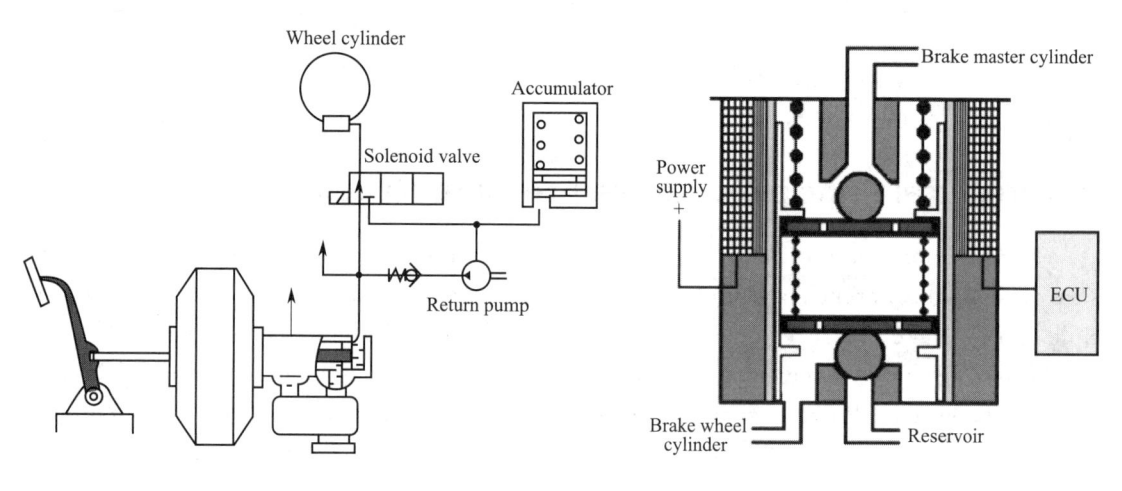

Fig. 1-44　Structure of circulating brake
pressure regulator

Fig. 1-45　Structure of three-position
three-way solenoid valve

Pressure holding state: As shown in Fig. 1-46, a small current (2A) is applied to the solenoid coil, resulting in small electromagnetic attraction force and less upward movement of the pull-in armature. However, the main spring can be properly compressed to close the inlet valve and release the auxiliary spring without opening the return valve.

Depressurization state: As shown in Fig. 1-47, large current (5A) is applied to solenoid valve coil, resulting in large electromagnetic attraction force and large upward movement of the pull-in armature. Meanwhile, main and auxiliary springs are compressed to keep the inlet valve closed and the return valve open.

This solenoid valve works in three states (pressurization, pressure holding and depressurization), which are called "three positions". The solenoid valve is externally provided

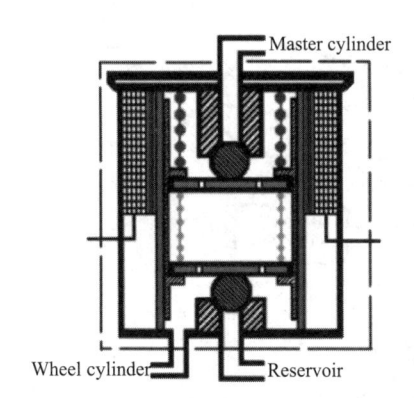 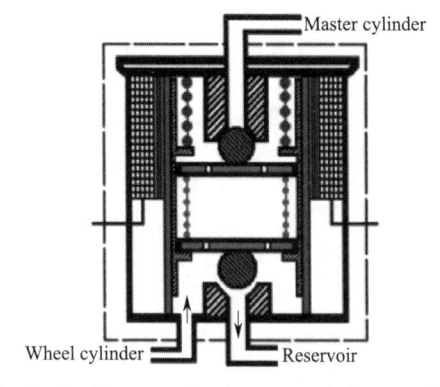

Fig. 1-46　Pressure holding state of three-position three-way solenoid valve

Fig. 1-47　Depressurization state of three-position three-way solenoid valve

with three interfaces (inlet, outlet and return port), which are respectively connected to master cylinder, wheel cylinder and reservoir, which is called "three ways". Therefore, this solenoid valve is called three-position three-way solenoid valve, which is usually written as 3/3 solenoid valve.

② Two-position two-way solenoid valve. The structure of two-position two-way solenoid valve is shown in Fig. 1-48, which is further divided into two-position two-way normally open solenoid valve and two-position two-way normally closed solenoid valve. The two kinds of solenoid valves are composed of valve, armature, solenoid coil, return spring, etc.

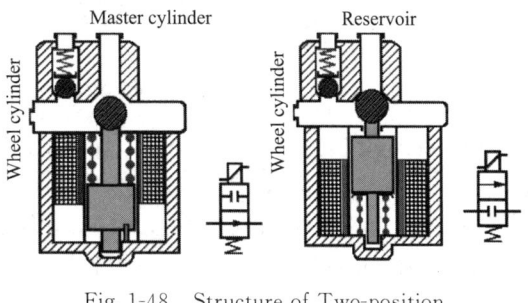

Fig. 1-48　Structure of Two-position Two-way Solenoid Valve

Under normal condition, the two-position two-way normally open solenoid valve opens under the action of spring tension, and the two-position two-way normally closed solenoid valve closes under the action of spring tension.

The two-position two-way normally open solenoid valve is used to control the brake fluid passage from the brake master cylinder to the brake wheel cylinder, also known as the two-position two-way normally open inlet solenoid valve.

The two-position two-way normally closed solenoid valve is used to control the brake fluid circuit from the brake wheel cylinder to the reservoir, also known as the two-position two-way normally closed outlet solenoid valve.

Two solenoid valves are used together to complete the task of adjusting brake pressure in ABS work together.

③ Two-position three-way solenoid valve. As shown in Fig. 1-49, the two-position three-way solenoid valve consists of two valves (the first ball valve and the second ball valve), armature, spring and solenoid coil, etc. The two-position three-way solenoid valve is mainly used as the main solenoid valve in TEVES MK II ABS.

The first ball valve (normally closed valve) is used to control the brake fluid passage between the booster chamber and the internal reservoir——high pressure control.

Item I　Maintenance of Automobile Electronic Control Active Safety System　**023**

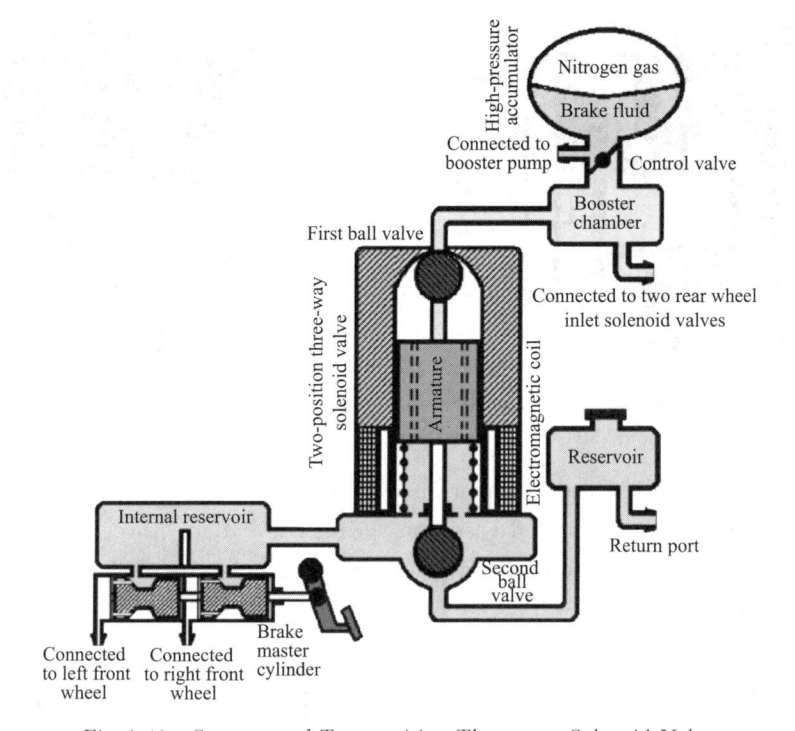

Fig. 1-49　Structure of Two-position Three-way Solenoid Valve

The second ball valve (normally open valve) is used to control the brake fluid passage between the reservoir cylinder and the internal reservoir——low pressure control.

The working process of two-position three-way solenoid valve is as follows.

When the brake pedal is stepped on and ABS does not work (the solenoid coil is not energized), the first ball valve is closed, the second ball valve is opened, and the internal reservoir is connected to the reservoir cylinder. The low pressure brake fluid flows from the brake master cylinder to the two front wheel brake cylinders to apply low pressure braking on both front wheels. Because the booster chamber stores high-pressure brake fluid while stepping on the brake pedal under the action of the control slide valve, high-pressure braking is applied to both rear wheels.

When ABS works (the solenoid coil is energized), the first ball valve opens to connect the high-pressure brake fluid passage between the booster chamber and the internal reservoir, and the second ball valve closes, cutting off the low-pressure brake fluid passage between the reservoir cylinder and the internal reservoir. At this time, both the front and rear wheels are under high-pressure braking.

During the braking, the conversion of pressurization, pressure holding and depressurization is controlled and regulated by the two-position three-way normally open inlet solenoid valve and the two-position three-way normally closed solenoid valve.

(2) Return pump and reservoir

When the solenoid valve is depressurizing, the brake fluid flowing from the brake wheel cylinder is pumped back to the brake master cylinder by the return pump through the reservoir.

The reservoir is divided into low-pressure reservoir and high-pressure accumulator according to the pressure of the brake fluid stored. They are respectively configured in different types of brake pressure regulating systems.

① Low-pressure reservoir and electric pump is shown in Fig. 1-50. The low-pressure reservoir is used to receive the brake fluid flowing back from the brake cylinder during ABS depressurization, while attenuating the pressure fluctuation of the return brake fluid to a certain extent.

There is a piston and a spring in the reservoir. When depressurizing, the return brake fluid compresses the piston downward against the spring tension, increasing the volume and temporarily storing the brake fluid.

Electric return pump consists of DC motor and plunger pump. The plunger pump consists of plunger, inlet and outlet valves and springs. When ABS works (depressurizes), according to the command output from ECU, DC motor drives the cam to rotate, and the cam will drive the plunger to move in the pump barrel. When the plunger moves upward, the brake fluid with certain pressure in the reservoir and the brake wheel cylinder enters into the plunger pump barrel. When the plunger descends, it presses and opens the inlet valve and the outlet valve at the bottom of the pump barrel to pump the brake fluid back to the outlet of the brake master cylinder.

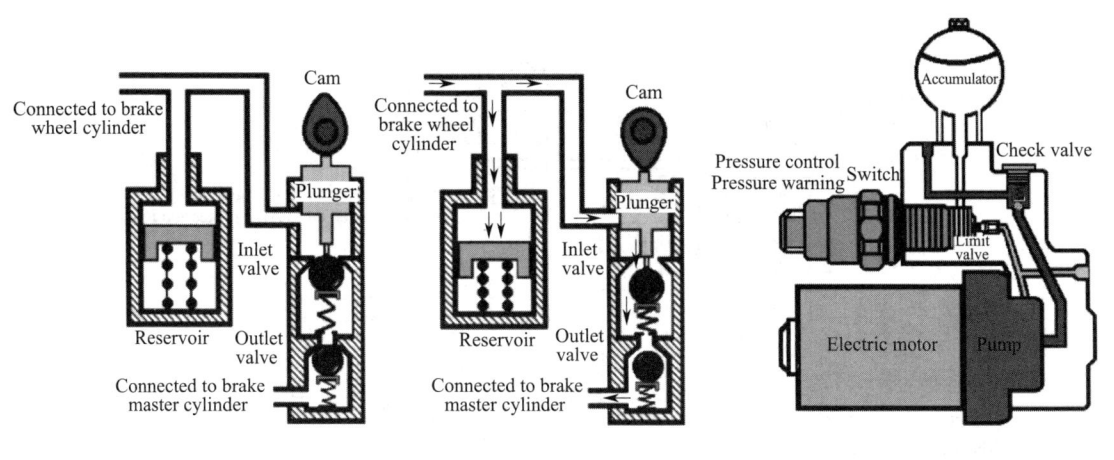

Fig. 1-50　Low Pressure Reservoir and Electric Pump

Fig. 1-51　High Pressure Accumulator and Electric Booster Pump

② High pressure accumulator and electric booster pump are shown in Fig. 1-51. A pressure control switch and a pressure warning switch are set at the lower end of the high-pressure accumulator to detect the brake fluid pressure in the lower chamber of the high-energy accumulator. When the pressure is lower than 15MPa, the switch is closed and the booster pump works. When the pressure reaches 18MPa, the switch opens and the booster pump stops working.

The high-energy accumulator is used to store high-pressure brake fluid required during braking or when the ABS is operating. Most high-pressure accumulators adopt black balloon-shaped spheres. The black balloon-shaped sphere is separated by a diaphragm into two non-communicating chambers. The upper chamber is an air chamber filled with nitrogen under

certain pressure. The lower chamber is a liquid chamber communicating with the liquid passage of the electric booster pump to contain the brake fluid pumped by the electric booster pump.

The pressure warning switch is provided with two pairs of switch contacts, one pair of normally open and one pair of normally closed. When the pressure of brake fluid in the lower chamber of the high-pressure accumulator is lower than 10.5MPa, the normally open contact is closed and the red brake warning light is turned on; meanwhile, the normally closed contact opens, and this signal is sent to ECU to turn off ABS and turn on yellow-brown ABS warning light.

The circulating brake pressure regulator operates as follows.

(1) Pressurization (normal braking) process

The pressurization process is shown in Fig. 1-52. Step on the brake pedal, since the inlet valve of the solenoid valve is opened and the return valve is closed, each solenoid valve will connect the passage between the brake master cylinder and each brake wheel cylinder, the brake fluid in the brake master cylinder will flow into each brake wheel cylinder through the inlet and outlet of each solenoid valve, and the brake fluid pressure of each brake wheel cylinder will increase with the increase of the brake fluid pressure output by the brake master cylinder.

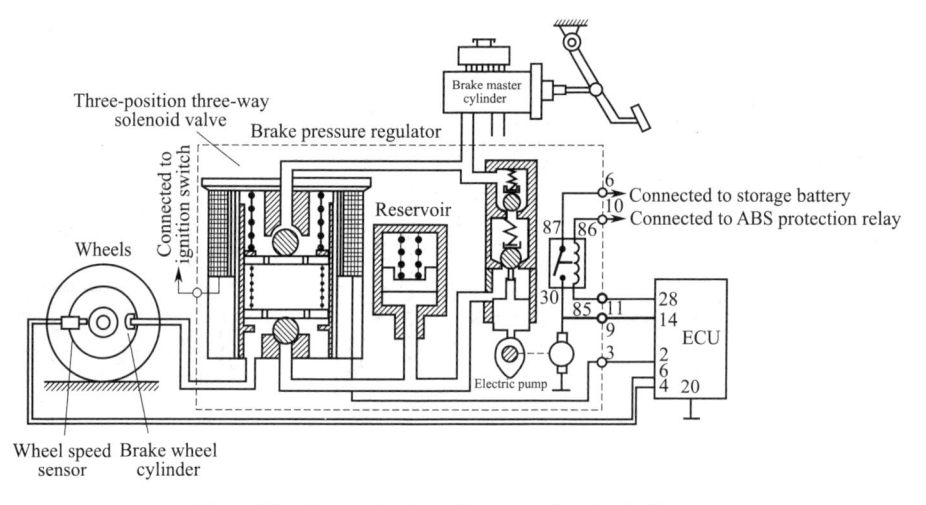

Fig. 1-52　Pressurization (Normal Braking) Process

(2) Pressure holding process

As shown in Fig. 1-53, when the slip ratio is close to 20% during braking of a wheel, the ECU outputs a command to control the solenoid coil to close the inlet valve of the solenoid valve (the return valve is still closed) through a small current (about 2A), so as to ensure that the brake pressure of the brake wheel cylinder in the control channel remains unchanged.

(3) Depressurization process

As shown in Fig. 1-54, when the slip ratio is greater than 20% during braking of a wheel, the ECU outputs a command to control the solenoid coil to pass a large current (about 5A) to close the inlet valve of the solenoid valve and open the return valve. The brake

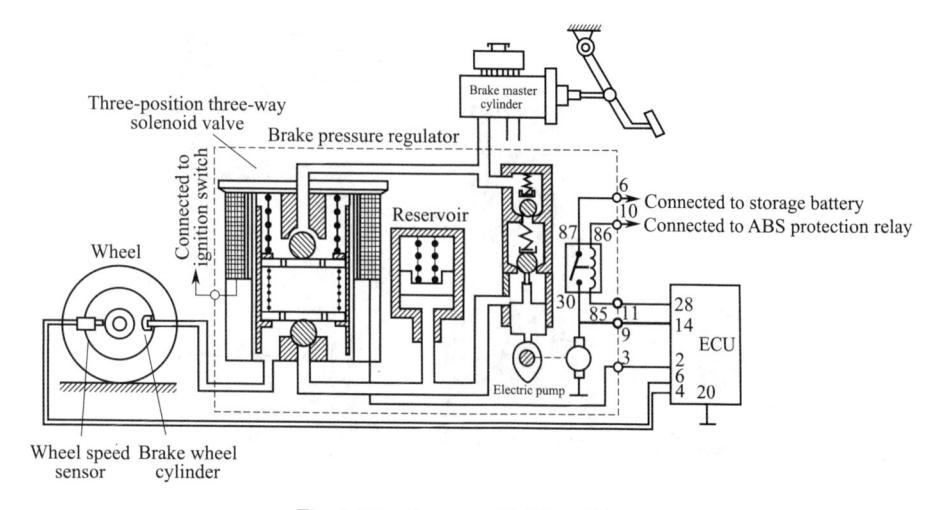

Fig. 1-53 Pressure Holding Process

fluid in the brake wheel cylinder will flow into the reservoir through the return valve to reduce the brake pressure.

At the same time, ECU controls the electric pump to operate with electricity to pump the brake fluid flowing into the reservoir back to the outlet of the brake master cylinder.

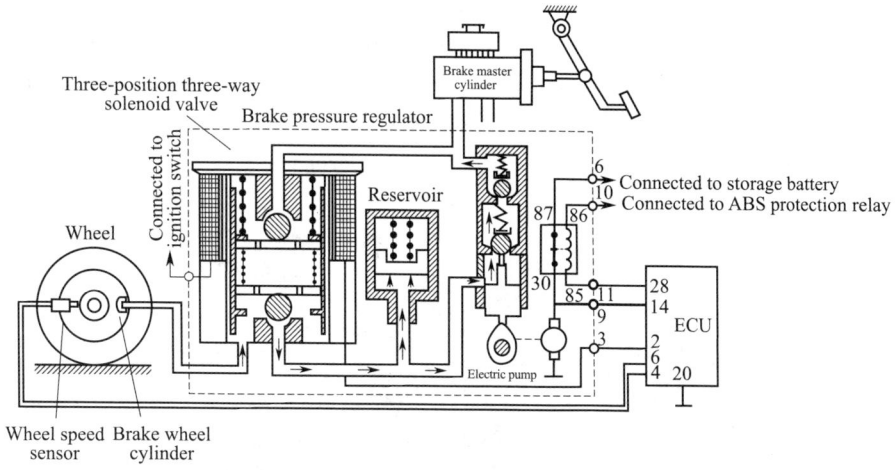

Fig. 1-54 Depressurization Process

2. Variable displacement brake pressure regulator

Hydraulic control variable displacement brake pressure regulator is shown in Fig. 1-55.

(1) Features

A set of hydraulic control device is added to the original brake system pipeline of automobile, which is used to change the volume of brake pipeline and realize the cyclic regulation of pressurization-pressure holding-depressurization. The hydraulic control circuit of the brake pressure regulation system and the brake fluid circuit of the ABS control are separated from each other.

(2) Application example of hydraulic control variable displacement pressure regulation mode (Honda Series ABS)

Item I   Maintenance of Automobile Electronic Control Active Safety System   **027**

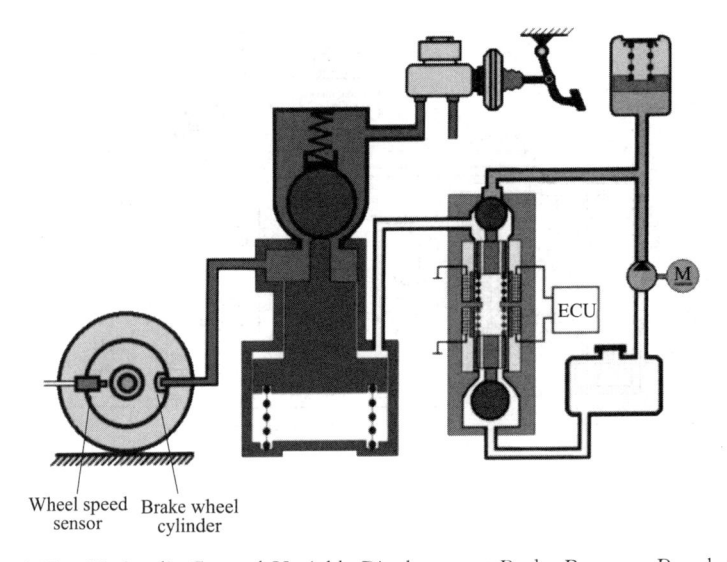

Fig. 1-55　Hydraulic Control Variable Displacement Brake Pressure Regulator

The application of hydraulic control variable displacement pressure regulation mode is shown in Fig. 1-56. Four sensors, four channels and four wheels are independently controlled. The brake pressure regulator consists of solenoid valve, pressure regulating cylinder, electric booster pump, accumulator and pressure switch.

The working process of hydraulic control variable displacement pressure regulation mode is as follows: Step on the brake pedal and brake fluid flows from brake pump→chamber A→switch valve→chamber B→brake wheel cylinder. The brake fluid pressure of the brake wheel cylinder will increase as the pedal force increases.

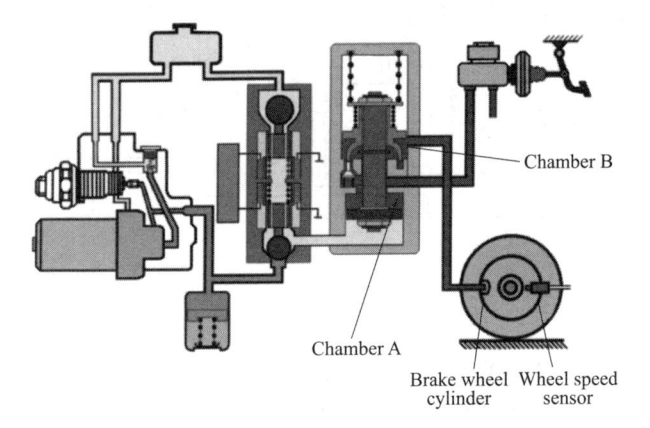

Fig. 1-56　Application example of hydraulic control variable displacement pressure regulation mode

When the slip ratio approaches 20%, the ECU controls the input solenoid valve to close after slightly energized, and the output solenoid valve to be energized and closed. The sliding piston produces displacement to close the switch valve, separate chamber A from chamber B, and keep the volume of chamber B unchanged, thus realizing the pressure holding process.

When the slip ratio is>20%, the ECU controls the input solenoid valve to be energized

028　Automotive Safety and Comfort System Maintenance

and open and the output solenoid valve to be energized and closed. The sliding piston moves upward under the action of control hydraulic pressure to increase the volume of chamber B and realize the depressurization process.

When the slip ratio is<20%, the ECU controls the input solenoid valve to be de-energized and closed and the output solenoid valve to be de-energized and open, controls the oil to drain into the reservoir, moves the sliding piston downward to reduce the volume of chamber B and realizes the pressurization process.

(3) Variable displacement brake pressure regulator controlled by micro-motor

The characteristic of the variable displacement brake pressure regulator controlled by micro-motor is that a set of control device is added to the original brake system pipeline of the automobile to control the change of volume in the brake pipeline. The adjustment mode of brake pressure is that the displacement of piston in the pressure regulating cylinder directly changes the volume of the brake pipeline, so as to realize the cyclic regulation of pressurization-pressure holding-depressurization. Its structure is shown in Fig. 1-57, mainly composed of pressure regulating cylinder and solenoid valve. The working process of ABS is that the check valve and the solenoid valve are closed and the piston moves in the pressure regulating cylinder to complete the process of pressurization, pressure holding and depressurization.

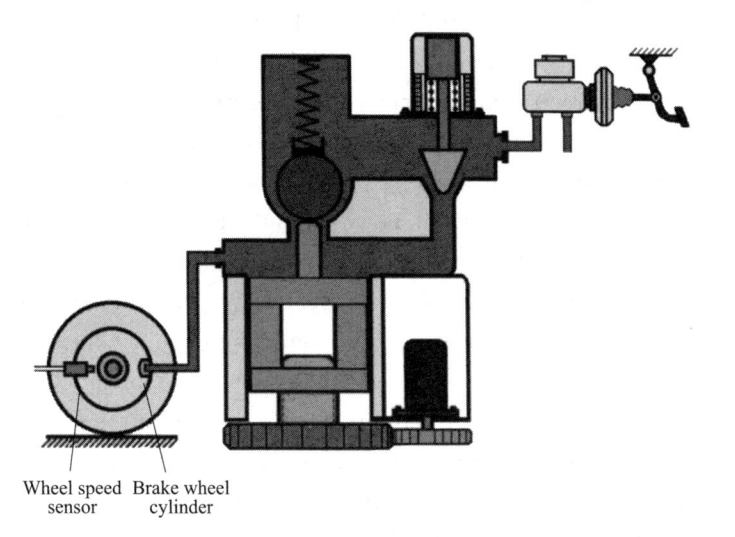

Wheel speed   Brake wheel
sensor   cylinder

Fig. 1-57   Variable Displacement Brake Pressure Regulator Controlled by Micro-motor

X. Electronic Control Unit (ECU)

Electronic control unit (ECU) is the control center of ABS system. It can receive the signal from the sensor and analyze it to judge whether the wheel is locked, and then send the brake pressure control command to the brake pressure regulator. In some models, in order to make the ABS system compact and reduce the number of plugs and wire harnesses, the ECU is mounted on the brake pressure regulator.

1. ECU functions

When ABS works, ECU monitors and controls the working condition of the braking system, i. e. ECU has the functions of "monitoring" and "controlling" on the braking system.

(1) Anti-lock braking control function

Anti-lock braking control of the braking system is the main function of the ECU. The ECU receives the input signals from each wheel speed sensor and other sensors, and then processes and calculates according to the preset control logic to form corresponding control commands to control the actuator, to adjust the brake pressure through the brake pressure regulator to prevent the wheels from locking.

(2) System monitoring function

Monitoring the braking system is the other function of the ECU. The ECU receives brake light switch, pressure switch and other various signals to monitor whether the ABS works normally. When the ECU detects that the ABS works abnormally, it will automatically stop the ABS operation and turn on the ABS warning light to avoid false control result caused by system failure. In the ABS partially utilizing hydraulic braking, the ECU also controls the operation of the electric hydraulic pump. Under normal conditions, after starting the engine, the ABS warning light shall go off automatically after several seconds, otherwise it indicates that ABS has fault.

2. Basic circuit of ECU

The internal circuit structure of the ECU mainly consists of input amplifier circuit, arithmetic circuit, solenoid valve control circuit and safety protection circuit.

The solenoid valve control circuit receives the solenoid valve control parameter signal sent from the arithmetic circuit, converts the digital control command into an analog control signal, amplifies the control signal and supplies different control currents to the solenoid coil of the solenoid valve to control the working position of the solenoid valve; The safety protection circuit mainly includes regulated power supply circuit, power monitoring circuit, fault memory circuit and relay drive circuit. The regulated power supply circuit converts the power supply voltage provided by vehicle storage battery or generator into the required stable voltage inside the ECU, and the power supply monitoring circuit monitors whether the power supply voltage is stable within the specified range; The fault memory circuit monitors the signals input to the ECU circuits (input circuit, arithmetic circuit and solenoid valve control circuit), and stores the detected faults in the memory in the form of DTCs so as to be retrieved when diagnosing faults; The relay drive circuit is actually an alarm circuit. When the fault memory circuit detects a fault, the alarm circuit drives the corresponding relay to cut off the ABS power supply circuit to make ABS stop working, the braking system switches to the normal braking mode, and lights up the ABS warning light to remind the driver of ABS failure.

3. Introduction to ECU Software

The software of the ABS electronic control unit mainly consists of anti-lock control and safety control. The anti-lock control is to sample, calculate and analyze the wheel speed signal pre-processed by input circuit, and form corresponding control command. The safety control is to monitor the working state of the system, store the fault conditions and shut down the system automatically.

XI. ABS Application Examples

ABS takes different forms, but is the same in two respects. On the one hand, the ABS working speed must reach a certain value before the anti-lock braking control adjustment is performed on the wheels which tend to lock up during the braking. On the other hand, the ABS has self-diagnosis function. Once the fault affecting the normal operation of the system occurs, the ABS will close automatically and the ABS warning light will light up at the same time, normal braking still works properly.

(Ⅰ) BOSCH ABS

1. Structural Features

The brake pressure regulator is separated and installed independently; the pressure regulating mode is circulating type; the control mode is that two front wheels are controlled independently and the two rear wheels are controlled together according to the principle of low selection; the solenoid valve is a three-position three-way solenoid valve.

2. Brake pressure regulating process

(1) Brake pressure increase

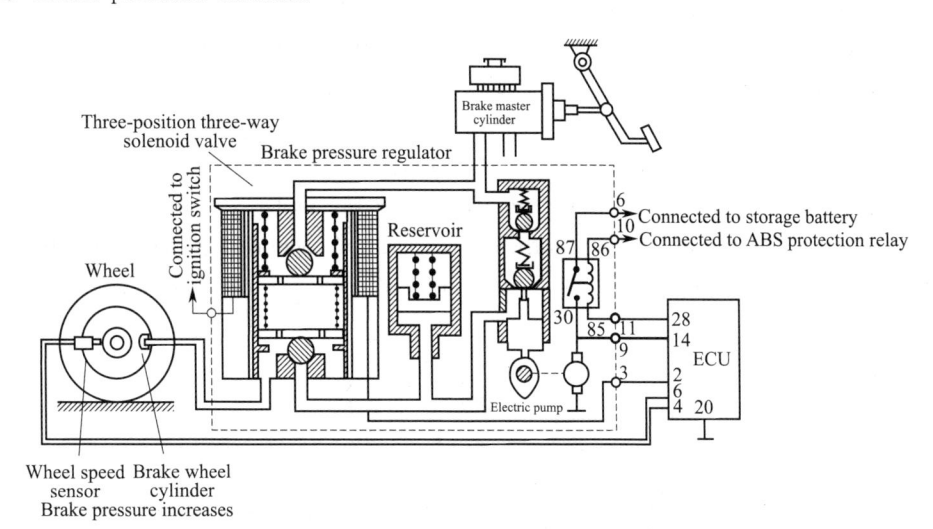

Fig. 1-58　Brake Pressure Increase Process

The increase process of brake pressure is shown in Fig. 1-58. Step on the brake pedal. As the inlet valve of the solenoid valve is opened and the return valve is closed, each solenoid valve will connect the passage between the brake master cylinder and each brake wheel cylinder. The brake fluid in the brake master cylinder will flow into each brake wheel cylinder through the inlet and outlet of each solenoid valve. The brake fluid pressure of each brake wheel cylinder will increase with the increase of brake fluid pressure output by brake master cylinder to realize the pressurization.

(2) Brake pressure holding

The brake pressure holding process is shown in Fig. 1-59. When the slip ratio is close to 20% during braking of a wheel, the ECU outputs a command to control the solenoid valve coil to close the inlet valve of the solenoid valve (the return valve is still closed) through a

Item Ⅰ　Maintenance of Automobile Electronic Control Active Safety System　**031**

small current (about 2A), so as to ensure that the brake pressure of the brake wheel cylinder in the control channel remains unchanged, thus realizing the pressure holding.

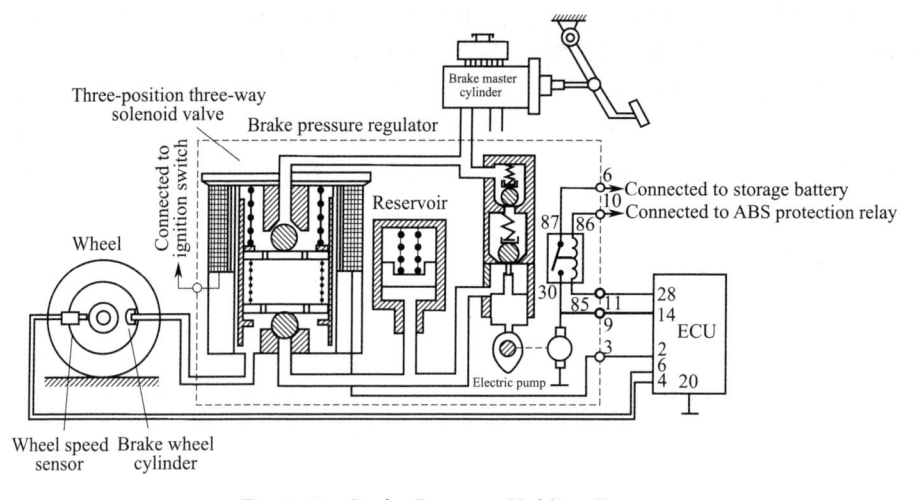

Fig. 1-59   Brake Pressure Holding Process

(3) Reduction of brake pressure

The brake pressure reduction process is shown in Fig. 1-60. When the slip ratio is greater than 20% during braking of a wheel, the ECU outputs a command to control the solenoid coil, to close the inlet valve of the solenoid valve through a large current (about 5A), and to open the return valve. The brake fluid in the brake wheel cylinder will flow into the reservoir through the return valve to reduce the brake pressure and realize the depressurization.

At the same time, the ECU controls the electric pump to operate with electricity to pump the brake fluid flowing into the reservoir back to the outlet of the brake master cylinder.

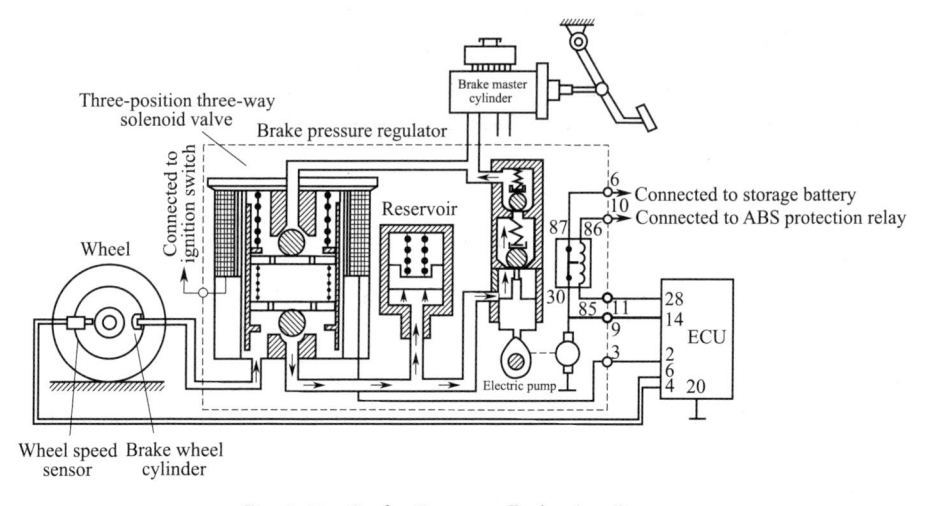

Fig. 1-60   Brake Pressure Reduction Process

3. Control process of electronic control system

The control process of the electronic control system shown in Fig. 1-61 is analyzed as follows.

(1) Turn on ignition switch, ECU enters self-check

ABS protection relay coil is energized: Battery voltage (12V) is sent to ECU terminal 1 via contact to trigger self-check for 3-5s. During self-check, ECU terminals 27 and 28 are not grounded, normally open contacts of electric pump relay and solenoid valve relay are not closed, electric pump and solenoid valve do not work.

(2) ABS warning light is on

There are two possible conditions when the ABS warning light is on: If the light is on for 3-5s and goes out, it indicates that the system is normal; if the light is on for 3-5s and does not go off, indicating that the system has fault. The ECU closes ABS, and the car only keeps normal braking.

(3) Self-check is normal, ABS waits for operation

ECU terminal 27 is grounded to turn on the solenoid relay coil circuit. The solenoid valve relay coil is energized, the iron core produces suction, normally closed contact (30→87A) is open, ABS warning light is off; normally open contact (30→87) is closed, battery voltage acts on three three-position three-way solenoid valve coils and ECU terminal 32.

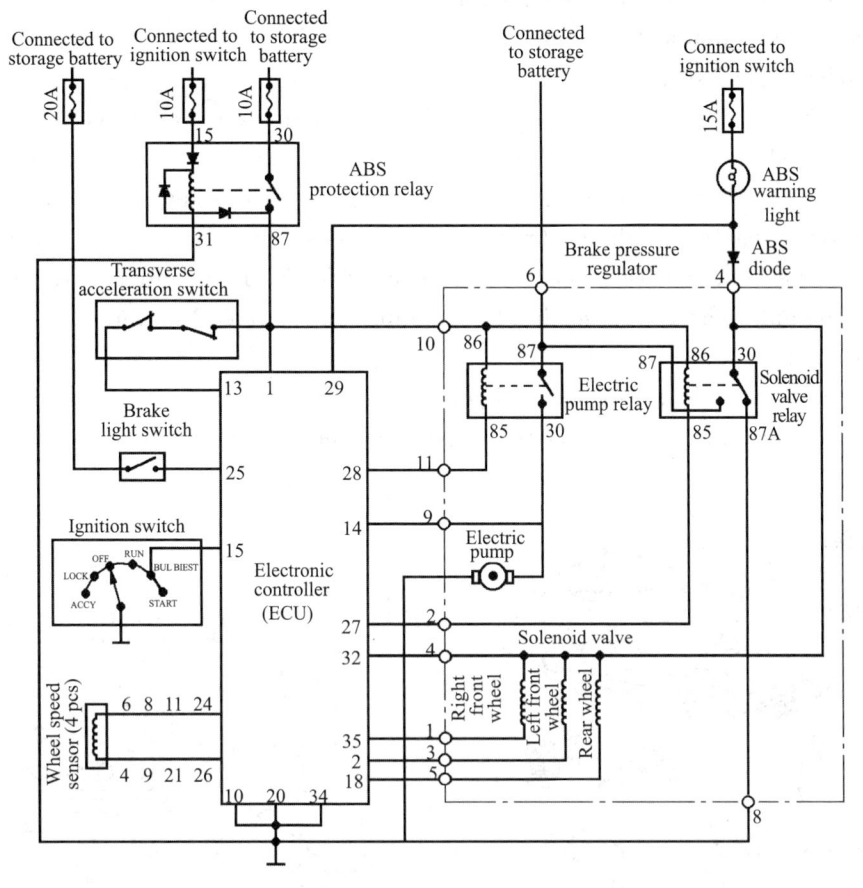

Fig. 1-61   BOSCH ABS Electronic Control System

(Ⅱ) TEVES MK20- Ⅰ ABS

TEVES MK20- Ⅰ ABS is a replacement product of TEVES MK Ⅱ ABS, which is a relatively new generation of ABS products in the world. The MK20- Ⅰ ABS used on SAN-

TANA 2000GSi car is taken as an example to illustrate its structural characteristics.

1. Structural features of MK20- I ABS

① Adopt modular structure design, integrate hydraulic control unit (reservoir, electric return pump, solenoid valve) and ECU into a whole to make its structure more compact.

② The solenoid valve coil is set inside the control unit to save connecting wires. The solenoid valve and return pump motor are directly driven by high-power integrated circuit, and the solenoid valve relay is omitted.

③ The ECU is equipped with fault memory, with fault diagnosis interface attached to the vehicle. The fault diagnosis can be conveniently carried out with the help of the DTC called by the scan tool.

④ MK20- I ABS adopts four-sensor and three-channel control system. Its control principle is to independently control the two front wheels and control the two rear wheels together according to the low selection principle.

The purpose is to ensure that the rear wheels do not lock before the front wheels during braking, so as to obtain good braking stability.

2. Main composition and structure

(1) Wheel speed sensor

SANTANA 2000GSi car is equipped with 4 magnetic induction wheel speed sensors, each wheel speed sensor is composed of sensor head and gear ring, as shown in Fig. 1-62.

The front wheel speed sensor ring gear (43 convex teeth) is embedded behind the brake disc and rotates together with the brake disc. The sensor head is mounted on the knuckle. The rear wheel speed sensor ring gear (43 convex teeth) is mounted on the hub and rotates with the hub, and the sensor head is mounted on the fixed bracket.

(2) Control module

The control module consists of a hydraulic control unit and an electronic control unit. The hydraulic control unit consists of reservoir, electric return pump, solenoid valve, etc, as shown in Fig. 1-63.

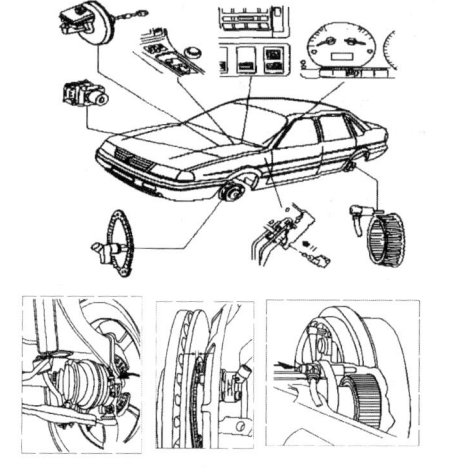

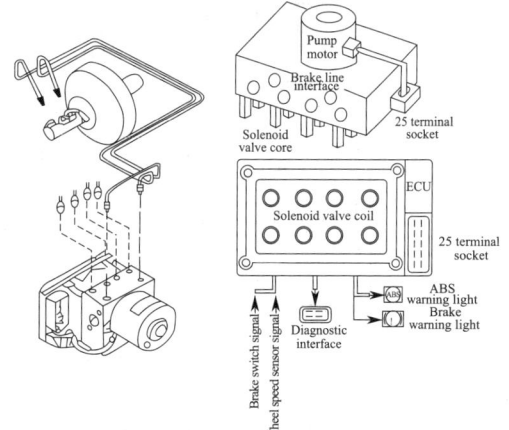

Fig. 1-62　Magnetic Induction Wheel Speed Sensor on SANTANA 2000GSi Car

Fig. 1-63　ABS Control Module of SANTANA 2000GSi Car

（3）Fault warning light

Two fault warning lights are installed on the instrument panel and the instrument panel accessories, one is ABS warning light（K47）and the other is brake device warning light（K118）.

After turning on the ignition switch, the ABS warning light turns off for about 2s, indicating that ABS has been started at the same time of self-check. If the ABS warning light is constantly on, it indicates that the ABS has failed.

3. Hydraulic control system

MK20-I ABS hydraulic control system adopted on SANTANA 2000GSi car is diagonal double circuit control system, as shown in Fig. 1-64.

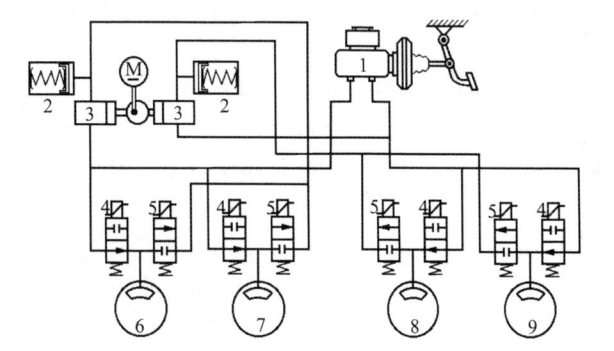

Fig. 1-64　MK20-I ABS Hydraulic Control System of SANTANA 2000GSi Car

 **Task Implementation**

I. Use and Maintenance of ABS

1. Use of ABS

（1）Some special phenomena easy to occur in vehicles equipped with ABS

① After the engine is started, there may be similar impact sound in the engine compartment.

② Some vehicles equipped with ABS will spring up when stepping on the brake pedal when the engine is started, but the brake pedal will sink when the engine stops.

③ When turning the steering wheel during braking, you will feel slight vibration of the steering wheel.

④ During braking, sometimes the brake pedal slightly sinks or vibrates, which is caused by frequent squeezing of high-pressure brake fluid when the brake wheel cylinder is retracted and released at high speed.

⑤ When driving at high speed and turning sharply, or driving on icy road, sometimes the brake warning light will be on.

⑥ When braking on the snowy road, the braking distance is sometimes long.

⑦ In the later stage of braking, the wheels of the vehicle equipped with ABS will also be locked, leaving a slippery mark on the ground, but it is different from that during conventional braking.

Item I　Maintenance of Automobile Electronic Control Active Safety System **035**

（2）Precautions for using vehicles equipped with ABS

① Keep enough braking distance.

② Do not step on the brake pedal repeatedly. When the brake pedal is depressed, the force applied to the brake pedal should be constant and stable.

③ When ABS is normal, hydraulic working noise and brake pedal vibration will be generated. This is normal. In case of emergency braking, the brake pedal shall be directly stepped on to the bottom without loosening.

④ Don't forget to control the steering wheel.

⑤ Pay attention to the ABS warning light on the instrument panel during driving. If it flashes or lights up for a long time, it means that ABS function is no longer available, but the conventional braking system still works, so you should go to the repair shop for maintenance as soon as possible.

⑥ Keep the sensor probe and the ring gear installed on the wheel clean.

⑦ The gas shall be filled strictly according to the specified tire pressure standard, and the pressure of coaxial tire shall be kept balanced. It is prohibited to use tires of different specifications.

⑧ ABS system has strict requirements for brake fluid. The brake fluid shall be added or replaced in strict accordance with the requirements in the vehicle operation manual, and it is prohibited to mix brake fluid of different models.

2. Matters needing attention when repairing ABS

① Failure of braking system is indicated by ABS warning light and brake device warning light. Sometimes the ABS warning light and the brake device warning light do not work, but the braking effect is still not ideal, the system may not be bled cleanly or there may be a malfunction in the normal braking system.

② In case of poor braking, firstly distinguish whether it is a mechanical fault or an ABS system fault. Identification method: Make the car work in the normal braking mode. If the poor braking fault disappears, it indicates ABS system fault; if the poor braking fault still exists, it is a mechanical fault.

③ After ABS fault is confirmed, the appearance of ABS shall be inspected first to check whether there is leakage of brake oil circuit, pump and valve, whether the terminal of wire and the connector are loose, and whether the battery is short of electricity. The fuse shall not be missed during line fault inspection.

④ If the appearance inspection is normal, check the DTC by fault scan tool or manual transfer to check the fault location.

⑤ Do not disassemble ECU and hydraulic control device easily. If it is suspected that there is any problem, replace it.

During disassembly and inspection of ABS hydraulic control device, pressure relief shall be carried out first to avoid personal injury caused by high pressure oil spurt. The pressure relief method is to turn off the ignition switch first and repeatedly step on the brake pedal for more than 20 times until the brake pedal force is obviously increased and becomes very hard.

⑥ Before starting maintenance, turn off the ignition switch and remove the negative wire from the battery. Pay particular attention that the ignition must be switched off before

pulling off the ABS electrical plug connection.

⑦ Before disassembly, thoroughly clean the connection point and support surface. Do not use gasoline, thinner and other similar cleaning agents during cleaning. The removed parts must be placed in a clean place and covered well.

⑧ After separating the ABS ECU from the hydraulic control unit, the hydraulic control unit must be placed on the special support to avoid damaging the valve body during transportation.

⑨ Do not use compressed air or move the vehicle after the brake system is opened.

⑩ If the removed parts cannot be repaired immediately, they must be carefully covered or sealed with plugs to ensure the cleanliness of the parts.

⑪ When replacing accessories, good quality accessories must be used. Accessories shall be removed from the package before installation.

⑫ Be sure to carry out installation and adjustment according to the requirements of the maintenance manual.

⑬ After repairing the ABS brake system, add brake fluid as required and bleed the system.

⑭ Emergency braking shall be carried out at least once during commissioning. When the ABS is working normally, a rebound is felt on the brake pedal, and a rapid and steady decrease in vehicle speed can be felt.

II. General Check Methods for ABS Faults

1. Inspection of vehicle speed sensor fault

(1) Fault phenomenon

In case that the wheel speed sensor breaks down, the sensor may not be damaged, the sensor head may be dirty, the air gap between sensor and ring gear may be too large or too small, or the sensor connector is loose.

(2) Inspection method

① Check the resistance value of the wheel speed sensor: Turn the ignition switch to OFF position; lift the car; remove the connectors of front and rear wheels and sensors respectively; according to the service manual of different vehicle models, use digital multimeter to check for abnormalities.

② Check the signal voltage of the wheel speed sensor: Lift the vehicle; place the ignition switch in the ON position; turn the wheel to be checked at a slow speed; check whether there is any problem with the digital multimeter corresponding to the service manual of different vehicle models. If there is any problem, replace it according to the requirements of the service manual of different models.

③ Check the ring gear of the wheel speed sensor: Check for deformation, broken teeth, soil, dirt, iron stone and other foreign matters blocking. Replace or clean according to different conditions.

2. Inspection of ECU

① Check whether ECU harness connector and connecting wire are loose.

② Check the voltage value, waveform or resistance of each terminal of ECU harness connec-

tor. If the voltage value and waveform or resistance are inconsistent with the standard values and the connected components and circuits are normal, replace the ECU and try again.

③ The replacement method is directly adopted for inspection, that is, if there is no fault of other components, the original ECU can be replaced by a new ECU. If the fault disappears, it is ECU fault.

3. Inspection of pressure regulator

(1) Common faults

Common faults of pressure regulator are bad coil of solenoid valve and leakage of valve.

(2) Inspection method

① Check the resistance of solenoid valve coil with ohmmeter. If the resistance is infinite or too small, the solenoid valve is faulty.

② Load the solenoid valve with its working voltage for test. If it fails to operate normally, replace it.

③ Check after disassembly.

4. Inspection of ABS control relay

(1) Common faults

Common faults of ABS control relay are poor contact of contact and bad coil of relay, etc.

(2) Inspection method

① Apply normal working voltage to the relay. If it can operate normally, then test the voltage and resistance between the relay contacts. Under normal circumstances, the voltage is zero when the contact is closed. The voltage is greater than 0.5V, indicating poor contact of the contact.

② The resistance of relay coil shall be within normal range.

Ⅲ. Adding and Supplementing ABS Brake Fluid

1. Requirement principles

① The brake fluid required by the manufacturer shall be selected.

② Brake fluid with oxidation resistance shall be selected.

③ Select the brake fluid with good lubrication effect on rubber parts, which shall not expand rubber parts.

④ The brake fluid with low corrosion to metal shall be selected.

⑤ The brake fluid with lower freezing point, higher boiling point and water absorption shall be selected, which must have good lubricating performance and adapt to the rubber and metal parts of hydraulic system.

2. Select brake fluid

For ABS brake fluid, DOT3 and DOT4 are generally selected. DOT5 silicon copper brake fluid cannot be used. Incorrect use of brake fluid may cause excessive wear of brake elements and other conditions.

3. Change interval of brake fluid

The brake fluid of the ABS system is recommended to be changed every two years.

Precaution: Check the fluid level in the brake fluid reservoir frequently. The liquid level

shall be between the maximum allowable level and the minimum level.

Ⅳ. Bleeding of ABS

1. Intuitive judgment of air permeated in ABS

If the brake pedal is pressed once, the brake pedal is weak. If the brake pedal is pressed for several times continuously, the brake pedal rises gradually, and the brake pedal feels very hard, which indicates that air is permeated into the ABS.

2. Hazard of air permeated in ABS

If there is air in the ABS, it will seriously interfere with the brake pressure regulation, so that the function of the ABS will be lost, resulting in the decrease of braking effect, slow braking response and even brake failure.

3. Bleeding of ABS

Bleed the ABS according to the regulations, and the bleeding sequence is as follows.

① Connect one end of the special rubber tube under a certain bleeding screw, and insert the other end into the glass bottle containing half bottle of brake fluid.

② Step on the brake pedal repeatedly, step on the brake pedal and hold it, open the bleeding screw of the brake wheel cylinder from far to near in sequence, and then tighten it immediately. There shall be bubbles in the glass bottle. Repeat this process for several times, with an interval of 2-5s each time until no bubble is generated in the glass bottle, and the brake pedal rises to the highest position (approximately flush with the accelerator pedal), as shown in Fig. 1-65.

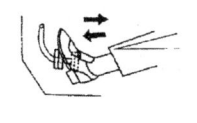 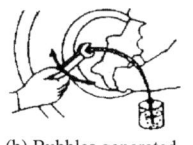 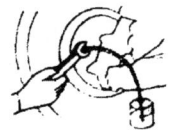

(a) Press the brake pedal repeatedly   (b) Bubbles generated   (c) No bubble generated

Fig. 1-65   Air Bleeding Process

③ Refill brake fluid.

4. Bleeding principle of ABS

The air bleeding principle of ABS is usually from far to near, from bottom to top, one wheel by one.

5. Bleeding sequence for ABS

The bleeding sequence is from the right rear wheel cylinder to the left rear wheel cylinder, from the left rear wheel cylinder to the right front wheel cylinder, and from the right front wheel cylinder to the left front wheel cylinder.

For example, the general procedure for bleeding Delco (Ⅵ) ABS is as follows.

① Find the front wheel bleeding screw.

② Install an oil drain pipe on the front wheel bleeding screw.

③ Slowly loosen the bleeding screw for 1/2-3/4 turn.

④ Brake fluid flows out. If there is no bubble, close it.

⑤ Find the rear wheel bleeding screw and perform bleeding according to the steps, as

shown in Fig. 1-66.

V. Fault Case Diagnosis Process of ABS

According to the fault phenomenon in the task data, firstly check the brake fluid level of the reservoir of ABS hydraulic regulator. If it is normal, set the ignition switch to OFF position, short-circuit the two ends of the diagnosis socket under the glove box, and then turn the ignition switch to ON position, read out the DTC, and no code is output.

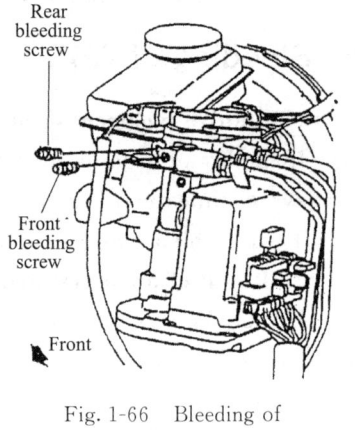

Fig. 1-66   Bleeding of
Delco (Ⅵ) ABS

Honda Accord ABS consists of ABS ECU, hydraulic regulator, wheel speed sensor, ABS warning light and diagnosis socket, etc. The hydraulic regulation adopts the variable volume principle. The hydraulic regulator is composed of oil pump, pressure accumulator, pressure switch, reservoir, 6 solenoid valves (3 input valves of inlet solenoid valves, 3 return solenoid valves) and 4 sliding piston groups. The inlet valve (input valve) is a normally closed solenoid valve and the return valve (output valve) is a normally open solenoid valve. During the whole braking process, the high-pressure oil produced by the oil pump does not communicate with the brake wheel cylinder. The pressure is regulated by the movement of the sliding piston. The movement of the sliding piston is controlled by the control piston, while the movement of the control piston is realized by the ECU commanding the solenoid valve to act to make the high-pressure oil enter or stop entering the lower of the control piston or return the high-pressure oil in the lower chamber of the control piston to the reservoir; in the normal braking state, the solenoid valve is not energized, and the pressure of the brake wheel cylinder rises with the pressure rise of the master cylinder; when both the inlet and return valves are energized, the pressure is reduced; when the inlet valve is powered off and closed, the pressure is maintained; ABS ECU determines whether the wheel is locked according to the signal from the wheel speed sensor, and then sends an command to the solenoid valve in the hydraulic regulator for anti-lock braking control. When the oil pressure is insufficient, the ABS ECU commands the oil pump motor to operate at the same time. The ABS ECU also monitors whether the ABS works normally through the brake light switch, hand brake light switch and pressure switch, and can conduct self-diagnosis.

Based on the above working principle, considering that the ABS oil pump motor runs for a long time after the vehicle is started each time, the ABS warning light lights up after the oil pump motor stops running. This suggests that there are two possibilities: Firstly, when the ABS oil pressure is insufficient during the initial startup, the oil pump motor runs and then starts after the engine shuts down, and the oil pump still needs to work, indicating that the oil pump failed to establish enough oil pressure for the system during the previous oil pump operation, which means that the oil pressure cannot be established when repeated starts are so; Secondly, the pressure switch can not be turned on when the oil pressure is high enough, the ABS ECU judges that the oil pressure is too low to make the oil pump operate for a long time after each engine start.

In order to determine whether the oil pressure is too low, unscrew the bleeding screw on the ABS hydraulic regulator and start the engine. At this time, the oil pump motor is running and only the oil column with a height of about 30mm can be ejected from the bleeding screw. After the oil pump works for a certain period of time, loosen the bleeding screw, and almost no oil flows out. Theoretically, the oil pump can generate pressure as high as about 20MPa, and there is a pressure accumulator, which can maintain enough oil pressure within a certain time even after the oil pump motor stops running. This condition indicates that the oil pressure is too low.

Observe that when the reservoir and the oil pump are running, no return oil be returned into the return port, but the inlet has backflow instead. The problem is most likely the inlet valve of the plunger oil pump itself or the plunger and plunger sleeve. Remove the hydraulic modulator assembly and disassemble the plunger pump. It is found that the steel ball and the valve seat of the inlet and outlet valves are worn, and the leather ring on the plunger is aging. Therefore, replace the plunger pump assembly, directly energize the oil pump motor and screw the bleeding screw. At this time, the oil column is discharged up to 200mm high. After reassembly, air shall be released, and the engine shall be started to eliminate the fault.

Originally, when the oil pressure of this type of ABS reaches the standard, the oil pump stops working. When the oil pressure is too low, the oil pump works. However, if the oil pressure is still insufficient after working for a certain period of time, the ABS ECU will command the oil pump to stop working and turn on the ABS warning light to warn the driver of ABS failure and repair. If such a malfunction occurs on a Honda car that is later shipped with this ABS, it is generally possible to read DTC 10.

Exercises

Choice questions

1. When the slip ratio is 100%, the lateral adhesion coefficient decreases to ( ) .
A. 100%　　　　　B. 50%　　　　　C. 0　　　　　D. They are all wrong.

2. To avoid dust and splashing water and mud affecting the operation of the sensor, fill the speed sensor before installation with ( ) .
A. Engine oil　　　B. Operating fluid　　C. Grease　　　D. ATF oil

3. The circulating brake pressure regulator is to install a solenoid valve between the brake master cylinder and the wheel cylinder in ( ), which directly controls the brake pressure of the wheel cylinder.
A. series connection　　　　　　　B. parallel connection
C. A and B are all correct　　　　　D. Neither is correct

Task Ⅱ Maintenance of Automobile Acceleration Slip Regulation

〔Learning Objectives〕

Knowledge requirements: Understand the function, composition, principle and main-

tenance method of ASR.

Capability requirements: Be able to perform basic inspection on ASR and diagnose and repair common faults of ASR by using common tools and measuring tools according to maintenance manual.

Task Import

Crown 3.0 sedan, ASR fault light on instrument panel is on normally. Through understanding, the fault phenomenon appears after the vehicle has been driven for a period of time, and the ASR fault light will be on at the same time; turn off the ignition switch and restart, the ASR fault light on the instrument panel will be off again; however, the ASR fault light will be on again after driving for a certain distance.

Knowledge Preparation

Ⅰ. Overview

1. Comparison between ASR and ABS

Both ABS and ASR are used to control the slip of the wheel relative to the ground to improve the adhesion between the wheel and the ground. However, ABS controls the "slip" of the wheels during braking, which is mainly used to improve the braking efficiency and the direction stability of the vehicle during braking, while ASR is to control the "slip" of the driving wheels when the vehicle is running, which is used to improve the traction force and ensure the driving stability when the vehicle starts, accelerates and runs on smooth road.

ASR can also control the sliding of the driving wheel relative to the ground by controlling the braking force of the wheel just like ABS, but ASR only controls the braking of the driving wheel.

ABS generally does not work at very low speeds (<5km/h), while ASR generally does not work at very high speeds (80-120km/h).

2. Slip Ratio and Its Relationship with the Adhesion Coefficient

During driving, the driving wheels may slip relative to the road surface. There is a close relationship between the slip ratio and the adhesion coefficient. Fig. 1-67 shows the relationship curve between the slip ratio and the adhesion coefficient. It can be seen from the figure that:

① Same as the slip ratio of the car during braking, the adhesion coefficient between the wheel and the road surface changes with the change of the slip ratio during the driving process of the vehicle.

② The adhesion coefficient varies greatly with the road surface. On dry or wet roads, the wheel has the maximum adhesion coefficient when the slip ratio is about 20%.

These trends are almost the same whether braking or driving. Therefore, ASR can also control the adhesion coefficient between the driving wheel and the road surface by controlling the slip ratio between them, so as to realize the anti-slip control during the driving process, so as to maintain the vehicle handling stability and the best driving performance during the

042 Automotive Safety and Comfort System Maintenance

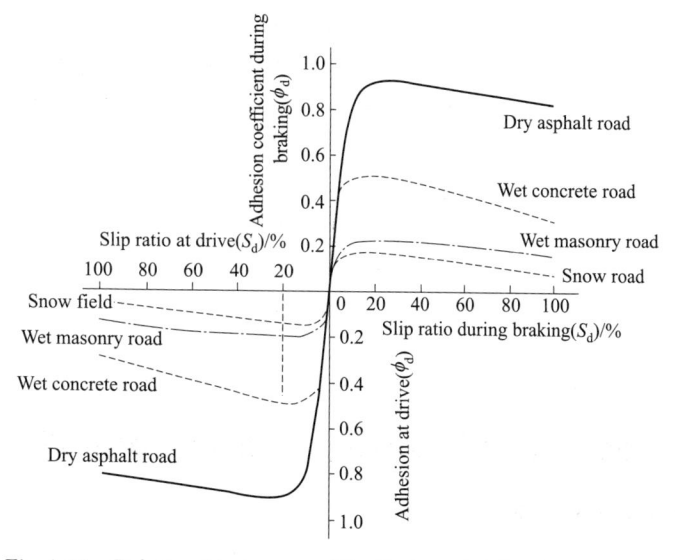

Fig. 1-67   Relationship between Slip Ratio and Adhesion Coefficient

driving process.

3. The role of ASR

Acceleration Slip Regulation (ASR) is an electronic control system used for anti-slip after ABS. ASR is used to prevent the slip of driving wheels when the vehicle starts, accelerates and runs on smooth road.

When the wheel rotates but the body does not move or the speed of the car is lower than the wheel rim speed, there is relative slip between the tire and the ground. This kind of slip is called "slip", so as to distinguish from the wheel "slip" caused by wheel lock during braking. Only driving wheels produce "slip" and all wheels (including driving and driven wheels) may "slip".

4. Types of ASR

ASR can be divided into differential braking control, engine output power control, integrated control of differential braking control and engine output power.

(1) Differential braking control

When the driving wheel slips unilaterally, the control computer outputs a control signal to make the differential brake valve and the brake pressure regulator act to apply braking force to the slip wheel to control the slip ratio of the wheel within the target range. At this time, the non-slip wheels still have normal driving force, thus improving the vehicle's starting and accelerating ability on slippery road surface as well as the stability of driving direction.

This control mode functions like a differential lock. When the driving wheel on the one side gets stuck in a mud pit or loses its driving ability completely, after braking, the driving wheel on the other side can still exert its driving force, so that the car can drive away from the mud pit. When the driving wheels on both sides slip, but the slip ratio is different braking force will be applied to the driving wheels on both sides.

(2) Engine output power control

If the accelerator pedal is pressed too hard when the vehicle starts and accelerates, the driv-

Item I   Maintenance of Automobile Electronic Control Active Safety System   **043**

ing wheels on both sides will slip due to too large driving force. At this time, the ASR control computer outputs a control signal to control the power output of the engine to restrain the slip of the driving wheels. Engine power control can be realized by changing the opening degree of throttle, adjusting fuel quantity of fuel injector and changing ignition time.

（3）Integrated control of differential braking and engine output power

ASR adopts the integrated control system combining differential braking control and engine output power control, and the control effect is more ideal. In the course of automobile driving, the road slippery condition is very different, the driving force status is also constantly changing, the integrated control system can take corresponding control measures according to the condition of engine and the actual situation of wheel slip.

Ⅱ. Basic Composition and Working Principle of ASR

1. Basic composition of ASR

The basic composition of ASR is shown in Fig. 1-68.

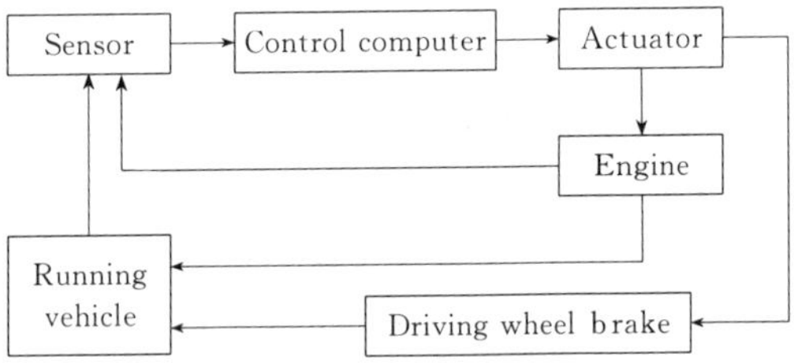

2. Working principle of ASR

ASR, also known as TCS (Traction Control System) or TRC, prevents the driving wheel from slipping during driving by regulating the driving torque and braking torque of the driving wheel.

The adjustment of the driving torque to the driving wheel can be realized by adjusting the

Fig. 1-68　Basic Composition of ASR

output torque of the engine, transmission ratio, differential locking coefficient, etc. At present, the methods of adjusting transmission ratio and differential locking coefficient are seldom used in ASR, but the output torque of engine can be realized by adjusting opening degree of throttle, ignition advance angle, fuel injection amount and interrupting fuel injection and ignition. Because the engine has been electronically controlled, the ignition and fuel supply of the engine can be controlled by the engine electronic control system, and then the output torque of the engine can be adjusted. At present, in ASR, the output torque of the engine is usually adjusted by controlling the opening degree of throttle and the ignition advance angle, so as to adjust the driving torque acting on the driving wheel.

Generally speaking, ASR can be realized by applying a certain braking torque to the driving wheel to reduce the rotational speed of the driving wheel quickly or to obtain different traction force on both driving wheels. In ASR, the wheel speed signal can be obtained by using the wheel speed sensor in ABS to determine whether the driving wheel is slipping or not. The ASR electronic control unit can be either stand alone or shared with ABS. The brake pressure regulator of ASR is commonly shared with the brake pressure regulator of ABS. In order to control the throttle opening degree, an electrically controlled auxiliary throttle and a throttle opening sensor are usually provided. The ignition advance angle is controlled by the engine electronic control system. Therefore, ASR is usually interwoven with ABS and engine electronic control system, and ASR also has ASR off indicator and ASR working indicator.

Fig. 1-69 shows a typical ABS/ASR anti-slip control system with both anti-lock braking and anti-slip functions. The ASR and ABS share the wheel speed sensor and electronic control unit. Only one ASR brake pressure regulator is added in the brake pipeline leading to the brake wheel cylinder of the driving wheel, an auxiliary throttle controlled by a stepping motor is added above the main throttle controlled by the accelerator pedal, and a throttle opening sensor is set at the main throttle and the auxiliary throttle, respectively, so that the anti-slip control can be realized.

For ASR in ABS/ASR shown in Fig. 1-69 during vehicle driving, the ABS/ASR electronic control unit determines the slip ratio of the driving wheel and the reference speed of the vehicle according to the wheel speed signal generated by each wheel speed sensor. When the ABS/ASR electronic control unit determines that the slip ratio of the driving wheel exceeds the set limit value, it turns the stepping motor driving the auxiliary throttle to reduce the opening degree of the auxiliary throttle. At this time, even if the opening degree of the main throttle does not change, the intake air amount of the engine decreases due to the decrease of the opening degree of the auxiliary throttle, so that the output torque of the engine decreases, and the driving torque on the driving wheel decreases accordingly. If the slip ratio of the driving wheel still does not decrease to the set control range, the ABS/ASR electronic control unit will control the ASR brake pressure regulator and ABS brake pressure device, apply certain brake pressure to the driving wheel, and the braking torque will act on the driving wheel.

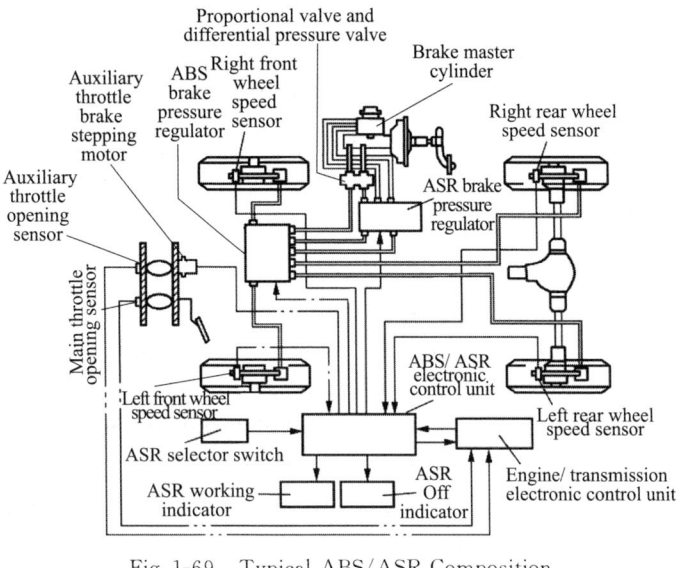

Fig. 1-69   Typical ABS/ASR Composition

The ASR brake pressure regulator in ABS/ASR shown in Fig. 1-70 mainly includes braking energy supply device and electromagnetic control valve assembly. The braking energy supply device is mainly composed of electric pump and accumulator, and the electromagnetic control valve assembly is mainly composed of three two-position two-way solenoid valves. They together with the ASR brake pressure regulator form the brake hydraulic system.

When the ABS/ASR electronic control unit determines that it is necessary to apply a

braking torque to the driving wheel, the ABS/ASR electronic control unit energizes the three two-position two-way solenoid valves in the ASR brake pressure regulator, the solenoid valve Ⅲ closes the brake pipeline from the brake master cylinder to the rear brake wheel cylinder, the solenoid valve Ⅱ connects the brake pipeline from the accumulator to the ABS brake pressure regulator, and the solenoid valve Ⅰ connects the brake pipeline from the ABS brake pressure regulator to the reservoir.

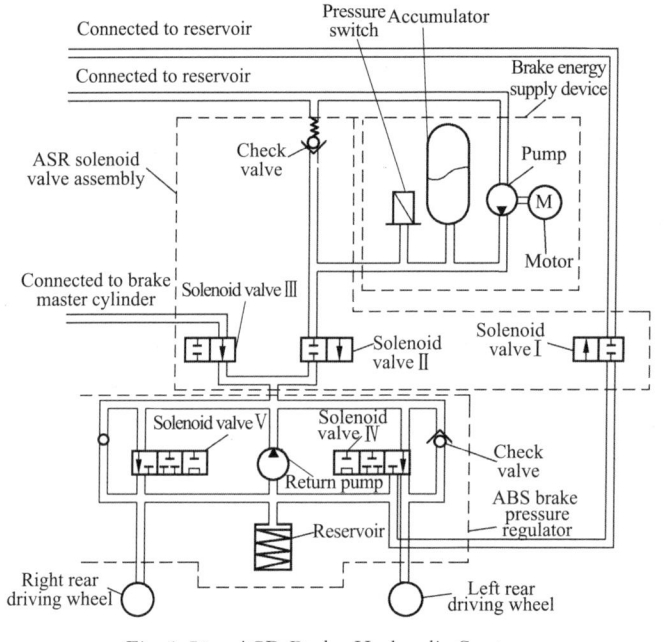

Fig. 1-70　ASR Brake Hydraulic System

The brake fluid with a certain pressure in the accumulator will enter the two rear brake wheel cylinders through the open solenoid valve Ⅱ and the solenoid valves Ⅳ and Ⅴ. The braking torque of the driving wheel increases with the increase of the brake pressure of the brake wheel cylinder. When the ABS/ASR electronic control unit determines that it is necessary to maintain the braking torque of the two driving wheels, the ABS/ASR electronic control unit makes the electromagnetic coils of the two three-position two-way solenoid valves Ⅳ and Ⅴ in the ABS brake pressure regulator pass a small current, so that the solenoid valves Ⅳ and Ⅴ are in the middle position, the inlet and outlet pipelines of the two rear brake wheel cylinders are closed, and the brake pressure of the two rear brake wheel cylinders is kept constant. When the ABS/ASR electronic control unit determines that it is necessary to reduce the braking torques of the two driving wheels, the electromagnetic coils of the solenoid valves Ⅳ and Ⅴ will pass a large current. The solenoid valves Ⅳ and Ⅴ respectively seal the inlet pipelines of the two rear brake wheel cylinders, and connect the outlet pipelines of the two rear brake wheel cylinders, and the brake fluid in the two rear brake wheel cylinders will flow back to the reservoir of the brake master cylinder through the solenoid valves Ⅳ and Ⅴ and the solenoid valve Ⅰ, and the brake pressure of the two rear brake wheel cylinders will be reduced. In the ASR brake pressure regulation process, ABS/ASR electronic control unit continuously monitors the movement state of the driving wheel according to the

046　Automotive Safety and Comfort System Maintenance

wheel speed signal input by the wheel speed sensor. By controlling the energization condition of solenoid valves IV and V, the brake pressure of the rear brake wheel cylinder is increased-maintained-decreased cyclically, so that the slip ratio of the driving wheel is controlled within the set ideal range. If that ABS/ASR electronic control unit determine that the braking torque of the two driving wheels need to be controlled differently, the ABS/ASR electronic control unit respectively controls the solenoid valves IV and V, so that the brake pressure of the two rear brake wheel cylinders is independently regulated.

When the ABS/ASR electronic control unit determines that anti-slip control is not required for the driving wheel, the ABS/ASR electronic control unit disenergizes each solenoid valve and returns each solenoid valve to the state shown in Fig. 1-70. The brake fluid in the rear brake wheel cylinder flows back to the brake master cylinder through the solenoid valves IV and V and the solenoid valve III, so that the braking torque of the driving wheel will be completely eliminated. At the same time, the ABS/ASR electronic control unit also controls the stepping motor to rotate to fully open the auxiliary throttle.

At present, the specific structures and working processes of ASR on different models are different, but they are the same in the following aspects.

① ASR can be selected by the driver through ASR selector switch whether it enters the working state. When ASR adjusts anti-slip, ASR working indicator will be on automatically. If ASR is turned off through ASR selector switch, ASR off indicator will be on automatically.

② When ASR is closed, auxiliary throttle will be in full open position automatically; ASR brake pressure regulator will not affect normal operation of the braking system.

③ If the driver steps on the brake pedal to brake during the anti-slip adjustment process of ASR, ASR will automatically exit the anti-slip adjustment process without affecting the braking process.

④ ASR usually adjusts the anti-slip rotation only within a certain speed range. When the vehicle speed reaches a certain value (such as 120km/h or 80km/h), ASR will automatically exit the anti-slip regulation process.

⑤ ASR usually has different priority selectivity within its working speed range, and at low vehicle speed, it is preferred to improve traction force. At this time, the braking torques applied to the two driving wheels can be different, i. e. the brake pressure of the two rear brake wheel cylinders is adjusted independently. When the vehicle speed is relatively high, it is preferred to improve the stability of the driving direction. In this case, the braking torques applied to the two driving wheels will be the same, that is, the brake pressure of the two rear brake wheel cylinders shall be adjusted together.

⑥ ASR has self-diagnosis function. Once there is any fault affecting the normal operation of the system, ASR will close automatically and send a warning signal to the driver.

III. Typical ASR System Structure

1. Structural characteristics of Toyota ASR System

ASR is called TRC in Toyota car system, and Toyota ABS/TRC anti-slip control system has the function of anti-lock braking and anti-slip driving. During the braking process, the anti-lock brake pressure of the four control channels is adjusted by means of circulating

pressure regulation. During the driving process, the anti-slip driving control is carried out by adjusting the opening of the throttle and braking the driving wheels.

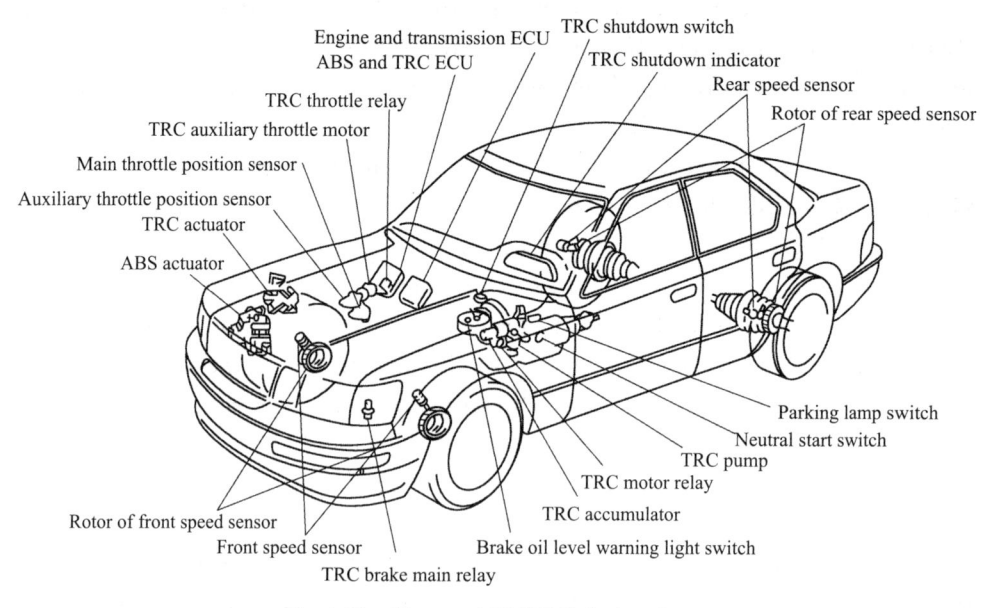

Fig. 1-71   Toyota ABS/TRC Composition

Toyota ABS/TRC mainly consists of wheel speed sensor, ABS/TRC electronic control unit, brake pressure regulator, TRC isolation solenoid valve assembly, TRC brake energy supply assembly, main and auxiliary throttle opening sensor, auxiliary throttle control stepping motor, etc., as shown in Fig. 1-71. Toyota ABS/TRC is equipped with an electromagnetic induction wheel speed sensor on each of the four wheels, which inputs the speed signal of each wheel into the ABS/TRC electronic control unit.

2. Working principle of TOYOTA TRC

During the driving process, if the ABS/TRC electronic control unit determines that the slip ratio of the driving wheel exceeds the control threshold value according to the wheel speed signal input by the wheel speed sensor, the ABS/TRC anti-slid control system enters into the driving anti-slip control process. The ABS/TRC electronic control unit will make the auxiliary throttle control stepping motor turn on, reduce the opening of the auxiliary throttle, reduce the air intake into the engine and reduce the output torque of the engine. When the ABS/TRC electronic control unit determines that it is necessary to brake the driving wheel, three isolation solenoid valves in the TRC isolation solenoid valve assembly will be energized to make the isolation solenoid valve of the brake master cylinder in a cut-off state, while the accumulator isolation solenoid valve and the reservoir isolation solenoid valve will be in flow state, and the brake fluid with pressure in the accumulator will enter the rear brake wheel cylinder, and the brake pressure of the rear brake wheel cylinder will increase accordingly. During the driving anti-slip braking, the ABS/TRC electronic control unit can increase, maintain and decrease the brake pressure of the two rear brake wheel cylinders by independently controlling the passing current of the two rear pressure regulating solenoid valves as in the case of anti-lock brake control.

Task Implementation

Ⅰ. Troubleshooting of ASR

1. Precautions for ASR overhaul

At present, most acceleration slip regulation have high working reliability, which usually does not require regular special maintenance. However, in the process of use, maintenance and overhaul, the following aspects shall be paid special attention to.

① When the ignition switch is in the ignition position, do not disassemble the electrical components and harness plugs in the system to avoid damaging the electronic control unit. Disconnect the ignition switch when removing and disassembling the electrical components and harness plugs in the system.

② Do not supply too high voltage to the electronic control unit, otherwise it will be easy to damage the electronic control unit. Therefore, do not start the engine with the charger, and do not charge the storage battery when it is connected with the electric appliance of the automobile.

③ The electronic control unit is also easy to be damaged by collision and knocking. Therefore, pay attention to prevent the electronic control unit from collision and knocking.

④ The electronic control unit is also easy to be damaged in high-temperature environment. Therefore, the electronic control unit shall be removed from the vehicle when painting the automobile. Also remove the harness plugs from the electronic control unit when welding electrical components or wiring in the system.

⑤ Do not let oil stain the electronic control unit, especially the terminal of the electronic control unit, otherwise the harness plug will be in poor contact and affect the normal operation of the system. Do not sandpaper the terminal of each plug in the system as this may cause poor contact.

⑥ When the storage battery voltage is too low, the system cannot enter into the working state. Therefore, pay attention to check the voltage of the storage battery, especially when the vehicle is started for the first time after long-term standstill.

⑦ Do not stain the wheel speed sensor and sensor ring gear with oil stain or other dirt; otherwise, the wheel speed signal generated by the wheel speed sensor may not be accurate enough, affecting the control accuracy of the system or even making the system unable to work normally. In addition, do not knock the speed sensor; otherwise, it is easy to cause demagnetization of the sensor, which will affect the normal operation of the system.

⑧ Since many braking systems with anti-slid braking function have accumulators to supply energy required for anti-lock brake pressure regulation, the high-pressure brake fluid in the accumulator shall be completely released to avoid personal injury caused by high-pressure brake fluid spouting during maintenance of the hydraulic system of such braking system. To release the high-pressure brake fluid from the accumulator, switch off the ignition, then repeatedly depress and release the brake pedal until the brake pedal becomes very hard. In addition, the ignition switch shall not be switched on until the brake hydraulic sys-

Item Ⅰ Maintenance of Automobile Electronic Control Active Safety System **049**

tem is fully installed to prevent the electric pump from being energized.

⑨ The special pipeline shall be used for the braking system with anti-slid control function, because the braking system often has very high pressure, and it is easy to be damaged if the non-special pipeline is used.

⑩ Wheel speed sensors, electronic control units and brake pressure regulators in most acceleration slip regulation are non-repairable and should be replaced as a whole if damaged.

⑪ After maintenance of the brake hydraulic system, or if the brake pedal is found to be soft during use, air shall be removed from the brake system in the required method and sequence.

⑫ Tyres recommended by automobile manufacturers shall be selected as much as possible. If tyres of other models are to be used, tyres with similar outer diameter, adhesion performance and moment of inertia shall be selected, but tyres of different specifications shall not be mixed, as this will affect the control effect of the anti-slid control system.

2. Reading and Clearing ASR Fault Codes

(1) Self-diagnosis and fail-safe function of the system

Most acceleration slip regulation have self-diagnosis and fail-safe function. When the ignition switch is in ignition position, the electronic control unit will automatically perform static test on itself, wheel speed sensor, electric components (such as solenoid valve, motor) and relay in the brake pressure regulator. During this period, the anti-lock warning light (or including the anti-slip warning light) will be on automatically, so that the anti-lock warning light and its wiring can be checked for faults. The duration of static self-test of the system is very short, generally only 3-5s. During the self-test, if the electronic control unit finds any fault in the system, the electronic control unit will store the memorized fault condition in the form of DTC, the anti-lock braking warning light will be on continuously, the anti-slid control system will not enter the working state, and the braking system of the car will be restored to the normal braking system. If the electronic control unit does not find a fault in the system during the self-test, the anti-lock warning light will automatically turn off after the self-test.

When the vehicle speed reaches a certain value, such as 5km/h or 8km/h, the electronic control unit of the acceleration slip regulation also needs to dynamically test some electrical components in the system (such as wheel speed sensor, solenoid valve and electric pump, etc.). During dynamic test, if any fault is found in the system, the electronic control unit will store the fault in the form of DTC, memorize the fault condition, and keep the anti-lock warning light on, and the braking system will be restored to the normal braking system.

In addition, the electronic control unit monitors the electrical components in the system during the working state of the system to check whether there is any fault in the system. Once a fault is found in the system, the electronic control unit will store the fault condition of the system in the form of DTC, and make the system exit from the working state, and the anti-lock warning light will be on continuously.

In a word, when the anti-lock warning light is on continuously, it indicates that the system has exited the working state due to fault, and the fault has been memorized in the

form of DTC. However, not all faults in the system can be detected by the electronic control unit, so it is necessary to check the system even if the anti-lock warning light does not turn on continuously, but the system is found to operate abnormally.

(2) Fault scan tools

In most acceleration slip regulation, the DTC can be read based on the flashing of the anti-lock warning light (or LED on the electronic control unit) by bridging the appropriate terminal in the diagnosis socket. Therefore, when reading DTCs, appropriate jumper wires are often required. A jumper wire is a section of wire with plug-in terminals at both ends, and some jumper wires are provided with fuse tubes in the middle, as shown in Fig. 1-72.

The DTC is only a series of numbers representing the fault condition. To know the fault condition exactly, it is also necessary to check the fault condition represented by the DTC according to the maintenance manual. In addition, the maintenance manual is also required to properly troubleshooting the system and is the most important tool in the process of fault diagnosis and maintenance.

When checking the acceleration slip regulation, a multimeter is a basic testing tool. Because the pointer multimeter can reflect the dynamic change of electrical parameters, it is more suitable for the circuit inspection of the anti-slid control system. In addition, some more special electrical parameter testing instruments (such as multi-trace oscilloscope, etc.) can also be used to more conveniently and deeply inspect the system.

In most cars, the terminals of the electronic control unit in the acceleration slip regulation are not labeled, which makes it difficult to determine the terminals to be tested, especially when voltage is applied to certain terminals. If the voltage is applied incorrectly, some electrical components in the system may be damaged. In addition, if the system is tested directly from the terminals of the harness plugs, it will not only affect the accuracy of test results, but also may cause deformation or damage to the terminals. For this purpose, the terminal box shown in Fig. 1-73 can be used. Because the number of terminals, terminal number arrangement and plug type in harness plugs of various acceleration slip regulation are different, the terminal boxes used are different.

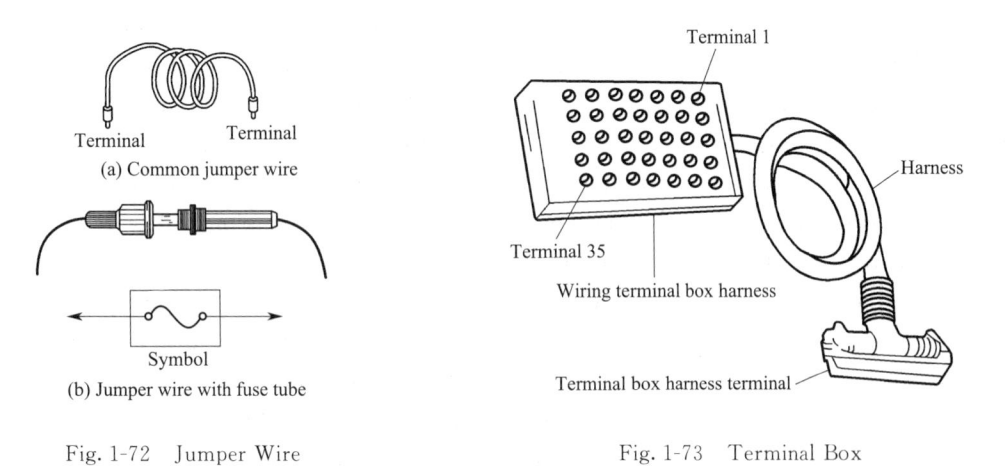

Fig. 1-72 Jumper Wire

Fig. 1-73 Terminal Box

As shown in Fig. 1-74, during the circuit test of the acceleration slip regulation, remove the harness plug of the system from the electronic control unit, and plug the harness

plug of the terminal box with the harness plug of the system, so that the terminal number on the terminal box corresponds to the terminal number in the system harness plug. Testing the terminals on the terminal box is equivalent to testing the corresponding terminals in the system harness plug.

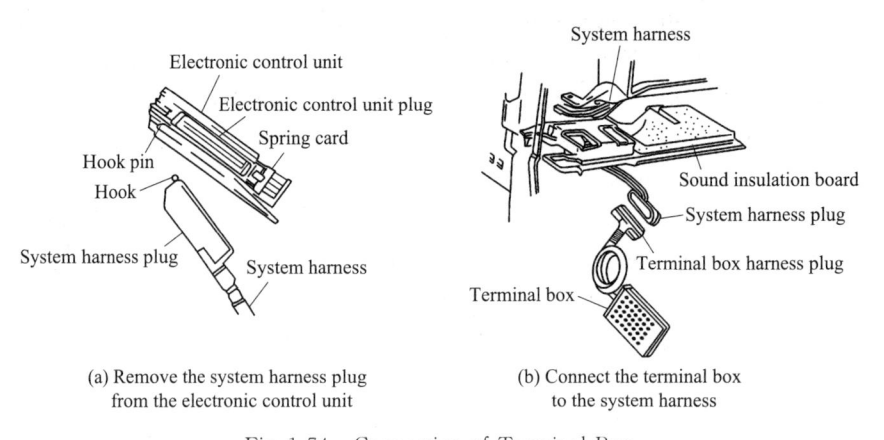

(a) Remove the system harness plug from the electronic control unit

(b) Connect the terminal box to the system harness

Fig. 1-74　Connection of Terminal Box

When checking the hydraulic unit of the acceleration slip regulation, it is sometimes necessary to use a pressure gauge, as shown in Fig. 1-75.

When fault diagnosis of the acceleration slip regulation is carried out, various diagnostic test instruments can also be used, and some systems can diagnose faults only by using special diagnostic test instruments. Special diagnostic test instruments can be divided into two categories, one of which can replace the electronic control unit of the system to check and simulate the working conditions of the system. Such instruments include ABS diagnostic tester shown in

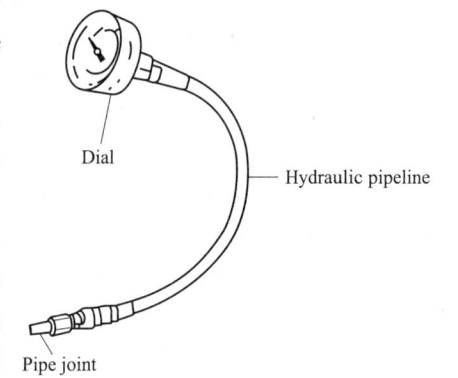

Fig. 1-75　Pressure Gauge

Fig. 1-76(a) and Toyota ABS diagnostic tester shown in Fig. 1-76(b), the other of which needs to read the fault information through two-way communication with the electronic control unit of the system. The electronic control unit of the system can read and decode the DTC, which is generally called decoder, as shown in Fig. 1-76(c) . The decoder can not only diagnose the acceleration slip regulation, but also can diagnose and test some other electronic control systems of the automobile just by choosing corresponding software.

(3) General steps for troubleshooting

When the warning light of the acceleration slip regulation (including anti-lock braking warning light and anti-slid warning light) is on continuously, or if the anti-slid control system is not working normally, troubleshooting shall be carried out timely for the system. In order to achieve good results, certain steps should be followed in troubleshooting. The general steps for troubleshooting are as follows.

① Confirm the fault condition and symptom.

② Visually inspect the system to check whether there are brake fluid leakage, wire

052　Automotive Safety and Comfort System Maintenance

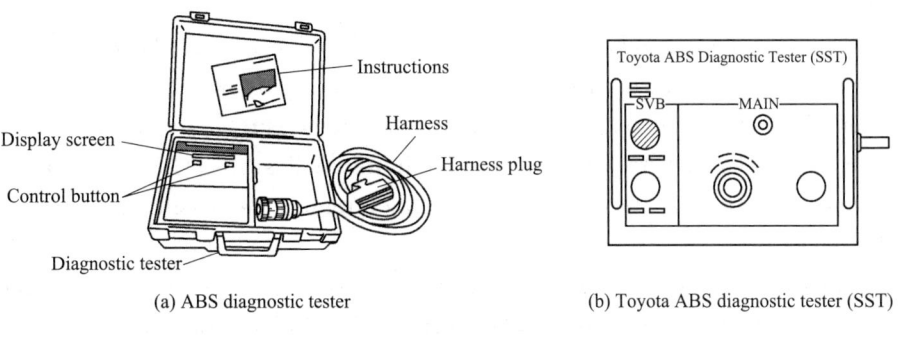

(a) ABS diagnostic tester   (b) Toyota ABS diagnostic tester (SST)

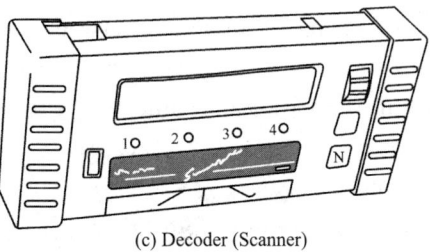

(c) Decoder (Scanner)

Fig. 1-76　Special Diagnostic Test Instruments

damage, plug loosening and low brake fluid level.

③ Read the DTC directly by the decoder or by the warning light, and then find out the fault condition represented by the DTC according to the maintenance manual.

④ According to the read fault situation, use necessary tools and instruments to conduct in-depth inspection on the fault position, and confirm the fault location and cause.

⑤ Eliminate the fault.

⑥ Clear the DTC.

⑦ Check whether the warning light is still on continuously. If the warning light is still on, it may be that there is still a fault in the system or that the fault has been eliminated but the DTC has not been cleared.

⑧ After the warning light is no longer on continuously, make a test drive to confirm whether the system recovers to normal operation.

In the process of fault diagnosis and maintenance, it should be noted that not only different models of cars may be equipped with different acceleration slip regulation, but also even cars of the same model may be equipped with different acceleration slip regulation due to different production years.

Most failures of the acceleration slip regulation are caused by loose or poor contact of wiring plug, open or short circuit of wire, open or short circuit of solenoid coil of solenoid valve, open or short circuit of electric pump circuit, open or short circuit of electromagnetic coil of wheel speed sensor, internal open or short circuit of relay, as well as abnormal operation of brake switch, liquid level switch and pressure switch, etc. In addition, too low battery voltage, too large clearance between wheel speed sensor and ring gear or dirt contamination, too low liquid level in reservoir may affect the normal operation of the system.

3. Maintenance of the main components of ASR

The following takes Toyota cars as an example to introduce the maintenance of the main

components of ASR.

Fault diagnosis of main relay circuit. Diagnostic Trouble Codes (DTC) are 11 and 12 when an open or short circuit occurs in the TRC main relay circuit.

① When TRC computer outputs ON signal to main relay, if the voltage of computer terminals SRC, SMC and SAC are 0V, the computer will store DTC 11, indicating that there is an open circuit fault in the TRC main relay circuit. The possible causes of the fault are as follows.

a. Poor TRC main relay (contact cannot be closed or contact is in poor contact).

b. Poor or loose wiring or connector between the TRC main relay and the computer.

c. Poor contact or loose of wiring or connector between the TRC main relay and the TRC brake pressure regulator.

d. Poor contact or loose in the wiring or connector between the TRC main relay and the battery.

e. Fault of the TRC computer.

② When the TRC computer does not output ON signal to the main relay, if the voltage of any one of the computer terminals SRC, SMC and SAC is battery voltage, the computer will store DTC 12, indicating that there is a short circuit fault in the circuit of the TRC main relay. The possible causes of the fault are as follows.

a. Poor TRC main relay (contact cannot open or the coil is short-circuited to the power supply).

b. Short circuit between the wiring and connector between the TRC main relay and the TRC brake pressure regulator and the power supply circuit.

c. Fault of the TRC computer.

③ The TRC main relay circuit is shown in Fig. 1-77, and the inspection method is as follows.

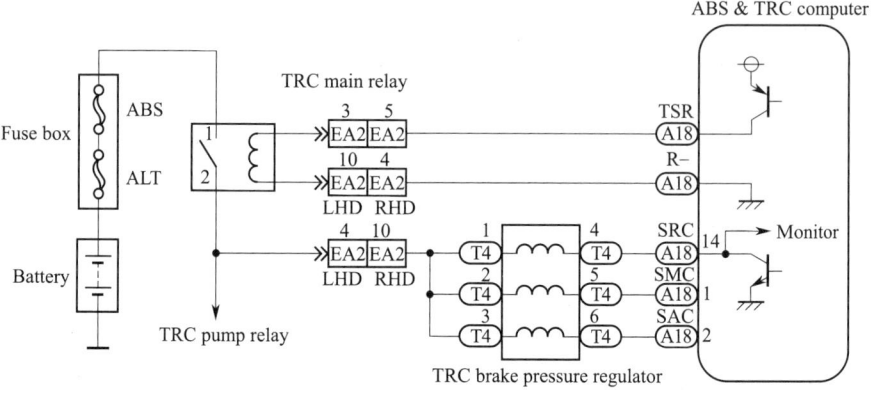

Fig. 1-77　TRC Main Relay Circuit

a. Check the voltage at the TRC main relay power terminal. Remove the TRC main relay connector. When the ignition switch is turned on, measure the voltage between No. 1 terminal of the TRC main relay connector (harness side) and ground with a DC voltmeter, as shown in Fig. 1-78. The normal voltage is battery voltage.

054　Automotive Safety and Comfort System Maintenance

If the voltage is abnormal, check the circuit, connector and relevant fuse between the TRC main relay and the battery. If the voltage is normal, check the main relay.

b. Check the TRC main relay. Measure the continuity between terminals of the TRC main relay connector. Normally, there is no conduction between terminals 1-2 (resistance ∞) and there is conduction between terminals 2-4 (small resistance).

Then apply battery voltage between terminals 2-4 of the relay, and then check whether there is continuity between terminals 1-2 of the relay, as shown in Fig. 1-79. Normally, it should be conductive.

If the above check results are abnormal, replace the TRC main relay. If the check results are normal, check the relevant circuit and connector of the TRC main relay, and check or replace the TRC/ABS computer if the wiring and connector are in good condition.

II. Fault Case Diagnosis Process of ASR

The ASR fault light on the instrument panel is always on, indicating that the ASR of this vehicle is faulty. ASR and ABS are generally integrated with each other, collectively referred to as automobile acceleration slip regulation.

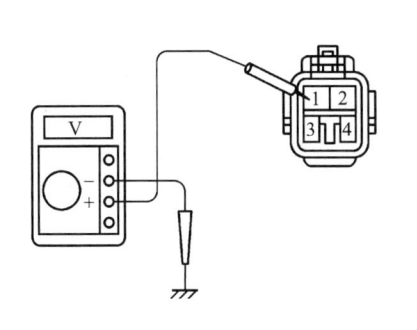

Fig. 1-78　Check the Voltage of Main
Relay Power Terminal

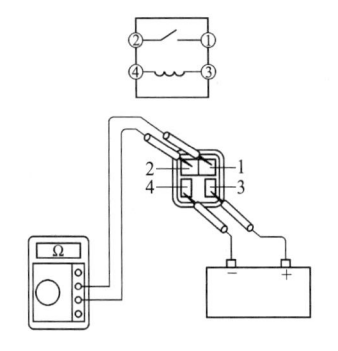

Fig. 1-79　Check the Conduction between
Main Relay Terminals

Firstly, the ASR DTC is called from the fault detection socket by using the onboard fault self-diagnosis function. The DTC displays: There is a problem in the signal transmission between the ASR computer and the EGAS (Electronic Throttle Control System) computer. Carry out fault self-diagnosis for EGAS, call DTC, but no information can be read. It is therefore suspected that there is a problem in the line. A careful examination of the line system of the EGAS computer does not reveal any anomalies. Turn on the EGAS computer and find that one of the integrated blocks in the EGAS computer has been burnt out. After replacement, test run, the ASR fault light is no longer on, but after a certain distance of road test, the ASR fault light is on again. Then the DTC of ASR is extracted by the on-board fault self-diagnosis system. The DTC indicates that the idle contact circuit is poor (the original ASR and EGAS signal transmission is poor).

Check the idle contact circuit (the MERCEDES-BENZ idling contact is installed under the accelerator pedal). If one wire of the idle contact circuit is found disconnected, plug the wire, test run, ASR fault light no longer lights up, and the fault is eliminated completely.

Exercises

Short Answer Question

Please analyze the similarities and differences between ASR and ABS.

Task Ⅲ Maintenance of Electronic Stability Program

[Learning Objectives]

Knowledge requirement: Understand the function, composition and principle of the Electronic Stability Program (ESP).

Capability requirement: Be able to diagnose and repair the Electronic Stability Program (ESP) according to the maintenance manual and using common tools and measuring tools.

 Task Import

A MERCEDES-BENZ ML500 SUV made in 2000 had a mileage of more than 80,000 km. Three instrument lights of ESP, ETS and ABS on the instrument panel were all on during driving. The vehicle has been inspected at the special maintenance station. After inspection, the maintenance personnel thought that ABS pump, lateral acceleration sensor and offset rate sensor were faulty, so it was necessary to replace the ABS pump, lateral acceleration sensor and offset rate sensor. The owner thought the repair price was too high, so he went to the repair shop to check.

 Knowledge Preparation

Ⅰ. Function of Electronic Stability Program

Electronic Stability Program (ESP) is developed by BOSCH and MERCEDES-BENZ. In February 1998, MERCEDES-BENZ for the first time installed the electrically-controlled vehicle stability system in its A-class mini-sedan in batches. It integrates the basic functions of the Electronic Anti-lock Braking System (ABS), Electronic Brake Force Distribution (EBD), and Acceleration Slip Regulation (ASR); it can identify unstable driving trends in milliseconds, eliminate them appropriately, and keep the vehicle on the desired driving route.

Ⅱ. Structure and Composition of ESP

ESP is developed on the basis of ABS, EBD and ASR. The electronic braking system consists of electronic control unit (ECU), hydraulic modulator assembly, wheel speed sen-

056 Automotive Safety and Comfort System Maintenance

sor, wheel speed sensor pulse ring, steering wheel angle sensor, yaw rate sensor and ESP control switch. The ECU and hydraulic modulator are integrated. The composition of ESP is shown in Fig. 1-80.

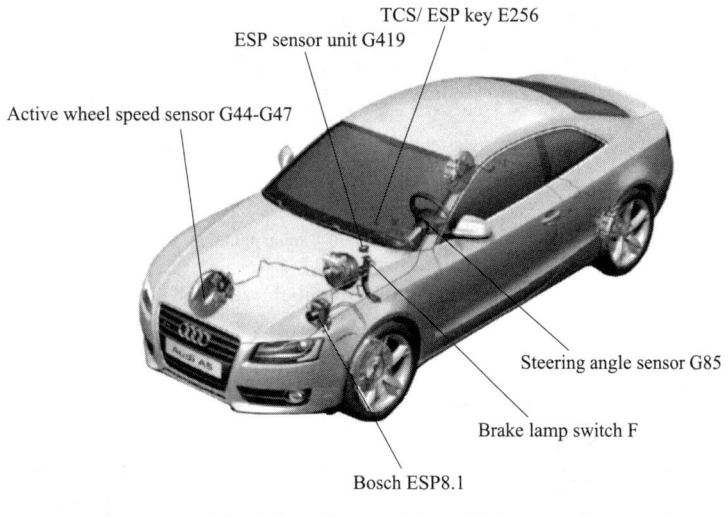

Fig. 1-80　Composition of ESP

1. Electronic control unit

The ECU is the control center of the ABS-ASR/ESP, which is integrated with the hydraulic modulator to form an assembly. Input signals continuously monitored and judged by the ECU are: battery voltage, wheel speed, steering wheel angle, yaw rate, ignition switch ON, stop lamp switch, serial data communication circuit, etc. Based on the received input signals, the ECU sends output control signals to the hydraulic modulator, the ECM, the instrument cluster, the serial data communication circuit, etc.

2. Hydraulic modulator assembly

The hydraulic modulator assembly is shown in Fig. 1-81. In order to independently control the brake circuit of each wheel, the system adopts a 4-channel circuit structure with front/rear separation. The hydraulic brake circuit of each wheel is isolated, so that the braking can be continued when a certain brake circuit leaks. The hydraulic modulator assembly adjusts the brake fluid pressure according to the control signal sent by the ECU. The hydraulic modulator assembly consists of return pump, motor, accumulator, inlet valve, outlet valve, isolation valve and rear start valve.

3. Front wheel speed sensor

The front wheel speed sensor, as shown in Fig. 1-82, is an electromagnetic sensor and is a part of the front wheel hub assembly, which is a permanent sealing device. The front left and right wheel hubs are equipped with wheel speed sensors and a 48-tooth magnetic pulse ring.

4. Rear wheel speed sensor

The rear wheel speed sensor, as shown in Fig. 1-83, is located on the bracket of the rear cover of the final drive and is also an electromagnetic sensor. The rear wheel speed sensor pulse ring is part of the inner axle flange of the final drive and cannot be repaired separately.

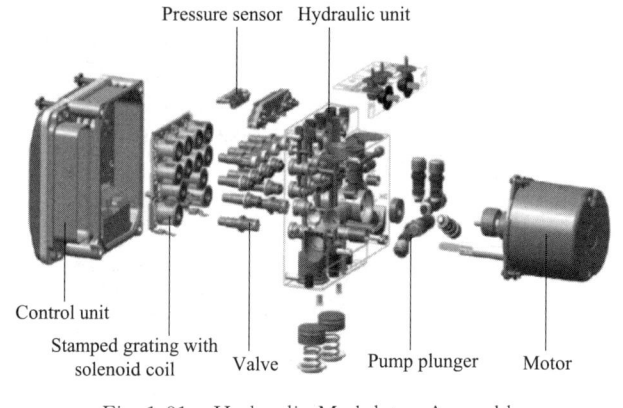

Fig. 1-81　Hydraulic Modulator Assembly

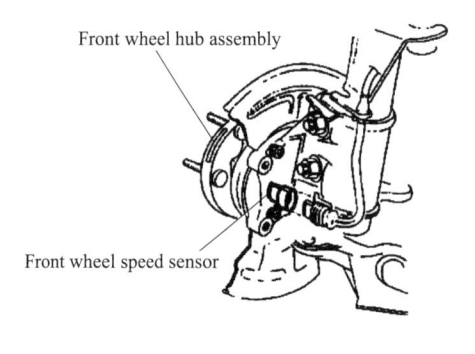

Fig. 1-82　Front Wheel Speed Sensor

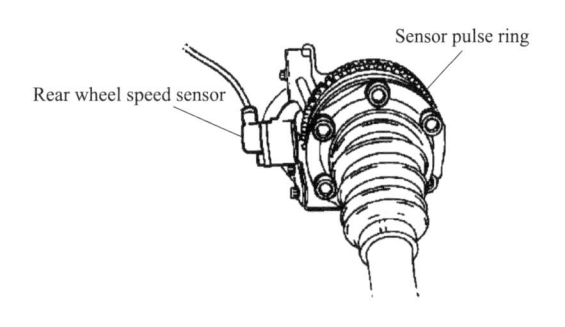

Fig. 1-83　Rear Wheel Speed Sensor

5. ESP switch

The ESP switch is located on the floor console. The switch is a momentary contact switch and the ESP switch is pressed once to turn the ESC from ON to OFF. When the ESP is turned off, the ABS-TCS system will still operate normally. When the ESP is in the OFF position, pressing the ESP switch again will turn on the ESC. Pressing the ESP switch for more than 60 seconds will be considered a short circuit, a DTC will be logged, and the ESP will be disabled during this ignition cycle. If no current DTC is logged for the TCS, the ESP will reset to the ON state on the next ignition cycle.

6. Steering wheel angle sensor

The steering wheel angle sensor is located under the steering wheel, as shown in Fig. 1-84. The steering wheel angle sensor provides an output signal indicative of the turning angle of the steering wheel. Because the number of teeth of the two measuring gears is different, two rotation angle signals with different phases are generated, i. e. an output signal indicating the rotation angle of the steering wheel of $\pm 760°$ can be generated. The ECU uses this information to calculate the direction requested by the driver. The control unit determines whether the actual driving trajectory of the vehicle is consistent with the driving requirements by comparing the signals of the steering wheel angle sensor and the yaw rate sensor, so as to determine the control target.

7. Yaw rate sensor

The yaw rate sensor is located under the instrument panel center console as shown in Fig. 1-85. The yaw rate sensor assembly consists of two components, a yaw rate sensor and a lateral acceleration sensor. The yaw rate sensor generates a corresponding output signal voltage based on the angle of rotation of the vehicle about its longitudinal axis; the lateral acceleration sensor generates a corresponding output signal voltage based on the amount of lateral wheel slip. The ESP control unit calculates the actual driving state of the vehicle by using the signals output by the yaw rate sensor and the lateral acceleration sensor, and determines the control target by combining the output signal of the wheel speed sensor and the serial data output signal of the steering wheel angle sensor.

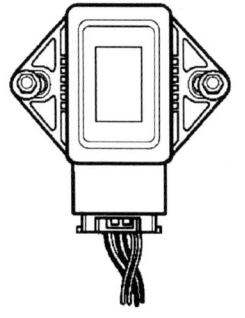

Fig. 1-84　Steering Wheel Angle Sensor　　　　Fig. 1-85　Yaw Rate Sensor

Ⅲ. Working Process of ESP Subsystem

The ESP is designed to provide optimum vehicle stability and directional control when cornering at high speed or driving on a slippery road. The ECU determines the driving direction desired by the driver through the steering wheel angle sensor, and calculates the actual driving direction of the vehicle through the wheel speed sensor and the yaw rate sensor. When the ESP detects that the vehicle's trajectory does not match the driver's requirements, the ESP first sends a serial data communication signal to the ECM requesting engine torque reduction using the engine torque reduction function in the TCS. If the ESP still detects lateral wheel slip, the ESP will ensure safety by rapidly overcoming the following operational deficiencies by applying braking intervention to more than one wheel of the front and rear axles based on the principle that all forces acting externally on the vehicle (whether braking force, propulsion force, or any kind of lateral force) will cause the vehicle to rotate around its center of gravity.

1. Operation to overcome understeer

The schematic diagram of understeer is shown in Fig. 1-86. The steering wheel angle sensor sends a signal to the ECU that the driver wants to steer in direction "A". The yaw rate sensor "B" detects that the vehicle begins to rotate while the front end of the vehicle starts to slip in direction "C", indicating that the vehicle is understeering and the ESP performs active brake intervention. The ESP uses the existing active braking control function of ABS-ASR system to brake the left rear wheel. At this moment, because the left rear wheel

is braked and the vehicle's center of gravity continues to move forward due to inertial action, the vehicle has to revolve around the left rear wheel as a fulcrum. In this way, the vehicle will turn towards the direction "A", i. e. toward the direction desired by the driver, and the operational defect of under-steering is overcome.

2. Operation to overcome oversteer

The oversteer diagram is shown in Fig. 1-87. The steering wheel angle sensor sends a signal to the ECU that the driver wants to steer in direction "A". The yaw rate sensor "B" detects that the vehicle begins to rotate while the rear end of the vehicle begins to slip toward direction "C", which indicates that the vehicle begins to oversteer and the ESP will perform active brake intervention. The ESP uses the existing active braking control function of ABS-ASR system to brake the right rear wheel. At this moment, the right rear wheel is braked and the vehicle's center of gravity continues to move forward due to inertial action, so the vehicle has to revolve around the right rear wheel as a fulcrum. In this way, the vehicle will turn towards the direction "A", i. e. toward the direction desired by the driver, and the o-ver-steering operation defect is overcome.

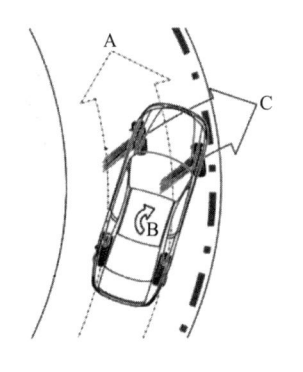

Fig. 1-86　Schematic Diagram of Understeer

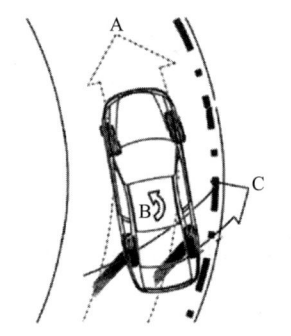

Fig. 1-87　Schematic Diagram of Oversteer

Task Implementation

Fault Case Diagnosis Process of Electronic Stability Program

Firstly, the scan tool STAR was used to check. After inquiring the ESP, a DTC C1402 was got, which means "high pressure return pump failure". The possible locations of this DTC are ABS pump, ESP control unit and associated circuits. The ABS pump on another vehicle was used for replacement test. After clearing the DTC, the test drive was carried out. After driving for a short distance, the ETS on the instrument panel was on. The DTC was called and still C1402, indicating that it was not the ABS pump fault. The ESP control unit of the MERCEDES-BENZ ML500 is located in the fuse box in the engine compartment, close to the engine control unit. In order to eliminate faults, the ESP control units of the two vehicles were switched. Because the ESP control unit was replaced, coding the control unit with the scan tool and activating the driving test found that the ETS light would still come on when starting and the ABS light would come on constantly after starting. A DTC C1200 is added in addition to DTC C1402, which means "driving test is activated". Originally, it did

060　Automotive Safety and Comfort System Maintenance

not exit after the activation of driving test. The DTC C1200 could not be cleared with the scan tool and the driving test was continued. At this time, the ESP, ETS and ABS lights on the instrument panel were all off. Turned on the ignition switch after the engine was turned off. Then it was found that all the fault lights on the instrument panel were off. The ignition switch was turned off for several minutes before turning on the ignition switch, and then the fault lights were all on again. Carefully observe the display of each instrument. The odometer did not display the mileage. The pointer of the fuel gauge rotated more than 300 degrees, and the tachometer pointer was abnormal.

In order to restore the instrument indication to normal, the maintenance personnel carried out several power-on and power-off tests, but with no effect. At this time, the owner reported that the car's meters had been calibrated, and weren't been adjusted properly in the first adjustment, the fuel gauge indication was abnormal after installation, later the gauge was calibrated again, the fuel gauge indication returned to normal. Based on this, the maintenance personnel decided to re-calibrate the instrument, find the backup data of the instrument, write the program again with the programmer, and the indication of each instrument returned to normal.

Problems with the ABS pump and ESP control unit can basically be eliminated through the above overhaul process. According to the ABS system circuit diagram, the maintenance personnel found that there were only two connecting wires on the high pressure return pump M1 of the ABS pump A7/3, one of which was grounded near the left headlamp and the other was controlled by the K25 relay. The K25 relay has 5 pins, pins 1 and 2 connected to pins 10 and 12 of the ESP control unit N47 respectively. Pin 5 is divided into two lines, one to pin 11 of the ESP control unit N47, the other to M1 high pressure return pump, and pin 3 to the constant power supply line. The maintenance personnel carefully checked the harness plugs on the ABS pump and ESP control unit and measured the relevant lines, but no problem was found. Because relay K25 plays an important role in the connection between ESP control unit and M1 high pressure return pump circuit, K25 relay was replaced. During the test drive, ETS lamp and ESP lamp were no longer on and DTC C1402 did not appear again. It seemed that the fault point really lied in relay K25. The ABS lamp that was constantly on due to the driving test activated by the scan tool STAR needs to be resolved next.

After following the instructions on the scan tool STAR, driving a distance after removing the diagnostic plug turned off the active driving test, but the ABS lamp remained on after a long drive distance. Instructions on driving test in MERCEDES-BENZ's WIS were found, and the car was driven according to the instructions, ABS light went out automatically. This fault was completely eliminated.

Exercises

Short Answer Questions

1. Briefly describe the working principle of ESP.
2. What are the components of ESP?

Item I　Maintenance of Automobile Electronic Control Active Safety System　**061**

Item Summary

With the application of electronic control technology, microcomputer processing technology and sensor technology, the vehicle control accuracy has been improved, and the safety technology has been greatly developed. The harmonious and integrated development of active safety technology and passive safety technology is an unstoppable development trend, which plays an important role in reducing the labor intensity of drivers and effectively protecting the safety of drivers, passengers and pedestrians in case of accidents.

Item Exercises

Ⅰ. Fill in the blanks

1. The main evaluation indexes for evaluating braking effectiveness are_____, _____ and_____.

2. Electronically controlled ABS consists of _____, _____ and _____.

3. The speed sensor mainly consists of _____ and _____.

Ⅱ. Single choice questions

1. The mounting position of the diamond pole axis sensor head is (   ).

A. Radial perpendicular to ring gear   B. Axial tangent to ring gear

C. Both are correct   D. Both are wrong

2. The installation position of the chisel pole axle speed sensor head is (   ).

A. Radial perpendicular to ring gear   B. Axial tangent to ring gear

C. Both are correct   D. Both are wrong

3. In order to ensure that there is no wrong signal output from the sensor, when installing the speed sensor, make sure that there is a certain air clearance between the sensor head and the ring gear, which is about (   ).

A. 5mm   B. 1mm   C. 0.01mm   D. $1\mu m$

Ⅲ. Explanation of Terms

1. Slip ratio

2. Direction stability of the vehicle during braking

Ⅳ. True or False

1. The evaluation indexes of braking performance mainly include braking efficiency and braking stability.

(   )

2. The braking efficiency mainly depends on the magnitude of the braking force, and the braking force is only related to the friction torque of the brake. (   )

Ⅴ. Short answer question

What types of ABS can be classified according to different classification methods?

Item II

Maintenance of Automobile Air Conditioning System

 **Item Guide**

Automobile air conditioning (A/C) system is a device which can cool, heat, ventilate and purify the air inside the car. It can provide comfortable riding environment for passengers, reduce fatigue strength of drivers and improve driving safety.

The A/C system has become one of the signs to measure whether the automobile functions are complete or not.

I. Composition of Automobile Air Conditioning System

1. A/C compressor

Automobile A/C compressor is generally installed beside the automobile engine, driven by the main engine or the auxiliary engine through the pulley. The A/C compressor extracts the refrigerant from the low-pressure zone and sends it to the high-pressure zone for cooling and condensation after being compressed. The refrigerant also changes from gaseous state to liquid state through heat dissipation fins to the air. The refrigerant flows from the high pressure zone to the low pressure zone and is injected into the evaporator through the expansion valve. The pressure drops suddenly, and the liquid refrigerant becomes gaseous immediately, absorbing a large amount of heat in the air through the fins. In this way, the A/C compressor will continuously absorb the heat at one end of the low pressure zone into the refrigerant, and then send it to the high pressure zone for emission to the air, thus playing the role of adjusting the temperature.

2. A/C condenser

The A/C condenser is used for refrigeration and air-conditioning system, in which the coolant in the tube is forced to exchange heat with the air outside the pipe, so as to achieve the effect of cooling air.

The condenser is the high-pressure equipment of the system when cooling (the cold-heating heat pump type is the low-pressure equipment in the heating state). It is installed between the compressor exhaust port and throttling device (orifice tube or expansion valve). The high-temperature and high-pressure gas discharged from the A/C compressor enters into the condenser and is cooled by heat dissipation through copper tube and aluminum foil. The air conditioner is equipped with axial cooling fan, which is of air-cooled type, so that the pressure of the refrigerant remains unchanged and the temperature is reduced, and

the refrigerant is converted into liquid during cooling and condensation.

The process of refrigerant change in the condenser can be regarded as isothermal change process theoretically. In fact, it has three functions: the first is that air takes away the superheated part of high-temperature air conditioning refrigerant gas sent by the compressor to make it become dry saturated vapor; the second is to liquefy under the condition of constant saturation temperature; and the third is to further cool the liquefied refrigerant to the same temperature as the surrounding air when the air temperature is lower than the condensation temperature to play a cooling role.

3. A/C evaporator

The function of the A/C evaporator is to make use of liquid low-temperature refrigerant easy to evaporate under low pressure, transform it into vapor and absorb heat of cooled medium, so as to achieve refrigeration purpose.

4. A/C expansion valve

Expansion valve is an important component in the refrigeration system. The expansion valve makes the liquid refrigerant with moderate temperature and high pressure become wet vapor with low temperature and low pressure through its throttling, and then the refrigerant absorbs heat in the evaporator to achieve refrigeration effect. The expansion valve controls the flow rate of the valve through the superheat change at the end of the evaporator to prevent under-utilization of evaporator area and cylinder knocking. Briefly speaking, the expansion valve is mainly used to automatically adjust throttling and control refrigerant flow according to the temperature change.

5. A/C receiver dryer

The receiver dryer has been continuously improved and renewed during the development of air conditioning. Its main function is storage and drying. With the development of modern refrigeration technology, the receiver dryer emerges as the times require. In refrigeration principle, refrigerant can absorb heat and release heat through transformation of physical form. When refrigerant is added into the A/C sealing system, it is inevitable to mix moisture in air and impurities in pipeline. During the transformation process of physical form, moisture will form solid ice, blocking the closed pipeline of the A/C system, thus affecting the flow of refrigerant, finally leading to refrigeration failure and even explosion in serious cases. The receiver dryer is used to suck away the moisture in the sealed A/C line and to filter out the tiny impurities in the pipeline.

II. Know the Connecting Lines

① High-pressure hose: The high-pressure hose is the connecting line between the compressor and the condenser.

② Liquid line: The liquid line is the connecting line between the condenser and the evaporator.

③ Return line: The return line is the connecting line between the evaporator and the compressor.

④ Heating line: The heating line is the connecting line between the engine and the heater radiator.

Ⅲ. Brief Description of Working Process of Air Conditioner

In order to analyze the thermodynamic cycle of the automobile air conditioning refrigeration system, the theoretical cycle of the automobile air conditioning refrigeration system must be analyzed first.

1. Compression process

The refrigerant gas at low temperature and low pressure is sucked by the compressor and compressed into refrigerant gas at high temperature and high pressure. The main function of this process is to compress and pressurize the gas to liquefy. This process is compensated by the consumption of mechanical work. In the compression process, the refrigerant state does not change, but the temperature and pressure increase continuously, forming superheated gas.

2. Condensation process

The refrigerant gas is discharged from the compressor and enters the condenser. The characteristic of this process is that the state of the refrigerant changes, that is, under the condition of constant pressure and temperature, the refrigerant gradually changes from gaseous state to liquid state. The condensed refrigerant liquid is in a state of high temperature and high pressure.

3. Throttling expansion process

The high-temperature and high-pressure refrigerant liquid enters the evaporator after being throttled by the expansion valve for temperature reduction and pressure reduction. The function of this process is to reduce the temperature and pressure of the refrigerant, regulate the flow rate and control the refrigeration capacity. Its characteristic is that when the refrigerant passes through the expansion valve, the pressure and temperature drop rapidly, from high-temperature and high-pressure liquid to low-temperature and low-pressure liquid.

4. Evaporation process

The refrigerant liquid enters the evaporator after being cooled down and depressurized by the expansion valve, and is sucked into the compressor from the evaporator outlet after absorbing heat and cooling. The characteristic of this process is that the refrigerant changes from liquid state to gas state, at which time the pressure does not change. After throttling, the low-temperature and low-pressure liquid refrigerant continuously absorbs the latent heat of vaporization in the evaporator, absorbing the heat in the vehicle and turning into low-temperature and low-pressure gas, which is sucked into the compressor and compressed again.

Task Ⅰ Automobile Air Conditioning System Identification

[Learning Objectives]

Knowledge requirements: Master the function, composition and classification of auto-

mobile air conditioning system.

Capability requirements: Be able to find all components of air conditioning system on the real vehicle, and obtain vehicle information by communicating with customers and consulting relevant maintenance technical data, etc.

 Task Import

In addition to using a control switch to regulate the temperature of the A/C system inside the car, can you find any other components of the A/C system in your car? The following is to help you understand the role, classification, composition and basic principles of the A/C system.

 Knowledge Preparation

Ⅰ. Functions of Automobile Air Conditioner

A/C is short for air conditioner. Modern car air conditioners have the following four functions, any of which is designed to make people feel comfortable.

① The A/C can control the air temperature in the compartment to a comfortable level.

② The A//C can remove moisture in the air.

③ The A/C can inhale fresh air and has ventilation function.

④ Some A/C can filter the air and remove the dust and pollen in the air.

Ⅱ. Main Indicators of Automobile Air Conditioner

The main indicators of the automobile A/C are temperature, humidity, flow rate and cleanliness.

1. Temperature

The comfortable temperature of human body is different in different seasons. The air outlet of the A/C shall be designed so that the cold air can be blown to the head of passengers and the hot air can be blown to the feet of passengers, i. e., the arrangement mode of "cool head and warm feet" shall be adopted.

2. Humidity

The most comfortable relative humidity is 50%-60% in summer and 40%-50% in winter. In this kind of humidity environment, people will feel comfortable. If the humidity is too high, moisture in the human skin can't be evaporated out, and people feel stuffy.

3. Flow rate

The air velocity is slightly higher in summer, and people are more comfortable in flowing air than in still air. High wind speed in winter will affect human body insulation, so it is desirable to keep the air flow as small as possible for winter heating, and it is better to keep the air velocity below 0.2m/s.

4. Cleanliness

The air in the cabin shall be clean, which requires the A/C system have a set of ventilation and filtration facilities and air purification equipment.

III. Composition and Classification of Automobile Air Conditioning System

1. Composition of Automobile Air Conditioning System

① Refrigeration system: The refrigeration system cools or dehumidifies the indoor air or the fresh air entering the vehicle from the outside to make the indoor air cool and comfortable.

② Heating system: The heating system is mainly used for heating, heating indoor air or fresh air entering from outside to achieve the purpose of heating and dehumidification.

③ Ventilation system: Fresh outside air is sucked into the vehicle for ventilation. At the same time, prevent the windshield from fogging.

④ Humidification system: When the air humidity is low, humidify the air inside the vehicle to increase the relative humidity of the air inside the vehicle.

⑤ Air purification system: The air purification system removes dust, peculiar smell, smoke and toxic gas from the indoor air of the vehicle.

⑥ Control system: The control system controls the temperature and pressure of the refrigeration and heating systems, and controls the indoor air temperature, air volume and flow direction to perfect the normal operation of the A/C system.

All or part of the above-mentioned parts are installed together on the automobile to form the automobile A/C system. In ordinary cars and freight cars, there are usually only refrigeration system, heating system, ventilation system and control system. In high-class cars and high-class buses, besides refrigeration system and heating system, there are also humidification system and PM2.5 air purification system.

2. Classification of Automobile Air Conditioning Systems

(1) Classification by function

Automobile A/C system can be divided into single-function automobile A/C system and combined automobile A/C system by function.

① Single-function automobile A/C system refers to the independent refrigeration system and heating system, which are generally used on large and medium-sized passenger cars.

② Combined automobile A/C system refers to the automobile A/C system in which refrigeration and heating share one blower and one set of operating mechanism. This kind of structure is divided into two work mode: refrigeration and heating work separately and refrigeration and heating can work at the same time, mostly used on cars.

(2) Classification by driving mode

Automobile A/C system is classified by driving mode into non-independent automobile A/C system and independent automobile A/C system.

① Non-independent automobile A/C system. The A/C refrigeration compressor is driven by the automobile engine. The refrigeration performance of the automobile A/C system is greatly affected by the working conditions of the automobile engine, and the working stability is poor. The refrigeration capacity is insufficient at low speed, and the refrigeration capacity is excessive at high speed, and the power consumption is large, which affects the dynamic performance of the automobile engine. This type of the automobile A/C system is gen-

erally used on small and medium-sized vehicles with relatively small cooling capacity.

② Independent automobile A/C system. The A/C refrigeration compressor is driven by a special A/C engine (also called auxiliary engine). The refrigeration performance of the automobile A/C system is not affected by the working condition of the automobile engine. It works stably and has large refrigeration capacity. However, due to the addition of an engine, not only the cost is increased, but also the volume and weight are increased. This type of the automobile A/C system is mostly used on large and medium passenger cars.

 ## Task Implementation

Train in groups to find the components of the A/C system on the real vehicle.

Exercises

Short Answer Questions

1. Briefly describe the working process of air conditioner.
2. Briefly describe the classification of air conditioner.

Task Ⅱ Maintenance of Automobile Air Conditioning Refrigeration System

〔Learning Objectives〕

Knowledge requirements: Master the structure, principle and maintenance method of each type of automobile air conditioning refrigeration system.

Capability requirements: Be able to make correct maintenance plan according to fault phenomenon. According to the maintenance manual, use the common maintenance tools to diagnose and repair the common faults of the automobile air conditioning refrigeration system.

 ## Task Import

A Shanghai GM Buick Lacrosse sedan is equipped with automatic A/C. When the A/C system works, intermittent non-cooling occurs. This fault often occurs when driving at high speed and idling sometimes. The higher the frequency of failure occurs in the hotter weather.

 ## Knowledge Preparation

Ⅰ. Structural Principle of Compressor in Automobile Air Conditioning Refrigeration System

Refrigeration compressor is the heart of the automobile A/C refrigeration system. It

compresses and transports refrigerant and ensures normal circulation of refrigerant. It is also the power to push refrigerant to circulate continuously in the cold-air system.

1. Crankshaft connecting rod compressor

Crankshaft connecting rod compressor is a kind of refrigeration compressor widely used. As shown in Fig. 2-1, the piston of the compressor constantly moves in the cylinder, changing the volume of the cylinder, thus playing the role of compressing and conveying refrigerant in the refrigeration system. The engine body of the crankshaft connecting rod compressor is composed of cylinder block and crankcase. The cylinder block is equipped with piston, and the crankcase is equipped with crankshaft. The crankshaft is connected with piston through connecting rod. An intake valve and an exhaust valve are installed on the top of the cylinder, which are connected with the suction pipe and exhaust pipe respectively through the suction chamber and the exhaust chamber. When the engine drives the crankshaft to rotate, the piston reciprocates up and down in the cylinder through the transmission of the connecting rod. With the cooperation of the suction and exhaust valves, it completes the task of sucking, compressing and conveying the refrigerant gas.

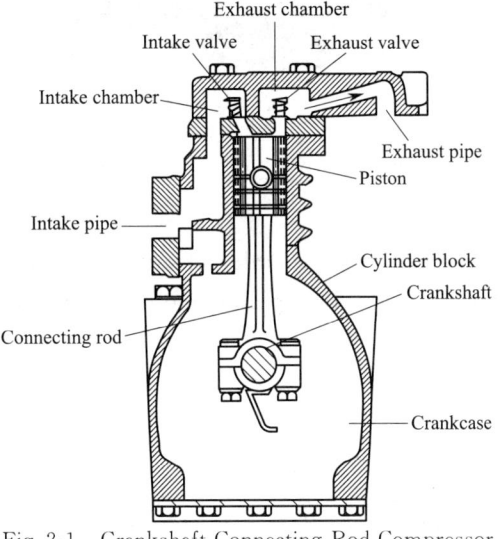

Fig. 2-1   Crankshaft Connecting Rod Compressor

2. Radial piston compressor

Radial piston compressor is a reciprocating piston compressor, it has two types.

One type is that four cylinders are located in the same radial plane, a connecting rod connects two pistons, and the crank slides in the connecting rod groove to convert the rotary motion of the crankshaft into linear reciprocating motion of the piston, as shown in Fig. 2-2, which is called a connecting rod radial piston compressor.

The other type is a non-connecting rod, called slip ring radial piston compressor, as shown in Fig. 2-3.

3. Swash plate compressor

The swash plate compressor is an axial piston compressor. Its main parts are main shaft and swash plate. The structure is shown in Fig. 2-4.

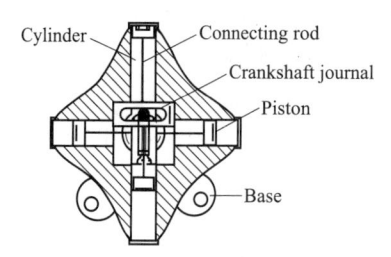

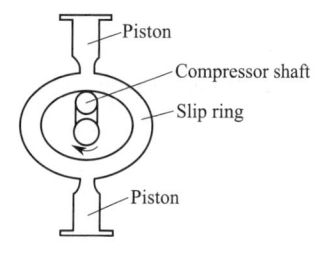

Fig. 2-2　Connecting Rod Radial Piston Compressor　　　Fig. 2-3　Slip Ring Radial Piston Compressor

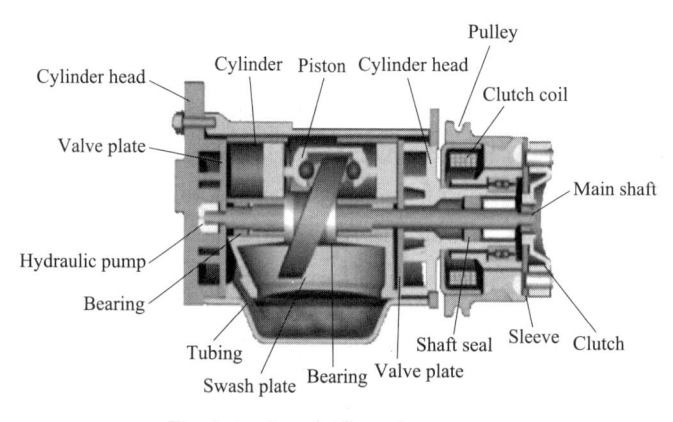

Fig. 2-4　Swash Plate Compressor

4. Compressor clutch

Automobile compressor clutch is generally electromagnetic type. The electromagnetic clutch has three main components: The pulley mounted on the bearing, the drive disc splined to the main shaft of the compressor and the electrical winding or coil that does not rotate, as shown in Fig. 2-5.

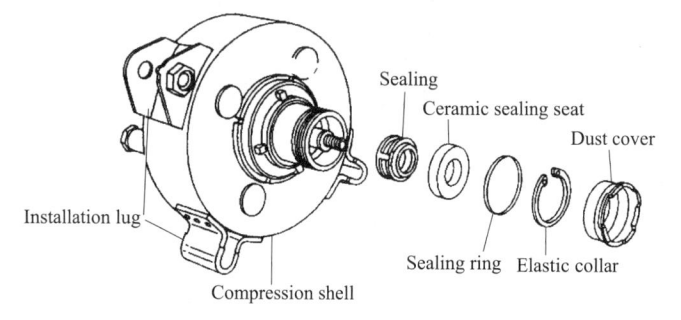

Fig. 2-5　Mechanism of Compressor Clutch

II. Expansion Valve of Automobile Air Conditioning Refrigeration System

Expansion valve, also called throttle, is the main component of the automobile A/C refrigeration system, installed at the evaporator inlet, as shown in Fig. 2-6. Expansion valve includes temperature-sensing expansion valve, H-type expansion valve, etc.

070　Automotive Safety and Comfort System Maintenance

1. Internal balance temperature-sensing expansion valve

Fig. 2-7 shows the structure of the internal balance expansion valve. Needle valve, seat and orifice are used to regulate refrigerant flow. Needle valve is driven by diaphragm.

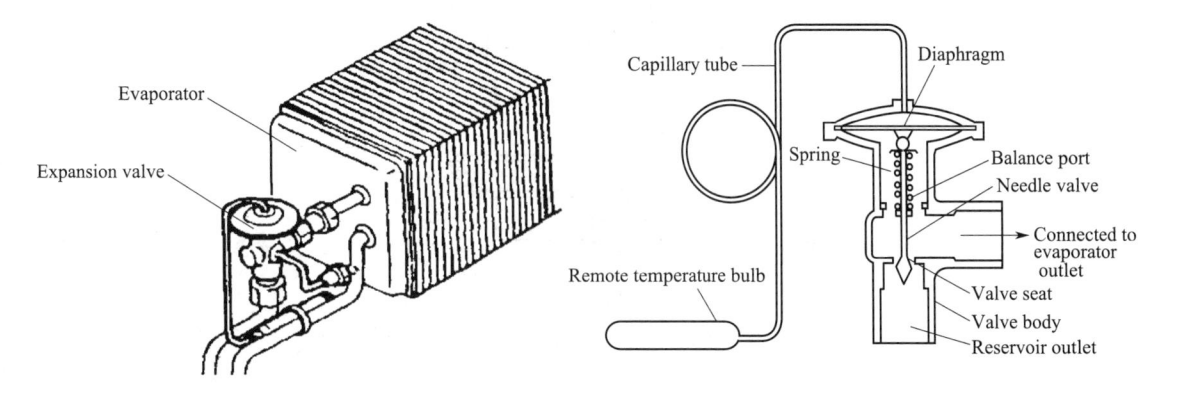

Fig. 2-6　Installation Position of Expansion Valve

Fig. 2-7　Internal Balance Temperature Sensing Expansion Valve

2. External balance temperature-sensing expansion valve

The structure of external balance temperature-sensing expansion valve is shown in Fig. 2-8.

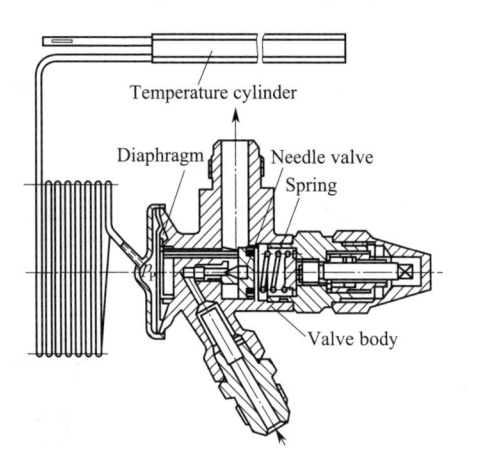

Fig. 2-8　External Balance Temperature Sensing Expansion Valve

3. H-type temperature-sensing expansion valve

The appearance of H-type temperature-sensing expansion valve is rectangular, named because its internal passage looks like the letter H. It has four connections to the car's A/C system, two of which are the same as the standard expansion valve, one to the receiver dryer outlet and the other to the evaporator inlet. It also has two interfaces, one connected to evaporator outlet and the other connected to compressor inlet, as shown in Fig. 2-9.

4. Orifice tube

The structure of orifice tube is shown in Fig. 2-10.

III . Automobile Air Conditioning Condenser

The condenser in the automobile A/C refrigeration system is a kind of heat exchanger

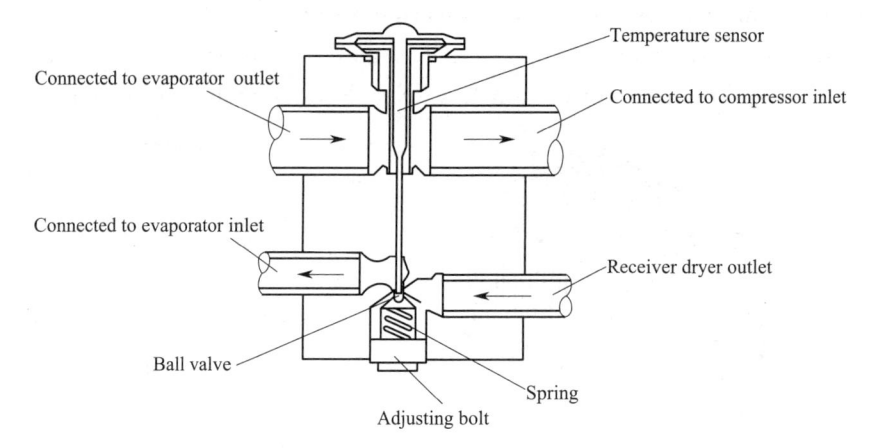

Fig. 2-9　H-Type Temperature Sensing Expansion Valve

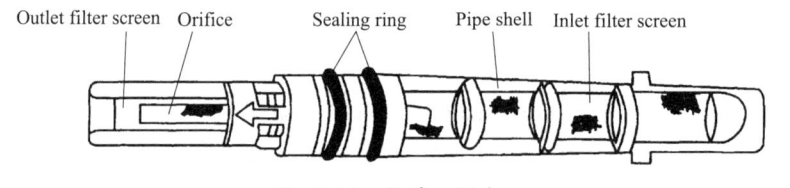

Fig. 2-10　Orifice Tube

composed of tubes and cooling fins. Generally, air-cooled structure is adopted, and its structural forms mainly include tube-belt type, tube-fin type and fin-type structures.

1. Tube-belt type

The structure of the Tube-belt type is shown in Fig. 2-11.

2. Tube-fin type

The structure of the Tube-fin type is shown in Fig. 2-12.

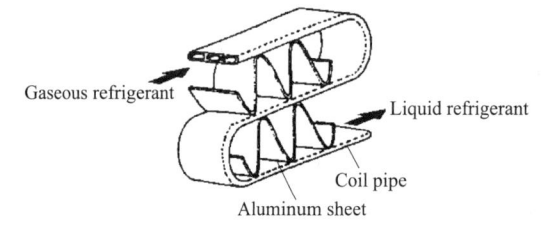

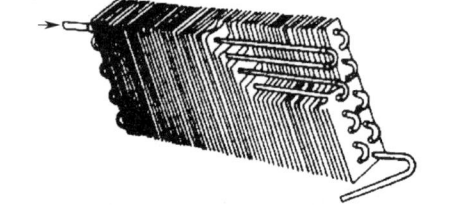

Fig. 2-11　Tube-Belt Condenser

Fig. 2-12　Tube-Fin Condenser

3. Fin condenser

Fin condenser is to mill fin cooling fins directly on the flat multi-way pipe surface, and then assemble into condenser, as shown in Fig. 2-13. Fin condenser is an advanced condenser for the automobile A/C.

Ⅳ. Receiver Dryer

The receiver dryer is simply called the reservoir, which is installed between the condenser and the expansion valve. The receiver dryer is composed of reservoir, dryer, access

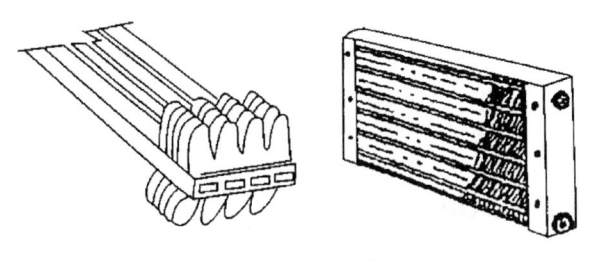

Fig. 2-13   Fin Condenser

window and safety device (see Fig. 2-14), assembled together or installed dispersed-ly. Fig. 2-15 shows the structure of receiver dryer.

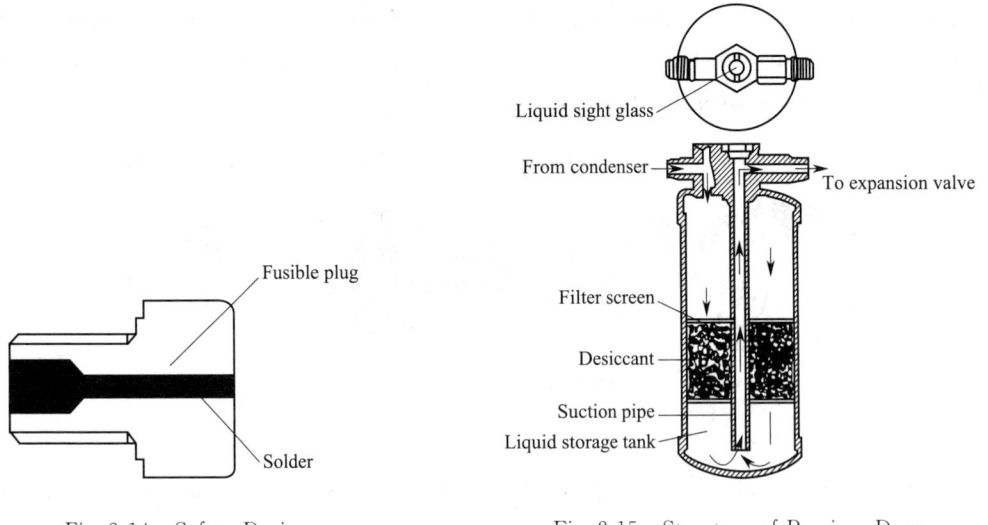

Fig. 2-14   Safety Device

Fig. 2-15   Structure of Receiver Dryer

The reservoir is generally installed near the condenser or other well-ventilated place for easy connection and installation and easy to observe the refrigerant flow from the top glass sight glass. For vertical reservoirs, the inclination shall not exceed 15° in case of deviation from the vertical direction. Before installing a new receiver dryer, the package of inlet and outlet nozzles shall not be opened too early to prevent moisture from entering the reservoir and system and losing its dehumidifying effect. Before installation, make sure the inlet and outlet ends of the reservoir to avoid incorrect installation. If the inlet and outlet are connected reversely, the refrigerant will be insufficient. The inlet and outlet ends of the reservoir are generally marked, for example, the inlet end is represented by the English letter IN, the outlet end is indicated by OUT, or an arrow is directly marked to indicate the inlet and out-let ends.

① Touch the inlet and outlet pipes of the receiver dryer with your hands, and observe the liquid glass. If the inlet is very hot and the outlet pipe is close to the air temperature, no or little refrigerant flows through the sight glass, or the refrigerant is cloudy with impuri-ties, it is possible that the strainer in the reservoir is blocked or the desiccant is scattered and the outlet is blocked. Generally, the drying agent is used for 3 months, and the mois-ture absorption capacity will be reduced by half. Therefore, the dryer shall be replaced every

Item II   Maintenance of Automobile Air Conditioning System   **073**

2 years.

② Check whether the fusible plug melts and whether there is oil stain at each joint.

③ Check whether the liquid sight glass has cracks and whether there are oil stains a-round it.

 Task Implementation

Ⅰ. Maintenance of Denso Compressor

Denso compressors may be equipped with Denso clutches or Warner clutch assemblies. Although the two clutches are similar in shape, their parts are not interchangeable. However, the entire clutch assembly is interchangeable on such compressors. The obvious difference between the two clutches is that the Denso clutch pulley (see Fig. 2-16) has two narrow single row bearings which are positioned with steel wire snap rings.

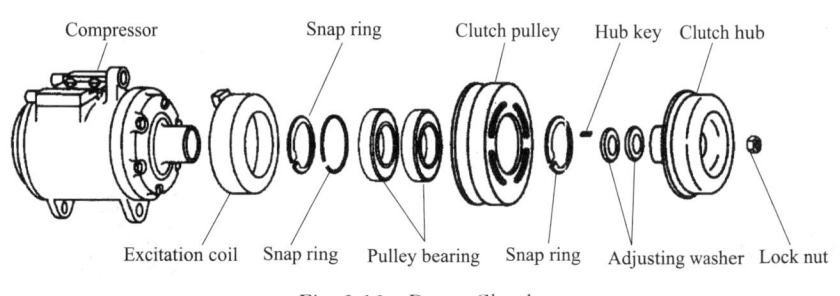

Fig. 2-16 Denso Clutch

The Warner clutch (see Fig. 2-17) has only one wide double row bearing, which is positioned by punching the flanging.

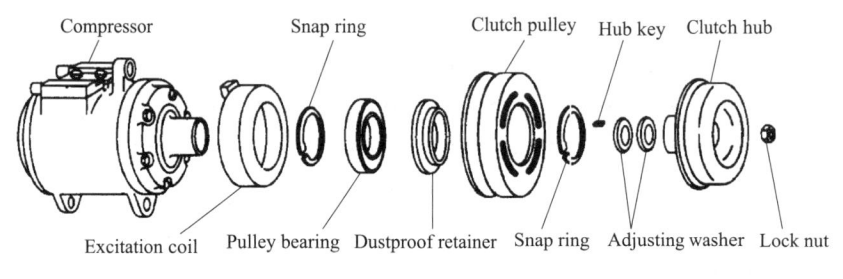

Fig. 2-17 Warner Clutch

① Use the clutch hub removal tool to disassemble the clutch hub, as shown in Fig. 2-18.

② Use snap ring pliers to disassemble pulley positioning snap ring, and then use three-jaw puller to remove pulley and bearing assembly, as shown in Fig. 2-19.

③ Use the snap ring pliers to disassemble the locating snap ring of excitation coil and take off the excitation coil from the compressor, as shown in Fig. 2-20.

④ Remove 6 tie-rods from the front cover with appropriate tools, as shown in Fig. 2-21.

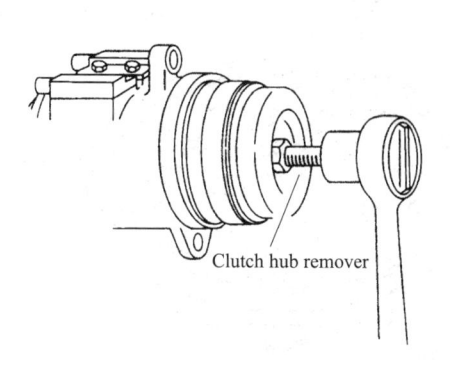

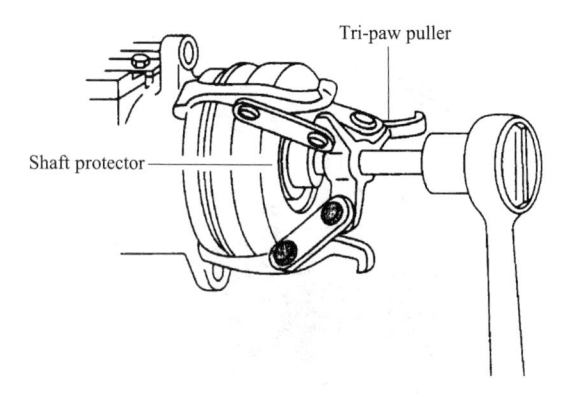

Fig. 2-18　Remove the clutch hub

Fig. 2-19　Remove the pulley and bearing assembly

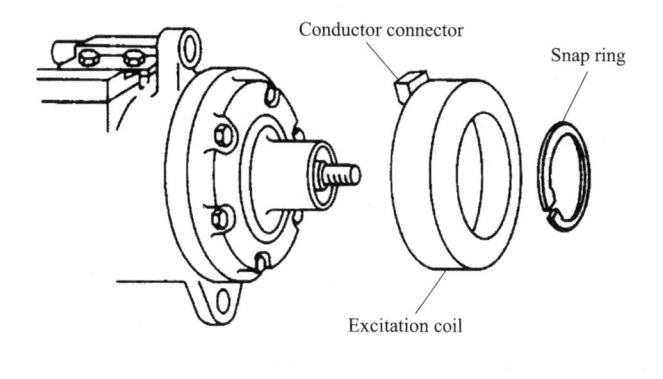

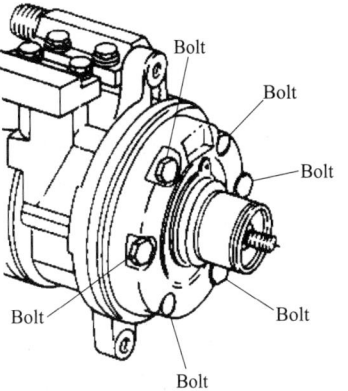

Fig. 2-20　Disassembly of Excitation Coil

Fig. 2-21　Remove Tie-Rod

⑤ Knock the front cover gently with a plastic hammer to separate the front cover from the compressor housing.

⑥ Remove O-ring between the compressor housing and the front cover and gasket between the front cover and the valve plate and discard them (disposable parts) .

⑦ Disassemble the shaft seal seat and the shaft seal with a shaft seal seat removal tool, as shown in Fig. 2-22.

⑧ Knock the rear cover slightly with a plastic hammer and remove the rear cover. Remove the O-ring between the rear lid and the housing and discard it (disposable part). Remove the valve plate using the valve plate removal tool, as shown in Fig. 2-23.

⑨ Knock the lug on the compressor housing to separate the front and rear shells.

⑩ Check whether the suction valve is damaged.

⑪ Inspect both exhaust valves for damage.

⑫ Inspect all mating surfaces for nicks and burrs.

⑬Check whether there are foreign materials in the piston cavity of the compressor and in the compressor body.

⑭ Lubricate all O-rings and gaskets thoroughly with clean mineral-based refrigerant oil or O-ring lubricant. Position front and rear housing O-rings and slide the housing halves together.

Item II　Maintenance of Automobile Air Conditioning System　**075**

Fig. 2-22 Disassembly of Shaft Seal

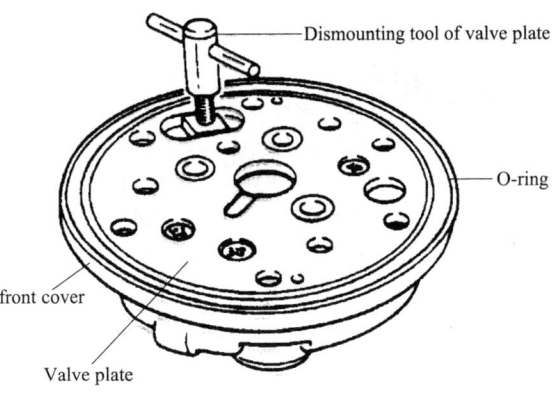

Fig. 2-23 Remove Valve Plate with a
Valve Plate Removal Tool

⑮ Install the rear cover to the valve plate gasket.

⑯ Install the exhaust valve plate and the suction valve plate. Ensure that the gasket and the valve plate are aligned with the positioning pins on the rear cover.

⑰ Install the rear cover O-ring and install the rear cover and the valve plate assembly to the compressor housing.

The positioning pin for the rear cover must be inserted into the corresponding hole on the compressor housing. Position the compressor on the rear cover and install the suction valve, exhaust valve and valve plate gasket, ensuring that the valve plate and the gasket are aligned with the positioning pins on the compressor housing. Install the compressor shaft seal ensuring that the shaft seal is turned into the crankshaft ring groove.

⑱ Fit O-rings on the front cover and the compressor housing and carefully slide the front cover onto the compressor housing.

Use six new brass washers (if required) to install the six compressor through bolts. Tighten these bolts to 29 N • m by using a 10 mm hex socket as required. Use alternate tightening (see Fig. 2-24) to tighten the bolts.

⑲ Install the excitation coil. Ensure that the positioning pin on the compressor is inserted into the hole on the clutch coil. Fit a snap ring. Ensure that the tapered edge of the snap ring is facing outward. Slide the rotor and the bearing assembly onto the cover. Use the bearing removal/ pulley installation tool (see Fig. 2-25) to lightly tap the pulley to install it on the cover.

⑳ Install the rotor and the bearing snap ring. The tapered edge of the snap ring must face outwards. Check the shaft and the hub keys to ensure they are properly seated. Align the keyway on the hub with the key on the shaft. Press the hub onto the compressor shaft using the hub installation tool, as shown in Fig. 2-26.

㉑ Check the clearance between the hub and the rotor with a non-magnetic feeler gauge, as shown in Fig. 2-27. Turn the shaft (hub) by half a turn and check the clearance again. If the clearance is incorrect, replace the appropriate adjusting washer as required. Install lock nut and tighten to 13. 6-19. 0 N • m.

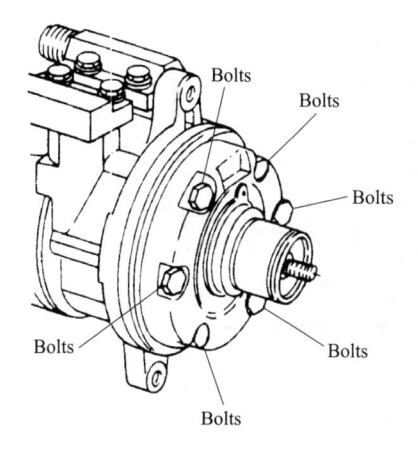

Fig. 2-24　Tighten Bolts

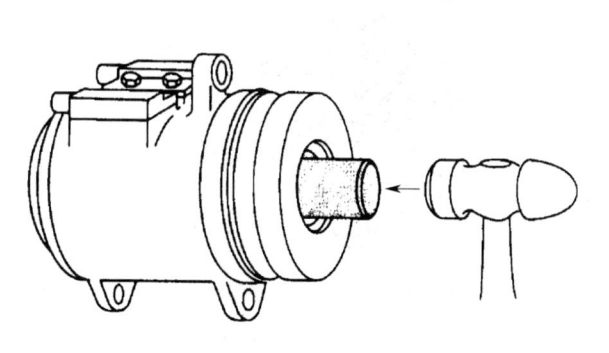

Fig. 2-25　Mount Pulley

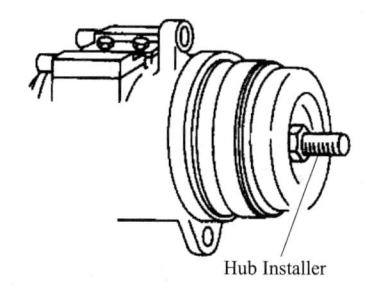

Fig. 2-26　Mount Hub

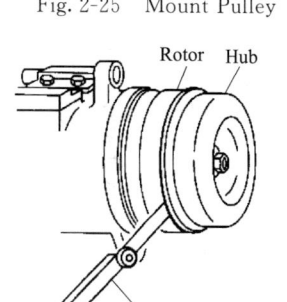

Fig. 2-27　Check Clearance

II . Maintenance of Expansion Valve on Air Conditioning Refrigeration System

1. Maintenance of L-type expansion valve

① Use two wrenches to remove the expansion valve, as shown in Fig. 2-28.

② Install the expansion valve on the manifold and the pressure gauge, and inject refrigerant, as shown in Fig. 2-29. Put the capillary tube of the expansion valve into the water tank, open the high pressure manual valve to make the pointer of the high pressure gauge reach 490 kPa, and the refrigerant is discharged as gas through the expansion valve.

③ Observe the change of water temperature in the water tank (abscissa) and the reading on the high pressure gauge (ordinate). The intersection of the two values shall fall between the two curves in Fig. 2-30, otherwise, replace the expansion valve.

2. Maintenance of the orifice tube of A/C refrigeration system

① Install the manifold pressure gauge set to the automobile A/C system.

② Start the engine and adjust the engine speed to 1000-1200r/min.

③ Turn all A/C control switches to MAX.

Operate the A/C system for 10-15min. Observe the low-pressure side pressure gauge. An abnormal reading on the low pressure side pressure gauge indicates that the orifice tube cannot allow enough refrigerant to enter the evaporator. Determine if the problem is caused by water in the system or by a blockage in the system. Place a warm cloth (about 52 ℃) around the fixed orifice tube and observe the low pressure side pressure gauge. If the pressure rea-

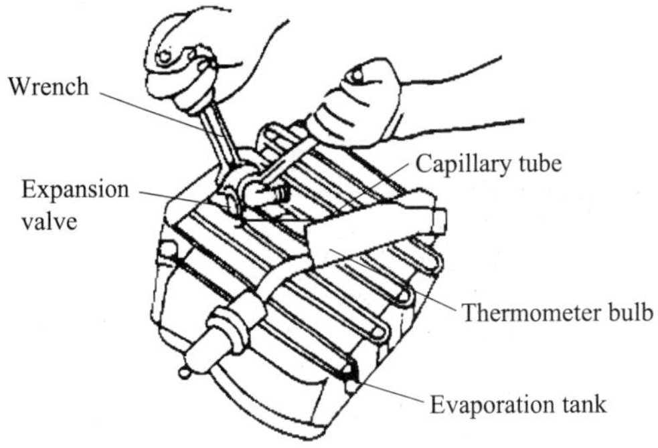

Fig. 2-28   Disassembly of Expansion Valve

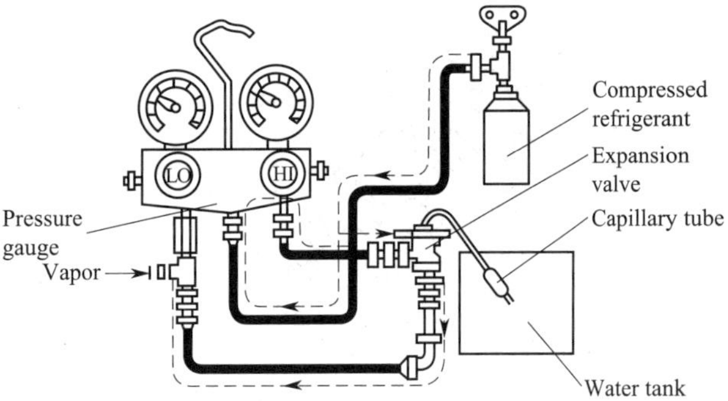

Fig. 2-29   Expansion Valve Connection

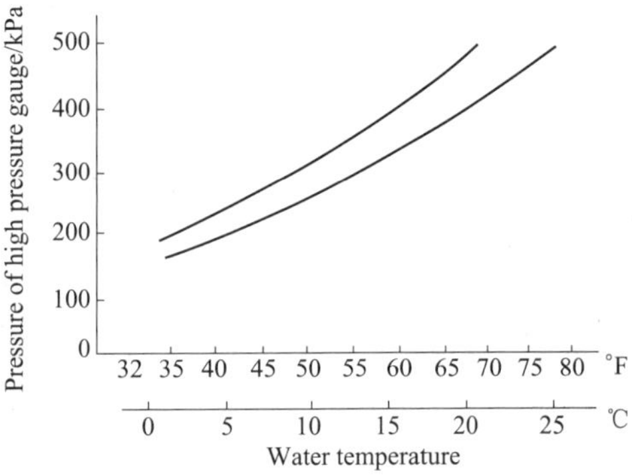

Fig. 2-30   Relationship between Water Temperature and Pressure of High Pressure Gauge

ding rises to the normal value or approaches the normal value, it indicates that there is moisture in the system. If there is moisture in the system, the reservoir must be replaced. If there is no change, the orifice tube may be blocked and the orifice tube must be replaced. When replacing the orifice tube, install the orifice tube removal tool onto the orifice tube, turn the T-shaped handle clockwise to make the tool just engage with the tongue piece of the orifice tube, hold the T-shaped handle, and turn clockwise the outer casing of the orifice tube removal tool to remove the orifice tube, as shown in Fig. 2-31.

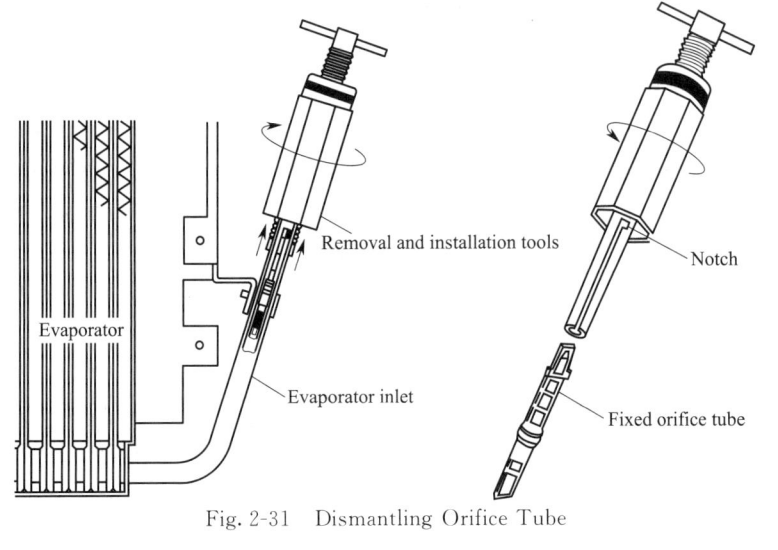

Fig. 2-31   Dismantling Orifice Tube

078   Automotive Safety and Comfort System Maintenance

Ⅲ. Maintenance of Automobile Air Conditioner Condenser

① Check whether there are debris, sundries and mud on the surface of the condenser and between the condenser and the engine water tank (shutdown inspection), and clean and wash with water.

② Check whether the condenser surface is painted off, and pay attention to timely touch-up paint to avoid corrosion.

③ Check whether there is oil stain on the condenser surface and pipe joint (including connector of reservoir). If yes, judge whether there is refrigerant leakage.

④ If the fin is bent, it shall be straightened carefully with pointed nose pliers or straightened with special fin comb.

⑤ If the condenser tube is bent, flattened or damaged due to external force such as stone, repair it in time.

⑥ Check whether the air guide cover is in good condition and whether the distance between the condenser and the water tank is reasonable (the distance between the two shall not exceed 5mm, otherwise the air circulating between them will generate turbulence and affect the heat dissipation).

Ⅳ. Fault Case Diagnosis Process of Automobile Air Conditioning Refrigeration System

In case of such fault (See Task Ⅱ Task Import), firstly check the system pressure with a manifold pressure gauge. If the high pressure is lower than 0.883 MPa and the low pressure is lower than 0.078 MPa, bubbles are found in the glass detection window, and the air from the air outlet is not cold, indicating insufficient refrigerant or serious leakage, so check and replenish the refrigerant. After maintenance, run the engine at the speed of 2000r/min until the bubble disappears. Check with the manifold pressure gauge. The pressure at the low pressure side shall be 0.118-0.216MPa, and the pressure at the high pressure side shall be 1.274-1.596MPa.

Then, check whether the system is dirty or blocked. Dirty blockage of the system refers to the mechanical impurities generated during the operation of the compressor and the impurities falling off due to the action of refrigerant on the inner wall of the system. These impurities block the receiver dryer or the expansion valve, blocking the refrigerant flow. For this, check with the manifold pressure gauge. If the low pressure side is vacuum, the pressure at the high pressure side is very low, at the same time, there is frost or icing on the pipes in front and back of the receiver dryer or the expansion valve, the air from the outlet is not cold, and there is no much change after the machine is shut down and turned on. This indicates that the system is dirty and blocked. Replace the receiver dryer or clean the expansion valve with alcohol.

The failure of the condenser fan is mostly caused by oil shortage of sliding bearing, burnout of bearing or open circuit or short circuit of motor winding. After inspection, if the bearing is short of oil, drill a small hole at the upper end containing oil felt of the slid-

ing bearing at the back of the motor and inject a few drops of No. 30 engine oil into the oil pot for lubrication; if the sliding bearing is burnt out, remove the rear cover of the motor and replace with a new bearing as required; if there is open circuit or short circuit fault in the motor winding, disassemble the motor for further maintenance or replace with a new fan.

Check with the manifold pressure gauge for poor air flow and poor cooling around the condenser. If the pressure at the high pressure side is relatively high and there is much dust and sundries accumulated at the cooling fin of the engine cooling system and the cooling fin of the condenser, the sundries and dust shall be removed and washed with tap water to ensure good ventilation and heat dissipation. If the evaporator ventilation duct is blocked by sundries and dust, the air conditioner can be turned on for inspection. If the air volume at the air outlet is small and the air from the air outlet is not cold, it indicates that the evaporator ventilation duct is blocked by dust and sundries. Remove the sundries, remove the dust, and install a piece of appropriate wire mesh on the air inlet side of the evaporator to prevent dust and sundries from being sucked in a large amount.

The compressor electromagnetic clutch slips, the engine can be started, and the air conditioner can be turned on for inspection. If there is abnormal sound or slipping of the electromagnetic clutch, remove the electromagnetic clutch for disassembly and inspection. If the wear of the clutch pressure plate and pulley working surface is not serious, it can be ground flat on the grinder; if the abrasion is serious, it shall be replaced with a new electromagnetic clutch. The compressor is damaged and has internal leakage, which can be checked with the manifold pressure gauge. If the pressure at the low pressure side is too high, the pressure at the high pressure side is too low, and there is abnormal knocking sound during operation of the compressor, and the temperature difference between the high pressure side and the low pressure side of the compressor is not large, indicating that the compressor has such faults as broken valve disc, damaged bearing or damaged sealing gasket, etc., the compressor shall be disassembled for maintenance or replaced.

If the external circulation damper is not closed, so that the hot air outside the vehicle enters into the vehicle, check whether the vacuum conduit on the vacuum solenoid valve is damaged or broken, so that the external circulation damper cannot be closed. Replace with a new vacuum tube if necessary.

Exercises

Fill in the blanks

1. In the condenser, the refrigerant is changed from _____ into_____ .

2. The high pressure in the high pressure part of the A/C system may be due to excessive _____ , or due to_____ in the system.

3. When the A/C system is replaced from R-12 to R-134a, the original receiver dryer should be replaced with a dryer containing_____ or_____ , because it contains_____ desiccant.

Task Ⅲ Maintenance of Automobile Air Conditioning Control System

【Learning Objectives】

Knowledge requirements: Master the structure and principle of automobile A/C control system, as well as the train of thought and method of fault diagnosis.

Capability requirements:

1. Be able to select correct detection and diagnosis equipment for fault diagnosis of the automobile A/C control system according to maintenance plan;

2. Be able to use multimeter, fault scan tool, refrigerant detector and common detection and diagnosis equipment to detect sensor, controller and actuator of automobile A/C system;

3. Be able to correctly record and analyze various test results and make fault judgment;

4. Be able to replace sensor, actuator and controller according to correct operating specifications, and perform system matching settings;

5. Be able to test, inspect and evaluate the repair quality of automobile A/C system;

6. Be able to correctly handle the auxiliary materials, waste liquid and damaged parts harmful to the environment and human body according to the environmental protection requirements.

 ## Task Import

A SMA car is equipped with R-134a refrigerant. When the A/C is turned on, the A/C does not cool. The electromagnetic clutch does not engage. Sometimes, it can be sucked in once, but it can be disengaged immediately, so it cannot work normally.

 ## Knowledge Preparation

Automobile A/C control system has compressor, condenser, expansion valve, evaporator, blower motor and other main components. The task of the automobile A/C circuit is to regulate and control the above-mentioned configuration, which is the basic characteristic of the automobile A/C circuit. Fig. 2-32 shows the electrical circuit diagram of the A/C device of a common car.

Ⅰ. Control of Power Supply

This part includes battery, ignition switch, fuse relay, blower motor switch, blower motor, pressure switch, electromagnetic clutch, etc. When the ignition switch is turned on, as long as the blower motor switch is closed, the A/C circuit starts to work normally. At this time, the electromagnetic clutch is engaged → the compressor operates → the re-

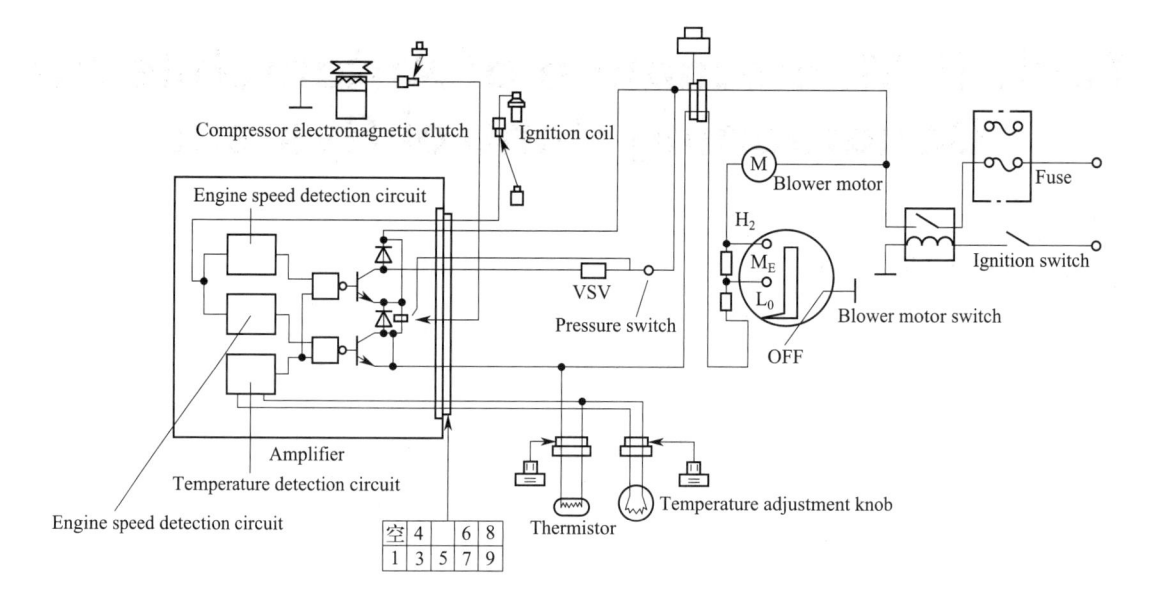

Fig. 2-32　Air Conditioning Circuit of Common Car

frigeration system circulates to start cooling. The air cooled by the evaporator is also fed into the compartment due to the operation of the blower motor.

II. Control of Compressor Electromagnetic Clutch

Because the compressor of the car is directly driven by the engine, the compressor will operate as power output when the electromagnetic clutch is engaged, and the electromagnetic clutch must be energized by its coil to generate electromagnetic attraction, so that the power pressure plate is attracted on the pulley, and then the compressor is driven to run through the pulley.

As the control circuit, as long as the ignition switch is in the ON position, the blower motor switch is turned on, and the blower motor circuit is turned on, an amplifying circuit current is supplied, and the electromagnetic clutch coil is turned on through the circuit to generate suction.

III. Pressure Switch Circuit

The pressure switch circuit is an essential circuit for the normal and safe operation of the refrigeration system. Because when the pressure of the refrigeration system rises for some reason, if there is no protection device, it will cause an operation accident of the refrigeration system. At this point, a pressure switch is used to disconnect the system and stop the compressor, thus protecting the compressor and the refrigeration system.

In the pressure switch, the pressure of the A/C system is generally introduced into the switch, and the contact of the switch is forcibly separated under the action of mechanical force, so as to cut off the switch circuit and to separate the electromagnetic clutch to stop the compressor.

082　Automotive Safety and Comfort System Maintenance

It can be seen from the above that in the whole circuit system, the basic components and circuits of the automobile A/C electrical system are mainly around the start-stop circuit of the compressor electromagnetic clutch as the control center.

IV. Typical Control Circuit in Automobile Air Conditioning Circuit

The circuit of general electric appliance are configured with various control circuits according to its various control functions, and so is the automobile A/C circuit.

V. Speed Control Circuit

The speed control circuit of the automobile A/C is mainly used to control the engine at idle speed and high speed to prevent excessive engine load and excessive cooling in the compartment.

 Task Implementation

I. Fault Detection and Troubleshooting Procedures for Air Conditioning Circuit of Toyota Corolla Car

1. Electronic control element position

The position of the electronic control components of the A/C circuit of Toyota Corolla Car is shown in Fig. 2-33.

2. Circuit inspection, calling and clearing of DTCs

① Turn ignition switch to ON position, press AUTO and R/F switch at the same time to check indicator. If the AUTO and R/F switch are not pressed simultaneously, cancel the check mode and start A/C control.

② After the inspection of indicator is finished, it will automatically enter into the continuous operation mode of DTC check (sensor check). In this mode, press R/F switch to enter regulator check continuous operation mode; press OFF switch to cancel check mode and start A/C control; press DEF switch to enter DTC check (sensor check) step-by-step operation mode.

③ In the step-by-step operation mode of DTC check (sensor check), press the R/F switch to enter the continuous operation mode of regulator check; press the AUTO switch to return to the continuous operation mode of DTC check (sensor check); press the DEF switch to perform step-by-step operation; press the OFF switch to cancel the check mode and start A/C control.

④ In the regulator check continuous operation mode, press AUTO switch to enter DTC check (sensor check) continuous operation mode; press OFF switch to cancel check mode and start A/C control; press DEF switch to enter regulator check step-by-step operation mode.

⑤ Under the step-by-step operation mode of regulator check, press the R/F switch to return to the continuous operation mode of regulator check; press the AUTO switch to return to the continuous operation mode of DTC check (sensor check); press the DEF switch to perform step-by-step operation; press the OFF switch to cancel the check mode and start

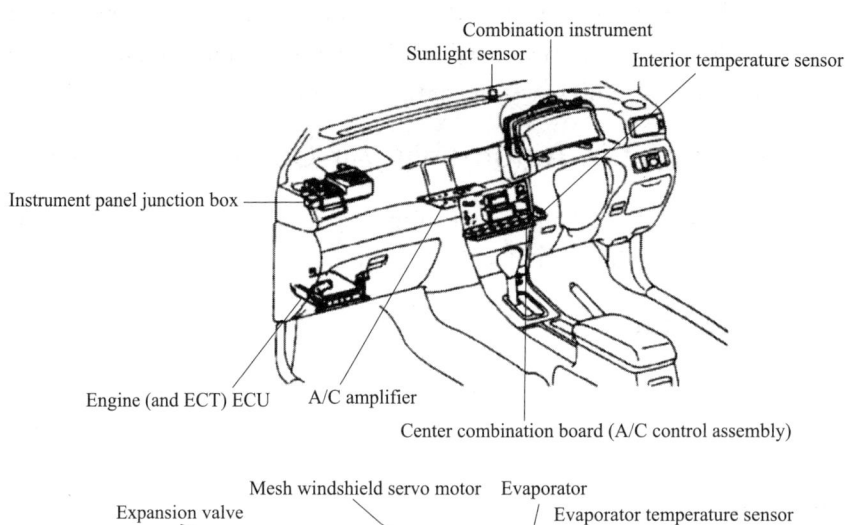

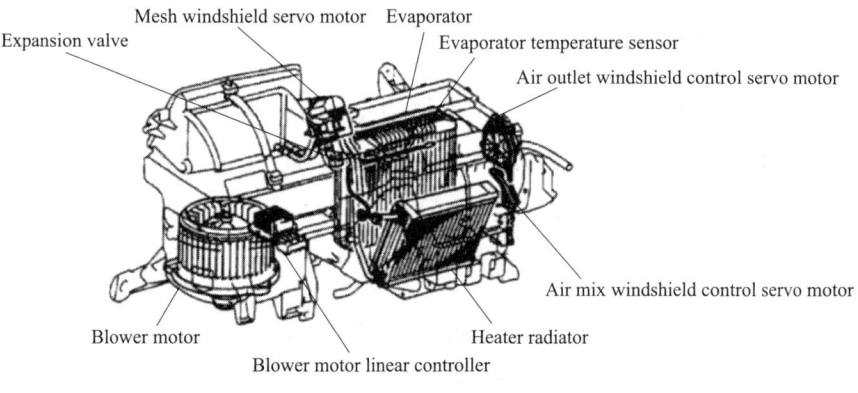

Fig. 2-33　Location of Electric Control Elements

A/C control.

⑥ Indicator inspection. Press AUTO and R/F switch at the same time, turn the ignition switch to ON position, all indicators shall be on and off for 4 times within 1s. When the indicator check is completed, the system automatically enters the DTC check mode.

⑦ DTC check (sensor check). After the indicator check is completed, the system automatically enters into the DTC check mode, at which time the DTC can be read through the control panel. If the display is required to slow down, press the DEF switch to switch to step-by-step operation. Every time DEF switch is pressed, DTC changes once.

⑧ Clear DTC.

a. During sensor inspection, press DEF switch and R/F switch simultaneously to clear DTC.

b. If the DOME fuse is pulled out from the relay box of the engine room for at least 20s or longer, the DTC can be cleared.

⑨ Check the regulator.

a. After entering the DTC check mode, press the R/F switch to enter into the regulator check mode.

b. Since each windshield, motor and relay are displayed in sequence on the temperature display screen at the interval of 1s, check the temperature and air flow by hand. If the display is required to slow down, press the DEF switch to switch to step-by-step opera-

tion. Every time the DEF switch is pressed, the display changes once.

⑩ A/C amplifier terminal voltage. Test the voltage between the terminals of the A/C amplifier, and the inspection result shall comply with the requirements in Table 2-1; otherwise, check the relevant sensors and electrical wiring. The A/C amplifier connector is shown in Fig. 2-34.

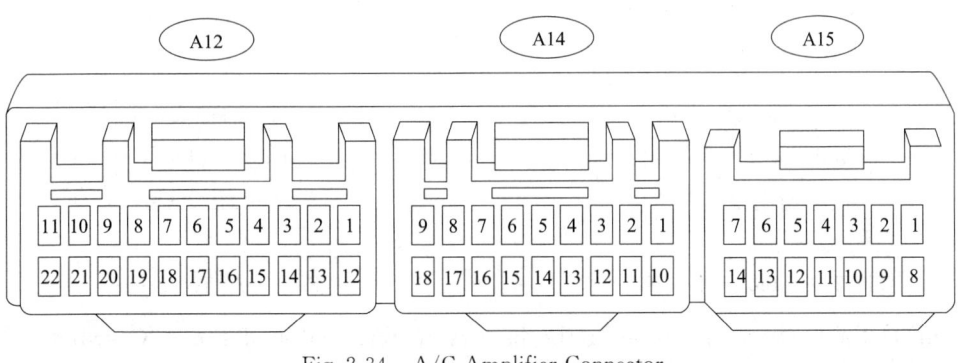

Fig. 2-34　A/C Amplifier Connector

Table 2-1　A/C Amplifier Terminal Voltage List

Test terminal	Wiring color	Test conditions	Standard value
TP—SG-1(A12-4—A12-12)	White blue-brown yellow	Ignition switch in ON, temperature switch coldest position → hottest position	3.5-4.5V→0.5-1.5V
TPM—SG-2(A12-5—A12-3)	Blue orange-blue yellow	Ignition switch in ON, air outlet FACE → DEF	3.5-4.5V→0.5-1.5V
S5-1—SG-1(A12-6—A12-2)	White red-brown yellow	Ignition switch in ON	4.5-5.5V
S5-2—SG-2(A12-7—A12-3)	Light green-blue-yellow	Ignition switch in ON	4.5-5.5V

3. Manual air conditioning component inspection

(1) Check the A/C amplifier circuit

Do not disconnect the connector of the A/C amplifier. Test the voltage between the terminals of the connector at the wiring side of the A/C amplifier. The inspection result shall meet the standard requirements; otherwise, check relevant sensors and electrical wiring. The rear side A/C amplifier connector is shown in Fig. 2-35.

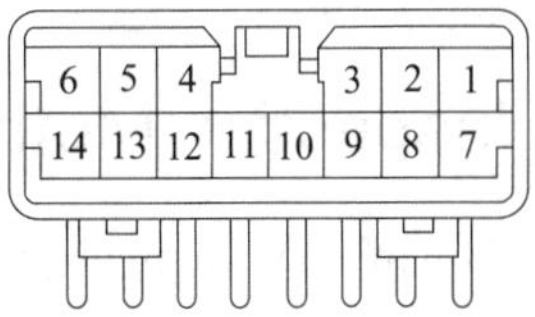

Fig. 2-35　Rear Side A/C Amplifier Connector

(2) Check the blower switch

Check the continuity of the blower switch. As shown in Fig. 2-36, when the blower switch is at OFF position, there shall be no conduction between terminals; when the blower switch is at LO position, the connection between terminals 1 and 8 shall be conducted; when the blower switch is at M1 position, the connection between terminals 1, 6 and 8 shall be conductive; when the blower switch is at M2 position, the connection between terminals 1, 5 and 8 shall be conductive; when the blower switch is at HI position, the connection between the terminals 1, 4 and 8 shall be conductive. If the con-

Item Ⅱ　Maintenance of Automobile Air Conditioning System　**085**

tinuity does not meet the requirements, replace the blower switch. Connect the positive electrode of the battery to the blower switch terminal 2 and the negative electrode to the terminal 3, and the lamp shall be on.

(3) Check the A/C switch

Check the continuity of the A/C switch. As shown in Fig. 2-37, when the A/C switch is pressed, the connection between terminals 2 and 5 shall be conductive. If the continuity does not meet the requirements, replace the A/C switch.

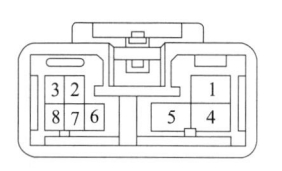

Fig. 2-36　Blower Switch

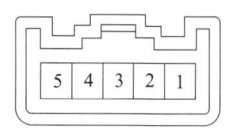

Fig. 2-37　A/C Switch

Connect the positive electrode of the battery to terminal 4 of the A/C switch and the negative electrode to terminal 3, and the lamp shall be on. If the lamp does not work, replace the A/C switch.

Connect the positive electrode of the battery to the terminal 2 of the A/C switch and the negative electrode to the terminal 1. Press down the A/C switch, and the A/C indicator shall be on. If the A/C indicator does not light up, replace the A/C switch.

When pressing down the A/C switch, connect the positive electrode of the battery to the A/C switch terminal 2, the negative electrode to the terminal 1, and then connect the battery positive electrode to the A/C switch terminal 4. The brightness of A/C indicator shall change. If the light does not change, replace the A/C switch.

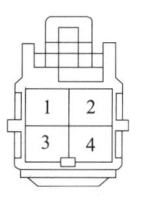

Fig. 2-38　Blower Resistor Connector

(4) Check the blower resistor

Test the resistance between the blower resistor terminals, 1.398-1.605 Ω between terminals 1 and 2, 0.465-0.535 Ω between terminals 1 and 3, and 3.069-3.531 Ω between terminals 1 and 4. The blower resistor connector is shown in Fig. 2-38.

Ⅱ. Inspection Method of Automobile Air Conditioner

During the inspection process of the automobile A/C, it is necessary to perform listening, looking, touching and checking.

Start the engine and stabilize it at about 1500r/ min, start the blower of the A/C system and set it to high gear, and set the function key to A/C gear. And move the temperature adjustment key from cold to hot, then from hot to cold slowly, to measure or feel the temperature change at the A/C air outlet and whether the operation of each control key is flexible and convenient.

1. Listening

The operating condition of the compressor is judged from the operating sound condition of the compressor.

① It is normal to hear the sound of light, brittle and uniform valve disc jumping from the compressor.

② Hearing the knocking sound, it indicates that the refrigerant has "liquid hammering" sound or the oil (excessive oil quantity) knocking the cylinder and other faults.

③ Serious friction sound is heard in the machine body and sometimes the clutch gives out friction sound, indicating heavy load of compressor, insufficient lubricating oil and slipping of clutch.

④ The external clap sound is heard, it is that V belt is too loose or seriously worn.

⑤ Listen to whether the fan in the air conditioner rotates or not. If there is a sound from the fan, it indicates that the blade collides with foreign matter, the fan bearing is worn or the fan is out of oil.

⑥ When the continuous impact sound of moving parts in the machine body can be heard more clearly during shutdown, the clearance between shaft and bearing, piston and cylinder body, and connecting rod and shaft caused by serious wear of internal moving parts is too large or loose.

2. Looking

① Observe whether the condenser surface is clean, because sundries and mud are attached to the condenser, which will affect the cooling effect. Always clean the condenser with water. However, care shall be taken not to damage the fins when cleaning the condenser. The deformed fins shall be carefully corrected with pointed nose pliers.

② The evaporator air inlet of the automobile A/C is usually equipped with air filter screen. Therefore, regularly observe the air filter screen.

③ Observe whether there are oil stains on all connecting parts of the A/C refrigeration system. Once there is oil stain, it indicates that there is refrigerant leakage here. At this time, use electronic leak detector or other kind of leakage detection device to check. Once the refrigerant leak is found or determined, the problem must be corrected immediately.

④ Check whether the compressor shaft seal leaks.

⑤ Carefully check each hose for wear, aging, bubbling, crack and leakage. Because a large number of rubber pipes are used in the cold and warm system of the automobile, it is easy to rub and wear with the car body during driving. It is easy to age due to high temperature in the engine room, and the refrigeration pipe is easy to crack in case of low temperature. As a result, the refrigerant and refrigerating lubricating oil leak, so that moisture, air and dust penetrate into the refrigeration system, causing damage to the compressor and all parts. Therefore, once the rubber pipe is found to be in contact with the engine, the rubber pipe shall be separated and fixed in time. When rubber pipe passes through metal plate, protective sleeve shall be provided generally, and the protective sleeve shall be firm, otherwise the metal will cut the rubber pipe.

3. Touching

Touch the temperature of the running A/C system pipeline and each component by hand. Under normal conditions, the pipeline temperature at the high pressure end shall be below 55 ℃, while the pipeline at the low pressure end is in low temperature state, so the components and pipelines at the low pressure end and the surface of the connecting part will

have water dew.

① Carefully touch the high pressure area, especially the metal parts at the high pressure end, such as outlet valve of compressor, condenser and receiver dryer with hands. These parts should be hot, normally hands feel warm but not hot. If it feels hot, check whether the cooling of the condenser is good, whether the surface of the condenser is clean and free of sundries, and whether the air volume of the fan is too small. At this time, you can try to use the large fan to blow against the condenser. If it is still hot, it may be too much refrigerant. If the feeling heat of the high pressure end is not enough, it means too little refrigerant; if there is no temperature, it means that the refrigerant has completely leaked.

② The feel of the low pressure pipe is cold with dew, but there should be no frost. If there is frost, the system is faulty. The expansion valve may be faulty or the refrigerant is filled too much and some of it needs to be discharged; or the temperature sensor or thermostat of the evaporator is faulty.

③ If frost or water dew appears on the receiver dryer, it indicates that the desiccant has been broken and blocked the refrigerant flow pipe, and the high-pressure area at the front end here is hot. At this point, eliminate the blockage problem as soon as possible and replace it with a new receiver dryer.

④ The temperature of the expansion valve felt by hand is special. Its refrigerant inlet connection is hot, while its outlet connection is cool with water dew.

⑤ Touch the air inlet and outlet of the compressor with both hands, and the hand feeling temperature shall be obviously different. If there is no temperature difference, it indicates that the refrigerant has completely leaked; if the difference is not large, it indicates that the refrigerant is insufficient.

⑥ Touch each connector with hand to check whether it is loose. Especially whether the connection of some electrical connectors is loose. These have great influence on the normal operation of the A/C system. Therefore, normal inspection must include fixing, fastening and cleaning of electrical connectors.

4. Checking

After the initial inspection of the system in the above three steps, further inspection is required to accurately determine the fault location of the A/C system.

① Check the tension of V-belt: The required tension is different with different diameter and center distance of the A/C pulley; the tension of a new V-belt and an old V-belt is also different; even the tension of the new V-belt will change greatly after 5 min of use. Therefore, the newly installed V-belt must be adjusted twice. After it is installed for the first time, adjust to the specified value. After 30min operation, the burrs on both sides of the new V-belt have been ground, and then the second adjustment shall be carried out.

② Check electromagnetic clutch: Switch on the clutch power switch, and the compressor shall run immediately; when the power supply is cut off, the compressor shall stop running immediately. If this is not the case, first check whether the switch is damaged and then check whether the solenoid coil is normal.

③ Check the speed governor of the fan motor: Turn on the switch of the fan motor and

adjust the speed from low gear to high gear to check whether the air volume sent out changes. If there is no change, the resistor of the governor may be damaged.

④ Check the high and low voltage protection switches and overheat protector: The function of the high and low pressure protection switches and the overheat protector is to protect the compressor and the refrigeration system from damage in case of failure of the refrigeration system. They are connected in series with the A/C switch and fan switch. When the working pressure of the system is too high, or when the ambient temperature is too low, refrigerant leaks too much. The high and low pressure switches disconnect the compressor clutch circuit.

⑤ Check the heating system: Firstly, ensure enough coolant. If the coolant is not clean or has rust or the liquid color turns yellow, drain off the coolant, clean the cooling system with chemical cleaning agent, clean it with clean water, and then fill up the coolant. Start the engine until the coolant temperature is normal. Turn the temperature control key to the heating position, and hot air shall be blown out from the air outlet.

⑥ Check expansion valve: The capillary tube of the expansion valve shall be firmly clamped and wrapped with insulating cloth at the outlet of the evaporator. Some capillary tubes shall be accurately inserted into the socket of the refrigeration pipeline and wrapped with temperature sensing package.

⑦ Check the sight glass: Automobile A/C is generally equipped with a sight glass to observe the flow of refrigerant inside the refrigeration system. Most cars are equipped with sight glasses at the outlet of the receiver dryer, and only the sight glasses of some cars or large and medium passenger cars are installed on the pipes between the receiver dryers and the expansion valves. The setting of the sight glass brings a lot of convenience to the maintenance of the automobile A/C. When checking the automobile A/C, you can observe the flow condition of refrigerant in the sight glass to determine whether the refrigeration working condition of the refrigeration system is normal. The steps to check the refrigeration conditions of the refrigeration system through the sight glass are as follows: Start the engine, stabilize the rotating speed at 1500-1700r/min, and let the refrigeration compressor operate for 5min; clean the glass of the sight glass, set the A/C function selection key to the maximum cooling state, and make the blower (including air conditioner and condenser blower) reach the maximum speed. At this time, the following conditions can be observed through the sight glass, as shown in Fig. 2-39.

a. Clarity: As shown in Fig. 2-39 (a), there is no bubble in the sight glass and no liquid flow can be seen. This condition indicates that the system has the following 3 faults.

(a) All refrigerant in the system has leaked. At this time, if you touch the air inlet and outlet of the compressor with your hand, there is no temperature difference, and the air temperature at the air outlet of the A/C is not low. At this time, immediately shut down the refrigeration system, check the reason for refrigerant leakage of the refrigeration system and carry out maintenance.

(b) Too much refrigerant. Touch the inlet pipe and exhaust pipe of the compressor with two hands respectively. The temperature difference is obvious, and the high-pressure side feels hot, and the low-pressure side can see frost; the temperature at the air outlet of the

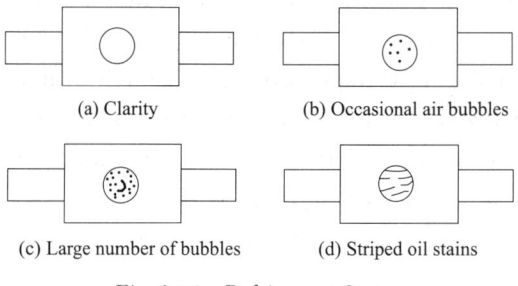

(a) Clarity   (b) Occasional air bubbles

(c) Large number of bubbles   (d) Striped oil stains

Fig. 2-39　Refrigerant Status

A/C is 3-5℃ higher than that of the normal refrigerant quantity; 45s after turning off the A/C system compressor, the sight glass is still clear without bubbles flowing through, it can be judged that there is too much refrigerant in the system, and the redundant refrigerant must be discharged at this time. Otherwise, problems such as cooling performance degradation and energy consumption increase may occur. At this time, measure the high pressure end with a pressure gauge, and its pressure exceeds the normal value.

（c）Appropriate amount of refrigerant. At this time, compared with excessive refrigerant, the first thing is that the high pressure does not burn and the temperature of the air outlet is low.

b. Occasional bubbles. Fig. 2-39（b）shows that a small amount of bubbles flow occasionally or slowly. This state indicates that the refrigerant is slightly insufficient or the desiccant of the refrigeration system is saturated, and moisture is mixed in the refrigerant. The way to distinguish these situations is as follows.

（a）When the expansion valve frosts and sometimes the color-changing desiccant can be seen on the sight glass, it indicates that the system refrigerant contains water, and the drying bottle shall be replaced immediately.

（b）When the expansion valve is not frosted, it indicates that the refrigerant is insufficient. An appropriate amount of refrigerant must be added, and check whether there is any leakage.

c. There is a large amount of bubbles or foams. As shown in Fig. 2-39（c）, this condition indicates that the refrigerant in the system is seriously insufficient, accompanied by a large amount of moisture and air entering the system. At this time, the refrigerant detector must be used for leakage detection and maintenance. Then vacuum the refrigeration system and add enough refrigerant oil and refrigerant.

d. Stripe-like oil stain or black oil-like foam on the glass of the sight glass. As shown in Fig. 2-39（d）, it indicates that the system has the following three faults.

（a）If there is obvious temperature difference between the inlet and exhaust pipes of the compressor, shut down the compressor of the A/C system at this time, and if the oil stain on the glass inside the sight glass is clean, it indicates that the amount of refrigerant in the system is small, but the refrigerant lubricating oil is too much. At this time, release some refrigerant lubricating oil from the system, and then add a proper amount of refrigerant.

（b）If there is obvious temperature difference between the inlet and exhaust pipes of the compressor, close the compressor of the A/C system at this time, and the oil stain left on

the glass is black or there are other sundries, which indicates that the refrigerant lubricating oil in the A/C system has deteriorated and polluted. At this time, after the refrigeration system is cleaned, the refrigerant lubricating oil and the refrigerant shall be refilled.

（c）If there is no obvious temperature difference between the inlet and exhaust valves of the compressor and no cool air comes out from the outlet of the A/C, it means that all the refrigerant has leaked out, and frozen lubricating oil is on the sight glass.

Ⅲ. Regular Maintenance of Automobile Air Conditioning System

（1）Refrigeration circulation system

① Check the high and low pressure pipes. The pipe codes of high and low pressure pipelines shall be complete, and the bolts shall be fastened without looseness. There shall be no blistering, aging or damage on the surface of the hose; there shall be no crack or leakage at the welding point of the rigid pipe. There is no collision interference with other parts. Use a leak detector to detect whether there is leakage at each pipe joint.

② Check the expansion valve. The expansion valve shall be free from blockage, the temperature sensing package shall function normally, and the expansion valve shall be able to automatically adjust the refrigerant supply amount according to the temperature change.

③ Check the filter of the receiver dryer. During normal operation of the refrigeration system, its surface shall be free from dewdrops or frost. Replace desiccant (detachable) or replace the filter assembly (non-detachable) of the receiver dryer as required.

④ Check and clean the evaporator and the condenser, and check all fixing bolts and nuts. Evaporator and condenser shall be free from leakage, cooling fins shall be free from bending, dust and sundries blocking; evaporator and condenser seats shall be free of crack; all fixing bolts and nuts shall be complete, tight and reliable.

⑤ Check the refrigerant. When the refrigeration system is working, observe the sight glass; there shall be no bubble flow. The working pressure of the system shall be 0.147-0.2MPa at the low pressure side and 1.4-1.5MPa at the high pressure side when the engine speed is 2000r/min, the blower rotates at the highest speed and the strongest gear is selected for cooling.

（2）Compressor

① Replace the lubricating oil of the compressor and clean or replace the oil filter screen. The height of the lubricating oil surface of the compressor shall reach the upper edge of the sight glass or the standard specified by the original factory. The oil filter screen shall be clean without sundries blocking or defect.

② Check the intake and exhaust valves. The intake and exhaust valves shall be opened and closed flexibly with normal functions.

③ Check the bushing. There shall be no leakage at the bushing.

（3）Electrical system

① Check the fans of the condenser and the evaporator. All fans shall operate normally without abnormal sound, blades shall be free from cracks, and fixing bolts and nuts shall be complete, firm and effective. There is no interference between the condenser fan and the condenser cooling fin.

② Check the high and low pressure switches. When the pressure is higher than 2. 2MPa，the high pressure switch can cut off the power supply to the electromagnetic clutch，and can automatically reset when the pressure is lower than 2MPa； when the pressure is lower than 0. 2MPa，the low pressure switch can cut off the power supply to the electromagnetic clutch，and when the pressure is higher than 0. 2MPa，it can automatically reset.

③ Check the electromagnetic clutch. The electromagnetic clutch shall clutch well without slipping，and the clutch bearing shall be free from deflection and drag during rotation.

④ Check whether the operation of forced draft fan is normal and reliable.

(4) Others

① Fastener：Check whether there is any damage，and fasten it if it is loose.

② V-belt：Check for tension and wear.

③ V-belt tension pulley：Check for smooth rotation.

④ Air filter screen：Replace the air filter screen if any blockage is found.

Ⅳ. Fault Detection of Automobile Air Conditioning System

① Use the decoder to detect the fault of the automobile A/C system and read the DTC.

② Analyze the measured fault content according to the DTC.

③ Carry out troubleshooting according to the maintenance manual.

Ⅴ. Fault Case Diagnosis Process of Automobile Air Conditioning Control System

Test after connecting the vehicle scan tool. During the test，it was found that the compressor did not engage when there was intermittent non-cooling. According to the analysis of the control principle of the automatic air conditioner of Buick car，besides the failure of the compressor itself，the failure of PCM，request signal of the A/C switch，pressure sensor signal and indoor/outdoor temperature sensor may cause failure of the compressor.

Connect the A/C pressure gauge and measure the pressure of the A/C pipeline. The result showed that the high pressure was 2000kPa and the low pressure was about 350kPa，which indicated that the pressure of the A/C system is normal. Open the relay box on the right side in the engine compartment and locate the compressor relay. Check the pull-in coil of the relay and no anomalies were found. Check the control line of the compressor relay with a multimeter (low potential when the relay was engaged and high potential when disconnected) and find that the control line from the PCM to the compressor relay had no low potential when the air conditioner was not cooled. Therefore，it can be concluded that the fault of intermittent non-cooling of the A/C system of this vehicle is not caused by the actuating part，but may be caused by the failure of PCM itself，abnormal signal or circuit related to the air conditioner.

Test the relevant line from the PCM to the compressor relay and find that there was no low potential signal in PCM line 39 when the fault is present. Connect the scan tool to monitor the A/C switch request signal，pressure sensor signal and indoor/outdoor temperature sensor signal of the A/C system. The result showed that the pressure sensor data was abnormal when there was a fault phenomenon，while the data of other sensors had no obvious

change. Based on the test results, the fault was judged to be intermittent binding of the pressure switch, which caused the PCM control compressor clutch to be intermittently engaged. After replacing the pressure switch, the intermittent non-cooling fault disappeared and the system returned to normal.

Exercises

Short Answer Question

Please demonstrate how to check the A/C system pressure.

Task Ⅳ Filling and Reclaiming Refrigerant for Automobile Air Conditioner

〔Learning Objectives〕

Knowledge requirements: Master the basic knowledge of automobile air conditioning refrigerant.

Capability requirements:

1. Be able to fill and reclaim refrigerant for automobile air conditioner.

2. Be able to use tools of filling and reclaiming automobile air conditioning refrigerant.

 Task Import

A Volkswagen Magotan car equipped with automatic A/C, the A/C outlet temperature is not too cold when the A/C is turned on.

 Knowledge Preparation

A certain amount of air will enter the refrigeration system during installation and maintenance of the A/C refrigeration system. The water vapor contained in the air will cause ice blockage of the expansion valve of the refrigeration system, increase of condensation pressure, corrosion of system components, etc. Therefore, the refrigeration system must be evacuated before filling with new refrigerant.

Ⅰ. Filling the Refrigerant of Automobile Air Conditioning System

The refrigerant can be filled into the refrigeration system only after the vacuum pumping of the refrigeration system meets the requirements and there is no leakage part in the refrigeration system through leak detection.

Vacuum pump is used for vacuuming after installation and maintenance of the refrigeration system to remove air and moisture in the system. Vacuum pumping does not draw out the water in the refrigeration system, but lowers the boiling point of water after vacuum is

Item Ⅱ Maintenance of Automobile Air Conditioning System **093**

generated in the refrigeration system. The water boils at a relatively low temperature and is extracted from the system in the form of vapor.

Commonly used vacuum pumps include slide valve type and blade type sealed with oil and water ring type sealed with water. The vacuum pump sealed with oil has high vacuum degree. The structure of the commonly used blade vacuum pump is shown in Fig. 2-40.

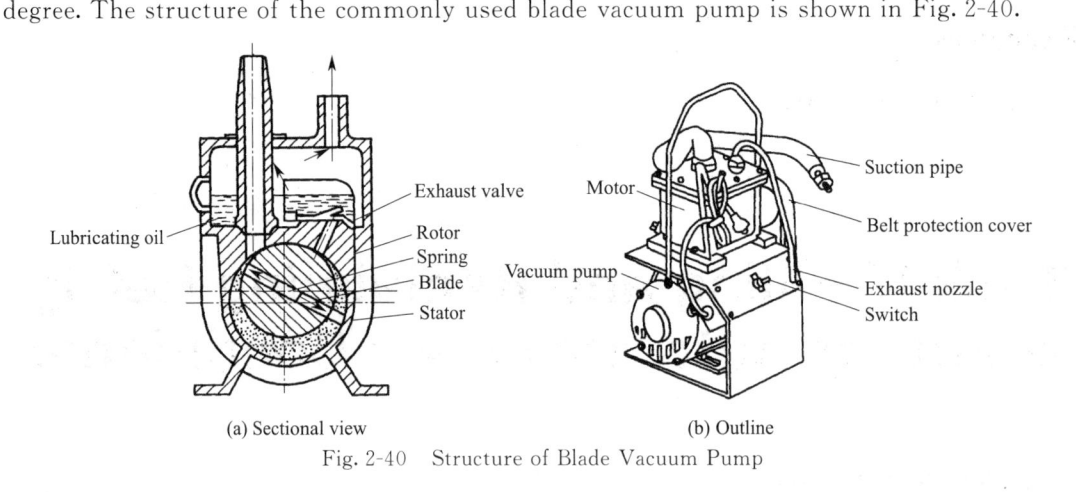

(a) Sectional view   (b) Outline

Fig. 2-40   Structure of Blade Vacuum Pump

It is mainly composed of stator, rotor, exhaust valve and blade, etc. During operation, the spring force makes two blades tightly adhere to the cylinder wall of the stator to ensure its tightness, while the inlet and outlet ports on the stator are divided into two parts by the rotor and the blade, forming the suction chamber and the compression chamber. When the rotor rotates, the volume of the inlet cavity gradually expands, and the pressure in the cavity decreases, thus the gas is sucked in. The volume of the compression chamber decreases gradually, the pressure rises, and the gas is discharged into the air from the exhaust valve. After repeated circulation, the air in the container is evacuated, so as to achieve the purpose of vacuum.

There are two methods to fill the refrigerant. One method is to fill the high-pressure end through the bypass hole (multi-purpose passage) of the compressor exhaust valve (high-pressure valve), which is filled with refrigerant liquid. This kind of filling method is safe, fast and suitable for the first filling of refrigeration system, that is, the system filling after leak detection and vacuumizing. However, when using this method, it must be noted that the compressor cannot be turned on during filling (engine stops) and the refrigerant tank is required to stand upside down, as shown in Fig. 2-41. The other method is to fill the low-pressure end through the bypass hole (multi-purpose channel) of the suction valve (low-pressure valve) of the compressor and fill with refrigerant gas. This filling method is slow in filling speed, which is suitable for the refrigeration system to replenish refrigerant. The filling method is shown in Fig. 2-42.

Before filling, the quantity of refrigerant injected must be determined. If the refrigerant is filled too much or too little, the cooling effect of the A/C will be affected. The nameplate of the compressor is generally marked with the type and charge amount of refrigerant used.

In order to facilitate the maintenance of the automobile A/C and carrying along with the vehicle, the refrigerant manufacturer has made a small tank of refrigerant (generally about 400g). If the refrigerant is to be injected into the refrigeration system of the automobile A/

C, the injection valve must be used. As shown in Fig. 2-43, the refrigerant injection valve pierces the refrigerant tank with the needle valve in front of the butterfly handle and introduces the refrigerant into the manifold pressure gauge set through the threaded joint.

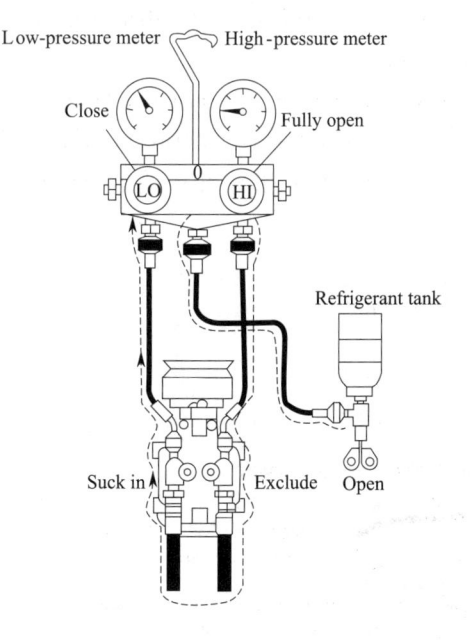

Fig. 2-41 Filling Liquid Refrigerant at High Pressure End

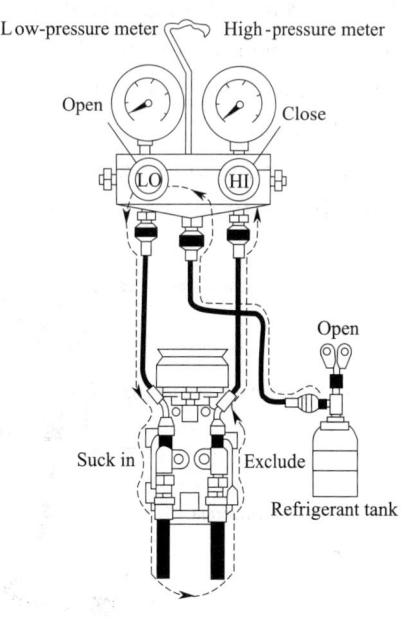

Fig. 2-42 Filling Gaseous Refrigerant at Low Pressure End

II. Replenishment and Discharge of Refrigerant for Automobile Air Conditioning Refrigeration System

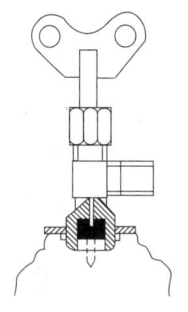

① Replenishment of refrigerant. After a period of operation of the automobile A/C system, the joints of some parts become loose due to bump and vibration of automobile, causing refrigerant leakage and poor refrigeration effect. Replenish refrigerant from the low pressure side to the system after leakage checking and eliminating, as shown in Fig. 2-44.

Fig. 2-43 Structure of Refrigerant Injection Valve

② Discharge of refrigerant. For repair or other reasons, the refrigerant in the system needs to be discharged in two ways: One is to put the refrigerant into the atmosphere, but this method pollutes the environment; the other is to recover the refrigerant, but there should be a recovery device. When discharging, the surrounding environment must be well ventilated and not close to open fire, otherwise toxic gas will be generated.

III. Filling Refrigeration Lubricating Oil of Automobile Air Conditioning Refrigeration System

The consumption of refrigerant lubricating oil of automobile A/C refrigeration system is

Item II   Maintenance of Automobile Air Conditioning System   **095**

very small，which can be replaced once every two years. Each replacement shall be filled according to the specified quantity（the model and quantity of lubricating oil are generally marked on the nameplate of the compressor）. Refrigerant lubricating oil of the same brand shall be used during filling. Mixed use of different brands of refrigerant lubricating oil will cause sediment pollution to the A/C refrigeration system.

Automobile A/C compressor is a high-speed running device，its normal operation depends on the lubrication. Too much lubricating oil will affect the refrigeration effect. When replacing the compressor and a certain part of the refrigeration system，it is necessary to check the oil quantity in the compressor.

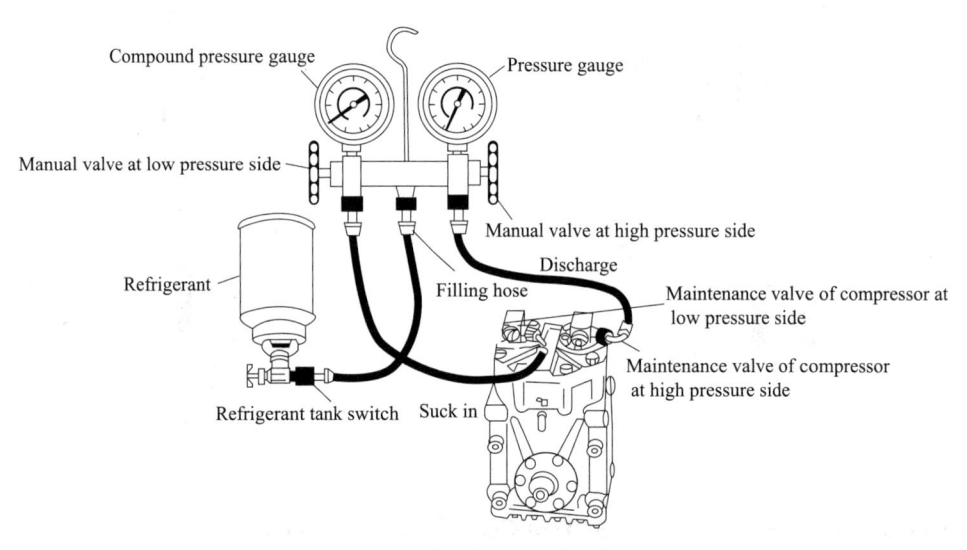

Fig. 2-44　Replenishment of Refrigerant

1. Check of refrigerant lubricating oil quantity of compressor

As shown in Fig. 2-45，remove the oil filler plug，inspect and rotate the clutch front plate through the oil filler plug hole，clean the dipstick and insert it into the compressor until the end of the dipstick touches the inner casing of the compressor. Take out the dipstick and observe the dip depth of the dipstick. When the quantity of refrigerant lubricating oil is appropriate，the oil level in the compressor shall be between the first 4-6 grids. If it is sufficient，it needs to be added，if more，it needs to be discharged，and then tighten the oil filler plug.

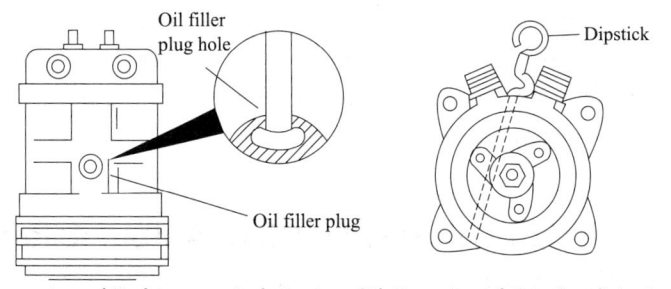

Fig. 2-45　Inspection of Refrigerant Lubricating Oil Quantity of Air Conditioning Compressor

096 Automotive Safety and Comfort System Maintenance

2. Filling of refrigerant lubricating oil

Refrigerant lubricating oil is not required to be added in the maintenance of the automobile A/C refrigeration system, but it must be replenished when replacing refrigeration system components and finding serious leakage in the system. There are two ways to replenish the refrigerant lubricating oil.

① Use the suction function of the compressor itself to suck the refrigerant lubricating oil from the low-pressure valve. At this time, the engine shall keep running at low speed.

② Fill the frozen lubricating oil by vacuum pumping.

Ⅳ. Reclaiming Refrigerant

Refrigerant itself is non-toxic and harmless to human beings, but it is an important pollution source for the environment. R-12 is the culprit responsible for the global ozone hole. Its substitute R-134a is not as serious as R-12, but it also pollutes the atmosphere.

The recovery unit is small and lightweight and is used only for those refrigerants designed for it. Its lubricating oil, hose and seal are suitable for a limited range of refrigerants. If used with mismatched refrigerants, the recovery unit can be damaged. See Fig. 2-46 for two recovery units for R-12 and R-134a. There are two methods to recover refrigerant: cooling method and compression method.

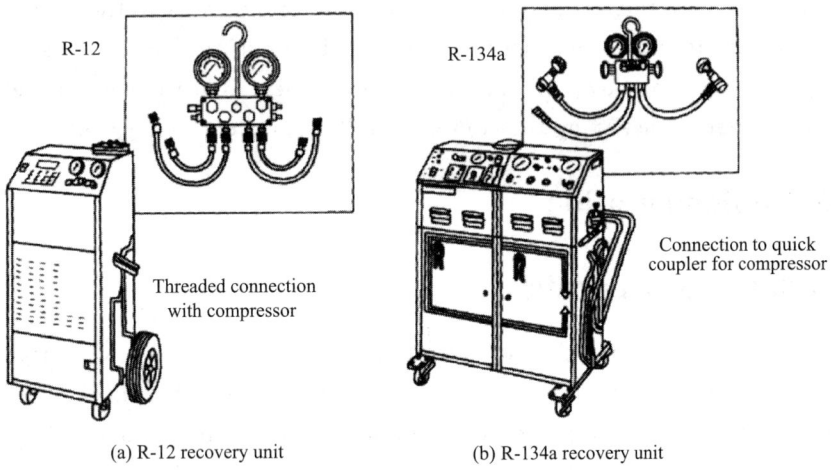

(a) R-12 recovery unit   (b) R-134a recovery unit

Fig. 2-46   Refrigerant Recovery Unit

① Cooling method. Cooling method is to cool and liquefy refrigerant vapor. During recovery, dry ice can be used to cool the refrigerant and recover it after liquefaction. The recovery container shall be cooled to −30℃. This method is suitable for clean refrigerant. Fig. 2-47 shows the schematic diagram of the recovery unit by cooling method. The cooling method has an independent refrigeration circulation system, in which the refrigerant in the recovery container condenses into liquid in the evaporator. The refrigerant discharged from the automobile A/C system passes through the filter dryer to remove moisture and impurities; and the oil separator removes the lubricating oil in the refrigerant. For the occasions where the refrigerant purity requirements are not strict, the recovered refrigerant can be recharged to the refrigeration system.

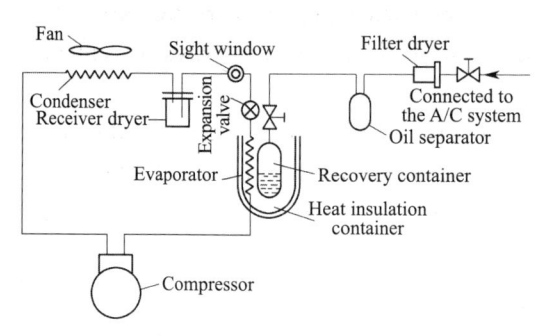

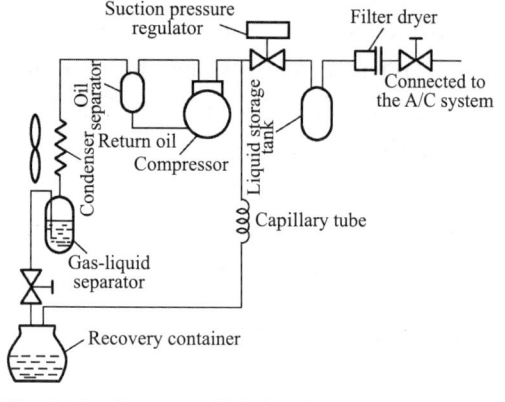

Fig. 2-47　Recovery Unit by Cooling Method　　　Fig. 2-48　Recovery Unit by Compression Method

② Compression method. Compression method uses compression to evaporate refrigerant into liquid. Its working principle is shown in Fig. 2-48. The refrigerant discharged from the A/C system passes through the filter dryer to remove moisture and impurities. Controlled by the suction pressure regulating valve, part of the liquid refrigerant remains in the liquid storage tank. The gaseous refrigerant enters the compressor and is compressed into high-temperature and high-pressure gas. When passing through the oil separator, the refrigerant lubricating oil mixed with the refrigerant is separated and flows back to the compressor, and the refrigerant enters into the condenser for cooling. Through the gas-liquid separator, the condensed liquid refrigerant flows to the recovery container, and the gaseous refrigerant in the recovery container is sucked by the compressor through the capillary tube.

 Task Implementation

Ⅰ. Precautions for Operation

① The consumption of refrigerant lubricating oil of automobile A/C refrigeration system is very small, so it can be replaced once every two years. When filling refrigerant, it shall be filled according to the type and charge amount of refrigerant marked on the nameplate of the compressor.

② If refrigerant is to be injected into the vehicle A/C refrigeration system, an injection valve must be used.

③ When the refrigerant is discharged, the surrounding environment must be well ventilated and not close to open flame, otherwise toxic gas will be generated.

Ⅱ. Operating Steps

1. Discharge of refrigerant

(1) Preparation

① Connect the pressure gauge set to the system.

② Start the engine and operate the automobile A/C system.

③ Adjust the engine speed to 1000-1200r/ min and operate for 5min.

（2）Discharge of refrigerant

① Restore the normal engine speed, and then shut down the engine.

② Slowly open the manual high-pressure valve to discharge the refrigerant through the middle hose. The open end of the middle hose should be wrapped with white cloth. If refrigerant oil is discharged, adjust the manual valve until there is just no refrigerant lubricating oil.

③ When the reading of the pressure gauge drops below 0.35MPa, slowly open the low pressure manual valve to discharge the refrigerant from both sides of high and low pressure at the same time.

④ Observe the reading of the pressure gauge and gradually open the manual high and low pressure valves as the pressure drops until the readings of high and low pressure gauges are zero.

2. Filling of refrigerant lubricating oil

Select a graduated cylinder to fill more refrigerant lubricating oil than the refrigerant lubricating oil to be replenished; screw down the low pressure hose connected to the compressor from the manifold pressure gauge and insert it into the cylinder containing the refrigerant lubricating oil, as shown in Fig. 2-49; start the vacuum pump, open the manual high pressure valve on the manifold pressure gauge, and replenish the refrigerant lubricating oil into the compressor from the low pressure side of the compressor; when the refrigerant lubricating oil reaches the specified amount, stop the suction of the vacuum pump and close the manual high pressure valve.

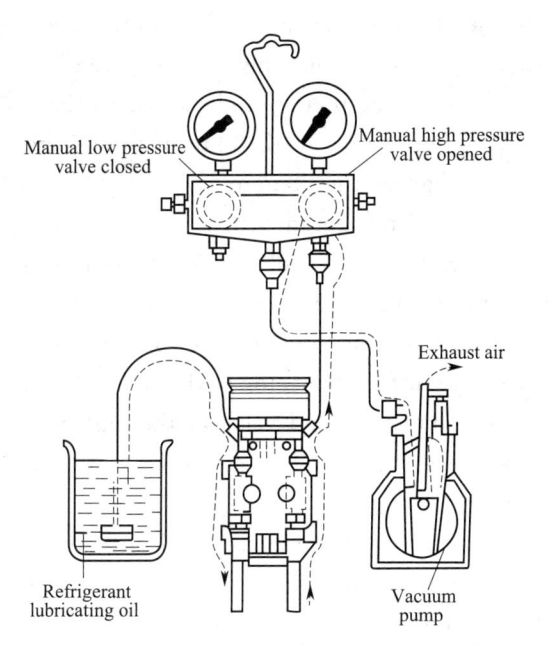

Fig. 2-49　Filling Refrigerant Lubricating Oil with Vacuum Extraction Method

3. System Vacuumizing

（1）Preparation

① Open the high and low pressure manual valves on the pressure gauge set, and connect the middle hose to the vacuum pump inlet.

② Remove the protective cover of vacuum pump exhaust port.

（2）vacuuming

① Start the vacuum pump.

② Observe the pressure gauge, the gauge needle should swing downward and show a slight vacuum.

③ After the vacuum pump operates for 10min, check whether the reading of the low pressure gauge is higher than 79.8kPa. If the vacuum degree is lower than 79.8kPa, close the high and low pressure manual valves, stop the vacuum pump, check whether there is

Item II　Maintenance of Automobile Air Conditioning System　**099**

leakage in the system, and repair it according to the situation.

④ Keep it for 5-10min. If the pressure rises, it indicates that there is leakage in the system. Check and eliminate it, and then carry out the vacuuming process.

⑤ If the pointer of the low-pressure gauge remains unchanged, continue vacuumizing for more than 30min, close the high-pressure and low-pressure manual valves, and then close the vacuum pump.

4. Filling of refrigerant

(1) Preparation

① Before installing the refrigerant injection valve on the refrigerant tank, firstly rotate the butterfly handle counterclockwise until the valve needle retracts, and then rotate the plate nut counterclockwise to the highest position.

② Install the injection valve into the threaded groove on the top of the refrigerant tank, and then turn the refrigerant injection valve clockwise until the injection valve is inserted into the refrigerant sealing plug.

③ Turn the plate nut clockwise to the end, and then fix the middle hose on the manifold pressure gauge to the joint of the injection valve.

④ Tighten the plate nut.

(2) Fill refrigerant when the system is stopped

① Rotate the handle clockwise to make the valve needle penetrate the sealing plug, and then rotate the handle counterclockwise to lift the valve needle.

② Loosen the middle hose connector on the gauge holder until refrigerant flows out and then tighten the connector (exhaust the air in the middle hose).

③ Open the hand valve at the high pressure side on the gauge holder and observe the low pressure gauge. The gauge needle shall be changed from vacuum range to pressure range.

④ Invert the refrigerant tank to allow the liquid refrigerant to enter the system.

⑤ Knock the bottom of the tank with your fingers. If there is a sound of empty cylinder, it indicates that the tank is empty. If the refrigerant is insufficient, the second tank should be filled from the low pressure side.

⑥ Close the manual valve at the high pressure side on the gauge holder, remove the injection valve from the middle hose, remove the pressure gauge set from the system, and recover all covers and caps.

(3) Fill refrigerant during system operation

① Connect the pressure gauge set to the system and start the engine, adjust the engine speed to 1250r/min, and ensure that the high and low pressure valves on the gauge holder are closed.

② Adjust the temperature key on the A/C control panel to the coldest position and the blower to the high speed.

③ Loosen the middle hose connector on the gauge holder until refrigerant flows out and then tighten the connector (exhaust the air in the middle hose).

④ Open the low-pressure manual valve on the gauge holder to allow gaseous refrigerant to enter the system.

⑤ Knock the bottom of the tank with your fingers. If there is a sound of empty cylinder, it indicates that the tank is empty. If the refrigerant is insufficient, refill another tank according to the above steps until the specified pressure is reached.

⑥ Close the manual valve at the low pressure side on the gauge holder, remove the injection valve from the middle hose; remove the pressure gauge set from the system, and cover all covers and caps again.

5. Performance test after filling refrigerant in air conditioning system

① As shown in Fig. 2-50, connect the pressure gauge set to the system. When connecting, close the high-pressure and low-pressure manual valves first, and exhaust the air in the pipe after connecting the pipe (otherwise, the air in the pipe will run into the refrigeration system).

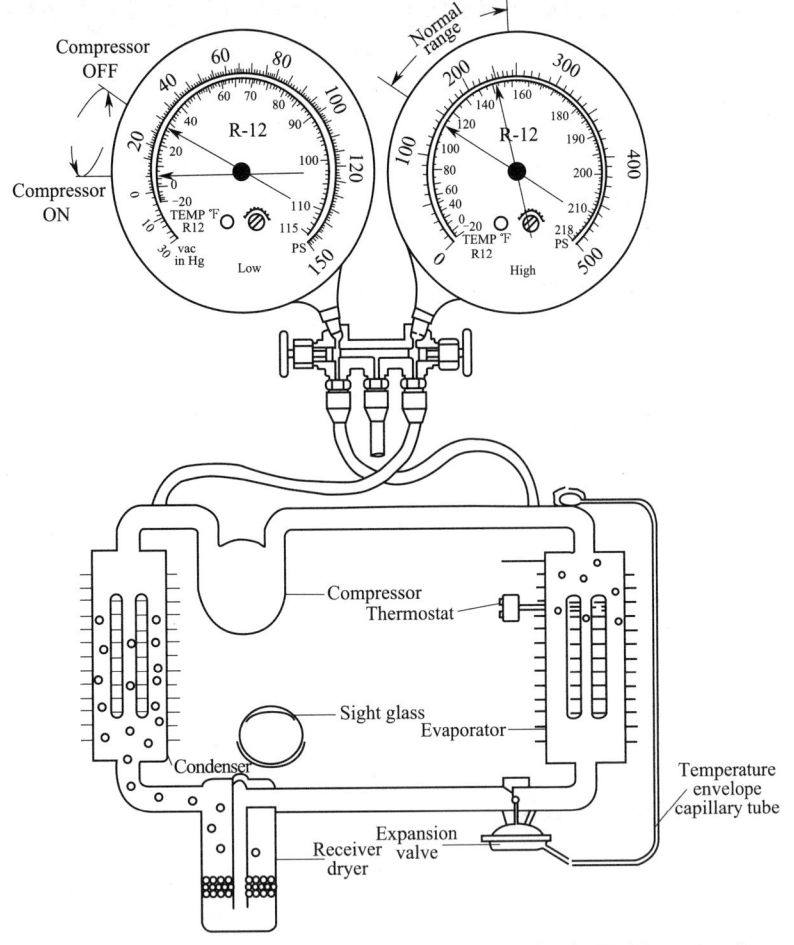

Fig. 2-50　Normal Value of High and Low Pressure of A/C Refrigeration System

② Start the engine, turn on the A/C and adjust the temperature key on the A/C control panel to the coldest position and the blower to the high speed.

③ Keep the engine speed at 2000r/ min.

④ Place the thermometer at the A/C outlet.

⑤ The psychrometer is placed at the air circulation inlet in the vehicle (Note: The bulb of the wet thermometer should be covered with cotton soaked in water).

⑥ Observe thermometer and psychrometer to test the working performance of the A/C system.

Exercises

Short Answer Question

What equipment should be used for vacuumizing refrigeration system? How to vacuumize?

Task V Maintenance of Automobile Air Conditioning Heating System

〔Learning Objectives〕

Knowledge requirements: Master the structure and principle of automobile air conditioning heating system as well as the train of thought and method of fault diagnosis.

Capability requirements:

1. According to the maintenance plan, select the correct detection and diagnosis equipment to diagnose the fault of automobile air conditioning heating system;

2. Be able to maintain, disassemble and assemble the main parts of automobile air conditioning heating system, and use multimeter and common testing equipment to test the air conditioning heating system;

3. Be able to correctly record and analyze various test results and make fault judgment;

4. Be able to test, inspect and evaluate the repair quality of automobile air conditioning heating system.

 Task Import

The air-conditioning outlet of a Volkswagen Passat sedan equipped with automatic air conditioning, after turning on the hot air in winter, has no hot air blowing out.

 **Knowledge Preparation**

Car heating is used to heat the carriage, which is generally in cold winter. According to the heat source used, the heating equipment can be divided into engine waste heat type and independent heat source type. According to the air circulation mode, it can be divided into internal circulation, external circulation and internal and external mixing. According to heat carrier, it can be divided into water heating type and air heating type.

Ⅰ. Engine Waste Heat Heating Device

1. Air heating device

The air heating system makes use of the exhaust waste heat of the engine to heat the carriage. About 36% of the heat can be carried away by the engine exhaust in gasoline en-

gines and 30% in diesel engines. The air heating system was one of the earliest forms of air conditioning. It uses an exhaust pipe to heat directly through the cabin, such as the early Beijing Jeeps and long-distance buses in the northern cold regions.

Fig. 2-51 shows the arrangement of the car air heating device. The heat exchanger 1 is connected to the engine, and the mixed gas is introduced into the heat exchanger for heating by the intake pipe 10. The heated air passes through the hot air exhaust pipe 3, and the heated air is sent into the cabin for heating by the blower 5.

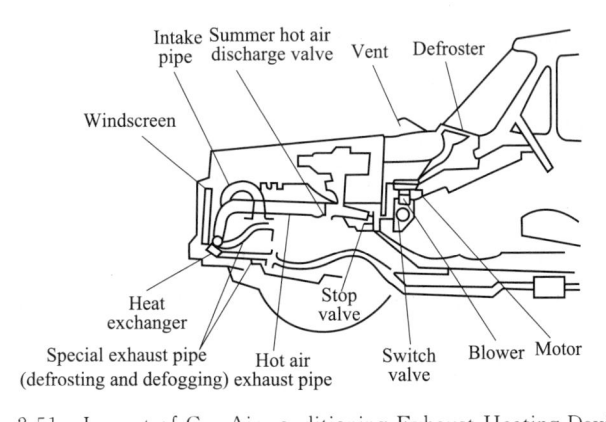

Fig. 2-51　Layout of Car Air-conditioning Exhaust Heating Device

The control panel is located on the instrument panel and changes the position of the damper to allow some hot air to enter defroster 7 to defrost the front window glass. If necessary, the rear window glass, side glass and feet can be heated through the special exhaust pipe 2. During cooling of air conditioner in summer, the temperature difference of cold air blown out from evaporator is large, which will make people feel uncomfortable. At this time, it can be mixed with hot air blown out by hot air discharging valve 9. The mixing ratio can be controlled by damper according to comfort requirements, so that comfortable cool air can be obtained. Stop valve 12 is used to shut off the hot air.

The heat source of the heat exchanger is the hot air after air cooling, which flows into the air side of the heat exchanger. The air at the tube side of the heat exchanger is heated and sent into the cabin. The heat transfer effect of the air heating device varies with vehicle speed. When the vehicle speed is high, the heat transfer effect is good; when the vehicle speed is low, the heat transfer effect is poor, as shown in Fig. 2-52.

The heat exchanger is cast into tubes with heat dissipation fins and installed on the exhaust pipe of the engine. On the one hand, the inner cavity is used as exhaust pipe; on the other hand, the air is heated outside and collected together and sent to the vehicle for heating. The structure of the heat exchanger is shown in Fig. 2-53.

Fig. 2-52　Effect of Air-Heating Heating Device

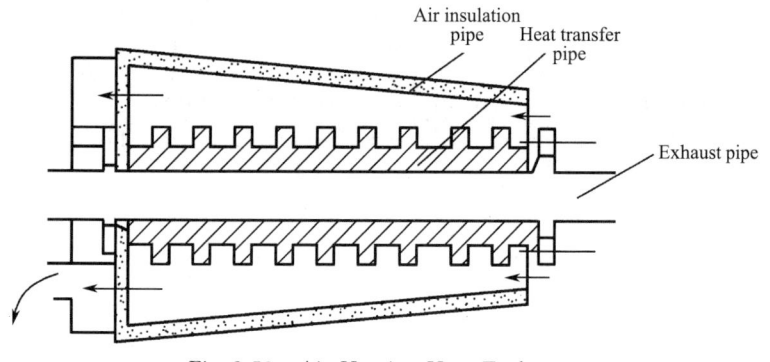

Fig. 2-53　Air-Heating Heat Exchanger

The schematic diagram of air heating device is shown in Fig. 2-54. A heat exchanger is installed on the exhaust pipe of the engine to heat the air. When working, close the valve leading to the muffler, and the exhaust gas enters into the heat exchanger for heating cold air outside the heat exchanger. After the cold air absorbs heat through the heat exchanger, its temperature rises and is blown into the cabin by the fan for heating and defrosting.

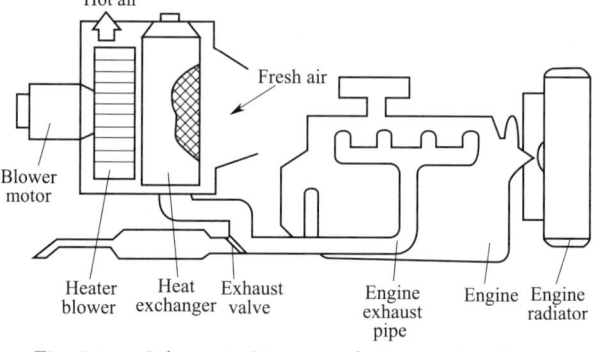

Fig. 2-54　Schematic Diagram of Air Heating Device

Because the exhaust of the engine has high heat content and can provide enough heating to regulate the temperature inside the vehicle, it is especially suitable for solving the heating problem of the car in the cold north. However, its heating effect is affected by vehicle speed and engine working condition, and the heating temperature is unstable. Secondly, because the exhaust contains corrosive gas and poisonous gas and particles, the heater must be made of corrosion-resistant materials, and the connection sealing must be reliable, otherwise once perforated, the consequences will be unthinkable. In addition, the heat exchanger installed in the exhaust pipe increases the exhaust resistance, which has certain influence on the working condition of the engine. Moreover, the structure of this device is complex and bulky, which limits its application to a certain extent.

2. Water heating device

In general, the water heating device uses coolant in the water-cooling engine cooling system as the heat source to introduce the coolant into the heat exchanger in the vehicle to exchange heat between the cabin air (internal air type) or outside air (external air type) sent by the blower and the coolant in the heat exchanger, and the blower sends the heated air into the cabin.

Sedans, trucks and small and medium-sized buses require less heat and can be heated directly by the waste heat of the engine coolant. The waste heat heating device is simple, safe and economi-

cal. However, its disadvantage is that the heat is relatively small, affected by the operating conditions of the car, when the engine stops running, that is, there is no heating.

The working principle of the water heating system is shown in Fig. 2-55. The coolant from the engine passes through the thermostat 11. When the temperature reaches 80℃, the thermostat is opened to allow the engine coolant to flow to the heater 5 of the heating system. A hot water switch 8 is provided between the thermostat and the heater to control the flow of hot water, and the other part of the coolant flows to the radiator. The coolant dissipates heat from the heater, heats the surrounding air, and then is sent to the vehicle by the fan 4. The coolant comes out of the heater, is sucked by the water pump 14, and then enters into the radiator of the engine again to cool the engine and complete a heating cycle.

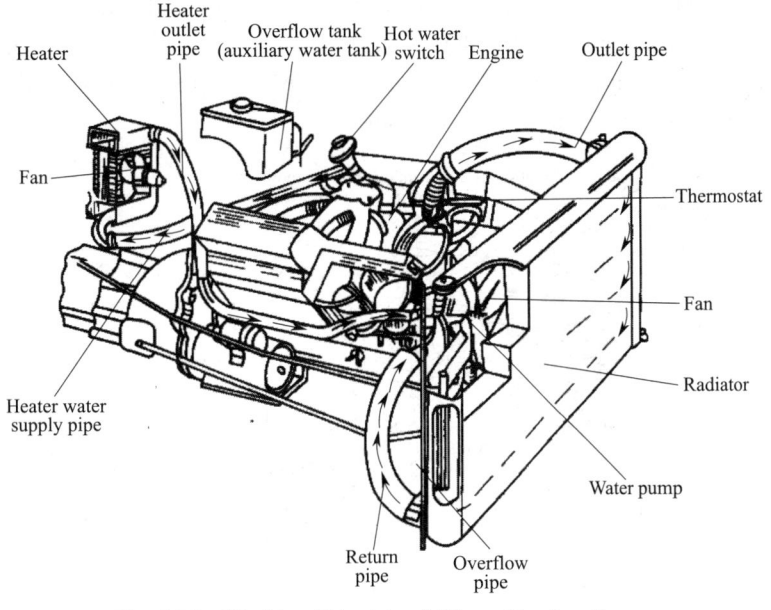

Fig. 2-55   Working Principle of Water Heating System

Fig. 2-56 shows the structure of a stand-alone water heating device, which consists of a complete assembly of hot air heat exchanger, fan and housing. The housing has an air outlet blowing to the feet and the front and an air outlet blowing to the window for defrosting. Such

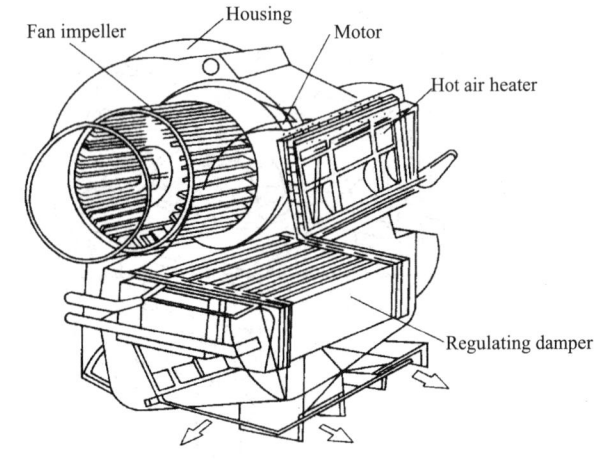

Fig. 2-56   Structure of Independent Water Heating Device

structures are commonly used in ordinary cars, trucks and minibuses.

At present, there are two types of structure of heater: tube-fin type and tube-belt type. The tube-belt heater has high heat dissipation efficiency, small volume and light weight, but its manufacturing process is more complicated; nowadays, the tube-fin type heater is mostly used, and measures such as reducing the tube wall thickness and grooving on the radiating fin can be adopted to improve its heat transfer efficiency.

Fig. 2-57 shows a water-heating internal and external mixed cycle heating device. The fresh air is sucked into the outside air inlet 7, and the internal air is sucked into the inside air inlet 5. After being mixed in the mixing chamber 4, the mixed air is fed into the air side of the heat exchanger 1 by the fan 8. The heat source is provided inside the heat exchanger tube by the circulating water of the engine. The mixed gas is heated and sent to the front seat foot and delivered to the front window for defrosting or defogging through the front window and side window defrosting connecting pipe. The heating device of this structure has a good effect and is generally used on medium and high-grade cars.

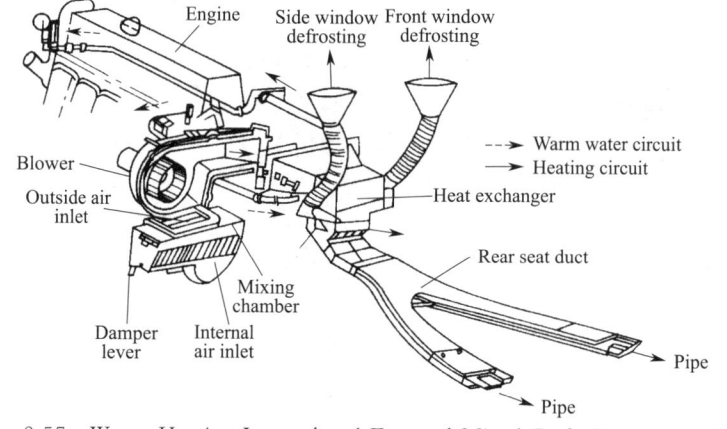

Fig. 2-57　Water Heating Internal and External Mixed Cycle Heating Device

Another structure is shown in Fig. 2-58. The heater and the evaporator are assembled in

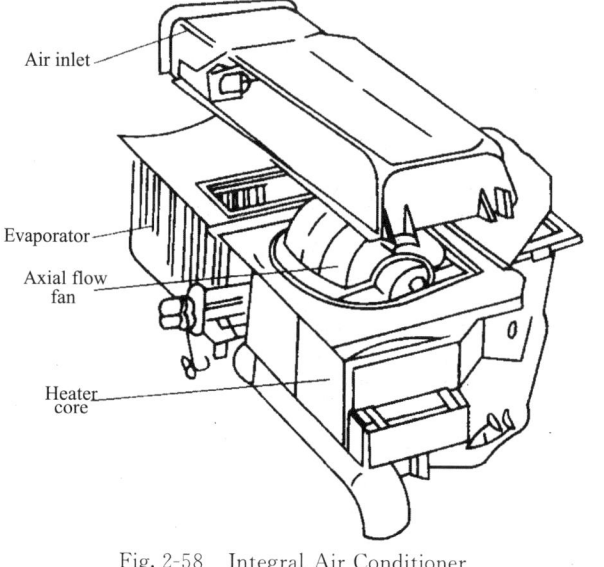

Fig. 2-58　Integral Air Conditioner

106　Automotive Safety and Comfort System Maintenance

a box and share a fan and shell，which can realize full-function air conditioning. Most luxury cars adopt this structure.

II. Independent Heat Source Heating Device

Special combustion heating devices are often used for tourist cars and vehicles in frigid regions. It has large heat supply and is not affected by engine power. Its combustion substances are gasoline，kerosene，light fuel oil，etc. The air or water is heated in the heat exchanger (the heating device is also divided into air heating type and hot water heating type). The burnt gas is discharged outside the vehicle after heat exchange without polluting the air inside the vehicle.

1. Hot water heating device

This device，also called boiling water type，is used as a pre-heater of the engine first to heat the cooling water of the engine to improve the startability and durability of the engine，and then as a heating device. The hot water heating type works well only when the engine power is low，and the fuel cost is less. Kerosene and light fuel oil are generally used as fuel. The calorific value is 1512-23260W，and the air flow rate is 80-800m³/h.

2. Air heating system

Fig. 2-59 shows the structure of air-heated independent combustion heater. When the

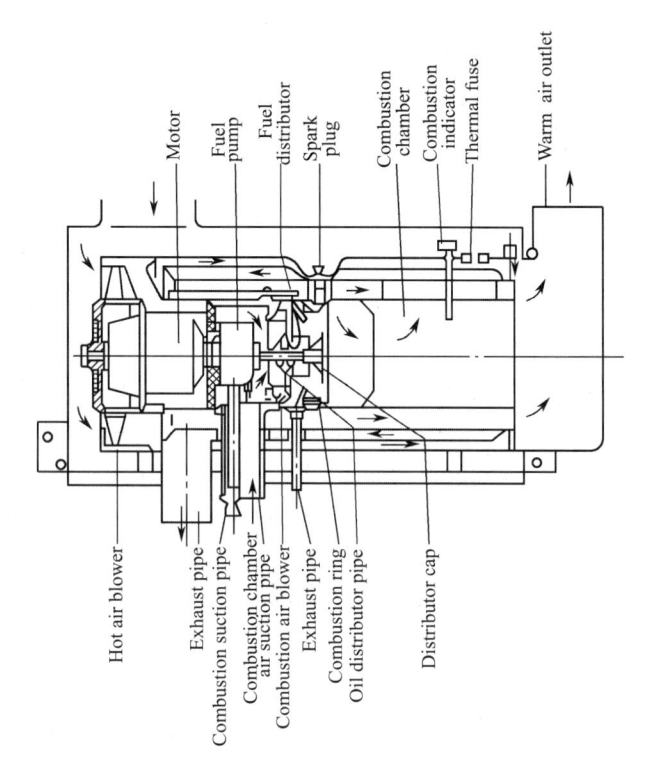

Fig. 2-59　Air-heated Independent Combustion Heater

running switch is turned on the "Ignition" position, the current turns on the spark plug 3. At this time, the front end of the nichrome wire is heated red, then the heater starts burning, and the motor 1 starts to run. The motor is equipped with fuel pump 2, fuel distributor 4, combustion air blower 12 and warming air blower 7. At the time of rotation of the blower 7, the fuel is sucked out from the fuel tank by the fuel pump 2 through the combustion filter and the solenoid valve combustion suction pipe 11. The fuel sucked by the fuel pump drops inside the distributor 4 and is dispersed and atomized by centrifugal force. When the air combusted is sucked by the blower 12 through the suction pipe 10 and mixed with the fuel, the fuel is ignited by a spark plug and burned in the combustion chamber 5. Once combustion begins, the spark plug is de-energized, after which the combustion chamber and the combustion ring 14 remain burning. The high-temperature gas after combustion is discharged into the atmosphere as exhaust through the exhaust pipe 8, and the air sent by the air blower installed at the front end of the motor shaft is heated through the combustion chamber, the outer cylinder partition wall and the outer side of the outer cylinder. The heated air is discharged through the warm air discharge port 16 and enters into the pipes inside the vehicle interior for heating.

3. Daily maintenance of heater

In winter, check the following items before starting to use the heater.

① Check whether there is fuel in the fuel tank.

② Check whether the inlet of heating air and the outlet of heating delivery pipe in the car are blocked.

③ Check whether there is air leakage in the fuel system. If yes, when the fuel pump sucks fuel, air will mix in from the leak, causing fuel interruption. When checking the leakage phenomenon, check carefully whether each connecting part of the fuel system is tightened and whether the pipeline is broken.

④ Check the fuel tank for leakage. Check whether there is oil leakage from oil tank cap, oil gauge hose, drain plug, etc. If any, it shall be repaired in time to avoid fire.

⑤ Check the fuel filter. It depends on whether there is accumulated water and sundries inside it. If yes, remove the filter glass for cleaning or replace the filter element. Replace the filter glasses if damaged. The sealing ring shall be replaced if it is aged.

⑥ Check the electrical circuit. Open the wiring cover and observe whether the wiring is damaged or detached. Repair if any. Screw out the glow plug and remove carbon deposit with wire brush to prevent poor ignition and poor insulation due to excessive carbon deposit, which may shorten the service life of glow plug.

⑦ Check the combustion air system. The combustion air intake pipe and exhaust pipe of the system must be checked frequently to see if there is reduced combustion air or poor combustion due to blockage of silt and dust.

Task Implementation

I . Structure of Passat Heating Device

Before carrying out repair on all electrical equipment, call up the anti-theft password of the radio, and then disconnect the ground wire of the battery. When the battery is reconnected, the equipment of the car (radio, hour hand, electric window lifter) shall be inspected.

The structure of Passat heating device is shown in Fig. 2-60.

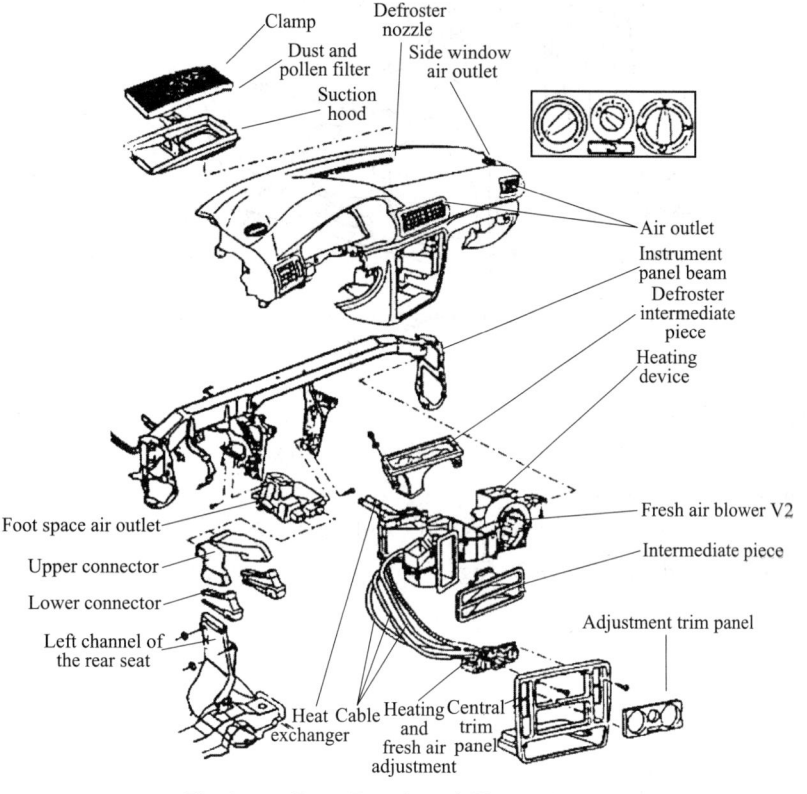

Fig. 2-60　Parts Drawing of Heating Device

II . Disassembly and Assembly of Passat Heating Device

1. Removal of fresh air blower

The removal of the fresh air blower V2 is shown in Fig. 2-61. Remove the oddments tray on the front passenger's side first, and then remove the blower.

2. Removal of heating and fresh air regulating device

The composition of the heating and fresh air regulating device is shown in Fig. 2-62.

The removal of the heating and fresh air regulating device is shown in Fig. 2-63. Push off the heating trim panel 3; remove the centre trim panel 2; pull the regulating device 1

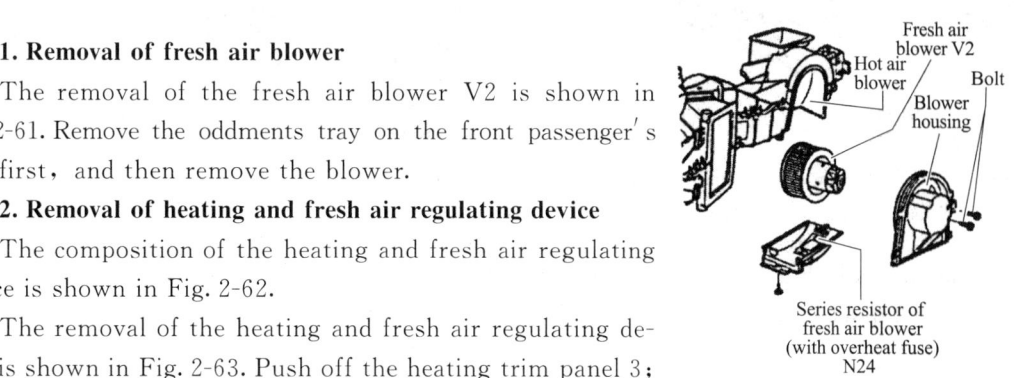

Fig. 2-61　Fresh Air Blower

Item II　Maintenance of Automobile Air Conditioning System **109**

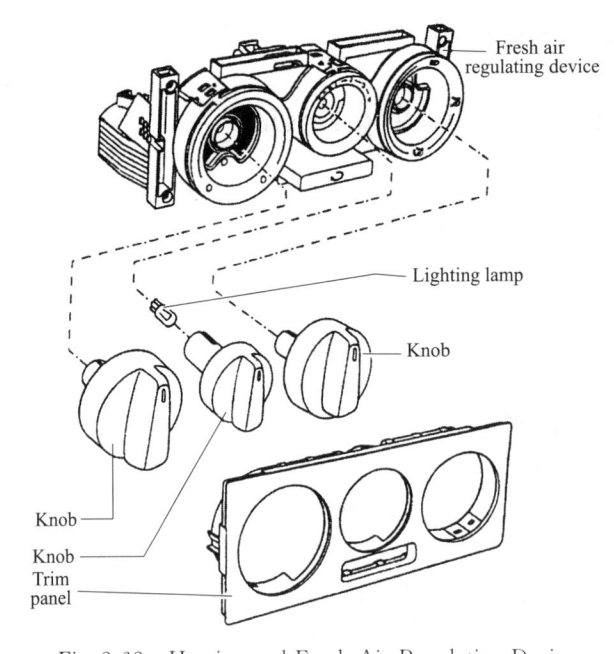

Fig. 2-62　Heating and Fresh Air Regulating Device

with the cable out of the instrument panel.

3. Removal of air outlet

① Remove the air outlet at the side window, as shown in Fig. 2-64. Pull out the air outlet at the side window edge with pliers.

② Remove the air outlet at driver's side and co-driver's side in the same way, except that one side is replaced. As shown in Fig. 2-65, pry off cover plate on side of the instrument panel with proper screwdriver and then take it out.

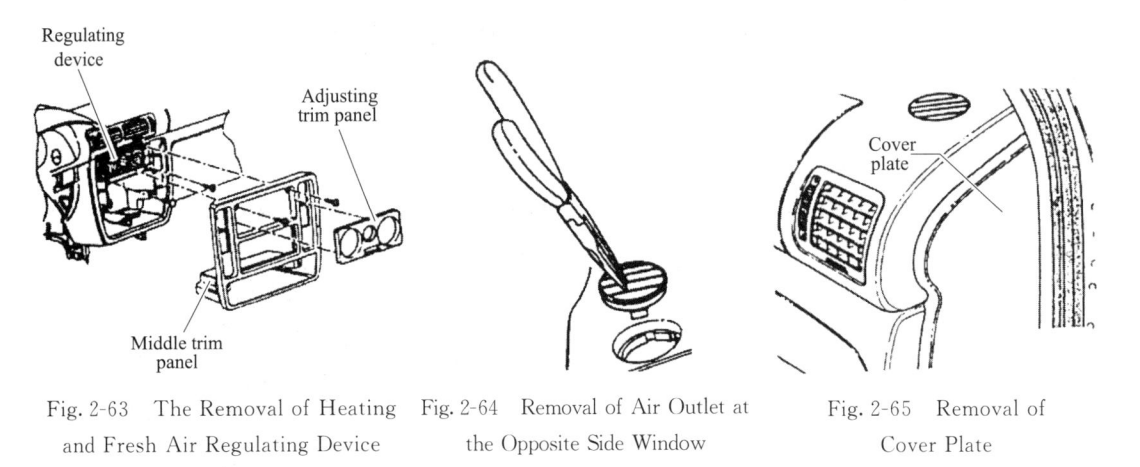

Fig. 2-63　The Removal of Heating and Fresh Air Regulating Device

Fig. 2-64　Removal of Air Outlet at the Opposite Side Window

Fig. 2-65　Removal of Cover Plate

As shown in Fig. 2-66, insert an applicable flat screwdriver between the air outlet and the seal component through holes A and B on the side alternately, and pry out the horizontal air outlet 1 in the direction C alternately with the screwdriver.

As shown in Fig. 2-67, when taking out the air outlet 1 along the direction C, separate

the connector 2 on the back side.

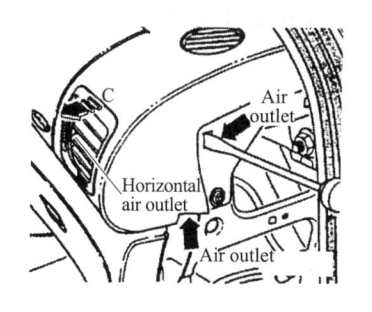

Fig. 2-66   Disassembly of Horizontal Air Outlet

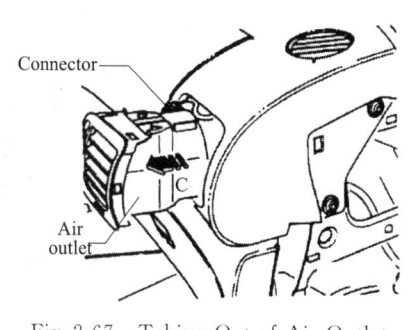

Fig. 2-67   Taking Out of Air Outlet

③ Remove the central air outlet as follows. As shown in Fig. 2-68, put the fingers of both hands on the lowermost horizontal bar A and press down the central air outlet 1 forcefully to release the locating hook B from its fixed position.

As shown in Fig. 2-69, after the central air outlet 1 is pulled out a little from the instrument panel, grab onto the point C with both hands, press the central air outlet in the direction D so that the locating hook below disengages and pull out the air outlet slightly.

As shown in Fig. 2-70, before taking out the air outlet in the direction of arrow, separate the connector of the central air outlet on the back side.

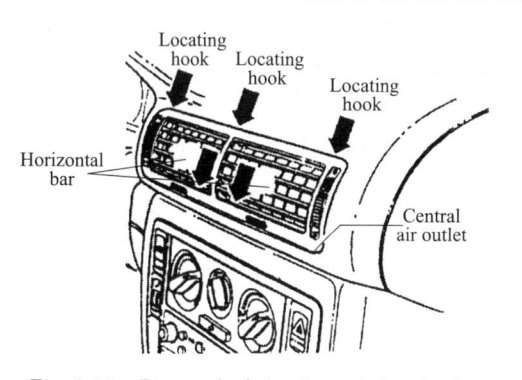

Fig. 2-68   Removal of the Central Air Outlet

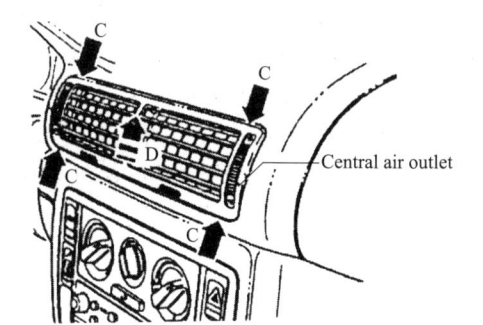

Fig. 2-69   Pull Out the Central Air Outlet

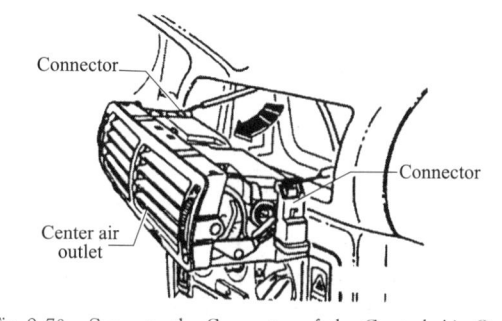

Fig. 2-70   Separate the Connector of the Central Air Outlet

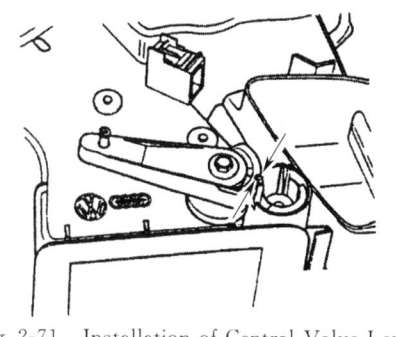

Fig. 2-71   Installation of Central Valve Lever

4. Installation and adjustment of lever for central valve

As shown in Fig. 2-71, there is an adjustment mark on the pinion of the central valve. When installing the lever, make sure that the adjustment mark of the lever is aligned with the adjustment mark on the pinion (as shown by the arrow in the figure.).

5. Installation and adjustment of cable

The installation and adjustment method of cable is shown in Fig. 2-72.

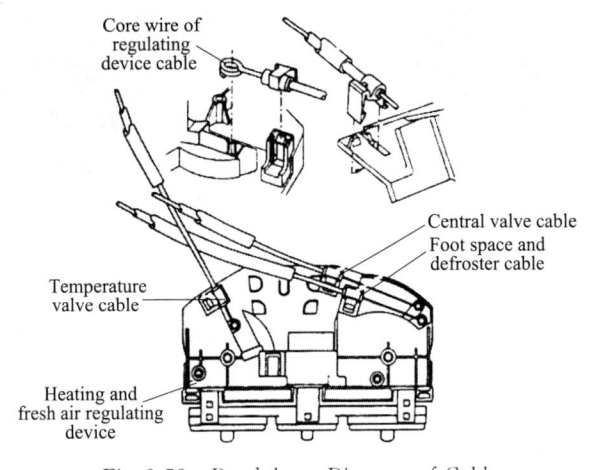

Fig. 2-72　Breakdown Diagram of Cable

Attention shall be paid to the following points during installation and adjustment of cable.

① Install the cable onto the removed adjusting device first, and then fix the cable to the heating device.

② The end of the cable sheath is marked with color. Shanghai Passat B5 foot space and defroster cable sheath holder are white; central valve cable sheath retainer is black; temperature valve cable sheath holder is red.

③ When rotating the knob, all valves must be able to hear to reach the stop position.

④ When inserting the cable core wire of the adjusting device, press the arrow at the end of the wire against the adjusting lever.

Exercises

Choice questions

1. Among the following automobile air conditioning components, (　　) is not heat exchanger.

A. Heating water tank　　　　　B. Condenser

C. Evaporator　　　　　　　　D. Blower

2. The intensity adjustment of the car heating capacity is generally adjusted by (　　).

A. Air volume　　　　　　　　B. Engine water temperature

C. Warm water valve　　　　　D. Vacuum capsule

Item Summary

There may be many kinds of fault phenomena of the automobile air conditioner, mainly caused by refrigerant failure (including too much or too little refrigerant filling, refrigerant moisture or air filling, etc.), pipeline system failure (including pipeline leakage, pipeline blockage), compressor and evaporator failure, etc. When dealing with various automobile A/C faults, you can check each system to eliminate them.

During the use of the automobile A/C system, the refrigerant in the system is drained or insufficient due to component damage or pipeline leakage, so it is necessary to refill or re-

plenish refrigerant to restore the normal working performance of the automobile A/C system. In the specific maintenance process of the automobile A/C refrigeration system, the basic operations such as refrigerant discharge or recovery, vacuumizing and filling are indispensable.

For the A/C system disassembled for repair or found to have too little refrigerant, completely evacuate the A/C system with vacuum pump before adding new refrigerant to remove the air and moisture in the A/C system. After completion of the vacuumizing, fill the A/C system with a fixed amount after confirming that there is no leakage in the system.

Fault phenomena of the automobile A/C heating system may appear in many ways, mainly caused by heating source failure (including too low coolant temperature of engine, water pump fault of engine cooling system) and pipeline system failure (including pipeline leakage and pipeline blockage). When handling the A/C heating system fault, check it in turn to eliminate the fault.

Item Exercises

Ⅰ. True or False

1. In the air conditioning refrigeration system, the more refrigerant, the stronger the refrigeration capacity. (   )

2. The lower the evaporator surface temperature, the better. (   )

3. Moisture in the refrigeration system will cause intermittent cooling of the system. (   )

Ⅱ. Single choice questions

1. When the air conditioning system is replaced with refrigerant, A says: The O-ring for R-12 does not need to be replaced; B says: The O-ring for the R-134a system can also be used for the R-12 system. Who's right? (   )

A. A is right   B. B is right   C. Both are right   D. None are right

2. A says: The vacuum pump is used to remove moisture from the system; B says: The vacuum pump is used to extract air from the system. Who's right? (   )

A. A is right   B. B is right   C. Both are right   D. None are right

3. When there is air in the air conditioning system, A says: The air will not be condensed; B says: Air will collect in the evaporator when the air conditioning cycle is stopped. Who's right? (   )

A. A is right   B. B is right   C. Both are right   D. None are right

Ⅲ. Short answer questions

1. What are the main components of the air conditioning system?

2. What is the working principle of the air conditioning system?

Item Ⅲ

Maintenance of Automobile Electronic Control Passive Safety System

 Item Guide

When the vehicle collides at a speed lower than 30km/h, the deceleration and inertial force generated by the collision are relatively small. The safety sensor and the central sensor send this signal to the airbag ECU, and the airbag ECU judges not to detonate the airbag, but only to activate the igniter of the safety belt tensioner. At the same time, send the ignition command to the left and right safety belt igniters to tighten the safety belts to prevent the driver and the passenger from being injured.

When the vehicle collides at a speed higher than 30km/h, the deceleration and inertial force generated by the collision are relatively large. The safety sensor and the central sensor send this signal to the airbag ECU, and the airbag ECU judges that the airbag and the seat belt tensioner need to be detonated to protect the driver and the passenger together. At the same time, send the ignition command to the left and right safety belt igniters and airbag igniter. When the safety belt is tightened, the airbag on the driver's side and the airbag on the passenger's side are opened at the same time, so as to protect the driver and the passenger.

Task Ⅰ Identification of Automobile Electronic Control Passive Safety System

【Learning Objectives】

Knowledge requirements: Master the function, composition and basic principle of automobile electronic control passive safety system.

Capability requirements: Be able to identify the components of automobile electronic control passive safety system on the real vehicle.

 Task Import

Automobile electronic control passive safety system is very important for driving safety. Can you find its components on the vehicle?

114 Automotive Safety and Comfort System Maintenance

Knowledge Preparation

When a traffic accident occurs, cars inevitably collide. There are two stages in a car collision: A collision between a vehicle and a vehicle or between a car and an obstacle in which no one is involved is the first stage of the collision. The first stage of collision will inevitably lead to deceleration of the vehicle, and the personnel in the vehicle will move towards the direction of the collision at a certain acceleration due to inertia. If the acceleration is large enough, it will cause collision between the personnel and the components in the vehicle. This collision is called the second stage of collision, i. e. the injury stage. The function of airbag is that between the first stage and the second stage of the collision, to rapidly generate an air cushion filled with gas between the personnel in the vehicle and the components of the vehicle. During the collision process, the kinetic energy of the passenger is absorbed through the damping exhaust of the airbag, so that the second stage of collision can be slowed down, so as to reduce the degree of injury to the personnel caused by the collision. The airbag belongs to the "passive safety protection device" of the automobile occupant. The safety belt plays an important role in the passive protection process, while the airbag belongs to the Supplemental Restraint System (SRS).

As an auxiliary configuration of passive safety of vehicle body, airbag has been paid more and more attention. When a car collides, a gas-filled air cushion is quickly opened between the occupant and the interior components before the "second collision", so that the passenger falls on the air cushion" when they move due to inertia, so as to mitigate the impact of the occupant and absorb the collision energy and reduce the injury degree of the occupant.

I. Function

When the car collides at a speed of more than 30km/h, the airbag will automatically inflate and spring open, filling a large airbag between the driver and the steering wheel instantly, so as to reduce the head and chest injury of the driver.

The driver side airbag assembly is located at the center of the steering wheel and the passenger side airbag assembly is located above the cargo bin on the right side of the instrument panel. The airbag on the driver's side is mostly made of nylon cloth coated with neoprene or silicone. The rubber coating provides sealing and protection, and there are 2 vent holes on the back of the airbag. The airbag on the passenger's side has no coating and is vented against the holes in the nylon cloth itself. See Fig. 3-1 for installation position and circuit connection of each component of airbag system on the vehicle.

II. Structure Classification

1. Collision sensor

The signal of vehicle collision intensity is detected and input into airbag ECU. The collision sensor installed in the front of vehicle is called front collision sensor; the collision sensor installed inside airbag ECU is called central sensor.

① Eccentric hammer type front collision sensor: It is installed between bumper and

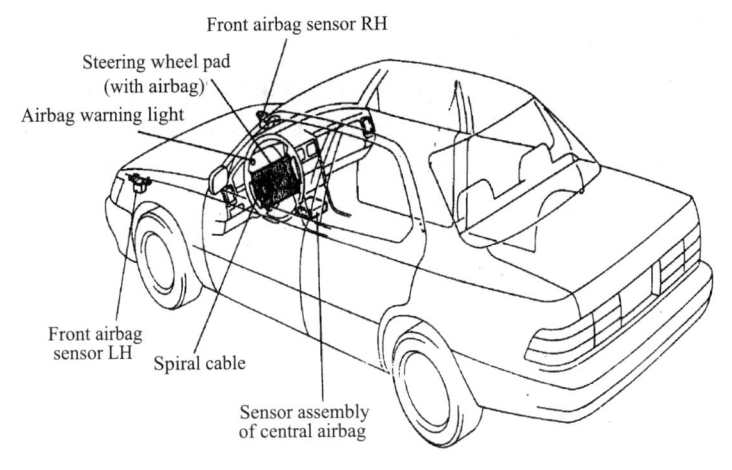

Fig. 3-1　System Layout

fender and installed in a shockproof protection box to sense low-speed collision signal.

② Strain gauge sensor: It's a sensor that changes that output voltage of a dynamic strain gauge due to the inertial force generated by the deceleration of the automobile cantilever. The greater the inertial force of the collision, the higher the output voltage.

③ Damping sensor: In case of strong impact, the steel ball sensor will close the contact and send out a collision signal.

2. Safety sensor

The safety sensor is used to prevent misoperation of the airbag caused by the system in case of non-collision. It is normally housed in a central controller and is mercury normally open switch. In the event of an impact, sufficient deceleration forces throw mercury on and switch on the electric detonator circuit. Instead of transmitting signals, the safety sensor directly controls the on/off of the power circuit required for airbag deployment.

III. Composition and Basic Principles

The airbag system is mainly composed of sensors, gas generators, igniters, airbag ECU and airbag SRS indicator. The sensor and microprocessor are used to judge the collision degree, transmit and send signals; the gas generator generates ignition action according to the signal indication, ignites the solid fuel and generates gas to inflate the airbag, so as to rapidly inflate the airbag. The airbag is installed in the steering wheel hub close to the cushion pad, with a capacity of 50-90L. The cloth used for the airbag has high tensile strength. Most of them are made of nylon material. The folded surface is attached with dry powder to prevent the airbag from sticking together and being broken in case of explosion; in order to prevent gas leakage, the inner layer of the airbag is coated with sealing rubber; meanwhile, the airbag is equipped with a safety valve, which will automatically release some gas when it is inflated excessively or the pressure inside the airbag exceeds a certain value, so as to avoid squeezing and injuring the passengers; the gas used in the airbag is mostly nitrogen.

1. Gas generator

The function of the gas generator is to produce gas in an effective time to allow the airbag to

116　Automotive Safety and Comfort System Maintenance

open. The gas generator consists of an upper cover, a lower cover, an inflating agent and a metal screen. A metal screen is installed on the inner surface of the gas generator to filter the slag particles generated by the combustion of the aerating agent and the igniting agent.

The gas generator uses thermal effect to generate nitrogen gas which fills in the airbag. At the moment the igniter detonates the igniting agent, the igniting agent will generate a large amount of heat, and the aerating agent will decompose immediately after heating to generate nitrogen and fill the airbag through the inflating hole. Although nitrogen is a non-toxic gas, minor amounts of sodium hydroxide and sodium bicarbonate (white powder) are by-products of the aerating agent. These substances are harmful, so keep good ventilation and take protective measures when cleaning inflated airbag.

2. Ignitor

The igniter is mainly composed of electric detonator, whose function is to detonate gunpowder after collision to produce a large amount of high temperature gas, impact or crush gas generating agent (sodium azide), and cool the high temperature gas and continue to generate gas.

3. Airbag ECU

The airbag ECU consists of central processor CPU, ROM, RAM, I/O interface, driver and other electronic circuits, as shown in Fig. 3-2. Meanwhile, there are safety sensor, standby power supply, voltage stabilizing circuit and fault self-diagnosis circuit inside the airbag ECU. The principle of airbag ECU electronic control system is shown in Fig. 3-3.

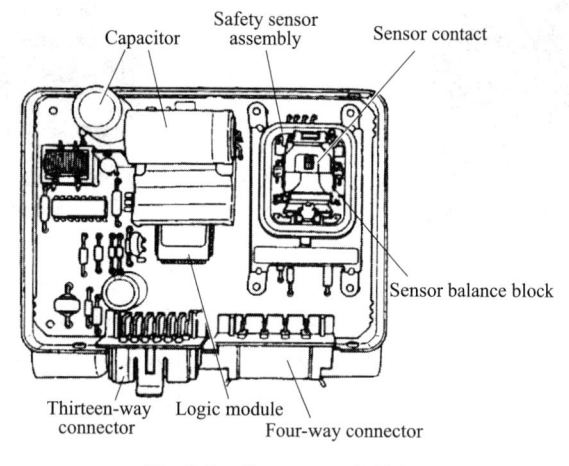

Fig. 3-2　Structure of Airbag

4. SRS indicator of airbag

The SRS indicator is located on the instrument panel. When the ignition switch is turned on, the diagnostic unit performs self-check on the system. If it turns on for 6s and goes out, it indicates that the airbag system is normal; if the SRS indicator still flashes or stays off after 6s, it indicates that the airbag system is faulty.

5. Composition of the safety system in the Audi A3 Sportback

(1) Airbag control unit J234

The airbag control unit is connected to the CAN drive data bus, as shown in Fig. 3-4.

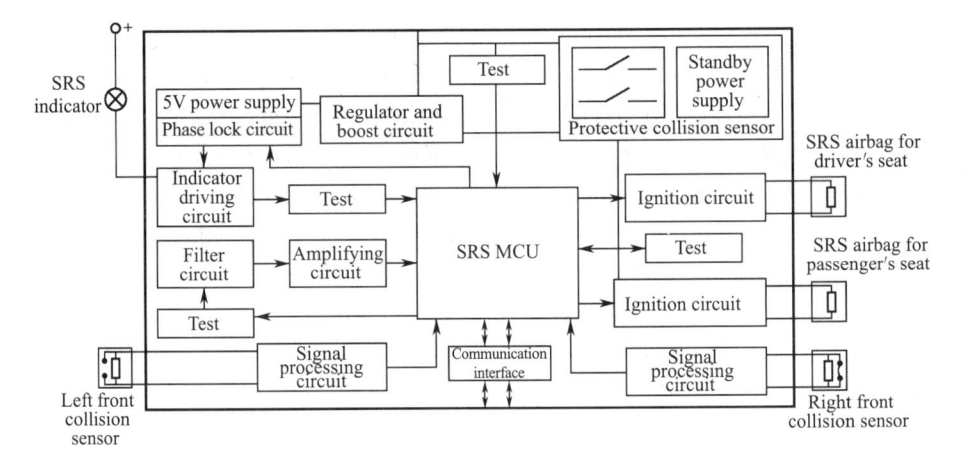

Fig. 3-3　Principle of Airbag ECU Electronic Control System

(2) Side restraint system collision sensor

Side airbag collision sensors G179 and G180 (at front door) are shown in Fig. 3-5.

Pressure sensors are installed in both front doors of the Audi A3 Sportback. In the event of a side collision, there will be a brief increase in air pressure in the door due to deformation of the vehicle. The sensor collects the information about the pressure rise and transmits it to the airbag control unit.

Fig. 3-4　Airbag Control Unit

Fig. 3-5　Side airbag Collision Sensor

The rear side airbag collision sensors G256 and G257 (C-pillar) are installed on the left and right of the C-pillar, respectively. The rear side airbag collision sensors G256 and G257 are conventional lighting sensors and are also installed on the 3-door Audi A3.

(3) Driver's airbag

A two-stage inflator is used on the driver's airbag. The airbag bounces open radially and is staggered with the ignition trigger time, so in the occurrence of traffic accident, the load on the driver will be reduced. Depending on the severity and type of accident, the airbag control unit controls the time interval between two ignitions. The time interval between the two ignitions may be 5-40 ms.

The airbag control unit activates the electronic trigger of the first inflator, as shown in Fig. 3-6. This ignites the igniter and triggers its own inflator again through the nozzle hole. Ignition of that inflator creates pressure in the gas generator. If the gas pressure exceeds the set limit, the gas generator deforms and access through the metal filter to the airbag is opened. The second inflator is ignited to deploy and inflate the airbag. After a certain period

of time, the airbag control unit supplies power to the second electronic igniter, and the igniter directly ignites the second inflator, as shown in Fig. 3-7. Over a certain pressure, the generated gas lifts the lid of the second stage and flows into the combustion chamber of the first stage, from where it passes through the filter into the airbag.

In contrast to the driver's airbag, the gas generator in the passenger's airbag works according to the principle of mixed gas technology, as shown in Fig. 3-8. The gas generator consists of two pyrotechnic inflators built into a high pressure gas cylinder. The airbag control unit activates the trigger and ignites the first inflator via the ignition device. If the pressure generated in the cylinder exceeds a set value, the safety diaphragm breaks and the gas mixture can fill the airbag. The gas generated after the second inflator is ignited will inflate the airbag again. The function of the coil spring is to ignite the inflator according to the set pressure.

A pyrotechnic tube gas generator is used as the gas generator. If the airbag control unit detects a side impact sufficient to trigger the airbag, power is supplied to the corresponding side airbag trigger. The main inflator is triggered by the igniter. The generated gas flows through the filter into the airbag.

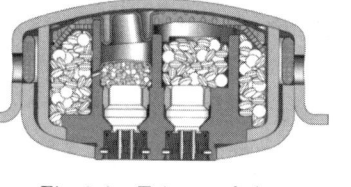  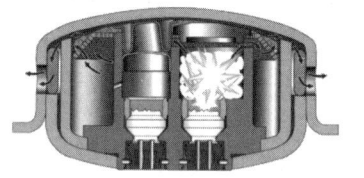

Fig. 3-6   Trigger of the First Inflator   Fig. 3-7   Trigger of the Second Inflator   Fig. 3-8   Passenger Airbag N131, N132

The side airbag is shown in Fig. 3-9, and the head airbag covers almost the entire side glass, as shown in Fig. 3-10. The gas mixture generator is mounted at the rear of the roof and inflates the airbag through an air duct. The strut is mechanically ejected from its position by igniting the inflator. The helium gas stored in the high-pressure gas cylinder at a pressure of 600 MPa causes rupture of the safety diaphragm. The gas flows through the filter into the gas injection tube connecting the airbag and the gas generator.

Fig. 3-9   Side Airbag N199, N200   Fig. 3-10   Head Airbag N251, N252

Task Implementation

Group training to find the components of automobile electronic control passive safety system on the real vehicle.

Exercises

Short Answer Questions

1. Briefly describe the classification of collision sensor.
2. Briefly describe the function of gas generator.

Task II Maintenance of Automobile Electronic Control Passive Safety System

【Learning Objectives】

Knowledge requirements: Master the train of thought and method of fault diagnosis of automobile electronic control passive safety system.

Capability requirements:

1. Be able to use multimeter, fault scan tool, oscilloscope and common detection and diagnosis equipment to detect the sensor, controller and actuator of automobile electronic control passive safety system;

2. Be able to correctly record and analyze various test results and make fault judgment;

3. Be able to replace sensor, actuator and controller according to correct operation specifications, and perform system matching settings;

4. Be able to test, inspect and evaluate the repair quality of automobile electronic control passive safety system.

Task Import

The airbag indicator of a Guangzhou Honda 2.3L Accord car is on, with a driving mileage of 32000 km.

Knowledge Preparation

All harnesses of the airbag system are wrapped in yellow bellows and integrated with the neck harness for easy differentiation. In order to ensure that the steering wheel has sufficient rotation angle without damaging the connecting harness of the driver's airbag assembly, spiral harness is adopted between the steering wheel and the steering column tube, that is, the harness is installed in the spiral spring, and then the spiral spring is put into the spring housing.

Electric horn harness is also installed in spiral spring. The spiral spring is installed between the steering wheel and the steering column. Pay attention to its installation position and direction during installation. Otherwise, spiral harness and the electric horn harness will be broken, the steering angle of steering wheel is insufficient or steering is heavy.

The spiral cable is used to ensure the connection of the power supply wiring. All harnesses of the airbag system are wrapped in yellow bellows and integrated with the neck harness for easy differentiation.

Task Implementation

I. Maintenance of Airbag System

Attention shall be paid to daily maintenance of airbag. The general inspection of the air-

bag shall be carried out according to the fault displayed in the DTC, which can be carried out by the driver or professional repairman in strict accordance with the operating instructions in the maintenance manual. Non-professional personnel are not allowed to disassemble and repair the airbag system.

1. Safety rules for airbag maintenance

The inspection, installation and maintenance of the airbag must be carried out by professional personnel. Test lamps, voltmeters and ohmmeters shall not be used for testing. Airbags can only be checked with special diagnostic instrument for automobile after installation. When checking the airbag, the battery ground wire must be disconnected. There is no need to wait after disconnecting the battery. When the airbag is connected to the power supply, there shall be no person in the vehicle. The airbag must be loaded immediately after being removed from the transport appliance. If it is necessary to stop working, put the airbag back into the transport appliance. Do not leave the airbag unattended. When storing and disassembling the airbag, the buffer surface shall face upwards. The airbag shall not be opened and repaired. New parts must be used. Airbags that have fallen onto hard ground or are damaged cannot be reused.

Procedure for replacing airbag: Remove the old airbag and place the cushion face upwards; take out the new airbag from the transport appliance and place it with the cushion face upwards; install the old airbag into the transport appliance; install the new airbag onto the vehicle.

The airbag has a certain service life (see sticker on B-pillar). If the airbag is replaced, remove the new sticker and attach it to the old sticker on the B-pillar. The airbag and sticker must be replaced every 14 years. If there is no sticker on the B-pillar, replace the airbag according to the maintenance manual.

The airbag shall not be stained with grease, detergent, etc., nor placed at the place with temperature above 100 ℃ (short time shall not be allowed).

2. Replacement and handling of airbag

(1) Replacement of airbag triggered after accident

In the event of a traffic accident, after the airbag and the seat belt tensioner work, the vehicle display will display a warning message "Airbag, front and side" or "Airbag, front and head". The airbag control unit can be used to control the triggering of up to 3 side/head airbags and/or tensioners.

After 3 triggers, the fault reader displays "Control unit defective". The airbag control unit must be replaced under the following conditions.

① Driver/co-driver airbag triggers once.

② The shell is damaged.

③ The channel within 200mm around the control unit is deformed.

④ After the airbag is triggered for 3 times.

⑤ All airbag assemblies are triggered.

⑥ If the co-driver's airbag has been triggered, replace the instrument panel.

⑦ The bracket on the co-driver's side has been deformed (secondary deformation is not allowed).

⑧ The lateral acceleration sensor is faulty (if the floor around the sensor is deformed).

⑨ After the driver's airbag is triggered, replace the return spring with slip ring and the safety belt triggered by the tensioner.

(2) Trigger airbag control unit

For the triggered front seat tensioner, the display shows "zu groß" (high resistance) and for the triggered rear seat tensioner, the display shows "zu groß" (high resistance).

(3) Replace the airbag control unit.

Query fault memory. For the triggered tensioner, the fault is recorded as "Tensioning Trigger—High Resistance". Replace all damaged parts if necessary (visual inspection).

(4) Handling of airbag not triggered after accident

If the airbag warning light K75 does not indicate a fault, it is not necessary to replace the airbag components and check the seat belt separately.

3. Storage and transportation of airbag

The airbag is a pyrotechnic device made of Grade I polyethylene, and its storage and transportation shall be treated as explosive dangerous articles (explosive management regulations). Airbag shall not be stored for more than 3 months.

4. Discard of airbag

Before the airbag is scrapped, it shall be triggered according to the corresponding safety regulations.

5. Assembly and disassembly of airbag components

(1) Installation position of the airbag

The installation position of main components of the airbag is shown in Fig. 3-11.

(2) Assembly and disassembly of driver's airbag

See Fig. 3-12 for the disassembly of the airbag on the driver's side.

① Removal of airbag on driver's side. Loosen the steering column adjusting device. Pull the steering wheel up and out as far as it will go. Place the steering wheel in the vertical position. Turn the Torx wrench (T30) 90 degree (clockwise as viewed from the front) in the direction of the arrow shown in Fig. 3-12 to loosen the locating detent 7. Turn back the steering wheel by half a turn to release the other locating detent. Pull off airbag plug 3 and plug 4 and position the airbag with the cushion face facing upwards.

② Installation of airbag on driver's side. When installing the airbag on the driver's side, ensure that the plug and the airbag are seated correctly (audibly). Pay attention that no person is inside the vehicle. Finally, switch

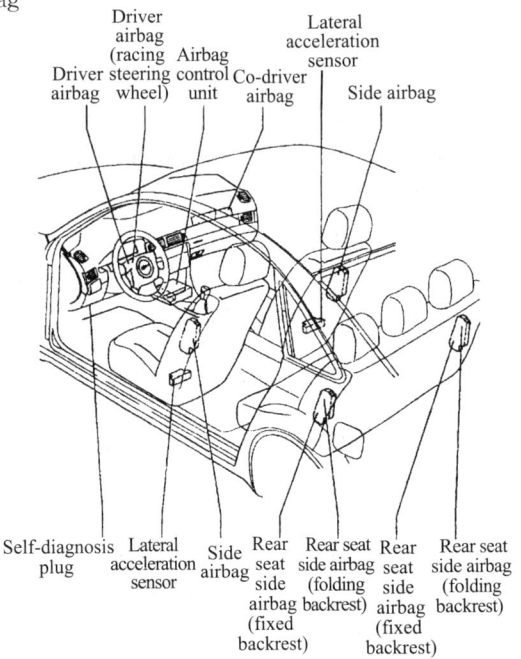

Fig. 3-11　Schematic Diagram of Installation Position of Airbag Components

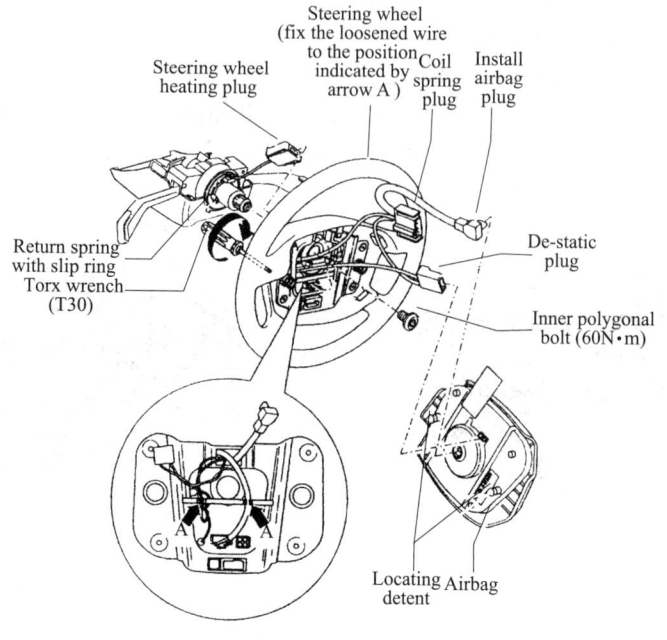

Fig. 3-12 Disassembly of Driver's Side Airbag

on the ignition switch and connect the battery ground wire.

③ Disassembly and assembly of steering wheel. When removing the steering wheel, remove the airbag first, place the steering wheel in the center position (wheels are aligned), unscrew bolt 5, pull off plug 2 and plug 10. When installing the steering wheel, install it when the steering wheel is in the center position (wheels are aligned). Make sure that the plug is seated correctly (audibly). Replace bolt 5, tighten it to 60N • m, and finally install the airbag.

（3）Disassembly and assembly of return spring with slip ring

Remove the driver airbag and the steering wheel. Pull the steering column fully out and down. As shown in Fig. 3-13, unscrew bolt 1 (two, tightening torque of 2. 8N • m) and remove clamp block 2.

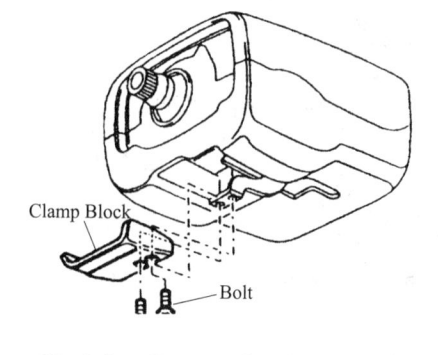

Fig. 3-13 Remove the Clamp Block

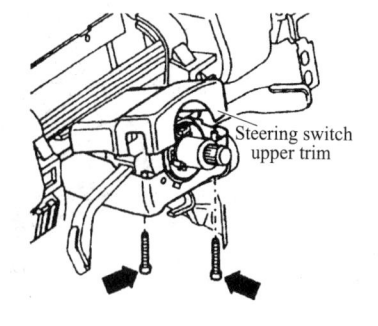

Fig. 3-14 Remove the Upper
Trim of the Steering Switch

Unscrew the two crosshead bolts as shown by the arrow shown in Fig. 3-14, and the tightening torque of the bolts is 0. 6N • m. Remove the steering switch upper trim. When in-

stalling, insert the upper half into the locating detent of the lower half, swing down and tighten, as shown in Fig. 3-14.

Unscrew bolt 2 (2 belts), and the tightening torque of the bolt is 0.6N • m. Remove the steering switch lower trim 3, as shown in Fig. 3-15. Pull off plug 1, release locating detent (arrow) and pull off the return spring with slip ring from steering switch, as shown in Fig. 3-16.

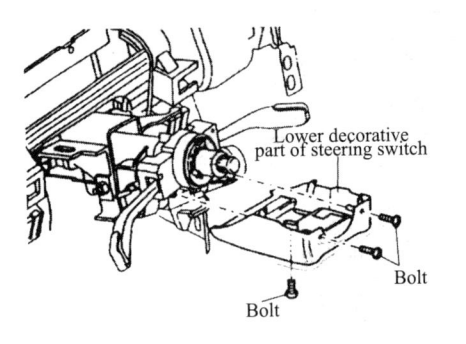 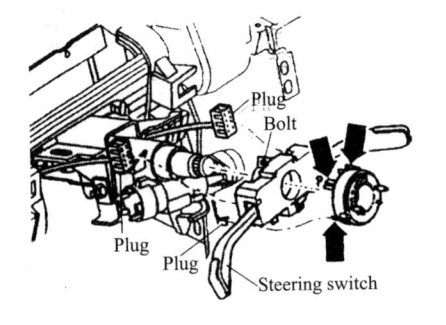

Fig. 3-15 Removing the Lower Trim of the Steering Switch

Fig. 3-16 Removing the Return Spring with Slip Ring

(4) Assembly and disassembly of co-driver's airbag

The breakdown of the co-driver's airbag is shown in Fig. 3-17. There are different models of co-driver's airbag, and the instrument panel shall match with the co-driver's airbag. When removing the co-driver's airbag, disconnect the ground wire of the battery, remove the glove box and pull off the plug 6. Be careful not to unplug the red foot plug on the co-driver's airbag. Unscrew nut 4 (4 nuts), remove the airbag, and place the airbag with cushion face upward.

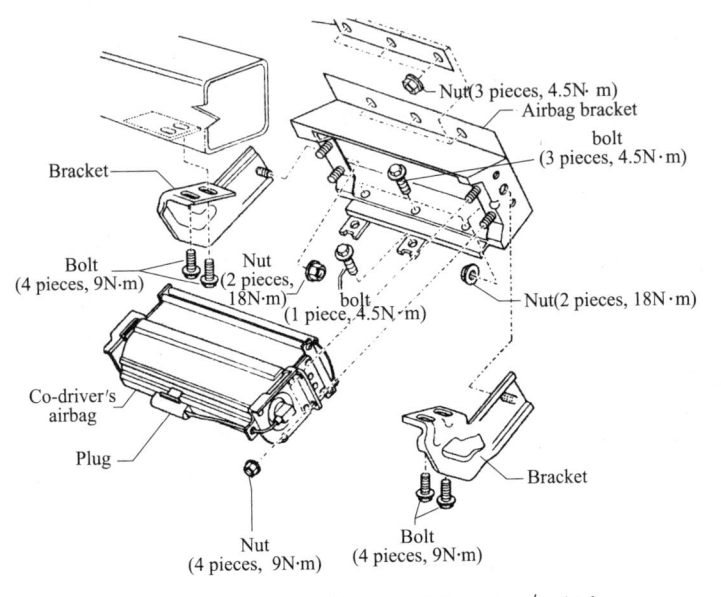

Fig. 3-17 Breakdown Diagram of Co-driver's Airbag

When installing the co-driver's airbag, make sure that the plug 6 is in place (audibly) and install the airbag. Turn on the ignition switch and connect the battery ground wire. Be

careful not to have anyone inside the vehicle during operation. Parts that must be replaced after triggering the airbag include bracket 2, nut 3 and nut 4, bolt 5 and airbag bracket 7.

As shown in Fig. 3-18, use a screwdriver to lift the retaining lug 2 of the plug 1 and pull off the plug in the direction of arrow 3. Disconnect battery ground wire. Remove front of centre floor console.

Remove insert for rear left and right rear foot air outlet deflector. As shown in Fig. 3-19, loosen the locating clip of plug 2, pull off plug 2 from control unit 1, unscrew bolt 3 (3 bolts) and remove the control unit. Re-coding is required after replacing the control unit.

(5) Disassembly and assembly of side airbag

The disassembly of side airbag is shown in Fig. 3-20. When removing the driver/co-driver side airbag, disconnect the battery ground wire, remove the backrest trim, loosen the mask around the side airbag 1, loosen the positioning of the plug 3, pull off the plug 3 from the side plug 1 and unscrew the two bolts 2. For clarity, the muffler pad is not shown in Fig. 3-20. Carefully loosen the locating detent 5 of the side airbag, remove the side airbag 1, and place the airbag with the cushion face upward.

When installing the driver/co-driver side airbag, do not cut the muffler pad around the locating detent 5, lift the muffler pad, enlarge the mounting hole by 5.5mm, spread the muffler pad onto the backrest bracket, fix the side airbag 1 to the muffler pad, insert the bolt 2, lift the muffler pad, install the nut and tighten it to 5.5N • m. Remove the sticker with service life from the airbag and attach it to the old sticker on the B-pillar. Remove the data label from the airbag and attach it to the seat label. Finally, connect the battery ground wire. Be careful not to have anyone inside the vehicle during operation.

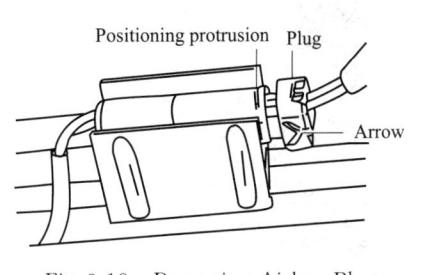

Fig. 3-18   Removing Airbag Plug

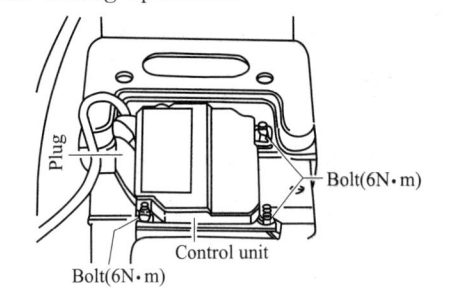

Fig. 3-19   Removing Airbag Control Unit

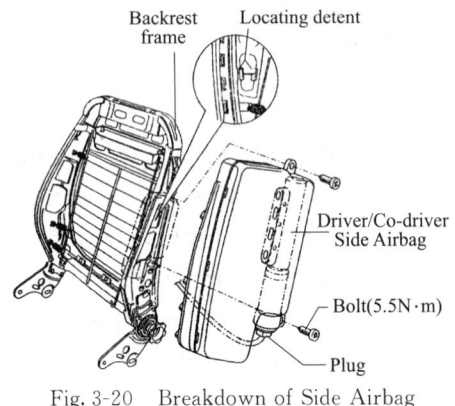

Fig. 3-20   Breakdown of Side Airbag

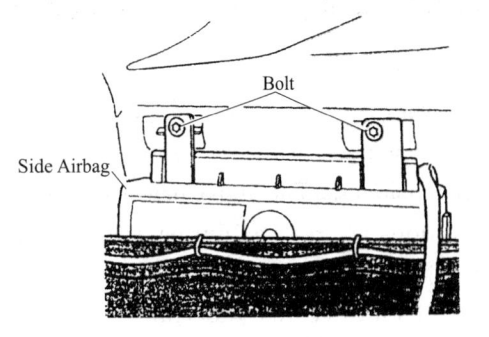

Fig. 3-21   Removing Rear Seat Side Airbag

(6) Disassembly and assembly of rear seat side airbag

Remove the rear seat as shown in Fig. 3-21. Unscrew bolt 2 (2 pieces) and remove side airbag 1.

(7) Disassembly and assembly of lateral acceleration sensor

The lateral acceleration sensors are installed on the front seats, one on the left and the other on the right, and the two sensors are the same. When installing, the arrow points outwards. Disconnect the battery ground wire, remove the front seat, remove the A-pillar lower trim panel, loosen the interior door sill trim, pull off the plug 2 of the lateral acceleration sensor 1, unscrew bolts 3 (2 pieces), and remove the lateral acceleration sensor, as shown in Fig. 3-22. The lateral acceleration sensor is installed in the reverse order of removal. Switch on the ignition switch, close the door and connect the battery ground wire. Be careful not to be manned in the vehicle.

(8) Disassembly and assembly of rear seat side airbag

① Disconnect the rear seat side airbag. Remove the rear seat. The left and right side airbags can only be cut off at the same time. It is impossible to cut off one air bag alone. The left and right C-pillars each have a plug, pull off locating protrusion 2 and plug 1 in the direction of arrow, as shown in Fig. 3-23. Secure the loosened plug connection with a tie-wrap. Install the rear seat and affix the disconnected side airbag label. Change airbag control unit coding from 204 or 206 to 104 or 106. Fill in the registration card and hand it over to the dealer for filing. Give the third copy of the registration card to the user and put it in the attached file.

② Connect the rear seat side airbag. Remove the rear seat. The airbags on the left and right sides can only be connected at the same time, and it is not allowed to connect only one airbag. The left and right C pillars should be connected with one plug each. Cut off plug tie-wrap.

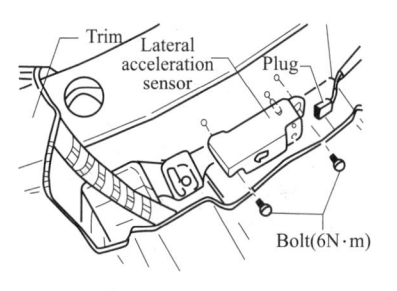

Fig. 3-22 Remove the Lateral Acceleration Sensor

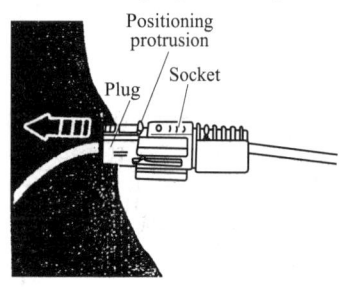

Fig. 3-23 Disconnect the Rear Seat Side Airbag

Ⅱ. Self-Diagnosis of Audi A6 Airbag System

1. Overview

Audi A6 airbag system consists of driver's airbag, co-driver's airbag, two front seat belt tensioners, two front side airbags, two rear seat side airbags and two or three rear seat belt tensioners. The above devices are triggered by the airbag control unit (J234) if the given conditions are reached during a crash. The co-driver's airbag can be turned off or turned on through self-diagnosis. After the airbag and the seat belt tensioner have been triggered, the control unit records the fault "Crash data saved" and the control unit needs to be replaced. Depending on the nature and intensity of the crash, the airbag control unit sends a "crash signal" to the central door lock control unit. This function has passive safety feature,

126 Automotive Safety and Comfort System Maintenance

i. e. when an airbag is triggered, the central door lock mechanism locks the door lock and trunk lock, locks the switch inside the vehicle, and the interior lighting lamp is turned on. The "crash signal" can be checked with actuator diagnostics. Coding is required before using a new airbag control unit. The airbag control unit (J234) must be replaced after the driver's or co-driver's airbag is triggered once, and the front seat belt tensioner or side airbag is triggered 3 times. Note that the wires of the airbag can only be visually inspected, and do not conduct electrical inspection on the triggering circuit. The ignition switch must be switched off when checking the wires.

2. Self-diagnosis function

(1) Self-diagnosis conditions

The following conditions shall be met during the self-diagnosis of the airbag system.

① Power supply and fuse of relevant system are normal.

② The fault reader V. A. G1551 has been connected.

③ The ignition switch has been turned on.

(2) Use of self-diagnosis function

A short-term fault is accidental and will be prompted with "/ SP" on the display screen. In order to correct these faults, clear the DTCs before repair.

① Turn off the ignition switch, connect the fault reader V. A. G1551, turn on the ignition switch, and press key 1 to select "fast data transmission".

② Address code of airbag system is 15, press key 1 and key 5.

③ Press the Q key to confirm the input.

④ 5s later, the screen displays the front airbag.

> 4B0959655G Airbag front + side 0001 →
> Code 01106 Service station code 06812

⑤ Press → key.

⑥ Press HELP key to print the list of optional functions.

Ⅲ. Fault Case Diagnosis Process of Automobile Electronic Control Passive Safety System

1. Read out DTC

Connect airbag short-circuit plug to left instrument panel service plug. The airbag indicator does not display any DTC, and the indicator is always on. The airbag indicator is always on, usually due to circuit failure of airbag indicator in the instrument assembly or short circuit or open circuit between plugs. In addition, in combination with the symptoms of this vehicle, it is possible that the fault of the airbag device itself or its power supply circuit device causes the fault lamp to be often on.

2. Clear DTC

Turn on the ignition switch. If the indicator is on and goes out after 6s, it indicates that the fault is intermittent, causing the fault lamp does not turn off. Turn off the ignition switch and check whether the No. 2 fuse 10A in the fuse/relay box under the instrument panel of the driver's seat is blown. The result is OK. After an SRS accident, the vehicle only re-

placed the airbag without replacing the SRS device. The new airbag components do not match with the original SRS device in the program setting, resulting in personal injury caused by airbag detonation when the vehicle should not be detonated. Failure to replace the SRS device may sometimes eliminate the DTC, but this has a great potential safety hazard. After replacing the matched SRS device, the fault lamp goes out and the SRS returns to normal.

Exercises

Short Answer Question
Briefly describe the function of the airbag system.

Item Summary

The airbag system can determine the type of collision that the vehicle is currently experiencing, providing the best protection for passengers. Intelligent and multi-airbags are the inevitable trend of airbag system development in the future.

Item Exercises

Fill in the blanks
1. The automobile safety system can be divided into two categories: the first kind of braking system belongs to _____ safety system; the second kind of airbag system belongs to _____ safety system.

2. The airbag system must be used together with _____ to effectively protect the safety of passengers.

Item IV

Maintenance of Automobile Electronic Control Suspension System

 ## Item Guide

With the improvement of people's requirements for vehicle maneuverability and comfort, as well as the rapid development of electronic technology, electronic control technology has been effectively applied to modern automobile suspension system. The greatest advantage of the electronic control suspension system is that it allows the suspension to react differently to different road conditions and driving conditions. It can not only make the ride comfort of the automobile reach the satisfactory state, but also make the handling stability of the automobile reach the best state.

Task I Identification of Automobile Electronic Control Suspension System

【Learning Objectives】

Knowledge requirements: Master the function, composition and basic principle of automobile electronic control suspension system.

Capability requirements: Be able to identify the components of the electronic control suspension system on the real vehicle.

 ## Task Import

To understand the auxiliary function of the electronic control suspension system in the driving process of the automobile, we should find out the difference between the electronic control suspension system and the traditional suspension system in terms of structure.

 ## Knowledge Preparation

Automobile suspension types can be divided into passive suspension, semi-active suspension and active suspension. Passive suspension is a mechanical suspension system composed of spring and shock absorber, while semi-active suspension and active suspension are all electronic control suspension systems.

Ⅰ. Functions of Electronic Control Suspension System

The basic function of the electronic control suspension system is to break through the limitation of the traditional passive suspension by controlling the stiffness and damping force of the suspension, so as to make the suspension characteristics adapt to the road condition and the driving state, so as to ensure that the ride comfort and handling stability of the vehicle can be satisfied. Its basic functions include the following aspects.

1. Height adjustment

No matter how much the vehicle's load, the vehicle height can be kept constant and the vehicle body level, so as to keep the headlamp beam direction unchanged; when the vehicle is driven on bad road surface, the vehicle height can be raised to prevent the axle from colliding with the road surface; when the vehicle is running at high speed, the vehicle height can be lowered to reduce air resistance and improve the handling stability.

2. Damper damping force control

By adjusting the damping coefficient of the shock absorber, the ride smoothness and handling stability can be improved by preventing the car from squatting at the rear of the car during rapid starting or acceleration; preventing the head sinking during emergency braking; preventing the vehicle body from shaking laterally when making a sharp turn; and preventing the longitudinal rocking of the vehicle body during gear shifting.

3. Spring stiffness control

As with shock absorber, the ride comfort and handling stability of automobile can be improved by adjusting the spring elastic coefficient under various working conditions.

Some models have only one or two of these functions, while others have all three.

Ⅱ. Types of Electronic Control Suspension Systems

There are many types of electronic control suspension systems used in modern cars.

1. Classification by different force transmission media

By the force transmission medium, the electronic control suspension system can be divided into pneumatic type and oil pressure type.

2. Classification by different control theory

By the different control theory, the electronic control suspension system can be divided into two kinds: semi-active and active. Among them, semi-active suspension is divided into two types: stage-semi-active (damping force can be adjusted in stages) and stageless semi-active (damping force can be continuously adjusted); active suspension can be divided into full active type (band width greater than 15 Hz) and slow full active (band width 3-6 Hz) by band width and energy consumption; and by different driving mechanism and medium, it can be divided into oil-gas active suspension driven by solenoid valve and air active suspension driven by stepping motor.

Stageless semi-active suspension can control the damping force of the suspension according to the driving state of the road and the response of the vehicle body, and the vibration response of the vehicle body is always controlled within a certain range within a few milliseconds. However, the damping force can not be effectively controlled under steering, starting

and braking conditions. Its advantage over full active suspension is that it does not need additional power source, consumes little energy and costs less.

Active suspension is a device that supplies and controls power sources (oil pressure, air pressure). Automatically adjust the stiffness, damping force of suspension and body height according to the changes of vehicle load, road condition, driving speed, starting, braking, steering and other conditions detected by various sensors. It can significantly improve the handling stability and ride comfort of the vehicle.

Ⅲ. Composition and Working Principle of Electronic Control Suspension System

The electronic control suspension system consists of sensor, electronic control unit (ECU) and actuator. The sensor converts the road conditions (vehicle vibration), vehicle speed, starting, acceleration, steering, braking and other working conditions of the vehicle into electrical signals, which are sent to ECU for comprehensive processing, and ECU outputs control signals for adjusting the stiffness, damping and body height of suspension. The actuator acts accurately according to the control signals of ECU, and timely adjusts the stiffness, damping coefficient of the suspension and body height, as shown in Fig. 4-1.

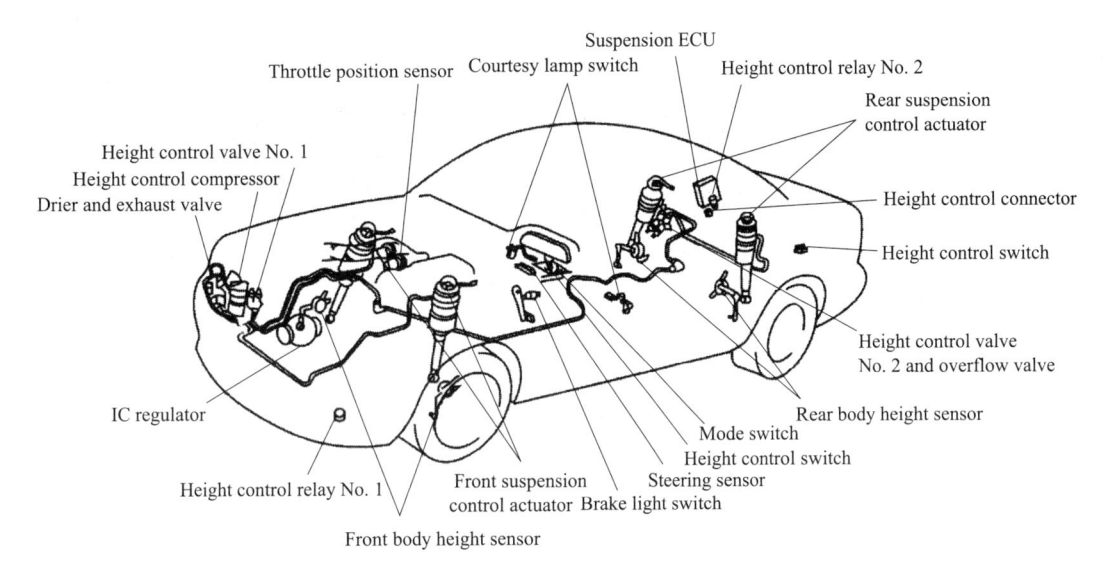

Fig. 4-1   Location of Electronic Control Suspension System Components on the Vehicle

1. Sensor

The function of the sensor is to send the signals of the vehicle speed, starting, acceleration, steering, braking and road condition, vehicle vibration condition and body height to the suspension ECU. The sensors used in the automobile suspension system mainly include body acceleration sensor, body height sensor, vehicle speed sensor, steering wheel angle sensor, throttle position sensor and so on. These sensors are described in detail below.

(1) Steering wheel angle sensor

The steering wheel angle sensor is used to detect the center position, rotation direction,

Item Ⅳ   Maintenance of Automobile Electronic Control Suspension System   **131**

rotation angle and rotation speed of the steering wheel. In the electronic control suspension, the suspension ECU judges the magnitude of the lateral force when the vehicle is steering according to the vehicle speed sensor signal and steering wheel angle sensor signal, so as to control the inclination of the vehicle body. The steering wheel angle sensor is used to detect the deflection direction of the automobile steering wheel.

Photoelectric steering wheel angle sensor is a commonly used steering wheel angle sensor in electric control suspension. Its structure and working principle are shown in Fig. 4-2. There are a certain number of narrow slots on the blocking disc pressed into the steering shaft, and there are two light emitting diodes and two photistors at both ends of the blocking disc respectively, forming two pairs of photocouplers (signal generators). When turning the steering wheel, the steering shaft drives the blocking disc to rotate. When turning to the narrow slot, the photistor senses the light emitted by the light emitting diode and outputs the "ON" signal; when the blocking disc is turned to other positions other than the narrow slot, the photistor does not feel the light of the light emitting diode and will output the "OFF" signal. In this way, with the rotation of the steering wheel, the output terminals of the two photocouplers will change "ON/OFF". The suspension ECU detects the steering speed of the steering shaft according to the "ON/OFF" conversion speed output by the two photocouplers. In addition, since the phases of the two photocouplers are shifted by about 90°, the rotation direction of the steering shaft can be detected by judging which blocking disc changes to "ON" state first.

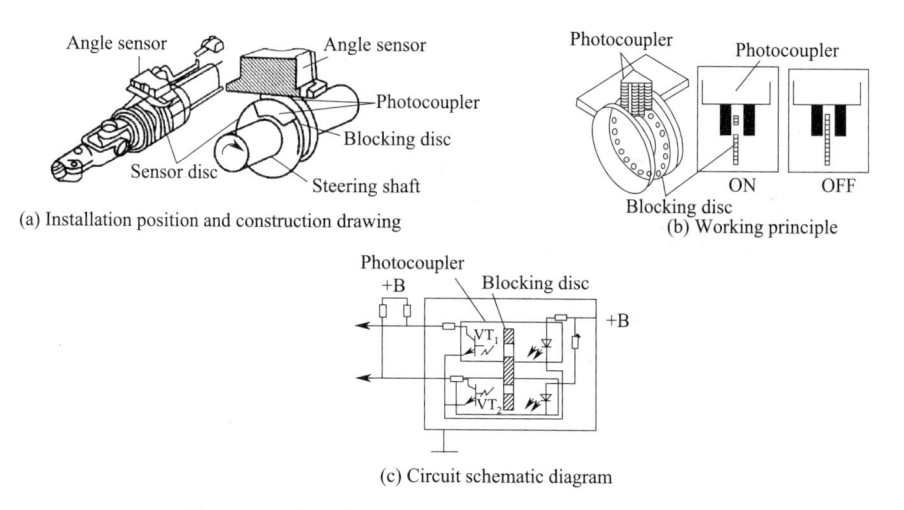

Fig. 4-2　Photoelectric Steering Wheel Angle Sensor

(2) Acceleration sensor

Generally speaking, the electronic control suspension system does not need to be equipped with a special acceleration sensor. The engine throttle position sensor signal is usually used to determine whether the vehicle is accelerating rapidly.

The sensors in the suspension system (vehicle speed sensor, height sensor, etc.) directly input the signal into the suspension ECU, but the throttle position sensor signal is input into the engine electronic control system, and then the engine electronic control system inputs this signal into the suspension ECU. When the vehicle is started or suddenly acceler-

ated, the power train control module generates an acceleration signal based on the throttle position sensor signal (the throttle opening is detected to be more than 90%) or the mass airflow sensor signal, and then provides the acceleration signal to the suspension ECU, which controls the actuator to switch to the hard damping state to reduce the "head up" ("sit-back") of the vehicle.

In rare cases, acceleration sensors are also used to collect acceleration signals, such as wheel slip. There are two kinds of acceleration sensors: differential transformer type and steel ball displacement type.

(3) Body height sensor

The function of the body height sensor is to convert the body height (the position of the vehicle suspension device) into an electric signal and send it to the suspension ECU. The number of height sensors depends on the type of electric control air suspension system equipped on the vehicle. One end of the height sensor is connected to the frame and the other end is mounted on the suspension system. On the electronic control suspension, the height sensor is used to collect body height information; on some ride comfort control systems, the height sensor is also used to detect suspension motion to determine if hard damping is required.

The body height sensor can be analog or digital; it can be linear or angular displacement.

Now the most widely used is the photoelectric digital body height sensor. There is a sensor shaft inside the sensor, the connecting rod installed at the outer end of the shaft is connected with the suspension arm, and a blocking disc with a certain number of narrow slots is fixed on the shaft. Four groups of light emitting diodes and photistors are symmetrically mounted on both sides of the blocking disc to form four pairs of photocouplers (signal generators). When the body height changes, the body and the suspension arm move relative to each other, and the connecting rod drives the sensor shaft and the blocking disc to rotate together. When the slot on the blocking disc is aligned with the coupler, the photistor senses the light emitted by the light emitting diode through the slot, and the photocoupler outputs ON signal, otherwise it outputs OFF signal. A combination of the four pairs of photocouplers on and off can be used to divide the vehicle body height change into 16 areas for detection as long as the slots on the blocking disc are properly distributed. The height sensor has a six-wire connector consisting of a power cord, a ground wire, and four signal wires.

Suspension ECU obtains body displacement information according to "ON" and "OFF" signals input by sensor. According to the amplitude and frequency of the body height change, the vibration condition of the vehicle body can be judged, and the body height can be judged according to the percentage of the body height in a certain area over a period of time (generally 10ms).

(4) Vehicle speed sensor

Suspension ECU can receive vehicle speed signal input from vehicle speed sensor, various other modules or multiplex network for various control functions of the system.

The output of the transmission, the drive shaft or the transfer case drives the speed sensor via gears. The vehicle speed sensor signal is an AC waveform signal. Its frequency and

voltage increase with the vehicle speed. The vehicle speed can be known from the signal frequency.

The vehicle speed signal can also be directly provided to the suspension ECU (directly connected) by other modules, and this signal is a DC change signal.

A vehicle speed signal may also be provided to the suspension ECU in the form of a data signal from the vehicle multiplex network.

(5) Door signal

The suspension ECU uses the door signal to perform some functions of the system, such as preventing exhaust when the door is open or maintaining the current driving height, etc. When the door is closed, the system resumes normal operation.

(6) Brake signal

When the car brakes, the brake switch sends a braking signal to the suspension ECU. After the suspension ECU receives the braking signal, the control actuator switches the suspension from soft to hard state to prevent the vehicle from "nodding" ("tail cocking").

(7) Suspension control switch

Suspension control switch includes suspension stiffness and LRC switch, height control switch and lock switch (height control ON/OFF switch). The first two switches are generally installed in the cab beside the gear selection control handle (see Fig. 4-3), and the lock switch is generally installed in the trunk (see Fig. 4-4).

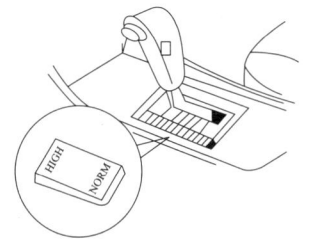 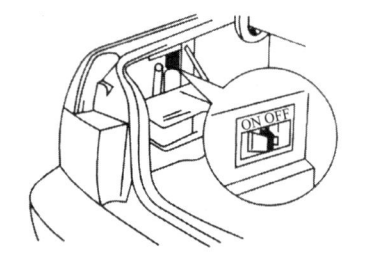

Fig. 4-3　Installation Position of Suspension Stiffness and
LRC Switch and Height Control Switch

Fig. 4-4　Installation Position of Locking
Switch (Height Control ON/ OFF Switch)

① Suspension stiffness and LRC switch. The LRC switch is used to select the stiffness and damping force parameters of the suspension. It has two gears: When the LRC switch is in the "NORM" position, the system enters "Normal Travel Automatic Control" and when the LRC switch is in the "SPORT" position, the system enters "High Speed Travel Control". In each mode, there are three states in order of stiffness and damping: low, medium and high. When the "NORM" and "SPORT" modes are selected by the LRC, the suspension ECU automatically adjusts the stiffness and damping coefficient among the low, medium and high states according to the input signal of the sensor.

② Height control switch. The height control switch also has two kinds of control modules, namely "NORM" and "HIGH". According to the order of height of vehicle body from low to high, each mode has three states of low, medium and high. In the "NORM" mode, the body height is always in the "Low" state, and the system carries out "normal value automatic control" for the body height; in the "HIGH" mode, the body height is often in the "High" state, and the system performs "high value automatic control" for the body height.

③ Lock switch (height control ON/OFF switch). The lock switch (height control ON/OFF switch) is generally installed in the trunk. When the lock switch is at "ON", the system will control the body height according to the mode selected by the driver through the height control switch; when the lock switch is at "OFF", the system will not adjust the body height.

2. Electronic Control Unit (ECU)

(1) Functions of ECU

The electronic control module (suspension ECU), which controls the suspension system, is the hub of the suspension control system and has a variety of functions.

① Amplification of sensor signal. The interference signal in the input signal (such as sensor signal and switch signal) is removed by the interface circuit, and then the extreme value is amplified, transformed, and compared to be converted into a signal suitable for input to the suspension ECU.

② Calculation of input signal. The suspension ECU calculates each input signal according to the program previously written in the ROM, compares the calculation result with the data in the memory, and sends the control signal to the actuator (motor, solenoid valve, relay, etc.). In addition to the switch signal, the signal input to the suspension ECU has voltage value, and A/D conversion shall also be performed.

③ Drive actuator. Suspension ECU amplifies the output drive signal with output driving circuit, and then sends it to various actuators, such as motor, solenoid valve, relay, etc., to realize the control of vehicle suspension parameters.

④ Fault detection. Suspension ECU uses fault detection circuit to detect fault of sensor, actuator and circuit.

(2) Structure of electronic control unit (suspension ECU) of electronic control air suspension system

The suspension ECU of electronic control air suspension system gives all input and output signals at the same time. The suspension ECU consists of an 8-bit microprocessor, input interface and output drive circuit as well as a failure safe circuit which is also used for the interface of the diagnostic module. The suspension ECU selects a pre-programmed control mode according to the received sensor signals.

(3) Working principle of electronic control unit (suspension ECU) of electric control air suspension system

The control program of the suspension ECU is written into ROM in advance. During the suspension control process, the calculation, analysis and comparison are carried out in the order specified by the control program.

After the system starts, firstly initialize the RAM and the actuator in the suspension ECU, then read all kinds of sensor input signals and various switch signals, calculate and analyze the input signals according to the system control mode selected by the driver, and send out control signals for vehicle driving attitude control, and then read various input signals, so as to repeat the cycle.

Because the signal processing speed of the suspension ECU is faster than the movement of the vehicle, the suspension ECU performs one calculation in microsecond order, so that there is no problem in control when processing in the above order.

3. Electronic Control Air Suspension Actuator

（1）Function of actuator

The function of the suspension actuator is to drive the air valve spools of the main and auxiliary air chambers and the rotary valve of the damping hole of the shock absorber to rotate，so as to control the suspension stiffness and damping parameters，as shown in Fig. 4-5.

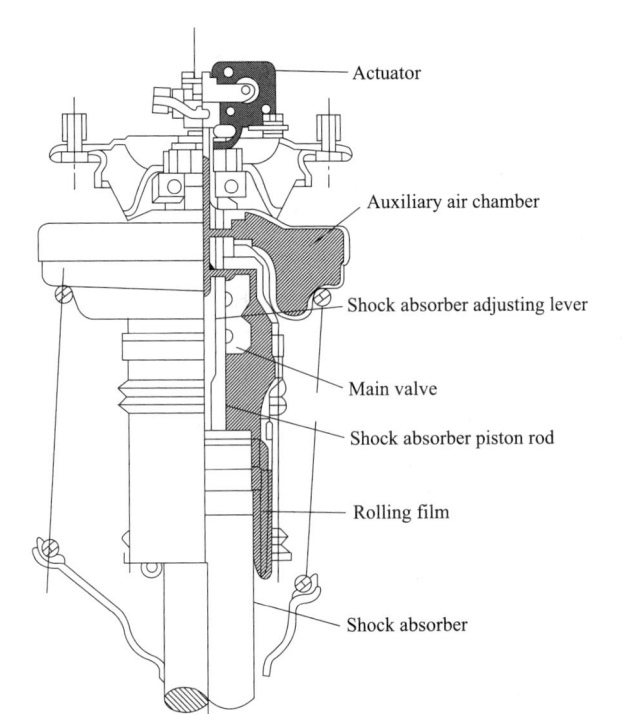

Fig. 4-5　Composition of Electric Control Suspension

The control function of the electric control air suspension system mainly includes the following three aspects of control.

① Speed and road sensing control. With the change of vehicle speed and road surface，this kind of control mainly changes the stiffness and damping coefficient of suspension to make it in low，medium and high states. There are three main types of vehicle speed and road sensing.

a. High speed sensing. When the vehicle speed is very high，the control module outputs the control signal to increase the stiffness and damping coefficient of the suspension correspondingly，so as to improve the handling stability of the vehicle at high speed.

b. Front and rear wheel correlation sensing. When the front wheel of a car encounters a single bump on the road surface，the control module outputs a control signal to reduce the stiffness and damping coefficient of the rear wheel suspension accordingly，so as to reduce the vibration and impact of the vehicle body.

c. Poor road sensing. The control module outputs control signal to increase the stiffness and damping coefficient of the suspension to control the vehicle body to generate great vibration when the vehicle runs on poor road surface.

② Body posture control. When a car starts，brakes and turns，it can cause a sharp change in the posture of the vehicle body. This kind of body posture change not only reduces

136　Automotive Safety and Comfort System Maintenance

the ride comfort of the car, but also makes the vehicle lose stability easily due to excessive tilting of the body, so it should be controlled. This kind of control mainly includes the following three aspects.

a. Body tilt control when steering.

b. Body nodding control when braking.

c. Backseat control of the body when starting or accelerating.

③ Body height control. Body height control is to control and adjust the height of the vehicle body when the vehicle speed and road surface change and the suspension ECU outputs the control signal to the executive element, so as to ensure the running stability and passage of the vehicle.

(2) Structure and working principle of electronic control air suspension system actuator

The structure of the actuator of the electronic control suspension system is shown in Fig. 4-6. When the suspension ECU controls the action of the stepping motor, it drives the pinion to rotate and the pinion drives the sector gear to rotate. The damping adjusting rod coaxial with the sector gear drives the rotary valve to rotate, thus changing the opening and closing number of damping holes to achieve the purpose of adjusting the damping of the shock absorber. At the same time, the damper adjusting rod drives the air valve control rod to rotate through the gear to rotate the air valve core. With the change of the rotation angle of the valve core, the stiffness of the air spring is also adjusted.

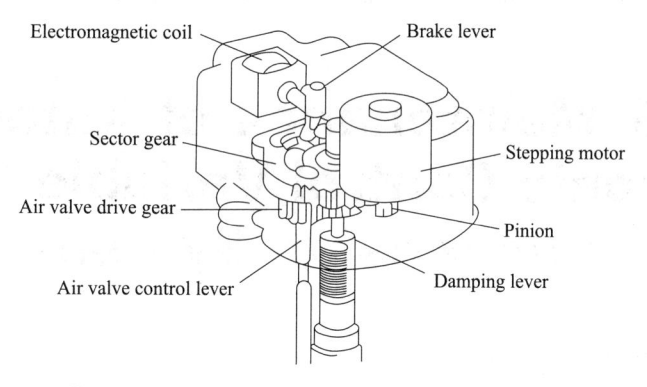

Fig. 4-6　Structure of Suspension System Actuator

There is also an electromagnetic coil on the actuator of the suspension system. When the solenoid coil is not energized, the brake switch controlled by it is released, the brake lever is in the sliding slot of the sector gear, and the sector gear can rotate; when the solenoid coil is energized, the brake switch is pulled in, the brake lever is pulled back, each gear is locked, and the damping adjusting lever and the air valve control lever cannot rotate. At this time, the stiffness parameters and damping parameters of the suspension are fixed, and the suspension system is in a relatively stable state.

(3) Classification of electronic control air suspension actuator

There are three common actuators of electronic control suspension system, namely 4-wire actuator, 3-wire actuator and 2-wire actuator.

① 4-wire actuator. The 4-wire actuator is a bi-directional DC motor. The actuator is mounted on top of the shock absorber and drives a shaft inside the shock absorber to change the shock absorber valve. Such actuators are controlled by the suspension ECU through a pair of components

called hard/soft relays. The 4-wire actuator can be removed from the shock absorber assembly and replaced separately, with a position sensor inside the 4-wire actuator.

② 3-wire actuator. The 3-wire actuator is a DC motor located on top of the shock absorber and can only rotate in one direction. When the motor rotates, the reduction gear assembly drives the shock absorber piston rod to change the vibration damping.

③ 2-wire actuator. The 2-wire actuator is an on/off solenoid valve. If the solenoid valve is in the off position, the shock absorber is hard damped; if the solenoid valve is in the on position, the shock absorber is soft damped. The 2-wire actuator is integral with the shock absorber and cannot be serviced separately.

Task Implementation

Students train in groups to find out the structural differences between electronic control suspension systems and conventional suspensions on real vehicles.

Exercises

Short Answer Questions

1. Briefly describe the function of electronic control suspension system.
2. Briefly describe the classfication of electronic control air suspension actutor.

Task Ⅱ Maintenance of Automobile Electronic Control Variable Height Suspension System

【Learning Objectives】

Knowledge requirements:

1. Understand the function, classification and composition of automobile electronic control variable height suspension system;

2. Master the structure, principle and maintenance of automobile electronic control variable height suspension system;

3. Understand the train of thought and method of fault diagnosis of automobile electronic control variable height suspension system.

Capability requirements:

1. Be able to obtain vehicle information through communication with customers and consulting relevant maintenance technical data;

2. Be able to formulate correct maintenance plan according to fault phenomenon;

3. According to the maintenance plan, select the correct detection and diagnosis equipment to diagnose the fault of automobile electronic control variable height suspension system;

4. Be able to use multimeter, fault scan tool, oscilloscope and common detection and

diagnosis equipment to detect the sensor, controller and actuator of automobile electronic control variable height suspension system;

5. Be able to replace the sensor, actuator and controller according to correct operation specifications, and perform system matching settings;

6. Be able to test, inspect and evaluate the repair quality of vehicle electronic control variable height suspension system.

  **Task Import**

A car instrument panel lighting system warning light is on, the suspension lift button LED on the central control panel flashes, and the electronic control air suspension lifting system does not work.

 Knowledge Preparation

Ⅰ. Functions and Classification of Body Height Control System

The main function of the body height control system is to automatically adjust the height of the vehicle body when the vehicle load or the driving speed of the vehicle changes, so as to stabilize the driving posture of the vehicle, thus improving the riding comfort and safety.

1. Automatic level adjustment

The system maintains the vehicle at a constant height level, regardless of the occupant and weight, and places the vehicle height in a normal or high position.

2. Regulation at high speed

When the vehicle suspension height switch is set to the SPORT position, the vehicle height is slightly lower than the normal position. This position improves stability and aerodynamics at high speeds.

3. Suspension position adjustment with ignition switch off

In order to prevent changes in vehicle height caused by changing the number of passengers and luggage weight after the ignition switch is turned off, the vehicle height position set can be adjusted. This function can improve the vehicle attitude when driving.

The body height control system is divided into two types, one is to control only two rear wheel suspensions and the other is to control the suspension height of all four wheels. The principles of both types of control are essentially the same.

Ⅱ. Composition of Variable Height Control Suspension System

At present, the automobile body height control system is composed of 4 height sensors (one under each shock absorber), control switch, EMS ECU, height adjusting actuator (including 4 pneumatic cylinders, two height control solenoid valves, air compressor, dryer and air pipeline).

Ⅲ. Control Process of Variable Height Control Suspension System

The variable height control suspension system automatically adjusts the body height

when the vehicle occupant or load changes. When the occupant or load increases, the system will automatically increase the body height; otherwise, when the occupant or load decreases, the system will automatically lower the body height.

1. Suspension system control process at constant body height

When the signal input from the body height sensor to ECU indicates that the body height is within the set height range, the ECU will give a command to stop the air compressor, keep the air quantity in the air damper unchanged, and keep the body height at the normal position.

2. Suspension system control process at lower body height

When the vehicle occupant or load increase causes the body height to be "low" or "too low", the height sensor inputs a signal of "low" or "too low" body to the suspension control EMS ECU. When the EMS ECU receives the signal that the body height decreases, it immediately sends the circuit connection command to the compressor relay and the height control solenoid valve. At the same time, connecting the relay circuit of the height control air compressor to operate the compressor, it connects the coil circuit of the height control solenoid valve to open the solenoid valve. The compressed air enters into the air pressure chamber (air chamber) of the air spring, and the increase of the charging volume of the air chamber will raise the height of the vehicle body.

When the relay contact of the air compressor is connected, the DC motor drives the air compressor to operate. The compressed air output from the compressor enters into the dryer for drying and then enters into the air tank. The gas pressure of the air tank is regulated by the pressure regulating valve.

3. Suspension system control process at elevated body height

When the vehicle occupant or load reduction causes the vehicle body height to be "high" or "too high", the height sensor will input a signal of body raised to the suspension control EMS ECU. When the EMS ECU receives the signal that the vehicle body height rises, it immediately sends the circuit cut-off command to the air compressor relay, and sends the circuit connection command to the exhaust valve and the height control solenoid valve. The compressor relay contact is quickly disconnected to cut off the motor circuit and stop the operation. The exhaust valve and the coil circuit of the height control solenoid valve are connected to open the solenoid valve. The air is discharged from the air pressure chamber of the shock absorber through the height control solenoid valve, air hose, dryer and exhaust valve. The air volume in the air pressure chamber decreases and the vehicle height decreases.

4. System protection measures

The air discharged from the shock absorber takes moisture away from the desiccant as it passes through the dryer. In this way, the desiccant will not become saturated with moisture after a period of use. This regenerative drying system for protecting desiccant is used in many electronic control suspension systems. The air pressure in the dryer shall be maintained at 55-165kPa to ensure a certain amount of air in the system. In this way, the air pressure chamber of the air spring will not collapse when the shock absorber is extended due to occupant or load reduction.

Task Implementation

Ⅰ. Maintenance of Electronic Control Variable Height Suspension System

1. Repair the fault of the electric control suspension after adjusting the height

A dedicated digital detector capable of displaying and translating DTCs shall be used for troubleshooting. Connect the dedicated detector to the detection interface of the suspension control and steering power control module to receive the DTC transmitted by the system control module self-test system, and complete the following diagnostic tests.

① Automatic/manual fault inspection.

② Fault code display.

③ Detailed inspection.

④ Function inspection.

In automatic/manual inspection, the control module self-test system detects if there is a fault with the system components. After checking for component failure, the controller raises and lowers the vehicle to check the status of the 3 height sensors. The height sensor is manually inspected after completion of the check. During this process, open the door several times, turn the steering wheel half turn to the left and right respectively, and the control module detects that the door switch and the steering sensor are working.

In the repair information provided by the manufacturer, a detailed check is provided for each type of DTC. The detailed check is performed using a voltmeter and an ohmmeter and determine the cause of the DTC.

A functional check is used at the end of an automatic/manual check to find the component represented by the DTC. Do not proceed to a functional check unless the detailed check indicates that a functional check is required. The functional check without such special instructions can cause damage to the control module. The manufacturer's maintenance manual provides procedures for the detailed check.

2. Operating procedures for inflation of air spring

① Lift the frame with the crane and slowly lower the crane until slight vehicle weight acts on the suspension.

② Turn the control switch of the electronic control suspension system to the ON state.

③ Keep the ignition switch from OFF to ON for 5s, open the driver's side door, close other doors and disconnect the ignition switch.

④ Connect the system detection diagnosis lead to grounding wire (grounding).

⑤ Step down the brake pedal and turn the ignition switch on.

⑥ When inflating the rear suspension spring, close and open the driver's door once respectively. After a delay of 6s, the rear suspension spring is inflated.

⑦ When inflating the front suspension spring, close and open the driver's door twice respectively. After a delay of 6s, the front suspension spring is inflated.

⑧ When the front and rear suspension springs need to be inflated, inflating the rear suspension spring first. After the rear suspension spring is inflated, close and open the door

at the driver's side once to inflate the front suspension spring.

⑨ If the diagnosis lead is separated from the grounding wire, the spring inflation state stops. If the ignition switch is turned off or the brake pedal is depressed, inflation will also stop.

Ⅱ. Fault Case Diagnosis Process of Electronic Control Variable Height Suspension System

The air suspension system was tested by connecting the fault detector, and the fault was found to be abnormal filling time of the central accumulator. The action test function of the fault detector was used to inflate the central accumulator and it was found that the command from the control unit could be issued but the inflator pump did not work. Based on the action test results, it can be determined that the cause of the fault may be either a circuit problem or a component problem. Firstly, check the power line of the inflator pump with the voltage gear of multimeter, and the test result is no working voltage. A line check against the circuit diagram found that the 40A fuse supplying the power supply had blown. However, it was found that there was no short circuit in the inflator pump and the circuit. Then replace the fused fuse and start the engine for test run, but the fault still exists after the test run. Therefore, the positive and negative pole power of the battery was directly led to the inflator pump with wire, and the inflator pump was found not working. Based on the above inspection results, it could be determined that the inflator pump was damaged. After replacing a new inflator pump, the lifting function of the suspension system resumed, the LED light on the lifting switch went out after the vehicle suspension reached the preset height, and the electric control air suspension system returned to normal.

Exercises

Fill in the blanks

1. Wheel and body conditions can only passively depend on the road surface and driving conditions as well as on the vehicle's elastic support elements, shock absorbers, and guiding mechanism suspensions are_____ suspensions.

2. According to the driving conditions, the stiffness of the suspension system, the damping force of the shock absorber and the height and attitude of the vehicle body can be adjusted at any time, the suspension that can keep the relevant performance of the vehicle in the best state is _____ suspension.

Task Ⅲ Maintenance of Automobile Electronic Control Variable Stiffness Suspension System

〔Learning Objectives〕

Knowledge requirements: Understand the train of thought and method of fault diagnosis of automobile electronic control variable stiffness suspension system.

Capability requirements:

1. According to the maintenance plan, select the correct detection and diagnosis equipment to diagnose the fault of automobile electronic control variable stiffness suspension system;

2. Be able to use multimeter, fault scan tool, oscilloscope and common detection and diagnosis equipment to detect the sensor, controller and actuator of automobile electronic control variable stiffness suspension system;

3. Be able to correctly record and analyze various test results and make fault judgment;

4. Be able to replace sensor, actuator and controller according to correct operation specifications, and perform system matching settings;

5. Be able to test, inspect and evaluate the repair quality of vehicle electronic control variable stiffness suspension system.

 # Task Import

The suspension system of a Mazda car can only operate in one mode regardless of the vehicle condition and cannot be adjusted according to the driving conditions. The car is equipped with Mazda electronic control suspension system TEMS. Under normal circumstances, the driver can select the control mode of suspension according to driving conditions, so as to determine the magnitude of damping force, but the vehicle can only operate in "normal manual mode".

 # Knowledge Preparation

I. Functions of Electronic Control Variable Stiffness Suspension System

One of the main factors affecting the ride comfort and driving safety is the stiffness of automobile suspension elastic element, which will directly affect the vibration intensity of vehicle body and the sensing degree of road condition and speed. At present, medium and high-grade automobiles tend to adjust the stiffness of elastic elements by adjusting the air pressure of these elements via adjustable stiffness air springs or hydro-pneumatic springs.

II. Composition of Electronic Control Variable Stiffness Suspension System

Electronic control variable stiffness suspension system is also composed of height sensor, control switch, EMS ECU, stiffness adjusting actuators (pneumatic cylinder, height control solenoid valve, air compressor, dryer and air pipeline), etc.

III. Adjustment Principle of Air Spring Suspension Stiffness

It is necessary to adjust the height of corresponding suspension and the damping of shock absorber to prevent or suppress phenomena such as "nodding", "rolling" and "backward sitting". For example, when the vehicle is in emergency braking, in order to suppress the nodding phenomenon, the EMS ECU of the suspension control will command the front air spring actuator to increase its air pressure according to the brake lamp switch ON signal

and the vehicle speed signal provided by the vehicle speed sensor, so as to increase the stiffness of the front air spring, and control the rear air spring actuator to deflate the rear air spring to reduce its stiffness. When the vehicle speed variation calculated by the control unit indicates that it is unnecessary to restrain the nodding control, the front and rear air springs will be restored to the original pressure.

In the electronic control suspension system used in some cars, off-road vehicles and large luxury buses, air springs and ordinary shock absorbers are used on each wheel. The stiffness of the air spring suspension can be changed by changing the pressure of the compressed air in the air spring chamber (actually changing the air density).

The air spring consists of shock absorber sealed with low pressure inert gas and adjustable damping force, rotary diaphragm, main air chamber, secondary air chamber and suspension actuating element. The volume of the main air chamber is variable. There is an oppositely extending diaphragm at the lower part of the main air chamber. When compressed air enters into the main air chamber, the height of the suspension can be increased, on the contrary, the height of the suspension

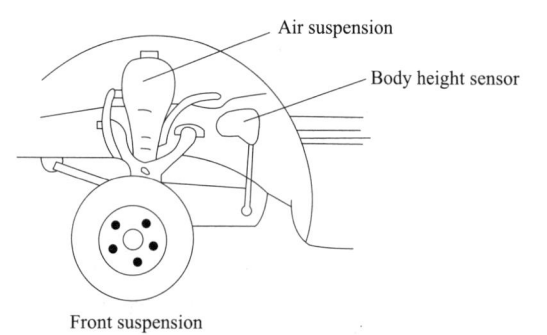

Fig. 4-7　Suspension Installation Position

can be lowered. The main and auxiliary air chambers are designed as a whole to save space and reduce weight. The upper part of the suspension is connected to the vehicle body and the lower part is connected to the wheel, as shown in Fig. 4-7. With the relative motion between the body and the wheel, the volume of the main air chamber is constantly changing. There is a passage between the main air chamber and the secondary air chamber, and the gas can flow through each other. The stiffness of the electronic control suspension can be changed by changing the size of the gas passage between the main and auxiliary air chambers. The piston of the shock absorber is connected to a DC stepping motor via a central rod (damping adjustment lever) and a gear train. The rotation of the stepping motor changes the size of the piston orifice, thus changing the damping coefficient of the shock absorber.

Principle of automatic adjustment of suspension stiffness: There are two major and minor passages on the air valve body between the main and auxiliary air chambers. Stepping motor drives the air valve control lever to rotate to rotate the air valve core by an angle and change the size of the gas passage, so as to change the gas flow between the main and auxiliary air chambers and change the stiffness of the suspension.

Suspension stiffness can be changed in low, medium and high states.

When the opening of the valve core is turned to align the low position shown in Fig. 4-8, the large bore of the gas passage is opened. The gas in the main air chamber passes through the middle hole of the valve core, and the side passage of the valve body communicates with the gas of the auxiliary air chamber. The larger the air flow between the two air chambers is, it is equivalent to the increase of the working gas volume, and the suspension stiffness is in a low state.

When the opening of the valve core is turned to align the medium position as shown in

144　Automotive Safety and Comfort System Maintenance

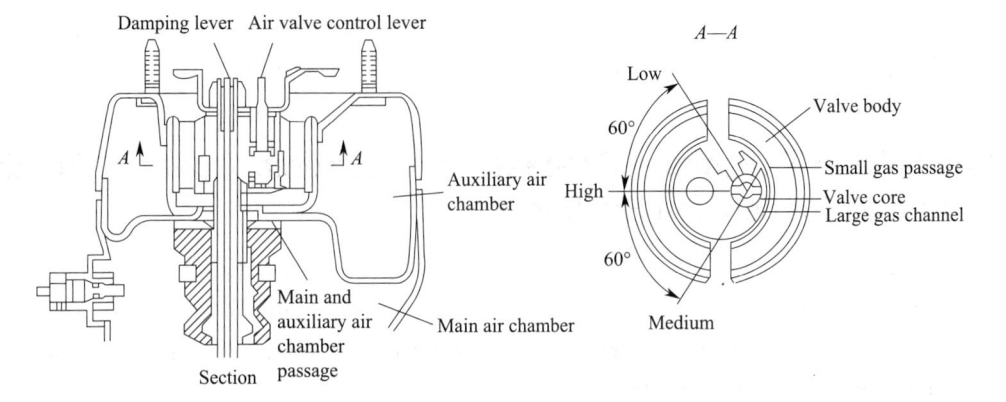

Fig. 4-8　Principle of Automatic Adjustment of Suspension Stiffness

Fig. 4-8, the orifice of the gas passage is opened, the flow between the two chambers is small, and the suspension stiffness is in the medium state.

When the opening of the valve core is turned to the high position shown in Fig. 4-8, all the gas passages between the two air chambers are sealed, and the gases between the two air chambers cannot flow each other, and compressed air can only enter into the main air chamber. During the vibration process of suspension, only the gas in the main air chamber undertakes the buffering work independently, and the suspension height is in the high state.

 Task Implementation

Ⅰ. Removal and Installation of Air Spring

Refer to the manufacturer's maintenance manual for assembly and disassembly of air spring. The general operation steps are as follows.

① Disconnect the electronic control suspension switch.

② After lifting the vehicle, the suspension will droop naturally, or jack up the vehicle and place the jack bracket under the frame to lower the vehicle on the bracket and make the suspension droop naturally.

③ Remove the nylon air pipe from the solenoid valve of the air spring. Turn the valve to the first gear to exhaust the air completely from the spring. Do not turn the valve to the second gear until the air is exhausted.

④ Remove the holder under the air spring and remove the spring from the frame.

⑤ Before installing the air spring, it should be folded correctly on the piston at the bottom of the leather chamber. Still fit the air spring on the frame and fit the holder under the spring. Ensure that the top of the spring is correctly installed in the spring and the spring must be positioned correctly when installing the suspension or suspension spring.

Note: The system control switch must be in the OFF position when repairing system components.

When removing the air spring valve, turn the valve to the first gear until the air in the air spring is completely discharged. Do not turn the valve to second gear until the air is completely discharged.

Item Ⅳ　Maintenance of Automobile Electronic Control Suspension System　**145**

The diagnosis and maintenance of many parts in the electric control air suspension system, such as shock absorber, stabilizer bar, etc., are carried out in the same way as in conventional suspension system.

II. Fault Case Diagnosis Process of Electronic Control Variable Stiffness Suspension System

During the maintenance, it was found that the vehicle had just been paved with ground glue. The mode selection switch of the vehicle is in front of the automatic transmission gear selector lever. If you want to apply ground glue, you need to remove the rubber around the mode selector switch and remove the switch guard board. Therefore, it was suspected that the cause of the failure was that the wiring of the mode selector switch was damaged during assembly and disassembly. Remove the mode select switch. The switch has 4 leads, including two leads to pin A1 and pin A13 of the electronic control unit in the suspension control system, one ground wire and the other to 20A fuse of the TEMS power supply. This wire remained energized after the ignition switch was turned on. However, the wire voltage was always 0 V when measured with a multimeter. Carefully inspect each pin and it was found that the part of the wire that extends into the plug had been disconnected. Connect the line, install the mode selection switch and conduct test run, and everything returned to normal. The suspension control system could automatically adjust "Normal Manual" "Normal Auto" "Motion Manual" and "Motion Auto" according to the corresponding selection no matter which mode selection switch button was pressed.

Exercises

True or False

1. The active suspension can control the damping force of the suspension according to the driving state of the road surface and the response of the vehicle body, and the vibration response of the vehicle body can be controlled within a certain range from the minimum to the maximum within a few seconds. ( )

2. The active suspension requires an external power source, which consumes a lot of energy. ( )

Task IV Maintenance of Automobile Electronic Control Variable Damping Suspension System

[Learning Objectives]

Knowledge requirements: Understand the train of thought and method of fault diagnosis of automobile electronic control variable damping suspension system.

Capability requirements:

1. According to the maintenance plan, select the correct detection and diagnosis equipment to diagnose the fault of automobile electronic control variable damping suspension system;

2. Be able to use multimeter, fault scan tool, oscilloscope and common detection and diagnosis equipment to detect the sensor, controller and actuator of automobile electronic control variable damping suspension system;

3. Be able to replace the sensor, actuator and controller according to correct operation specifications, and perform system matching settings;

4. Be able to test, inspect and evaluate repair the quality of vehicle electronic control variable damping suspension system.

 **Task Import**

When the electric vehicle is running, the suspension stiffness and damping coefficient are not adjusted according to the driving conditions, road conditions and vehicle attitude changes.

Knowledge Preparation

Ⅰ. Functions and Control Modes of Variable Damping Suspension System

Among electronic control suspension systems, variable damping suspension systems are most commonly used. The variable damping suspension systems have a number of advantages over suspension systems using air springs, the most prominent being the light mass. The variable damping suspension system adds only the mass of the electronic control elements and the actuator elements that change the shock absorber damping.

The variable damping suspension system adopts the following three control modes.

① Control according to the driving condition of the vehicle.

② Control according to the operation mode selected by the driver.

③ Control according to the driving condition of the vehicle and the operation mode selected by the driver.

Ⅱ. Structural Features of Damping Control Mechanism of Shock Absorber

1. Operation Mode Selector Switch

The working mode selector switch that electronically controls the shock absorber damping of the suspension system, also known as the operation mode selector switch, is used to select the working mode of shock absorber damping. The shock absorber damping state is different depending on the working mode selected by the driver. The damping state of the shock absorber is generally "standard" "medium hardness" and "hard" .

2. Variable Damping Actuator

The actuator of the TOYOTA electronic adjustable suspension system is mounted on top of the shock absorber strut.

Ⅲ. Control Process of Damping Adjustment of Shock Absorber

1. Damping "Standard" Control Process

When the EMS ECU determines that the damping is in the "standard" state according to

the sensor and control switch signals, the control unit sends a control command to the stepping motor to rotate the motor clockwise, so that the pinion drives the sector gear to rotate in the counterclockwise direction until one side of the sector gear groove abuts against the stopper.

2. Damping "Medium" Control Process

When the ECU determines that the damping is in the "medium" state according to the sensor and control switch signals, the control unit sends the control command to the stepping motor to rotate the motor in the counterclockwise direction, so the pinion drives the sector gear to rotate clockwise until the other side of the sector gear groove is against the stopper (calculated from the "soft" position, the angle is about 120°). At the same time, the sector gear drives the rotary valve control lever and rotary valve to rotate, to make the damping hole on the rotary valve correspond to the damping oil hole on the piston rod. Because only the damping hole on the second section is open and the flow of damping fluid through the piston is not quick and not slow, the shock absorber can expand and contract at a slow rate, leaving the damping in a "medium" state.

3. Damping "Hard" Control Process

When the ECU determines that the damping is in "hard" state according to sensor and control switch signals, the control unit will send a control command to the stepping motor and the solenoid coil at the same time to make the stepping motor and the sector gear rotate about 60° from the extreme position of "soft" or "medium" damping (rotate clockwise 60° from the limit position of "soft", rotate anticlockwise 60° from limit position of "medium"), turn on electromagnetic coil current, and its electromagnetic suction force will draw the stopper out and make the stopper enter into a pit in the middle of the groove of sector gear. At the same time, the sector gear drives the rotary valve control lever and rotary valve to rotate, to make the damping hole on the rotary valve correspond to the damping oil hole on the piston rod. Because all 3 damping holes are closed, the damping fluid cannot flow, so the shock absorber retracts very slowly, leaving the damping in a "hard" state.

4. Control of Indicator of Variable Damping Suspension System

In addition to sending control signals to the actuating elements, the ECU also sends out control commands to the three indicators of the suspension system on the instrument panel. When the shock absorber is in the "soft" damping state, one indicator on the left side is on; when the shock absorber is in the "medium" damping position, the indicators on the left and the middle are on; when the shock absorber is in the "hard" damping position, all three indicators are on. When the ignition switch is turned on, the indicator of the suspension system lights up for about 2s and then goes out, so that the driver can check whether the indicator and its wiring are in good condition. If the control unit finds that there is a problem with the system, these indicators will flash to alert the driver that the system is faulty.

The electronic control module of the electronic control suspension generally has a self-diagnosis and detection function. During maintenance, it is required to carry out inspection and maintenance according to the corresponding vehicle maintenance manual and the inspection process. In addition, some basic tools are required, such as common hardware tools, jacks, jack brackets, rulers, etc.

Task Implementation

Ⅰ. Basic Steps for Diagnosis of Electronic Control Variable Damping Suspension System

If the warning light of the electronic control suspension is on under engine operating conditions, the control module has detected a fault in the electronic control suspension system. The fault diagnosis and maintenance procedures of the electronic control suspension system vary according to different vehicle models, and maintenance shall be carried out according to the procedures described in the maintenance manual provided by the manufacturer.

When there is a fault in the electronic control suspension warning light display system of LINCOLN CONTINENTAI car, the diagnosis steps are as follows.

① Ensure that the electronic control suspension system switch is in the ON position.

② Turn on the ignition switch and turn it off after 5s. Open the door on the driver's side and close the other doors.

③ Ground the diagnostic lead near the control module, close the door on the driver's side and lower the window glass.

④ Turn on the ignition switch, and the warning light will flash continuously at 1.8 times/s, indicating that the system enters into fault diagnosis state.

Ⅱ. Maintenance and Detection of Electronic Control Variable Damping Suspension System

1. Test run detection

The test run can display the DTC of the last driving. The test run can detect faults that cannot be detected in other checks (some faults are intermittent).

The test run shall be carried out at different speeds and road conditions until at least 5 km or the mode signal lights in the instrument panel are on. After the test run, the vehicle shall be directly driven to the maintenance site, and then the ignition switch shall be disconnected after stopping, the DTC is stored in the control module of the electronic control suspension within 1h after the ignition switch is turned off (or until the ignition switch is on again). If the ignition switch is turned on after 1h, the DTC will be deleted from the memory of the electronic control suspension control module. During the test, the switch of the electronic control suspension must remain in the "ON" state.

Connect a tester capable of performing the electric control suspension test to the diagnostic interface near the control module. The test shall be carried out according to the procedures in the vehicle manufacturer's maintenance manual and the operating instructions of the tester. The tester displays a "PASS" code or one or more DTCs. Note down the DTCs for use in troubleshooting.

2. Hierarchical diagnostic test

(1) Automatic/manual diagnostic test

In the automatic/manual test, the electronic control suspension control module performs a self-test and checks other system parts. After this check, the manual check allows the maintenance personnel to check the various inputs of the control module.

(2) DTC display

After the automatic/manual check has been completed, the DTC can be displayed by pressing the corresponding tester button. Each DTC is displayed for approximately 15s and continues to be displayed until the next detection mode is entered. The fault signal obtained during the test run shall be compared with the DTC in the maintenance bay test. When one kind of signal appears in both states, it indicates that the fault is "real" fault; if the fault signal only appears during train operation and test run test, the fault is "intermittent" fault.

(3) Detailed inspection

Detailed inspection is a specific troubleshooting process, which should be carried out in order of priority. DTCs are provided according to priority. After troubleshooting a fault, be sure to check the system again. The computers in some system modules may store only a certain number of codes by priority. If only one DTC is displayed, there may be another DTC with a lower priority in the system.

3. Spring inflation diagnosis

The inflation diagnosis of the spring allows maintenance personnel to charge or exhaust each air spring using the electronic control suspension control module.

This procedure displays a part that has failed, such as an air spring solenoid valve or a corresponding trigger circuit. Maintenance personnel can detect air lines for leakage during spring inflation.

Exercises

Fill in the blanks

1. Switches used in automobile electronic control suspension systems are_____, _____, _____ and_____.

2. The actuating mechanism of automobile electronic control suspension system includes_____, elastic elements which can adjust spring height and elasticity, etc.

Item Summary

Electronic control suspension represents the development direction of automobile suspension at present, and semi-active suspension system is the main development direction in the future. It is necessary for semi-active suspension to develop an adjustable damping shock absorber with reliable performance and convenient adjustment.

Item Exercises

Ⅰ. Fill in the blanks

1. Active suspension can be divided into_____ and ____ by different frequency band and energy consumption. It can be divided into _____ and_____ by different driving mechanism and medium.

2. The automobile electronic control suspension system consists of various sensors sensing the operating condition of the car, switches, _____ and ____.

Ⅱ. True or False

1. A car equipped with an electronic control suspension system can maintain a certain height and keep the body level, regardless of the vehicle load.   (   )

Item V

Maintenance of Automobile Anti-theft System

Item Guide

The automobile anti-theft system is a device installed on the vehicle to increase the difficulty of vehicle theft and prolong the time of vehicle theft. It can prevent the vehicle from being stolen, violated and protect the vehicle by connecting the anti-theft system and the automobile circuit together. With the development of science and technology, people have developed various kinds of anti-theft devices with different structures to deal with the ever-increasing means of car theft.

Task I Cognition of Automobile Anti-theft System

【Learning Objectives】

Knowledge requirements: Understand the types and functions of the automobile anti-theft system.

Capability requirements: Be able to identify various types of anti-theft systems on the vehicles.

Task Import

What are the types of the automobile anti-theft systems? What are the differences between the anti-theft systems of different cars?

Knowledge Preparation

At present, the automobile anti-theft device has been developed into high-tech products such as electronic password, remote control for help and information alarm from the initial mechanical control. The early anti-theft device was mainly used to control the interlocking mechanism such as door lock, door and window. With the development of science and technology, the automobile anti-theft device is becoming more and more strict and perfect. At present, the anti-theft device can be divided into five categories by its structure and func-

tion: mechanical type, electronic type, network type, biometrics type and chip type, each having its own advantages and disadvantages, but the development direction of automobile anti-theft is chip type and network type with higher intelligence.

Ⅰ. Mechanical Anti-theft Device

Mechanical anti-theft device refers to various kinds of anti-theft locks made of metal materials, including steering column lock, steering wheel lock, gear lever lock, pedal lock (clutch pedal lock, brake pedal lock), wheel lock, etc. The function of these anti-theft locks is to lock the control parts of the automobile, so that the thief cannot drive the car away. Early automobile anti-theft equipment is mainly mechanical anti-theft lock, only anti-theft not alarm.

Ⅱ. Electronic Anti-theft Device

Electronic anti-theft device, also called microcomputer anti-theft device, mainly includes plug-in type, push button type and remote control type. The anti-theft device adopts concealed installation, with complete functions, wireless remote control and easy operation.

1. Anti-theft alarm function

The electronic anti-theft device controls the starting and ignition circuits of the automobile through the electronic equipment. After the whole system is started, if there is illegal movement of the car, illegal open of door, fuel tank door, engine cover and trunk cover and illegal connection of the ignition circuit, the anti-theft device will immediately enter the alarm state, control the vehicle light to flash, sound the horn, cut off the starting circuit, ignition circuit, fuel injection circuit, fuel supply circuit and even cut off the automatic transmission circuit, so as to make the car completely paralyzed. The disadvantage of electronic anti-theft system is high false alarm rate.

2. Door ajar safety prompt function

When the vehicle door is not closed properly, the warning light will flash for several seconds continuously. After stopping the car and locking the door remotely, if the door is not closed properly, the lights will flash continuously and the horn will sound until the door is closed.

3. Car-hunting function

When the vehicle owner uses the remote controller to search for his/her car, the horn chirps intermittently, accompanied by flashing lights.

4. Remote central door lock

When the remote controller sends the correct signal, the central door lock automatically opens or closes. The remote controller and electronic key of the electronic remote control anti-theft device have corresponding password. The transmitting part of the remote controller adopts microwave/infrared system. Use the remote controller to send the password signal to the vehicle, then the vehicle door lock system works.

Ⅲ. Network Anti-theft System

The network car anti-theft system is a new anti-theft method which is more popular and more advanced and practical in the world at present. There are two main types: One is GPS anti-theft system, the other is GSM mobile anti-theft device.

1. GPS anti-theft system

GPS, i. e. global position system, belongs to a network anti-theft device. It is an active monitoring anti-theft device. It determines the position of vehicle through GPS, and then transmits the position and alarm information to the alarm center. If that GPS anti-theft device is disassemble illegally, it will send out alarm information, and at the same time, it can track and locate the car in real time. By use of GPS positioning function, the position of the stolen vehicle can be found quickly and accurately.

The disadvantage of GPS anti-theft system is that the service charge is often paid, and the power of system operation is large.

2. GSM mobile anti-theft device

Based on GSM communication network, GSM mobile anti-theft device is used for intelligent linkage of mobile phone and car against theft. It has many functions such as anti-theft, monitoring, remote control, remote alarm, positioning and anti-hijacking. . It is an effective means to maintain social security and protect the interests of vehicle owners. Compared with similar products, this system also has more concealed installation, more advanced technology, more reliable performance and other characteristics. GSM mobile anti-theft device has the advantages of no base station and no distance limit for alarm.

The disadvantage of GSM mobile anti-theft device is that it needs to pay the monthly rent of GSM number and depend on the coverage of GSM network. The thief may use the signal jammer to prevent the vehicle from contacting with the alarm center, making the anti-theft system invalid.

Ⅳ. Biometric Anti-theft Device

At present, the biometric anti-theft system applied to the vehicle is car fingerprint recognition and anti-theft system, which is also the best anti-theft system. The downside of the biometric anti-theft device is that it's expensive, and there's an extra fingerprint comparison before starting the car.

Ⅴ. Chip Anti-theft Device

Chip digital anti-theft device is the focus of the development of modern automobile anti-theft device. Most cars adopt this kind of anti-theft method as original anti-theft device. The basic principle of the chip anti-theft device is to lock the circuit and oil circuit of the car's engine so that the vehicle cannot be started without the chip key. Digitized passwords have extremely low repeated code rate, and can be unlocked only by touching the password recognition coil on the vehicle with the password key, thus eliminating the possibility of being scanned. Now many mid-and high-end models have been equipped with the original chip anti-

theft system.

 Task Implementation

Students are grouped to identify each type of vehicle anti-theft system.

Exercises

Questions

1. The function of electronic anti-theft system.

2. The classfication of network anti-theft system.

Task Ⅱ Maintenance of Automobile Anti-theft System

〔Learning Objectives〕

Knowledge requirements：

1. Understand the function, classification and composition of automobile anti-theft system；

2. Master the structure, principle and maintenance of automobile anti-theft system；

3. Understand the train of thought and method of fault diagnosis of automobile anti-theft system.

Capability requirements：

1. Be able to obtain vehicle information through communication with customers and consulting relevant maintenance technical data；

2. Be able to formulate correct maintenance plan according to fault phenomenon；

3. Be able to select correct detection and diagnosis equipment for fault diagnosis of anti-theft system according to maintenance plan.

 Task Import

A Toyota Corolla sedan cannot be started. Turn on the ignition switch and observe that all instruments and warning lights work normally. However, when starting, it is detected that there is no ignition and fuel injection in the engine, and at the same time, it is found that the security indicator of the anti-theft system is on. Based on this phenomenon, it is basically determined that the fault is a malfunction of the vehicle anti-theft system.

Knowledge Preparation

At present, the automobile anti-theft system has developed into the fifth generation. The fifth generation anti-theft system not only has more effective anti-theft effect than

the previous anti-theft system, but also has other advanced points. The unique radio frequency identification technology can ensure that the driver can be identified correctly in any situation. When the driver approaches or is far away from the vehicle, it can automatically identify his/her identity, automatically open or close the vehicle.

Ⅰ. Type of Automobile Anti-theft System

The structure of the individual anti-theft system control unit is shown in Fig. 5-1; the anti-theft system control unit can be integrated in the combination instrument, as shown in Fig. 5-2; the anti-theft system control unit can also be integrated into the comfort system control unit, as shown in Fig. 5-3.

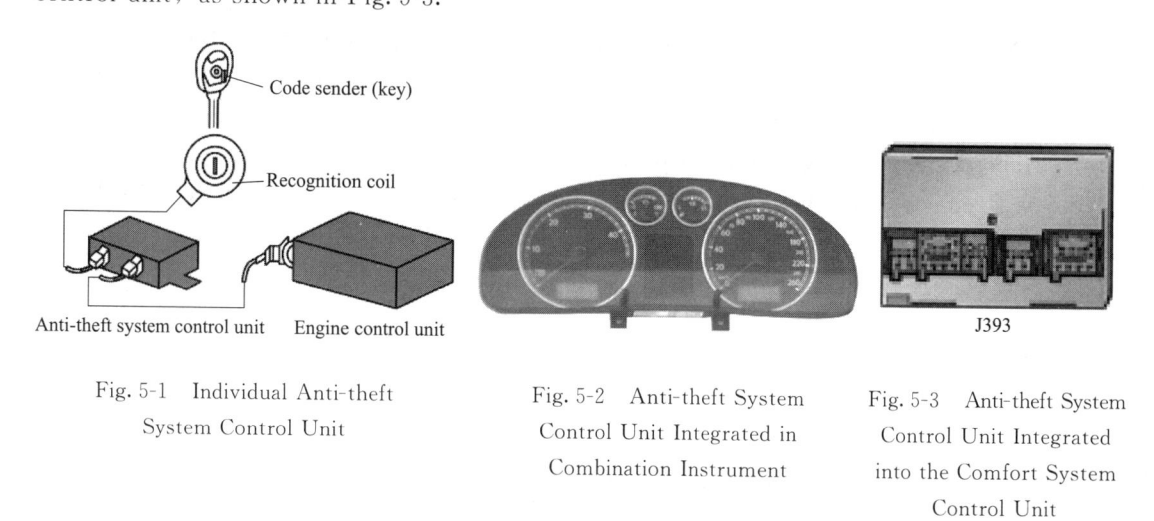

Fig. 5-1　Individual Anti-theft System Control Unit

Fig. 5-2　Anti-theft System Control Unit Integrated in Combination Instrument

Fig. 5-3　Anti-theft System Control Unit Integrated into the Comfort System Control Unit

The second and third generation anti-theft system consists of ignition code sender (key), identification coil (antenna) on ignition switch, anti-theft system control unit in instrument, engine control unit (only involved in calculation of anti-theft code on the third generation system) and fault warning light on instrument panel, as shown in Fig. 5-4.

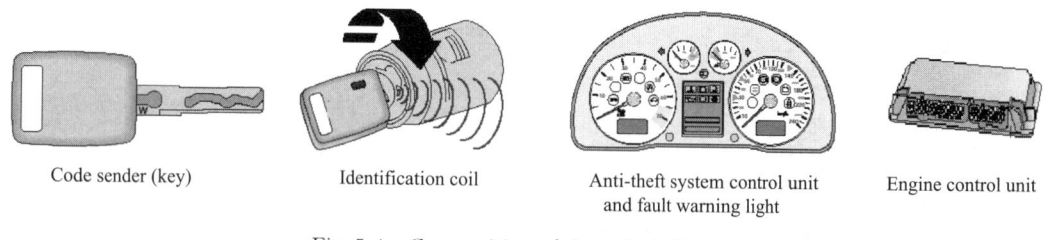

Code sender (key)　　Identification coil　　Anti-theft system control unit and fault warning light　　Engine control unit

Fig. 5-4　Composition of Anti-theft System

Ⅱ. Features of the Third Generation Anti-theft System

The engine control unit of the third generation anti-theft system is part of the anti-theft system, and the key is locked after adaptation and cannot be used in other vehicles. The third generation anti-theft system provides functional support for the second generation anti-theft system, and the data is transferred through CAN bus.

III. Composition and Working Principle of the Third Generation Anti-theft System

The anti-theft device consists of the following components: anti-theft control unit completed adaption (integrated on instrument panel), one fault warning light on combination instrument panel, one readout coil on ignition lock, engine control unit completed adaption, ignition key equipped (with pulse transponder).

The anti-theft device control unit is integrated with the combination instrument. If the control unit is damaged, the combination instrument must be replaced. The pulse transponder code is composed of a fixed code and a variable code. This code is changed every time the car is started to prevent others from copying the key. In addition, each anti-theft device also has a set of variable code calculation rules, which remain unchanged during the service life. When the car key is fitted, the anti-theft device writes the calculation rules into the pulse transponder of the key and learns the fixed code of the corresponding pulse transponder. The fixed code identifies each different key, so that a lost key can be locked. Each time the ignition switch is turned on, the anti-theft device readout coil reads the pulse transponder fixed code in the key, then reads the variable code and checks whether the key is qualified to start.

When using an authorized key, the warning light comes on briefly (max. 3s) and then goes off. When an unauthorized key is used or there is a fault in the system, for example, turning on the ignition switch, the alarm stays on.

1. Fixed code transmission (from key to anti-theft system control unit)

As shown in Fig. 5-5, after the ignition switch is turned on, the anti-theft system control unit queries the transmitted data of code sender (key) by changing the magnetic field energy in the antenna. At this point, the key sends back its fixed code (which is stored in the anti-theft system control unit in the first match). The transmitted fixed code is compared with the code stored in the anti-theft system control unit, and if the same, the variable code is transmitted.

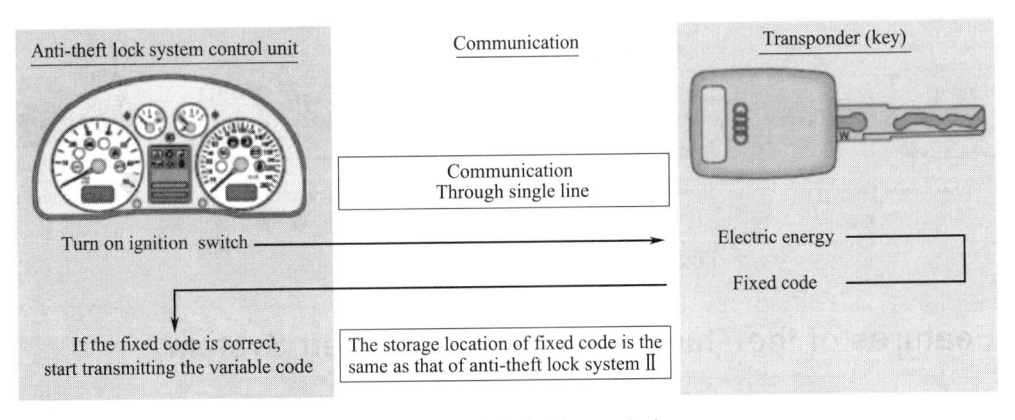

Fig. 5-5　Fixed Code Transmission

2. Variable code transmission (from anti-theft system control unit to key)

As shown in Fig. 5-6, the anti-theft system control unit randomly generates a variable

code. Within the key and in the anti-theft system control unit there is a formula table and an identical and non-rewritable SKC (secret key code). The key and the anti-theft system control unit respectively calculate the result, and the key sends the result to the anti-theft system control unit, which compares the result with its own calculation result. If the two are same, key confirmation is complete.

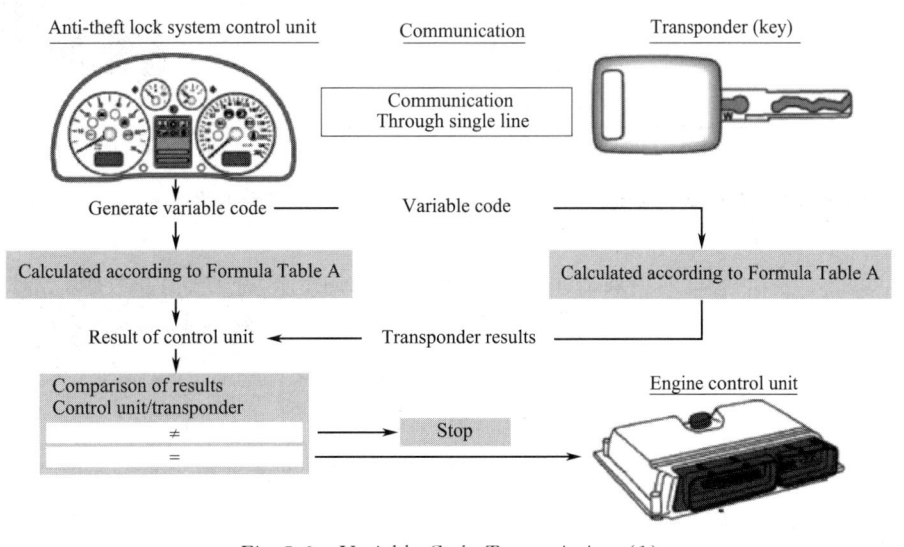

Fig. 5-6   Variable Code Transmission (1)

3. Variable code transmission (from engine control unit to anti-theft system control unit)

As shown in Fig. 5-7, the engine control unit randomly generates a variable code. There is another formula table and an identical SKC (formula indicator) in the engine control unit and in the anti-theft system control unit. The anti-theft system control unit returns this calculation result to the engine control unit for comparison with its calculation result. This data is also transmitted via the CAN bus. If the results are the same, the engine is allowed to start. After each engine start, the engine control unit generates a variable code according to the principle of random selection, and stores the variable code in the engine control unit and in the anti-theft system control unit for calculation at the next engine start.

Ⅳ. Working Principle of the Fourth Generation Anti-theft System

The fourth generation anti-theft system is not a conventional and simple vehicle anti-theft control system, but an anti-theft system with network data exchange function. The most important part of the fourth generation anti-theft system is the Fahrzeugauskunft-und Zentrales Identifikations-Tool, FAZIT.

1. Features of the fourth generation anti-theft system

① The function form is the same as that of the third generation anti-theft device, except that all components related to the anti-theft device shall be matched online.

② Data can be transmitted safely, quickly and reliably to the vehicle only through "online inquiry" of the scan tool. Check by fax whether the PIN code of the anti-theft device exists.

③ All vehicle keys (including those re-ordered) are coded for a vehicle before leaving

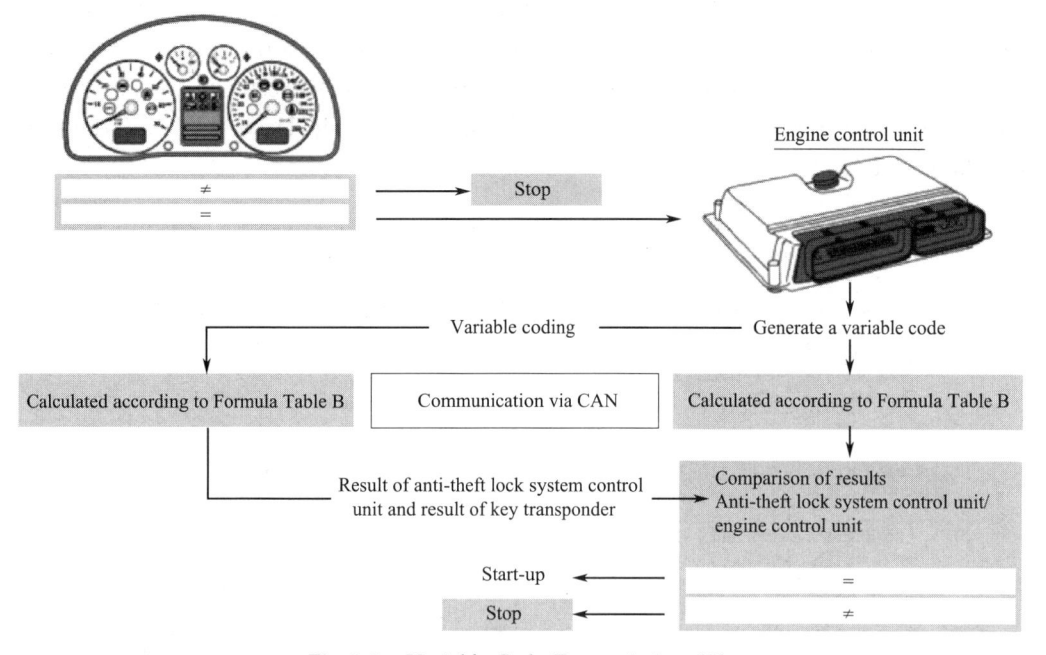

Fig. 5-7　Variable Code Transmission（2）

the factory, so these keys can only be adapted to that vehicle.

2. Composition of the fourth generation anti-theft system

（1）Anti-theft system control unit

Currently, some of the vehicle anti-theft control units are equipped independently, and some are installed in the combination instrument assembly. The fourth generation anti-theft system is a combination of the two.

（2）Engine control unit

All engine control units are part of the anti-theft system and must be connected online.

（3）Vehicle key

The key has a mechanically coded key tooth, which can only be used at the lock core (driver's door, trunk lid). The key transmitter is integral with the electronic components and operates without voltage from the key battery. This advanced key adds an electronic component which enables wireless two-way communication with the entry and start permission control unit.

（4）Entry and start permission switch

A fourth-generation anti-theft car is equipped with an unusual ignition switch. The entry and start permission switch is not a mechanically coded key. The switch is equipped with a reading coil which transmits the password data transmitted by the ignition key to the entry and start control unit via a two-way data cable. The entry and start permission switches do not need to be fitted into the anti-theft system.

（5）Steering wheel lock actuator

The steering wheel lock actuator is controlled by the entry and start permission switch. It locks or unlocks the steering wheel.

158 Automotive Safety and Comfort System Maintenance

(6) Other parts

All other electronic components, such as door handles, antennas, start/stop buttons, etc., are not equipped with microcontrols and are not part of the WFS anti-theft system and component protection system.

 Task Implementation

The Corolla anti-theft system (engine shutdown system) uses the transponder key ECU assembly to store the authorized ignition key code. If an unauthorized key is attempted to start the engine, the transponder key ECU will send a signal to the engine computer ECM to inhibit fuel supply and ignition, thereby effectively inhibiting engine operation.

Transponder key coil/amplifier: When a key is inserted in the ignition lock core, the key coil receives a key code. The amplifier then amplifies the ID code and outputs it to the transponder key ECU assembly.

Corolla anti-theft system is shown in Fig. 5-8.

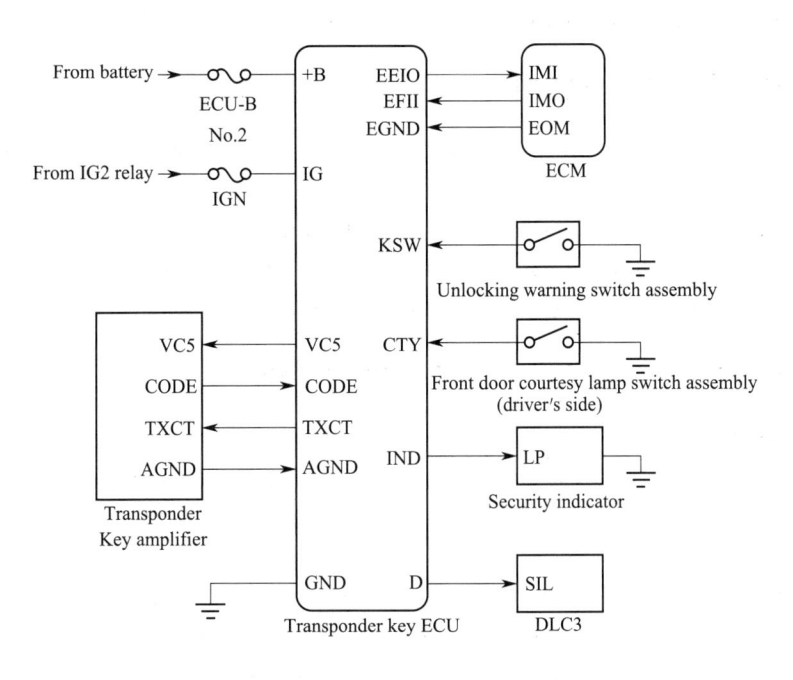

Fig. 5-8　Carolla Anti-Theft System

The function of the unlock warning switch assembly is to check whether a key is inserted into the ignition lock core and output the result to the transponder key ECU assembly.

The function of ECM is to receive ID code from transponder key ECU assembly, verify whether the ID code is a legal code, verify whether the ECU is a legal component, and decide to start or stop the engine after calculation.

Depending on the operation of the transponder key ECU assembly, the interior security indicator is on or starts flashing. When the transponder key ECU assembly detects that the key unlocking warning switch is set to the ON position, the ECU supplies current to the

transmitter key coil and generates an electric wave. After receiving the electric wave, the transmitting and answering chip in the key handle outputs a key identification code signal. The signal is amplified by the transponder key amplifier, received by the transmitter key coil, and sent to the ECU.

The ECU matches the key identification code with the vehicle identification code previously registered in the ECU and sends the result to the ECU. The engine start control enters the ready mode (fuel injection control and ignition control) after the identification result shows that the key identification code matches the vehicle identification code and the ECU has confirmed the match. At the same time, ECU sends an indicator off command to turn off the safety indicator.

I . Precautions for Maintenance

Connect the scan tool OBD2 plug to the vehicle diagnostic seat, turn on the ignition switch and turn on the scan tool power switch. The key is a precision device, so do not drop or strike the key during operation and keep it away from high temperatures, magnets or magnetized objects. Operate according to the provisions of the maintenance manual.

II . Technical Requirements

Understand the components, installation position and working condition of the anti-theft system through practice, and be familiar with the system detection method. Master the operation method of extracting DTC, clearing DTC and data stream of the scan tool, and refer to the detection method provided in maintenance manual according to the information provided by scan tool, so as to eliminate faults accurately.

III . Maintenance of Corolla Anti-theft System

1. Usage of scan tool

Find the vehicle diagnostic seat on the lower left side of the instrument panel, as shown in Fig. 5-9. Connect the diagnostic connector of the scan tool to the vehicle diagnostic seat, as shown in Fig. 5-10. Turn on the power switch of the scan tool and select the model system, as shown in Fig. 5-11. Select "Model System" option, as shown in Fig. 5-12. Select "Anti-theft System' option, as shown in Fig. 5-13. Use the "Read DTC" function, as shown in Fig. 5-14. Select "Data List" to read the data stream, as shown in Fig. 5-15.

Fig. 5-9   Vehicle Diagnostic Seat

Fig. 5-10   Connect Vehicle Diagnostic Seat

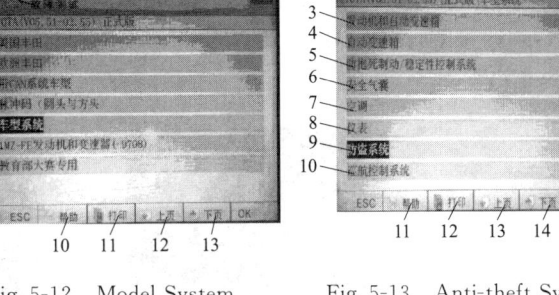

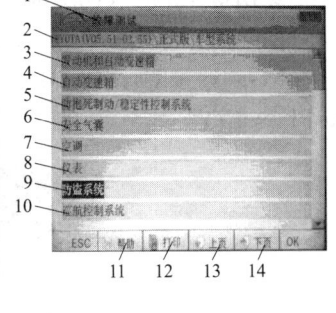

Fig. 5-11　Select Model System

1—Fault test；2—Chinese car models；

3—American car models；

4—European car models；

5—Japanese car models；

6—Korean car models；

7—Service assistance

Fig. 5-12　Model System

1—Fault test；2—Official version；

3—TOYOTA，USA；4—TOYOTA EUROPE；

5—Vehicle models with CAN system；

6—Pulse code（round head and square head）；

7—Vehicle model system；

8—1MZ-FE engine and

transmission（9708）；

9—Special for the competition

of the Ministry of Education；

10—Help；11—Print；12—Previous

page；13—Next page

Fig. 5-13　Anti-theft System

1—Fault test；2—Official version

\ vehicle model system；

3—Engine and automatic transmission；

4—Automatic transmission；

5—Anti-lock brake/stability

control system；

6—Airbag；7—Air conditioning；

8—Meter；9—Anti-theft system；

10—Cruise control system；11—Help；

12—Print；13—Previous page；

14—Next page

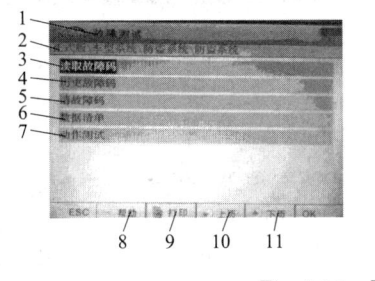

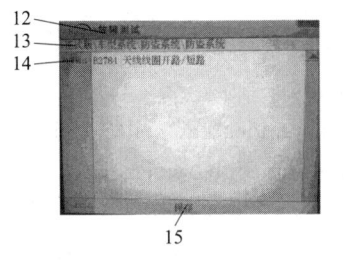

Fig. 5-14　Read DTC

1，12—Fault test；2，13—Official version/ Model system/ Anti-theft system/ Anti-theft system；3—Read out DTC；

4—History DTC；5—Clear DTC；6—Data list；7—Action test；8—Help；9—Print；10—Previous page；

11—Next page；14—DTC；1；B278 antenna coil open/ short circuit；15—Save

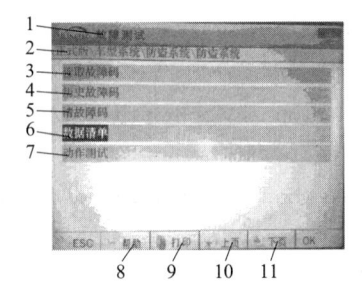

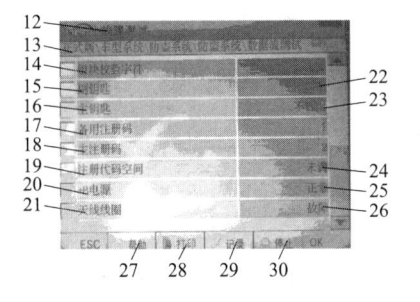

Fig. 5-15　Read Data Stream

1，12—Fault test；2，13—Official version/ Model system/ Anti-theft system/ Anti-theft system；3—Read out DTC；

4—History DTC；5—Clear DTC；6—Data list；7—Action test；8，27—Help；9，28—Print；10—Previous page；

11—Next page；14—Chunk check character；15—Secondary key；16—Master key；17—Alternate registration code；

18—Master registration code；19—Registration code space；20—＋B power supply；21—Antenna coil；

22，23—Mismatch；24—Not full；25—Normal；26—Fault；29—Record；30—Stop

Item Ⅴ　Maintenance of Automobile Anti-theft System　**161**

2. Disassembly procedures

Remove the steering column bushing, as shown in Fig. 5-16.

Remove the transponder key coil amplifier harness connector under the ignition switch, as shown in Fig. 5-17.

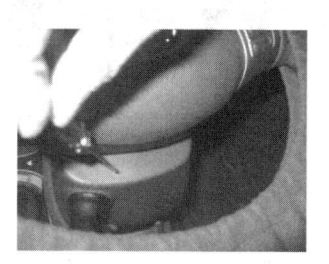

Fig. 5-16   Remove the Steering Column Bushing

Fig. 5-17   Transponder Key Coil Amplifier Harness Connector

3. Test method

Test the transponder key coil amplifier, as shown in Fig. 5-18.

Test the resistance between E29-7 ♯ — body grounding wire, which is always less than 1 Ω. If the test result does not comply with the specification, it is possible that there is a problem on the harness side. The next step is to reconnect the transponder key coil amplifier connector E29, and detect according to the following values.

Fig. 5-18   Transponder
Key Coil Amplifier

When the key is not in the ignition lock core, the voltage between E29-1 ♯ — E29-7 ♯ is lower than 1V; when the key is in the ignition lock core, the voltage is 4. 6-5. 4V.

The voltage between E29-4 ♯ — E29-7 ♯ is less than 1V when the key is not in the ignition lock core.

The voltage between E29-5 ♯ — E29-7 ♯ is less than 1V when the key is not in the ignition lock core.

Use the "Clear DTC" function, as shown in Fig. 5-19.

Select "Data list" to read the data stream and confirm troubleshooting, as shown in Fig. 5-20.

Ⅳ. Fault Case Diagnosis Process of Automobile Anti-Theft System

After the fault scope is determined through the fault phenomenon, the system structure

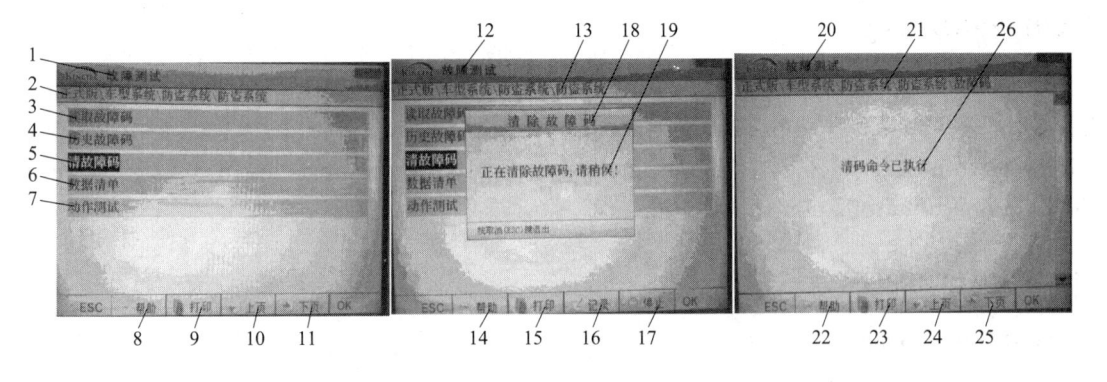

Fig. 5-19　Clear DTC

1，12，20—Fault test；2，13，21—Official version/ Model system/ Anti-theft system/ Anti-theft system；

3—Read out DTC；4—History DTC；5—Clear DTC；6—Data list；7—Action test；

8，14，22—Help；9，15，23—Print；10，16，24—Previous page；11，17，25—Next page；18—Clear DTC；

19—Clearing DTC，please wait！；26—Clear code command executed

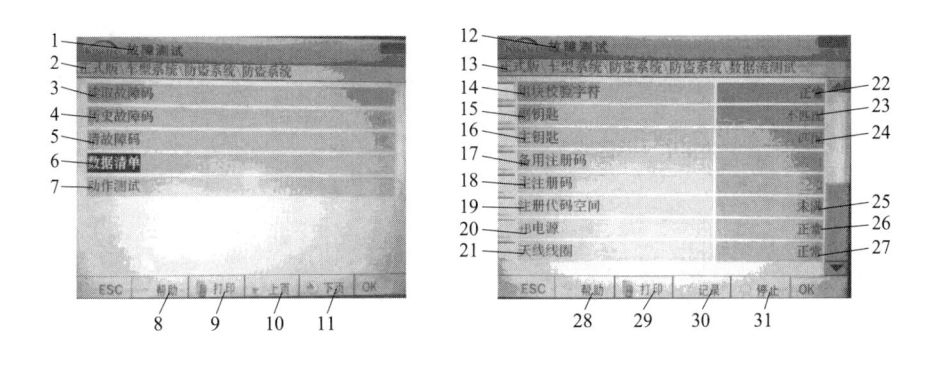

Fig. 5-20　Read Data Stream

1，12—Fault test；2，13—Official version/ Model system/ Anti-theft system/ Anti-theft system；

3—Read out DTC；4—History DTC；5—Clear DTC；6—Data list ；7—Action test；

8，28—Help；9，29—Print；10，30—Previous page；11，31—Next page；Help；Print；Previous page；Next page；

14—Chunk check character；14—Secondary key；16—Master key；17—Alternate registration code；

18—Master registration code；19—Registration code space；20—＋ B power supply；21—Antenna；

22，26，27—Normal；23—Mismatch；24—Match；25—Not full

and control principle of the fault must be understood thoroughly to analyze and diagnose the fault accurately. Since the malfunction of this vehicle indicates that it is caused by the anti-theft system，it is necessary to understand the structure，composition，working principle and circuit diagram of the anti-theft system of this vehicle. These must be clarified before diagnosing this fault. During the maintenance process，the fault point can be determined quickly and accurately by inquiring the maintenance manual and relevant maintenance data and using the fault scan tool and detection tools reasonably.

Exercises

Short Answer Question：

What are the components of the Audi A3 anti-theft system?

Item V　Maintenance of Automobile Anti-theft System　**163**

Item Summary

Aiming at the rising trend of automobile theft cases in the world, the automobile manufacturers are constantly improving the anti-theft technology, especially with the progress of micro-electronics technology, the automobile theft-proof technology has developed towards the direction of automation and intelligence.

Item Exercises

Fill in the blanks

1. The computer-controlled central door lock system consists of_____, _____ and_____.

2. The signal input device consists of _____, _____, _____, _____, _____, _____ and_____.

Item VI

Maintenance of Automobile Cruise Control System

 Item Guide

When a car runs on the highway for a long time, the driver operates the accelerator pedal for a long time, which is easy to cause leg muscle fatigue. The automobile cruise control system was born to solve this problem. The automobile cruise control system has gone through several processes such as mechanical control system, transistor system, analog integrated circuit control system and microcomputer control system. The vehicle cruise control system controlled by microcomputer has been developed rapidly since it was applied to automobile in 1981. Nowadays, the new cars basically adopt the cruise control system controlled by microcomputer.

Task I Structure and Working Principle of Automobile Cruise Control System

[Learning Objectives]

Knowledge requirements: Understand the composition, structure and principle of automobile constant speed cruise system.

Capability requirements: Be able to identify the components of the cruise control system on the vehicle.

 Task Import

On a 2007 Camry sedan, the CRUISE indicator is on when the cruise control system switch is pressed, but the vehicle speed cannot be set.

 Knowledge Preparation

I. Classification and Function of Cruise Control System

Cruise Control System (CCS) is an electronic control unit which uses advanced electronic technology to automatically adjust the vehicle's driving speed, so as to realize driving

at the preset speed. Turn on the cruise control switch, and the cruise control system will automatically increase or decrease the throttle opening without controlling the accelerator pedal according to the change of driving resistance. With this device, the driver will not be tired due to controlling the accelerator pedal for a long time to stabilize the vehicle speed when driving on the expressway for a long time. At the same time, the times of stepping on the accelerator pedal and brake pedal can be reduced due to the constant speed driving after using the speed stabilizing device, so that the cooperation between the vehicle fuel supply and engine power can be optimized, effectively reducing fuel consumption and reducing harmful gas emission.

1. Classification of the cruise control system

At present, CCS is generally divided into two categories, one is the electronic cruise control system, the other is the electronic vacuum control cruise control system. The former is mainly composed of command switch, vehicle speed sensor, electronic controller and accelerator actuator. The latter is generally composed of control switch, vacuum system and control circuit.

2. Functions of the cruise control system

(1) Setting function

When the main switch is turned on and the vehicle is running within the range of cruise control speed (40 ~ 120km/h), if the cruise control switch is turned on, the cruise control ECU will store the vehicle speed in ECU memory and keep the vehicle running at this speed.

(2) Manual cancellation function

When the vehicle is driven in cruise control mode, the cruise control mode is deactivated if the stepping motor actuator disengages the solenoid clutch.

(3) Automatic cancellation function

When the vehicle is driven in the cruise control mode, when the brake pedal is pressed down or the driving current of the stepping motor is too large, and the stepping motor always rotates towards the throttle opening direction, the vehicle speed set in the memory will be cleared, the cruise control mode will be canceled and the main control switch will be closed at the same time.

(4) Recovery function

When the traffic flow on the road can run stably again, press the "Resume" function switch, so that the vehicle automatically runs stably and evenly at the speed set above.

(5) Vehicle speed lower limit control function

The lower limit of vehicle speed is the lowest speed that can be set by the cruise control, and its value is 40km/h. The cruise control shall not be lower than this speed. When the vehicle is driven in cruise control mode, if the vehicle speed drops below 40km/h, the cruise control is automatically cancelled and the vehicle speed set in the memory is cleared.

(6) Vehicle speed upper limit control function

The upper limit of vehicle speed is the maximum speed that can be set by the cruise control, generally not exceeding 200km/h. When the car is driven in the cruise control mode, the vehicle speed shall not exceed 200 km/h even if the acceleration switch is operated for safety.

(7) Constant speed control function

ECU compares the actual vehicle speed with the set vehicle speed. If the vehicle speed is higher than the set vehicle speed, the control actuator will reduce the throttle appropriately; if the vehicle speed is lower than the set vehicle speed, the control actuator will appropriately increase the throttle.

(8) Set speed adjustment function

When the vehicle is driven in the cruise control mode, if the acceleration or deceleration switch is operated, the actuator will increase or decrease the throttle appropriately to change the vehicle speed. The cruise control ECU memorizes the changed vehicle speed and performs cruise control according to the changed vehicle speed.

(9) Automatic transmission control function

When the vehicle with automatic transmission is driven in the cruise control mode, if the transmission is in the overdrive when uphill and the vehicle speed drops to over 4km/h lower than the set vehicle speed, the cruise control ECU sends an overdrive cancellation signal to the automatic transmission ECU to cancel the automatic transmission overdrive; when the vehicle speed rises to 2km/h lower than the set vehicle speed, the cruise control ECU sends an overdrive recovery signal to the automatic transmission ECU to resume the automatic transmission overdrive.

Ⅱ. Working Principle and Composition of Cruise Control System

The working principle of the CCS is that the cruise control component reads the pulse signal sent by the vehicle speed sensor and compares it with the set speed, so as to control the actuator to adjust the increase or decrease of the throttle opening. The throttle position sensor sends the throttle opening signal to the engine ECU, and the engine ECU controls the fuel injection amount to keep the vehicle at the set speed.

The CCS is mainly composed of ECU, sensor, control switch and actuator.

1. CCS ECU

The CCS ECU is the center of the control system and is usually installed in a closed case made of metal sheet. Its main function is to calculate and judge according to the input signals of sensors, control switches, etc. When the CCS ECU judges that the actual vehicle speed deviates from the target vehicle speed, it sends a control signal to the actuator (motor or solenoid coil of the pressure control valve) that controls the throttle opening, controls the actuator action, adjusts the throttle opening to change the vehicle speed, and finally controls the error between the actual vehicle speed and the target vehicle speed within the allowable range. The ECU adopted by the CCS can be used by cruise system alone or share a ECU with other control systems. In addition, the CCS ECU also plays the role of memorizing the set cruise speed and self-diagnosing the fault of the CCS. See Fig. 6-1 for the principle block diagram of the CCS ECU.

The CCS ECU consists of linear amplifier and integral amplifier, as shown in Fig. 6-2. It has two input signals, one is the feedback signal of the actual vehicle speed, which is detected by the vehicle speed sensor and fed back to the controller; the other is that the driver directly sets the vehicle speed as required. After the controller detects and identifies different

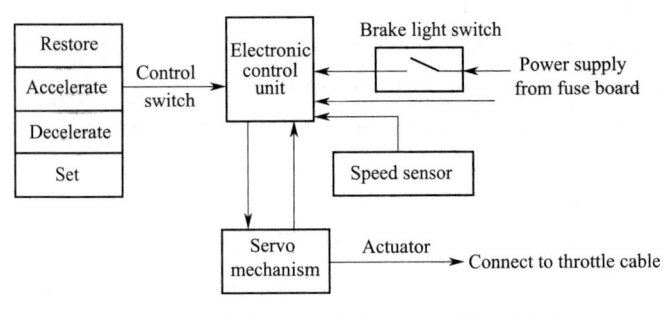

Fig. 6-1　Principle Block Diagram of CCS ECU

signals, a control signal is sent to the throttle actuator. The throttle actuator adjusts the o-pening of engine throttle according to the received signal to ensure the stability of vehicle speed. As the core component of CCS, the control technology adopted by ECU directly determines the control result.

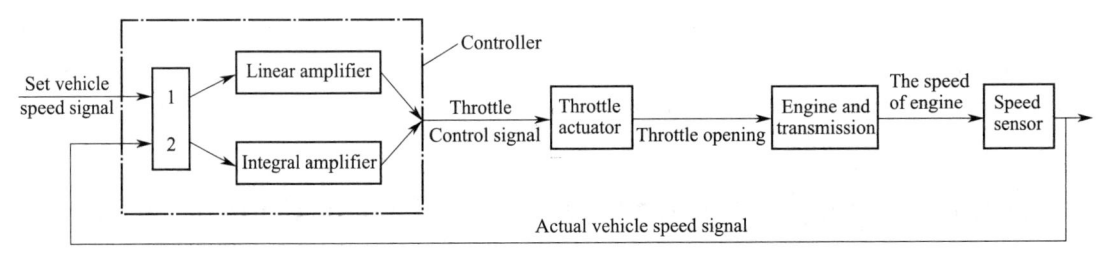

Fig. 6-2　Composition of CCS ECU

2. CCS Sensor

The sensors used in the CCS mainly include vehicle speed sensor, throttle position sensor and throttle control rocker arm position sensor. The CCS ECU controls the throttle opening and stabilizes the vehicle speed according to these signals.

(1) Vehicle speed sensor

The speed sensor is normally mounted on the transmission output shaft because the actual vehicle speed is proportional to the transmission output shaft speed. The speed sensor has magnetic induction type, Hall type, photoelectric type and other structural forms, the commonly used is magnetic induction type. The function of the vehicle speed sensor is to convert the actual vehicle speed into an electrical signal and send it to the CCS ECU.

(2) Throttle position sensor

The signal from the throttle position sensor can be used simultaneously for engine control, automatic transmission control and cruise control. The function of the throttle position sensor in the CCS is to convert the change of throttle opening into an electrical signal and send it to the CCS ECU.

(3) Throttle control rocker arm position sensor

The function of the throttle control rocker arm position sensor is to convert the position of the throttle control rocker arm into an electrical signal and send it to the CCS ECU.

3. CCS control switch

The control switch of the CCS is used by the driver to operate the vehicle to enter or

cancel the cruise system. It mainly consists of master switch, brake switch, neutral start switch, clutch switch, parking brake switch, etc. It is mainly used to start and shut down the CCS and adjust the working state of the CCS.

(1) CCS master switch

The CCS master switch is generally a lever switch mounted on the steering column easily accessible to the driver, or the combination switch is designed on the steering wheel. Most switches have 3 gears: SET/COAST, CAN or CEL and RES/ACC. Normally, when the vehicle speed exceeds 40km/h, the vehicle will remember the current speed and keep driving at constant speed by pressing the SET key. When the CAN or CEL key is pressed, the constant speed driving will stop immediately. The RES/ACC is used to re-drive the vehicle at the set speed after braking or disconnecting the circuit. When the car is in the state of automatic cruise control, the vehicle speed can be increased by pressing the ACC key, or the vehicle speed can be reduced by pressing the COAST key.

(2) Brake switch

The brake switch is used to transmit the brake signal (i. e. the signal that the driver presses the brake pedal) to the CCS ECU so that the vehicle can quickly exit the cruise control state.

(3) Neutral start switch

The neutral start switch is used to send a neutral signal to the CCS ECU (i. e. the signal that the transmission control lever is in the neutral position) so that the vehicle can immediately exit the cruise control state.

(4) Parking brake switch

When the parking brake lever is pulled up, the parking brake switch is turned on, and the ON signal is transmitted to the CCS ECU to exit the cruise control state.

(5) Clutch switch

When the clutch pedal is depressed, the switch is turned on, and the ON signal is sent to the CCS ECU to exit the cruise control state.

4. Actuator

The actuator is also called servo, which is driven by the CCS ECU to drive the guyed disk in parallel with the throttle cable. It is used to adjust the opening of throttle so as to accelerate, decelerate and drive the vehicle at constant speed. Actuators are usually divided into electric type and vacuum type (pneumatic type).

(1) Vacuum actuator

The structure of the vacuum actuator is shown in Fig. 6-3. The seal cylinder contains a diaphragm, a diaphragm spring, two air solenoid valves and a vacuum solenoid valve. The grounding wires of the vacuum solenoid valve and the air solenoid valve are respectively connected to the terminals of the CCS ECU. When grounding inside ECU, the solenoid valve works. Inside the vacuum solenoid valve, there is a vacuum tube connector which is connected to the intake manifold via a rubber tube. A cable that pulls the throttle is installed in the middle of the diaphragm. The vacuum actuator utilizes the vacuum degree of the engine intake manifold to attract the diaphragm. Through the throttle cable, the throttle opening is increased and the fixed position can be maintained. If the air solenoid valve is opened, the

throttle cable is released due to the elastic force of the diaphragm spring and the throttle opening decreases.

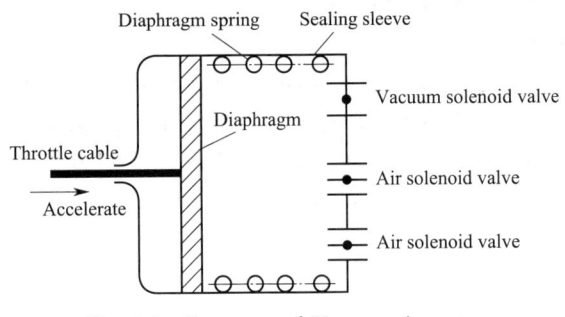

Fig. 6-3   Structure of Vacuum Actuator

Fig. 6-4 shows the structural principle of the vacuum CCS. When the CCS is not working, the vacuum solenoid valve remains closed, the air solenoid valve is opened, and the seal cylinder is open to atmosphere. When the car accelerates, the vacuum solenoid valve opens and communicates with the intake manifold, while the two air solenoid valves are closed, the vacuum degree in the sealing cylinder increases, the diaphragm is attracted to overcome the spring force, and the throttle opening is increased through the cable to accelerate the vehicle. When accelerating to a certain vehicle speed, the vacuum solenoid valve and the air solenoid valve are closed at the same time. At this time, the vacuum degree in the sealing cylinder remains unchanged, and the car keeps running at a constant speed. When the automobile decelerates, the air solenoid valve returns to the open state. At this time, the air enters into the sealing cylinder, the diaphragm spring presses the diaphragm back to the original position, the throttle opening decreases, and the automobile decelerates.

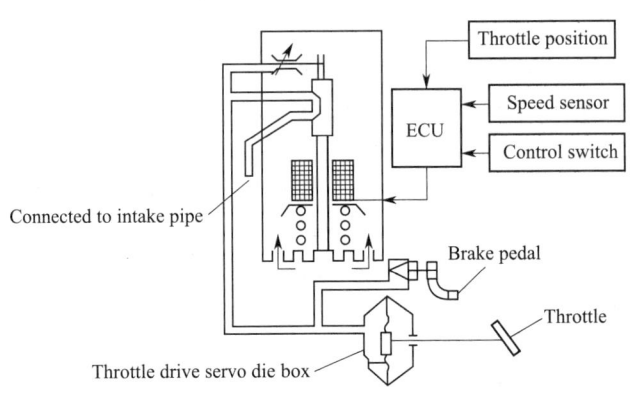

Fig. 6-4   Structural Principle of Vacuum CCS

(2) Electric actuator

Electric actuator mainly consists of motor, safety electromagnetic clutch and position sensor. The motor adopts DC permanent magnet motor, which can change the rotation direction of throttle by changing the current direction in the motor. When the motor rotates, it can drive the actuating element control arm to rotate, and the control arm changes the throttle opening through the control cable. To limit the rotation angle of the control arm, the motor circuit is equipped with a limit switch. A safety electromagnetic clutch is installed be-

tween the motor and the control arm. When cruise control is performed, the safety electromagnetic clutch is engaged, and the rotation of the motor can change the throttle opening. If the actuator or vehicle speed sensor fails during the cruise control driving phase, the safety electromagnetic clutch is disengaged immediately. The electric actuator is also equipped with a position sensor, which is a potentiometer composed of a sliding rheostat to detect the rotation position of the actuator control arm and input the signal into the CCS ECU.

 Task Implementation

Camry CCS is controlled by the vehicle ECM. When the CCS operates, when the ECM receives the ON signal from the master switch of the CCS, the ECM will illuminate the CRUISE main indicator in the combination instrument, and the CCS will start to operate. The ECM compares the travel vehicle speed transmitted by the vehicle speed sensor with the stored vehicle speed set by the CCS master switch. When the travel speed is greater than the stored vehicle speed, the ECM controls the throttle motor in the throttle assembly to decrease the throttle opening; when the travel speed is less than the stored vehicle speed, the ECM controls the throttle motor in the throttle assembly to increase the throttle opening. If the position of the transmission shift lever is moved from D to N while the CCS is operating, the ECM receives the park/neutral position switch signal and the ECM will cancel the operation of the CCS.

The principle of Camry CCS is shown in Fig. 6-5.

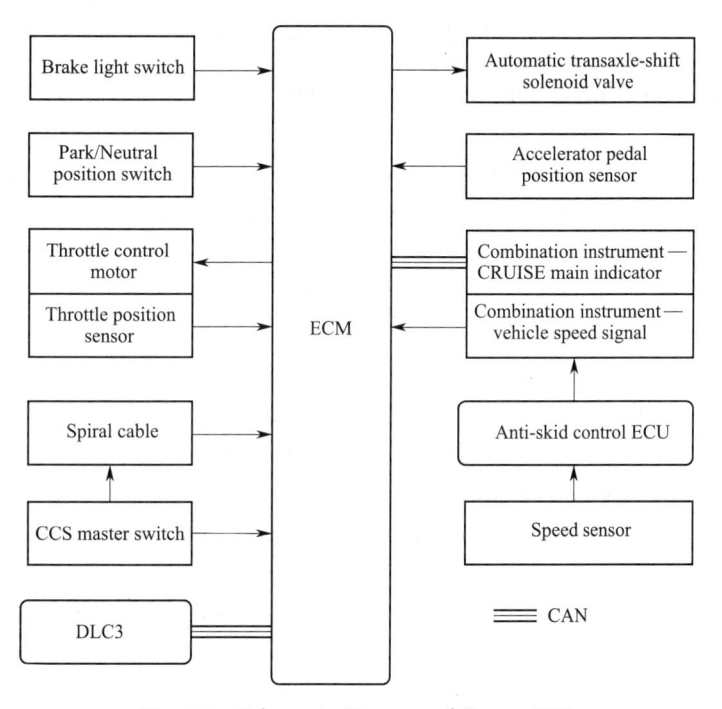

Fig. 6-5　Schematic Diagram of Camry CCS

① Connect the scan tool to detect P0571 DTC.

② Refer to the maintenance manual. The DTC means brake light switch A circuit. The

possible fault location is brake light switch, brake light circuit or ECM.

③ Analyze the brake switch circuit diagram according to the maintenance manual, as shown in Fig. 6-6. The CCS will not operate when 12V power is received at the STP terminal of the ECM.

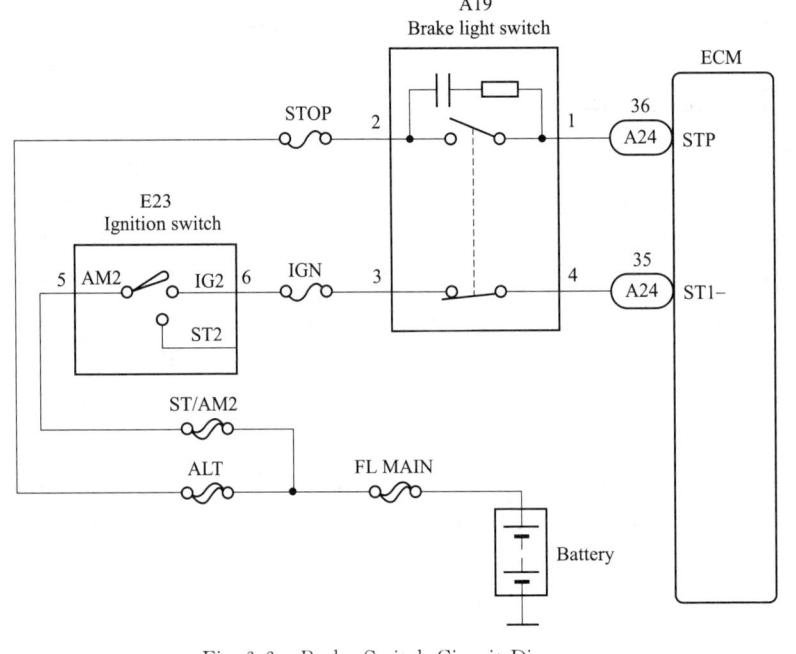

Fig. 6-6　Brake Switch Circuit Diagram

④ Enter the data flow test function of the scan tool and find that the signal of brake light switch S1 is always ON when the brake pedal is stepped down and released.

⑤ Disconnect A19 harness terminal from brake light switch, and use the multimeter voltage gear to detect the voltage between No. 2 pin of terminal A19 and negative pole of vehicle body as 12V. Turn on the ignition switch to ON to detect that the voltage between pin 3 of terminal A19 and the negative pole of vehicle body is 12V. According to the test results, the brake light switch power circuit has no fault.

⑥ When removing the brake light switch, use the multimeter resistance gear to check the resistance between pin 1 and pin 2 of the brake light switch to be 0.8Ω when the switch pin is pressed and not pressed. Test that the resistance between pin 3 and pin 4 is infinite when the switch pin is not depressed, and the resistance is 0.6Ω when pin is depressed. Based on the test results, it is analyzed that pin 1 and pin 2 of the brake light switch are short-circuited.

According to the above test, it is determined that the cause of the fault is the short circuit of the brake light switch. As soon as the STP terminal of ECM receives 12V voltage from the brake light switch directly, the ECM will consider the vehicle to be in braking condition after receiving the signal, so the ECM program will cancel the constant speed cruise control.

172　Automotive Safety and Comfort System Maintenance

Exercises

Short Answer Question

What is the working principle of the CCS?

Task II Maintenance of Automobile Adaptive Cruise Control System

【Learning Objectives】

Knowledge requirements: Understand the composition, structure and working principle of adaptive cruise control system.

Capability requirements: Be able to identify the components of the adaptive cruise control system on the vehicle.

 Task Import

When selecting the adaptive cruise control system with the instrument multi-function menu on a MAGOTAN car, the instrument indicates "Fault adaptive cruise" and AC cannot be used.

 Knowledge Preparation

The adaptive cruise control system (also called active cruise control system, abbreviated as ACC) is a newly developed driver assistance system. Compared with the traditional vehicle speed control system, it has a great expansion in function.

I. Advantages of Adaptive Cruise Control System

① Through the feedback signal of the vehicle distance sensor, the ACC control unit can judge the road condition according to the moving speed of the object approaching the vehicle and control the running state of the vehicle; through the force applied by the driver on the pedal sensed by the feedback accelerator pedal, the ACC control unit can decide whether to execute the cruise control to alleviate the driver's fatigue.

② The ACC normally operates at speeds greater than 25 km/h and requires manual control by the driver when the vehicle speed drops below 25 km/h. With system software upgrades, the ACC enables a "stop/start" function to cope with frequent stops and starts when driving in cities. This extension of the ACC allows the vehicle to maintain a set distance from the vehicle ahead at very low speeds. After the front vehicle has started, the ACC alerts the driver that the driver can start driving by pressing the accelerator pedal or pressing a button to give a signal.

③ The ACC makes formation travel easier. The ACC control unit can set the automatic

tracking vehicle. When the vehicle follows the preceding vehicle, the ACC control unit can adjust the vehicle speed to be the same as that of the preceding vehicle.

④ At the same time, keep a constant vehicle distance, and this distance can be selected through the setting button on the control lever near the steering wheel.

Ⅱ. Limitations of Adaptive Cruise Control System

① The ACC is a driver assistance system, not a safety system. This system does not allow fully automatic driving.

② The ACC can only play a control role in the speed range of 30-200 km/h.

③ The ACC cannot sense stationary objects.

④ The sensing effect of radar may be deteriorated by the influence of rain, water spray and melting snow.

⑤ At small turning radius, the system function will be affected due to the limitation of radar detection area.

Ⅲ. Working Principle of Adaptive Cruise Control System

The basic function of the ACC is to maintain the driver's chosen distance from the vehicle in front. Therefore, the ACC is the further development of the CCS. The vehicle is equipped with a radar sensor that measures the distance between the vehicle and the vehicle ahead and the speed of the vehicle in front. If the distance is greater than the value set by the driver, the vehicle will accelerate until the vehicle speed reaches the vehicle speed set by the driver. As shown in Fig. 6-7, the driver of the blue car activates the ACC and sets the desired speed v and the desired distance D_w. The vehicle accelerates all the way to the set desired speed. If the distance is less than the value set by the driver, the vehicle will decelerate. The deceleration can be achieved by reducing the output power, shifting gears or applying braking if necessary. As shown in Fig. 6-8, the blue car identifies a red vehicle traveling in the same lane ahead. The system reduces the speed of the blue car by reducing the throttle and braking if necessary, so that the distance between the two cars is adjusted to the desired distance. For comfort reasons, the braking effect can only reach 25% of the braking system's maximum braking deceleration capacity. When the distance to the preceding vehicle is increased to a safe distance, the ACC control unit controls the vehicle to drive at the set speed. If greater deceleration is required, the ACC control unit sends an audible and visual signal to inform the driver of the active braking action.

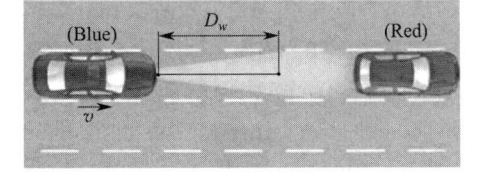

Fig. 6-7   Acceleration to Set Desired Speed

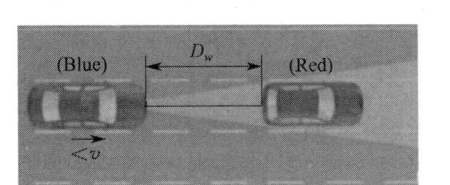

Fig. 6-8   Deceleration to Set Desired Speed

Although the ACC controls vehicle speed automatically, the driver can actively acceler-

ate or brake at any time. When the driver brakes under the cruise control status, the ACC control unit will terminate the cruise control; when the driver accelerates under the cruise control status and stops the acceleration, the ACC control unit will conduct cruise control at the originally set vehicle speed. This adjustment reduces the driver's exertion and thus indirectly improves driving safety.

IV. Composition of Adaptive Cruise Control System

The ACC mainly consists of radar sensor, wheel speed sensor, steering angle sensor and ACC control unit. The wheel speed sensors (shared with ABS system) are installed on the front and rear wheels to sense the driving speed of the vehicle; the steering angle sensor is used to judge the driving direction of the vehicle.

1. Radar sensor

The key component of the ACC is radar sensor, which is usually installed in radiator grille or inside of front bumper, which can detect the distance of 200m from the front of the car. Its main function is to measure the distance of the target vehicle, the speed of the vehicle and determine the position of the vehicle ahead.

(1) Distance measurement

The frequency difference between the transmitted signal and the received (reflected) signal depends on the distance between the objects. The larger the distance between the objects, the longer the time the reflected signal runs before it is received, and thus the greater the difference between the transmission frequency and the reception frequency.

(2) Vehicle speed measurement

To determine the speed of the preceding vehicle, a physical effect, known as the Doppler effect, needs to be applied. There is an essential difference between whether a reflected wave is at rest or in motion relative to a wave-emitting object. The frequency of the reflected wave increases if the distance between the object emitting the wave and the object reflecting the wave decreases, whereas if the distance increases, the frequency decreases. The electronic device analyzes this frequency change to get the speed of the vehicle ahead.

(3) Measurement of the position of the vehicle ahead.

Radar detection signals are emitted as lobes. The signal strength decreases as the distance from the transmitter increases, as shown in Fig. 6-9. To confirm the position of the vehicle ahead, a message must be attached about the angle at which the vehicle ahead moves in front of the vehicle. This information can be obtained by using a three-beam radar detection technique. The angle information can be determined by the amplitude (signal strength) relationship of the received (reflected) signal of each radar lobe, as shown in Fig. 6-10.

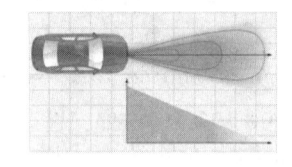

Fig. 6-9　Lobe Detection Signal

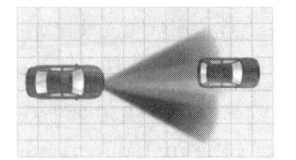

Fig. 6-10　Three-beam Radar Detection

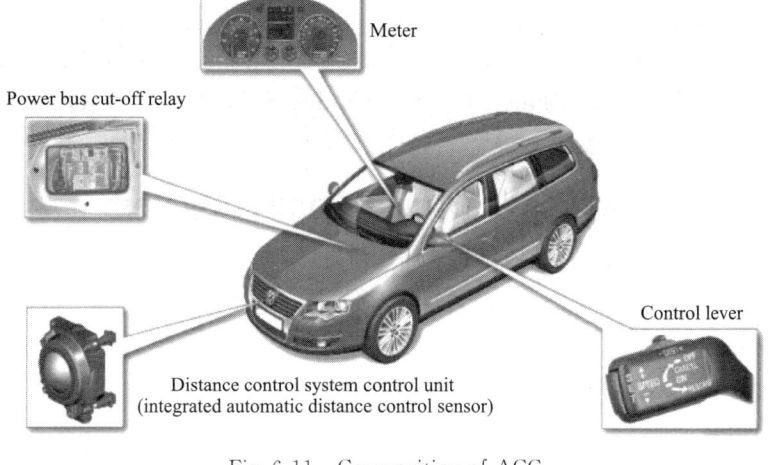

Fig. 6-11 Composition of ACC

2. ACC control unit

ACC control unit is the central processing unit of the ACC and is the core part of the system. It is responsible for processing the data (including relative distance and relative speed) sent by the sensor, then calculating according to the control algorithm, and finally forming instructions to control the operation of the actuator. It mainly includes the calculation of the target headway to determine the distance between the vehicle and the vehicle ahead; the headway controller, which calculates and obtains the vehicle speed and acceleration command of the target headway; and the vehicle speed controller, which determines the operation of the brake actuator and the throttle actuator.

3. Other components

Other components include cruise control switch, speed setter, distance setter, status display, alarm, etc.

Task Implementation

Fault Diagnosis and Repair of Adaptive Cruise Control System

1. Composition of adaptive cruise control system

The composition of the ACC of the Volkswagen model is shown in Fig. 6-11.

(1) ACC sensor

The Magotan sedan ACC sensor is used to determine the distance away from and relative speed of the front car, if the distance is larger than the set distance, the vehicle is accelerated to the set vehicle speed of the driver. If the distance is less than the set distance, the ACC automatically reduces the engine torque and, if necessary, applies the necessary braking to adjust the distance between the two vehicles to the driver's preset value, which is time-controlled. For safety reasons, the braking deceleration is limited to $0.3g$ (approximately 3m/s^2). If such deceleration fails to brake and stop the vehicle, the system will sound through the instrument and send a text prompt requiring the driver to intervene.

The transmission frequency of ACC sensor is 76.5GHz, the detectable range is 150m, the horizontal viewing angle is 12°, the vertical viewing angle is ±4°, and the vehicle speed

176 Automotive Safety and Comfort System Maintenance

detection range is 30-210km/h, as shown in Fig. 6-12.

(2) ACC control lever

The ACC control lever has different functions in different positions, as shown in Fig. 6-13. When the ACC control lever is in the ACC OFF position, the ACC function is off. When the ACC control lever is in the CANCEL position, it represents "standby mode" and the desired vehicle speed value is stored in memory. When the ACC control lever is in ACC ON position, it means that ACC is always in "ON" state. Press ON/OFF button to switch to "standby mode". When ACC control lever is in RESUME position, it means the vehicle speed is restored to the preset speed. The vehicle speed increases by 1 km/h every time the ACC lever is pulled backward.

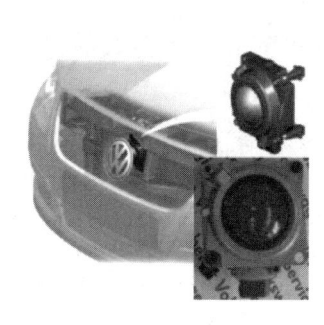

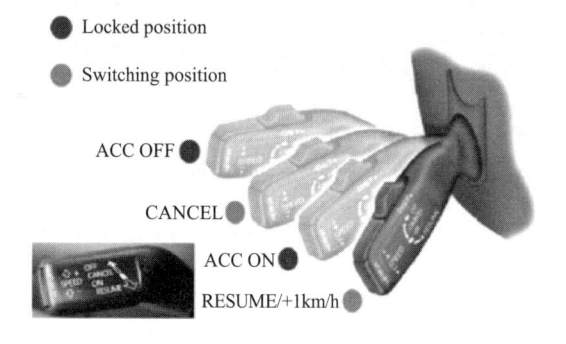

Fig. 6-12　ACC Sensor　　　　　　Fig. 6-13　ACC Lever Function

2. Functions of ACC

When the traveling speed of the Magotan equipped with ACC reaches 30km/h or above, the ACC starts to work. If there is no vehicle within the detection range of the ACC sensor, drive at the set speed, as shown in Fig. 6-14.

If a slow vehicle is running in the same lane ahead of the vehicle, the engine torque is reduced and if necessary, the vehicle applies gentle braking measures to adjust the distance between the two vehicles to the driver's preset value, which is time-controlled. The braking intervention is through ABS hydraulic pump. For calculation reasons, only the case of driving in the same direction can be selected as reference, as shown in Fig. 6-15.

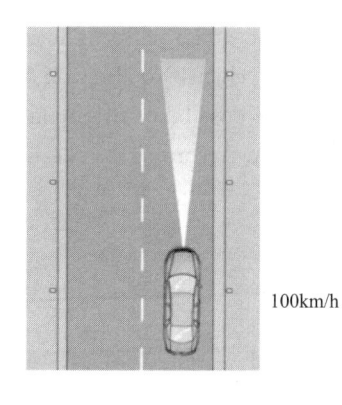

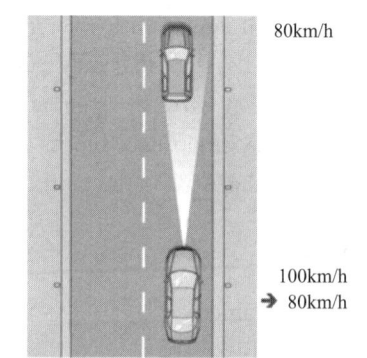

Fig. 6-14　Driving at Set Speed　　　　Fig. 6-15　Reducing Vehicle Speed

Item Ⅵ　Maintenance of Automobile Cruise Control System　**177**

3. Fault detection

Using VAS5052A to carry out detection，for engine and ACC fault，fault display is shown in Fig. 6-16 and Fig. 6-17.

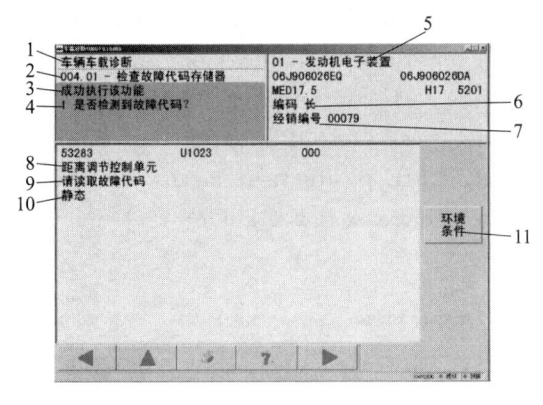
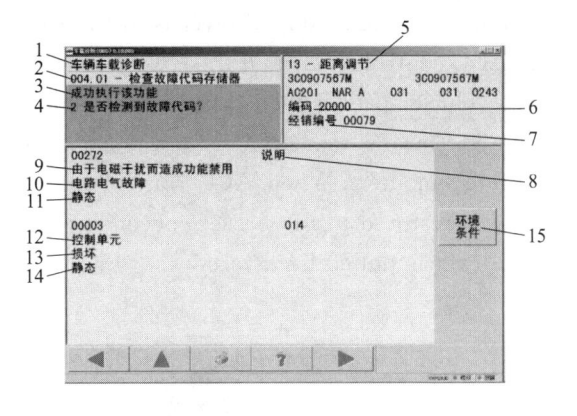

Fig. 6-16　Engine System Fault

1—Vehicle on-board diagnosis；

2—004. 01 - check DTC memory；

3—Successfully executed this function；

4—Is a DTC detected?；

5—01-Engine electronic device；

6—Code length；7—Distribution No. ；

8—Distance adjustment control unit；

9—Please read out the DTC；

10—Static state；11—Environmental conditions

Fig. 6-17　ACC Fault

1—Vehicle on-board diagnosis；

2—004. 01 - check DTC memory；

3—Successfully executed this function；

4—Is a DTC detected?；5—13-Distance adjustment；

6—Coding；7—Distribution No. ；8—Description；

9—Function disabled due to electromagnetic interference；

10—Electrical fault of circuit；11—Static state；

12—Control unit；13—Damage；14—Static state；

15—Environmental conditions

Analyze the fault. The fault stored in the engine system is caused by malfunction of ACC，so it is only necessary to eliminate the fault of ACC. There are several possible causes of ACC malfunction.

① Signal interference of other lines or electrical appliances.

② ACC circuit fault.

③ ACC radar sensor error adjustment.

④ ACC radar sensor fault.

4. Fault judgment

Check relevant circuit with reference to circuit diagram，and no abnormality is found，especially for the sound system that may cause signal interference on the vehicle. No abrasion of wires or short circuit between wires or open circuit is found. Therefore，the possibility of circuit failure is ruled out. Read the group data blocks of ACC 006 with VAS5052A. According to the inspection，the root cause of the ACC is the fault of ACC radar sensor.

Exercises

Fill in the blanks

The ACC mainly consists of _____ ，_____ ，_____ and_____ .

Item Summary

Nowadays，the requirement of intelligent automobile is more urgent. The automatic

ACC can effectively relieve the fatigue of long-distance driving, which is one of the important ways to improve comfort and interest, so the ACC will become the mainstream in the future.

Item Exercises

Ⅰ. Fill in the blanks

1. The control switch of the CCS mainly consists of_____ , _____ , _____ , _____ , _____ .

2. Most cruise control master switches have 3 gears, including _____ , _____ and _____ .

Ⅱ. True or False

1. The control switch of the CCS is used by the driver to operate the vehicle to enter or cancel the cruise system.　　　　　　　　　　　　　　　　　　　　　　　　　　　( )

2. The CCS will automatically increase or decrease the throttle opening according to the vehicle's driving resistance, without controlling the accelerator pedal.　　　　　　　( )

Item VII

Maintenance of Automobile Electric Power Steering

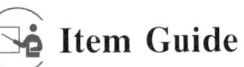 Item Guide

The power steering system can assist the driver to adjust the direction of the vehicle and reduce the strength of driving the steering wheel. Compared with the traditional mechanical and hydraulic power steering, the electric power steering (EPS) has the advantages of sensitive steering, low energy consumption, good compatibility with the environment, low cost and so on. Many high-end cars are equipped with EPS, so developing EPS has great practical significance and commercial value.

Task Structure and Working Principle of Electric Power Steering

[Learning Objectives]

Knowledge requirements: Understand the composition, structure and principle of automobile electric power steering.

Capability requirements: Be able to identify the components of the electric power steering on the vehicle.

 Task Import

A 2011 Corolla turns with heavy steering wheel and electric power steering trouble light on the instrument panel is on.

Knowledge Preparation

I. Classification of Power Steering

1. Hydraulic power steering

Hydraulic Power Steering (HPS) is generally composed of hydraulic pump, oil pipe, pressure flow control valve body, V-type drive belt, oil storage tank, etc. The system works whether the vehicle is turning or not, and at low speeds and at large steering angle,

180　Automotive Safety and Comfort System Maintenance

the hydraulic pump is required to output more power to obtain greater assistance. Therefore, resources are wasted to some extent. When the vehicle is equipped with hydraulic power steering, when turning at a low speed, the steering wheel is relatively heavy and the engine power loss is relatively large. Because the pressure of hydraulic pump is very large, it is also easy to damage the assist system. Also, the hydraulic power steering consists of a hydraulic pump, a pipeline and an oil cylinder. In order to maintain the pressure, the system is always in a working state regardless of whether steering assistance is required, so the energy consumption is high.

2. Electric power steering

Electric Power Steering (EPS) uses the power generated by an electric motor to assist the driver in power steering. EPS generally consists of torque (steering) sensor, electronic control unit, motor, reducer, mechanical steering gear, and battery power supply. EPS can be divided into hydraulic EPS and electric EPS by different power source. The hydraulic EPS is based on the traditional HPS, and adds solenoid valve to control the fluid flow, vehicle speed sensor and electronic control unit. The electronic control unit controls the solenoid valve to make the steering power magnification continuously adjustable according to the detected vehicle speed signal, so as to meet the steering assistance requirements at high and low speeds. Electric EPS uses DC motor as power source, and electronic control unit controls the magnitude and direction of motor torque according to steering parameters and vehicle speed signals. The torque of the motor is decelerated and increased by the electromagnetic clutch through the deceleration mechanism, and then applied to the steering mechanism of the automobile to obtain a steering force suitable for the working condition.

EPS can reduce steering force at low speed to improve steering system maneuverability; at high speed, it can appropriately increase steering force to improve handling stability. The hydraulic EPS adds electronic control unit on the basis of the traditional HPS. According to different control modes, the hydraulic EPS can be divided into three types: flow control type, reaction force control type and valve sensitivity control type.

3. Electric Hydraulic Power Steering

Electric Hydraulic Power Steering (EHPS) is the same as mechanical hydraulic power, but the biggest difference between EHPS and mechanical hydraulic power is that the hydraulic pump driven by the motor through belt is not used, but the electric pump is used instead. Its main components include oil storage tank, power steering control unit, electric pump, steering gear, power steering sensor, etc. The power steering control unit and the electric pump are integral structures.

The EHPS overcomes the disadvantages of traditional hydraulic power steering system. The hydraulic pump is no longer driven directly by the engine belt, but driven by an electric pump. All the working states of the hydraulic pump are the most ideal states calculated by the electronic control unit according to the vehicle's driving speed, steering angle and other signals.

When the automobile is steering at a low speed and large angle, the electronic control unit drives the electronic hydraulic pump to output large power at high speed so that the driver can turn the direction with less effort; when the automobile is running at a high

speed, the hydraulic control unit drives the electronic hydraulic pump to operate at a lower speed, which saves part of engine power while not affecting the high-speed steering demand.

The advantages of the EHPS are firstly reflected in the energy consumption. The electronic pump driven by electric energy, using the electric energy output from the generator and the battery, no longer consumes the power of the engine itself, and the startup and shutdown of the electronic pump are all controlled by the electronic system. When the steering action is not performed, the electronic pump is closed. Unlike the mechanical hydraulic booster pump, the electronic pump is always linked with the engine to further reduce energy consumption. Secondly, the electronic control unit of the EHPS can change the steering assist force by changing the flow rate of the electronic pump in real time through the information processing of sensors such as vehicle speed sensor, lateral acceleration sensor, steering angle sensor, etc., that is, the variable power function with speed. Of course, it is not only the EHPS that can achieve variable power with speed.

Features of EHPS: No matter from the aspect of technology, function or economy, the EHPS is more advantageous than the mechanical hydraulic power system, but at present, the EHPS can not replace the mechanical hydraulic power, mainly because the EHPS has higher cost, less reliability than the mechanical hydraulic power and limited power assistance force.

II. Composition and Working Principle of Electric Power Steering

1. Advantages of electric power steering

Compared with conventional hydraulic power steering, the EPS has the following advantages.

① The motor provides power only when steering, which can significantly reduce fuel consumption. Traditional hydraulic power steering system uses the engine to drive steering oil pump, no matter steering or not, it will consume part of engine power. However, the EPS is powered by the motor only when steering, and does not consume energy when it is not steering.

② The magnitude of steering power can be adjusted by the software in ECU, which can give consideration to steering portability at low speed and handling stability at high speed, with good returnability.

The magnitude of power provided by the EPS can be adjusted by the software in the ECU. At low speed, the EPS can provide greater steering power and ease of steering of the vehicle; with the increase of vehicle speed, the steering power provided by the EPS can be gradually reduced, and the steering force required by the driver during steering will gradually increase, so that the driver will feel the obvious "road feel" and improve the vehicle stability.

③ Compact structure, light weight, good assembly of production line and easy maintenance. The EPS eliminates hydraulic steering oil pump, oil cylinder, hydraulic pipeline, oil tank and other components, and the motor and deceleration mechanism can be integrated with steering column and steering gear, making the steering system compact, light, good assembly in production line, saving assembly time and easy maintenance.

④ Through the program setting, the EPS is easy to match with different vehicle models, which can shorten the period of production and development.

2. Type of EPS

According to the arrangement mode of auxiliary motor, EPS can be divided into Column-assist type EPS, Pinion-assist type EPS and Rack-assist type EPS.

(1) Column-assist type EPS (C-EPS)

The C-EPS consists of a torque sensor, an electric motor, a clutch and a steering power mechanism, which is mounted on the steering column. It is characterized by compact structure and good responsiveness of motor power. However, as the motor is installed in the cockpit, limited by space arrangement and noise, the motor is small and has small output torque, which is generally only used on small and compact vehicles, as shown in Fig. 7-1.

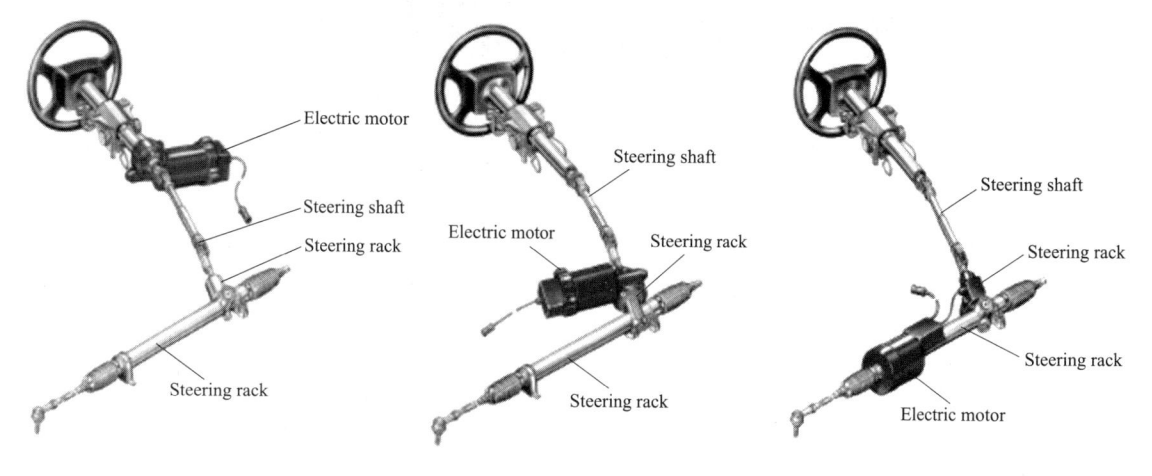

Fig. 7-1 Column-assist Type EPS   Fig. 7-2 Pinion-assist Type EPS   Fig. 7-3 Rack-assist Type EPS

(2) Pinion-assist type EPS (P-EPS)

The torque sensor, motor, clutch and steering power mechanism of the P-EPS are still integrated, but they are installed on the steering gear, which can directly assist the gear, so as to obtain greater steering force. It can be used in medium-sized vehicles to provide large power values. This form can make the arrangement of each component more convenient, but when a universal transmission device is installed between the steering wheel and the steering gear, the acquisition of torque signal is not in the same straight line with the power wheel, so it is difficult to ensure the accuracy of the power control characteristics, as shown in Fig. 7-2.

(3) Rack-assist type EPS (R-EPS)

The torque sensor of the R-EPS is separately installed at the steering gear, and the motor and the steering power mechanism are installed at the rack at the other end of the steering gear to assist the rack. The power assist unit of the R-EPS in shown in Fig. 7-3.

3. Composition of EPS

EPS mainly consists of torque sensor, speed sensor, motor, deceleration mechanism and ECU. The sensor detects the magnitude and direction of the torque or angle generated by the steering wheel during the steering operation of the driver, converts the required informa-

tion into digital signals and inputs it to the control unit. Then the control unit calculates these signals to obtain a torque corresponding to the driving condition, and finally sends out the instruction to drive the motor to work, and the output torque of the motor is assisted by the action of the transmission device. EPS is shown in Fig. 7-4.

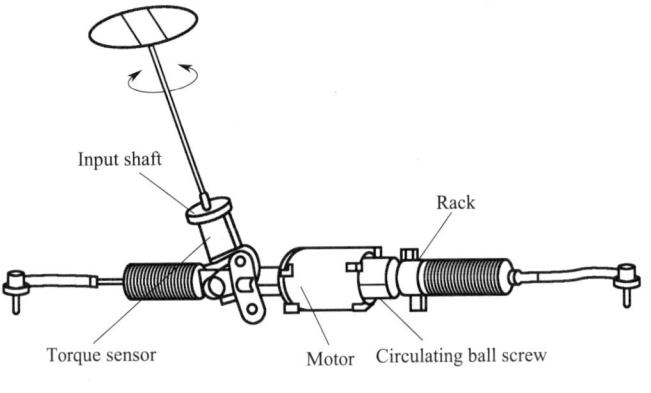

Fig. 7-4　Structure of EPS

4. Operating principle of EPS

Although the structural components of EPS differ from vehicle to vehicle, the basic principle is the same. It is generally composed of a torque (steering) sensor, an ECU, an electric motor, an electromagnetic clutch and a deceleration mechanism.

Its basic working principle: When the steering shaft rotates, the torque sensor converts the detected torque signal into an electric signal and sends it to the ECU. Then the ECU calculates the torque signal, vehicle speed signal and axle load signal to obtain the magnitude of steering and assist current of the power motor, and completes the steering power control. When the ignition switch of the car is closed, the ECU starts to carry out self-test on the EPS system. After the self-test is passed, the relay and clutch are closed, and the EPS system starts to work. When the steering wheel rotates, the steering angle sensor and torque sensor on the steering shaft transmit the measured angular displacement on the steering wheel and the torque acting on it to the ECU. The ECU controls the motor to generate corresponding power according to these two signals and in combination with the vehicle speed and other information, so as to achieve the best control within the full speed range: When driv-

ing at low speed, the steering force is reduced to ensure the vehicle steering is flexible and portable; When driving at high speed, damping control shall be appropriately added to ensure stable and reliable steering wheel operation. The working schematic diagram of EPS is shown in Fig. 7-5.

（1）Electric power steering ECU

The whole system is powered by on-board 12V battery. When the ECU is working, the signals collected by sensors such as

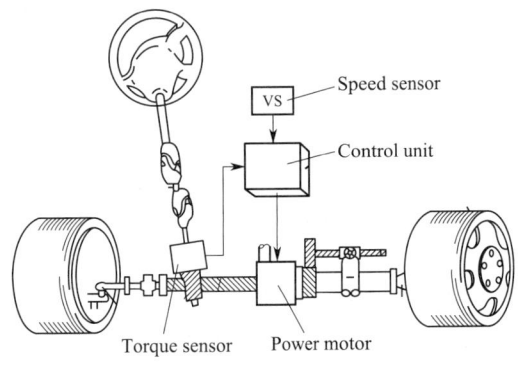

Fig. 7-5　Working Principle of EPS

torque, angle, speed and temperature are processed by input interface circuit and then sent to the corresponding port of MCU. The MCU analyzes and processes these data according to the system power characteristic and corresponding algorithm to determine the magnitude and direction of power current, and sends out pulse command through PWM port of the MCU and commutation command from corresponding commutation control port, and controls the DC motor to work through driving circuit and H bridge circuit. A current sensor is set on the driving circuit of the motor. The sensor feeds back the actual working current of the motor to the MCU through the current detecting circuit, which realizes the closed loop control of the motor according to the corresponding control algorithm. If that EPS system work abnormally, the MCU will drive the EPS light to give an alarm prompt, disconnect the relay and clutch at the same time, exit the electric power working mode and switch to manual power mode.

(2) Torque sensor

Torque sensor is used to detect the magnitude and direction of steering wheel torque and steering wheel angle. It is one of the control signals of the EPS. There are two main types of torque sensors: contact type and non-contact type. There are three types of commonly used contact sensors (mainly potentiometer type): swing arm type, double-row planetary gear type and torsion bar type, while non-contact torque sensors mainly include photoelectric type and magnetoelectric type. The former has low cost, but it is easy to drift under the influence of temperature and wear, and its service life is low. It is difficult to realize the measurement of absolute rotation angle and angular velocity due to the compromise between manufacturing accuracy and torsion bar stiffness. The latter has small volume, high precision, strong anti-jamming ability and relatively high rigidity, so it is easy to realize the measurement of absolute rotation angle and angular velocity, but the cost is high.

① Photoelectric torque sensor. The photoelectric torque sensor consists of two obscuring discs with holes and an elastic torsion bar. The disk rotates with the steering wheel, and each obscuring disc is composed of a LED and a photosensitive transistor, as shown in Fig. 7-6. They are installed facing each other, and the torsion bar is elastically connected between them. When the steering wheel rotates, due to the existence of steering resistance, the torsion bar is deformed, and the photoelectric signal values between the two photoelectric elements will appear the difference, which is the measurement value of the steering power. The greater the steering torque, the greater the torsion bar deformation, the greater the difference angle. The torque

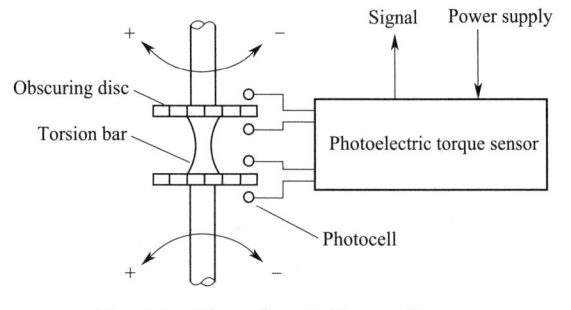

Fig. 7-6　Photoelectric Torque Sensor

and direction signals are transmitted to the ECU. According to the vehicle speed sensor signal and vehicle status signal (static or dynamic), the ECU is programmed to provide quantitative steering power control through the power motor.

② Magnetoelectric torque sensor. There are two pairs of magnetic pole rings in the magnetoelectric torque sensor, which are installed opposite to each other to connect the input shaft and output shaft. The elastic connected torsion bar is replaced by magnetic connection. It is a non-contact torque sensor with small volume and high accuracy of output signal value. When the torsional angle difference between the input shaft and the output shaft occurs, the air gap between the pole rings will change, resulting in the change of magnetic induction quantity in the electromagnetic induction coil, which is the measurement value of steering power. This signal is output to EPS/ ECU as the basis for steering power, as shown in Fig. 7-7.

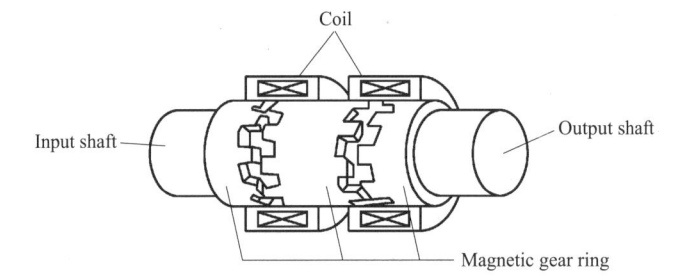

Fig. 7-7   Magnetoelectric Torque Sensor

(3) Motor

The motor outputs proper torque according to the instruction of the ECU. The brushless permanent magnet motor is generally adopted. The brushless permanent magnet motor has the characteristics of no excitation loss, high efficiency and small volume. The motor is one of the key parts of the EPS, which has great influence on the EPS performance. Because the control system needs to produce different power torque according to different working conditions, has good dynamic characteristic and is easy to control, all these require the motor to have linear mechanical characteristic and speed regulation characteristic. In addition, it also requires low speed and large torque, small fluctuation, small moment of inertia, small size, light mass, high reliability and strong anti-interference ability.

(4) Electromagnetic clutch

The electromagnetic clutch is to ensure that electric power only works within a predetermined range. When the vehicle speed and current exceed the specified maximum value or the steering system fails, the clutch will automatically cut off the power supply to the motor and resume manual steering control. In addition, without assistance, the clutch can also eliminate the effect of inertia of the motor on steering. To reduce that difference in the feel of a vehicle when driven without steering power, the clutch not only has hysteresis output characteristic, but also has a half clutch state region.

(5) Deceleration mechanism

The deceleration mechanism is used to increase the torque transmitted by the motor to the steering gear. It comes in two main forms: planetary gear deceleration mechanism and

worm deceleration mechanism. Because the deceleration mechanism has great influence on the working performance of the system, it is required to reduce the noise, improve the efficiency and the symmetry of the left and right steering operation.

 Task Implementation

The Corolla EPS is operated by electric motor and reduction gear installed on steering column. The power steering system generates torque to increase steering torque. According to the vehicle speed signal and the torque sensor signal built into the steering column assembly, the power steering ECU determines the direction of auxiliary power and the magnitude of steering torque. Therefore, the steering torque is controlled to be small during low-speed driving, and appropriately increased during high-speed driving.

The composition of the Corolla EPS is shown in Fig. 7-8.

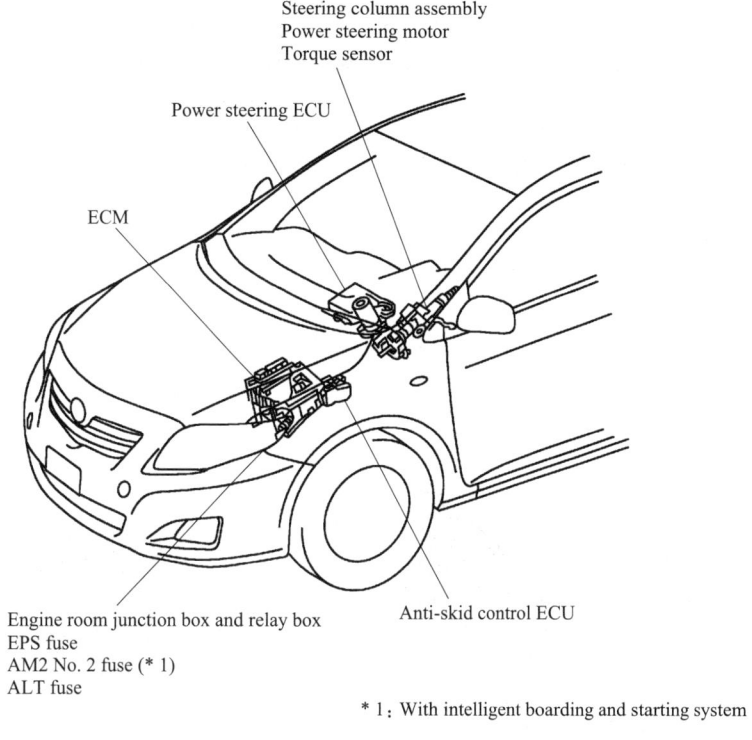

Fig. 7-8 Composition of Corolla EPS

Power steering ECU: Based on the steering torque signal from the torque sensor and the vehicle speed signal from the anti-skid control ECU, the power steering ECU calculates auxiliary power.

Power steering motor: The power steering motor is activated by current from the power steering ECU and generates torque to assist the steering torque.

Ⅰ. Precautions

① The connection sequence of the scan tool: Connect the OBD2 plug of the scan tool to the vehicle diagnostic seat → turn on the ignition switch → turn on the power switch of the

scan tool.

② Do not touch the terminal of the vehicle connector during operation to prevent terminal deformation or failure caused by static electricity.

③ Avoid striking the steering column assembly during operation, especially the motor or torque sensor.

④ When disconnecting the connector related to EPS system, turn the ignition switch to the ON position and make the steering wheel back, and then turn the ignition switch to the OFF position and then disconnect the connector.

⑤ During operation, refer to the maintenance manual and operate according to the provisions of the maintenance manual.

II . Technical Requirements

Understand the components, installation position and working condition of the EPS through practice, and be familiar with the system detection method under static and dynamic state. Master the change of voltage and current when the torque amplification sensor works and the detection method of the motor to eliminate the faults accurately.

III . Maintenance of Corolla Power Steering System

1. Usage of scan tool

Find the vehicle diagnostic seat on the lower left side of the instrument panel, as shown in Fig. 7-9.

Connect the scan tool to the vehicle diagnostic seat, as shown in Fig. 7-10.

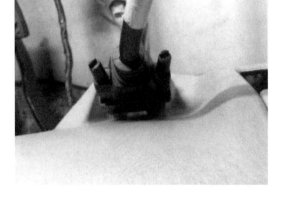

Fig. 7-9 Vehicle Diagnosis Seat　　　　Fig. 7-10 Connecting Scan Tool

Turn on the power switch of the scan tool and select the vehicle model, as shown in Fig. 7-11. Select "Vehicle Model System" option, as shown in Fig. 7-12.

Select "Electronic Auxiliary Power Steering", as shown in Fig. 7-13.

Use the "Active DTC" function to read the current DTC, as shown in Fig. 7-14.

Use "Clear DTC" function, as shown in Fig. 7-15. Select "Electronic Power Steering" to read the data stream.

Item Ⅶ Maintenance of Automobile Electric Power Steering **189**

Fig. 7-11 Turn on the Scan Tool
1—Fault test; 2—Chinese car models;
3—American car models; 4—European car models;
5—Japanese car models; 6—Korean car models;
7—Service assistance

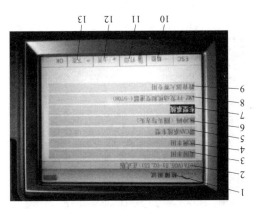

Fig. 7-12 Select Vehicle Model
1—Fault test; 2—Official version; 3—TOYOTA, USA;
4—TOYOTA EUROPE;
5—Vehicle models with CAN system;
6—Pulse code (round head and square head);
7—Vehicle model system;
8—1MZ-FE engine and transmission (9708);
9—Special for the competition of the Ministry of Education;
10—Help; 11—Print; 12—Previous page; 13—Next page

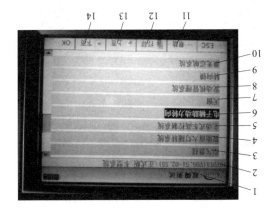

Fig. 7-13 Selection System
1—Fault test; 2—TOYOTA (V05, 51-02, 55) \ Official version \ Vehicle model system;
3—Air suspension; 4—Intelligent headlamp running system;
5—Active vehicle height control system;
6—Electronic power steering; 7—Sunroof;
8—Engine management system; 9—Steering lock;
10—Laser cruise system; 11—Help;
12—Print; 13—Previous page; 14—Next page

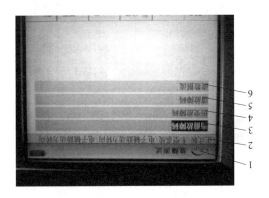

Fig. 7-14 Read Current DTC
1—Fault test; 2—Official version \ Vehicle model system \ Electronic power steering;
3—Active DTC; 4—History DTC; 5—Clear DTC;
6—Read data stream

Observe the output voltage of torque sensors 1、2 and 3 under the condition that the vehicle stops and the steering wheel does not move (no load), and judge whether it is the standard value according to the maintenance manual, as shown in Fig. 7-16.

190 Automotive Safety and Comfort System Maintenance

Fig. 7-15 Clear DTC

1—Fault test; 2—Official version \ Vehicle model system \ Electronic power steering \ Electronic power steering;
3—Active DTC; 4—History DTC; 5—Clear DTC;
6—Read data stream; 7—Help; 8—Print;
9—Previous page; 10—Next page

Fig. 7-16 Observe Torque Sensor

1—Fault test; 2—Electronic power steering \ Electronic power steering \ Data stream test; 3—Torque sensor 1 output;
4—Torque sensor 2 output; 5—Torque sensor 3 output;
6—Torque 1 zero value; 7—Torque 2 zero value;
8—Torque 3 zero value; 9—Motor positive voltage;
10—Motor negative voltage; 11—Help; 12—Print;
13—Record; 14—Stop

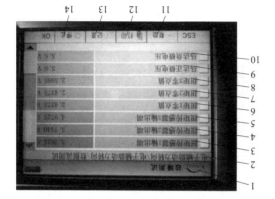

When the vehicle stops, turn the steering wheel to the right, observe the output voltage of torque sensors 1, 2 and 3, and judge whether it is the standard value according to the maintenance manual, as shown in Fig. 7-17.

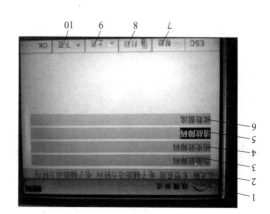

Fig. 7-17 Observe the Torque Sensor When Turning the Steering Wheel to the Right

1—Fault test; 2—Electronic power steering \ Electronic power steering \ Data stream test;
3—Torque sensor 1 output; 4—Torque sensor 2 output;
5—Torque sensor 3 output; 6—Torque 1 zero value;
7—Torque 2 zero value; 8—Torque 3 zero value;
9—Motor positive voltage; 10—Motor negative voltage;
11—Help; 12—Print; 13—Record; 14—Stop

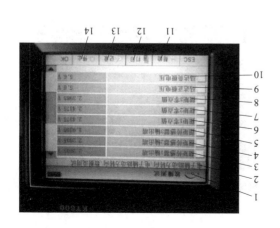

Fig. 7-18 Observe the Torque Sensor When Turning the Steering Wheel to the Left

1—Fault test; 2—Electronic power steering \ Electronic power steering \ Data stream test;
3—Torque sensor 1 output; 4—Torque sensor 2 output;
5—Torque sensor 3 output; 6—Torque 1 zero value;
7—Torque 2 zero value; 8—Torque 3 zero value;
9—Motor positive voltage; 10—Motor negative voltage;
11—Help; 12—Print; 13—Record; 14—Stop

When the vehicle stops, turn the steering wheel to the left, observe the output voltage

of torque sensors 1, 2 and 3, and judge whether it is the standard value according to the maintenance manual, as shown in Fig. 7-18.

2. Inspection and maintenance methods

Remove the screw fixing the instrument with a cross screwdriver, as shown in Fig. 7-19.

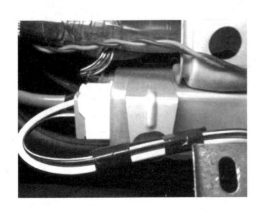

Fig. 7-19 Screw Position   Fig. 7-20 Power Steering ECU

Remove the instrument to find the power steering ECU, as shown in Fig. 7-20. The schematic diagram of power steering ECU terminals is shown in Fig. 7-21.

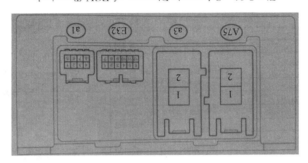

Fig. 7-21 Schematic Diagram of ECU Terminals

Check the voltage or resistance of each terminal with a multimeter according to the maintenance manual, as shown in Fig. 7-22.

Terminal Number (Symbol)	Wiring color	Terminal description	Status	Specified status
a75-1(PIG)-A75-2 (PGND)	L-W-B	Power supply	Always	11-14 V
a75-2(PGND)-ground itself	W-B-self grounding	Power supply grounding	Always	Less than 1Ω
a3-1(M1)-A75-2 (PGND)	R-W-B	Power steering motor	Turn the steering wheel to the left when the ignition switch is in the ON(IG) position	11-14V
			Turn the steering wheel to the right when the ignition switch is in the ON(IG) position	Less than 1V

Fig. 7-22

Terminal Number (Symbol)	Wiring color	Terminal description	Status	Specified status
a3-2(M2)-A75-2 (PGND)	B-W-B	Power steering motor	Turn the steering wheel to the left when the ignition switch is in the ON(1G) position	Less than 1V
			Turn the steering wheel to the right when the ignition switch is in the ON(1G) position	11-14V
E32-1(CANH)- E32-72(CANL)	SB-W	CAN communication line	Turn the ignition switch to the OFF position	54-69Ω
E32-6(IG)- A75-2(PGND)	L-W-B	IG power supply	Turn the ignition switch to the ON(1G) position	11-14V
a1-5(TR01)- A75-2(PGND)	W-W-B	Phase moment sensor signal	Turn the steering wheel to the left and right when the ignition switch is in the ON(1G) position	0.3-4.7V
a1-6(TROV)- A75-2(PGND)	R-W-B	Phase moment sensor supply voltage	Turn the ignition switch to the ON(1G) position	7.5-8.5V
a1-7(TR02)- A75-2(PGND)	Y-W-B	Phase moment sensor signal	Turn the steering wheel to the left and right when the ignition switch is in the ON(1G) position	0.3-4.7V
a1-8(TROG)- A75-2(PGND)	B-W-B	Phase moment sensor grounding	Always	Less than 1Ω

Fig. 7-22   Data of each terminal

Exercises

Short Answer Questions

1. What is the composition of the EPS?
2. What are the advantages of the eletric power steering?

Item Summary

With the maturity of electronic control technology and the reduction of cost in recent years, EPS has been paid more and more attention, and has rapidly stepped into the application field because of its incomparable advantages compared with traditional power steering system, and partially replaced hydraulic power steering (HPS). EPS will become the ideal upgrade product of automobile traditional steering system.

Item Exercises

Short Answer Questions

1. What are the components and functions of the magneto-electric torque sensor?
2. What are the advantages of the electric power steering?
3. What are the characteristics of electronic hydraulic power steering?